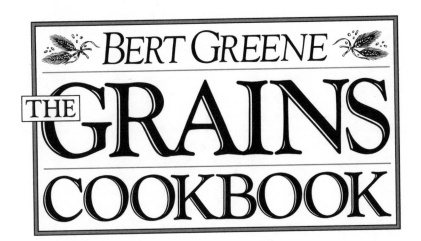

BERT GREENE

THE GRAINS COOKBOOK

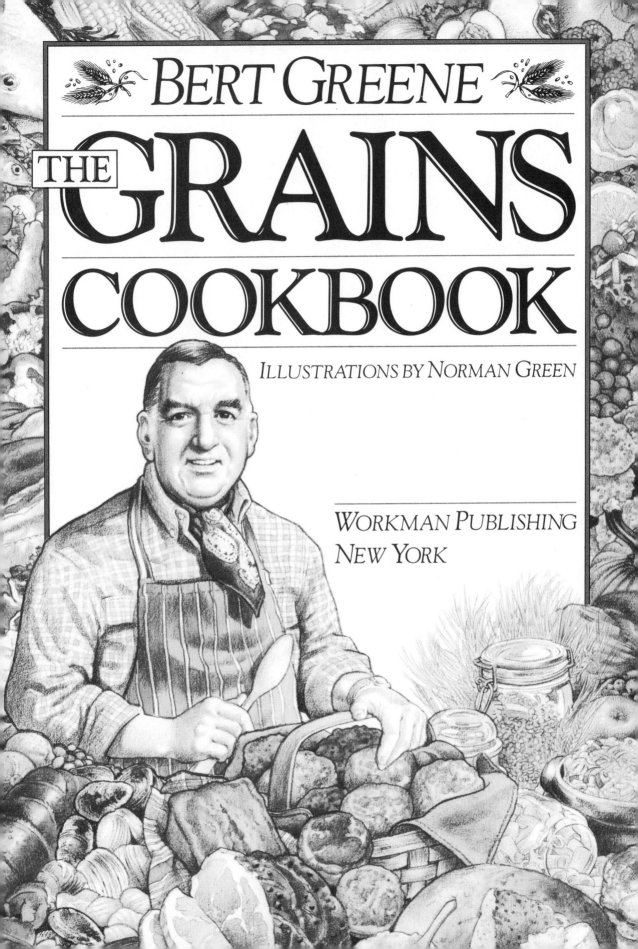

BERT GREENE

THE GRAINS COOKBOOK

ILLUSTRATIONS BY NORMAN GREEN

WORKMAN PUBLISHING
NEW YORK

Publisher's Thanks

To Phillip S. Schulz
for his generous help in getting
The Grains Cookbook
from manuscript to book.

*Library of Congress Cataloging-in-Publication
Data*

Greene, Bert.
The grains cookbook.
Includes index.
1. Cookery (Cereals) I. Title.
TX808.G735 1988   641.6'31   88-40223
ISBN 0-89480-610-6
ISBN 0-89480-612-2 (pbk.)

Cover and book illustrations: Norman Green

The recipe for From-Scratch Buckwheat
Noodles originally appeared in *Better Than
Store-Bought*, by Helen Witty and Elizabeth
Schneider Colchie. Copyright © 1979 by
Helen Witty and Elizabeth Schneider Colchie.
Reprinted by permission of Harper & Row.
The recipe for Marion's Semolina Seed Cake
originally appeared in *The Fanny Farmer Baking
Book*, by Marion Cunningham. Copyright ©
1984 by Marion Cunningham. Reprinted by
permission of Alfred A. Knopf.

Workman Publishing Company, Inc.
708 Broadway
New York, NY 10003

Manufactured in the United States of America

First printing October 1988

10 9 8 7 6 5 4 3 2 1

CONTENTS

REMEMBERING BERT

Shortly after completing the manuscript for *The Grains Cookbook*, Bert Greene died—it was a great loss for his friends and colleagues. Bert brought a tremendous amount of energy to the American cooking community. His spirited classes, cookbooks, and articles gained him millions of fans who enjoyed his accessibility and his unpretentious approach to food.

It was my good fortune to be the editor of Bert's last two cookbooks. It was a real pleasure to work closely with him—Bert's expertise was astounding, and his love of food was infectious—"Suzanne, dear heart, you will learn to love kasha, I promise." He was an editor's dream—a writer with the rare talent to make each recipe perfect and the ability to fill his stories with warmth and humor.

Bert made friends wherever he went. Everyone who read his personable books and articles felt they knew him. But the people who respected his contributions and talents most were his companions in the food community. A few of the many join me in a heartfelt tribute to this terrific man.

Suzanne Rafer

Bert Greene did so much for us all, first with his pioneering store in the Hamptons, which pointed the good direction for so many who came after him. His books and his newspaper column gave inspiration to the hordes of followers who are good cooks today because of his encouraging approach. He was a generous and imaginative friend, a fine teacher, and thank heaven he didn't take off without leaving us his last word—this splendid typically perfectly wonderfully Bert Greene book.

Julia Child

Bert, whom I knew for many years during his stay in the Hamptons, was an inspired and inventive cook. He was a quiet man, a gentle man, and he lives on vibrantly through his recipes.

Craig Claiborne

Bert was a big man—big in size, generosity, laughter, and knowledge. I remember, vividly, walking down a Village street one day between Bert and Jim Beard, feeling like a happy dwarf. If Bert had one particular gift, it was making people feel comfortable with food that challenged them. They sensed his contagious enthusiasm and warmth and were encouraged to cook—the best reward for a food writer.

Barbara Kafka

Bert had a great gift for taking his work but not himself seriously. He was a big, stylish bear of a man who drew people to him with warmth and grace. I treasured him because he was truly cultured in an uncultured age, but even more because he never fell victim to the pomposity and inflated sense of self-importance that afflicts so many who achieve stardom in the kingdom of food. What I remember most is the laughter we shared over the years. What I think the world will best remember is Bert as the friendly voice, the encourager of other less-than-expert cooks. From the early days of his career, he made the kind of real, full-flavored, unfussy food that we are once again learning to appreciate in this country. Bert Greene left an important and substantial legacy.

Ila Stanger

What I like about Bert Greene's work is the unpretentiousness of it. He had a rare gift for describing the way things really are, always with clear vision, embracing generosity, and unfailing good humor. I will surely miss this master of American cooking.

Paula Wolfert

There was a poignant last line in Bert's obituary in *The New York Times*: "There were no survivors." It was wrong. There are thousands of survivors and we need only read his vibrant words to know that he will always be with us—encouraging, helping, and inspiring. His own pleasure in sharing good food with good friends has ensured him a permanent place at our table.

Irena Chalmers

Bert Greene had more style and more taste than almost anyone I know. He also had more love to give. You can savor all of these qualities when you make a Bert Greene recipe. Even if you never had the great pleasure of knowing him and loving him back, as soon as you dig into one of his dishes you recognize the care, skill, and concern that went into devising it. It is always enormously delicious, comforting, nurturing, honest food, informed by Bert's meticulous historical, social, nutritional, and culinary research. But it is also inventive food created by a man whose sensibilities never allowed him to do anything without putting his stamp on it.

Arthur Schwartz

Bert did everything with enthusiasm and panache whether it was moderating a seminar, writing a cookbook, demonstrating a dish, or cooking dinner for friends. He was fun, funny, and a friend.

Jean Hewitt

Bert struck me as being a very warm and gentle man. One of his most attractive qualities was his strong advocacy of newcomers to the food world. He was constantly searching out exciting recipes and people. Whenever we ate together in a restaurant, we'd always go into the kitchen to visit the chef. Bert was inquisitive without being pedantic, and never flaunted his vast knowledge or who he was.

Jacques Pépin

It was typical of Bert to embrace an idea, a cause, a person with spontaneous gusto—then slowly grow into the depth and breadth of his commitment. Such was the case with grains, which he had once enjoyed as mere gravy-holders, then understood to be nutritional blessings, then began to perceive as culinary delights: flavorful, defined, distinct, delicious—worthy of his considerable attention.

Elizabeth Schneider

Bert Greene was a strong writer who never seemed to lose his way. He always knew exactly what good was. His taste grew from a love of home cooking— nothing fancy, just things he liked. His food is impressive and hospitable without trying to be.

Marion Cunningham

Bert Greene's work was very personal in that he never tried to be trendy, but wrote about what he believed in. He was a sincere, generous, charming man who knew the proper flavor boundaries of the foods he wrote about. Bert has left us a body of recipes solidly rooted in tradition. Their homespun quality makes them seem as sincere as he was.

Mimi Sheraton

Bert was a giant of a man. His laughter and wit, and love of life and food, filled a room as well as the pages of his books. His great gift of life lives on in his writing, where those of us who love him can

find his voice as we turn the pages and cook his food.

Nathalie Dupree

Bert Greene was a very wise man. He had an innate knowledge and appreciation of flavor which even the greatest chefs do not always possess. This is probably the wisest of all his books.

M.F.K. Fisher

Bert was one of the truly great human beings with an enormous capacity for life and for love and I loved him with a whole heart. He was honest, intelligent, loyal, caring, passionate, and kind, and his friendship enriched my life. I know that of all Bert's work he was especially proud of *Grains*. I am so grateful he lived to complete it.

Rose Levy Beranbaum

There's no mysterious, mystical aspect to Bert's cooking. The magic is Bert himself. He understood better than any other the palate and cuisine of America. He won our hearts with a warm honest message that came across loud and clear. Bert was truly eclectic and this was reflected in his food, which is made up of a daring alliance of ingredients. The dishes he prepared were robust and rustic, creating downright satisfying flavors. We associate such food with love and warmth shared with family and friends. Bert Greene was a true maverick of his time.

Julie Sahni

Bert and I were friends over the last few years. I always admired how he approached his work with warmth and enthusiasm. His knowledge of food and what tasted good was dominant throughout his cooking classes and demonstrations. When Bert taught, you learned.

Bradley Ogden

His marvelous sense of humor, his great gifts, his warmth, always make you rush to try his mouthwatering recipes. This book is a must.

Guiliano Bugialli

Bert Greene was a dear friend—a gentle giant of a man who touched my heart with his tremendous capacity for sharing himself with others. This multi-talented man brought a full measure of magic to whatever he did, leaving a loving imprint on thousands of lives. Bert once said that "books are a writer's children." Indeed, he breathed life into each and every one of his literary offspring with his warm, candid style, liberally laced with wit, humor, and to use a *Bertism*, a healthy dose of "stovetop logic." And, though the man is gone, his magic will be with us forever because he left us all with a priceless legacy—seven of his progeny to read and treasure and remember him by. Thank you, dear friend.

Sharon Tyler Herbst

GREENE ON GRAINS

When I first decided to write a book about grains, it was with decided misgivings. These "high-fiber foods," as nutritionists call them, were being ignored by much of the population, yet they were being touted in every newspaper and magazine as major sources of complex carbohydrates, fiber, and vitamins—what we all need to protect against heart disease, cancer, and digestive distress. But it was no wonder they were being overlooked. For though I remembered how deliciously grains could be prepared by good old-fashioned cooks, I also knew how they tasted at many a modern health food restaurant: *Boring!*

My late grandmother, no mean hand at stirring a pot of grains, had a philosophy on the subject that made me her kitchen convert the moment I heard it espoused.

"Things that are supposed to be good for you," I recall her saying, "should keep the secret of their good intentions strictly to themselves!"

And so say I. My feelings about grains are exactly the same as my feelings about the other wonderful foods that I have written of in the past. "Does it taste good?" is the only prerequisite for a dish's inclusion in my books. If it does not, I pass it by—no matter what vitamin valhalla is promised as my just reward. For food, like love, must never be a joyless experience.

My prejudice against conspicuously joyless consumption harks back to the late 1960s when as a sort of experiment, I elected to give up all the foods I normally ate (like meat, fish, fowl, eggs, cream, milk, butter, and cheese) for a strict regimen of grains and greens alone.

The meals were taken at an urban commune in New York City's East Village and were prepared by a group of very young men and women who viewed my age and ample size with ill-concealed mistrust.

What I recollect best of that dim excursion into self-denial is not the meals (which, to be kind, were rudimentary) but the attitude of my fellow diners who so righteously consumed them. To a man and woman, every young person ate just what was placed before them—without salt, pepper, or any genuine relish. They all might have been denizens at some correctional facility, for there were tin plates and plastic forks and no conversation whatsoever. Since food is not (and never was) a penance to me, I left this cold commune fast.

Of course, by the early '80s, I had returned to greens with renewed interest and a happier approach, and turned out recipes for dishes that my friends have since enjoyed. Now it seems to me that the time is ripe to enlist grains in dishes that brim with exciting flavors.

When I started dipping and sifting into grains, I literally fell in love with the subject. And, like all infatuated men before me, became obsessed with the nuances and diversities of each and every one that ever existed—from barley to wild rice and even beyond. Grains boring? Certainly no longer!

It has been a four-year labor of love that I sometimes thought would never be completed. But here it is, Greene's colossus of fact, lore, and nutrition. And, naturally, splendid recipes.

A cookbook of fiber-rich, complex-carbohydrate foods that taste delicious. My grandmother would have been proud!

Bert Greene

BARLEY

The Wholesome, Low-Gluten Grain

Barley is a grain I have associated with a steaming soup kettle for most of my life. Most, but not all. And therein lies a tale, of course.

My redoubtable grandmother, Minna Cohn, had a weakness for nursing. "The Jewish Florence Nightingale" is how my grandfather jocularly referred to his wife (usually behind her back). Not without a kernel of truth too, for this lady actively sought to nurture and nourish the ailing, whether they resided in her own bailiwick or somewhere up the block. And her husband's bantering never deterred her from what she considered her appointed rounds.

"People could call me worse things"—she would say as she shrugged elaborately—"than a *maidel* with a lamp!"

The important thing was keeping the world at large vital and vertical, and to this end she made soup—very often barley soup—three quarters of every calendar year.

I can clearly recall how she would part the curtain of her kitchen window, sniffing like a bird-dog and peering at the sky for significant weather signs. From November to May, any sudden mass of cumulus clouds floating over the garage roof sent her scurrying to the pantry and icebox like a shot.

Scooping up a handful of barley and a packet of dried mushrooms here, a carrot and a can of tomatoes there, she would assemble those ingredients together with a beef bone and compose the most stirring antitoxin one could ever imagine—without a written recipe or a side trip to the greengrocer or butcher! Instinct and common culinary sense produced her pottage. And I am sorry to report that none of her four daughters, or their progeny either, inherited that masterful art.

But barley in my grandmother's kitchen, inspiring as it might be in a soup spoon, was sharply limited to that use alone. I never knew there were other strings to the grain's bow until I went to Russia over forty years later.

The trip was part of a cultural exchange between the U.S. and the U.S.S.R. back in the early 1970s, during an unexpected thaw in international relations. Members of the tour had obviously been handpicked for this view of life behind the Iron Curtain, because the group was certainly composed of disparate types: businessmen, teachers, a painter, a union official, a therapist, and a Methodist minister. Plus a cook! A collection of fellow Americans politically limp—without a hint in any of our heads of what life in Russia would truly be like.

The travelers met (warily) for the first time at Kennedy Airport an hour before the scheduled flight time. Aloof at first, we became somewhat less reserved—one might say almost familial—during the next half dozen hours, as delay after delay prolonged our departure.

Initially we killed time saluting the good fortune that bound us together by chugging expensive Russian vodka at every cocktail bar in the airport. Later, ravenously hungry and hung over by turns, we chewed stale candy bars and antacid tablets aboard the stalled liner itself—a chill haven (an Aeroflot jet) that we had eventually been shepherded into by a crew of clearly disapproving flight attendants. Two of whom, female, inexplicably sprayed the air with cologne as each unsteady passenger groped for his or her seat in the semi-dark.

The scent they atomized (which we came to know very well indeed in the weeks that followed) is one of two aromas that pervade all public buildings and vehicles in the Soviet Union. Known as "Moscow Nights," this fragrance hangs in the air like an impenetrable fog from Tashkent to Kiev, recalling nothing so much as the floribundant deodorants used in latrines all over the world.

The other smell, rather more inviting to the nostrils, is scorched barley.

This heady essence, always inhaled outdoors, rises from blackened iron pots hung from tripods on street corners in every Russian city. At these urban islands, crews of construction workers—uniformly women of indeterminate age and overwhelming size—stir their breakfast, lunch, and sometimes even dinner over banked fires.

These middle-aged-to-very-ancient women perform all manner of manual labor. With incredible physical strength and endurance, they haul blocks of concrete out of the pavement with their bare hands and manipulate trip-hammers, steamrollers, even monster industrial cranes, without so much as dislodging a lock of hair from their babushkas.

It came as something of a surprise, my second day in Moscow, to come upon a band of these Amazons laying down their shovels to take turns stirring a pot of barley over the fire. And more of a shock to observe them spooning the

grains—seasoned with nothing except singed onion or garlic—into dainty bowls which they then passed around to one another like cakes at a tea party.

Barley is obviously the pause that refreshes in Russia.

In light of my aromatic memories, it is not surprising to discover that the Union of Soviet Socialist Republics is the world's leading barley grower. Point of fact: Over 20 million tons of this grain are produced (and shortly thereafter consumed) on Russian soil each year. But then, *Hordeum vulgare*, as barley is formally known, has a long and laureate history as fodder for woman, man, and beast.

The Grain's Genesis

Humans have been eating barley for years. How long? Agronomists and archeologists seem not to concur, but traces of Stone Age cakes, devised of wheat and barley baked in the sun, indicate clearly that the amount of barley grain in the prehistoric dinner pail outweighed the wheat kernels by a ratio of five to one. No mere jot of culinary trivia, that preponderance reveals an important fact: barley has always been one of *Homo sapiens'* handy sources of supply.

A versatile crop that farmers love, with its short growing season and excessively robust leaf stalks, barley is also one of the hardiest perennials around, able to withstand drought, flood, frost, and in a pinch, pestilence too. If that doesn't explain its popularity with the green-thumbed set, try this: In one form or another, barley can be harvested from the upper reaches of the Arctic to the tropic plains of the Equator! In both climes, its wholesome, low-gluten grain has been a chief source of intestinal fortitude (in cereal and flour) as well as intemperate behavior (in beer and malt spirits) for literally a millennium.

The Chinese (who always seemed to be the first to eat anything) are generally credited as being the earliest barley eaters. Shards of Hsia Dynasty pottery, dated circa 1520 B.C., clearly depict the end of a great famine, with hulled barley falling like rain out of the heavens directly into a peasant family's rice bowl.

Which may not be as mythic as it appears. In the green pockets of northern Asia four thousand years ago, this plant grew wild. But the untended crop came to seed so precipitately that food gatherers were forced to set up tents at the field's edge, to watch the ripening kernels lest they shattered unexpectedly and sent their spoils blowing in the wind.

Barley was not just a movable feast in China; it became, in time, the basis for formal agriculture all over Asia when flimsy tents were replaced with solid farm dwellings and itinerant gleaners turned into domesticated planters.

From the beginning, man always knew he would not want for sustenance as long as his barley crop sprouted. He also learned to grind the grain to make flour for bread and malt for brew. And while low-gluten barley made a rather bitter quaff and a loaf only the strong-toothed could chew, the muscle-men who built the Pyramid of Cheops thrived on both. Their allotment for a day's labor? Three loaves of bread and a ration of beer. Both, needless to say, fortified with barley because it was cheap and available!

Barley is still a bargain, one cup of dried expanding to four times that amount in a saucepan.

Some Plain Grain Talk

Barley kernels are tough buds. Each kernel is protected by three layers of skin: two inedible husks that harbor the germ (or embryo) of the plant, and another delicate covering known as the *aleurone*, which shields the endosperm, a nubbin that gives barley its starchy bulk.

Unfortunately when barley is refined for human consumption (animals eat it in the rough), the husks, aleurone, and embryo are washed away in the polishing process—leaving only the endosperm (or pearl), which is the white barley that consumers are accustomed to finding on supermarket shelves.

Without aleurone, a healthy margin of barley's nutritional composition is seriously diminished, including loss of protein, valuable fiber, and B vitamins. However, in passing it must be noted that a cup of cooked pearl barley still offers the same amount of protein as a glass of milk, along with hearty increments of niacin, thiamine, and potassium.

Another plus for pearl barley: Scientists at the University of Wisconsin recently announced that a substance that inhibits cholesterol production in the blood has been traced (contrary to all expectation) to the nonfibrous portion of the grain.

How to Buy It

*T*here are several options available to barley buyers: whole hulled barley, pressed barley, and pearl barley. *Whole hulled barley*, brownish gray in color and decidedly gritty to the tooth, can be found only at health food stores or natural food emporiums. Approximately double the cost of pearl barley, it is nutritionally the higher rated. However, hulled barley's excessively fibrous texture and the necessity to soak it overnight prior to cooking will, I suspect, keep all but the deepest-dyed grain lovers at bay.

Asian *pressed barley* (hato mugi) is a grain in common currency in traditional Japanese cookery as well as macrobiotic circles. Slightly larger in size and gummier in texture than conventional white barley, hato mugi is compressed and minimally vitamin-enriched. It is available at Japanese groceries or may be mail-ordered from suppliers who stock Asian products. But in my prejudiced opinion, it is scarcely worth the effort.

With one exception, all the barley recipes in this collection were tested with off-the-shelf *pearl barley*. Pearl barley is not only the most dependable form on the market, it is also a staple with a long pantry life: six to nine months in an airtight container is the manufacturer's guarantee—and longer still if your pantry's temperature hovers around 68°.

How to Cook It

*M*y rule of thumb is to cook pearl barley in boiling water (or broth) at a ratio of 3 cups liquid to 1 cup grains. Cooking time: 35 to 40 minutes. To speed up the cooking process somewhat, and in passing achieve a remarkably fluffy kernel, consider presoaking pearl barley in twice the amount of water as grains for a period of 5 hours or overnight. Cooking time for presoaked barley: 15 minutes flat.

Another tonic cooking method for pearl barley is to parboil it first and steam it later (see below).

I always soak whole hulled barley overnight and use more liquid in the cooking (4 to 4½ cups to 1 cup of grains). Cover the pot and extend the cooking time to 60 minutes. Be sure to check the pot after half the cooking time has elapsed, however, for more liquid is often required.

Like rice, barley may be stirred into a remarkably creamy form of risotto, but never attempt this version with any barley except pearl barley.

HOT STEAMED BARLEY

2 quarts water
Salt to taste
1 cup pearl barley

1. Bring the water to a boil, add salt, and add the barley. Stir once with a wooden spoon so the barley does not stick to the bottom of the pot. When the water returns to boiling, reduce the heat and simmer, uncovered, until barely tender, 20 minutes. Drain in a colander.

2. Place the colander over several inches of boiling water in another pot. (Do not let the bottom of the colander touch the water.) Lay a single layer of paper towels on top of the barley, and steam for at least 30 minutes. Barley can be held this way for several hours without harm.

Serves 4

BARLIED BEEF GRANDMOTHERLY STYLE

*T*o many diners in the Western world, barley's most familiar guise is in a soup bowl. My own first contact with the grain was my grandmother's bespoke pottage, prepared with alacrity whenever I looked peaked or sneezed twice in a row. No matter the state of my health, I never objected to her pharmacopeia, for it was literally the most comforting food I'd ever tasted.

The barley soup that my grandmother stirred up (heavy on the beef, mushrooms, and tomatoes) was a dish that could be eaten with a spoon at the first sitting only. A night's layover in her icebox caused it to become so thick and dense that family members always attacked it with a knife and fork at successive meals. A comparable amalgam of my own—based on my forebear's marvelous concoction—never pretends to be anything other than the stew (or stoup) it actually is!

2 tablespoons vegetable oil
2 to 2¼ pounds beef brisket
2 cloves garlic
7 cups water
½ ounce dried mushrooms, sliced
½ cup water, boiling
1 small onion, chopped
2 medium carrots, peeled and chopped
2 medium parsnips, peeled and chopped
3 medium turnips, peeled and chopped
1 rib celery, finely chopped

5 large fresh mushrooms, coarsely chopped
1 can (14 ounces) plum tomatoes with their juice
3 cups homemade chicken stock (see page 376) or canned broth
3 cups homemade beef stock (see page 377) or canned broth
⅓ cup pearl barley
Pinch of dried thyme
Salt and freshly ground black pepper to taste

1. Heat the oil in a large heavy pot over medium-high heat. Add the meat and sauté it until well browned all over. Remove the brisket to a plate. Add the garlic and 1 cup of the water to the pot, scraping the sides and bottom with a wooden spoon. Return the meat to the pot, and add the remaining 6 cups water. Heat to boiling. Reduce the heat and simmer, covered, skimming the surface occasionally to remove excess fat, 1 hour and 40 minutes.

2. Meanwhile, place the dried mushrooms in a medium-size mixing bowl. Cover them with the boiling water, and let stand 30 minutes. Drain.

3. Discard the garlic from the pot and skim the surface of any remaining fat. Add the onion, carrots, parsnips, turnips, celery, both mushrooms, tomatoes, chicken and beef stock, barley and thyme. Bring to a boil. Reduce the heat and simmer, partially covered, until the meat is very tender, about 1½ hours.

4. To serve: Remove the meat from the pot and cut it into pieces. Return the pieces to the stew. Season with salt and pepper.

Serves 6

GEORGIAN YOGURT AND BARLEY SOUP

A barley soup of a somewhat paler hue than my grandmother's, the following is a residual of my 1970s trip to the U.S.S.R. This seminal dish varies with the sector of the Russian geography in which it is stirred. The most conspicuous version I slurped came from the mountainous region of the Caucasus, where the peasants are all remarkably long in the tooth and credit that longevity to—you guessed it—yogurt and barley!

2 tablespoons unsalted butter
1 large onion, finely chopped
1 clove garlic, minced
⅓ cup pearl barley
4½ cups homemade chicken stock (see page 376) or canned broth
2 eggs, lightly beaten
1 tablespoon all-purpose flour
1½ cups plain yogurt
1 teaspoon chopped fresh mint, or ¼ teaspoon dried
1 teaspoon chopped fresh cilantro (Chinese parsley)
1 teaspoon chopped chives or scallion tops
Salt and freshly ground white pepper to taste

1. Melt the butter in a large heavy pot over medium-low heat. Add the onion; cook 1 minute. Add the garlic; cook 4 minutes longer. Add the barley, tossing well to coat with the onion mixture. Then stir in the chicken stock and heat to boiling. Reduce the heat and simmer, covered, 1 hour. Remove the cover and reduce the heat to low.

2. Combine the eggs with the flour, yogurt, mint, cilantro, and chives in a medium-size bowl. Slowly stir this into the soup. Warm the soup through, but do not allow it to boil. Season with salt and white pepper.

Serves 6

WINTER VEGETABLE AND BARLEY CHOWDER

*B*arley has always been a true cereal of champions. In ancient Athens, according to Pliny the Elder, a mite of barley grains—never less than the amount that would half fill a warrior's helmet—was allotted to every participant in the Olympics. In time, serious gladiators in Thessaly lived on a diet of root vegetables and barley, and the effect of that regimen was so spectacular in hand-to-hand combat that the crowds named them "barley eaters."

Barley and root vegetables are still a heck of a team at the table. For winning evidence, see the unconventional chowder that follows—a champion first course or one-dish dinner.

BARLEY TRIVIA, ANCIENT-STYLE

Back in prebiblical days, Egyptians were cannibals—just like the crocodiles with whom they shared the Nile. In time, however, the former got religion and were persuaded by the goddess Isis along with her brother-husband, Osiris, to dine on barley and wheat instead of their fellow man. But never the crocodiles! As a matter of fact, grain consumption merely made the Egyptians more appetizing to them. It's a wonder that barley, let alone civilization, survived the crunch!

But both did, obviously. Aside from nourishment, the ancient Egyptians also believed that barley had all manner of mystical and medicinal powers. Snakebite, they divined, could be averted by feeding even the most venomous reptile a porridge of barley mixed with honey and wine. There is no report on the survival rate, but as the same cure was claimed to be a prophylactic against hangover, it was probably considerable. As the old Egyptian saying goes . . . You pays your piaster and you takes your choice!

½ cup pearl barley
1 cup water
3 tablespoons unsalted butter
1 cup diced smoked ham
1 large onion, finely chopped
3 cloves garlic, minced
1 medium carrot, peeled and diced
1 medium parsnip, peeled and diced
1 cup diced peeled rutabaga (about ½ small rutabaga)
1 leek, white part only, rinsed well and chopped
1 cup finely shredded cabbage
6 cups homemade chicken stock (see page 376), or one 46-ounce can chicken broth
1 cup heavy or whipping cream
Salt and freshly ground black pepper
Pinch of dried thyme
¼ teaspoon freshly grated nutmeg
⅓ cup freshly grated Parmesan cheese

1. Soak the barley in the water for 6 hours or overnight.

2. Melt the butter in a large heavy pot over medium-low heat. Add the ham; cook until the edges turn gold, about 5 minutes. Stir in the onion; cook 2 minutes. Add the garlic; cook 3 minutes longer. Add the carrot, parsnip, rutabaga, leek, and cabbage. Cook, covered, 10 minutes. Add the chicken stock and heat to boiling. Reduce the heat and simmer, partially covered, 30 minutes.

3. Add the barley and cook for 15 minutes more.

4. Reduce the heat to low, and slowly stir the cream into the chowder. Warm the chowder through, but do not allow it to boil. Add salt and pepper to taste, the thyme, and the nutmeg. Just before serving, sprinkle the surface of the chowder with the cheese.

Serves 6 to 8

BEEF SAUTE WITH BARLEY AND RICE

*B*ecause it never dies, barley is sometimes accorded the happy designation "a grain of resurrection." It has also been dubbed (in the Bible) "a fruit of the Lord." For, as the Good Book implies, when there are barley grains in a pot no man goes hungry. For some practical verification of that thought, I suggest you glance at this recipe—a fortuitous amalgam of protein and cereal that amply feeds four to six on a scant pound of meat!

1 pound boneless beef sirloin, trimmed
1 tablespoon unsalted butter
5 to 6 tablespoons olive oil
1 medium onion, finely chopped
1 shallot, finely chopped
½ teaspoon crushed dried hot red peppers
2 cloves garlic, minced
4 shiitake mushrooms (about 2 ounces),
*   sliced*
½ cup pearl barley
½ cup Italian arborio rice (see page 258)
3 cups homemade beef stock (see page 377)
*   or canned broth*
Salt and freshly ground black pepper to
*   taste*
¼ teaspoon chopped fresh sage, or a pinch
*   dried*
1½ tablespoons chopped fresh parsley

1. Cut the sirloin into strips 2 inches long, ¼ inch thick, and ½ inch wide. Set them aside.

2. Heat the butter with 1 tablespoon of the oil in a 5- to 6-quart heavy pot or Dutch oven over medium heat. Add the onion, shallot, and dried red peppers; cook 1 minute. Add the garlic; cook 4 minutes longer. Using a slotted spoon,

*L*ike most grains, barley has had many ups and downs in kitchen popularity over the years. As a baker's staple (way back in biblical times), it lost favor to wheat early on because the minimal amount of protein in barley flour contained such a low percentage of gluten that the loaves devised of it were frankly tooth-shattering to all but the hardiest diners. Of a consequence, barley was relegated to porridges and stews that all those less well-molared could digest. In one form or another, soft-cooked barley is still very much a staple at stoves, hearths, and campfires all over the world.

transfer the mixture to a plate.

3. Add 2 tablespoons of the oil to the same pot. Sauté the mushrooms until golden, about 5 minutes. Using a slotted spoon, transfer them to the plate with the onions.

4. Add 2 more tablespoons of the oil to the same pot. Sauté the beef strips, one third at a time, over medium-high heat until browned on all sides. (Add more oil to the pot if needed.) Transfer the beef to a separate plate.

5. Reduce the heat under the pot to medium-low. Add the barley and rice, and stir well. Add the stock, scraping the sides and bottom of the pot with a wooden spoon. Add the reserved onion-mushroom mixture, and heat to boiling.

Then reduce the heat and simmer, covered, over medium-low heat until the barley and rice are tender and almost all the liquid has been absorbed, about 35 minutes.

6. Add the sautéed beef strips and cook, tossing constantly, over medium heat until warmed through, about 5 minutes. Season with salt and pepper, then stir in the sage and parsley.

Serves 4 to 6

CHOLLENT

Chollent is a Jewish pot roast that is generally baked alongside beans, and more often than not, barley. The following is loosely based on a recipe in Fanny Sylverstein's *My Mother's Cookbook*. I first met Fanny, who is a true fan of mine, in 1987. I quickly became a fan of hers, after reading that guileless memoir of her adventures as an immigrant girl on New York's Lower East Side. As an adult she became personal chef to the head of Paramount pictures. Her recipes are as adventurous as her life.

3 tablespoons vegetable oil
1 thick boneless beef chuck roast (3½ to 4 pounds)
1 medium onion, finely chopped
1 clove garlic, minced
1 teaspoon salt
¼ teaspoon freshly ground black pepper
2 teaspoons hot Hungarian paprika
½ teaspoon ground ginger
2 quarts homemade beef stock (see page 377) or canned broth
1 cup dried pink beans
1 cup pearl barley
Chopped fresh parsley, for garnish

1. Preheat the oven to 250°F.

2. Heat the oil in a large Dutch oven over medium-high heat until hot but not smoking. Brown the roast well on all sides, 8 to 10 minutes. Remove the roast to a plate. Reduce the heat under the Dutch oven to medium.

3. Add the onion to the Dutch oven and cook, scraping the bottom and sides of the pot with a wooden spoon, 3 minutes. Add the garlic; cook 2 minutes longer. Stir in the salt, pepper, paprika, and ginger. Stir well, and add the beef stock. Heat to boiling, and then stir in the beans and barley. Bring the mixture to a boil, and add the roast.

4. Place the covered pot in the oven and cook 2½ hours. Stir the mixture, and then continue to cook, partially covered, until the meat is very tender, about 1½ hours longer. Remove the cover completely if the mixture is too wet.

5. To serve: Remove the meat and slice it. Spoon the bean and barley mixture into a large shallow serving dish, and place the meat slices over the top. Sprinkle with parsley.

Serves 6 to 8

BARLEY AND BLACK BEAN CHILI

Chili in startling black and white—literally. A wonderfully festive and flavorful dish for cold, cold weather.

½ pound dried black turtle beans
½ cup diced salt pork (about 3 ounces)
2 cups cubed smoked ham (about ¾ pound)
2 onions, chopped
2 cloves garlic, minced
1 hot green pepper, seeded, deveined, and minced
2 tablespoons olive oil
2½ cups cubed pork (about 1¼ pounds)
2 tablespoons chili powder
¼ cup dark rum
1 tablespoon hot Hungarian paprika
1 teaspoon ground cumin
1 teaspoon chopped fresh oregano, or ¼ teaspoon dried
1 teaspoon chopped fresh basil, or ½ teaspoon dried
4½ cups homemade beef stock (see page 377) or canned broth
1 cup pearl barley
1 tablespoon finely chopped pickled jalapeño peppers
¾ teaspoon crushed dried hot red peppers
Salt and freshly ground black pepper to taste
1 hard-cooked egg, chopped
1 large onion, finely chopped

1. Place the beans in a large pot, and cover with cold water. Heat to boiling; boil 2 minutes. Remove the pot from the heat and let stand 2 hours.

2. Cook the salt pork in boiling water to cover for 2 minutes. Drain, and pat dry with paper towels.

3. Sauté the salt pork in a large heavy ovenproof pot or Dutch oven over medium heat until lightly golden. Raise the heat slightly and add the ham cubes. Continue to sauté until the salt pork is crisp and the ham is lightly browned, about 4 minutes. Transfer with a slotted spoon to a bowl.

4. Add the onions to the pot, and cook over medium-low heat 1 minute. Add the garlic and hot green pepper. Cook 4 minutes. Transfer to the bowl with the ham and salt pork.

5. Add the olive oil to the pot and sauté the pork pieces over medium-high heat 1 minute. Sprinkle the pork pieces with the chili powder and cook 3 more minutes. Stir in the rum, scraping the bottom and sides of the pot. Add the paprika, cumin, oregano, basil, 4 cups of the beef stock, and the black beans. Heat to boiling. Reduce the heat and simmer, covered, 1 hour.

6. Preheat the oven to 350°F.

7. Add the barley and the remaining ½ cup stock to the bean mixture. Cover, transfer the pot to the oven, and bake until the barley is tender and all liquid

Though barley's strong suit is not immediately apparent in an oven, the same Egyptians who regularly rejected it for bread always baked it into decorative cakes on festival days. There was a good reason, of course: Pliable barley formed into animal shapes (pigs, oxen, even hippopotamuses) was an economy measure, allowing the lower classes to simulate the live animal sacrifices of their betters, without the mess or undue stress on their purse strings.

has been absorbed, 35 to 40 minutes. (Remove the cover and cook for 10 minutes if the mixture is too thin.) Add the jalapeño pepper, dried red peppers, and salt and pepper. Bake 10 minutes longer. Serve topped with the chopped egg and finely chopped onion.

Serves 6

BARLEY-CRAMMED ROAST CHICKEN

Barley is a grain often described as having mystical powers. According to my friend Pliny (the best and only early food scribe), ancient soothsayers would scratch the letters of the alphabet in sand, place a grain of barley in each initial, then wait till a wandering bird passed by and pecked at the grains. The letters the bird chose would then be juggled and jawed over until a reasonable meaning could be justified. If we were speaking of the following dish, two words are required: EAT HEARTY.

FOR THE STUFFING

1 ounce pancetta or thick bacon, chopped (about ¼ cup)
1 large shallot, minced
1 teaspoon unsalted butter
1 clove garlic, minced
2 medium tomatoes, seeded and coarsely chopped
1 teasoon chopped fresh basil, or ¼ teaspoon dried
2 cups cooked barley
¼ teaspoon chopped fresh rosemary, or a pinch dried
Dash of hot pepper sauce
Salt and freshly ground black pepper to taste

FOR THE CHICKEN

1 chicken, about 3½ pounds, well rinsed and dried
1 clove garlic, bruised
1 teaspoon unsalted butter, at room temperature
1 slice pancetta or thick bacon
1½ cups homemade chicken stock (see page 376) or canned broth

FOR THE TOMATO GRAVY

1 medium tomato, peeled and seeded
½ teaspoon chopped fresh basil, or ¼ teaspoon dried
1 tablespoon all-purpose flour
Salt and freshly ground black pepper to taste

1. Make the stuffing: Sauté the pancetta in a medium-size saucepan over medium-low heat until it is soft and all grease has exuded, about 4 minutes. Add the shallot; cook 1 minute. Add the butter and garlic; cook 2 minutes longer. Stir in the tomatoes and basil. Raise the heat to medium-high, and cook until the sauce has thickened, 4 to 5 minutes. Remove the pan from the heat, and add the barley, rosemary, hot pepper sauce, and salt and pepper. Toss well and set aside.

2. Roast the chicken: Preheat the oven to 375°F.

3. Wipe the chicken inside and out with a damp paper towel, then pat it dry. Rub the chicken inside and out with the bruised garlic. Spoon the barley stuffing into the cavity; sew and truss the chicken. Rub the breast area with the butter. Cut the slice of pancetta in half, and place the halves over the chicken breast. Roast on a rack 20 minutes, basting often with the chicken stock. Reduce the heat to 350°F and continue to roast, basting occasionally with more stock, until the juices run yellow when the chicken is pricked with a fork, about 1 hour longer. Transfer the chicken to a roasting platter and remove the trussing string. Let it stand 10 minutes. Degrease the pan juices and set them aside.

4. Make the tomato gravy: Place the tomato, basil, and flour in the container of a food processor or blender. Process until smooth and thick. Transfer the mixture to a small saucepan, place it over medium heat, and cook 1 minute. Stir in 1 cup of the pan juices. Whisk over medium-low heat until slightly thickened. Season with salt and pepper. Serve with the chicken and stuffing.

Serves 2 to 4

JIM-DANDY JAMBALAYA

A jambalaya like this is not to be found in Cajun country, but it sure is jim-dandy.

1 red bell pepper
4 large (about 1 pound) hot Italian sausages
1 cup pearl barley
1 tablespoon unsalted butter
1½ cups chopped scallions, white bulbs and green tops
1 large clove garlic, minced
1 jalapeño pepper, seeded, deveined, and minced, or ⅛ teaspoon crushed dried hot red pepper
3 cups homemade chicken stock (see page 376) or canned broth
¼ teaspoon chopped fresh thyme, or a pinch dried
½ pound thick-sliced smoked ham, cubed
1 pound medium shrimp, shelled and deveined
1 pound bay scallops or quartered sea scallops
Salt and freshly ground black pepper to taste
1 tablespoon chopped fresh parsley

1. Preheat the oven to 350°F.
2. Using a long-handled fork, roast the bell pepper over a gas flame until it is blackened all over; or roast the pepper under a broiler, turning until crisp on all sides. Carefully wrap the pepper in paper towels and place it in a small plastic bag. Set it aside to cool. Then rub the burned peel off with paper towels. Core and seed the pepper, and set it aside.

3. Sauté the sausages in an oil-rubbed 3- to 4-quart Dutch oven over medium heat until well browned on all sides, about 5 minutes. Transfer the sausages to a plate and set aside to cool. Then cut them into ½-inch-thick slices.

4. In the same Dutch oven, sauté the barley over medium heat until lightly browned, about 4 minutes. Add the butter and scallions; cook 1 minute. Add the garlic and jalepeño pepper; cook 5 minutes longer.

5. Place the peeled bell pepper in the container of a food processor or blender. Add 1 cup of the chicken stock and process until smooth. Stir this mixture into the barley mixture, along with the remaining 2 cups stock, the thyme, ham, and sausages. Heat to boiling. Transfer the pot to the oven and bake, covered, 35 minutes.

6. Remove the pot from the oven, and stir in the shrimp and scallops. Return it to the oven and bake, covered, 15 minutes. Remove the cover and bake 5 minutes longer. Remove the pot from the oven and let it stand for 5 minutes. Then add salt and pepper. Before serving, sprinkle with parsley.

Serves 6

STUFFED PEPPERS

*T*his is a variation of my sister's favorite stuffed pepper recipe that substitutes barley for the expected rice.

¾ cup water
Salt to taste
¼ cup pearl barley
4 large red bell peppers
6 sweet Italian sausages (1¼ pounds)
1 onion, finely chopped
1 clove garlic, minced
1 tablespoon Dijon mustard
1 teaspoon hot Hungarian paprika
½ teaspoon salt
⅛ teaspoon freshly ground black pepper
1 egg, lightly beaten
1 teaspoon fresh bread crumbs
2 teaspoons freshly grated Parmesan cheese
2 teaspoons olive oil
Chopped fresh parsley, for garnish

1. Bring the water to a boil in a medium-size saucepan. Add salt to taste and the barley, and simmer, uncovered, until tender, about 35 to 40 minutes. Drain, and set aside in a large mixing bowl.

2. Preheat the oven to 375°F.

3. Trim the tops off the peppers, and remove the cores and seeds. Cook the peppers in boiling salted water to cover for 1 minute. Set aside to drain.

4. Remove the sausage meat from the casings and sauté, breaking up the lumps with a wooden spoon, in a heavy skillet over medium heat until lightly browned, about 8 minutes. Transfer with a slotted spoon to the large mixing bowl and stir together with the barley.

5. Add the onion to the same skillet and cook, scraping the bottom and sides of the pan, over medium-low heat for 1 minute. Add the garlic; cook 4 minutes. Add this to the barley mixture in the bowl.

6. Add the mustard, paprika, salt, pepper, and beaten egg to the barley mixture and mix thoroughly. Fill each pepper cavity with the stuffing, mounding the tops.

7. Place the peppers in a heatproof baking dish that holds them snugly. Sprinkle the top of each pepper with ¼ teaspoon bread crumbs. Then sprinkle each with ½ teaspoon Parmesan, and finally drizzle each with ½ teaspoon olive oil. Bake 50 minutes. Remove from the oven and sprinkle with the parsley.

Serves 4

ANDALUSIAN BARLEY

*F*rom Granada. I first tasted the following dish as an adjunct to a plate of *anguilas* (tiny baby eels fried in garlic) after a long, hot, dusty ride on an American Express tourist excursion from Madrid. Proof of the pudding is that I cannot remember a single sight or sound of the splendid cathedral we drove hours to visit, but the barley is printed on my brain forever.

2 chorizos (Spanish sausages) or other spicy
    sausage (about ½ pound), chopped
1 tablespoon unsalted butter
1 medium onion, minced
¼ teaspoon chopped fresh thyme, or a
    pinch dried
1 cup pearl barley
3 cups homemade chicken stock (see page
    376) or canned broth
Salt and freshly ground black pepper to
    taste
½ cup sliced green olives
Chopped fresh parsley, for garnish

1. Sauté the chopped chorizos in a large saucepan over medium-low heat until they are lightly browned and all oil has exuded. With a slotted spoon, transfer the sausages to a dish and set aside.

2. Add the butter to the saucepan and sauté the onion for 2 minutes. Stir in the thyme and barley, tossing well to coat with the onion. Add the stock and chorizos. Heat to boiling. Reduce the heat and simmer, covered, until all the liquid has been absorbed and the barley is tender, 35 to 40 minutes.

3. If the barley seems too chewy, add more broth and continue to cook. If it is too wet, uncover, raise the heat, and cook until the liquid is absorbed. Then add salt and pepper.

4. To serve: Remove the saucepan from the heat. Stir in the olives, and sprinkle with parsley.

Serves 4 to 6

WARM ISLAND SALAD
(Ensalada Isleña)

*B*arley on the light side—in a seafood salad—to be served any time you need a touch of summer.

3½ cups water
Salt
1 cup pearl barley
1 cup clam juice
¼ cup dry white wine
½ lemon, sliced
1 sprig fresh thyme, or a pinch dried
1 sprig parsley
3- to 4-ounce lobster tail
¼ pound shrimp
½ pound bay scallops or quartered sea
    scallops
4 scallions, white bulbs and green tops,
    chopped
1 cucumber, peeled, seeded, and diced

1 small zucchini, diced
½ cup sliced radishes (about 1 bunch)
2 tablespoons minced red bell pepper
2 tablespoons chopped fresh basil
1 clove garlic, crushed
1 teaspoon Dijon mustard
¼ cup olive oil
1 tablespoon fresh lemon juice

1. Bring 3 cups of the water to a boil in a medium-size saucepan. Add salt to taste and the barley, and simmer, uncovered until just tender, 35 to 40 minutes. Drain, and set aside.

2. Combine the clam juice, wine, remaining ½ cup water, lemon slices, thyme, and parsley in a medium-size heavy saucepan. Heat to boiling, then reduce the heat. Add the lobster tail and gently poach until pink and firm, 3 to 5 minutes. Using a slotted spoon, transfer it to a plate. Add the shrimp to the saucepan; cook 3 minutes. Transfer them to the plate. Add the scallops to the saucepan and poach until barely firm, about 3 minutes. Transfer them to a bowl. Raise the heat under the saucepan and reduce the stock to ¼ cup. Strain and reserve.

3. Clean and devein the shrimp and cut each in half crossways. Clean the lobster tail and cut into pieces.

4. In a large bowl, combine the barley, scallions, cucumber, zucchini, radishes, red bell pepper, basil and the seafood. Toss well.

5. In another bowl, use the back of a spoon to mash the garlic and ½ teaspoon salt together to form a paste. Stir in the mustard and the reserved fish stock. Whisk in the oil and lemon juice. Pour this dressing over the barley-seafood mixture, and mix well.

Serves 6 to 8

GREEN BARLEY

*F*rom The Marches of northern Italy. In spring, the farmers' wives there stir barley (or rice) into a *brodo* made of any strong-flavored greens they can find growing outside their kitchen doors. It purifies the sluggish winter blood—that's the claim—but it also rejuvenates the slack tongue after a night on the town.

2 tablespoons unsalted butter
1 medium onion, finely chopped
1 clove garlic, minced
2 cups finely chopped Swiss chard and arugula leaves, mixed
1 cup pearl barley
1 slice prosciutto, minced
3 cups homemade chicken stock (see page 376) or canned broth
⅛ teaspoon freshly grated nutmeg
¼ cup chopped fresh parsley
2 tablespoons chopped chives or scallion tops
Salt and freshly ground black pepper to taste

1. Melt the butter in a large saucepan over medium-low heat. Add the onion; cook 1 minute. Add the garlic; cook 2 minutes longer. Stir in the chopped greens, tossing to coat with the onion mixture. Add the barley, prosciutto, chicken stock, and nutmeg. Heat to boiling. Reduce the heat and simmer, covered, until all the liquid has been absorbed and the barley is tender, 35 to 40 minutes.

2. If the barley seems too chewy, add more broth and continue to cook. If it is too wet, uncover, raise the heat slightly, and cook until the liquid is absorbed. Then stir in the parsley and chives, and add salt and pepper.

Serves 4 to 6

CZECH BARLEY AND PEAS

An absolutely unforgettable taste from Prague. Proper Czech housewives, incidentally, mate their barley with dried peas, but to my tongue, fresh (or frozen) *petit pois* are the grain's true-blue partner.

3 cups water
Salt to taste
1 cup pearl barley
2 strips bacon
⅓ cup julienned smoked ham
1 medium onion, finely chopped
1 package (10 ounces) frozen peas
2 tablespoons homemade chicken stock (see page 376) or canned broth
4 fresh sage leaves, minced, or ¼ teaspoon dried
½ teaspoon minced fresh marjoram leaves, or a pinch dried
Freshly ground black pepper to taste

1. Bring the water to a boil in a medium-size saucepan. Add salt and the barley, and simmer, uncovered, until just tender, 35 to 40 minutes. Drain.

2. Meanwhile, sauté the bacon in a large heavy skillet over medium heat until crisp. Drain on paper towels, leaving the fat in the skillet. Crumble and reserve the bacon.

3. Add the ham to the skillet. Sauté it until the edges are lightly browned, about 4 minutes. Transfer with a slotted spoon to a plate, and set aside.

4. Add the onion to the drippings in the skillet. Cook over medium heat 2 minutes. Add the frozen peas and cook, stirring constantly, until the peas are thawed, 2 to 3 minutes. Stir in the reserved ham and barley. Add the chicken stock, and cook over medium-low heat until warmed through. Stir in the sage and marjoram leaves, and season with salt and pepper to taste.

Serves 4 to 6

If you are of the impression that *barleycorn* is something to be gulped neat, or with a chaser of H_2O, you're only half right!

Though the name came to be synonymous with malt spirits over the years, a barleycorn (which is the seed of the barley plant) was once a standard measure of length. In the early 14th century, in fact, a royal fiat of the House of Tudor resolved: *All metric units be standardized as one inch being equal to three grains of barleycorn, laid end to end.*

The same decree also designated the running foot as being equal to 39 barleycorns, and the linear yard as being equal to 117 barleycorns. Presumably still end to end.

Curious as all that may seem, the next fact is even more bizarre: Barleycorn remained the basis of all metric calibration in Great Britain, and in America as well, for the next four hundred years. In 1888, when the U.S. shoe industry was first formally consolidated in Lynn, Massachusetts, a press statement announced that the established shoe size 13, or 39 barleycorns, would be the largest regularly manufactured last.

Apparently no allowance was made for any extremity that exceeded the limitation. But that's when the other barleycorn probably came into the picture: gulped neat, to ease aching feet!

STIR-FRIED BARLEY

*F*rom Stockton, California, not Shanghai. This Asian mixture was demonstrated for me at a TV studio, after a stove-top appearance on a local morning show a while back. Whole hulled barley in the wok gives this stir-fry a very different, nutty quality. But lightly toasted pearl barley (stirred over medium heat in a dry pan until golden prior to boiling) will approximate the bite. If you use pearl barley, omit the soaking step.

½ cup whole hulled barley
6 cups water
Salt to taste
1 tablespoon olive oil
1 large shallot, minced
½ teaspoon crushed dried hot red peppers
2 teaspoons unsalted butter
2 teaspoons chopped fresh basil, or ½ teaspoon dried
½ teaspoon tomato paste
Pinch of beef bouillon powder
Freshly ground black pepper to taste

1. Soak the barley overnight in 3 cups of water. Drain.

2. Bring the 6 cups water to a boil in a medium-size saucepan. Add salt to taste and the barley, and simmer, uncovered, until tender, about 1 hour. Drain, and set aside.

3. Heat the oil in a wok or large skillet over medium heat. Add the shallot and dried red peppers. Cook 2 minutes. Stir in the butter and the barley. Cook, tossing constantly, until warmed through. Stir in the basil, tomato paste, and bouillon powder. Cook 1 minute. Season with salt and pepper to taste.

Serves 4

BARLEY GOATEE

*F*rom Provence, France. A dish invented by an American friend turned into a thrifty French housewife by marriage. No mean chef, the lady devised this casserole without forethought—from only the barest ingredients in her minuscule refrigerator—when a guest from the U.S. (yours truly) arrived unexpectedly for lunch. The dish's name? Another improvisation, this one concocted after two bottles of local wine.

1½ cups water
Salt to taste
½ cup pearl barley
2½ tablespoons unsalted butter
1 medium onion, finely chopped
1 clove garlic, minced
2 tablespoons minced red bell pepper

¼ teaspoon crushed dried hot red peppers
3 egg whites
Pinch of salt
Pinch of sugar
1⅓ cups coarsely grated aged goat cheese
Freshly ground black pepper to taste

1. Bring the water to a boil in a

medium-size saucepan. Add salt to taste and the barley, and simmer, uncovered, until just tender, 35 to 40 minutes. Drain, and set aside.

2. Preheat the oven to 425°F.

3. Melt the butter in a medium-size skillet over medium-low heat. Add the onion; cook 1 minute. Add the garlic, red bell pepper, and dried red peppers; cook 4 minutes longer.

4. Add the barley to the skillet, tossing well to coat it with the onion mixture. Cook, stirring occasionally, 5 minutes. Transfer to a bowl.

5. In a large bowl, beat the egg whites with the salt until soft peaks form. Sprinkle with the sugar, and beat until stiff but not dry. Stir one third of the egg whites into the barley mixture. Then fold in the remaining whites. Fold in 1 cup of the goat cheese.

6. Spoon the mixture into a well-buttered shallow ovenproof casserole or pie plate. Sprinkle the top with the remaining ⅓ cup goat cheese, then sprinkle with black pepper. Bake until golden, 18 to 20 minutes.

Serves 4

GREEN BEAN AND BARLEY CAKES

*B*arley is a grain much prized as a green. In the Middle Ages the tender stalks were traditionally woven into bridal wreaths. Before that, in Rome, barley sprig motifs were common currency on ancient coins, and they appeared often as symbols of replenishment on Greek temple architecture. Why? Because barley never withers; as soon as one stalk is reaped another takes its place—literally evergreen. Speaking of which, have one of my favored barley alliances, wreathed in very green beans.

¼ pound string beans, trimmed
1 cup cooked pearl barley, chilled
1 tablespoon minced shallot
1 teaspoon minced jalapeño pepper
1 egg, lightly beaten
1 cup grated Monterey Jack cheese (about 4 ounces)
1 cup fresh bread crumbs
3 to 4 tablespoons vegetable oil
Salt and freshly ground black pepper to taste

1. Preheat the oven to 225°F.

2. Cook the string beans in boiling salted water until tender, 5 minutes. Drain, and set aside to cool. Then finely chop the beans.

3. In a large bowl, combine the beans with the barley, shallot, jalapeño pepper, egg, and cheese. Mix well.

4. Spread the bread crumbs on a plate. Scoop up 1 tablespoon of barley mixture and using your finger, push it from the spoon into the crumbs. Pat the crumbs into both sides of the cake. Transfer it to a plate, and repeat until you have used up all the barley mixture.

5. Heat 3 tablespoons oil in a large heavy skillet over medium-low heat. Sauté the barley cakes until golden brown and crisp, about 4 minutes per side. Keep them warm in the oven until all the cakes have been sautéed. (Add more oil to the skillet if needed.) Before serving, sprinkle the barley cakes with salt and pepper.

Serves 4

WILD MUSHROOM AND BARLEY RISOTTO

A switch on the familiar rice dish. Barley gives a slightly more chewy texture to risotto and should be served with nothing more than a leafy green salad.

2 tablespoons unsalted butter
1 teaspoon olive oil
¼ pound fresh shiitake, pleurotte, chanterelle, or oyster mushrooms (or any combination of wild mushrooms), sliced
1 large shallot, minced
1 small clove garlic, minced
⅓ cup dry white wine
½ cup pearl barley
3½ cups homemade chicken stock (see page 376) or canned broth, heated
Chopped fresh parsley, for garnish
Freshly grated Parmesan cheese (optional)

1. Melt 1 tablespoon of the butter with the oil in a large heavy skillet over medium-high heat. Add the mushrooms; cook, tossing constantly, until lightly browned, 4 minutes. Transfer to a bowl, using a slotted spoon, and set aside.

2. Reduce the heat under the skillet to low. Add the remaining 1 tablespoon butter and stir in the shallot; cook 1 minute. Add the garlic; cook 4 minutes longer. Stir in the wine, scraping the bottom and sides of the pan. Heat to boiling; boil until slightly syrupy, about 4 minutes. Reduce the heat to medium-low, add the barley and mushrooms, and stir until well coated with shallot mixture. Stir in 1 cup of the hot stock. Cook, stirring frequently, until all liquid has been absorbed, about 15 minutes. (If the liquid absorbs too quickly, reduce the heat.)

3. Stir in another cup of stock and continue to cook, stirring frequently, until all liquid has been absorbed, about 15 minutes.

4. Add another cup of stock and continue to cook, stirring frequently, until all liquid has been absorbed, about 15 minutes.

5. Add the remaining ½ cup of stock and continue to cook until the barley is tender and all liquid has been absorbed, about 15 minutes. Raise the heat slightly if the mixture is too wet. Sprinkle with parsley, and serve with Parmesan cheese if desired.

Serves 4

BARLEY DUMPLINGS

*F*irst cousin to Italian gnocchi rather than any American pot kin, the following snowy morsels are not only delectable but salubrious to one's well-being in the bargain. For the record—and putting the butter and cheese topping aside—a cupful of these dumplings is tabbed at less than 100 calories per serving! You can, by the way, literally put the butter and cheese aside and serve these dumplings with a tomato sauce.

1½ cups water
Salt
½ cup pearl barley
¼ teaspoon freshly ground black pepper
1 egg yolk
¼ teaspoon finely minced jalapeño pepper
½ cup grated Monterey Jack cheese
4 tablespoons freshly grated Parmesan
  cheese
1 cup all-purpose flour
2 extra-large egg whites
3 tablespoons unsalted butter, melted
Freshly grated Parmesan cheese, for garnish
  (optional)

1. Bring the water to a boil in a medium-size saucepan. Add salt to taste and the barley, and simmer, uncovered, until very tender, about 1 hour. Drain, and set aside to cool. Then cover and refrigerate the barley.

2. Preheat the oven to 375°F.

3. Place the chilled barley in the container of a food processor, and process until smooth. Add ¼ teaspoon salt, the pepper, egg yolk, jalapeño pepper, Monterey Jack cheese, and 3 tablespoons of the Parmesan cheese. Process briefly. Add ¼ cup of the flour and process until just mixed. Transfer the mixture to a large bowl.

4. Beat the egg whites until stiff but not dry. Fold them into the barley mixture. Fold in ¼ cup of the flour.

5. Place the remaining ½ cup flour in a shallow bowl. With a spoon (about 2 tablespoons in size), scoop up the barley dough and drop it into the flour, scraping the dough from the spoon with your finger. Lightly roll the dough in flour, and then transfer it to a plate. Repeat until you have used up all the dough.

6. Cook the dumplings, about six at a time, in a deep pot of boiling salted water, 1 minute. Remove the dumplings with a slotted spoon, and lightly drain them on paper towels. Transfer the cooked dumplings to a buttered baking dish that is large enough to hold them in a single layer. When all the dumplings have been cooked, drizzle them with the melted butter, and sprinkle with the remaining 1 tablespoon Parmesan cheese. Bake 20 minutes. Serve with extra Parmesan cheese, if desired.

Serves 4 to 6

ITALIAN-STYLE BARLEY TORTE

A dense fruited confection, this is dubbed "Italian-style" because it is based on a classic Venetian rice cake of similar texture and taste. Serve it with freshly whipped cream flavored with a dab of sour cream.

6 cups water

2 cups milk

¾ cup pearl barley

½ cup plus 2 tablespoons sugar

2 tablespoons fresh bread crumbs

2 jumbo eggs, separated

1 jumbo egg, lightly beaten

8 tablespoons (1 stick) unsalted butter, melted

¾ cup all-purpose flour

1 teaspoon baking powder

2 tablespoons hazelnut liqueur

½ teaspoon vanilla extract

2 dried pineapple slices, finely chopped

6 dried apricots, finely chopped (about ¼ cup)

1 teaspoon finely slivered orange zest

1 teaspoon finely slivered lemon zest

1 tablespoon unsalted butter, at room temperature

1. Heat the water and milk to boiling in a large pot. Stir in the barley. Reduce the heat and simmer, uncovered, stirring occasionally, 1 hour. Raise the heat slightly and stir until the mixture is thickened and creamy. Remove the pot from the heat, and immediately stir in the ½ cup sugar. Let the mixture stand 10 minutes, then transfer it to a large bowl.

2. Preheat the oven to 375°F.

3. Butter a 10-inch glass or ceramic quiche dish, and dust it with bread crumbs. In a small bowl, beat the egg yolks with the whole egg, and stir this into the barley mixture. Add the melted butter, flour, baking powder, hazelnut liqueur, vanilla, pineapple, apricots, and orange and lemon zests. Mix well.

4. Beat the egg whites until stiff but not dry. Fold them into the barley mixture.

5. Pour the barley mixture evenly into the prepared quiche dish. Sprinkle the top with the 2 tablespoons sugar, and dot with the 1 tablespoon butter. Bake until slightly puffed and firm to the touch, about 40 minutes. Serve slightly warm.

Serves 8

THE FLOURING OF THE GRAIN

Barley flour has been used in bread making since ancient times. Early on, it was recognized as a high-energy, low-fat ingredient—generally turned into somewhat dense, chewy flatbreads that were not only filling for the workers in the fields, but just as important, kept almost indefinitely.

Today, barley flour is used mainly as a flavoring agent. Slightly sweet, with a mild malty undertaste, it gives new dimensions to old standbys, adding moisture to a dish along the way. However, since barley flour is very low in gluten, it must be mixed with a high-protein wheat flour for use in baking. A general rule of thumb is to substitute ½ cup of barley flour for an equal amount of whole-wheat or bread flour in any of your favorite bread recipes. You will have a healthier, more flavorful loaf of bread as a result.

Barley flour is generally made from ground whole hulled barley, which is then sieved to remove the tough outer shell.

BARLEY SCOTCH EGGS

Barley flour, when used instead of wheat flour or bread crumbs in the sausage coating for Scotch eggs, keeps the mixture from drying out. These eggs may be served hot or at room temperature as an appetizer or party fare.

¾ pound country-style sausage meat
6 tablespoons barley flour
4 hard-cooked eggs, peeled and halved
    lengthwise
1 egg, lightly beaten
½ teaspoon salt
½ teaspoon freshly ground black pepper
Oil for deep-frying

1. Place the sausage meat in a medium-size bowl. Add 2 tablespoons of the flour; mix thoroughly. Place the sausage between two sheets of wax paper, and roll it out until it is about ⅛ inch thick. Remove the top layer of wax paper, and using a sharp knife, cut the sausage into eight sections (without cutting through the bottom layer of wax paper).

2. Place 2 more tablespoons of the flour in a bowl. Dip each cooked egg half in the beaten egg, and then roll it in the flour. Place each egg half on a sausage section, and roll the sausage around the egg, pressing the edges together to seal it tightly.

3. Heat about 3 inches of oil in a small heavy saucepan until it is hot but not smoking.

4. Place the remaining 2 tablespoons flour in a bowl. Add the salt and pepper; mix well. Roll the sausage-coated eggs in the seasoned flour, and deep-fry (about four at a time) in the hot oil until crisp, about 2 minutes. Drain on paper towels.

Serves 4

BARLEY FLATBREAD

The Scots have their scones, the Welsh their *haidd*. This version of the Welsh bread is best served straight from the oven and slathered with butter and/or honey. The bread mixture is more like a thick crepe batter than dough. I make it in a 12-inch non-stick pizza pan. Leftovers may be toasted and served for breakfast the next day.

3 tablespoons olive oil
1 medium onion, chopped
1 clove garlic, minced
¼ teaspoon crushed dried hot red peppers
1½ cups barley flour
1¼ cups milk
¼ cup water
1 tablespoon sugar
½ teaspoon salt

1. Place an oven rack in the upper third of the oven. Preheat the oven to 500°F.

2. Heat 1 tablespoon of the oil in a medium-size skillet over medium heat. Add the onion; cook 1 minute. Add the garlic and dried red peppers; cook, stirring often, until dark golden, about 5 minutes. Remove the skillet from the heat.

3. Place the barley flour in the container of a food processor. Add the milk, water, sugar, salt, and the remaining 2 tablespoons oil. Process until smooth.

Combine this with the onion mixture, and pour into a well-buttered 12-inch non-stick pizza pan. Bake for 15 minutes. Cut into wedges and serve immediately.

Serves 4 to 6

JULIE SAHNI'S GARLIC-DILL BREAD

*T*he favorite bread of the Patels, a Hindu sect in the Indian state of Gujarat, these skillet flatbreads go perfectly with diced or shredded spicy lamb, pork, or chicken dishes. Adapted from Julie Sahni's remarkable tome, *Classic Indian Vegetarian and Grain Cooking*, the breads may be served buttered, warm from the pan. Or to enhance the flavor even further, use tongs to pass the breads over a gas flame for 8 to 10 seconds before they go to table. The breads will crisp and puff up.

1 boiling potato (6 ounces)
1 hot green pepper, seeded, deveined, and finely minced
1 large clove garlic, crushed
2½ tablespoons vegetable oil
½ teaspoon salt
2 tablespoons chopped fresh dill
¾ cup barley flour
½ cup all-purpose flour

1. Cook the potato in boiling salted water to cover until tender, about 20 minutes. Drain.

2. While the potato is still hot, peel it, and mash it until smooth. Add the hot green pepper and garlic. Let the potato mixture stand until cool.

3. Add the oil, salt, and dill to the potato mixture. Stir in the barley flour, and then work in the all-purpose flour to form a soft dough. Transfer to a lightly floured surface, and knead for 2 minutes. Divide the dough in half, and roll each half into a rope 6 inches long. Cut each rope into six pieces. Form each piece of dough into a ball, and roll it out with a

floured rolling pin to form a 6-inch round. Stack the dough rounds between layers of paper towels as you roll them out.

4. Heat an oil-rubbed cast-iron skillet over high heat for 3 minutes. Reduce the heat to medium, and place one round of dough in the skillet. Cook until the underside is spotted, 1 minute. Remove the bread from the skillet with a spatula. Continue with the remaining rounds. Stack the breads between layers of paper towels as you cook them. Reheat (in the paper towels) in a 175°F oven (if your oven isn't reliable this low, heat to 225°F and watch the breads closely) for 10 minutes before serving.

5. Serve the Garlic-Dill Bread wrapped in a warm towel, in a large bowl or basket. Each person fills a bread with whatever dish it is accompanying and rolls it up like a tortilla.

Makes 12 small flatbreads; serves 4 or 6

SCOTCH BARLEY STOVE-TOP SCONES

*B*arley breads, in the form of scones or bannocks (large rounds), have been made in Scotland for centuries. These moist, cakey quick breads are the perfect foil for a "rasher of bacon" with eggs—or even a steaming hot bowl of cock-a-leekie soup. The following scones are not as thick as traditional ones, so be prepared—they disappear twice as fast!

½ cup raisins
2 tablespoons unsalted butter, melted
1 cup barley flour
1 cup bread flour
¼ teaspoon salt
½ teaspoon baking soda
1 teaspoon cream of tartar
¼ cup maple syrup
1 egg, lightly beaten
⅔ to ¾ cup milk

1. Place the raisins in a small bowl. Pour the melted butter over them, and let stand until softened, about 10 minutes.

2. Combine the barley flour, bread flour, salt, baking soda, and cream of tartar in a medium-size bowl. Mix well, and stir in the maple syrup, egg, and just enough of the milk to make a very thick batter. Stir in the raisin/butter mixture.

3. Heat a greased cast-iron skillet or griddle over medium heat. When it is hot, spoon the batter, 1 large tablespoon for each scone, into the skillet. Cook (three or four at a time) until golden on both sides and puffed up, 3 to 4 minutes per side. Keep warm in a 225°F oven while cooking the remaining scones.

Makes 16 scones

*H*ere is another barley legend. The fable concerns Christopher Columbus. After discovering the New World and taking corn kernels back to Spain as a legacy of his journey, he resolved to return the favor—by bringing wheat and barley from the crowded European fields to the open spaces of "the Indies."

But neither bounty impressed the natives as much as the fancy pantaloons, colored parasols, and assorted bangles that were also part of his cargo. Of a consequence, the bales of wheat from the ship's hold withered and dried on the shore. The barley grains, however, had a somewhat more felicitous fate. Part of the cereal blew into the mountains, where it flourished untended for a hundred years or longer—until some intrepid islander finally cracked a kernel between his teeth, and promptly added it to his rice pot. Another part of the barley floated out to sea on the tide along with Columbus's departing vessels. It did *not* take root in the water, but it certainly fattened Caribbean shrimp and crab to incredible dimensions from that day forward.

At least, that's how the story was told to me.

BARLEY FRUITCAKE

Barley flour, added to fruitcake, adds moisture and density to the cake that reportedly allows it to last (tightly wrapped, that is) for years. I have never tried it, but can attest that a fruitcake made in September is at its prime served in December.

2 pounds fruit (about 4 cups):
¼ pound dried cherries
¼ pound dates
¼ pound dried figs
9 ounces raisins
1 package (11 ounces) mixed dried
*　　fruits*
1 cup (2 sticks) unsalted butter, at room
*　　temperature*
1 cup sugar
1 teaspoon vanilla extract
1 teaspoon finely slivered orange zest
5 eggs
½ cup sherry
1½ cups all-purpose flour
½ cup barley flour
½ teaspoon salt
1 cup chopped walnuts
1 cup chopped pecans
¼ cup fresh orange juice
¼ cup Grand Marnier

1. Preheat the oven to 300°F.

2. Pit any fruits that require it. Finely chop all the fruits and combine them in a bowl.

3. In the large bowl of an electric mixer, beat the butter until light. Slowly beat in the sugar; beat until light and fluffy. Beat in the vanilla and orange zest. Add the eggs, one at a time, beating thoroughly after each addition. Slowly beat in the sherry.

4. Sift the all-purpose flour with the barley flour and salt into a bowl. Slowly stir into the cake batter. Stir in the chopped fruits and the nuts.

5. Spoon the batter into a buttered and floured 10-inch tube pan. Bake until a toothpick inserted in the center comes out clean, about 1½ hours. Cool in the pan on a rack for 10 minutes.

6. Combine the orange juice with the Grand Marnier. Lightly prick the top of the cake, and spoon the liquid over the surface. Remove the cake from the pan. Cool thoroughly, and store in an airtight container for at least 1 month before serving.

Serves 10 to 12

BRAN
Not Just Wheat but Oat Bran, Too

I met my first authentic bran lover (a madcap heiress) when I was twenty-three. She was considerably older, no great beauty, and tightfisted into the bargain. And not, even by the kind light of memory, typical of what I had been led to expect (from the movies) as a high-spirited, freewheeling prototype of the rich. In real life, the rich seemed petty, imperious, and wholly self-concerned. Still, I was utterly transfixed by them.

My madcap heiress was Peggy Guggenheim, who, as she announced in a somewhat breathy anglicized voice, was "between husbands and lovers and in New York City for the duration."

It was the close of World War II when we met. Peggy, then in her late forties, was running Art of This Century, a celebrated gallery of surrealist art, during the day and collecting material for her memoirs, *Out of This Century*, at night. I confess that I longed to be considered worthy of a paragraph (or at least a sentence) in her romantic chronicles.

It is important to state at the outset that I was highly impressionable at the time. And that the fabled Guggenheim hauteur affected me the way a magnet agitates base metal. I was drawn to her at first sight. I called her every day, sent flowers often, and flagrantly spent my first hard-earned paychecks taking her to restaurants far beyond my means—hostelries where she most often caused consternation, not only because of her curious dress code (bobby sox, sneakers, and sable) but also because of her bad manners, vilifying the waiters and busboys who danced attendance upon her as "blackguards and ne'er-do-wells willing to be seduced by tips"!

I remember Peggy best barefoot (because her shoes hurt) in a posh French restaurant, despotically waving away the wine steward with a command to bring us "*vin ordinaire*, if you please! We want to drink only what you drink in the kitchen!" And in an aside, assuring me that the wine cooks drink is infinitely superior to a *grand cru*!

When the wine was served (in water glasses), it was, I would have sworn, pure red vinegar. But Peggy delightedly drank four glasses to prove her point.

Peggy's food habits were erratic at best. The only serious meal she ate every day was what she called a "nursery breakfast," taken at about four in the afternoon, composed of a soft-boiled egg, tea with lots of milk, and muffins (bran muffins) slathered with butter and honey or jam.

She would very often eat this meal in her fabulous art gallery with myriad Jackson Pollock paintings on its curving walls, seated at a desk near the entrance, collecting admissions as she chewed a muffin. In those days, no art gallery in New York charged an entrance fee. But Peggy was adamant on the subject. "If they come here to laugh," she said, "Let 'em pay an amusement tax!"

She imposed the tariff of one dollar per person, making change herself. There was no need for her to do this—any one of her employees could have done it for her. But Peggy explained, with a little sigh, that making money reminded her of her grandfather.

My involvement with Peggy was short and sweet, terminated by mutual disinterest and her decision to leave America once the armistice was signed, to open a new gallery in Venice—Palazzo Venier dei Leoni.

Before she left, she undertook to give me a birthday present. I was informed, by one of her aides at the gallery, that she contemplated bestowing upon me a large Jackson Pollock painting. Horrified, for I never truly appreciated Pollock's style (and he was far from famous at the time), I suggested that a dozen oxford-cloth Brooks Brothers shirts would be more appreciated. A gift I duly received on October 16.

When Peggy's departure date drew near, I wanted to reciprocate. I toyed with the idea of some small trinket she might consider wearing (for her taste in jewelry was highly erratic too), and though I browsed for hours at Cartier, nothing seemed appropriate or, parenthetically, affordable.

Through the same go-between who had alerted me to the possibility of the Pollock painting came a suggestion: "Peggy says it will be a long journey. The *Ile de France* is only recently returned to passenger service, and the food will be execrable. Could you manage to find her a dozen bran muffins for nursery breakfast?"

In an act of supreme sacrifice (for rationing was still on), I borrowed all the coupons for butter and sugar I could. For two days, I baked batches of bran muffins: with raisins, with nuts, with bananas, with dates. There were six dozen in all, wrapped in cardboard cartons that usually housed champagne.

Peggy gave me a decidedly platonic kiss at the gangplank, as she whispered in my ear, "Your muffins are di-vine, darling. But in the future, never add *fruit* of any kind. Lilies were not meant to be gilded!"

The Grain's Genesis

By and large, trenchermen are not neutral on the subject of bran. They either love or loathe it out of hand, despite any benefit this so-called miracle fiber has for a body's well-being.

The truth of the matter is, for centuries the only real bran eaters were slaves and assorted serfs, peasants of one sort or another whose diet was composed of everything their betters considered unfit for civilized human consumption. As a result, the underdogs in history flourished while the honchos waxed and ultimately waned, victims of overrefinement at the fork end which may be traced directly to a lack of roughage (bran) in their diet.

To set the issue straight, bran is neither a cereal nor a grain. It is the tough outermost covering of a seed. Any seed. The ancients called bran "chaff" and gave it short shrift in the Bible, where wheat chaff is compared to "the ungodly who the wind driveth away."

That's a bad rap for any dish, and it took bran almost two thousand years (and the aid of a latter-day prophet, Dr. Sylvester Graham) to clear its reputation and achieve a new and squeaky clean image: life preserver on a plate!

The late Dr. Graham (whose name graces my favorite wheaten cracker) was one of a quirky band of 19th-century food crusaders who railed against the bad eating habits of the American bourgeoisie—in particular the middle-class penchant for soft white bread (which was proof of status to anyone in the New World whose forefathers had subsisted on loaves of a darker hue in the old one). Graham was an advocate of wheat bran in the diet: at least once a day was his prescription. Because, he maintained, as bran is composed of almost wholly indigestible cellulose, a cupful could sweep the system free of waste in just three hours.

Graham was such a successful evangelist for fiber that he terrified his constipated countrymen into a total change of eating habits within two decades. By the time of his death in the 1920s, over half the households in the U.S. had eschewed the notion of a hearty breakfast with a capital B (syrup-drenched flapjacks or sizzling rashers of bacon with eggs) for a healthier one—cereal in a bowl with a lower-case b (for bran) added. Though it must be told, it was often added in far less than the hoped-for cathartic doses. But for better or worse, fiber had entered the American diet at last!

Some Plain Grain Talk

The word "bran" springs from the Middle French or older Gaulish word *brenno*, which means "unattested." Earlier the Celts had another word for it, *bren*, which they used to describe broken or split coats of armor. It makes sense if one realizes that bran, in edible form, stems from a split outer cover.

The bran overcoat is well insulated. It is made of six protective layers of primarily noncaloric dietary fiber, notably vitamin B, vitamin B_6, niacin, pantothenic acid, riboflavin, and thiamine. Everything, in fact, alleged to keep us in tip-top shape.

However, dietary fiber is a complex substance. As bran is essentially composed of bulk, the human body—even with its complex enzyme system—cannot digest more than a fraction of the

amount it consumes. Most of the bulk, therefore, is "passed through" undigested.

For years we have known that this unassimilated bulk has a proven value in relieving constipation and preventing any diverticular-type diseases that develop in weak areas of the intestines. But according to Cornell University's recent scientific studies on the subject, dietary fiber may also have a tonic effect in regulating serum cholesterol and in lowering blood sugar levels for diabetics. Some studies (the research is ongoing) lean toward the notion that high fiber consumption may offer protection against cancer of the colon and rectum. And, on a less threatening note, promote healthy weight loss too!

The Health Handle

*B*ran's earliest appearance at the American table was in a cereal bowl. After Dr. Graham's passionate philippics on the subject, it was introduced to the home (packaged by the Kellogg Company) in 1916. Nowadays, it is still a best-seller, though not necessarily consigned to breakfast food alone.

Most bran sold in the U.S. today is made of wheat. That is *processed* ("refined") *wheat bran*—the outer covering, separated from the germ and endosperm of the kernel, milled, toasted, and in some instances cooked under high pressure for a greater degree of "chewability." Flavorings as well as sugar, salt, and replacement vitamins are added. *Unprocessed wheat bran* is essentially a raw ingredient of little savor outside a muffin! *Unprocessed oat bran* has of late begun to appear on supermarket shelves (packaged by Quaker) as an alternative to unprocessed wheat bran.

Processed and unprocessed bran differ remarkably as to flavor, crunch, and degree of dietary fiber. For instance, a cupful of Bran Flakes cereal may in actuality contain only 6.5 grams of crude dietary fiber, while a like portion of untreated unprocessed bran will contain twice that amount, 13 grams. A cupful of unprocessed oat bran, on the other hand, is conspicuously low in crude fiber (1.5 grams), but bulk is not its particular virtue in terms of health.

Which bran type is most therapeutic? That's a loaded question—much depending upon one's physical condition and need. For while large portions of insoluble, unprocessed wheat bran indubitably have a tonic effect on the alimentary canal, nutritionists claim it is water-soluble oat bran that effectively reduces blood levels of LDL cholesterol.

In my opinion, it is the sensible combination of both brans in processed and unprocessed forms (sometimes mixed but more often used singly) that gives the cook the option of adding dietary fiber to most dishes without advertising any therapeutic motive at the dining-room table!

How to Buy It

*U*nprocessed *bran* until very recently could be purchased only at health food stores. Today, however, it is possible to buy it in supermarkets as well, packaged (by Quaker) in 8-ounce cartons that are conspicuously emblazoned: "For adding Fiber to Baked Goods, Breads, Toppings & More."

Among *processed brans*, All-Bran is a top choice. Cooked under steam pressure, then baked in a low oven to reduce moisture, this shredded cereal is a trial to chew, but it combines felicitously with other flours and nuts when it is cooked or baked. All-Bran contains approximately 9 grams of dietary fiber in every serving. Bran Buds, while similarly processed, is extruded and cut into nugget-size fragments that may easily be converted to coarse flour or crumbs in a food processor. However, a package of

Bran Buds does have a higher sugar content and a slightly lower endowment of dietary fiber, about 8 grams per serving. For the record, most crispy (wheat) bran flake cereals contain a mere 4 grams of dietary fiber per serving.

Oat bran (Quaker's product), packaged in 16-ounce cartons and promoted as a "Creamy High-Fiber Cereal" with no salt, no sugar added, contains a slim 0.5 grams crude fiber per ounce.

As a yardstick for the health-concerned, it might be worth noting that fruits and vegetables usually contain between 0.4 and 6.0 grams of dietary fiber per serving. A loaf of whole wheat bread contains a good deal less than 2 grams per slice.

Bran is a grain with a reasonable shelf life, as long as the package is well sealed and moisture free. Exposed bran (like most cereals) proves a hospitable breeding ground for ants and maggots. If you live in a damp climate, it is a good idea to store an open carton in a self-seal plastic bag in the freezer to inhibit any insect population rise. I keep unprocessed bran in the pantry, packed into a quart canning jar with an airtight screw-top lid, and store open cartons of processed bran in several layers of sealed self-lock storage bags.

If you are not a heavy bran user, it's a good idea to inscribe the date of purchase on the package with a felt-tip pen.

Bran often loses its bonus of minerals and vitamins after one year's time.

How to Cook It

*T*here is no hard and fast rule for cooking with bran, but there *are* ways of varying its anonymous flavor and somewhat fibrous texture.

To enhance the taste of unprocessed bran, consider toasting it in a medium-hot heavy skillet, stirring often until the mixture takes on a decided amber-to-brown hue.

Preheating processed bran in a warm (300° F) oven for 10 to 15 minutes will likewise give it a stronger flavor and more toothsome bite.

It is important to note that both unprocessed and processed bran may be ground to a variety of textures, from a flour-like powder to rough crumbs, in a food processor or blender.

Bran makes an admirable substitute for bread crumbs in most recipes, and mixing crushed bran crumbs with sugar and a modicum of butter will provide a delicately nutty flavored topping for cakes and pastries. Unprocessed oat bran, substituted for a portion of wheat bran in baking recipes, will produce moister, decidedly more silken hot breads, pancakes, and cookies.

To my mind, bran's most durable and beloved guise is the muffin.

HI-FI MEATLOAF

*T*he acronym stands for high fiber as much as culinary high fidelity. This recipe (supplemented with All-Bran cereal) is the most succulent loaf I think I have ever sampled—and I've sampled a goodly number in my time.

¾ cup All-Bran cereal
2 teaspoons unsalted butter
1½ pounds ground beef
¾ pound ground veal
¼ pound ground pork
2 shallots, minced
1 large canned green chile, minced
1 egg, lightly beaten
⅛ teaspoon dried thyme
1 tablespoon minced fresh parsley
Dash of hot pepper sauce
½ cup homemade chicken stock (see page 376) or canned broth
½ teaspoon salt
¼ teaspoon freshly ground black pepper
2 teaspoons Dijon mustard
2 tablespoons chili sauce
2 strips bacon
Chopped fresh parsley, for garnish

1. Preheat the oven to 375°F.

2. Place the All-Bran in the container of a food processor and process until it has the texture of coarse crumbs.

3. Melt the butter in a heavy skillet over medium heat. Stir in the bran. Cook, stirring constantly, 2 minutes.

4. Transfer the bran to a bowl, and add all the ingredients through the black pepper. Mix thoroughly and form into a loaf on a shallow baking dish.

5. Combine the mustard and chili sauce in a small bowl. Mix well and spread over the top and sides of the meat loaf. Lay the bacon strips over the top. Bake 1 hour and 15 minutes. Sprinkle with extra parsley before serving.

Serves 6 to 8

BRAN-NEW OVEN-FRIED CHICKEN

*U*nprocessed bran is prominent in the crisp and crackling upholstery of this baked bird. So delicious, it gives health food a new image! Warning: this dish is hot. If you're timid, reduce the amount of hot pepper sauce to 1 teaspoon.

1 large chicken (about 4 pounds), cut into serving pieces
2 cups buttermilk
⅛ teaspoon crushed whole allspice
2 teaspoons hot pepper sauce
1 tablespoon soy sauce
1 teaspoon salt
4 tablespoons (½ stick) unsalted butter
½ cup plus 2 tablespoons homemade chicken stock (see page 376) or canned broth

6 tablespoons unprocessed wheat bran
¼ teaspoon freshly ground black pepper
¼ teaspoon freshly grated nutmeg
1 tablespoon all-purpose flour

1. Place the chicken pieces in a large bowl. Combine the buttermilk, allspice, hot pepper sauce, soy sauce, and salt in another bowl, and pour the mixture over the chicken. Cover, and refrigerate overnight.

2. About 2 hours before serving, place the chicken in a colander and let it stand until well drained. Reserve the buttermilk mixture.

3. Preheat the oven to 375°F.

4. Heat the butter with the ½ cup chicken stock in a small saucepan. Keep warm.

5. Place the bran in the container of a food processor and process until fairly smooth. Transfer to a paper bag and add the pepper and nutmeg. Shake to mix well.

6. Pat the chicken pieces dry with paper towels, and add them to the bag with the bran mixture. Shake the bag well to coat the pieces evenly.

7. Place the chicken pieces, skin side down, on a rack covering a roasting pan. Bake, basting every 5 minutes with the butter-stock mixture, 30 minutes. Turn the chicken over and continue to bake, basting every 5 minutes with the pan juices, until the coating is crisp and the juices run yellow when the meat is pricked with a fork, about 30 minutes longer. Transfer the chicken pieces to an ovenproof platter and keep warm in a 225°F oven.

8. Place the roasting pan over medium-low heat. Add the flour. Cook, stirring constantly, 2 minutes. Whisk in the reserved buttermilk in three additions, scraping the sides and bottom of the pan. Stir in the 2 tablespoons chicken stock and cook until slightly thickened, about 4 minutes. Pass the gravy with the chicken.

Serves 4

BRANNED BITKI

I never ate bran in any form whatsoever in the Soviet Union, but *bitki* (tiny highly seasoned fried meat cakes) appeared in one guise or another at almost every meal I consumed there. My favorite version, spiked with unprocessed bran, is a domestic translation.

½ cup unprocessed wheat bran
½ cup fresh bread crumbs
1¼ pounds ground veal
¼ pound cooked ham, ground
¼ cup milk
1 onion, finely chopped
1 clove garlic, minced
½ teaspoon caraway seeds
3 tablespoons chopped fresh dill
1 teaspoon chopped fresh parsley
1 egg, lightly beaten
3 tablespoons unsalted butter
1 teaspoon oil
2 teaspoons all-purpose flour
1 cup homemade chicken stock (see page
    376) or canned broth

1 cup sour cream, at room temperature
¼ teaspoon freshly grated nutmeg

1. Combine the bran and bread crumbs in a large bowl. Mix well and transfer half the mixture to a large plate.

2. To the mixture in the bowl, add the veal, ham, milk, onion, garlic, caraway, 1 tablespoon of the dill, parsley, and egg. Mix thoroughly and shape into 1½-inch balls. Using the palm of your hand, flatten them slightly into cakes. Press the cakes into the remaining bran-crumb mixture to coat on both sides.

3. Heat 2 tablespoons of the butter with the oil in a 9- or 10-inch non-stick

skillet over medium heat. Sauté the meat cakes in two or three batches until golden brown on both sides, adding more butter if needed. Transfer to a plate.

4. In the same pan, melt the remaining 1 tablespoon butter over medium-low heat. Stir in the flour. Cook, stirring constantly, 2 minutes. Whisk in the chicken stock, scraping up any meat cake crumbs that remain on the sides and bottom of the pan. Heat to boiling. Reduce the heat and simmer 2 minutes. Transfer the mixture to a 2-quart saucepan. Whisk in the sour cream and cook over medium-low heat 2 minutes. Add the nutmeg, 1 tablespoon of the dill, and the meat patties. Cook over low heat until the patties are warmed through, about 10 minutes. Sprinkle with the remaining 1 tablespoon dill.

Serves 4 to 6

F ifty years ago in the "sticks," as the nether parts of New York City were known, the brans most denizens ate were made by a company called Dugan's, which hand-delivered the product to one's door daily. That these cakes were made in factory ovens was somewhat dispiriting to a generation of home bakers, but the fresh taste (and convenience) shortly won over the most doubtful Thomases on the turf— including my highly prejudiced grandmother.

Dugan's (the name emblazoned in a dark blue cursive script on every carton) soon became as familiar a symbol in Queens as the American flag or the Empire State Building looming on the horizon. And no breakfast table was laid nor coffee percolator placed on a stove until the familiar thump-whinny-stamp-of-hooves down the block announced the presence of "The Dugan Man" with his horse and cache of still-warm baked goods.

They were prodigious muffins: raisined or plain, baked in fluted paper nests, with a perfume more intoxicating than attar of roses. And a flavor so irresistible that a true muffin addict (like me) could chomp down three before any other family member tucked a napkin into place.

When I began to cook out of necessity during the Depression, my first serious ambition at the stove was to bake. Specifically, bran muffins. Because, I reasoned, it would save our budget a serious weekly outlay. I was ten years old and a dollar seemed a fortune in those days.

My mother and grandmother were somewhat skeptical about this aspiration, and less than enthusiastic after tasting the results.

"Why is it man's nature to tamper with perfection?" I recall my grandmother asking rhetorically as she took an initial bite. My mother's observation was more direct.

"Some have a knack for cooking. Others bake well. Don't push your luck!"

Needless to say, I gave up the idea of ever producing a bran muffin again— until many years later when attrition or fickle public taste forced Dugan's to shutter their doors. Then I spent a month at the oven, baking brans day after day. Whether I mastered the art or not is a matter of conjecture. You will simply have to decide for yourself. (Muffin recipes begin on page 39.)

BRAN-HERBED WEAKFISH

Bran and seafood are highly compatible partners. For evidence, have the next rendering blanketed in herbed bran crumbs. Serve with an amendment of tartar sauce.

1 cup Bran Flakes cereal, ground fine in a food processor
½ cup fresh bread crumbs
1 tablespoon finely chopped fresh basil, or 1 teaspoon dried
1 tablespoon minced fresh parsley
¼ cup all-purpose flour
⅓ cup milk
1½ pounds weakfish (sea trout) or other white fish, cut into serving pieces
1½ tablespoons unsalted butter
2 to 3 tablespoons vegetable oil
2 tablespoons malt vinegar
Chopped fresh parsley, for garnish
Tartar Sauce (see facing page)

1. Preheat the oven to 400°F.
2. Combine the ground Bran Flakes with the bread crumbs, basil, and parsley in a shallow bowl. Place the flour on a plate. Place the milk in another shallow bowl.

3. Pat the fish dry with paper towels. Dip the fish first in flour, shaking off the excess, then in milk, and finally in the bran mixture. Place on a plate.

4. Heat 1 tablespoon of the butter with 2 tablespoons of the oil in a large skillet over medium heat. Sauté the fish, a few pieces at a time, adding more butter and oil as needed, until golden, about 3 minutes per side. Transfer to an ovenproof platter and bake 10 minutes. Sprinkle with the vinegar and parsley, and serve with Tartar Sauce.

Serves 4

BRAN-BATTERED FISH AND SHRIMP

This batter of unprocessed bran and beer is best served up accompanied by malt vinegar. A sprinkling on the crispy hot fish and you've got perfection.

½ cup unprocessed wheat bran
½ cup cake flour
2 teaspoons English dry mustard
¼ teaspoon freshly grated nutmeg
½ teaspoon salt
1 cup beer
4 eggs, separated
2 teaspoons Dijon mustard
1½ pounds fish filets (flounder, sole, fluke), quartered
1 pound shrimp, shelled and deveined

¼ cup fresh lemon juice
⅓ cup all-purpose flour (approximately)
Vegetable oil for frying
Malt vinegar
Lemon wedges
Tartar Sauce (recipe follows)

1. Place the bran in the container of a food processor and process 30 seconds. Add the cake flour; process 10 seconds. Add the dry mustard, nutmeg, and salt.

Process briefly, and then add the beer, egg yolks, and Dijon mustard. Process until smooth. (If you do not have a food processor, place the bran in a blender container and blend until fairly smooth, about 30 seconds. Transfer to a bowl, and stir in the remaining batter ingredients.) Transfer to a bowl and refrigerate, covered, 8 hours.

2. Sprinkle the fish filets and shrimp with the lemon juice; let stand 30 minutes.

3. Drain the fish and shrimp. Pat them dry with paper towels and dust lightly with the all-purpose flour.

4. Beat the egg whites until stiff; fold them into the batter.

5. Heat about 1 inch of oil in a heavy skillet until very hot. Dip the fish into the batter, and then fry in the hot oil, about 5 pieces at a time, until golden brown on both sides, 2 to 3 minutes per side. Drain the cooked pieces on paper towels, then transfer them to a heatproof platter and keep warm in a 225°F oven while frying the remaining fish. When the fish is cooked, fry the shrimp, about 1½ minutes per side. Drain the shrimp on paper towels and add to the platter with the fish. Serve with malt vinegar, lemon wedges, and Tartar Sauce.

Serves 4

Tartar Sauce

1 cup mayonnaise, preferably homemade
    (see page 379)
½ cup sour cream
½ teaspoon Dijon mustard
1 small shallot, minced
3 small sour gherkins or cornichons, finely
    chopped
1 teaspoon finely chopped fresh parsley
1 tablespoon chopped fresh dill
¼ teaspoon fresh lemon juice
1 teaspoon Pernod liqueur
Salt and freshly ground black pepper to
    taste

SOME BRAN TRIVIA

Back in the 18th century, no American of sensibility even remotely considered the idea of *eating* bran. Nonetheless, the cereal held a conspicuous corner in every townsman's household. Reticules filled with bran, dried flowers, and herbs (or pine needles if the homeowner was poor) scented linen presses, hope chests, and high- and lowboys throughout the thirteen colonies. In the scullery, bran husks were sprinkled on live coals to bank fires, and were used with sand to scour pot bottoms blackened by cooking!

Bran surfaced even more artfully in the American West a hundred years after. At "bran dances" held in barns, country stores, and even open fields, the floor was covered with a thick carpet of "wagon dust" (dried wheat bran). The bran was always raked at least 3 or 4 inches deep and well dampened before the pioneer folk attempted to try out the shoe leather.

Bran dances vanished before the end of the century, when worldliness hit the Chisholm Trail and dance halls replaced church socials and "caledonians." There are, however, some notable accounts of these rustic jollifications in diaries and dance cards of the day. According to one partner's early account: "A bran-nied pasture is right pleasant to reel or schottische upon at first. But heaven preserve us if it is danced *dry*! Sneezes and wheezes for hours afterward!"

Whisk the mayonnaise with the sour cream in a medium-size bowl. Whisk in the remaining ingredients. Refrigerate, covered, until ready to serve.

Makes about 1½ cups

EGGPLANT CANNOLI

Cannoli are calorie-rich Italian pastries. My branned version borrows little of the original except great taste, name, and shape. Serve it as a first course.

1 large eggplant (about 1¼ pounds), cut
    into ¼-inch-thick slices
Salt
⅓ cup all-purpose flour
⅔ cup unprocessed wheat bran
2 eggs
1 teaspoon water
3 tablespoons olive oil
2 tablespoons peanut oil
1 clove garlic, unpeeled
⅓ cup diced Italian hard salami
3 tablespoons chopped fresh parsley
3 tablespoons freshly grated Parmesan
    cheese
1½ cups ricotta cheese
Freshly ground black pepper to taste
Chile-Flecked Tomato Sauce (recipe
    follows), warmed
Chopped fresh parsley, for garnish

1. Place the eggplant slices in a colander, and sprinkle them generously with salt. Let stand 30 minutes. Brush off the salt with damp paper towels.

2. Place the flour and the bran in the container of a food processor or blender. Process 1 minute. Transfer to a plate.

3. Beat the eggs with the water in a shallow bowl. Dip the eggplant slices into this mixture, shaking off any excess, and then dip into the flour-bran mixture. Transfer to a large plate.

4. Combine the oils in a small bowl and heat half the mixture in a large heavy skillet over medium heat. Sauté the eggplant slices, a few at a time, adding more oil as needed, until golden brown on both sides, 2 to 3 minutes per side. Drain the cooked eggplant on paper towels. When half the eggplant is done, place the garlic clove at one edge of the pan, and continue cooking the egg-

plant. Remove the garlic when it is well browned and set it aside to cool.

5. Preheat the oven to 400°F.

6. Peel and mince the cooked garlic. Place it in a medium-size bowl and add the salami, parsley, Parmesan, and ricotta. Mix well and season with salt and pepper.

7. Place about 1½ teaspoons filling mixture down the center of each eggplant slice. Roll them up like cannoli, secure the tops with wooden toothpicks, and place them snugly together in a baking dish. Bake 12 to 15 minutes. Remove the toothpicks, drizzle with the tomato sauce, and sprinkle with parsley.

Serves 6 to 8

Chile-Flecked Tomato Sauce

1 tablespoon unsalted butter
1 tablespoon olive oil
6 scallions, white bulbs and green tops,
    chopped
1 small clove garlic, minced
1 small green chile, seeded, deveined and
    minced
1½ cups chopped, seeded tomatoes
Pinch of sugar
Pinch of dried oregano
Pinch of ground mace

Heat the butter with the oil in a medium-size saucepan over medium-low heat. Add the scallions; cook 1 minute. Add the garlic and green chile; cook 4 minutes longer. Stir in the remaining ingredients and raise the heat slightly. Cook, stirring occasionally, until slightly thickened, about 10 minutes.

Makes about 1¼ cups

SPINACH-BRAN PIZZA WITH CHEESE AND SAUSAGE

*T*o a concerned member of the stove-top health club, the most positive aspect of any bran fiber is its mutability. I use bran to enrich pie crusts, to extend meat loaves and patties, and to delectably "bread" whatever cutlet, croquette, or other crunchable comes to roost in my sauté pan. And in my pizza or tart pan, to boot!

FOR THE TOMATO BASE

2 tablespoons olive oil
1 small onion, minced
1 clove garlic, minced
1 cup chopped, seeded tomatoes
Pinch of sugar
½ teaspoon chopped fresh oregano, or
*   ¼ teaspoon dried*
⅛ teaspoon ground allspice
1 teaspoon unsalted butter
Salt and freshly ground black pepper to
*   taste*

FOR THE CRUST

1 tablespoon olive oil
1 small onion, minced
1 clove garlic, minced
1 package (10 ounces) frozen chopped
*   spinach, thawed and squeezed dry*
1 large canned green chile, minced
1 cup All-Bran cereal, processed fine in a
*   food processor*
½ cup freshly grated Parmesan cheese
⅛ teaspoon crushed dried hot red peppers
¼ teaspoon salt
¼ teaspoon freshly ground black pepper
1 egg, lightly beaten

FOR THE TOPPING

2 large sweet Italian sausages, cut into ½-
*   inch-thick slices*
½ cup crumbled goat cheese
1¼ cups coarsely grated mozzarella (about
*   5 ounces)*

1. Make the tomato base: Heat the oil in a medium-size saucepan over medium-low heat. Add the onion; cook 1 minute. Add the garlic; cook 4 minutes. Stir in the tomatoes, sugar, oregano, and allspice. Cook, uncovered, stirring occasionally, until thick, about 30 minutes. Stir in the butter and season with salt and pepper. Set aside to cool.

2. Meanwhile, make the crust: Preheat the oven to 400°F. Lightly butter a 9- or 10-inch loose-bottom tart pan.

3. Heat the oil in a medium-size heavy skillet over medium-low heat. Add the onion; cook 1 minute. Add the garlic; cook 4 minutes. Stir in the spinach and the chile and raise the heat slightly. Cook, stirring constantly, until all moisture has evaporated, about 4 minutes. Remove the skillet from the heat.

4. Place the All-Bran in a medium-size bowl and add the spinach mixture. Mix well, and stir in the Parmesan cheese, dried red peppers, salt, black pepper, and egg. Mix thoroughly. Spread this mixture evenly over the bottom of the prepared tart pan. Bake 10 minutes. Cool slightly.

5. Sauté the sausage slices in a dry heavy skillet until lightly browned and partially rendered of fat, about 4 minutes.

6. Spread the tomato mixture evenly over the cooled spinach crust. Dot the top with goat cheese. Place the sausage slices over the top, and sprinkle with the mozzarella. Bake 20 minutes.

Serves 4 to 6

CAILLE
(Bran-Crammed Swiss Chard)

*T*he next recipe has a mysterious antecedence. I encountered it on a South Carolina menu as "Louisiana-style quail," though it clearly was not fowl. The notion of poaching a grain-and-meat mixture in a nest of greens is indubitably Middle European, yet the tag was decidedly French. No matter, *caille* is a very good dish to have in anyone's culinary repertoire—whatever its point of origin.

1 large head Swiss chard (about 10 leaves)
1 cup ground ham
1 egg, lightly beaten
½ cup milk, scalded and cooled
1 cup fresh bread crumbs
1 cup Bran Flakes cereal, ground fine in a
*   food processor*
1 cup grated Monterey Jack cheese with
*   jalapeño peppers*
2 tablespoons chopped fresh parsley
⅛ teaspoon ground mace
⅛ teaspoon freshly grated nutmeg
½ teaspoon salt
¼ teaspoon freshly ground black pepper
2 cloves garlic
1 cup homemade chicken stock (see page
*   376), or canned broth, warmed*
1 tablespoon unsalted butter
1 large tomato, seeded and chopped
Pinch of sugar
Chopped fresh parsley, for garnish

1. Preheat the oven to 350°F.

2. Rinse the Swiss chard and trim off most of the heavy white ribs. Cook the chard leaves in boiling salted water to cover until just wilted, 2 to 3 minutes. Drain.

3. Place the ham in a large bowl and add all the ingredients through the black pepper. Mix thoroughly. Place about 1½ tablespoons ham mixture on the rib side of each leaf. Roll it up, folding in the ends like an envelope.

4. Place the chard envelopes seam side down in a lightly buttered baking dish. Place the garlic cloves on the bottom of the dish. Pour the chicken stock over the chard, and bake, covered, 25 minutes.

5. Remove the baking dish from the oven, and carefully drain off all liquid into a bowl, reserving the garlic. Keep the chard warm, uncovered, in a 225°F oven.

6. Melt the butter in a medium-size saucepan over medium heat. Add the cooked garlic and mash it with a fork. Stir in the tomato, sprinkle with the sugar, and then stir in the reserved cooking juices. Heat to boiling and boil rapidly until thickened, about 10 minutes. Spoon the sauce over the chard, and sprinkle with parsley.

Serves 4

*A*ccording to the late food savant Waverley Root, "Bran is a health-promoting constituent of wheat, which nature puts in and man diabolically takes out!"

HONEY-ORANGE BRAN MUFFINS

*F*rom California come these muffins of remarkable flavor and prodigious size. They're "sun kissed," like other good gifts of the Golden West!

¼ cup firmly packed light brown sugar
4 tablespoons (½ stick) unsalted butter,
    melted
⅔ cup buttermilk
2 eggs, lightly beaten
¼ cup honey
Finely slivered zest of 1 orange
1 cup all-purpose flour
1 cup unprocessed wheat bran
1 tablespoon baking powder
¼ teaspoon salt

1. Preheat the oven to 350°F. Lightly grease a 12-cup muffin tin.

2. Place the brown sugar in a large bowl. Pour the melted butter over it, and mix well with a wooden spoon. Stir in the buttermilk, eggs, honey, and orange zest.

3. Combine the flour, bran, baking powder, and salt in another bowl. Mix well, and stir into the buttermilk mixture. Mix until just smooth.

4. Fill each prepared muffin cup about two-thirds full with batter. Bake until golden and firm, about 25 minutes. Remove the tin from the oven and let it stand 5 minutes. Then loosen the edges of the muffins with a knife and unmold.

Makes 12 muffins

APPLESAUCED BRANS

*T*his recipe is absolutely best when the applesauce is homemade. However, the silken muffins are a decided breakfast asset, no matter what the ingredient's lineage.

⅓ cup firmly packed light brown sugar
4 tablespoons (½ stick) unsalted butter,
    melted
⅔ cup Homemade Applesauce (recipe
    follows)
2 eggs, lightly beaten
⅓ cup light cream or half-and-half
1 cup all-purpose flour
1 cup unprocessed wheat bran
1 tablespoon baking powder
¼ teaspoon salt
¼ teaspoon ground cinnamon
⅛ teaspoon ground ginger
¼ cup raisins
¼ cup chopped walnuts

1. Preheat the oven to 350°F. Lightly grease a 12-cup muffin tin.

2. Place the brown sugar in a large bowl. Pour the butter over it, and mix well with a wooden spoon. Stir in the applesauce, eggs, and light cream.

3. Combine the flour, bran, baking powder, salt, cinnamon, and ginger in another bowl. Stir the dry ingredients into the applesauce mixture, and mix until just smooth. Add the raisins and walnuts.

4. Fill each prepared muffin cup about two-thirds full with batter. Bake until golden and firm, about 25 minutes.

Remove the tin from the oven, and let stand 5 minutes. Then loosen the edges of the muffins with a knife and unmold.

Makes 12 muffins

Homemade Applesauce

6 to 8 tart red apples (such as Winesap or
  Jonathan)
¼ cup water
2 lemon slices, each ½ inch thick
½ to 1 cup sugar
½ teaspoon ground cinnamon
⅛ teaspoon freshly grated nutmeg
Juice of 1 lemon

1. Core, peel, and cut the apples into sixths. Place them in a heavy saucepan and add the water and lemon slices. Cook, covered, over medium-high heat until very tender, about 12 minutes. Discard the lemon slices.

2. Mash the apples in the saucepan with a vegetable masher. Add sugar to taste, and then stir in the cinnamon, nutmeg, and lemon juice. Cook, uncovered, over medium heat for 3 minutes. Store in sterilized jars.

Makes about 2½ pints

THE FOUR SEASONS' OLYMPIC BRANS

One of my favorite bran muffins comes from the extensive repertoire of Helmut Pedevilla, pastry chef at the Four Seasons Olympic Hotel in Seattle, Washington. I stayed at this elegant northwestern hostelry three times one year, and made up my mind after the second visit that I could not possibly sleep without the chef's highly salubrious muffin recipe as a security blanket. Pedevilla's creation is a wake-up call no man of good appetite can resist.

½ cup raisins
½ cup walnut halves, chopped
1 cup plus 2 tablespoons sifted pastry or
  cake flour
1 egg
¼ cup vegetable oil
6 tablespoons light brown sugar
1 cup buttermilk
5 tablespoons honey
1½ cups Bran Flakes cereal
1¼ teaspoons baking soda
½ teaspoon salt

1. Preheat the oven to 400°F. Lightly grease a 12-cup muffin tin.

2. Place the raisins and walnuts in a medium-size bowl and toss with the 2 tablespoons flour. Set aside.

3. Lightly beat the egg in a large bowl. Slowly beat in the oil. Then beat in the brown sugar, buttermilk, honey, and Bran Flakes.

4. Sift the remaining 1 cup flour with the baking soda and salt. Stir the flour into the bran mixture, then add the raisins and walnuts.

5. Fill each prepared muffin cup about two-thirds full with batter. Bake until golden and firm, about 25 minutes. Remove the tin from the oven, and let it stand for 5 minutes. Then loosen the edges of the muffins with a knife and unmold.

Makes 12 large muffins

HOT-TEMPERED BRAN MUFFINS

*T*he following is a dinner (rather than breakfast) muffin, dedicated to the state of Texas, where the denizens' internal temperature is a direct result of their pepper consumption. Be advised, however—these are relatively mild mannered.

2½ cups Bran Flakes cereal
1 cup milk
1 egg, lightly beaten
⅓ cup unsalted butter, melted
½ cup honey
2 teaspoons hot salsa
1 pickled jalapeño pepper, seeded,
    deveined, and minced
1 tablespoon minced pickled sweet pepper
    or pimiento
1 cup all-purpose flour
1 tablespoon baking powder
½ teaspoon salt

1. Preheat the oven to 400°F. Lightly grease a 12-cup muffin tin.

2. Place the Bran Flakes in the container of a food processor, and process until smooth. Transfer the bran to a large bowl, and pour the milk over it; let stand 3 minutes.

3. Add the egg, butter, honey, salsa, jalapeño pepper, and sweet pepper to the bran mixture, and stir until smooth.

4. Combine the flour, baking powder, and salt in another bowl. Mix well, and stir into the bran mixture until just smooth.

5. Fill each prepared muffin cup about two-thirds full with batter. Bake until golden and firm, about 25 minutes. Remove the tin from the oven, and let it stand 5 minutes. Then loosen the edges of the muffins with a knife and unmold.

Makes 12 muffins

ANNA TEEL BARLOW'S HEAVENLY BRANS

"*H*eavenly" is no random compliment for the next dispensation—two packaged bran breakfast cereals in one sublime amalgam. Mrs. Barlow is so generous a recipe-giver that she also included her method for whipping up "baker's secret," an unguent that ensures any muffin's quick release from the clutches of a sticky pan.

Baker's Secret (see Box, page 42)
⅓ cup chopped pitted dates
½ cup walnut halves, chopped
1 cup plus 2 tablespoons all-purpose flour,
    sifted
1 egg
¼ cup vegetable oil

6 tablespoons sugar
1 cup buttermilk
½ cup water, boiling
1 cup All-Bran cereal
1¼ teaspoons baking soda
½ teaspoon salt
½ cup Bran Flakes cereal

BAKER'S SECRET

Here is Anna Teel Barlow's recipe for Baker's Secret: Combine ¼ cup solid vegetable shortening, ¼ cup vegetable oil, and ¼ cup all-purpose flour. Beat until creamy. Store in a jar in the refrigerator. Use to grease cake pans, bread pans, and muffin tins. It will keep indefinitely.

1. Preheat the oven to 400°F. Lightly grease two 9- or 12-cup muffin tins with Baker's Secret.

2. Place the dates and walnuts in a medium-size bowl and toss with the 2 tablespoons flour. Set aside.

3. Lightly beat the egg in a large bowl. Slowly beat in the oil. Then beat in the sugar and buttermilk.

4. Pour the boiling water over the All-Bran in a small bowl. Stir this into the buttermilk mixture.

5. Sift the remaining 1 cup flour with the baking soda and salt. Stir the flour into the buttermilk mixture and add the Bran Flakes and reserved dates and walnuts.

6. Fill each prepared muffin cup about two-thirds full with batter. Bake until golden and firm, about 25 minutes. Remove the tins from the oven, and let them stand for 5 minutes. Then loosen the edges of the muffins with a knife and unmold.

Makes 15 to 16 muffins

BELTANE RANCH BRANS

*R*osemary Wood is the donor here. I first sampled Ms. Wood's exceptional handiwork, slathered with butter and homemade strawberry jam, at breakfast under a live oak tree, when I was a paying guest at her rambling colonial ranch in Glen Ellen, California. After I professed my admiration, she produced the recipe. It came with some good advice, too: The batter may be prepared (and kept covered in the fridge) up to four weeks ahead with no apparent diminishment of flavor or texture. Knowing you have batter at the ready allows you to make great muffins any time you get the urge. Now that's a true bran-lover's bonus!

1 box (1 pound) Bran Flakes cereal
3 cups sugar
5 cups all-purpose flour
5 teaspoons baking soda
2 teaspoons salt
1 cup vegetable oil
4 eggs, lightly beaten
1 quart buttermilk

1. Preheat the oven to 375°F. Lightly grease up to four 12-cup muffin tins.

2. Combine the Bran Flakes, sugar, flour, baking soda, and salt in a large bowl. Mix well, and add the oil, eggs, and buttermilk. Stir until smooth. Store, well covered, in the refrigerator until needed, up to four weeks' time.

3. Fill each prepared muffin cup about two-thirds full with batter. Bake until golden and firm, 15 to 20 minutes (or a few minutes longer if batter was not brought to room temperature). Remove the tins from the oven, and let them stand for 5 minutes. Then loosen the edges of the muffins with a knife and unmold.

Makes about 48 muffins

A Beltane Dozen

If you are as shy of refrigerator room as I am, you may wish to subdivide the recipe. Here's how to get a single batch.

2¾ cups Bran Flakes cereal
¾ cup sugar

1¼ cups all-purpose flour
1¼ teaspoons baking soda
½ teaspoon salt
¼ cup vegetable oil
1 egg, lightly beaten
1 cup buttermilk

Follow steps 1 through 3, above, greasing only one 12-cup muffin tin.
Makes 12 muffins

BUTTERMILK BRAN BREAD

The recipe for my favorite bread to toast and slather with peanut butter and honey.

2 packages dry yeast
½ cup lukewarm water
1 cup buttermilk, at room temperature
2 tablespoons safflower oil
¼ cup molasses
¼ cup honey
1 teaspoon coarse (kosher) salt
1 cup unprocessed wheat bran
1 cup whole-wheat flour
5 cups all-purpose flour (approximately)
Cornmeal
1 tablespoon unsalted butter, melted

1. Place the yeast in a large bowl and sprinkle it with the water. Let it stand a few minutes to soften; then stir in the buttermilk, safflower oil, molasses, honey, salt, and bran. Let stand for 5 minutes.

2. Slowly beat in the whole-wheat flour with a heavy wooden spoon, and then about 3½ cups of the all-purpose flour, enough to form a slightly sticky dough. Transfer the dough to a lightly floured surface. Knead the dough for 10 minutes, incorporating about 1 more cup of the all-purpose flour. When the dough is elastic, place it in a large lightly greased bowl. Turn the dough so that it is lightly greased all over. Cover tightly, and let it rise until doubled, 2½ hours.

Though dentists do not assiduously recommend it, bran is good for the teeth too!

Despite a tendency of its particles to lodge between molars, wheat bran makes such a dandy dentifrice that natives of the Ural mountains have been chewing it for years. Hundreds of years, actually—and these denizens have remarkably white choppers to show for any wear and tear.

Likewise, in Outer Mongolia tribesmen always chomp rice bran to toughen up flaccid gums.

And while I do not suggest the practice for most city dwellers (chewing bran involves much expectoration), it's a good idea to remember that wheat bran is so high in vitamin B (which promotes the formation of healthy body tissues) that it contains twice the mineral content of the wheat grain itself.

Parenthetically, bran also makes an excellent staple for bread makers who enjoy a degree of dental exercise at the dinner table. Like me!

3. Punch the dough down and divide it in half. Knead each half briefly on a lightly floured board, forming them into round loaves. Place the loaves on a cornmeal-sprinkled baking sheet, cover with a flour-rubbed tea towel, and let stand 1 hour.

4. Preheat the oven to 375°F.

5. Brush the tops of the loaves with the melted butter. Bake in the top third of the oven until golden brown and hollow-sounding when tapped with your finger, about 30 minutes.

Makes 2 loaves

SHARON TYLER HERBST'S BRAN WAFFLES

Sharon Tyler Herbst is one of a small contingent of San Francisco cookbook writers who eschew what is trendy for what is tried and true at the table. More important, her recipes never fail. The following bounty is borrowed from her excellent book *Breads*.

3 eggs, separated
¾ cup sour cream
¾ cup milk
⅔ cup unsalted butter, melted
½ cup Bran Flakes cereal
2 teaspoons molasses
½ teaspoon vanilla extract
1½ cups all-purpose flour
2 teaspoons baking powder
½ teaspoon baking soda
¼ teaspoon salt
2 tablespoons sugar

1. Lightly beat the egg yolks in a medium-size bowl. Whisk in the sour cream, milk, butter, Bran Flakes, molasses, and vanilla.

2. Combine the flour, baking powder, baking soda, salt, and sugar in another bowl. Stir into the bran mixture.

3. Beat the egg whites until stiff, and fold them into the waffle batter. Cook the waffles in a preheated waffle iron, following manufacturer's directions. Keep the waffles warm on a wire rack in a 200°F oven while you cook the remaining batter.

Serves 4

Aside from cereal at the breakfast table, bran makes a positive contribution to any health-minded cook's collection of hotcakes, flapjacks, and waffles—adding a distinctive taste (like toasted nuts) as well as a nutritive embellishment.

BRAN-GRAHAM CRACKER CRUST

*T*o my tongue, bran's most surprising alliances are all on the sweet side. For starters, consider it as the architecture of a splendidly simple pastry.

This mixture is devised of crushed wheat crackers and toasted unprocessed wheat bran. Use it for any unctuous filling you have a letch for—or try either of the sweet-toothed suggestions that follow.

⅓ cup unprocessed wheat bran, toasted (see page 30)
1¼ cups graham cracker crumbs (about 11 graham crackers)
⅓ cup sifted confectioners' sugar
1 teaspoon ground cinnamon
7 tablespoons unsalted butter, melted

1. Preheat the oven to 300°F. Lightly butter a 9-inch pie plate.

2. Place the bran in the container of a food processor or blender, and process as fine as possible, 3 to 5 minutes.

3. Combine the bran, cracker crumbs, confectioners' sugar, and cinnamon in a medium-size bowl. Pour the melted butter over the mixture, and blend thoroughly. Press the crumb mixture over the bottom and sides of the prepared pie plate. Bake 15 minutes. Cool thoroughly before using.

Makes crust for one 9-inch pie

PEANUT BUTTER PIE

*T*he handiwork of Susan Alper, a talented young chef at The Lamb & The Lion Restaurant in Elmont, New York. Her pie is a cold, crunchy, creamy crowd-pleaser. But better than ever when bedded on bran.

¼ pound cream cheese, at room temperature
1 cup chunky-style peanut butter, at room temperature
1 cup confectioners' sugar, sifted
⅓ cup milk
2 teaspoons vanilla extract
1 teaspoon dark rum
1½ cups heavy or whipping cream
1 Bran-Graham Cracker Crust (see above)

1. Combine the cream cheese and peanut butter in the large bowl of an electric mixer. Beat until smooth. Add the confectioners' sugar; beat until fluffy. Beat in the milk, vanilla, and rum.

2. Beat the cream until stiff. Stir one third of the cream into the peanut butter mixture. Fold in the remaining cream. Spoon into the prepared pie shell. Refrigerate 4 hours before serving.

Serves 8

NEW YORK LIME PIE

A distant cousin of a classic Florida Key lime pie, this chiffony creation is made with store-bought citrus and lots of imagination.

3 eggs, separated
1 cup granulated sugar
Juice of 3 limes (½ cup)
Finely grated zest of 2 limes
2 tablespoons light rum
1 tablespoon unflavored gelatin
¼ cup cold water
1 cup heavy or whipping cream
1 tablespoon confectioners' sugar
1 Bran-Graham Cracker Crust
    (see page 45)

1. Beat the egg yolks with the granulated sugar and lime juice in a large bowl until light. Slowly beat in the lime zest and rum.

2. Combine the gelatin and the cold water in a small bowl, and set aside to soften, 1 minute. Place the bowl over hot water and stir until the gelatin has dissolved. Stir it into the lime juice mixture. Transfer to the top of a double boiler and cook, stirring often, over simmering water for 10 minutes. Set aside to cool for 5 minutes, and then refrigerate until the mixture begins to set, about 40 minutes.

3. Beat the cream with the confectioners' sugar until thick. Fold it into the lime mixture. Beat the egg whites until stiff; fold them into the lime mixture. Refrigerate 15 minutes, then fold the mixture lightly and refrigerate another 10 minutes. (Do not allow the mixture to set completely.) Spoon the filling into the prepared pie shell. Refrigerate 3 hours.
    Serves 6 to 8

CRAN-BRAN BETTY

*B*rown Betty is a fruited American classic traditionally made of sliced apples, layered between sheets of crumbs and sugar and baked in a casserole. My version, on the tart side, is strictly Cape Cod in derivation. Serve it with cinnamon ice cream.

¾ pound cranberries, picked over and
    rinsed
1½ cups sugar
¼ cup honey
Finely slivered zest of 1 large orange
¼ teaspoon freshly grated nutmeg
½ teaspoon ground cinnamon
¼ teaspoon salt
3 tablespoons Grand Marnier
2 pounds sweet apples
½ cup all-purpose flour

½ cup unprocessed wheat bran, toasted
    (see page 30)
4 tablespoons plus 2 teaspoons unsalted
    butter, chilled
Cinnamon Ice Cream (recipe follows)

1. In a large mixing bowl, combine the cranberries, 1 cup of the sugar, the honey, orange zest, nutmeg, cinnamon, salt, and Grand Marnier. Let stand 15 minutes.

2. Preheat the oven to 350°F. Lightly butter a shallow baking dish.

3. Peel, core, and slice the apples, stirring the slices into the cranberry mixture as you work.

4. Combine the remaining ½ cup sugar, the bran, and the flour in another bowl. Add the 4 tablespoons butter and blend with a pastry blender until the mixture has the texture of coarse crumbs.

5. Place a third of the cranberry-apple mixture over the bottom of the prepared baking dish. Sprinkle with a third of the bran mixture. Continue to layer, ending with bran mixture. Dot the top with the 2 teaspoons butter. Bake until crisp, about 45 minutes. Serve slightly warm, with Cinnamon Ice Cream.

Serves 8

Bran is saddled with some highly disparate cognomens across the globe. Health-concerned Frenchmen call it *son*, which means a "ring" or "cover." Germans dub it *Kleie*. Nutrition-minded Italians spoon their bran as *crusca*, which may be translated as "rough stuff," while the Spanish call it *salvado*, or "salvation," which bespeaks bran's value in a diet more eloquently than any tract of Dr. Graham and friends.

Cinnamon Ice Cream

Cinnamon (to my mind) is the cranberry's most stalwart flavor alliance. For concrete evidence, treat yourself to the joy of the following seductive cinnamon ice cream, allowing it to melt on the warm pudding's surface. It is the handiwork of Karl Dauner, a brilliant young German-born, New York-practicing chef-caterer.

2 cups heavy or whipping cream
¾ cup milk
2 cinnamon sticks
7 egg yolks
½ teaspoon ground cinnamon
½ cup sugar

1. Combine the cream with the milk and cinnamon sticks in a glass or ceramic bowl. Cover, and let stand at room temperature for 4 hours.

2. Transfer the cream, milk, and cinnamon sticks to a medium-size noncorrosive saucepan. Slowly heat just to the boiling point. Remove the pan from the heat, and let it stand until cool. Discard the cinnamon sticks. (Scoop any film from the surface if necessary.)

3. In a large bowl, beat the egg yolks with the ground cinnamon and sugar until light and fluffy. Add the cooled cream/milk mixture. Pour into the canister of an ice cream maker and process according to manufacturer's directions.

Makes about 1 quart

ORIGINAL SIN FRUITCAKE

What a surprise to discover that all the healthy goodness of carrots, dates, and bran can produce such a decadent meal ending!

FOR THE CAKE

2 eggs
1⅓ cups granulated sugar
⅔ cup vegetable oil
1½ teaspoons vanilla extract
⅔ cup fresh orange juice
2 teaspoons finely slivered orange zest
⅓ cup unprocessed wheat bran
1⅔ cups cake flour, sifted
1 teaspoon baking soda
½ teaspoon baking powder
¼ teaspoon salt
1½ teaspoons ground cinnamon
⅔ cup coarsely chopped walnuts
½ cup chopped pitted dates
1½ cups loosely packed grated carrots

FOR THE ICING

1 cup confectioners' sugar
2 tablespoons fresh orange juice
1 teaspoon heavy or whipping cream

1. Preheat the oven to 325°F. Lightly butter and flour an 8- to 10-cup bundt pan.

2. Beat the eggs with the sugar in a large bowl until light. Beat in the oil, vanilla, orange juice, and orange zest.

3. Combine the bran, flour, baking soda, baking powder, salt, and cinnamon in another bowl. Mix well; then stir into the egg mixture. Let stand 10 minutes. Stir in the walnuts, dates, and carrots.

4. Pour the batter into the prepared bundt pan. Bake until a toothpick inserted in the center of the cake comes out clean, about 1 hour. Cool completely in the pan on a rack before unmolding.

5. To make the icing, combine the confectioners' sugar with the orange juice and cream; beat until smooth. Drizzle over the cake.

Serves 8 to 10

FORT KNOX BARS

*T*he name says it all. These honey-bran-pecan squares are like 48-carat gold on the tongue and equally worthy of serious hoarding. But store them in a freezer after baking, not in a safe deposit vault, please.

FOR THE CRUST

5 tablespoons unsalted butter, at room
    temperature
¼ cup sugar
¼ cup solid vegetable shortening
2 egg yolks
1 teaspoon bourbon
1½ cups all-purpose flour
½ teaspoon baking powder
⅛ teaspoon salt

FOR THE FILLING

1 cup (2 sticks) unsalted butter
½ cup honey
1¼ cups firmly packed light brown sugar
¼ cup granulated sugar
1 teaspoon vanilla extract
2 teaspoons bourbon
¼ cup heavy or whipping cream
3 cups coarsely chopped pecans
1 cup All-Bran cereal

1. Make the crust: In a medium-size bowl, beat the butter with the sugar and shortening until light. Beat in the egg yolks and bourbon.

2. Sift the flour with the baking powder and salt into another bowl. Stir into the butter mixture with a wooden spoon. Cover, and chill in the freezer for 30 minutes.

3. Preheat the oven to 350°F.

4. Remove the dough from the freezer and roll it out between sheets of wax paper to form a 10 by 13-inch rectangle. Carefully remove the top sheet of wax paper and flip the dough over into a 9 by 12-inch baking pan. Press any broken edges together. Prick the dough all over with a fork. Bake 10 minutes, then cool on a rack.

5. Make the filling: Combine the butter, honey, both sugars, and vanilla in a medium-size saucepan. Heat to boiling. Reduce the heat and simmer, stirring often, 3 minutes. Remove the pan from the heat. Stir in the bourbon, cream, pecans, and All-Bran. Mix well, and spoon over the prebaked crust. Bake until firm, about 25 minutes. Cool completely before cutting into 1¼-inch squares.

Makes about 60 bars

OAT BRAN VARIATIONS

When the word "bran" crops up, the designation most often implies wheat. But of late, manufacturers of oat products (like Quaker) have been making a serious bid to turn consumer awareness to oat bran.

Functionally, the difference between one bran and another boils down to degrees of stove-top malleability. The unprocessed fiber of oat bran is water-soluble, whereas the fiber of unprocessed wheat bran is not. In cooking, oat bran has an inherent creaminess while wheat bran has a crisp bite.

More important than texture, however, are the two brans' distinguishing health characteristics. Oat bran has been found to reduce blood levels of LDL cholesterol (the type associated with fatty arterial deposits). Scientists maintain that while cholesterol reduc-tion is not entirely absent with other brans, only oat has a proven track record—just as wheat bran has no peer in the area of digestive and intestinal regulation.

If you consider substituting oat bran for wheat in any recipe, note at the outset that oat bran will be moister and more dense than its more familiar wheat counterpart.

The following side dishes (or first courses) are meant to flesh out a spare meal or to replace meat, poultry, or fish as an entrée on occasion. Devised specifically for oat bran, they taste so good that even diners without particular health concerns will find them utterly irresistible. The oat variations on muffins and biscuits are equally healthful and delicious.

OAT BRAN MUFFINS

*U*sing pure oat bran makes for a heavy muffin, so combine it with cake or soft wheat flour. For a variation that is super-potassium-enriched, substitute chopped bananas for the golden raisins.

1 cup oat bran
1 ¼ cups cake or soft wheat flour
1 tablespoon baking powder
½ teaspoon salt
¼ cup firmly packed dark brown sugar
⅔ cup milk
¼ cup honey
2 tablespoons vegetable oil
2 eggs, lightly beaten, or ½ cup egg substitute
½ cup golden raisins
½ cup chopped nuts

1. Preheat the oven to 425°F. Lightly grease a 12-cup muffin tin.

2. Combine the oat bran with the flour, baking powder, and salt in a large bowl. Add the brown sugar, and mix with your fingers or a pastry blender until well blended. Stir in the remaining ingredients.

3. Fill each prepared muffin cup about three-quarters full with batter. Bake until golden brown and firm, 15 to 18 minutes. Let the tin stand for 5 minutes, then loosen the edges with a knife and unmold the muffins.

Makes 12 muffins

COATED OAT BISCUITS

A healthy turn on a favorite Southern recipe. The biscuit dough is beaten and then coated in flour before baking. These are best served straight from the oven, with lots of honey.

1 ¾ cups cake or soft wheat flour
1 cup oat bran
1 tablespoon baking powder
½ teaspoon salt
½ cup solid vegetable shortening, chilled
1 cup milk (approximately)

1. Preheat the oven to 425°F. Lightly rub a baking sheet with oil.

2. Place ¼ cup of the flour in a small bowl and set it aside.

3. Combine 1 cup of the flour with the oat bran, baking powder, and salt in a large bowl. Cut in the vegetable shortening with a knife or a pastry blender

until well mixed. Stir 1 cup milk into the mixture, and let it stand 3 minutes to allow the bran to soften. The mixture will be slightly loose.

4. Beat the remaining ½ cup flour into the batter until the mixture is smooth and thick. It will resemble a smooth paste. (Add more milk if it is too thick.) Scoop up about 2 tablespoons of the dough on a spoon, then using your finger, push the dough off the spoon, dropping it into the reserved flour. With your fingers spread apart, lightly toss the dough to coat it well with flour. Do not

worry about the excess flour. Gently place the dough on the prepared baking sheet, and repeat with the remaining dough. Bake until lightly browned, 15 to 18 minutes.

Makes 12 biscuits

TOMATO-OAT BRAN PUDDING

Almost like a thick vegetable porridge, this super-healthful dish is delicious when matched with plain broiled chicken and a green vegetable.

2 tablespoons olive oil
1 medium onion, chopped
1 clove garlic, minced
1 can (28 ounces) imported plum tomatoes
    (about 3¼ cups)
1 teaspoon chopped fresh basil, or ½
    teaspoon dried
1 teaspoon chopped fresh thyme, or ¼
    teaspoon dried
¼ teaspoon sugar
1 cup oat bran
¼ teaspoon salt
¼ teaspoon freshly ground black pepper
⅛ teaspoon crushed dried hot red peppers
½ cup grated Gruyère cheese
2 tablespoons freshly grated Parmesan
    cheese

1. Preheat the oven to 350°F.

2. Heat the oil in a medium-size saucepan over medium-low heat. Add the onion; cook 1 minute. Add the garlic; cook 3 minutes (do not brown). Stir in the tomatoes, breaking them up with a wooden spoon. Add the basil, thyme, and sugar. Heat to boiling. Reduce the heat and simmer, uncovered, until reduced to 3 cups, about 8 minutes.

3. Stir the oat bran into the tomato mixture. Cook, stirring frequently, until thick, about 6 minutes. Stir in the salt, black pepper, dried red peppers, Gruyère, and 1 tablespoon of the Parmesan. Spoon the mixture into a lightly buttered 1½-quart soufflé dish. Sprinkle the top with the remaining 1 tablespoon Parmesan. Bake 20 minutes.

Serves 4

SPINACH AND OAT BRAN SOUFFLE

I often serve this green-flecked soufflé with sliced cold meats and a plate of fresh sliced tomatoes alongside for a light dinner.

1½ tablespoons olive oil
1 large shallot, finely chopped
1 clove garlic, minced
⅛ teaspoon crushed dried hot red peppers
1 package (10 ounces) frozen chopped
    spinach, thawed and squeezed dry
⅔ cup oat bran

2 cups milk or skim milk
1 egg yolk
⅛ to ¼ teaspoon hot pepper sauce
Salt and freshly ground black pepper to
    taste
5 egg whites
1 teaspoon freshly grated Parmesan cheese

1. Preheat the oven to 400°F.

2. Heat the oil in a medium-size skillet over medium-low heat. Add the shallot; cook 1 minute. Add the garlic and dried red peppers; cook 2 minutes longer. Stir in the spinach and cook, stirring often, until most of the liquid has evaporated, about 4 minutes. Set aside.

3. Place the bran in a medium-size saucepan. Pour the milk over it and heat it slowly, stirring often, to boiling. Reduce the heat and simmer until thick, about 3 minutes. Remove the pan from the heat and beat in the egg yolk. Stir in the spinach mixture, hot pepper sauce, and salt and pepper.

4. Beat the egg whites until stiff. Fold them into the spinach-bran mixture. Spoon into a lightly greased 1½-quart soufflé dish, and sprinkle the top with the Parmesan. Bake until puffed and golden, 30 minutes.

Serves 6

CREAMY CARROTY OAT BRAN PUREE

Another hearty, healthy side dish, best served with simply prepared meat or fish. Vegetarians should feel free to substitute a strong vegetable stock for the chicken stock.

½ pound carrots, peeled and sliced
1 onion, sliced
3 cups homemade chicken stock (see page 376) or canned broth
1 cup oat bran
½ teaspoon freshly grated nutmeg
Salt and freshly ground black pepper to taste
1 teaspoon chopped fresh chives

1. Combine the carrots, onion, and chicken stock in a medium-size saucepan. Cover and heat to boiling. Reduce the heat and simmer, covered, until the vegetables are tender, about 15 minutes. Drain over another saucepan. (You should have 3 cups liquid; add water to make that amount, if necessary.)

2. Place the cooked onion and carrots in the container of a food processor or blender. Process until smooth.

3. Heat the reserved cooking broth to boiling; then reduce the heat. Whisk in the oat bran and cook, whisking constantly, over medium-low heat until smooth and thick, about 4 minutes. Stir in the carrot-onion mixture. Add the nutmeg, and season with salt and pepper. Keep warm over low heat, or in the top of a double boiler over simmering water. Stir in the chives before serving.

Serves 6

WILD-OAT BRAN RISOTTO

Wild, because of the mushrooms. Risotto, because the combination of the creamy oat bran and cooked rice reminds me of the velvety smoothness of the Italian classic.

2 tablespoons olive oil
1 medium onion, finely chopped
1 clove garlic, minced
¼ pound large mushroom caps (shiitakes if possible), sliced
3 cups defatted homemade chicken stock (see page 376) or canned broth
1 cup oat bran
¼ cup chopped prosciutto
1 cup cooked long-grain rice (see page 217), warmed
Freshly ground black pepper to taste
Chopped fresh parsley, for garnish

1. Heat the oil in a large saucepan over medium-low heat. Add the onion; cook 1 minute. Add the garlic; cook 4 minutes.

2. Push the onions to the edge of the pan and raise the heat to medium. Add the sliced mushrooms and cook, stirring often, until lightly browned, about 4 minutes. Stir in the chicken stock, scraping the sides and bottom of the pan. Whisk in the oat bran, and cook, whisking constantly, until thick, about 3 minutes.

3. Stir the prosciutto and cooked rice into the bran mixture. Season with pepper, and sprinkle with parsley.
Serves 4

RICE HAS A BRAN TOO!

Rice bran is the oily brown coating found under the hard outer shell of rice grains.

Up until the 1980s, no one outside the Orient had found any serious use for rice bran except as animal food. But there is a very recent development in the heart of southern Louisiana's rice belt: the cultivation of many new commercial products from rice bran—notably a polyunsaturated oil that is high in vitamin E and fiber and totally allergen-free.

BUCKWHEAT
A Great Source of Complex Carbohydrates

The next tale is about buckwheat pancakes, basketball, and my father, in reverse order.

From middle age until his death, my father's life was not a conspicuously happy one. A self-made man with a handsome wife and two healthy children, S. M. Greene (as he liked to be called) had had a thriving business and a well-deserved reputation as "the fastest electrical contractor in the fastest-growing suburb of New York City" until the Depression slowed him down.

He was also a man who liked to sing. And though not particularly gifted with mellow vocal chords, he used to sing, hum, and whistle all the time. When the stock market crash halted the building industry, my father managed to stay in good voice, for he had saved enough for what he always called "a rainy day." Even after the banks failed in 1932, he warbled, albeit uneasily, "Let's have another cup'a coffee and let's have another piece'a pie." Besides, S. M. was a man of high hopes. He voted for Roosevelt and Repeal with real optimism, and crooned "Happy days are here again . . ." on Election Day in eager anticipation.

But as one unhappy day ran into another, his capital dwindled, his investments were devalued, and his friends—to whom he had often lent money in the past—deserted him. So my father stopped singing.

These disappointments sent him into a kind of torpor that little could dispel, except two things: food and sports. I remember my father at breakfast, demolishing pancakes with one hand while holding the sports section of the paper in the other, roundly cursing the losing team he had backed. Each morning he would seek out the back page before glancing at the headlines. Even on the day war was declared in Europe.

Like the ballpark figures and knockout scores, what he was served also caused my father to give vent to his emotions.

"What the heck is this I am eating?" he would inquire. And he would be little mollified at the answer, for S. M. Greene was not an easy man to please. His eating habits were parochial, and he hungered after dishes of his youth that I could never prepare to his satisfaction.

"Son, we will have to find you a better cookbook," he announced one day after I had failed at the task again. "Or find us a new chef!"

That was a joke, of course, since I had become the family cook by default when my mother went to work "temporarily"—I stayed at the job almost a decade.

Actually as I approached adolescence I grew so tall and robust that I sensed my parent viewing me in a new and unexpected light—as potential brawn for the playing fields. However, I hadn't the slightest aptitude for sports. I either fumbled the ball, dropped the bat, or missed the pass!

If he was discouraged, my father kept it to himself. But then, I said he was a hopeful man. Rather than upbraiding me for physical shortcomings, he concentrated on refining my culinary skills. An avowed lover of the dark, pungent flavor of buckwheat, he would leave pancake recipes (torn from newspapers) on my dresser or pillow, with terse notes penciled in the margin: "Sound good?" or "Thought this might be worth a try."

A dutiful son, I attacked every recipe my father pressed upon me, but none pleased his demanding tongue. A memory of ethereal buckwheat cakes consumed somewhere, sometime long ago, always outclassed my lumpish efforts. And Bert's score at the griddle remained resolutely zero.

This story has a happier end than you would suppose. After Pearl Harbor, my father applied for war work at a naval base in Rhode Island, where he was hired (at maximum security) to install heavy-duty electrical equipment in destroyers and submarines. Through hard labor he regained his pride, a small bank account, and a special commendation from the President of the United States. The fact that he had been *chosen* altered his perception of himself. He even began to hum again.

His son's college days, if anything, strengthened my father's vibrato. By the time I arrived at William and Mary, almost all the varsity men had been drafted. So it was really not surprising that the coach of the basketball team signed me up to play center at first sight—without a tryout and over my mild protests—merely because I was an awesome size!

My father never saw me play. Few did, in fact, for I did not last long into the season. But parental pride was obviously contagious. After reading a letter from home, the coach who had benched me made me team manager instead.

It was a high-spirited man who drove to Williamsburg at the end of freshman year to fetch his son home. What made my father so exuberant was not sports alone, but the fact that someone in the South knew how to make his beloved buckwheat cakes.

After consuming a plateful of these airy pancakes at the hotel where he and my mother spent the night, my father immediately dispatched me to the kitchen to procure the recipe.

Through amazing grace—for I was actually a shy kid—I convinced the tall black man at the huge stove to part with his secret, and S. M. Greene's cup literally ranneth over.

He had not sung in years, but on that long drive home from dappled Virginia to dusty New York, my father would turn to grin at me (the almost athlete) and then croon back at the windshield: "Yessir, that's my baby now!"

The Grain's Genesis

*T*echnically speaking, buckwheat is no grain at all but a fruit of the *Fagopyrum* genus, a distant cousin of garden-variety rhubarb. Like its spiky kin, buckwheat is a veritable magnet for honeybees and a mild inhibitor of cutworms and white flies. But there the family resemblance ends. Despite the corolla of papery white blossoms and delicate vernal perfume, it is buckwheat's seed rather than its stem that is the plant's strong point. A three-cornered shell, when dried and split it reveals a pale kernel that is known as a "groat." In one form or another, groats have been keeping man on the straight and narrow since the 10th century B.C. Maybe even before, buckwheat pharmacopeia being somewhat on the scanty side.

One thing is certain, however: The first buckwheat groat blossomed in Central Asia. To this day, in fact, Manchurian legends persist of giants who roamed the earth, leaving mountains and valleys wherever their footprints fell, and who were nourished by seeds of night-flowering trees. It is no coinci-

dence that for centuries buckwheat was erroneously called "beech-wheat" in China because the seed was much like the nut of a flowering beech tree.

Food scouts tell us that buckwheat's first harvest took place near Lake Baikal, a body of water that forms a natural border between Manchuria and Siberia, giving both the Chinese and the Russians license to claim it as a natural resource. And rather more pertinently, the incentive to stir generous helpings into their native cuisines. Despite the prandial enthusiasm, buckwheat remained virtually untasted by Europeans until well into the Middle Ages.

Some pundits claim that buckwheat was a souvenir of Tartar raids on northern Europe in the 1400s. Others, equally emphatic, state that buckwheat entered southern Europe with the invading Moors. Which may be a shade closer to the mark, since Italians, Spanish, and French to this day refer to buckwheat as *sarrasin*, or "Saracen grain."

It was the Dutch who gave buckwheat its rightful name. In 1549 they officially dubbed it *boek weit* (book wheat) to honor the Scriptures whose auspices, they claimed, brought it to flower on their shores. It's a simile not too far-fetched. Like the Bible, buckwheat's survival has been a saga of resistance to adversity. It thrives on poor soil and inhospitable climate, and has been known to survive drought, frost, and even a flood from time to time.

Buckwheat made its way west to the New World as part of a Dutch settler's dowry, when his *vrouw*'s family, short on guilders, pressed groats instead. The seed took root in the rich soil of the Hudson Valley almost immediately, so the story appears to have had a rather happy ending.

A 1627 logbook of farmer H. T. Van Cortland in the colony of Niew Amsterdaam listed a yield of over "137 zaks boek weit vrucht" after a first summer harvest. But as buckwheat was planted only as a "catch crop" (where odds and ends of a field are sown together), the burgher fed most of it to his Holstein cows, realizing little profit other than *pannekoek* flour!

And it is only in recent history—since the rise of the health food movement, in fact—that buckwheat farming has proven to be financially viable.

Today the grain-that-is-not-a-grain is cultivated like a patchwork quilt from Maine to the Midwest, with a high proportion of the crop grown and milled in the small town of Penn Yan, in the lakes region of western New York State. Buckwheat's hardiness is its chief asset to farmers as well as a prime selling point to natural foodies, because it is one of the few commercially grown U.S. crops that requires no chemicals in the field or in the processing plant.

Some Plain Grain Talk

The proteins in buckwheat are the best-known source of complex carbohydrates. The fuel acquired by consuming these complex carbohydrates (found only in plant kingdom starches) produces what nutritionists call a "protein-sparing effect," which can be compared to an interest-bearing bank account: it allows the body to meet its energy requirements without dipping into its protein reserves. Any excess that the body accrues are reserved, like interest, to be called upon for cell building and tissue repair if the body malfunctions.

To give the health picture an even rosier glow, buckwheat also contains a high proportion of all eight amino acids (lysine, leucine, isoleucine, methionine, tryptophan, threonine, phenylalanine, and valine), which the body does not manufacture but are nonetheless deemed absolutely essential for keeping it in tip-top shape. All this makes buckwheat closer to being a "complete protein" than

any other plant source—even soybeans!

How to Buy It

By and large buckwheat is not generally found on supermarket shelves, and a shopper must make tracks to a natural foods store to find a supply of the uncommon varieties—with one notable exception: *kasha*, which is actually roasted hulled buckwheat kernels.

To lessen consumers' confusion, let me state at the outset that while all buckwheat is groats, there are two basic forms on the market: whole white buckwheat and roasted buckwheat (or kasha). And while both are virtually the same in texture after cooking, the flavor is as different as day and night. Roasted buckwheat (kasha) is toasted in an oven and tossed by hand until the kernels acquire a deep tan color, a nutlike flavor, and an ever-so-slightly-scorched aroma. Whole white buckwheat, on the other hand, is naturally dried and has a delicate flavor that makes it an admirable stand-in for rice or pasta.

Kasha is packaged four ways: whole, coarse, medium, and fine-ground. I generally use the whole or coarse form (interchangeably) in most dishes. Medium and fine-ground kasha cook somewhat more quickly and are decidedly less chewy.

Whole white buckwheat is packaged two ways: hulled groats, the form I most often opt for at the stove, and cream of buckwheat, a stone-ground grits-like cereal from the heart of the kernel.

Birkett Mills, of Penn Yan, New York, is the major processor and packager of buckwheat in the U.S. Birkett Mills' kasha is sold in most supermarkets under the "Wolff's" trademark, while whole white buckwheat is sold as "Pocono" brand in health food stores. For more information, see the list of major suppliers and mail-order sources at the back of the book.

Buckwheat has a long shelf life in the kitchen. Store it, well covered in glass or airtight plastic containers, out of the direct sunlight for best results.

How to Cook It

*P*rior to cooking, kasha is traditionally coated with beaten egg (1 egg to 1 to 2 cups of kasha) and then stir-toasted in a heavy skillet over medium heat until dry, about 3 minutes. There are several reasons for this egg wash. European cooks insist it adds nutrients, but a more logical explanation is that when buckwheat is heated, the starch in the granules swells and ruptures, turning the cooked kernels mushy. A dried egg "polish" helps keep the grains separate and crisp even after long cooking periods.

My standard method for cooking kasha is to add the coated, toasted grains to a seasoning (such as sautéed onion) along with water or broth, cooking uncovered over fairly high heat until the mixture boils. Then reduce the heat to low and cook, covered, for 15 minutes. Stir once, and turn off the heat and allow the pan to stand, covered, 10 minutes longer.

Whole white buckwheat groats do not require an egg wash or any toasting beforehand. My standard precept for cooking groats is very simple. Merely combine groats with any seasoning until well coated, then add liquid and cook until the mixture boils. Reduce the heat to low and cook, covered for about 20 minutes.

KASHALLEGIANCE

Being "American" has a different connotation today than it did when I was a boy. These days it stands for pride in one's past. Back in the 1930s, when I was growing up, few Americans celebrated their ethnic roots, and there was shame in the admission that one's mother or father was foreign-born. Mine were not, but my maternal forebears came from Russia and Poland. They spoke in broken English and to my acute embarrassment sometimes lapsed into their mother tongue (Yiddish) in front of my friends.

To the chauvinist I was, even more mortifying than their accent was my grandparents' appetite. From time to time, one or the other would hanker after a dish from "the old country," like kasha—which, despite a highly exotic ring to its nomenclature, was so utterly alien in flavor and aroma that not one of their progeny or their progeny's star-spangled issue would even consider sampling a forkful! I guess we assumed that if we did, our taste buds would be branded un-American in the narrow eyes of our more Yankee compatriots.

If Louis and Minna Cohn were disturbed by their four grandchildren's snobbery, they never betrayed it. They ate their kasha (burnished by onions and braised with lamb or oxtails) as part of the inalienable rights bestowed by Miss Liberty herself (a lady who, I must report, my grandmother often confused with the poet Emma Lazarus, whose immortal words are inscribed on the statue's base, for she inevitably referred to her as "that Jewish girl in the harbor").

BASIC KASHA AND ONIONS

*T*his is the simplest and easiest way to prepare kasha.

1 cup whole or coarse-ground kasha
1 large egg, lightly beaten
2 tablespoons unsalted butter
1 medium onion, finely chopped
4 scallions, white bulbs and green tops
  chopped separately
1 large clove garlic, minced
½ teaspoon ground mace
½ teaspoon chopped fresh thyme, or a
  pinch of dried
2 cups homemade beef stock (see page 377)
  or canned broth
Chopped fresh parsley, for garnish

1. Stir the kasha with the egg in a medium-size bowl until well mixed. Transfer to a medium-size skillet and place over medium heat. Stir the kasha with a fork until it is dry and the grains are separated, about 3 minutes.

2. Melt the butter in a medium-size saucepan over medium-low heat. Add the onion and the scallion bulbs; cook 1 minute. Add the garlic; cook until lightly browned, about 5 minutes.

3. Stir the kasha into the onion mixture, and add the mace, thyme, and beef stock. Heat to boiling. Reduce the heat and cook, covered, over low heat for 15 minutes. Stir once, turn off the heat, and let stand, covered, 10 minutes. Stir in the scallion tops, and sprinkle with parsley.

Serves 4 to 6

GRANDMOTHER'S SOUP

*T*his soup is *not* an inheritance from either of my forebears. It is a receipt of Middle European persuasion, however, that, like the best of grandmothers' soups all over the world, cooks a long time but requires little or no attention until it's almost done.

1 cup white beans
1½ tablespoons olive oil
4 leeks, white bulbs with 1 inch of green
  stems, well rinsed and coarsely chopped
1 medium onion, chopped
3 large cloves garlic, chopped
1 large carrot, finely chopped
1 ham bone with meat on it
1 lamb bone with meat on it
4 large tomatoes, seeded and chopped
½ teaspoon sugar
1 tablespoon chopped fresh basil, or
  1 teaspoon dried
1 fresh sage leaf, minced, or a pinch dried

6 cups homemade chicken stock (see page
  376) or canned broth
4 cups water
½ cup whole white buckwheat groats
1 small jalapeño pepper, seeded, deveined
  and minced
2 small zucchini, finely chopped (about
  1 cup)
3-inch strip of lemon zest
Chopped fresh parsley, for garnish

1. Soak the beans overnight in cold water to cover. (Or place them in a medium-size saucepan and cover with cold water; heat to boiling and boil 2 minutes. Then let stand 1 hour.) Drain.

2. Heat the oil in a large saucepan over medium-low heat. Add the leeks and onion; cook 1 minute. Add 2 cloves of the garlic and the carrot; cook 4 minutes longer. Add the ham and lamb bones, the white beans, tomatoes, sugar, basil, sage, chicken stock, and water. Heat to boiling. Reduce the heat and gently simmer, covered, until the beans are tender, about 2 hours.

3. Remove the bones from the soup; remove the meat from the bones. Skim the surface of the soup of all fat (or cool and place in the refrigerator until grease congeals on the surface, then remove it). Return the meat to the soup and return to boiling.

4. Add the groats to the soup along with the jalapeño pepper. Reduce the heat and cook, covered, over low heat for 20 minutes. Add the zucchini; cook, uncovered, 5 minutes.

5. Meanwhile, mince the lemon zest together with the remaining clove of garlic. Add to the soup, sprinkle with parsley, and serve.

Serves 8 to 10

BLACKENED PORK CHOPS WITH RED-FACED GROATS

*T*his dish was invented for one of my TV appearances, on *Hour Magazine* with Gary Collins. The pork chops I used were the cheapest cut I could find at my supermarket, so a good meat tenderizer became a prerequisite prior to putting them in the skillet. If you buy prime pork, it's an option you may gloss over with my blessing.

4 pork chops, each about ¾ inch thick
2 teaspoons natural meat tenderizer
1 clove garlic, bruised
1 medium onion, finely chopped
1 clove garlic, minced
1 medium red bell pepper, cored, seeded and finely chopped
1 tablespoon tomato paste
½ teaspoon hot Hungarian paprika
1 cup whole white buckwheat groats
2 cups homemade beef stock (see page 377) or canned broth, heated
Chopped fresh parsley, for garnish

1. Preheat the oven to 350°F.

2. Sprinkle the pork chops on both sides with tenderizer. Pierce the meat with a fork, then rub it with the bruised garlic.

3. In a heavy ovenproof saucepan, large enough to hold the chops in one layer, sauté the meat, fatty edges first, until well browned on all sides, about 8 to 10 minutes. Remove the chops to a plate. Discard all but 1 tablespoon fat from the pan.

4. Add the onion to the saucepan and sauté over medium-low heat for 1 minute. Add the minced garlic and the bell pepper; cook 3 minutes longer. Stir in the tomato paste, paprika, groats, and stock. Arrange the chops on top of the groats mixture, cover, and transfer to the oven. Bake until the chops are tender and all liquid has been absorbed, about 20 minutes. Remove the pan from the oven and let it stand, still covered, for 5 minutes before serving. Sprinkle with parsley.

Serves 4

ALSATIAN PORK WITH BUCKWHEAT DUMPLINGS

*I*n Alsace-Lorraine this dish is known as *porc avec quenelles blé noir*—literally, pork with black hay dumplings, "black hay" being buckwheat's name in French. And it is worthy of duplication at your stove, no matter how the appellation strikes you.

Use fine-ground kasha for the dumpling recipe. If you can't find some in your nearest natural foods store, grind your own by whirling whole kasha in a food processor or blender until it has the texture of percolator coffee grounds. This takes about 1½ to 2 minutes.

FOR THE PORK

2 tablespoons unsalted butter
1 tablespoon vegetable oil
2½ pounds boneless pork (from short ribs, spare ribs, thick-cut chops)
3 pounds sauerkraut, rinsed in cold water and drained
1 large tomato, peeled, seeded, and chopped (about 1 cup)
½ teaspoon caraway seeds
4 juniper berries, crushed
3 fresh sage leaves, chopped, or ¼ teaspoon dried
3 fresh basil leaves, chopped, or ¼ teaspoon dried
½ teaspoon anchovy paste
1 cup homemade chicken stock (see page 376) or canned broth
1½ cups Riesling wine (Alsatian, if possible)
8 cloves garlic
1 pound smoked sausage (such as kielbasa or bratwurst), cut into large pieces

FOR THE DUMPLINGS

¼ cup fine-ground kasha
½ cup water
½ teaspoon salt
1 teaspoon unsalted butter
1 egg, lightly beaten
½ cup milk
1 cup cake flour
2 teaspoons baking powder
2 teaspoons chopped fresh chives
1 teaspoon chopped fresh parsley

SOME FLAVOR NOTES ON GROATS

If you ask me to describe the difference between whole white buckwheat groats and roasted buckwheat groats (kasha), I will have to refer you to an epigram by the late-19th-century Russian gastronome, Curnonsky. "Cuisine," he wrote, "is when things taste like *themselves!*"

So it is with buckwheat. The difference between the passive sapidity of whole white groats (almost fated to be mated with other ingredients) and the dark, enveloping tincture of kasha (dominating every seasoning it meets) is as classic as yin and yang. For while the textures are identical (they were grown on the same branch, after all), a first bite of whole white groats can form an instant bond at a fork end, whereas kasha is an acquired taste that some, in fact, never ever truly acquire!

Greene's advice to the kashawary is to sample it prudently, beginning with the cabbage rolls, cornsticks, and dumplings.

1. Preheat the oven to 350°F.

2. To make the Alsatian pork, melt 1 tablespoon of the butter with the oil in a large ovenproof pot or Dutch oven over medium heat. Sauté the pork pieces until brown on all sides, about 10 minutes. Transfer the pork to a plate.

3. Pour off the grease from the pot, but do not wipe it out. Add the remaining tablespoon of butter and place over medium-low heat. Stir in the sauerkraut, tomato, caraway seeds, juniper berries, sage, basil, and anchovy paste. Mix well. Add the chicken stock and wine. Heat to boiling. Place the sautéed pork on top of the sauerkraut mixture, add the garlic cloves, and cover. Transfer the pot to the oven and bake for 1 hour and 10 minutes. Add the sausage and bake, covered, 20 minutes longer.

4. Meanwhile, make the dumplings. In a small saucepan combine the kasha with the water, salt, and butter. Heat to boiling. Reduce the heat and cook, covered, over low heat until tender, about 10 minutes. Transfer to a medium-size bowl and stir in the beaten egg, milk, cake flour, baking powder, chives, and parsley. Mix thoroughly.

5. Remove the pot from the oven. Cut the pork into bite-size pieces and slice the sausage. Return the meats to the pot and mix them into the sauerkraut. Place the dumpling batter, in large tablespoonfuls, over the top. Cover the pot, return it to the oven, and bake until the dumplings are firm, about 18 minutes.

Serves 6

GLOBE TROTTERS GROATS AND SAUSAGES

Of a decidedly mixed-up lineage, the next recipe makes a remarkably straightforward one-dish supper. I serve it with just a green salad, a crusty loaf of bread—and an icy cold beer.

9 sausages (3 sweet Italian, 3 hot Italian, and 3 Spanish chorizos), about 1¾ pounds total
2 medium onions, halved and sliced
1 tablespoon olive oil
1 medium green bell pepper, cored, seeded, and cut into strips
1 medium red bell pepper, cored, seeded, and cut into strips
1 medium yellow bell pepper, cored, seeded, and cut into strips
1½ cups whole white buckwheat groats
1 cup dry white wine
1½ cups homemade chicken stock (see page 376) or canned broth
½ cup sliced black olives (Niçoise or Kalamata)
Chopped fresh parsley, for garnish

1. Sauté the Italian sausages in a large saucepan over medium heat until well browned on all sides, 8 to 10 minutes. Transfer to a plate. Add the chorizos to the pan and sauté until well browned on all sides, 8 to 10 minutes. Transfer to the plate with the Italian sausages. Drain all but 1½ tablespoons of fat from the pan.

2. Add the onions to the pan and cook over medium heat until lightly browned, about 8 minutes. Transfer to a bowl.

3. Add the olive oil to the pan. Add all the peppers and toss over medium-high heat for 2 minutes. Return the onions to the pan and stir in the groats, wine, and stock, scraping the sides and bottom of the pan. Press the chorizos into the mixture, and top with the Ital-ian sausages. Heat to boiling. Reduce the heat and cook, covered, over low heat for 20 minutes. Remove the sausages and slice, on the angle, into 2-inch pieces. Return the sausage pieces to the pepper mixture and toss in the olives. Sprinkle with parsley.

Serves 4 to 6

CLARA B. LESS'S STUFFED CABBAGE ROLLS

Clara B. Less, a long-time denizen of Dearborn, Michigan, is probably one of the great unheralded cooks of the nation, and I am doing my best to put her on the map! A reader who became a pen pal, over the years she has sent me innumerable recipes that have worked their way (like inchworms) into books, articles, and newspaper columns. Her splendid-yet-salubrious dish that follows originally called for a tin of canned soup in the ingredients list, plus a pithy comment: "Bert, I know you hate cream of mushroom soup but the dish is *delicious!*" No question about it, Clara dear. But in my opinion better yet with a homemade blanket of béchamel sauce and mushrooms! Cheating cooks may use their own judgment in the matter. Just don't tell *me* about it, please!

With Mrs. Less's remarkable cabbage rolls, I usually serve an accompanying boat of tomato sauce. It's another option. The sauce of choice—heavy, heavy on the garlic—comes from another brilliant chef, Karl Dauner, currently at the helm of one of New York's best and brightest catering establishments, Custom Cuisine.

2 large eggs
1 cup whole or coarse-ground kasha
2 ounces salt pork, diced (about ½ cup)
1 medium onion, chopped
1 cup long-grain rice
2 tablespoons pearl barley
½ teaspoon salt
¼ teaspoon freshly ground black pepper
2 cups water
1 large head cabbage (about 3 pounds), leaves separated

¾ pound ground beef
½ pound ground veal
¼ pound ground pork
2 tablespoons chopped fresh parsley
Salt and freshly ground black pepper to taste
Béchamel Sauce with Mushrooms (recipe follows)
Karl Dauner's Garlic-Zapped Tomato Sauce (recipe follows; optional)

1. Lightly beat one of the eggs in a medium-size bowl. Stir in the kasha until well mixed. Transfer to a medium-size skillet and place over medium heat. Stir the kasha with a fork until it is dry and the grains are separated, about 3 minutes.

2. Cook the salt pork in a medium-size saucepan over medium heat until lightly browned, about 4 minutes. Add the onion; cook until lightly browned, about 3 minutes. Stir in the rice, kasha, barley, salt, pepper, and water. Heat to boiling. Reduce the heat and cook, covered, over low heat for 15 minutes. Stir once; then turn off the heat and let stand, covered, 10 minutes. Remove the cover and cool to room temperature.

3. Meanwhile, cook the cabbage leaves in boiling water to cover until just wilted, about 1 minute. Rinse under cold running water; then drain and pat dry with paper towels.

4. Preheat the oven to 350° F.

5. Combine the meats with the remaining egg, parsley, and cooled grain mixture in a large bowl. Season with salt and pepper, and mix well.

6. Fill the cabbage leaves generously with meat mixture, and roll them up. Place the rolls, seam side down, in a lightly greased large shallow baking dish. Chop any remaining cabbage and place it around and between the rolls. Spoon the Béchamel Sauce over the top and bake, covered, 1½ hours. Serve with Garlic-Zapped Tomato Sauce, if desired.

Serves 6 to 8

Béchamel Sauce with Mushrooms

4 tablespoons (½ stick) unsalted butter
¾ pound mushrooms, finely chopped
3 tablespoons all-purpose flour
1½ cups homemade chicken stock (see page 376) or canned broth
½ cup heavy or whipping cream

1. Melt 2 tablespoons of the butter in a large skillet over medium-high heat. Sauté the mushrooms until golden brown, about 5 minutes.

2. Melt the remaining 2 tablespoons butter in a medium-size saucepan over medium-low heat. Stir in the flour. Cook, stirring constantly, 2 minutes. Whisk in the chicken stock and the cream. Cook, whisking occasionally, until thick, about 8 minutes. Stir in the mushrooms.

Makes about 2¼ cups

Karl Dauner's Garlic-Zapped Tomato Sauce

¼ cup olive oil
4 to 5 cloves garlic, finely chopped
1 can (28 ounces) imported Italian plum tomatoes, with juice
2 teaspoons chopped fresh basil, or 1 teaspoon dried
¼ teaspoon crushed dried hot red peppers
Salt and freshly ground black pepper to taste

1. Heat the oil in a medium-size saucepan over medium-low heat. Add all but ½ teaspoon of the garlic; sauté until golden, about 4 minutes.

2. Add to the saucepan the tomatoes, all but ½ teaspoon of the basil, and the dried red peppers. Cook, uncovered, over high heat until all liquid has evaporated and the sauce is very thick, about 20 minutes. Add salt and pepper to taste. Remove from the heat and allow to cool slightly. Then stir in the remaining garlic and basil.

Makes about 2½ cups

LAMB STUFFED WITH EGGPLANT AND KASHA

A very different stuffed lamb dish, moist and rich with flavor, and perfect for a company dinner.

1 small eggplant (about ¼ pound)
Salt
½ cup whole kasha
1½ tablespoons lightly beaten egg
3 tablespoons olive oil
1 large onion, chopped
1 large clove garlic, minced
1 teaspoon crushed dried hot red peppers
1 cup homemade chicken stock (see page 376) or canned broth
¾ cup white wine
4 pounds boned and butterflied leg of lamb (from a 6- to 8-pound leg)
1 large clove garlic, slivered
Chopped fresh parsley, for garnish

1. Cube the eggplant, place it in a colander, and sprinkle it generously with salt. Let it stand 1 hour. Then brush the salt off with damp paper towels.

2. Meanwhile, stir the kasha with the egg in a medium-size bowl until well mixed. Transfer to a medium-size skillet and place over medium heat. Stir the kasha with a fork until it is dry and the grains are separated, about 3 minutes.

3. Heat 2 tablespoons of the oil in a medium-size saucepan or Dutch oven over medium-low heat. Add the onion; cook 3 minutes. Add the minced garlic and cook 2 minutes longer. Stir in the eggplant cubes and dried red peppers. Cook until the eggplant is soft and lightly colored, about 8 minutes. Stir in the kasha, and toss until it is coated with the onion/eggplant mixture. Stir in ½ cup chicken stock and ½ cup wine, and heat to boiling. Reduce the heat and simmer, covered, over low heat for 15 minutes. Stir once, then turn off the heat and let it stand, covered, 10 minutes. Cool slightly.

4. Preheat the oven to 400°F.

5. Spread the eggplant/kasha mixture over the lamb, and gently roll the lamb up like a jelly roll. Tie it in several places to secure it; then fold up the ends and tie lengthwise. Tuck the slivers of garlic under the strings on top of the rolled lamb. Roast the lamb on a rack in a roasting pan for 1 hour.

6. Reduce the heat to 325°F. Pour the remaining chicken broth and wine in the bottom of the pan and cook 20 minutes longer for medium rare.

7. Remove the lamb and let it stand for 8 minutes. Meanwhile, strain the pan juices and serve with the lamb. Sprinkle the lamb with parsley before serving.

Serves 6 to 8

OXTAILS WITH KASHA AND RICE

*T*his *Mittel Europa michati* is Czech—a dish of succulent oxtails stewed in a pot with kasha and rice and everything nice. Need I add, absolutely satisfying into the bargain? If you've given heed to my earlier advice about complex carbohydrates, you'll also note that each portion is like money in the body's "bank account"!

Take note that this dish is juicy. It is necessary to stir the mixture well during the last minutes of cooking so the kasha absorbs the liquid.

1 strip thick-cut bacon, diced
¼ cup all-purpose flour
½ teaspoon salt
½ teaspoon freshly ground black pepper
4 pounds oxtails, cut in pieces
2 tablespoons olive oil
1 tablespoon plus 1 teaspoon unsalted
    butter
1 medium onion, finely chopped
2 cloves garlic, minced
1 small carrot, finely chopped
1 small parsnip, finely chopped
2 large ribs celery, finely chopped
1 teaspoon chopped fresh thyme, or
    ¼ teaspoon dried
1 bay leaf
4 whole allspice, crushed
2 cups homemade chicken stock (see page
    376) or canned broth
2 cups dry white wine
2 cups water
1 cup whole kasha
1 large egg, lightly beaten
⅓ cup long-grain rice
½ teaspoon tomato paste
Chopped fresh parsley, for garnish

1. Preheat the oven to 350°F.

2. Cook the bacon in boiling water to cover for 5 minutes. Drain, and pat dry with paper towels.

3. Combine the flour with the salt and pepper in a shallow bowl. Lightly coat the oxtails with this mixture.

4. Heat 1 tablespoon of the oil with the 1 tablespoon butter in a large heavy pot or Dutch oven over medium heat. Sauté the oxtails in batches until brown on all sides, 5 minutes per batch. Using a slotted spoon, transfer them to a plate. Pour off the grease and wipe out the pot.

5. Add the remaining 1 tablespoon oil to the pot and sauté the bacon over medium-low heat for 3 minutes. Add the onion; cook 1 minute. Add the garlic; cook 2 minutes longer. Stir in the carrot, parsnip, celery, thyme, bay leaf, allspice, stock, wine, and water. Return the oxtails to the pot and heat to boiling, skimming the surface of fat. Cover the pot, transfer it to the oven, and cook until the meat is tender, about 2 hours and 15 minutes.

6. Meanwhile, stir the kasha with the egg in a medium-size bowl until well mixed. Transfer to a medium-size skillet and place over medium heat. Stir the kasha with a fork until it is dry and the grains are separated, about 3 minutes.

7. When the oxtails are tender, remove them from the pot and keep warm in a 225°F oven. Remove the bay leaf from the pot, and stir in the kasha and rice. Heat to boiling over medium-high heat. Reduce the heat and cook, covered, over low heat until tender, about 20 minutes. Remove the cover and stir in the tomato paste. Cook, stirring constantly, until all liquid has been absorbed, 4 to 5 minutes. Arrange the kasha on a platter, surrounded by the oxtails. Place the 1 teaspoon butter in the center of the kasha, and sprinkle with parsley.

Serves 4 to 6

TOMATO, CHEESE, AND GROATS SUPPER

"Groats" is a Middle English word with Druid antecedents, amended from *greot*, the same linguistic taproot that gave us "grit" and "grist"—all of which describe fragments of grain which promise little gratification in a bowl of porridge.

Quite on the contrary, the groats connection in the next quasi-Italian dish (devised of two kinds of tomatoes and three kinds of cheese) not only promises, it delivers: *satisfaction plus*.

2 tablespoons unsalted butter
1 medium onion, finely chopped
1 clove garlic, minced
1 cup whole white buckwheat groats
1 can (28 ounces) imported Italian
  tomatoes, with juice, coarsely chopped
¼ teaspoon salt
¼ teaspoon freshly ground black pepper
¼ teaspoon crushed whole allspice
1 package (15 ounces) ricotta cheese
1½ cups grated Gruyère cheese (about
  6 ounces)
¼ pound goat cheese, crumbled
1 egg, lightly beaten
½ cup sun-dried tomatoes in oil, cut into
  strips
¼ cup freshly grated Parmesan cheese

1. Preheat the oven to 350°F. Lightly butter a 2-quart round casserole dish.

2. Melt the butter in a medium-size saucepan over medium-low heat. Add the onion; cook 1 minute. Add the gar- lic; cook until lightly browned, about 5 minutes. Remove the pan from the heat.

3. Stir the groats into the onion mixture, tossing well to coat. Add the tomatoes, salt, pepper, and allspice. Heat to boiling. Reduce the heat and cook, covered, over low heat for 20 minutes.

4. Layer half the groats mixture over the bottom of the casserole dish.

5. Combine the ricotta, Gruyère, and goat cheese in a medium-size bowl. Beat in the lightly beaten egg. Dot the groats with half the cheese mixture. Place half the sun-dried tomato strips over the top. Add the remaining groats mixture. Dot with the remaining cheese mixture, and then the remaining tomato strips.

6. Bake 30 minutes. Sprinkle the top with Parmesan cheese, and bake 5 minutes longer.

Serves 6

KASHA AND RADISH SALAD

Strictly speaking, *kasha* is the word for "cereal" in most Slavic tongues. And while it has become virtually synonymous with long-cooked fricassees, goulashes, *suppes*, and *gedämpfte brusts* (depending upon the geography of the stove), that is not the whole story. Have a French provincial *salade de radis* to prove my point: kasha is simply not parochial provender!

1 cup whole kasha
1 large egg, lightly beaten
4 sprigs parsley
3 sprigs thyme
5 fresh sage leaves
2 cups water
¼ cup plus 1 teaspoon red wine vinegar
¾ teaspoon salt
¼ teaspoon freshly ground black pepper
1 clove garlic, crushed
2 teaspoons Dijon mustard
2 tablespoons fresh lemon juice
½ cup olive oil
½ cup thinly sliced radishes
2 tablespoons chopped fresh parsley

1. Stir the kasha with the egg in a medium-size bowl until well mixed. Transfer to a medium-size skillet and place over medium heat. Stir the kasha with a fork until it is dry and the grains are separated, about 3 minutes.

2. Tie the parsley and thyme sprigs with the sage leaves in a cheesecloth bag to make a bouquet garni. Combine the water, ¼ cup vinegar, ½ teaspoon of the salt, the pepper, and the bouquet garni in a medium-size saucepan. Stir in the kasha, and heat to boiling. Reduce the heat and cook, covered, over low heat for 15 minutes. Stir once, then turn off the heat and let stand, covered, 10 minutes. Cool to room temperature.

3. Mash the garlic with the remaining ¼ teaspoon salt in a small bowl until a paste is formed. Stir in the mustard, lemon juice, and the 1 teaspoon vinegar. Slowly whisk in the oil.

4. Place the kasha in a medium-size bowl and pour the vinaigrette dressing over it. Toss well. Lightly toss in the radishes and 1 tablespoon of the parsley. Sprinkle the remaining 1 tablespoon parsley over the top. Serve lightly chilled or at room temperature.

Serves 6

GROATS AND BLUE CHEESE FRITTERS

Have a change in fritters next time you're looking for a tasty aside to chicken or pork. These will give the more typical corn or apple varieties a real run for the money.

1 tablespoon unsalted butter
1 shallot, minced
1 clove garlic, minced
1 cup whole white buckwheat groats
2 cups homemade chicken stock (see page 376) or canned broth
½ pound aged (tangy) blue cheese, crumbled
¼ teaspoon freshly ground black pepper
1 cup fresh bread crumbs
¼ cup freshly grated Parmesan cheese
1 large egg
2 tablespoons water
Peanut oil for frying
Salt

1. Melt the butter in a medium-size saucepan over medium-low heat. Add the shallot; cook 1 minute. Add the garlic; cook until lightly browned, about 5 minutes. Stir in the groats and chicken stock, and heat to boiling. Reduce the heat and cook, covered, over low heat for 20 minutes. Add the blue cheese and the pepper, and stir until the cheese has melted and is incorporated into the groats.

2. Lightly grease a 9-inch cake pan. Spoon the groats mixture evenly into the pan. Cool, and then refrigerate for 1 hour.

3. Combine the bread crumbs with the Parmesan cheese in a shallow bowl. Blend the egg and the water in another shallow bowl.

4. Cut the groats mixture into pieces about 1 inch wide and 1½ inches long. Carefully dip them in the egg mixture, and then coat with the bread crumb mixture.

5. Heat ¼ inch of peanut oil in a heavy skillet. Sauté the fritters (about six at a time) until crisp and golden, about 2 minutes per side. Remove with a slotted spoon and pat dry on paper towels. Keep warm in a 225°F oven while cooking the remaining fritters (or reheat for 10 minutes in a 400°F oven). Sprinkle with salt before serving.

Serves 6

ROSE LEVY BERANBAUM'S KASHA VARNISHKES

My grandparents had not the slightest inkling of buckwheat's health properties. They ate kasha simply because it gave them gratification. I suggest you do the same, starting with this dish: a highly untraditional rendering of an "old country" canon that was donated to my collection by one of the great bakers of the world, Rose Levy Beranbaum. Rose is not only a past-mistress of cake decoration but also a cook with real soul. Her notable *kasha varnishkes* with dried porcini mushrooms (yet) might have shocked my grandparents initially, but only until the first bite. It is a kasha variation to die for!

½ ounce dried porcini mushrooms
¼ cup hot water
1 cup coarse-ground kasha
1 large egg, lightly beaten
5 tablespoons unsalted butter
2 cups chopped onions
1 teaspoon sugar
1 pound large white mushrooms, including stems, sliced
2 large cloves garlic, minced
1 teaspoon salt
1½ teaspoons freshly ground black pepper
1 tablespoon chopped fresh oregano, or 1 teaspoon dried
1½ cups (approximately) homemade chicken stock (see page 376) or canned broth, heated
2 cups bow-tie noodles
Chopped fresh parsley, for garnish

1. Soak the dried mushrooms in the hot water in a small bowl until soft, about 15 minutes. Drain, reserving the liquid. Chop the mushrooms and reserve.

2. Meanwhile, stir the kasha with the egg in a medium-size bowl until well mixed. Transfer to a medium-size skillet and place over medium heat. Stir the kasha with a fork until it is dry and the grains are separated, about 3 minutes.

3. Melt 4 tablespoons of the butter in a large saucepan over medium heat. Add the onions, sprinkle with the sugar, and cook, stirring often, until well browned, about 8 minutes. Add the sliced white mushrooms and the garlic. Cook, covered, stirring occasionally, until the mushrooms release their liquid, about 4 minutes. Uncover and continue to cook until all the liquid has evapo-

rated, 8 to 10 minutes.

4. Stir the kasha into the onion-mushroom mixture, and cook 2 minutes. Add the reserved porcini mushrooms, salt, pepper, and oregano. Add enough hot chicken stock to the reserved mushroom liquid to make 1¾ cups. Stir this into the kasha mixture and heat to boiling. Reduce the heat and cook, covered, over low heat for 15 minutes. Stir once, turn off the heat, and let stand, covered, about 10 minutes.

5. Meanwhile, cook the noodles in boiling salted water until just tender, about 12 minutes. Drain, and return to the pan. Toss with the remaining 1 tablespoon butter, cover, and keep warm over low heat.

6. Transfer the kasha mixture to a flameproof dish. Place under a preheated broiler, and broil, stirring often, to brown the kasha. Toss with the cooked noodles, and sprinkle with parsley.

Serves 6

GREEN BRUMUS

Kasha is obviously one of man's movable feasts. Green Brumus (it means "midnight snack") stems from the upper regions of Newfoundland, where it is eaten only in the summer months. Presumably by the light of the midnight sun . . . Serve it year round to accompany your favorite pot roast.

½ pound string beans, trimmed (cut large
    beans in half)
⅓ cup whole kasha
1 tablespoon lightly beaten egg
1 cup homemade chicken stock (see page
    376) or canned broth
¼ teaspoon salt
⅛ teaspoon freshly ground black pepper
2 tablespoons unsalted butter
3 scallions, white bulbs and green tops,
    chopped
½ bunch watercress, with 2 inches of stem,
    separated
¼ cup red wine vinegar
Salt and freshly ground black pepper to
    taste
Chopped fresh parsley, for garnish

1. Cook the beans in boiling salted water to cover until crisp-tender, about 3 minutes. Rinse under cold running water; drain.

2. Stir the kasha with the egg in a medium-size bowl until well mixed. Transfer to a medium-size saucepan and place over medium heat. Stir the kasha with a fork until it is dry and the grains are separated, about 3 minutes. Stir in the stock, salt, and pepper. Heat to boiling. Reduce the heat and cook, covered, over low heat for 15 minutes. Stir once and keep warm, partially covered, over low heat.

3. Melt the butter in a large heavy skillet over medium-high heat. Add the scallions; cook 2 minutes. Add the beans, tossing well to coat with scallions. Stir in the watercress and vinegar. Cook, tossing constantly, until almost all liquid has evaporated, about 3 minutes. Reduce the heat to medium-low and stir in the cooked kasha. Add salt and pepper to taste, and sprinkle with the parsley.

Serves 4

KASHA CORNSTICKS

Kasha and cornmeal fused into 40-carat cornsticks that are the best meal-stretcher a breakfast, lunch, or dinner could have. The formula has been around for years; I found it on a box of Wolff's kasha! There's no egg wash in this recipe, as the kasha is meant to season the cornbread, not dominate it.

1 cup milk
½ cup whole kasha
4 tablespoons (½ stick) unsalted butter, cut into bits
1 cup plus 2 tablespoons all-purpose flour
½ cup yellow cornmeal
4 teaspoons baking powder
½ teaspoon salt
¼ teaspoon freshly ground black pepper
¼ cup honey
2 tablespoons toasted sesame seeds (see Note)
1 egg, lightly beaten

1. Preheat the oven to 425°F.

2. Heat the milk in a medium-size saucepan to the scalding point; remove the pan from the heat. Stir in the kasha and butter. Let stand until lukewarm.

3. In a large mixing bowl, combine the flour with the cornmeal, baking powder, salt, and pepper. Add the kasha mixture to the flour mixture along with the honey, sesame seeds, and egg. Stir only until mixed; do not overwork.

4. Pour the batter into a well-greased cornstick pan (see Baker's Secret, page 42). Bake until firm to the touch, 15 to 20 minutes. Let stand 10 minutes before unmolding.

Makes about 2 dozen cornsticks

Note: To toast sesame seeds, spread the seeds in a skillet and place them over medium heat, stirring several times until they turn golden brown, 6 to 8 minutes.

DAY-AFTER HUSH PUPPIES

I love prandial residuals (a high-falutin term for leftovers). The terrific breakfast (or lunch or dinner) dish that follows requires little more than one vital ingredient: a cup of leftover Cream of Buckwheat and Garlic. So be a generous cook the night before!

1 cup cold leftover Cream of Buckwheat and Garlic (see page 72)
3 tablespoons fresh bread crumbs
1 tablespoon unsalted butter
1 teaspoon vegetable oil

1. Form the leftover buckwheat mixture into patties, using 1½ tablespoons for each. Roll them in the bread crumbs.

2. Heat the butter with the oil in a large heavy skillet over medium heat. Sauté the hush puppies until golden brown and warmed through, about 3 minutes per side.

Makes 6 patties

CREAM OF BUCKWHEAT AND GARLIC

Cream of Buckwheat is a commercial cereal ground from the heart of buckwheat grains. It is pale in color and highly palliative in flavor. Slosh Cream of Buckwheat with cream and sugar, or for a side dish, amend the velvety texture with practically any seasoning that comes to mind. My mind elected garlic in this recipe. Serve it next time you roast a chicken.

15 cloves garlic, unpeeled
2 tablespoons plus 2 teaspoons unsalted
    butter
3 cups milk
½ cup Cream of Buckwheat (see Note)
2 tablespoons freshly grated Parmesan
    cheese
Salt and freshly ground black pepper to
    taste

1. Drop the garlic cloves into boiling water; cook 2 minutes. Drain, cool slightly, and peel.

2. Melt the 2 tablespoons butter in a heavy saucepan. Add the garlic. Cook, covered, over low heat until tender, about 30 minutes (do not allow to brown).

3. Mash the garlic with a fork, adding ¼ cup of the milk, until a paste is formed. Add the remaining milk and heat to boiling. Add the Cream of Buckwheat and simmer, stirring frequently, until thickened, 10 to 12 minutes. Add the 2 teaspoons butter, the Parmesan cheese, and salt and pepper. Serve immediately.

Serves 4

Note: Cream of Buckwheat is available at most natural foods stores or may be mail-ordered from Pocono Mills, Penn Yan, New York. See the list of suppliers and mail-order sources at the back of the book.

BUCKWHEATRIVIA

Over the years, buckwheat has bloomed in America under some highly chequered colloquial aliases. In the anthropomorphic Northeast, it has been harvested and milled under such colorful tags as Dog Tongue, Antelope Brush, and Bee's Bonnet. In the South, black farmers have picked it as Napkin Ring, Indian Tobacco, and Sulphur-and-Molasses Blossom—the latter most probably because of its therapeutic effect on the system after being hulled. But who knows for sure? Middle-Western pioneer settlers called buckwheat Whisk Broom, Umbrella Plant, and Spotted Turban—the last handle obviously a reference to the plant's variegated pink and white flora. In the Southwest, where it has never flourished in homesteaders' fields with any constancy, buckwheat's monikers reflect a true touch of agrarian chauvinism: Desert Strumpet and Witch's Weeds for starters.

BITECKY

What's up next is a Russian dish of long and highly polished credentials. This version of bitecky (there are as many variants in Kiev as there are chicken cutlets) is special because of the healthy mite of mushrooms in the dish. If I am feeling lavish as a czar, I whip it up with porcini or shiitake mushrooms. If I'm feeling a pinch in the pocket, I make my bitecky with anything the supermarket has on sale. And the bitecky fans never know the difference!

2 tablespoons unsalted butter
2 large shallots, minced
1¼ cups finely chopped mushroom caps
    (about 4 ounces)
1 cup whole white buckwheat groats
1 cup heavy or whipping cream
1 cup homemade chicken stock (see page
    376) or canned broth
½ cup freshly grated Parmesan cheese
Salt and freshly ground black pepper to
    taste
Chopped fresh parsley, for garnish

1. Melt the butter in a medium-size saucepan over medium-low heat. Add the shallots; cook 1 minute. Raise the heat to medium-high and stir in the mushrooms. Cook, stirring constantly, until lightly browned, about 4 minutes.

2. Stir the groats into the mushroom mixture, tossing well to coat. Add the cream and chicken stock. Heat to boiling. Reduce the heat and cook, covered, over low heat for 20 minutes. Stir in the cheese. Season with salt and pepper, and sprinkle with parsley.

Serves 6

BUCKWHEAT LACE

For further proof of whole white buckwheat groats' mutability, have a lovely old southern recipe for a super-crunchy cookie.

1 cup whole white buckwheat groats
1 egg
½ teaspoon vanilla extract
8 tablespoons (1 stick) unsalted butter,
    melted
1 cup firmly packed light brown sugar
½ cup walnut halves, chopped

1. Preheat the oven to 375°F.

2. Place the groats in the container of a food processor. Process until fairly fine.

3. Beat the egg with the vanilla and the butter in a large bowl until smooth. Beat in the brown sugar, groats, and walnuts.

4. Lightly butter an aluminum foil–lined baking sheet. Drop the batter by generous teaspoonfuls onto the foil, placing them far apart. Spread each spoonful of cookie batter out flat; do not mound. Bake until golden brown, about 8 minutes. Remove the foil from the baking sheet, and let the cookies cool completely before peeling them off the foil. Repeat until all the batter is used up.

Makes about 30 cookies

THE FLOURING OF THE GRAIN

Nutrition-minded bakers may grind buckwheat flour at home or purchase it, packaged, at natural foods stores.

To grind your own: process 1 cup of white or roasted whole buckwheat groats in a food processor or blender until it is finely pulverized, about 3 minutes.

My rule of thumb for adding buckwheat flour to any standard baking recipe is to substitute ⅓ to ½ cup of buckwheat flour per cup of a higher-gluten flour. Since buckwheat flour contains virtually no gluten (which gives baked goods their essential lightness), I most often combine it with all-purpose, whole-wheat, or bread flour—the last being the most gluten-rich.

Commercially ground buckwheat flour comes in two types: dark and light. Both are 100 percent buckwheat, but the dark variety has a more pungent flavor and contains a higher percentage of the fine-milled particles of seed hulls.

FROM-SCRATCH BUCKWHEAT NOODLES

After pancakes, I would certainly nominate pasta as buckwheat flour's crowning achievement. The Japanese have a very special place in their cuisine for a super-healthy pasta devised of buckwheat flour, known as soba noodles. Soba noodles are available at Oriental groceries, but I would seriously advise any creative cooks with a spot of time on their hands to consider making buckwheat pasta from scratch.

It's easiest to prepare the dough in a food processor, though I prefer to roll it out in an old-fashioned hand-cranked pasta machine, myself.

This recipe is only slightly altered from the one to be found in *Better Than Store-Bought*, by my good friends Helen Witty and Elizabeth Schneider.

2 large eggs
1 cup buckwheat flour
½ cup bread flour
½ cup all-purpose flour
½ teaspoon coarse (kosher) salt
2 or 3 tablespoons water

1. Place the eggs in the container of a food processor. With the motor running, add the flours, salt, and enough water to make a firm dough, allowing the motor to run until the sides of the container come clean and the dough forms a ball.

2. Transfer the dough to a lightly floured surface. Knead by hand for 5 minutes. Let the dough stand, loosely covered, for 5 minutes. Then roll it out by hand or with a pasta machine until very thin. Cut into noodles. Hang the noodles over a broom handle or the back of a chair until dry. Store in airtight plastic bags.

Makes about 10 ounces dry pasta

PIZZOCHERI

What follows is a little-known (so far) Italian buckwheat pasta dish that stems from the Valtellina region of Lombardy. It is called *pizzocheri*, and it is a generous bequest from one of the best pastry makers and teachers in New York, Nick Malgieri.

Nick states that many versions of *pizzocheri* exist, but all share a common ingredients list. There must be sage, potatoes, and some form of green (cabbage, spinach, or Swiss chard) to cloak the buckwheat pasta; and there must be two cheeses, Parmesan and a soft melting type (Taleggio, Fontina, or French Vacherin). His preferences are chard for earthy flavor and Taleggio for earnest richness.

½ pound (about 2 medium) new potatoes
¾ pound Swiss chard (red variety, if possible)
3 tablespoons unsalted butter
1 medium onion, halved and thinly sliced
1 large clove garlic, minced
1½ tablespoons chopped fresh sage, or 1½ teaspoons dried sage leaves rubbed together
½ pound dry From-Scratch Buckwheat Noodles (see facing page)
½ pound Taleggio, Fontina, or Vacherin cheese, cubed
⅓ cup freshly grated Parmesan cheese
Salt and freshly ground black pepper to taste
Chopped fresh parsley, for garnish

1. Peel, halve, and cut the potatoes into ¼-inch-thick slices. Cook the potato slices, uncovered, in boiling salted water to cover for 5 minutes. Cover and remove from the heat; let stand until cooked through, about 15 minutes longer. Drain.

2. Meanwhile, trim the stems from the chard and cook them in boiling salted water to cover for 2 minutes. Add the leaves and cook until wilted, about 2 minutes more. Drain and chop.

3. Melt the butter in a large saucepan over medium-low heat. Add the onion; cook, covered, 5 minutes. Add the garlic and sage. Cook, uncovered, 1 minute. Remove the pan from the heat.

4. Cook the pasta in a large pot of boiling salted water until just tender, about 3 minutes for homemade, about 8 for commercially prepared. Drain.

5. Return the saucepan with the onions to low heat. Add the potato slices and toss lightly to warm through. Add the cooked pasta, the Swiss chard, and both cheeses. Toss lightly until the cheese has melted. Season with salt and pepper and sprinkle with parsley.

Serves 4 to 6

JAMES RIVER STYLE PASTA WITH CLAMS

Years and years ago, when I was in college in Virginia, we would often cut classes and go clamming in the tidewater where the James River and Atlantic Ocean almost meet. The result of these aquatic expeditions was a dish devised of clams, Smithfield ham, and a shot of bourbon, served on noodles.

Half a lifetime later, it is still a favorite comfort food—best when some other daredevil does the clamming, however. Buckwheat noodles are right at home here, and look into Surrey Ham (see the source list) for their not-too-salty confederate.

3 dozen small clams, washed well
½ teaspoon cornstarch
2½ tablespoons unsalted butter
1 medium onion, finely chopped
1 large clove garlic, minced
1 cup homemade chicken stock (see page 376) or canned broth
¼ cup white wine
8 ounces dry From-Scratch Buckwheat Noodles (see page 74)
½ cup finely chopped smoky country ham
½ cup chopped fresh parsley
¼ teaspoon freshly ground black pepper
1 teaspoon bourbon

1. Place the clams in a large bowl. Add cold water to cover, and stir in the cornstarch. Let stand 15 minutes. Rinse several times under cold running water; drain. This will effectively clean the clams.

2. Melt 1½ tablespoons of the butter in a large saucepan over medium-low heat. Add the onion; cook 1 minute. Add the garlic; cook 4 minutes longer. Add the cleaned clams, the stock, and the wine. Heat to boiling. Reduce the heat and cook, covered, until the clams open, about 5 to 8 minutes.

3. Remove the clams from the broth and place them in a bowl. Remove the clam meat from the shells, catching all juices. Add the juices to the broth and boil until reduced by about one third, about 5 minutes. Coarsely chop the clams.

4. Meanwhile, cook the pasta in a large pot of boiling salted water until just tender, about 3 minutes for homemade, about 8 minutes for commercially prepared. Drain.

5. When the clam broth has reduced sufficiently, stir in the ham, pasta, and parsley. Toss until warmed through. Toss in the pepper and bourbon.

Serves 4

BRAWNY BREAD

Brawny, because this is one bread loaded with goodness. Coffee and molasses add dark rich flavor to the loaf, while whole groats add a bit of crunch. It makes a wonderful sandwich bread.

¾ cup whole white buckwheat groats
1¾ cups lukewarm water
2 tablespoons dry yeast
½ cup brewed coffee, lukewarm
¼ cup molasses
¼ cup honey
1 cup light buckwheat flour
5 tablespoons unsalted butter, melted
1½ cups bread flour
2½ to 3 cups stone-ground whole-wheat
    flour
1 egg white

1. Heat a large non-stick skillet over medium heat. Add the groats, and sprinkle with ¼ cup of the water. Stir the groats with a fork until they are dry and lightly toasted, about 5 minutes. Set the skillet aside.

2. Sprinkle the yeast over the lukewarm coffee in a large bowl. Stir in the molasses and honey. Let stand until the yeast begins to bubble, 10 minutes.

3. Add the remaining 1½ cups water to the yeast mixture. Using a heavy wooden spoon, stir in the buckwheat flour, 3 tablespoons of the butter, ½ cup of the toasted groats, and the bread flour. Then stir in the whole-wheat flour, about ½ cup at a time, until a stiff dough is formed. Turn onto a floured board and knead, adding more whole-wheat flour if needed, until smooth and elastic, about 10 minutes.

4. Place the dough in a large greased bowl. Cover, and let rise in a warm place until doubled in bulk, about 1½ hours.

5. Punch down the dough. Knead it on a lightly floured surface for 5 minutes. Return the dough to the bowl, cover, and let rise until doubled in bulk again, about 1 hour.

6. Punch down the dough once more. Knead it briefly, and divide it in half. Roll each half lengthwise into a sausage shape about 10 inches long. Beat it flat with your hands, and fold the dough into thirds. Brush each loaf with egg white, and roll them in the remaining toasted groats. Place each loaf in a buttered bread pan measuring about 9 by 5 by 3 inches. Cover them with flour-rubbed tea towels and let stand until the dough rises over the edge of the pans, about 1 hour.

7. Preheat the oven to 375°F.

8. Bake the bread until the loaves sound hollow when tapped, 35 to 40 minutes. Turn the loaves out onto racks, and brush the tops with the remaining melted butter to give them a sheen.

Makes 2 loaves

CAMPTON PLACE'S CRANBERRY BUCKWHEAT MUFFINS

*B*uckwheat's best breakfast utility (aside from pancakes) is indubitably in muffin form. The best I know are served up at the fabled Campton Place Hotel in San Francisco. These quintessential hot breads are the handiwork of Bradley Ogden, one of the most talented chefs to be found in America. For evidence of that extravagant statement, whip up a batch at once!

1⅓ cups fresh cranberries, picked over
¾ cup sugar
3 tablespoons fresh orange juice
1¼ cups all-purpose flour
1 cup light buckwheat flour
1½ tablespoons baking powder
½ teaspoon baking soda
1 teaspoon salt
2 eggs
8 tablespoons (1 stick) unsalted butter, melted
½ cup buttermilk (approximately)

1. Combine the cranberries with ½ cup of the sugar and the orange juice in a medium-size bowl. Let stand for 30 minutes.

2. Preheat the oven to 375°F.

3. Grease a twelve-cup muffin tin.

4. Combine the flours, remaining ¼ cup sugar, baking powder, baking soda, and salt in a bowl.

5. In a separate bowl, beat the eggs with the butter until smooth. Stir in the cranberries, with all their liquid. Beat in the dry ingredients. Stir in enough buttermilk to make a soft batter. Do not overbeat.

6. Fill the muffin cups about seven-eighths full. Bake until firm and golden brown, about 15 minutes. Cool the tin on a rack for 10 minutes before unmolding the muffins.

Makes 12 muffins

OLD-FASHIONED BUCKWHEAT CAKES

This is the best buckwheat pancake recipe extant: light yet velvety-rich flapjacks, invented by the talented Phillip Stephen Schulz. I am just sorry my father isn't around to sample a batch!

Serve them with butter and maple syrup, or honey thinned with warm water.

2½ cups milk
2 tablespoons molasses
1½ teaspoons dry yeast
1⅓ cups buckwheat flour
⅔ cup all-purpose flour
½ cup fine-ground cornmeal
½ teaspoon salt
1 teaspoon sugar
1 teaspoon baking soda
½ cup lukewarm water
2 tablespoons unsalted butter, melted
2 egg yolks, lightly beaten
3 egg whites

1. Eight to 12 hours before serving, scald the milk and stir in the molasses. Let the mixture cool to lukewarm, then stir in the yeast and let stand until the yeast begins to bubble, 10 minutes. Transfer to a large bowl.

2. Using a wooden spoon, stir the buckwheat flour into the molasses mixture. Stir in the all-purpose flour, cornmeal, and salt. Beat until smooth. Cover, and let stand at room temperature 8 to 12 hours.

3. Just before serving, dissolve the

sugar and baking soda in the lukewarm water in a small bowl. Stir this into the prepared batter, then whisk in the butter and egg yolks.

4. Beat the egg whites in a large bowl until stiff. Fold them into the batter.

5. Pour about ⅓ cup batter for each cake on a preheated griddle or into a non-stick skillet. Cook over medium heat until bubbles form on top and the underside is nicely browned, about 1 minute. Turn the cake over and brown the other side.

Makes about 18 pancakes

BIGWIG BLINI

A pancake of another stripe. These are Russian, and still the most welcome course in dietary *détente* the Soviets have to offer. Traditionally, blini are served with two bowls on the side: one filled with caviar, the other heaped with sour cream. The caviar is meant to be spooned inside the warm pancake, and a dab of sour cream covers that. The blini is then folded in half and sluiced with melted butter. If you can't spring for Beluga or Sevruga for your blinis, don't despair; smoked salmon, thinly shaved, makes an excellent substitute.

This recipe, I might add, did not come into my hands from the KGB. It is the sterling creation of W. Peter Prescott, affable Entertaining Editor of *Food & Wine* magazine.

As these pancakes require at least 4½ hours pre-preparation, a batch may be made partially in advance (through step 3) and refrigerated. Remember to let the batter come to room temperature before continuing, however. Timing makes the difference between a delicate blini and a dud ICBM!

1 teaspoon dry yeast
½ teaspoon sugar
1¼ cups buttermilk, lukewarm
½ cup sifted buckwheat flour
½ teaspoon baking soda
5 tablespoons unsalted butter, melted and
  cooled
2 eggs, separated
½ cup sour cream
¾ cup sifted all-purpose flour
½ teaspoon salt
¼ cup milk

1. Combine the yeast with the sugar and ¼ cup of the buttermilk in a large bowl. Let stand until the yeast begins to bubble, 10 minutes.

2. Stir the buckwheat flour, baking soda, and the remaining 1 cup buttermilk into the yeast mixture. Cover with a tea towel and let stand in a warm place until doubled in volume, about 2 hours.

3. Whisk 3 tablespoons of the butter with the egg yolks and sour cream in a medium-size bowl until smooth. Stir this into the buckwheat mixture. Then stir in the all-purpose flour, salt, and milk. Cover, and let stand in a warm place until doubled in volume, about 2 hours.

4. Beat the egg whites until stiff but

not dry. Fold them into the buckwheat mixture, and cover loosely with plastic wrap. Let stand 30 minutes.

5. Pour about 2 tablespoons batter for each blini onto an oil-rubbed preheated griddle or non-stick skillet. Do no more than four at a time; the blini should be no more than 3 inches in diameter. Cook over medium heat until lightly browned on the bottom and the surface is covered with bubbles, about 1 minute. Turn over and lightly brown the other side. Place the blini on a plate and brush lightly with melted butter. Keep warm in a 225°F oven while you cook the remaining batter.

Serves 6 to 8 as an appetizer (makes about 32 blini)

PANCAKECCLESIA

If you will recall, it was my father's buckwheat proclivity that began this chapter in the first place. His love of buckwheat was obviously a genetic legacy, for I have the craving too—though neither Greene could claim singularity in the predilection.

Washington Irving, for instance, once confided that his dream breakfast would be "two dozen dainty slapjacks of buckwheat covered with a pitcher each of honey and treacle and soaked by a hogshead of butter"! Diamond Jim Brady was another prodigious buckwheat fancier. Brady's trencherman appetite for pancakes was so enormous (fifty per sitting) that he once caused a major maple syrup shortage at Rector's restaurant in New York City by appearing there for breakfast twice in the same day.

Have another pair of buckwheat addicts: Gary Cooper and Ernest Hemingway. It is reported in Ketcham, Idaho, that these two outdoorsmen friends held an informal pancake-eating duel in the 1940s to determine whose capacity was the greater. Cooper, the movie star who had to watch his weight, stopped after the twelfth serving. Hemingway, the writer who prided himself on an unbridled appetite in all things, won the contest by downing seventeen. But according to scuttlebutt, he lost by default, as he was forced to "unswallow" shortly after laying down his fork. The world's champion pancake eater is probably the least well known, outside *The Guiness Book of Records*, that is. Peter Dowdeswell of Northampton, England, consumed sixty-two buckwheat cakes (6 inches in diameter) in 6 minutes 58.5 seconds on February 9, 1977. And kept them down too.

FRACTURED FUDGE CAKE

I like every chapter to end on a sweet note. The chocolate cake that follows is one of the most satisfying you will ever swallow—and somewhat healthier than most, for the existence of buckwheat flour in its devise.

I received the recipe from a friend in Washington, along with a brief description: "Rich!" she wrote. "And remarkably fudgy!" she amended.

Being a hopeless recipe fiddler (never able to leave well enough alone), I tried making it with buckwheat flour. *Disaster!*

Lucky to have Rose Levy Beranbaum (the cake baker's first aid) as a friend, I called for help. Scientist that she is, Rose analyzed the problem at once: it was the lack of gluten in buckwheat flour that turned the cake flat. She also suggested a cure; substituting high-gluten bread flour for two thirds of the buckwheat. The cake worked like a charm, and it is now the prize of my chocolate repertoire. I told you I like happy endings!

I call this cake "Fractured Fudge" because the top rises nobly in the oven and then fissures slightly as it cools. Don't give it another thought. Cover the fracture with lots of whipped cream and give thanks to Rose, as I do, with every forkful.

12 ounces semi-sweet chocolate
5 tablespoons brewed espresso or very
*   strong coffee*
1 cup (2 sticks) unsalted butter, at room
*   temperature*
2 cups sugar
6 eggs, separated
⅔ cup bread flour
⅓ cup dark buckwheat flour

1. Preheat the oven to 350°F. Lightly butter and flour a 9-inch springform pan.

2. Combine the chocolate and the coffee in the top of a double boiler, and stir over simmering water until the chocolate has melted and the mixture is smooth. Set aside to cool.

3. In the large bowl of an electric mixer, slowly beat the butter with the sugar until light and lemon-colored. Beat in the egg yolks, one at a time, beating thoroughly after each addition.

4. On low speed, beat in the cooled chocolate mixture, and then both flours.

5. Beat the egg whites until stiff, and fold them into the cake batter. Pour the batter into the prepared springform pan. Bake until the top is crusty and the cake is fairly firm, 65 to 70 minutes. Cool on a rack before unmolding. (The top will be very crusty. If the outer edges do not separate from the pan, tap the pan lightly with the side of a knife, then unmold.)

Serves 8

BULGUR

Has Kept Man Vital Since the Dawn of Time

Bulgur came into my life under mildly shocking circumstances: I first sampled it at a bordello in Paris. And while stranger initiations must surely have taken place in houses of ill repute, none, I suspect, ever had a more profound effect on the sampler's taste buds.

I journeyed to France for the first time when I was over forty and overanxious about new experiences—that is to say, totally unprepared for culture shocks. France was a country I had yearned to visit all my life. From the time I was twelve and decided someday I would live in an atelier in Montmartre, painting pictures like Utrillo, I'd prepared myself for the experience. I learned all the street names by heart. I knew which bridge across the Seine was closest to the Louvre (where my pictures would hang). I was an unmitigated francophile—but scared to go there.

Experienced travelers warned me not to be too optimistic about the French. Looks were deceiving, these friends cautioned. The French could be very testy with those who were not fluent in their language.

At the last moment I flew to England instead, for what, I rationalized, would be a week's introduction to Europe in one's native tongue. But the atmosphere (and language) of the British was so comfortable that the week soon extended to a month, while the visa to France wilted in my wallet. Finally the departure date could no longer be postponed.

It is a brief hop from England to France, but on arrival at the airport in Paris, I was beset with a paralyzing sense of long distance. The high school French I'd hoped to redress with months of tutoring proved hopeless the moment I quizzed an airline employee about *les hôtels*.

I had left London so precipitately that there had been no time to arrange accommodations. Unfortunately, my arrival coincided with an international automobile show in Paris. Every hotel I had ever heard about was completely booked when I telephoned for a reservation. Growing dispirited, I made my way to the French equivalent of Travelers' Aid.

The young woman in charge was extremely attractive but totally detached. She responded to my translated dilemma with a survey of her polished fingernails and a perfect command of English.

"What a pity you did not inquire about commercial activities in the city beforehand," she chided. "Though next week would not be better. There is a major fabric fair being held." Then, noting my look of desperation, she consulted first a large portfolio and then a small telephone.

After dialing and exchanging a flurry of indecipherable French with someone on the phone, she turned to me with a thin smile, inquiring: "Is a private bath a necessity? An elevator a prerequisite?" When I shook my head no, she shook hers as well, murmuring, *"D'accord.* There is a small establishment on Rue de Bruyard. Reputedly more commercial than residential but..."—here she lowered her lids—"to tell you frankly, sir, there has been no update on its status in my files for some years. Two hundred francs a night."

"I'll take it."

The driver of the taxi, edging through the late-day traffic of Paris, was even less edifying when I tried to quiz him (in French of course) about the hotel's location. "Is it a quiet street?" I managed after some mental gymnastics.

"Tranquille?" He was plainly being diplomatic. "Perhaps in the early morning hours, monsieur."

The hotel on Rue de Bruyard was less than a block from the infamous Place Pigalle. The building was small and nondescript, old but not old enough to be considered antique. There was no lobby, just a greasy counter backed with a rack displaying just one key. The clerk, who was eating a bowl of aromatic stew or soup, did not rise as I entered. Primed for my appearance, however, he stopped chewing long enough to pluck the key from its nest, collect my payment, and hand over the register to be signed. The smell of what he was eating was intoxicating, but I was aware as I scrawled my name that while every room was supposedly occupied, no other guests had registered.

The room I was assigned was five flights up a winding staircase that grew narrower at each landing.

To my dismay, I had to carry my luggage up the steps in the dark, as the hall lights unpredictably extinguished (to save power) every few seconds and had to be switched on again at the next landing.

Banging about in the gloom gave me some insight into the true nature of this establishment. At one landing, a tall man, adjusting his trousers as he closed a door, smiled in complicity before making his descent. At another, two young women wearing the briefest pants I'd ever seen sat on the steps counting money and arguing wildly, paying no attention whatsoever as I passed between them.

When I reached the room I had been assigned, it turned out to be a swollen dormer jutting over the roof. A naked light bulb hanging over the bed was burned out, and while there was a rusty sink in one corner, no towels could be found.

In high dudgeon, I marched down the stairs again, almost colliding with half a dozen sailors so drunk they collapsed on the landing like dominoes.

"What kind of place is this anyway?" I shouted in flawless French at the taciturn clerk, still eating his stew.

"Algerian" was his only explanation. Unruffled, he wiped his moustache. "You want a reduction in price? Here..." He handed me a worn fifty-franc note. "But be quiet. No questions asked. Do not call the police!"

"You don't seem to understand," I stammered. "There are no towels in my room. And the light bulb..."

"Ah, a little girl will take care of those details directly. Go to your room, monsieur." He smiled, mollifying me like a cranky child who is offered a lollipop. Like a fool I did as I was told.

As I climbed the stairs again, the smell of the dish he was eating seemed to pervade the entire building—like a

smoky but not unpleasant perfume. As I sat on the lumpy bed, I realized that I had not eaten since breakfast in London and was very, very hungry. From the window I could—by bending my head to my shoulder—observe a sliver of the Eiffel Tower like a crescent moon, illuminating the inky violet sky.

Presently there was a knock at the door. The promised "little girl," who was at least twenty-five and exceedingly well endowed, stood in the semi-gloom carrying two thin towels and a plate of the same dish the clerk had been eating, both of which she handed over sullenly.

"What's this?" I asked, accepting the bowl. She shrugged and started down the steps. If a man did not know a bribe when he saw one, he was obviously not worth her time.

"Wait," I cried. She halted at the first step. "What is this called?"

"*Bourgouri.*" She spat the word out. "Supposed to make a man..." She did not attempt to finish the sentence, but her gestures explicitly described great virility.

Sitting on the bed, I ate the *bourgouri*, which was delicious. I don't know if it had any effect on my manhood. I left the hotel the next morning and never pursued the question. But it decidedly gave me a letch—for bulgur.

The Grain's Genesis

Bulgur, the parched, steamed, and dried berries of wheat, has kept man vital and vertical since the dawn of time. Maybe even longer. According to Arab folklore, the forbidden tree in the Garden of Eden was no blooming apple at all but a high-rise stalk of wheat—a plant so enormous that every kernel was the size of Adam's head and so wide that the snake God had placed there to guard it could not possibly span the trunk's circumference. Literally at loose ends, this reptile convinced Eve to prune the of-

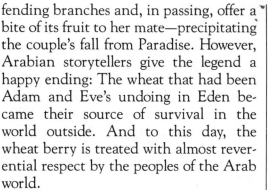

fending branches and, in passing, offer a bite of its fruit to her mate—precipitating the couple's fall from Paradise. However, Arabian storytellers give the legend a happy ending: The wheat that had been Adam and Eve's undoing in Eden became their source of survival in the world outside. And to this day, the wheat berry is treated with almost reverential respect by the peoples of the Arab world.

The Middle East was indubitably the landscape where bulgur was born, but it spread soon afterward in every possible direction. As far back as 1000 B.C., Stone Age Laplanders amended their diet of raw meat with an uncooked wheat gruel, and they'd probably be chomping it still if evolving ice caps had not made grain cultivation in Arctic geography a horticultural bust.

If I tell you that bulgur survived the prevailing winds of change, it is no overstatement. Evidence of this grain in China predates the birth of Christ by about 2,800 years. It was introduced by the Emperor Shen Nung, who declared the five sacred crops of China to be soybeans, rice, barley, millet, and wheat. However, dried cooked wheat did not become a popular food in the Orient until the ascension of the Qin ruler Shih Huang-ti in 221 B.C. Almost four centuries after Shen's pronouncement, Shih banned noodles (which he claimed induced softness of character) and instituted a regimen of barely cooked grains and wheat porridges meant to toughen his countrymen for the struggle for independence.

According to all reliable data—which is scanty at best—Shih's ordinance lasted a mere decade. During that short time, however, consumption of wheat (in dishes not unlike bulgur) swept all of China and then spread to Japan and India as well.

Traces of cooked sun-dried wheat grains have been found in Egyptian tombs, Etruscan urns, and Hun saddle-bags. The Romans even had a word for bulgur. They called it *cerealis*, after the goddess of harvests, Ceres. Ancient Israelites had their own name, *dagan*, which means "bursting kernels of grain."

Some Plain Grain Talk

*T*he most persistent myth about bulgur is that it is simply cracked wheat. Not so. Both bulgur and cracked wheat are indeed compounded of whole wheat berries, but there the similarity ends.

Cracked wheat, as its name implies, is uncooked wheat that has been dried first and cracked apart later, by coarse milling. Bulgur, on the other hand, is wheat that has been steamed, then dried (whole or partially debranned) before being crushed into various grinds.

Since bulgur is only marginally processed, it is a grain that is vitamin-high. Each quarter pound of bulgur contains over 11.2 grams of protein, 75.7 grams of carbohydrates, 338 milligrams of phosphorus, and 229 milligrams of potassium, as well as healthy doses of calcium, iron, thiamine, riboflavin, and niacin. Or as many nutrients as one will find in a whole loaf of 100 percent whole-wheat bread!

The differences between bulgur and cracked wheat are most apparent at the stove. Bulgur requires a mere presoaking when it is used for salads like tabbouleh, and only minimal cooking when it is to be the basis of a pilaf or stew. Cracked wheat is something else again. Dried raw, essentially, it requires an extended period of boiling before it is even barely digestible. And while a gung-ho cook can convert a cup of cracked wheat into a reasonably accurate facsimile of bulgur when the occasion demands, bulgur and cracked wheat are definitely *not* interchangeable in the recipes that follow.

How to Buy It

*U*ntil recently bulgur was not an easy item to find at most American supermarkets. Prior to the mid-1960s, it was eaten exclusively by transplanted émigrés from the Middle East, and it was only an intrepid cook with a taste for tabbouleh or falafel who made tracks to an Armenian, Lebanese, or Syrian neighborhood grocer for the ingredients.

Happily, times have changed and packaged bulgur can now be found on most supermarket shelves—sandwiched between barley, buckwheat, and wild rice. Better news still is that bulgur may also be purchased in bulk (at considerably reduced prices) from natural foods stores and mail-order sources.

When you are shopping for bulgur, note that packaged and bulk varieties come in three different grades: *Coarse grind*, which has a rice-like texture, is most often used for pilafs and stuffings. *Medium grind* (or all-purpose) is the one I choose for cold salads and cooked vegetable side dishes. *Fine grind*, the most delicately milled of all, is the one I specify for bread and dessert recipes. In the recipes that follow, I rarely specify the grind of bulgur. It's the cook's choice, but keep in mind the above guidelines.

Storing bulgur, however, is another matter entirely, and I have lots of suggestions about that.

To maximize this grain's shelf life in the pantry, I strongly recommend the use of a large glass canning jar—preferably one that is absolutely airtight, with a hinged lid and rubber ring—as protection against heat spoilage and insect invasion.

No matter what the container, bulgur should be kept out of direct sunlight and stored below 60°F. If you have room, this grain will also keep for months in the refrigerator and for up to a year in the freezer. If a glass container is too cumbersome, consider airtight plastic bags for refrigerator or freezer storage.

A friend of mine places several herbal tea bags in the old-fashioned apothecary jar that holds her bulgur. She claims the tea retards weevils. While I cannot verify that, I do know that the delicate scent of camomile and such gives the grains one memorable bouquet.

How to Cook It

*T*astes differ as to the proper degree of munch and crunch in a dish of bulgur, so I offer no hard and fast rules for its preparation, only basic techniques (which are absolutely fail-safe for even a neophyte to grains cookery). Basic bulgur may be prepared four ways:

The Non-Presoak Method. Place 1 cup bulgur with 2½ cups liquid in a covered heavy saucepan over low heat. As it cooks, the grain will absorb all the liquid—about 20 to 25 minutes. (Cooking times will vary with the grind of bulgur used. A fine-milled grind will take considerably less time than a coarse or medium grind.) When the liquid is entirely absorbed, remove the pan from the heat and allow the bulgur to stand, still covered, for an additional 10 minutes. This allows the flavors to meld and the grains to dry out and separate. Fluff the cooked bulgur with a fork before serving.

The Hot Presoak Method. Place 1 cup bulgur in a heatproof bowl. Cover it with 3 to 4 cups of boiling salted water and let stand 40 minutes or longer. Line a colander with cheesecloth, place it in the sink, and drain the bulgur in it. Then twist the cheesecloth around the bulgur and squeeze until all moisture is extracted. At this point, the bulgur requires no extra cooking.

The Cold Presoak Method. Follow the hot presoak procedure, using cold water. However, cold-water soaking takes twice as much time: 2 to 2½ hours.

Some bulgur aficionados insist that the long soaking allows the grains to absorb liquid very slowly and consequently the bulgur has a more toothsome quality.

The Boiled Method. Bulgur may also be boiled like rice. Place 1 cup of bulgur in a large pot filled with 3 or 4 quarts of boiling salted water. Bring back to the boil, reduce the heat, and simmer 20 minutes. Then drain the bulgur in a strainer and press the grains dry with a spoon before it is served.

TEN-LAYER VEGETABLE SOUP

*B*ulgur's virtue in the kitchen, aside from its significant nutritional bonus, is its taste, faintly reminiscent of whole-wheat toast—a taste that even newcomers to grain-grazing find familiar and comforting.

From a cook's point of view, bulgur has another prime asset: mutability. This is a grain that can bow to assertive seasonings without losing a jot of its individuality. Consider the following quickly made soup devised of any and every veggie a fridge or freezer can yield, plus an increment of bulgur to fuse the flavors. It is a recipe, incidentally, very loosely based on a Tuscan garden soup from the redoubtable Nika Hazelton's collection.

2 tablespoons olive oil
2 medium tomatoes, cut into ¼-inch-thick slices
2 medium onions, cut into ¼-inch-thick slices
¼ teaspoon crushed whole allspice
2 cloves garlic, minced
1 large head romaine lettuce, shredded
½ cup bulgur
1 cup chopped fresh parsley
½ cup chopped fresh basil, or 2 tablespoons dried
1 large zucchini or yellow squash, cubed
¼ teaspoon crushed dried hot red peppers
1 package (10 ounces) frozen peas
1 package (10 ounces) frozen baby lima beans
2 teaspoons mixed chopped fresh herbs (sage, rosemary, chives, thyme)

1½ cups homemade chicken stock (see page 376) or vegetable stock (see page 378) or canned chicken broth
Salt and freshly ground black pepper to taste
Freshly grated Parmesan cheese

1. Spread the oil over the bottom of a large soup pot and layer all the ingredients, starting with the tomatoes and through the lima beans, in the pot. Cover, and cook over medium-low heat for 15 minutes.

2. Remove the cover, stir in the herbs and stock, and heat to boiling. Reduce the heat and simmer, uncovered, for 30 minutes. Season with salt and pepper. Pass the Parmesan cheese on the side.

Serves 6

PERSIAN LAMB SHANKS WITH BULGUR

This dish of lamb shanks and bulgur, cooked in wine and dappled with currants, may taste like a pasha's party fare, but it's not. The only thing Persian about it, in fact, is the rug it was named after!

4 lamb shanks, about 12 ounces each
2 large cloves garlic, slivered
Salt and freshly ground black pepper to
*　　taste*
Hot Hungarian paprika
3 tablespoons all-purpose flour
*　　(approximately)*
2 tablespoons unsalted butter
2 tablespoons olive oil
1 large onion, halved and thinly sliced
¼ teaspoon chopped fresh rosemary, or a
*　　pinch of dried*
¾ cup red wine
1¼ cups water
¼ cup dried currants
2 cups homemade beef stock (see page 377)
*　　or canned broth*
1⅓ cups bulgur
Chopped fresh parsley, for garnish

1. Preheat the oven to 375°F.

2. With an ice pick or a sharp knife, make five or six holes in the flesh of each lamb shank. Insert a sliver of garlic into each hole. Sprinkle each shank with salt, pepper, and paprika to taste. Dust the shanks with the flour.

3. Heat the butter with the oil in a large pot or Dutch oven over medium heat. Sauté the lamb shanks until golden on all sides, about 10 minutes. Transfer the lamb shanks to a plate. Add the onion to the pot; cook until golden, about 4 minutes. Stir in the rosemary.

4. Return the lamb shanks to the pot. Add the wine and water, and heat to boiling. Cover, transfer the pot to the oven, and bake 1½ hours.

5. Reduce the heat to 350°F and remove the pot from the oven. Transfer the shanks to a plate. Stir the currants into the cooking juices. Add the stock, scraping the sides and bottom of the pot.

Bulgur is a grain with more aliases than a shifty sheik. Depending upon which side of the Persian Gulf a cook's forebears were born on, you will find it spelled as *bulghur, bulgor, bulgar, boulgar, boulghour, borgul, borgol, burghul,* or *burghoul.*

And if you think that's confusing, let me tell you that one man's bulgur is definitely *not* another's borghul! The product found on the shelves of your supermarket is a far cry from any grain seller's offering in the Casbah.

For starters, American bulgur, which has been steamed and dried in rotary drums, is a deep russet-to-umber color and generally comes from hard winter wheat grown in Kansas, Nebraska, or Texas.

Middle Eastern bulgur, grown in the wheat fields of Afghanistan, Syria, and Lebanon, is a much lighter shade and almost always milled from soft summer wheat. Moreover, since it is parboiled and sun-dried, authentic bulgur retains a slight grassy aftertaste that true bulgurophiles recognize and dote upon.

Stir in the bulgur. Place the pot over medium heat, and heat to boiling. Return the shanks to the pot, cover, return it to the oven, and bake until the bulgur is tender and all liquid has been absorbed, 20 to 25 minutes. Before serving, fluff the bulgur with a fork and sprinkle with parsley.

Serves 4

OTTOMAN MEATBALLS IN TOMATO SAUCE

*B*ulgur is added to the meat mixture here to give the meatballs a slightly nutty flavor. I serve this dish over rice, but spaghetti does nicely as well.

FOR THE TOMATO SAUCE

4 tablespoons (½ stick) unsalted butter
1 medium onion, finely chopped
1 clove garlic, minced
1 small rib celery, finely chopped
4 large ripe tomatoes, peeled, seeded, and chopped
1 teaspoon chopped fresh basil, or ½ teaspoon dried
1 teaspoon chopped fresh oregano, or ¼ teaspoon dried
Pinch of dried thyme
2 teaspoons sugar
¼ teaspoon grated orange zest
Salt and freshly ground black pepper to taste

FOR THE MEATBALLS

½ cup homemade beef stock (see page 377) or canned broth
¼ cup bulgur
2 teaspoons unsalted butter
1 small onion, finely chopped
1 clove garlic, minced
1 pound 5 ounces ground beef
10 ounces ground veal
5 ounces ground pork
2 eggs, lightly beaten
½ cup chopped fresh parsley
½ cup freshly grated Parmesan cheese
½ teaspoon salt

¼ teaspoon freshly ground black pepper
2 tablespoons olive oil (approximately)
Chopped fresh parsley, for garnish

*B*ulgur is not exclusive to the Middle East. This grain came to European tables as early as 1470, a souvenir of the Ottoman rulers who branched out after their conquest of Turkey. At its high point, during the reign of Sultan Suleiman the Magnificient, the Ottoman Empire stretched from the Bosporus clear across the Balkans to Vienna, not counting outposts in Africa and Asia Minor. And Ottoman influences in fashion, furnishings, and food reverberated all over the Western World during its five hundred years of dominance—even crossing the Atlantic at one point. It is reported that, to finance his second trip to the New World, Columbus acceded to Queen Isabella's wishes and planted Ottoman wheat. And he remained there, rooted to the spot, until the first seedlings sprouted.

1. Make the tomato sauce: Melt the butter in a large saucepan over medium-low heat. Add the onion; cook 1 minute. Add the garlic and celery; cook 4 minutes. Stir in the tomatoes, basil, oregano, thyme, sugar, and orange zest. Cook, uncovered, stirring occasionally, until thick, about 45 minutes. Season with salt and pepper, and set aside.

2. Make the meatballs: Place the stock in a small saucepan and heat to boiling. Stir in the bulgur and reduce the heat. Cook, covered, over low heat until the bulgur is almost tender and all liquid has been absorbed, 15 to 20 minutes. Set aside, covered, until cool.

3. Melt the butter in a medium-size skillet over medium-low heat. Add the onion; cook 1 minute. Add the garlic;

cook 4 minutes longer. Set aside.

4. Combine the beef, veal, and pork in a medium-size bowl. Add the cooked bulgur, the onion mixture, and the eggs, parsley, Parmesan cheese, salt, and pepper. Mix thoroughly and form into small meatballs.

5. Heat the oil in a heavy skillet over medium heat. Sauté the meatballs, a few at a time, adding more oil if needed, until well browned, about 5 minutes. As the meatballs are sautéed, set them aside on a plate.

6. Heat the tomato sauce over medium heat until hot. Add the meatballs, and reduce the heat to medium-low. Cook, uncovered, for 30 minutes. Before serving, sprinkle with parsley.

Serves 6

TWIN ROASTED CHICKENS WITH GARLICKY BULGUR DRESSING

Don't be put off by the forty cloves of garlic—the long, slow sautéeing removes the sting. The bulgur will be slightly crunchy when you stuff the birds, but it will steam in the cavities as the chickens roast.

FOR THE STUFFING

2 large heads garlic, cloves separated,
    unpeeled (about 40 cloves)
4 tablespoons (½ stick) unsalted butter
1½ cups homemade chicken stock (see page
    376) or canned broth
1¼ cups bulgur
2 tablespoons chopped fresh parsley
1 teaspoon chopped fresh sage, or
    ¼ teaspoon dried
½ teaspoon salt
¼ teaspoon freshly ground black pepper

FOR THE CHICKEN

2 small chickens (2½ to 3 pounds each)

4 tablespoons (½ stick) unsalted butter, at
    room temperature
2 tablespoons Dijon mustard
¼ cup fresh bread crumbs

1. Make the stuffing: Cook the garlic cloves in boiling water to cover for 2 minutes. Drain and peel.

2. Melt the butter in a large saucepan over low heat. Add the garlic cloves. Cook, covered, until the garlic is very tender, about 20 minutes. Do not allow it to brown.

3. Using a fork, mash the garlic into a paste. Add the chicken stock and heat

to boiling. Stir in the bulgur and reduce the heat. Cook, covered, over low heat until all liquid has been absorbed, about 15 minutes. Remove the pan from the heat and add the parsley, sage, salt, and pepper. Allow the stuffing to cool slightly.

4. Preheat the oven to 375°F.

5. Spoon the stuffing into the cavities of the chickens. Sew securely and truss. Pat the chickens dry with paper towels, and place them on a rack in a roasting pan, breast side up.

6. Combine the softened butter with the mustard and bread crumbs, and mix until smooth. Spread this mixture evenly over the tops and sides of the chickens. Place the chickens in the oven and roast until they are crisp and the juices run yellow when pricked with a fork, about 1½ hours. Remove the trussing strings before serving.

Serves 4 to 6

ARMENIAN-STYLE CHICKEN WITH BULGUR

*F*rom the northeastern region of Turkey, this hearty dish is basically a bulgur-thickened stew. Walnuts and honey in its devise give a whiff of the exotic land from which it comes.

2 tablespoons olive oil
1 teaspoon unsalted butter
1 chicken (3½ pounds), cut into serving
    pieces
½ teaspoon salt
¼ teaspoon freshly ground black pepper
½ teaspoon chopped fresh thyme, or
    ¼ teaspoon dried
1 medium onion, chopped
2 cloves garlic, minced
1 small hot red pepper, seeded, deveined,
    and minced
2 cups homemade chicken stock (see page
    376) or canned broth
1 cup bulgur
½ cup broken walnut pieces
1 tablespoon honey
1 teaspoon chopped fresh mint, or
    ¼ teaspoon dried
1 teaspoon chopped fresh basil, or
    ½ teaspoon dried

1. Heat the oil with the butter in a large cast-iron skillet over medium heat. Sprinkle the chicken pieces with the salt, pepper, and thyme, and sauté, a few pieces at a time, until golden brown, about 10 minutes. Transfer the pieces to a plate as they are done.

2. Remove all but 1 tablespoon fat from the skillet. Add the onion and cook over medium-low heat, scraping the sides and bottom of the pan, for 2 minutes. Add the garlic and hot pepper; cook 4 minutes longer.

3. Return the chicken pieces to the skillet, stir in the stock, and heat to boiling. Reduce the heat and simmer, covered, for 20 minutes.

4. Using tongs, remove the chicken pieces to a plate. Stir the bulgur into the cooking juices, and add the walnuts and honey. Mix well and return the chicken pieces. Continue to cook, covered, until the chicken and bulgur are tender and

all liquid has been absorbed, about 20 minutes longer. Turn off the heat and let the skillet stand, covered, for 10 minutes. Before serving, fluff the bulgur with a fork, and sprinkle with the mint and basil.

Serves 4

PAKISTANI CHICKEN WITH BULGUR RICE

From Pakistan, a more traditional stew. Serve it on a large platter, surrounded with the mixture of bulgur and rice to sop up the juices.

½ cup bulgur
½ cup long-grain rice
1 tablespoon unsalted butter
2 teaspoons vegetable oil
1 chicken (about 3½ pounds), cut into pieces
1 large clove garlic, minced
1 teaspoon fennel seeds
½ teaspoon cayenne pepper
½ teaspoon turmeric
¼ teaspoon ground cumin
½ teaspoon salt
¼ teaspoon freshly ground black pepper
1 medium onion, chopped
½ teaspoon paprika
½ cup water
Chopped fresh parsley, for garnish

1. Cook the bulgur in a large pot of boiling salted water for 10 minutes. Add the rice; boil 12 minutes longer. Drain in a colander.

2. Place the colander over 2 inches of boiling water in another pot. Do not let the bottom of the colander touch the water. Cover the bulgur/rice mixture with a single layer of paper towels. Steam for at least 15 minutes. (The mixture can be held this way for several hours without harm.)

3. Meanwhile, heat the butter with the oil in a large heavy skillet over medium heat. Sauté the chicken pieces, a few at a time, until well browned, about 10 minutes. Transfer the chicken to a plate.

4. While the chicken is browning, place the garlic, fennel seeds, cayenne pepper, turmeric, cumin, salt, and black pepper in a small bowl and mash with the back of a spoon until smooth.

5. When all the chicken pieces are sautéed, drain all but 1 tablespoon fat from the skillet. Add the onion; cook over medium-low heat, scraping the bottom and sides of the pan, for 3 minutes. Stir in the mashed garlic and spice mixture; cook 2 minutes longer. Sprinkle the mixture with the paprika. Stir in the water and return the chicken pieces to the skillet. Heat to boiling. Reduce the heat and simmer, covered, basting occasionally, until the chicken is tender, about 40 minutes.

6. To serve, fluff the bulgur/rice mixture with a fork and arrange it around the edge of a serving platter. Spoon the chicken mixture into the center, and garnish with parsley.

Serves 4

BERBER CHICKEN AND TOMATO SALAD

*F*rom Morocco, a wonderfully simple salad that, on its native shores, is often made with couscous. I like it best at room temperature.

1 cup bulgur
1 cup chopped, seeded, peeled tomatoes
*   (about 2 medium)*
2 cups boneless skinless cooked chicken
*   pieces*
3 tablespoons chopped fresh basil
1 teaspoon chopped fresh mint
2 cloves garlic, minced
⅓ cup olive oil
3 tablespoons red wine vinegar
Salt and freshly ground black pepper to
*   taste*

Chopped fresh parsley, for garnish

1. Cook the bulgur in a large pot of boiling salted water until tender, 20 to 25 minutes. Drain, and set aside to cool.

2. In a large bowl, combine the cooled bulgur, tomatoes, chicken, basil, mint, and garlic. Lightly toss, then add the oil, vinegar, and salt and pepper. Sprinkle with parsley.

Serves 4 to 6

PEPPERED PAILLETTE

A paillette is a spangle used for ornamenting decorative costumes. In this case, it's green salsa that turns a leftover turkey dish into a joyous occasion.

2 tablespoons olive oil
1 medium onion, chopped
1 clove garlic, minced
1 medium red bell pepper, cored, seeded,
*   and chopped*
2 cups cooked turkey or chicken
½ cup hot green salsa
1½ cups homemade chicken stock (see page
*   376) or canned broth*
1 cup bulgur
Salt and freshly ground black pepper to
*   taste*
Chopped fresh parsley, for garnish

1. Heat the oil in a medium-size

saucepan over medium-low heat. Add the onion; cook 1 minute. Add the garlic and bell pepper; cook 4 minutes longer.

2. Add the turkey to the pepper mixture and toss to coat. Stir in the salsa and chicken stock, and heat to boiling. Stir in the bulgur, reduce the heat, and cook, covered, over low heat until the bulgur is tender and all liquid has been absorbed, 20 to 25 minutes. Turn off the heat and let the pan stand, covered, for 10 minutes. Fluff the bulgur with a fork, and season with salt and pepper. Before serving, sprinkle with parsley.

Serves 4 to 6

TOMATO BULGUR WITH SCRAMBLED EGGS

*T*his combination of creamy bulgur topped with even creamier scrambled eggs makes a perfect brunch dish with nothing more than a green salad on the side. The eggs must be cooked *slowly* to obtain a smooth, velvety texture.

FOR THE TOMATO BULGUR

2 tablespoons olive oil
1 medium onion, chopped
2 cloves garlic, minced
1 can (14 ounces) imported Italian plum
    tomatoes, with juices, chopped
1 cup chopped, seeded, peeled fresh
    tomatoes (2 medium)
Pinch of sugar
⅛ teaspoon dried thyme
⅛ teaspoon dried oregano
1 tablespoon chopped fresh basil, or 2
    teaspoons dried
½ teaspoon anchovy paste
8 crushed whole allspice
1 tablespoon unsalted butter
1½ cups homemade chicken stock (see page
    376) or canned broth
¾ cup bulgur
Salt and freshly ground black pepper to
    taste

FOR THE SCRAMBLED EGGS

1 tablespoon unsalted butter
2 tablespoons heavy or whipping cream
4 eggs, lightly beaten
Salt and freshly ground black pepper to
    taste
Chopped fresh parsley, for garnish

1. Make the tomato bulgur: Heat the oil in a medium-size saucepan over me-dium heat. Add the onion; cook 2 min-utes. Add the garlic; cook 2 minutes longer. Stir in the canned and fresh tomatoes, sugar, thyme, oregano, basil, and anchovy paste. Cook, uncovered, until the tomatoes are soft and the sauce is fairly thick, about 15 minutes. Add the crushed allspice and the butter. Cook 5 minutes longer.

2. Add the stock to the tomato mix-ture, and heat to boiling. Stir in the bulgur and reduce the heat. Cook, cov-ered, over low heat until the bulgur is tender and all liquid has been absorbed, 20 to 25 minutes. Turn off the heat and let the pan stand, covered, for 10 min-utes. (If the mixture seems too wet, re-move the cover and stir over medium-low heat until it is creamy in texture.) Add salt and pepper.

3. Meanwhile, make the scrambled eggs: Melt the butter in a large skillet over low heat. Whisk the cream into the eggs and pour the mixture into the skil-let. Cook over low heat, stirring fre-quently, until soft curds form, about 20 minutes. Add salt and pepper.

4. To serve, arrange the tomato bul-gur in a warm serving dish. Spoon the eggs evenly over the top. Sprinkle with parsley.

Serves 4 to 6

IRAQI TABBOULEH

W hile the precise meaning of *tabbouleh* changes with the landscape on which it is made, most denizens of the Middle East agree that it translates as "good table dish"!

1 cup bulgur
1 medium onion, finely chopped
6 scallions, white bulbs and green tops, finely chopped
1½ cups chopped fresh parsley
½ cup finely chopped fresh mint
¼ cup olive oil
¼ cup fresh lemon juice
Salt and freshly ground black pepper to taste
2 medium tomatoes, seeded and chopped
Lettuce or fresh grape leaves, for serving
Marinated artichoke hearts, olives, hard-cooked eggs, or nasturtium leaves or flowers, for garnish
Toasted pine nuts, for garnish

1. Place the bulgur in a medium-size bowl. Cover with cold water, and let stand until softened, 2 to 2½ hours. Line a strainer with a double layer of cheese-cloth, and pour in the bulgur. Twist the cloth around the bulgur and squeeze until all moisture has been extracted.

2. Transfer the bulgur to a large bowl. Mix in the onions and scallions with your hands. Stir in the parsley, mint, olive oil, and lemon juice. Season with salt and pepper, and toss in the tomatoes. Refrigerate, covered, for at least 2 hours before serving.

3. To serve, mound the mixture in a shallow bowl or on a platter. Surround it with lettuce or grape leaves. Add any of the garnishes, and sprinkle the pine nuts over the salad.
Serves 6 to 8

TEXAS TABBOULEH

T his Texas rendering (high on the jalapeños) is not an absolutely authentic tabbouleh, but a great version, nonetheless. It is the handiwork of talented Michael McLaughlin, chef-owner of The Manhattan Chili Company in New York City.

1 cup bulgur
1 large red bell pepper
2 jalapeño peppers: 1 seeded, deveined, and minced; 1 seeded, deveined, and coarsely chopped
2 small tomatoes, seeded and chopped
2 medium zucchini, chopped
4 scallions, white bulbs and green tops, chopped
1 tablespoon chopped fresh basil
2 cloves garlic, coarsely chopped
½ cup fresh cilantro (Chinese parsley) leaves
½ cup fresh mint leaves
¼ cup white wine vinegar
¾ cup olive oil
Salt and freshly ground black pepper to taste
Lettuce leaves, for serving
8 ounces goat cheese, crumbled
Chopped fresh parsley, for garnish

1. Cover the bulgur with boiling salted water in a heatproof bowl. Let it stand 40 minutes.

2. Meanwhile, roast the bell pepper over a gas flame, turning until it is charred all over (or place it under a broiler until charred). Carefully wrap the pepper in paper towels and place in a plastic bag. Let it stand until cool. Then rub the charred skin from the pepper with paper towels, and chop the pepper.

3. Line a strainer with a double layer of cheesecloth, and pour in the bulgur. Twist the cloth around the bulgur and squeeze until all moisture has been extracted. In a mixing bowl, combine the chopped bell pepper and the bulgur with the minced jalapeño pepper, the tomatoes, zucchini, scallions, and basil. Toss well.

4. Place the coarsely chopped jalapeño pepper, garlic, cilantro leaves, mint leaves, vinegar, and oil in the container of a food processor or blender. Process until smooth. Pour over the bulgur mixture, and season with salt and pepper.

5. Arrange lettuce leaves over the bottom of a salad bowl. Mound the bulgur mixture in the center, and dot the top with the goat cheese. Sprinkle with parsley.

Serves 4 to 6

LEBANESE BORGHOL

A salad, borghol (another name for bulgur) stems from Lebanon, where it is eaten hot or cold, for breakfast, lunch, or dinner, as a side dish to meat, fowl, fish, or simply a plate of fresh greens. Unlike tabbouleh, borghol is cooked, and not presoaked.

⅓ cup olive oil
1 medium onion, chopped
2 large cloves garlic, minced
1 cup chopped, seeded, peeled tomatoes
1 tablespoon chopped fresh basil, or 1 teaspoon dried
1 cup bulgur
1½ cups homemade beef stock (see page 376) or canned broth, heated
1 tablespoon honey
1 tablespoon tomato paste
½ teaspoon salt
½ teaspoon freshly ground black pepper
2 tablespoons chopped fresh parsley

1. Heat the oil in a medium-size saucepan over medium heat. Add the onion; cook until lightly browned, about 3 minutes. Add the garlic; cook 1 minute longer. Stir in the tomatoes and basil. Cook 2 minutes longer.

2. Stir the bulgur into the tomato mixture, making sure that the bulgur is well coated. Stir in the beef stock. Reduce the heat to low and cook, covered, for 5 minutes.

3. Add the honey, tomato paste, salt, and pepper to the bulgur mixture. Continue to cook, covered, until the bulgur is tender and all liquid has been absorbed, 15 to 20 minutes. Turn off the heat and let the pan stand for 10 minutes. Then use a fork to toss in 1 tablespoon of the parsley. Sprinkle the remaining parsley over the top before serving. Serve hot or cold.

Serves 4 to 6

KEYMA
(Lentils with Bulgur)

K*eyma* is supposedly an Indian dish, or so it was noted when this recipe came to me umpteen years ago. Lentils and bulgur make a remarkably tonic combination. I am happy to make a whole lunch of just this dish.

1 cup lentils
3 tablespoons unsalted butter
1 teaspoon vegetable oil
1 large onion, chopped
1 clove garlic, minced
Pinch of ground cloves
1 jalapeño pepper, seeded, deveined, and
  minced
¼ pound cooked ham, chopped
2 tablespoons plus ¼ cup chopped fresh
  parsley
2 cups homemade chicken stock (see page
  376) or canned broth
1 cup bulgur
2 tablespoons red wine vinegar
Salt and freshly ground black pepper to
  taste

1. Cook the lentils in a large pot of boiling salted water until partially tender, about 20 minutes. Drain.

2. Heat the butter with the oil in a large saucepan over medium-low heat. Add the onion; cook 1 minute. Add the garlic and sprinkle with the cloves; cook 4 minutes longer. Stir in the jalapeño pepper, the ham, and the 2 tablespoons parsley. Continue to cook 5 minutes.

3. Add the lentils to the onion mixture. Stir in the stock and heat to boiling. Stir in the bulgur and reduce the heat. Cook, covered, over low heat until the bulgur is tender, 20 to 25 minutes. Turn off the heat and let the pan stand, covered, for 10 minutes. Then add the vinegar, salt and pepper to taste, and the ¼ cup parsley, fluffing the bulgur with a fork.

Serves 4

HERBED ORZO AND BULGUR PILAF

Orzo is a rice-shaped Greek pasta that matches up well with bulgur. Serve this next time you roast a leg of lamb.

4 tablespoons (½ stick) unsalted butter
2 large scallions, white bulbs and green
  tops, finely chopped
½ cup orzo
2 cups lamb stock (see page 378)
1 cup bulgur

1 tablespoon minced fresh rosemary, or 1
  teaspoon dried
1 tablespoon minced fresh basil, or 1
  teaspoon dried
1 tablespoon minced fresh parsley
1 teaspoon minced garlic

1. Melt the butter in a medium-size saucepan over medium heat. Add the scallions; cook 1 minute. Stir in the orzo; cook 4 minutes. Add the lamb stock and heat to boiling. Stir in the bulgur and reduce the heat. Cook, covered, over low heat until the bulgur is tender and all liquid has been absorbed, 20 to 25 minutes. Turn off the heat and let the pan stand, covered, for 10 minutes.

2. Stir the herbs and garlic into the bulgur mixture, fluffing it with a fork. Serve immediately.

Serves 4 to 6

TRIPLE-THREAT ONION PILAF

Yellow onions, leeks, and shallots add pizzazz to a basic pilaf. This goes well with fowl of all sorts.

3 tablespoons unsalted butter
1 teaspoon olive oil
1 medium onion, finely chopped
2 medium leeks, rinsed well and finely chopped
1 shallot, minced
1 large clove garlic, minced
1 cup bulgur
2½ cups homemade beef stock (see page 377) or canned broth, or 1½ cups beef stock with 1 cup chicken stock (see page 376)
¼ cup chopped fresh parsley
Salt and freshly ground black pepper to taste
¼ cup freshly grated Parmesan cheese

1. Heat the butter with the oil in a large heavy saucepan over medium-low heat. Add the onion; cook 1 minute. Stir in the leeks, shallot, and garlic. Reduce the heat to low and cook, covered, for 30 minutes.

2. Add the bulgur to the onion mixture, tossing to coat the grains. Add the stock and heat to boiling. Reduce the heat and cook, covered, over low heat until the bulgur is tender and all liquid has been absorbed, 20 to 25 minutes.

Turn off the heat and toss in the parsley. Let the mixture stand, covered, 10 minutes. Then season with salt and pepper, fluffing the bulgur with a fork. Sprinkle with the Parmesan cheese.

Serves 4

A BULGUR CAVEAT!

Since bulgur is precooked, *do not overcook it!*

A good rule of thumb is to remove a grain or two from the pot after 20 minutes of cooking time has elapsed. It will not be done, but the texture should be "toothsome" enough to allay any fears, and then the dish can be completed with utter confidence.

And remember: The final 10 minutes resting time, off the heat, is when the bulgur becomes dry and light.

TURKISH "FOREIGN RICE"
(Ecnebi Pirinc)

*T*his is a side dish served in the dining car of the Orient Express on its last lap, from Venice to Istanbul. *Ecnebi pirinc* (foreign rice) is also a slang expression for "small change"—which this definitely is not!

2 tablespoons olive oil
1 medium onion, chopped
1 clove garlic, minced
¼ teaspoon chopped fresh thyme, or a
*   pinch of dried*
1 teaspoon chopped fresh basil, or
*   ½ teaspoon dried*
2 medium tomatoes, peeled, seeded, and
*   chopped (about 1¼ cups)*
½ cup cubed hard salami (preferably
*   Italian or Hungarian)*
1¼ cups homemade chicken stock (see page
*   376) or canned broth, heated*
1 cup bulgur
½ cup ricotta or cottage cheese
Chopped fresh parsley, for garnish
Freshly grated Parmesan cheese (optional)

1. Heat the oil in a large saucepan over medium heat. Add the onion; cook until lightly browned, about 3 minutes. Add the garlic; cook 1 minute longer. Stir in the herbs and tomatoes. Reduce the heat to medium-low and cook, covered, until the tomatoes are very soft and juicy, about 10 minutes. Add the cubed salami; cook, covered, 2 minutes longer.

2. Remove the cover from the saucepan, add the chicken stock, and heat to boiling. Stir in the bulgur and reduce the heat. Cook, covered, over low heat until the bulgur is tender and all liquid has been absorbed, 20 to 25 minutes. Turn off the heat and let the pan stand, covered, for 10 minutes. With two forks toss in the ricotta or cottage cheese, and sprinkle with parsley. Serve with Parmesan cheese, if desired.

Serves 4

BULGUR WITH FENNEL AND PEAS

I admit to being an addict of anything that tastes of licorice. Fennel and Pernod are teamed with peas in the following pilaf to satisfy like cravings.

2 tablespoons unsalted butter
¾ cup chopped scallions (about 9), white
*   bulbs and green tops*
1 small clove garlic
1 small fennel, trimmed and chopped
*   (2½ cups), fronds chopped and reserved*
1½ cups homemade chicken stock (see
*   page 376) or canned broth*
¾ cup bulgur
10 ounces (2 cups) fresh peas
1 tablespoon Pernod liqueur
Salt and freshly ground black pepper to
*   taste*

1. Melt the butter in a large saucepan over medium-low heat. Add the scallions; cook 1 minute. Add the garlic; cook 2 minutes longer.

2. Stir the chopped fennel and the chicken stock into the scallion mixture and heat to boiling. Reduce the heat and cook, covered, for 5 minutes. Stir in the bulgur and cook, covered, over low heat until the bulgur is tender, 20 to 25 minutes. Stir in the peas; cook, covered, 1 minute. Turn off the heat and let the pan stand, covered, for 10 minutes. Add the Pernod and season with salt and pepper, fluffing the bulgur with a fork.

Serves 4

BULGUR TIANS

A tian is basically a gratin that includes Swiss chard or spinach. This contains both. The bulgur is presoaked in boiling water. This is merely a time-saving step and has no effect on the flavor of the finished dish.

½ cup bulgur
2½ tablespoons unsalted butter
2 tablespoons olive oil
1 large onion, finely chopped
3 cloves garlic, minced
½ medium red bell pepper, cored, seeded and chopped
¼ teaspoon crushed dried hot red peppers
2 small zucchini, finely diced
8 ounces fresh spinach, trimmed and chopped
1 pound Swiss chard, including stems, chopped
½ cup chopped fresh basil
⅓ cup chopped fresh parsley
1 teaspoon salt
¼ teaspoon freshly ground black pepper
3 eggs, lightly beaten
⅓ cup freshly grated Parmesan cheese
⅓ cup grated Jarlsberg cheese
3 tablespoons soft bread crumbs

1. Cover the bulgur with boiling water in a heatproof bowl. Let stand 15 minutes. Drain.

2. Preheat the oven to 375°F.

3. Heat the butter with the oil in a large saucepan over medium-low heat. Add the onion; cook 1 minute. Add the garlic and bell pepper; cook 2 minutes. Add the dried red peppers and zucchini; cook, stirring constantly, 2 minutes longer.

4. Add the spinach and chard to the saucepan. Toss well, then cover, and cook 5 minutes. Stir the bulgur into the greens mixture. Add the basil, parsley, salt, and pepper. Cook, covered, 5 minutes. Remove the cover and continue to cook, stirring often, 5 minutes longer. The mixture should be fairly dry; raise the heat slightly if it is too wet.

5. Transfer the bulgur mixture to a well-buttered 8- to 10-cup casserole. Lightly fluff the mixture with a fork. Pour the eggs over the top. Sprinkle with both cheeses, and then with the bread crumbs. Bake until golden, 25 to 30 minutes.

Serves 6

"SCROLL"
(Bulgur Pilaf with Escarole)

Greens and grains. This hearty pilaf is matched with pork in my house.

2 tablespoons vegetable oil
1 small onion, chopped
2 large cloves garlic, minced
1 whole head escarole, sliced (about 4 cups)
1½ cups homemade chicken stock (see page 376) or canned broth
1 cup bulgur
Salt and freshly ground black pepper to taste

1. Heat the oil in a large saucepan over medium-low heat. Add the onion; cook 1 minute. Add the garlic; cook 4 minutes longer.

2. Stir the escarole and stock into the onion mixture, and heat to boiling. Stir in the bulgur and reduce the heat. Cook, covered, over low heat until the bulgur is tender and all the liquid has been absorbed, 20 to 25 minutes. Turn off the heat and let the pan stand, covered, for 10 minutes. Then season with salt and pepper, fluffing the bulgur with a fork, and serve.

Serves 4

SAUTEED BULGUR WITH SOUR CREAM AND DILL

My favored method for cooking bulgur. I serve it as an adjunct to poultry or lamb.

4 tablespoons (½ stick) unsalted butter
1 large onion, chopped
1 large carrot, chopped
1 large rib celery, chopped
1 large parsnip, chopped
2½ cups homemade chicken stock (see page 376) or canned broth
1 cup bulgur
Salt and freshly ground black pepper to taste
2 tablespoons plus ¾ cup sour cream
¼ cup chopped fresh dill

1. Melt the butter in a large saucepan over medium-low heat. Add the onion; cook until golden, about 5 minutes. Stir in the carrot, celery, and parsnip; cook 2 minutes. Cover, and cook 10 minutes longer.

2. Add the stock to the vegetable mixture. Heat to boiling, then stir in the bulgur and reduce the heat. Cook, covered, over low heat until the bulgur is tender and all liquid has been absorbed, 20 to 25 minutes. Turn off the heat and let the pan stand, covered, for 10 minutes. Then season with salt and pepper, fluffing the bulgur with a fork. Add the 2 tablespoons sour cream and the dill. Pass the remaining sour cream on the side.

Serves 4

BULGUR NICOISE WITH ROSY CREAM

A Mediterranean-inspired dish with a pure Greene embellishment. The rosy whipped cream melts like butter on the hot bulgur—and it makes a smashing first course.

3 tablespoons olive oil
8 ounces fresh shiitake mushrooms, sliced
1 tablespoon unsalted butter
1 large onion, chopped
1 clove garlic, minced
1½ teaspoons chopped fresh oregano,
    or ½ teaspoon dried
1 teaspoon crushed dried hot red peppers
⅔ cup chopped pitted black olives (oil-
    cured are best)
2 cups homemade chicken stock (see page
    376) or canned broth
1 cup bulgur
½ cup heavy or whipping cream
1 teaspoon tomato paste
Salt and freshly ground black pepper to
    taste
1 tablespoon chopped fresh parsley
2 tablespoons chopped fresh basil

1. Heat the oil in a large saucepan over medium-high heat. Add the mushrooms and sauté until golden, 5 minutes.

2. Add the butter to the pan and reduce the heat to medium-low. Stir in the onion; cook 1 minute. Add the garlic, oregano, and dried red peppers; cook 1 minute longer. Stir in the olives and chicken stock, and heat to boiling. Then stir in the bulgur and reduce the heat. Cook, covered, over low heat until the bulgur is tender and all liquid has been absorbed, 20 to 25 minutes. Turn off the heat and let the pan stand, covered, for 10 minutes.

3. Meanwhile, beat the cream with the tomato paste in a large bowl until stiff. Transfer to a serving bowl.

4. Season the bulgur with salt and pepper, fluffing it with a fork. Sprinkle with the chopped parsley and basil. Pass the rosy cream on the side.

Serves 4

BULGUR-STUFFED TOMATOES

These herby stuffed tomatoes go well with just about anything, and are just as good when tomatoes are not at their prime.

4 ripe medium tomatoes
¼ cup strong homemade chicken stock (see
    page 376)
2 tablespoons olive oil
1 medium onion, finely chopped
1 large clove garlic, minced
1 teaspoon sugar
½ cup bulgur
1 teaspoon chopped fresh basil, or ½

teaspoon dried
½ teaspoon chopped fresh thyme, or ¼
    teaspoon dried
½ teaspoon salt
¼ teaspoon freshly ground black pepper
⅛ teaspoon hot pepper sauce
2 tablespoons freshly grated Parmesan
    cheese

1. Slice the tops off the tomatoes and scoop out the interiors with a spoon, leaving about ¼-inch-thick walls. Turn the scooped-out tomatoes upside down on paper towels to drain. Place the tomato pulp and seeds in the container of a food processor or blender, and process until smooth. You should have about 1¼ cups liquid. Add enough chicken stock to make 1½ cups total liquid.

2. Heat the oil in a medium-size saucepan over medium-low heat. Add the onion; cook 1 minute. Add the garlic; cook 3 minutes longer. Stir in the tomato mixture and add the sugar, bulgur, basil, thyme, salt, pepper, and hot pepper sauce. Heat to boiling. Then reduce the heat and cook, covered, over low heat until the bulgur is tender and all liquid has been absorbed, 20 to 25 minutes. (Remove the cover and continue to cook if the mixture seems too wet.) Turn off the heat and let the pan stand, covered, for 10 minutes.

3. Stuff the bulgur mixture into the tomato shells, mounding it high. Sprinkle with the Parmesan cheese. Place under a preheated broiler and cook until the tops are golden and the tomatoes are warmed through, about 5 minutes.

Serves 4

MAKING BULGUR FROM SCRATCH

Store-bought bulgur is not a pricey ingredient, yet it is simple and thrifty to make bulgur on your own. A better reason for doing it yourself than saving either time or money is that currently no commercially packaged bulgur is processed from organically grown wheat, even though organic wheat berries are in evidence at natural foods stores everywhere.

First pick over the whole wheat berries for any loose fragments or dust. A light rinse under cold running water won't hurt. Then combine 1 cup wheat berries in a large pot with 2 cups liquid. (Plain water is fine, but strained stock or vegetable juice will impart more flavor.) Bring the liquid to the boil, reduce the heat to medium-low, and simmer, covered, for 1 hour.

In a colander, drain off any liquid the berries have not absorbed. Then, using a large fork, spread them over a baking sheet or metal tray and toast in a low (225°F) oven until the berries are dry to the touch and separate easily, about 1 hour. Stir the berries from time to time as they toast. Allow the dried berries to cool completely. Then place about ¼ cup of the cooled berries in a zipper-lock-type plastic bag, seal the bag, and crush the berries with a rolling pin until you have the desired "grind." Repeat with the remaining berries. This will yield 1 to 1¼ cups medium-ground bulgur.

If you are using homemade bulgur for tabouleh and want to use the cold presoak method (see page 86), add another 30 to 60 minutes' soaking time.

BUTTERMILK BULGUR BREAD

*T*his is a very old-fashioned whole-wheat bread (the kind your grandmother served when you stayed over). It has minimal crunch but maximum flavor, dappled with tomato and drizzled with honey. Try it toasted, please!

1 package dry yeast
¼ cup warm water
3 tablespoons honey
2 teaspoons tomato paste
½ cup fine-ground bulgur
1½ cups buttermilk, warmed
⅓ cup unsalted butter, melted
1 teaspoon coarse (kosher) salt
2 cups whole-wheat flour
2 cups bread flour (approximately)
Cornmeal

1. Place the yeast in a large bowl. Cover with the water, and let stand until the yeast begins to soften, about 3 minutes. Add the honey and tomato paste, and whisk until smooth. Stir in the bulgur and buttermilk; let stand 20 minutes.

2. Stir the butter and salt into the bulgur mixture. Then stir in the whole-wheat flour and about 1½ cups bread flour to make a stiff dough. Turn out onto a lightly floured surface. Knead for 15 minutes, adding more bread flour if necessary to keep the dough from sticking. Transfer the dough to a lightly greased bowl, cover, and let rise in a warm place until doubled in volume, about 1½ hours.

3. Turn the dough out onto a lightly floured surface; punch it down and divide in half. Roll and pull each half until it resembles a loaf of French or Italian bread.

4. Sprinkle a baking sheet with cornmeal, and place the loaves on the sheet. Brush the loaves lightly with water, cover loosely with a towel, and let rise in a warm place until doubled in volume, 45 minutes to 1 hour.

5. Preheat the oven to 400°F.

6. With a sharp knife, slash the surface of the loaves four or five times, then brush them again with water. Bake until crisp and hollow-sounding when tapped with your finger, about 25 minutes. Cool on a rack.

Makes 2 loaves

BULGUR MUSHOSH

*T*he last recipe in my bulgur bouquet is a silken apricot pudding known as *mushosh* in the Middle East, where it is also called "Beirut Wedding Cake."

If you are thinking of eliminating the sensuous and velvety vanilla sauce to cut calories—*don't!*

½ cup chopped dried apricots (about
    4 ounces)
⅔ cup granulated sugar
1 cup fresh orange juice
1 cup water
1 teaspoon finely slivered orange zest
½ cup fine-ground bulgur
1 tablespoon unsalted butter
2 eggs, separated
6 tablespoons heavy or whipping cream
1 tablespoon Grand Marnier
2 tablespoons light brown sugar
Classic Vanilla Sauce (recipe follows)

1. Combine the apricots with the granulated sugar, orange juice, water, and orange zest in a medium-size saucepan. Heat to boiling, then reduce the heat. Simmer, partially covered, until the apricots are very tender, about 10 minutes.

2. Stir the bulgur into the apricot mixture and heat to boiling. Reduce the heat and cook, covered, over low heat until the bulgur is very tender, about 45 minutes. (Add more water if needed to complete cooking.) Turn off the heat and let the pan stand, covered, for 10 minutes. Stir in the butter until melted.

3. Preheat the oven to 350°F.

4. Beat the egg yolks with the cream in a medium-size bowl. Slowly beat in the bulgur mixture, then stir in the Grand Marnier.

5. Beat the egg whites until stiff, and fold them into the bulgur mixture.

Transfer the mixture to a shallow 1- to 1½-quart baking dish.

6. Place the brown sugar in a fine-mesh strainer, and holding the strainer over the apricot mixture, press it through with the back of a spoon. Place the baking dish in a roasting pan and add ½ inch boiling water to the pan. Bake for 30 minutes, then cool on a rack. Serve at room temperature or well chilled, with Classic Vanilla Sauce.

Serves 6 to 8

Classic Vanilla Sauce

3 extra-large egg yolks
½ cup sugar
1¼ cups milk, scalded
1 teaspoon vanilla extract
1 tablespoon kirsch
⅓ cup heavy or whipping cream

1. Beat the egg yolks with the sugar in the top of a double boiler until smooth. Whisk in the milk and cook, stirring constantly, over simmering water until it is thick enough to coat a wooden spoon, 20 to 25 minutes. Whisk in the vanilla. Cool to room temperature.

2. Whisk the kirsch into the custard. Beat the cream until stiff and fold it into the custard. Chill thoroughly before serving.

Makes 2½ to 3 cups

CORNMEAL
The Grain with a World-Feeding Potential

My cornmeal connection involves a railroad stop, a celebrated writer, and the loss of a job.

When I graduated college I hadn't the slightest clue what I wanted to be. Trained as an art teacher, I quit the classroom cold after the first week. Unable to either maintain discipline or keep my eye off an ominous wall clock ticking the hours away, I decided to try my hand as a writer-illustrator of children's books instead.

Armed with a new blue suit and a huge portfolio, I wandered from publisher to publisher, often eliciting a mea-

sure of praise for a sketch or a smile at a clever line, but no assignments whatsoever.

An editor finally told me why. "You have no experience," he said. "Talent is not enough in this field. One needs to know the nuts and bolts of how a book is put together. It's all mechanics..."

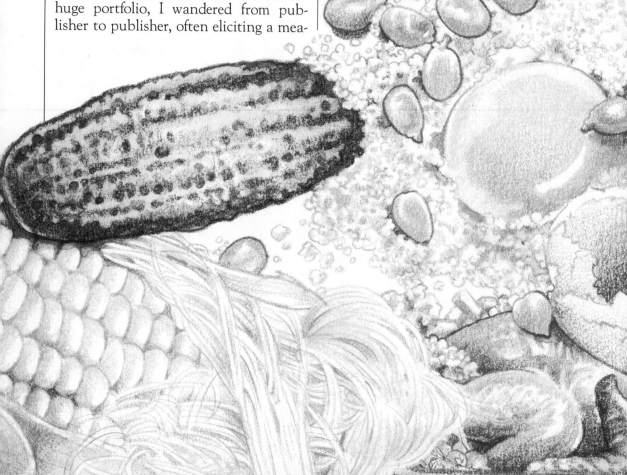

Not being mechanically inclined, my heart sank. But this kind man wrote me a letter of introduction to one of the best literary agents around. "Perhaps he can give you some straight advice."

The agent in question had a faultless reputation, which I will not sully here, but nothing about him was even faintly "straight." After weeks of broken appointments, he finally saw me in his lair—a huge neo-Renaissance studio in an area of New York grown somewhat shabby.

I could tell he was impressed neither by my graphic nor by my literary abilities. But my size obviously riveted his attention. A man of a certain age, molded in the Noël Coward style, he wore nubby tweeds and a tattersall vest, and smoked cigarettes in a long holder that flicked ashes on his clothing, desk, and my portfolio too.

"Undeniably you have talent," he rasped, turning the pages. "But it needs honing...refinement. For a person with the right sensibilities I would consider making an opening in my personal staff. Not writing or illustrating books, you understand, but performing chores vital to the publishing industry, immersing yourself in arts and letters."

If I had a moment's hesitation about his offer, all qualms disappeared as I observed the signed photographs on his desk: F. Scott Fitzgerald and Ludwig Bemelmans.

I took up the gauntlet and was shown by a tall, dark, and disapproving female (his personal secretary) where to hang my coat. The first immersion required my moving a cabinet of rejected manuscripts to the mail room. Besides myself there were three others in the office's employ, and I inherited all the nasty jobs they refused.

After a week's labor, I was rewarded with a special title: "Our Mr. Greene." Whenever a disputed matter arose, my employer would announce grandly that he'd have to consult with Our Mr. Greene before making any judgment. In truth he never consulted me about anything, except perhaps the postage required for letters to London or Paris.

Why did I stay at this odious job? A shallow reason. I enjoyed contact with America's literati, even though the proximity was usually secondhand.

One famous figure whom I did get to know was the critic and bon vivant Lucius Beebe. Beebe was the first man I ever heard described as a *gourmet*. Hopelessly devoted to the high life, he ate and drank prodigiously, wore a sable-lined coat, and tipped headwaiters so extravagantly that he was often forced to call our office for cab fare home. He also constantly demanded cash advances for articles not yet written. These payments were usually delivered to the Stork Club or El Morocco (where he wrote a newspaper column in the early morning). Everyone in the office took turns messengering money to Beebe.

Arriving at work one morning, I was met by the secretary, who thrust an envelope in my hand. Before she could speak, our employer appeared, highly agitated.

"Rush this to Beebe at once," he said.

"To the Stork Club?"

"No, no. Some place in the country. The name is written on the envelope, with instructions how to get there. Buy a round trip ticket at Grand Central—and don't dawdle. Beebe needs this fast!"

The departing train was a local and so devoid of passengers at that hour of the day that I had an entire car to myself, except for the times a conductor popped in to call out the next stop.

It was a long, lulling ride. To keep myself awake, I held the envelope to the light and tried to make out the amount within. Failing, I very carefully removed the tape that sealed it. It was a check for five thousand dollars, the largest sum I had ever seen in any form. I remember

thinking that checks like that would be mine someday, and if I fell asleep it was because of those blissful thoughts. When I heard the conductor call out the name of Beebe's town, I almost tripped in my rush down the iron steps.

Beebe was waiting—behind a driver—in an open car that made other cars at the station pale by comparison.

He sniffed at me as if I were an untried cheese, and slowly held out his hand for the check. Which, for some inexplicable reason, was no longer in the envelope. Envelope yes. Check no!

I was unable to speak. Beebe began to quiz me, mildly at first and then somewhat vexed as I fabricated answers to his questions.

"Did you *see* the check?"

"No. Yes."

"On the train?"

"I don't remember. Maybe."

"Oh sweet Jesus!" Like an angry god, he ordered the driver to take us home.

When we arrived, Beebe went directly to the telephone. My heart sank, for I was certain he was calling my office. Unexpectedly, however, he dialed the railroad. Glancing at his watch, he ascertained exactly what time and at which station the train would next stop, and made a plan. Before replacing the receiver he dispatched his driver to a depot five miles away. Then, facing me squarely for the first time, he asked a totally improbable question.

"Do you like corn bread?"

I was so taken off guard I could not answer. Beebe shrugged. Then, turning on his heel, he made his way to the kitchen. When I attempted to follow, he held up his hand.

"No, big boy," he said with a tinge of irony. "You go to the dining room table."

I did. Chagrined, I sat there in torment, waiting for the next terrible thing to happen. When Beebe returned, he was carrying a large tray in one hand and a pitcher in the other. On the tray were two china soup bowls and a plate piled high with freshly made corn bread, so warm it made the air shimmer.

As I watched, he placed a slice in each of the bowls and handed over the pitcher. When I hesitated, wondering whether to pour or not, he shook his head.

"Don't worry—it's milk, not hemlock!" Beebe smiled at his joke. "Unpasteurized rich milk. Though I have the feeling you've never eaten corn bread with milk before. Philistines sprinkle it with sugar, but you and I are going to be pure today."

We ate the golden cake in silence—I more greedily than he. Noting my relish, Lucius Beebe relaxed his handsome features into a sly half smile. "You should always tell the truth," he said, "and life will reward you with good corn bread like this every so often. As a just reward."

I did not have to answer, for the phone began to ring. When Beebe answered it, I knew from his tone and air of relief that the missing swag was recovered. When he returned to the table, we both had another helping.

Beebe spoke in a cool, detached tone. "You like railroad trains, don't you? I know, because I do too. As a train lover, I'd say you were so *seduced* by the sound of the whistle blowing and the hum of the wheels rolling that you didn't even know you took a peek at that *enormous* check. Right?"

My mouth filled with regret and corn bread, I merely shook my head.

"I thought so," said Beebe. "Well, this adventure will be our little secret."

We never shook hands on it. But I knew, sure as I was sitting there eating lunch with the gastronome of the western world, that the story could not end there. Like the corn bread, it was too good not to be passed on.

So before I could be fired, I quit!

The Grain's Genesis

Corn is the only grain that can lay claim to solid American roots. In late December 1492, Roderigo de Jeres and Luis Torres, two of Christopher Columbus's crewmen, went on a reconnaissance mission into the interior of what is now Cuba. They returned four days later, swollen red with mosquito bites but more enflamed still with tales of huge green stalks, over ten feet tall, abloom with a curious yellow and white fruit the Indians called *maiz*. According to Jerez and Torres, "This maiz is a kernel-berry that was well tast'd raw or cook'd. But could also be bak'd, dry'd and ground into a flour."

To prove their point, they filled four saddlebags with maize, which in time made its way back to the Spanish court along with the other New World oddities (including potatoes, tomatoes, and squash) that Columbus crammed into the holds of his ships.

Almost five hundred years have passed since Queen Isabella and King Ferdinand tasted maize for the first time and adjudged that pleasantly nutty grain to be a minor treasure, equal to if not greater than any vagrant spice the Genoan explorer sought to traffic in their name.

And those four saddlebags of maize produced a harvest high, wide, and handsome enough to yield roughly five thousand ears of corn by 1495, not to mention ten thousand bushels of cornmeal.

The corn that Jerez and Torres uncovered was probably the scantiest crop in the New World. In parts of Central America (Aztec territory), corn grew to the height of small forests. And the stalks were so densely crammed wth spiky cobs that the fields were described by Cortes's mounted troops as being "impenetrable as a stone wall. A strong man takes his life in his hands if he attempts to cross an Aztec field of maize."

Some Plain Grain Talk

To bend an old saying toward the kitchen stove, let me say that cornmeal is not just another pretty taste!

On the contrary, this grain is one of the few complex carbohydrates that has the potential of feeding the entire world. In point of fact, it is expected that by the middle of the 21st century, two thirds of all proteins consumed on earth will be some form of cornmeal derivative.

The corn kernel that is milled to form cornmeal is composed of a rough hull covering twin layers of hard and soft starch deposits. At the heart of this package is a protein-high, naturally oil-rich germ that gives cornmeal its nutritive value.

Cornmeal is processed in two ways: *stone-ground* and *enriched-degerminated*. The latter is a modern process that entails kiln-drying the kernels first, then grinding them between massive steel rollers. Most commercially processed cornmeal is produced this way because it is cost-efficient. Unfortunately, the steel rollers that pulverize the kernels also break down and filter out the healthy fiber in the hull, and they remove the germ entirely, which causes the final product to have a dry and somewhat granular texture. Stone-ground cornmeal, on the other hand, is not heated at all. The kernels are ground by water-powered millstones, which crush the germ, hull, and the hard and soft starch layers as well. This cornmeal has a somewhat unctuous feel and a rich and intense flavor. In fact, both stone-ground and enriched-degerminated cornmeal are enriched to be brought up to USDA standards.

It is important to understand cornmeal's serious food deficiencies as well as its nutritive virtues. While a cup of cooked cornmeal is high in carbohydrates as well as containing 0.44 milligrams of thiamine, 0.26 milligrams of riboflavin, and 3.52 milligrams of niacin —not to mention whopping amounts of potassium and magnesium—it is *not* considered a "whole food" because of the fact that it lacks two essential amino acids, lysine and tryptophan.

However, when it is combined with other grains, legumes, and judicious amounts of animal protein—even butter, milk, and cheese products—cornmeal acquires enough of the aforementioned amino acids to keep a cornmeal lover bright and bushy-tailed.

How to Buy It

*A*ll the recipes in this chapter, with one or two exceptions, were tested with two kinds of cornmeal: Quaker Enriched-Degerminated and Indian Head Stone Ground. Both are highly acceptable, but the more gratifying results were obtained using Indian Head Stone Ground, which is slightly higher priced than Quaker but is equally accessible in supermarkets.

A glance at the resource list at the back of this book will reveal names of excellent small stone-ground flour producers around the country, whose products are available at natural foods stores or by mail order.

It is important to note that yellow cornmeal contains a higher degree of beta carotene (one of the substances that maintains the balance of the body's immune system) than white cornmeal. However, white cornmeal is so much a part of many great regional dishes (like southern spoonbread) that I for one would pass on the beta carotene rather than fly in the face of tradition!

How to Store It

*B*ecause of its high oil content, stone-ground cornmeal has a relatively brief shelf life in any pantry over 45°F. It may be kept in airtight, self-seal plastic bags in the refrigerator for up to three months, and twice that time in the freezer. Enriched-degerminated cornmeal has somewhat longer staying power. Unfortunately the cool temperature of refrigerator and freezer, while inhibiting insect infestation and retarding rancidity, also increases vitamin loss and encourages oxidation.

How to Cook It

*T*here is no single rule for cornmeal preparation, so my suggestions vary with the recipes.

Though many health-food faddists decry the addition of any flour (whole-wheat or otherwise) to straight cornmeal in a tin of corn sticks or a pan of corn bread, I disagree. I find that tempering the mixture actually makes a softer, lighter, and, yes, more digestible offering in the final analysis.

*I*n Texas, where cornmeal arrived in 1836 as a victory spoil of independence from Mexico, they still have some mighty colorful corn associations. *Corn twisters*, for instance, are dry spells. In *corn weather* you can sleep "nekkid," for it's hot. *Corn wind* means no wind at all and *corn lightning* is merely thunder. A *corn in the ear* implies you are deaf as a post, while *corn on the tongue* means you are looking for a wife— preferably one who's a *cornmeal patter* (a good cook) or a *corn shaker* (so well endowed physically that the corn stalks shake whenever she's near)!

OVER-EASY GREEN CHILE ENCHILADAS

*I*n Mexico, where corn is a staple, maize was known as *panizo*, or "panic grass." That moniker was bestowed upon the plant by early 16th-century Spanish settlers who had grave misgivings about depending on an annual-growing grain for their subsistence. They needn't have worried—there has never been a corn famine in Central or Latin America, or the U.S. either.

To this day, Mexicans consider corn their staff of life. They pound *panizo* (maize, cornmeal, masa harina) into a rough flour that they combine with water and cook over high heat until it becomes the tortilla we all know and love.

Recently I came upon a wonderfully salubrious (if very inauthentic) version of the tortilla made of everyday cornmeal. These quasi-tortillas are better than any of the commercial varieties you will find on a supermarket shelf and easier to make than scrambled eggs. Moreover, it takes less than half an hour to whip up a big batch. Yes, they freeze!

2 tablespoons olive oil
1 small yellow onion, chopped
2 cloves garlic, minced
1 tablespoon chopped canned jalapeño
   peppers
2 cans (4 ounces each) mild green chile
   peppers, chopped
2 tomatoes, peeled, seeded, and chopped
   (about 1 cup)
½ teaspoon cumin seeds, ground
1 teaspoon finely chopped fresh cilantro
   (Chinese parsley)
1 cup shredded cooked pork or chicken
Vegetable oil
10 Phony Tortillas (recipe follows)
1 cup grated Monterey Jack cheese
Sour cream
Shredded lettuce

1. Preheat the oven to 350°F.
2. Heat the oil in a large skillet over medium-low heat. Add the onion; cook 2 minutes. Add the garlic and jalapeño peppers; cook 3 minutes longer. Stir in the mild peppers, tomatoes, cumin, and cilantro. Raise the heat to medium and cook, stirring occasionally, 5 minutes. Stir in the meat; cook 2 minutes. Re-move the skillet from the heat.
3. Heat 1 inch of vegetable oil in another large skillet over medium heat. Carefully dip each Phony Tortilla into the hot oil for a few seconds only. Transfer the fried tortillas to paper towels.
4. Fill each tortilla with the meat mixture and roll up. Place them in a lightly greased baking dish. Sprinkle with the cheese, and bake 10 minutes. Serve with sour cream and shredded lettuce.

Makes 10 enchiladas

Phony Tortillas

1 cup yellow cornmeal
½ teaspoon salt
½ cup bread flour
1 egg, lightly beaten
2 cups water

1. Combine the cornmeal, salt, and flour in a large bowl. Stir in the egg and water until smooth.
2. Heat a lightly greased 6-inch non-stick skillet over medium heat. Spoon 3 to 4 tablespoons batter into the hot pan.

Turn and twist immediately to cover the bottom of the pan. Cook 30 seconds, then flip and cook the other side. Do not brown the tortilla. Place the cooled tortilla on a sheet of paper towels. Continue the process, layering the cooked tortillas in paper towels, until all the batter is used up.

Makes about 20 tortillas

Note: These tortillas may be stored for several days in a plastic bag in the refrigerator.

SOUTHWEST BEAN CAKE

All trendy restaurants these days seem to serve some version of bean cake. This dish makes great party fare, as well as a tasty brunch or supper dish. I often serve it just with a green salad.

½ pound string beans
5 tablespoons plus 1 teaspoon unsalted butter, at room temperature
1 teaspoon vegetable oil
1 medium onion, finely chopped
1 clove garlic, minced
½ pound chorizos (Spanish sausages), thinly sliced
2 large ripe tomatoes, seeded and chopped
1 tablespoon chopped fresh basil, or 1 teaspoon dried
1 hot green pepper, seeded, deveined, and minced
1 red bell pepper, cored, seeded and finely chopped
2 eggs
1 cup buttermilk
½ cup heavy or whipping cream
1 cup yellow cornmeal
½ cup all-purpose flour
½ teaspoon baking soda
½ teaspoon baking powder
Pinch of sugar
½ teaspoon salt
¼ teaspoon freshly ground black pepper
⅛ teaspoon sweet Hungarian paprika
2 teaspoons chili powder or ground dried mild chiles
¼ cup sliced black olives
1 cup grated Monterey Jack cheese
Dash of hot pepper sauce

1. Preheat the oven to 350°F.

2. Cut the string beans French style—in half lengthwise. Cook in boiling salted water until tender, about 8 minutes. Rinse under cold running water, drain, and set aside.

3. Melt 2 tablespoons of the butter with the oil in a large heavy skillet over medium heat. Add the onion; cook 2 minutes. Add the garlic and sliced chorizos. Continue to cook until the chorizos are lightly browned, 5 to 6 minutes.

4. Add the tomatoes, basil, hot green pepper, and red bell pepper to the sausage mixture. Continue to cook, stirring occasionally, until the tomatoes are soft, about 12 minutes. Toss in the reserved beans and cook 10 minutes longer. Remove the skillet from the heat.

5. Beat the eggs wth 3 tablespoons of the butter in a large bowl until smooth. Beat in the buttermilk and cream. Stir in the cornmeal, flour, baking soda, baking powder, sugar, salt, pepper, paprika, and chili powder. Mix well. Stir in the reserved chorizo / bean mixture, the

olives, cheese, and hot pepper sauce.

6. Rub a 10-inch cast-iron skillet with the remaining 1 teaspoon butter. Spoon the batter into the skillet, and bake until firm and golden brown, about 35 minutes. Cut into wedges and serve.

Serves 6 to 8

RED-HANDED CHILI

In this unusual stew made with Spanish sausages, chicken, and shrimp, the cornmeal is essential as a thickener. Serve the chili over rice.

2½ tablespoons olive oil
½ pound chorizos (Spanish sausages), sliced ¼ inch thick
1 whole chicken breast, skinned, boned, and cut into 1-inch pieces
1 large onion, finely chopped
2 cloves garlic, minced
1 Italian frying pepper (Cubanelle), seeded and finely chopped
3 large canned mild green chile peppers, chopped
¼ cup yellow cornmeal
1½ tablespoons chili powder
½ teaspoon ground cumin
½ teaspoon crushed dried hot red peppers
2 medium tomatoes, seeded and chopped (¾ cup)
1 can (14 ounces) imported Italian tomatoes, with juice
1½ cups homemade chicken stock (see page 376) or canned broth
1 pound shrimp, shelled and deveined
Chopped fresh parsley, for garnish
3 cups cooked rice, heated

1. Preheat the oven to 350°F.

2. Heat 1 tablespoon of the oil in a large Dutch oven over medium-low heat. Add the chorizos; cook, stirring occasionally, until lightly browned, about 10 minutes. Using a slotted spoon, transfer the chorizos to a bowl..

3. Add half the chicken pieces to the skillet and sauté over medium heat until lightly colored, about 4 minutes. Transfer to a separate bowl. Sauté the remaining pieces and add them to the bowl. Wipe out the pot.

4. Heat the remaining 1½ table-

*C*orn at first was a catchall term for all loose grains—rice, wheat, barley.

Until Linnaeus set everybody straight, Turks called wheat "Syrian corn" and Syrians called millet "Turkish wheat." The Chinese called opium seeds "rainbow corn." Count your blessings that they never tried making that into cornmeal!

In America, where cornmeal is native fodder, there are still cultural differences. The South traditionally chooses white cornmeal for cooking, while the North invariably opts for yellow. In the Southwest, Indians have immemorially grown a blue corn, and in the Northeast, farmers harvest a red corn for silage. Trendy restaurateurs and chic chefs find the blue and red irresistible. Not I!

spoons oil in the Dutch oven. Add the onion; cook over medium-low heat 1 minute. Add the garlic, frying pepper, and green chiles. Cook 2 minutes. Stir in the cornmeal, chili powder, cumin, and dried red peppers. Cook, stirring constantly, 2 minutes. Stir in both tomatoes, the chicken stock, and the reserved chorizos. Heat to boiling. Cover the pot and transfer it to the oven. Bake, stirring occasionally, 50 minutes. (The dish may be prepared ahead to this point.)

5. Stir the reserved chicken pieces into the chili. Cover, and bake for 5 minutes. Add the shrimp and bake, covered, 5 minutes longer. Sprinkle with parsley, and serve with rice.

Serves 4 to 6

HUSH PUPPY FRIED CHICKEN

*T*he story goes: A Southerner, after an outdoor fish fry, threw some batter into the fire to feed to his yapping dogs—which he gave them, saying, "Hush, puppies." I use a hush puppy batter for frying chicken, and I assure you, you will *not* want to throw it to the dogs.

½ cup sour cream
¼ teaspoon cayenne pepper
1 chicken (about 3½ pounds), cut into
  pieces
3 strips bacon
¼ cup cornmeal, white or yellow
¼ cup all-purpose flour
¼ teaspoon freshly grated nutmeg
¼ teaspoon salt
⅛ teaspoon freshly ground black pepper
Pinch of hot Hungarian paprika
4 tablespoons (½ stick) unsalted butter
Chopped fresh parsley, for garnish

1. Combine the sour cream and the cayenne pepper in a small bowl. Place the chicken in a large bowl, and toss with the sour cream mixture until well coated. Let stand 20 minutes.

2. Preheat the oven to 300°F.

3. Sauté the bacon strips in a large heavy skillet until crisp. Drain on paper towels, then crumble and reserve. Reserve the drippings in the skillet.

4. Combine the cornmeal with the flour, nutmeg, salt, pepper, and paprika in a large bowl. Roll the chicken pieces in this mixture, and place them on a plate.

5. Heat the bacon drippings in the skillet over medium-low heat. Add 2 tablespoons of the butter. Sauté the chicken, half the pieces at a time starting with the dark meat, until golden brown on both sides, about 10 minutes per side. Transfer to a baking dish and place in the oven as the pieces are done. Add more butter to the pan as needed. When all the pieces are sautéed, keep in the oven no longer than 30 minutes. Sprinkle with parsley before serving.

Serves 3 or 4

OLD-TIMEY CHICKEN STEW WITH CORNMEAL DUMPLINGS

In times past, cornmeal was reputed to have singular curative powers. One mid-16th-century medico believed a poultice of cornmeal and white wine could cure cataracts and kept his patients in the dark for weeks, adding a few grains or a few drops to the mask daily. Results? Lost in the passage of time, I'm afraid.

A couple of centuries later, Marie Antoinette, worried over her "spotty" complexion, allowed her face to be baked daily in a mixture of cornmeal and cream. Her skin, according to court gossip, improved immeasurably—until she lost her head, and one cannot blame that on cornmeal.

As late as the early 20th century, doctors in New England prescribed cornmeal baths for rheumatism.

The best cornmeal restorative I know is an edible one. At the first sign of a sneeze, try this chicken stew with gilded dumplings. The patient will be up on his feet the day after—more than likely foraging for a second helping!

FOR THE STEW

2 tablespoons unsalted butter
3 tablespoons vegetable oil
1 chicken (3½ to 4 pounds), cut into pieces
1 yellow onion, finely chopped
1 clove garlic, minced
1 medium carrot, diced
1 medium parsnip, diced
1 medium turnip, diced
1 rib celery, diced
⅛ teaspoon chopped fresh thyme, or a pinch of dried
½ teaspoon freshly ground black pepper
½ cup white wine
½ cup homemade chicken stock (see page 376) or canned broth

FOR THE DUMPLINGS

½ cup yellow cornmeal
½ cup cake flour
1½ teaspoons baking powder
½ teaspoon salt
1 egg, lightly beaten
⅓ cup milk
½ teaspoon Dijon mustard
1 tablespoon deviled ham

1. Make the stew: Heat the butter with the oil in a large saucepan or Dutch oven. Sauté the chicken, a few pieces at a time, until very well browned, about 10 minutes. Transfer the cooked chicken to a plate.

2. Discard all but 2 tablespoons drippings from the pan. Add the onion; cook, scraping the bottom and sides of the pan with a wooden spoon, 2 minutes. Add the garlic; cook 2 minutes longer. Stir in the carrot, parsnip, turnip, celery, thyme, pepper, wine, and stock. Heat to boiling. Reduce the heat, return the chicken pieces to the pan, cover, and cook over medium-low heat 30 minutes.

3. Meanwhile, make the dumplings: Combine the cornmeal, flour, baking powder, and salt in a large bowl. Mix well, and stir in the egg, milk, mustard, and deviled ham. Mix well.

4. After the chicken has cooked for 15 minutes, spoon the dumpling batter over the chicken in large spoonfuls. Cook, covered, until just firm, about 15 minutes.

Serves 4

ROAST TURKEY WITH CORN BREAD DRESSING

You don't have to be a Southerner or love okra to savor this meal. The dressing adds dash and flavor to traditional fare.

1 fresh turkey (16 to 18 pounds)
2 large cloves garlic
Salt and freshly ground black pepper to
    taste
Corn Bread, Sausage, and Okra Dressing
    (recipe follows)
3 strips bacon
1/3 cup dry white wine
1 quart water
1 medium onion
1 rib celery with its leaves, broken
3 sprigs parsley, plus additional for
    garnishing the turkey
1/4 teaspoon salt
4 peppercorns
1 1/2 tablespoons unsalted butter
1 1/2 tablespoons all-purpose flour
1/4 cup heavy or whipping cream

1. Preheat the oven to 325°F.

2. Remove the giblets from the turkey; reserve the giblets, except the liver. (You may wish to reserve the liver for another purpose.) Wipe the turkey inside and out with a damp cloth.

3. Bruise 1 garlic clove and rub the turkey well, inside and out, with the bruised garlic, and season with salt and pepper. Stuff the cavity with the dressing, and truss. Place the turkey on a rack in a roasting pan, and lay the bacon strips across the breast. Cut a piece of cheesecloth large enough to fit over the turkey. Soak the cheesecloth in the wine and place it over the turkey. Pour any remaining wine over the turkey, and roast 30 minutes.

4. Meanwhile, combine the giblets (not the liver), water, onion, celery, the remaining garlic clove, 3 sprigs parsley, salt, and peppercorns in a large saucepan. Heat to boiling, then reduce the heat. Simmer, uncovered, until the liquid is reduced to 2 cups, 30 minutes. Strain the giblet stock.

5. Baste the turkey with the giblet stock. Roast, basting with stock every 30 minutes, until the legs move freely and juices run clear when the inner thigh is pierced with a fork, about 5 to 5 1/2 hours total. For the last half hour of roasting, remove the cheesecloth. (First wet the turkey with basting juices. It should lift off easily.) Raise the oven heat to 375°F to crisp the skin. Then transfer the turkey to a carving board, and let it stand 15 minutes.

6. Meanwhile, strain the turkey drippings, degreasing them if necessary. Melt the butter in a medium-size saucepan over medium-low heat. Whisk in the flour. Cook, stirring constantly, 2 minutes. Whisk in the drippings and cream; simmer 5 minutes. Taste, and adjust the seasonings as necessary. Garnish the turkey with the remaining parsley sprigs. Serve with the gravy and corn bread dressing.

Serves 8 to 10

Corn Bread, Sausage, and Okra Dressing

½ cup wild rice
1 cup water
6 tablespoons (¾ stick) unsalted butter
½ recipe Vermont Corn Bread (see page
    125), cooled and cubed
½ pound sweet Italian sausage
1 large onion, chopped
1 Italian frying pepper (Cubanelle), seeded
    and finely chopped
½ teaspoon crushed dried hot red peppers
1 teaspoon minced fresh sage, or
    ¼ teaspoon dried
¼ pound small okra, cut into ½-inch-thick
    slices

1. Combine the wild rice with the water in a small saucepan and heat to boiling. Reduce the heat and cook, covered, over low heat until tender, 30 minutes. Drain, and transfer to a large bowl.

2. Melt 2 tablespoons of the butter in a large heavy skillet, and sauté a third of the corn bread cubes until golden. Transfer to the bowl with the rice. Continue to sauté the corn bread cubes until all butter and cubes are used up.

3. Sauté the sausage in the same skillet over medium heat until well browned, about 8 minutes. Drain on paper towels, cool slightly, and cut into ½-inch-thick slices. Add them to the bowl with the corn bread.

4. Drain all but 2 tablespoons grease from the skillet. Add the onion; cook over medium-low heat 2 minutes. Add the frying pepper and dried red peppers. Cook 3 minutes longer. Transfer the onion mixture to the bowl, add the sage and okra, and mix well.

Makes about 7 cups

SIASCONSET SEAFOOD SPOON BREAD

A southern recipe that found its way to Nantucket. White cornmeal is the requirement here, please!

¼ pound shrimp, shelled and deveined
½ pound bay scallops
5½ tablespoons unsalted butter
6 scallions, white bulbs and green tops
    separated, thinly sliced
1 clove garlic, minced
½ red bell pepper, cored, seeded, and
    minced (about ⅓ cup)
1 small hot green pepper, seeded, deveined,
    and minced
1 tablespoon dry white wine or vermouth
Salt and freshly ground black pepper to
    taste
2⅓ cups light cream or half-and-half
1 teaspoon sugar
½ teaspoon salt
1 cup white cornmeal
4 egg yolks
1 teaspoon baking powder
6 egg whites

1. Cut the shrimp into chunks the size of the scallops. Set aside.

2. Melt 1 tablespoon of the butter in a medium-size skillet over medium-low heat. Add the green scallion tops; cook 1 minute. Add the garlic; cook 2 minutes longer. Stir in the peppers and cook 4 minutes longer.

3. Raise the heat to medium-high and add ½ tablespoon of the butter. When the butter has melted, stir in the scallops and shrimp, and toss constantly until the shrimp have turned lightly pink, about 2 minutes. Then stir in the wine. Continue to cook until almost all liquid has evaporated, about 1 minute. Season with salt and pepper, and set aside to cool.

4. Preheat the oven to 400°F. Lightly butter a 2-quart soufflé or casserole.

5. Combine the remaining 4 tablespoons butter with the cream in a medium-size saucepan. Cook over low heat until the butter has melted. Do not allow it to boil. Stir in the sugar and salt. Whisk in the cornmeal, and cook over medium-low heat, stirring constantly, until the mixture is very thick, 4 to 5 minutes. Transfer the cornmeal mixture to a large heatproof bowl and immediately beat in the egg yolks, one at a time, beating thoroughly after each addition. Add the baking powder and the seafood.

6. Beat the egg whites until stiff. Stir one third of the whites into the cornmeal mixture. Fold in the remaining whites. Pour into the prepared soufflé dish or casserole, and with a teaspoon, make a circular indentation in the top about ½ inch from the rim. Sprinkle the top with additional black pepper and place the dish in the oven. Immediately reduce the heat to 375°F. Bake until puffed and golden, 35 minutes. Serve immediately.

Serves 4 to 6

AUSTRO-HUNGARIAN CORNMEAL MUSH WITH PORK

*T*his is my loosely adapted version of a dish Paul Kovi wrote about in *Transylvanian Cuisine*. Mr. Kovi is one of the owners of the prestigious Four Seasons restaurant in New York. His book, however, is full of wonderful homey recipes from his childhood. I serve poached eggs over the top.

2 tablespoons vegetable oil
2 to 2½ cups chopped cooked pork
1 small onion, finely chopped
1 large carrot, chopped
2-inch celery rib (white part), trimmed and chopped
1 small potato, diced
¼ cup chopped fresh parsley
3½ cups homemade chicken stock (see page 376) or canned broth
1 cup yellow cornmeal
Salt and freshly ground black pepper to taste

1. Heat the oil in a large heavy skillet over medium heat. Stir in the pork and cook until well browned on all sides, about 5 minutes. Stir in the onion; cook 2 minutes longer.

2. Reduce the heat to medium-low and add the carrot, celery, potato, and 2 tablespoons of the parsley. Cook 2 minutes. Add 2 cups of the stock and heat to boiling. Reduce the heat, cover, and cook over medium-low heat 10 minutes.

3. Remove the cover and add the remaining 1½ cups broth. Return to boiling and stir in the cornmeal. Reduce the heat and cook, uncovered, over medium-low heat until slightly thickened but not stiff, about 10 minutes. Add salt and pepper to taste.

4. Sprinkle with the remaining 2 tablespoons parsley before serving.

Serves 6 to 8

CORN BREAD AND HAM HASH

This dish is wonderful for a glamorous brunch or for a Sunday night supper.

4 tablespoons (½ stick) unsalted butter
2 cups cubed stale corn bread (½-inch cubes)
1 medium onion, chopped
1 clove garlic, minced
½ cup diced red bell pepper
2 cups cubed ham
½ cup chopped seeded tomatoes
1 cup fresh corn kernels (from 2 large ears)
4 allspice berries, crushed
Dash of hot pepper sauce
Salt and freshly ground black pepper to taste
1 teaspoon finely chopped fresh sage

1. Preheat the oven to 375°F.
2. Melt 1½ tablespoons of the butter in a large ovenproof skillet over medium heat. Add 1 cup of the corn bread cubes, and sauté until golden brown on all sides, 4 minutes. Transfer them to a bowl. Repeat the process with another 1½ tablespoons butter and the remaining 1 cup corn bread cubes.

3. Wipe out the skillet and melt the remaining 1 tablespoon butter in it over medium-low heat. Add the onion; cook 1 minute. Add the garlic; cook 3 minutes longer. Stir in the bell pepper, ham, and tomatoes. Cook, covered, 5 minutes. Stir in the corn and allspice. Cook, covered, 5 minutes longer.

4. Remove the cover and gently toss the corn bread cubes into the mixture. Add the hot pepper sauce, and season with salt and pepper. Transfer the skillet to the oven and bake, uncovered, 15 minutes. Sprinkle with sage and serve.

Serves 4

GLAZED HAM LOAF

Ham loaf is one of those budget stretchers that housewives relied on in the 1940s and '50s. I view this one as a treat because it calls for corn bread!

FOR THE HAM LOAF
2 pounds cooked ham, ground
½ pound pork sausage meat
1 cup crumbled leftover corn bread
1 small onion, finely chopped
1 clove garlic, minced
¼ cup finely chopped red bell pepper
¼ cup chopped fresh parsley
½ cup pineapple juice
2 eggs, lightly beaten
1 teaspoon dark brown sugar
½ teaspoon dry mustard

½ teaspoon salt
¼ teaspoon freshly ground black pepper
¼ teaspoon freshly grated nutmeg

FOR THE GLAZE
1 cup firmly packed dark brown sugar
2 teaspoons tarragon vinegar
2 teaspoons Dijon mustard
¼ cup pineapple juice

Chopped fresh parsley, for garnish

1. Preheat the oven to 350°F.

2. Combine all the ingredients for the ham loaf in a large bowl. Mix well. Shape into a loaf in a shallow baking dish. Bake 15 minutes.

3. Meanwhile, combine all the ingredients for the glaze in a small saucepan. Heat to boiling; boil 1 minute.

4. After 15 minutes, baste the ham loaf with the glaze. Continue to bake, basting with the glaze and pan juices, 1 hour. Let stand 10 minutes. Sprinkle with parsley before serving.

Serves 8

GOLD-BRICKED MACARONI AND CHEESE

This updated version of macaroni and cheese is very soul-satisfying to the kid in all of us. Cornmeal adds new texture to an old standby.

½ pound elbow macaroni
5 tablespoons unsalted butter
¼ cup cornmeal, white or yellow
⅛ teaspoon crushed dried hot red peppers
3 tablespoons all-purpose flour
1 cup homemade chicken stock (see page 376) or canned broth, heated
½ cup heavy or whipping cream
2 teaspoons fresh lemon juice
¼ teaspoon freshly grated nutmeg
½ teaspoon salt
¼ teaspoon hot pepper sauce
¼ cup freshly grated Parmesan cheese
¼ pound grated semi-mild Cheddar cheese (such as Mimolette)
¼ pound grated Swiss or Jarlsberg cheese
2 medium tomatoes (about ¾ pound), seeded and chopped

1. Cook the macaroni in boiling salted water until tender, about 8 minutes. Rinse under cold running water until cool. Drain, and set aside.

2. Meanwhile, melt 2 tablespoons of the butter in a small skillet over medium heat. Stir in the cornmeal and dried red peppers. Cook, stirring constantly, until lightly browned, about 4 minutes. Set aside.

3. Melt the remaining 3 tablespoons butter in a medium-size saucepan over medium-low heat. Stir in the flour. Cook, stirring constantly, 2 minutes. Whisk in the chicken stock and cream. Cook, whisking constantly, until very thick, 1 minute. Whisk in the lemon juice, nutmeg, salt, and hot pepper sauce. Remove from the heat and stir in 2 tablespoons of the Parmesan cheese. Fold in the cooled macaroni.

4. Preheat the oven to 350°F. Lightly butter a 2-quart casserole dish.

5. Place one third of the macaroni mixture in the prepared casserole. Sprinkle with one third of the Cheddar and one third of the Swiss cheese. Spoon one third of the tomatoes over the top. Repeat layering two more times, ending with tomatoes.

6. Combine the remaining 2 tablespoons Parmesan cheese with the cornmeal mixture. Sprinkle over the top of the macaroni mixture. Bake 30 minutes.

Serves 4

WHITE AND BLACK BEAN PIE

*T*his bean pie is a show-stopper: refried beans in a cornmeal crust, topped with melting white cheese. It goes well with all manner of braised meats and poultry.

FOR THE BEAN FILLING
1 pound dried black beans
8 ounces bacon
2 medium onions, finely chopped
2 cloves garlic, minced
3 fresh jalapeño peppers, seeded, deveined, and minced
2 cups homemade chicken stock (see page 376) or canned broth
Salt and freshly ground black pepper to taste

FOR THE CRUST
½ cup yellow cornmeal
⅔ cup cold water
1⅓ cups boiling water
1½ tablespoons unsalted butter

¼ pound Monterey Jack cheese, grated (about 1 cup)

1. Pick over the beans and remove any debris. Place the beans in a pot, cover with cold water, and let stand, covered, overnight.

2. Drain the beans and cover once more with cold water. Heat slowly to boiling; then reduce the heat. Simmer, uncovered, until tender, about 1 hour. Drain, and set aside to cool.

3. Sauté the bacon in batches in a large heavy skillet until crisp. Drain on paper towels. Crumble and reserve.

4. Discard all but ¼ cup bacon drippings from the skillet. Add the onions and cook over medium-low heat 1 minute. Add the garlic and jalapeño peppers. Cook 5 minutes longer. Using a slotted spoon, transfer the onion mixture to a bowl. Reserve the skillet.

5. Place half the beans and half the onion mixture in the container of a food processor. Add 1 cup of the chicken stock. Process, using the pulse button, until thick but still chunky. Transfer to the skillet. Repeat with the remaining beans, onion mixture, and stock. Cook, stirring constantly, over medium heat until very thick, about 15 minutes. (Be careful: black beans burn easily.) Remove the skillet from the heat and add the salt and pepper.

6. Make the crust: Stir the cornmeal into the cold water. Stir this mixture into the boiling water in a small saucepan. Return to boiling. Stir in the butter, and reduce the heat. Cook, covered, stirring occasionally, 30 minutes. Set aside to cool slightly.

7. Preheat the oven to 400°F. Lightly rub a 10-inch glass or ceramic quiche pan with butter.

8. Spread the cornmeal over the bottom and sides of the pan, forcing the mixture up the sides as it cools. Bake 5 minutes. Remove the dish from the oven, and reduce the heat to 350°F.

9. Sprinkle a third of the reserved bacon over the bottom of the crust. Spoon in the bean mixture. Sprinkle with another third of the bacon. Sprinkle with the cheese, and add the remaining third of the bacon. Bake 30 minutes. Let stand 10 minutes before serving.

Serves 6 to 8

BERT'S BASIC POLENTA

Cornmeal recipes abound in a clutch of surprising cuisines. Italians, for example—who would never consider chomping corn on the cob—dote on a dish called *polenta*, which is basically nothing more than cornmeal mush carried to gastronomic heights.

In northern Italy there is a great mystique about the shape of the pot in which polenta is stirred; a U-shaped copper pan is adjudged the ideal utensil. However, not being Italian, I merely use any heavy-bottomed saucepan. And for a creamier texture, I prefer milk to water.

2½ cups milk
¾ cup cornmeal, yellow or white

1. Slowly bring the milk to a boil in a medium-size heavy saucepan, and then gradually add the cornmeal. Whisk them together over medium-low heat until the polenta is smooth and thick, 5 minutes.

2. Using a bowl scraper, pour the mixture into a lightly buttered pie plate. Cool on a wire rack, and then refrigerate for 1 hour.

3. At this point, polenta may be sliced into wedges and either dusted with Parmesan cheese and baked, or lightly sautéed in butter.

Serves 6 to 8

MUSHROOM POLENTA

The mushrooms here must be wild. The commercially grown white ones just won't do in this dish.

5 tablespoons unsalted butter
½ tablespoon olive oil
2 shallots, minced
¼ pound wild mushrooms, such as shiitakes, finely chopped
2½ cups milk
¾ cup yellow cornmeal
¼ teaspoon crushed dried hot red peppers
3 tablespoons freshly grated Parmesan cheese
Salt and freshly ground black pepper to taste

1. Heat 1 tablespoon of the butter with the oil in a large heavy skillet over medium-high heat. Add the shallots and cook until golden, about 2 minutes. Stir in the mushrooms, raise the heat slightly, and cook, stirring constantly, until they are golden and any juices have evaporated, about 3 minutes. Set aside.

2. Slowly heat the milk to boiling in a medium-size heavy saucepan over medium-low heat. (Do not allow it to scorch.) Gradually beat in the cornmeal with a wire whisk. Beat in the dried red peppers and 1½ tablespoons of the cheese. Continue to beat until the mixture is smooth and thick, 5 minutes. Add the mushroom mixture and salt and pepper to taste, and pour into a lightly buttered 9-inch pie plate. Cool on a wire rack. Refrigerate 1 hour.

3. Preheat the oven to 375°F. Melt the remaining 4 tablespoons butter.

4. Cut the polenta into wedges and place them on a buttered baking dish. Drizzle with the melted butter. Sprinkle with the remaining 1½ tablespoons cheese, and bake 15 minutes.

Serves 6 to 8

LEEK POLENTA

*T*his is one of my favorite dishes. Of course, I happen to love leeks. They add a sweetness to this polenta that goes nicely with the cheese.

6 tablespoons (¾ stick) unsalted butter
2 tablespoons olive oil
4 to 6 large leeks, white parts rinsed, dried, and finely chopped (about 4 cups)
¼ cup dry white wine
Pinch of ground cloves
Pinch of ground mace
2½ cups milk
¾ cup yellow cornmeal
¼ cup grated Fontina cheese
Salt and freshly ground black pepper to taste

1. Heat 2 tablespoons of the butter with the oil in a large heavy skillet over medium-low heat. Add the leeks; cook 4 minutes. Sprinkle with the wine, cloves, and mace. Continue to cook, stirring occasionally, until the leeks are tender, 12 to 15 minutes. Raise the heat slightly and cook until all liquid has evaporated. Set aside.

2. Slowly heat the milk to boiling in a medium-size heavy saucepan over medium-low heat. (Do not allow it to scorch.) Gradually beat in the cornmeal with a wire whisk. Continue to beat until the mixture is smooth and thick, 5 minutes, then beat in 2 tablespoons of the cheese and the leek mixture. Season with salt and pepper, and pour into a lightly buttered 9-inch pie plate. Cool on a wire rack, then refrigerate 1 hour.

3. Preheat the oven to 375°F. Melt the remaining 4 tablespoons butter.

4. Cut the polenta into wedges and place them on a buttered baking dish. Drizzle with the melted butter, and sprinkle with the remaining 2 tablespoons cheese. Bake 15 minutes.

Serves 6 to 8

SAUSAGE AND PEPPER POLENTA

*T*his almost makes a meal in itself. Just add in a green salad and a glass of white wine, and I am happy.

1 tablespoon olive oil
1 small onion, chopped
½ medium green bell pepper, cored,
    seeded, and cut into small strips
½ medium red bell pepper, cored, seeded,
    and cut into small strips
½ pound sweet Italian sausage, chopped
2½ cups milk
¾ cup yellow cornmeal
1 tablespoon chopped fresh basil, or 1
    teaspoon dried
Dash of hot pepper sauce
3 tablespoons freshly grated Parmesan
    cheese
Salt and freshly ground black pepper to
    taste
4 tablespoons (½ stick) unsalted butter,
    melted

1. Heat the oil in a large skillet over medium-low heat. Add the onion; cook 2 minutes. Add the peppers; cook 3 minutes longer. Raise the heat slightly and stir in the sausage meat. Continue to cook, stirring often, until the meat loses its pink color and is thoroughly cooked, about 5 minutes. Set aside.

2. Slowly heat the milk to boiling in a medium-size heavy saucepan over medium-low heat. (Do not allow it to scorch.) Gradually beat in the cornmeal with a wire whisk. Continue to beat until the mixture is smooth and thick, 5 minutes. Stir in the sausage mixture, the basil, hot pepper sauce, and 1½ tablespoons of the cheese. Season with salt and pepper, and pour into a lightly buttered 9-inch pie plate. Cool on a wire rack, then refrigerate 1 hour.

3. Preheat the oven to 375°F. Lightly butter a large baking dish.

4. Cut the polenta into wedges and place them on the prepared baking dish. Drizzle with the melted butter, and sprinkle with the remaining 1½ tablespoons cheese. Bake 15 minutes.

Serves 4 to 6 as a main course

KANSAS CITY CORN BREAD

I discovered this bread on one of my many trips to Kansas City. It is part of a collection put out by the Kansas City Junior League in their beautiful book, *Beyond Parsley*—a remarkable step forward in Junior League cookbooks.

12 ounces bacon
1 cup stone-ground yellow cornmeal
1 cup whole-wheat flour
⅓ cup sugar
2½ teaspoons baking powder
¼ teaspoon salt
1 cup buttermilk
6 tablespoons (¾ stick) unsalted butter,
    melted
1 egg, lightly beaten

1. Preheat the oven to 400°F.
2. Sauté the bacon, a third at a time, in a heavy skillet until crisp. Drain on paper towels, then crumble and reserve. Lightly brush an 8-inch square cake pan with bacon drippings.

3. Combine the cornmeal with the flour, sugar, baking powder, and salt in a large bowl. Stir in the buttermilk, butter, and egg. Beat in the crumbled bacon.

4. Pour the batter into the cake pan. Bake until golden, about 25 minutes. Serve warm, cut into pieces.

Serves 4 to 6

VERMONT CORN BREAD

In Vermont they serve corn bread with maple syrup. This is my all-purpose version, which I picked up in Brattleboro.

1½ cups yellow cornmeal
½ cup all-purpose flour
1 tablespoon baking powder
½ teaspoon baking soda
¾ teaspoon salt
1½ cups buttermilk
1 egg, lightly beaten
3 tablespoons bacon drippings, warmed
3 tablespoons maple syrup
1 tablespoon unsalted butter, melted

1. Preheat the oven to 425°F. Lightly grease an 8-inch square cake pan.

2. Combine the cornmeal, flour, baking powder, baking soda, and salt in a large mixing bowl. Stir in the buttermilk, egg, bacon drippings, and maple syrup. Mix well.

3. Pour the batter into the prepared cake pan. Brush with the melted butter. Bake until golden, 15 to 20 minutes. Serve warm, cut into pieces.

Serves 4 to 6

PUMPKIN CORN BREAD

My friend Kate Almand tells me that Lucius Beebe had it all wrong! Corn bread is to be eaten in a bowl of *buttermilk*, not "sweet" milk. This pumpkin corn bread does just fine either way.

1 cup yellow cornmeal
1 cup all-purpose flour
3 tablespoons sugar
1 tablespoon baking powder
1 teaspoon baking soda
½ teaspoon salt
Pinch of ground ginger
Pinch of ground cinnamon
Pinch of ground white pepper
2 eggs
1 cup puréed fresh or canned pumpkin
1 cup sour cream
8 tablespoons (1 stick) unsalted butter, melted

1. Preheat the oven to 425°F. Lightly grease a 9-inch square cake pan.

2. Combine the cornmeal, flour, sugar, baking powder, baking soda, salt, ginger, cinnamon, and white pepper in a mixing bowl.

3. In a large mixing bowl, beat the eggs with the pumpkin, sour cream, and 7 tablespoons of the melted butter until smooth. Add the cornmeal mixture, and stir until smooth.

4. Pour the batter into the prepared cake pan. Brush with the remaining 1 tablespoon melted butter. Bake until golden brown, 15 to 20 minutes. Serve warm, cut into pieces.

Serves 4 to 6

SPINACH-FLECKED CORN BREAD

You may substitute turnip greens if you are a true-blooded Southerner. This green and gold bread looks as attractive on a plate as it is good to eat—especially with pork or chicken.

4 tablespoons (½ stick) unsalted butter
1 shallot, minced
4 cups coarsely chopped rinsed fresh
    spinach leaves (about 6 ounces)
1½ cups cornmeal
½ cup bread flour
2 teaspoons baking powder
¼ teaspoon baking soda
½ teaspoon salt
¼ teaspoon freshly ground black pepper
¼ teaspoon freshly grated nutmeg
1 cup milk
½ cup sour cream
1 egg, lightly beaten
1 tablespoon unsalted butter, melted

1. Preheat the oven to 425°F.
2. Melt 3 tablespoons of the butter in a 9-inch cast-iron skillet over medium-low heat. Add the shallot; cook 1 minute. Add the spinach with just the water that clings to the leaves. Cook, covered, stirring occasionally, until soft, about 10 minutes. Remove the cover and raise the heat to medium. Cook until most of the liquid has evaporated, 1 minute longer. Remove the skillet from the heat.
3. Combine the cornmeal with the flour, baking powder, baking soda, salt, pepper, and nutmeg. Stir in the milk, sour cream, and egg. Mix well, and stir in the spinach mixture. Wipe out the skillet.
4. Melt the remaining 1 tablespoon butter in the skillet over medium heat. Pour the batter into the skillet, remove it from the heat, and brush with the melted butter. Transfer the skillet to the oven, and bake until the bread is golden, 15 to 20 minutes. Serve warm, cut into wedges.
Serves 4 to 6

ROSY CORN BREAD

Corn bread seems to have a real affinity for pork, as Italians and Southerners know. Try this with a sautéed ham steak, or with country-cured ham in red-eye gravy.

1½ cups yellow cornmeal
½ cup all-purpose flour
1 tablespoon baking powder
½ teaspoon baking soda
¼ teaspoon salt
3 eggs, lightly beaten
¾ cup ricotta cheese

¾ cup tomato juice
½ cup grated Cheddar cheese
4 tablespoons (½ stick) unsalted butter,
    melted
1 tablespoon freshly grated Parmesan
    cheese

1. Preheat the oven to 425°F. Lightly

grease an 8-inch square cake pan.

2. Combine the cornmeal, flour, baking powder, baking soda, and salt in a large bowl.

3. In another bowl, beat the eggs with the ricotta, tomato juice, Cheddar, and 3 tablespoons of the butter.

4. Combine the two mixtures and pour into the prepared cake pan. Brush with the remaining 1 tablespoon melted butter, and sprinkle with the Parmesan cheese. Bake until golden brown, about 20 minutes. Serve warm, cut into pieces.

Serves 4 to 6

TIJUANA CORN BREAD

*T*ijuana is a dusty Mexican border town full of booze and peppers. No booze can be found in this corn bread, but there are plenty of peppers. Try this with beef *fajitas*.

3 tablespoons unsalted butter
2 scallions, white bulbs and green tops, chopped
½ medium red bell pepper, cored, seeded, and finely chopped
½ medium green bell pepper, cored, seeded, and finely chopped
½ cup fresh corn kernels (from 1 large ear)
1½ cups yellow cornmeal
1 cup self-rising cake flour
½ teaspoon salt
2 tablespoons sugar
1 teaspoon baking powder
½ teaspoon baking soda
1 cup buttermilk
2 eggs, lightly beaten
2 teaspoons unsalted butter, melted

1. Preheat the oven to 425°F. Lightly butter an 8-inch square cake pan.

2. Melt the 3 tablespoons butter in a heavy skillet over medium-low heat. Add the scallions and peppers; cook until soft, about 5 minutes. Stir in the corn; cook 2 minutes longer. Remove the skillet from the heat.

3. Combine the cornmeal, flour, salt, sugar, baking powder, and baking soda in a large bowl. Stir in the buttermilk and eggs. Then stir in the vegetable mixture.

4. Spoon the batter into the prepared cake pan. Brush the top with the melted butter. Bake until puffed and golden, about 20 minutes. Serve warm, cut into pieces.

Serves 4 to 6

PROSCIUTTO AND PARMESAN CORN BREAD

*T*his makes a perfect starter to any meal—or serve it along with a salad for brunch.

1½ cups yellow cornmeal
½ cup all-purpose flour
1 tablespoon baking soda
¼ teaspoon salt
¼ teaspoon freshly ground black pepper
1½ cups heavy or whipping cream
2 eggs, lightly beaten
2 ounces thinly sliced prosciutto, chopped
    (about ½ cup)
2 tablespoons chopped fresh chives
½ cup freshly grated Parmesan cheese
4 tablespoons (½ stick) unsalted butter,
    melted

    1. Preheat the oven to 425°F. Lightly grease an 8-inch square cake pan.

    2. Combine the cornmeal, flour, baking soda, salt, and pepper in a large mixing bowl. Stir in the cream, eggs, prosciutto, chives, all but 1 tablespoon of the Parmesan cheese, and 3 tablespoons of the melted butter.

    3. Pour the batter into the prepared cake pan. Brush with the remaining 1 tablespoon melted butter, and sprinkle with the reserved 1 tablespoon Parmesan cheese. Bake until golden, about 20 minutes. Serve warm, cut into pieces.

    Serves 4 to 6

PERFECTLY PEACHY CORN BREAD FRENCH TOAST

*F*or me, one of the joys of making corn bread for Saturday night supper is having some left over for Sunday morning breakfast!

    The best French toast in my not inconsiderable repertoire of hot breads is this one. It is an invention the chef conceived after downing several morning eye-openers—a drink known as a Fuzzy Navel, compounded of orange juice and Peachtree Schnapps. One thing led to another, and before I knew it, Perfectly Peachy Corn Bread French Toast was born.

    I advise using leftover Vermont, Pumpkin, or in a pinch Kansas City corn bread (pages 124 and 125) for this dish. And for those allergic to alcohol, peach nectar makes an admirable stand-in for the booze!

½ cup fresh orange juice
2 tablespoons Peachtree Schnapps, or
    ¼ cup peach nectar
2 eggs, separated
¼ cup granulated sugar
¼ teaspoon ground cinnamon
⅛ teaspoon freshly grated nutmeg
½ cup heavy or whipping cream
12 slices leftover corn bread
8 tablespoons (1 stick) unsalted butter
    (approximately)
Confectioners' sugar
Orange Peach Syrup (recipe follows) or
    maple syrup

    1. Combine the orange juice, schnapps, egg yolks, sugar, cinnamon, nutmeg, and cream in a large bowl. Mix well. Beat the egg whites until stiff, and fold them into the orange juice mixture.

    2. Preheat the oven to 250°F.

    3. Place the corn bread slices in the orange juice mixture, making sure they are well-covered with the mixture. Leave

them in the mixture until they are soaked but not mushy, 2 to 3 minutes.

4. Melt 4 tablespoons of the butter in a heavy skillet and heat until foamy. Remove the bread slices from the juice mixture, shaking off any excess. Sauté them, three or four at a time, on both sides until golden brown, adding more butter as needed. Transfer the slices to an ovenproof platter and dust with confectioners' sugar. Keep warm in the oven until all slices have been sautéed. Dust once more with confectioners' sugar, and serve with Orange Peach Syrup or maple syrup.

Serves 4

Orange Peach Syrup

½ cup fresh orange juice
½ cup sugar
1 teaspoon finely slivered orange zest
¼ cup Peachtree Schnapps or peach nectar

1. Combine the orange juice and sugar in a small saucepan, and cook over medium heat until the mixture boils. Add the slivered orange zest; cook 1 minute longer. The mixture will be slightly thick.

2. Remove the pan from the heat and immediately stir in the schnapps. Allow the mixture to stand for 5 minutes for the flavors to blend properly. Serve warm or at room temperature.

Makes about 1¼ cups

CAMPTON PLACE'S DOUBLE-CORN CORN STICKS

Corn-crammed corn stick that was whipped up one lazy afternoon by chef Bradley Ogden at the dining spot known as Campton Place, in San Francisco.

Baker's Secret (see page 42)
½ cup yellow cornmeal
½ cup all-purpose flour
2 tablespoons sugar
1¼ teaspoons baking powder
½ teaspoon salt
1 cup heavy or whipping cream
1 egg yolk
3 tablespoons unsalted butter
½ cup fresh corn kernels (from 1 large ear)
2 egg whites

1. Preheat the oven to 425°F. Lightly grease a corn stick mold with Baker's Secret.

2. Combine the cornmeal with the flour, sugar, baking powder, and salt in a large bowl. Stir in the cream and egg yolk. Set the batter aside.

3. Melt the butter in a medium-size saucepan over medium-low heat. Stir in the corn kernels, and toss to warm through. Stir the corn into the batter.

4. Beat the egg whites until stiff. Fold them into the batter.

5. Spoon the batter evenly into the prepared mold. Bake until firm and golden, 15 to 20 minutes. Serve hot.

Makes 22 small corn sticks

PHILLIP STEPHEN SCHULZ'S LACE CAKES

*L*ace Cakes are a real Yankee bequest to this cornmeal collection and the most ethereal pancakes I have ever consumed. (And I must admit I have consumed a lot.) The best rendering I know comes from ex-Coloradoan Phillip Stephen Schulz, who could certainly give Aunt Jemima a run for the money when it comes to a duel at the griddle.

2 eggs
2 cups milk (approximately)
1 cup fine yellow cornmeal
1 teaspoon sugar
½ teaspoon salt
6 tablespoons (¾ stick) unsalted butter, melted

1. Using a whisk, beat the eggs in a large bowl until light. Whisk in the remaining ingredients until smooth.
2. Heat a lightly greased griddle or heavy skillet over medium heat. Pour about 3 tablespoons batter for each cake on the griddle, and cook until the underside is golden brown, 3 to 4 minutes. Turn over and lightly brown the other side, another 3 to 4 minutes. Stir the batter well before making each cake, as the cornmeal will thicken up. Add more milk if the batter becomes too thick. Serve with maple syrup or jam.

Makes twelve 5-inch cakes

APPALACHIAN SPOON AND FORK CAKE

*I*f you thought cornmeal was just another stick-to-the ribs ingredient, take a squint at this Appalachian coffee cake. It is the most toothsome (sweet-nutty-raisined) confection extant.

1 cup chopped pecans
¾ cup firmly packed dark brown sugar
1 teaspoon ground cinnamon
⅔ cup raisins
8 tablespoons (1 stick) unsalted butter, melted and cooled
2 cups cake flour
1 cup yellow cornmeal
¾ cup granulated sugar
1 teaspoon baking powder
½ teaspoon baking soda
¼ teaspoon salt
3 eggs, lightly beaten
1 cup sour cream
1 teaspoon vanilla extract

1. Preheat the oven to 350°F. Lightly butter and flour a 9-inch springform pan.

2. Combine the pecans, brown sugar, and cinnamon in a medium-size bowl. Mix well. Remove ½ cup of this mixture and set it aside. Add the raisins and ¼ cup of the melted butter to the remaining pecan mixture. Set aside.

3. Combine the flour, cornmeal, granulated sugar, baking powder, baking soda, and salt in a large bowl. With a heavy wooden spoon, beat in the eggs, sour cream, remaining ¼ cup butter, and vanilla until smooth.

4. Spread half the batter over the bottom of the prepared springform pan. Sprinkle the raisin mixture over the top. Carefully spread the remaining batter over the raisin mixture, and sprinkle with the reserved ½ cup nut mixture. Bake until a toothpick inserted in the center of the cake comes out fairly clean, 45 to 50 minutes. Cool on a wire rack before removing the sides of the pan.

Serves 8

GINGERED PUMPKIN PIE

*T*his pie is a staple in my holiday dessert book because it is easy to make and smashing to taste. It nests in a gilded cornmeal pie crust. I suggest you flag the crust recipe for lots of other uses. It's a winner!

1 Gilded Cornmeal Pie Crust (recipe
   follows)
1 cup puréed cooked pumpkin, canned or
   fresh
½ cup firmly packed light brown sugar
½ cup heavy or whipping cream
½ cup milk
2 tablespoons cognac
3 eggs, lightly beaten
¼ cup finely slivered candied ginger
1 teaspoon ground cinnamon
⅛ teaspoon ground cloves
¼ teaspoon freshly grated nutmeg
¼ teaspoon salt

1. Preheat the oven to 350°F.

2. Roll out the pie crust dough and line a 9-inch pie plate with it. Trim and flute the edges.

3. Place the pumpkin in a large bowl, and whisk in the remaining ingredients. Pour the filling into the prepared pie shell. Bake until set in the center, about 45 minutes.

Makes one 9-inch pie

Gilded Cornmeal Pie Crust

1¼ cup all-purpose flour
½ cup yellow cornmeal
¼ teaspoon salt
6 tablespoons solid vegetable shortening,
   chilled
2 tablespoons unsalted butter, chilled
3 to 4 tablespoons cold water

Combine the flour, cornmeal, and salt in a large bowl. Cut in the shortening and butter with a pastry blender until the mixture has the texture of coarse crumbs. Add just enough cold water to form a fairly soft dough. Refrigerate 1 hour before using.

Makes enough for one 9- to 11-inch single-crust pie

MRS. HITE'S GEORGIA LEMON PECAN PIE

I used to work with Mrs. Hite's son, John, during my days as promotion art director for *Esquire* magazine. He pressed this recipe into my hands one day, and I have been making it ever since, taking the liberty to combine the filling with my aforementioned Gilded Cornmeal Pie Crust. Unbeatable!

1 Gilded Cornmeal Pie Crust (see page 131)
4 eggs
2 cups sugar
¼ cup milk
1 tablespoon yellow cornmeal
1 tablespoon all-purpose flour
Finely slivered zest of 1 lemon
Juice of 1 lemon
¾ cup chopped pecans
8 tablespoons (1 stick) unsalted butter, melted

1. Preheat the oven to 325°F.

2. Roll out the pie crust dough and line a 10-inch glass or ceramic quiche dish with it. Trim and flute the edges.

3. Beat the eggs in a large mixing bowl until light. Slowly add the sugar, beating until the mixture is light and fluffy. Beat in the remaining ingredients. Pour the filling into the prepared pie shell, and bake until it is golden brown and firm, about 45 minutes.

Makes one 10-inch pie

THE FLOURING OF THE GRAIN

Cornstarch, that old pantry familiar in the rectangular box, is actually a flour, finely milled of a high-starch corn hybrid.

Why and when does one use cornstarch? Cornstarch is a light thickener of sauces (notably in Oriental and Latin American dishes) and adds just the right degree of density to puddings, soups, custard sauces, and mousse bases that flour very often turns viscous. Cornstarch is also an invaluable aid when making pie fillings of super-acidy fruits:

A delicate sprinkling as the fruit is layered will keep the juices from running out of the pie shell as it bakes.

Cornstarch does come with a few caveats, however. It lumps unless it is well mixed with liquid before being added to a dish on the stove. And it has a raw taste if it is cooked over too high a heat. It is also essential to remember not to overbeat cornstarch-based recipes, for that breaks down the starch's delicate balance and thins it irremediably.

JOCKEY CREPES

Cornstarch's finest hour! This unique crêpe recipe (printed on the Argo cornstarch box back in the 1960s) contains no flour whatsoever, which means that the batter flows out of your blender and into your pan in minutes. (Most crêpe batters sit in the fridge for hours, waiting for the gluten in the flour to relax and produce a delicate pancake—but not these feather-light treats.)

Fill them with anything you like, but this seafood amalgam will knock your socks off—you have my word on it.

5 tablespoons unsalted butter
1½ tablespoons minced shallots
½ cup dry white wine
1 pound bay scallops
½ teaspoon minced hot red pepper, or ¼ teaspoon crushed dried hot red peppers
1 teaspoon minced fresh cilantro (Chinese parsley)
⅛ teaspoon anchovy paste
2 tablespoons all-purpose flour
1 cup heavy or whipping cream
Freshly ground black pepper to taste
½ cup freshly grated Parmesan cheese
12 Cornstarch Crêpes (recipe follows)

1. Preheat the oven to 350°F. Lightly butter a large baking dish.

2. Melt 3 tablespoons of the butter in a heavy saucepan over medium-high heat. Add the shallots; cook until lightly browned, about 2 minutes. Raise the heat and add the wine; cook 1 minute. Add the scallops along with the hot red pepper, cilantro, and anchovy paste. Cook, tossing gently, over high heat until the scallops turn white, 2 to 3 minutes. Drain the scallops, reserving the liquid. Place the scallops in a bowl and keep warm.

3. Melt the remaining 2 tablespoons butter in a heavy saucepan over medium-low heat. Whisk in the flour. Cook, stirring constantly, 2 minutes. Whisk in the reserved scallop liquid and raise the heat. Cook, stirring occasionally, over medium-high heat until very thick, about 6 minutes. Beat in the cream until smooth. Season with pepper, and remove from the heat.

4. Add two thirds of the sauce to the reserved scallops. Stir in two thirds of the cheese. Fill the crêpes, roll them up, and place them seam side down on the prepared baking dish. With a teaspoon, drizzle the remaining sauce over the crêpes. Sprinkle with the remaining cheese. (Crêpes may be made ahead to this point.) Bake for 8 to 10 minutes.

Makes 12 filled crêpes

Note: Crêpes may also be prepared, filled, and frozen; allow 15 to 20 minutes in a 400°F oven if frozen.

Cornstarch Crêpes

These crêpes refrigerate, and freeze, remarkably well.

2 eggs
¾ cup milk
6 tablespoons cornstarch
1 tablespoon vegetable oil
2 teaspoons sugar
¾ teaspoon baking powder
⅛ teaspoon salt

1. In the order given, place all the ingredients in the container of a blender. Blend on high speed until very smooth, about 1 minute. Transfer the batter to a bowl.

2. Heat a greased 6-inch crêpe or omelet pan until it is very hot. Pour about 2 tablespoons of the batter onto the center of the pan. Turn and twist the pan immediately to coat the bottom. Cook over medium-high heat until the crêpe is lightly browned and the top is dry around the edges, about 30 seconds. Carefully turn the crêpe over and cook several seconds. Transfer to a paper towel. Repeat with the remaining batter, stacking the crêpes, with a paper towel in between, on top of each other. When through, invert the stack so the golden sides are down.

Makes 12 crêpes

Note: These crêpes may be made in advance and stored, refrigerated, in a plastic bag.

OLD-FASHIONED PRUNE WHIP

A venerable comfort food that does not show its age one jot.

¾ cup chopped pitted prunes
¼ teaspoon almond extract
¼ cup boiling water
3 eggs, separated
¼ cup granulated sugar
¼ teaspoon vanilla extract
1½ tablespoons cornstarch
¾ cup milk, scalded
1 cup heavy or whipping cream
3 tablespoons confectioners' sugar

1. Place the prunes in a heatproof bowl. Sprinkle them with the almond extract, then pour the boiling water over them. Set aside.

2. Whisk the egg yolks with the granulated sugar in the top of a double boiler until smooth. Whisk in the va- nilla, cornstarch, and scalded milk. Place over simmering water and cook, stirring constantly, until thickened, about 10 minutes. Remove from the heat and allow to cool.

3. Place the prunes with all their liquid in the container of a food proces- sor. Process, using the pulse button, un- til smooth. Transfer to a large bowl, and fold in the cooled custard.

4. Beat the cream with the confec- tioner's sugar until stiff. Fold into the prune mixture.

5. Beat the egg whites until stiff and fold them into the prune mixture. Trans- fer to a serving bowl and chill well before serving.

Serves 8

ROTHE GRUETZE

*T*his Danish fruit dessert (which we always called "red grits" when I was a kid) makes a comeback as a fruit soup appetizer, splashed with vodka if you like, or as a light ending to a summer meal.

8 ounces Italian or red plums
¼ cup water
1 pint fresh strawberries, rinsed and hulled
1 package (10 ounces) frozen raspberries in syrup, thawed
¾ cup sugar
3 tablespoons cornstarch
1 cup cranberry-raspberry juice (not drink)

1. Cut the plums in half and remove the pits. Place them in a medium-size saucepan, add the water, and heat to boiling. Reduce the heat and cook, covered, over low heat 15 minutes. Add the strawberries, and raspberries with syrup. Heat to boiling, reduce the heat, and simmer, uncovered, 10 minutes longer.

2. Using a wooden spoon, press the fruit through a sieve into the top of a double boiler. You should have 2½ cups. Stir in the sugar and cook, stirring occa-sionally, over simmering water until the sugar has dissolved, 1 to 2 minutes.

3. Place the cornstarch in a medium-size bowl and whisk in ¼ cup of the cranberry-raspberry juice until very smooth. Whisk in the remaining juice. Add this mixture to the fruit mixture and cook, stirring constantly, 8 minutes. Cover, and continue to cook until it is slightly thickened and you can no longer taste the cornstarch, 10 to 12 minutes. Do not overcook. Remove the pan from the heat and cool, stirring occasionally, to room temperature. Chill well before serving.

Serves 4 to 6

CHOCOLATE NATILLA

A wondrous chocolate pudding for all seasons. The recipe comes from Clive DuVal, talented chef-owner of Tila's, the best Gringo-Mex restaurant in Houston, and now in Washington, D.C., too.

1 ounce semi-sweet chocolate
½ cup sugar
Pinch of salt
1¾ cups milk
1 tablespoon fresh orange juice
2 tablespoons golden rum
3 tablespoons cornstarch
½ teaspoon vanilla extract
1 tablespoon Kahlua

1. Melt the chocolate in the top of a double boiler over simmering water.

2. Combine the sugar, salt, and 1½ cups of the milk in a small saucepan. Heat almost to boiling. Whisk into the melted chocolate, then stir in the orange juice and rum.

3. Place the cornstarch in a small bowl. Whisk in the remaining ¼ cup milk until smooth. Stir this mixture into the chocolate mixture and cook, stirring constantly, 8 minutes. Cover and continue to cook, stirring once or twice, until it is thickened and you can no longer taste the cornstarch, 10 to 12 minutes. Do not overcook. (When removing the cover, be careful that the accumulated moisture does not trip into the natilla.) Remove from the heat, add the vanilla and Kahlua, and cool, stirring occasionally, to room temperature. Chill thoroughly before serving.

Serves 4

ROSE LEVY BERANBAUM'S GENOISE

Cornstarch is not used much for cake or pastry. However, one exception (devised by the brilliant cake baker-teacher Rose Levy Beranbaum in her book, *Cake Bible*) is the following classic genoise cake, in which flour is leavened with cornstarch and added slowly to a zabaglione-like mixture of warm eggs and sugar for an utterly silken result.

I must warn you, this is a very special cake. Make it only when you have sufficient time and when the telephone answering machine is taking your calls!

I think this genoise gets better as it sits. Plan on baking it the night before the dinner party, please.

4 tablespoons (½ stick) unsalted butter
1 teaspoon vanilla extract
4 large eggs
¾ cup plus 1½ teaspoons sugar
½ cup sifted cake flour
½ cup plus 1 tablespoon cornstarch (lightly spooned, not packed)
½ cup water
2 tablespoons liqueur (such as kirsch or Grand Marnier)
Chocolate Buttercream Frosting (recipe follows)

1. Preheat the oven to 350°F. Butter a 9-inch springform pan and line it with parchment paper. Butter and flour the paper.

2. Melt the butter in a small skillet over medium heat and cook, stirring frequently, until browned. Do not burn it. Cool the butter slightly, and strain it through cheesecloth. You should have 3 tablespoons clarified brown butter. Place the butter in a small pan and add the vanilla. Place over medium-low heat until almost hot (110° to 120°F). Set aside and keep warm.

3. Place a large heatproof bowl over a pan of simmering water. Add the eggs and ½ cup of the sugar. Beat with a hand-held electric mixer until tripled in volume, 8 to 10 minutes.

4. Remove a scant cup of the egg mixture and whisk it into the brown butter mixture. Set aside.

5. Sift the flour with the cornstarch, and sift half of this mixture over the beaten eggs, folding it in gently with a slotted spoon. Fold in the remaining flour mixture. Fold in the brown butter mixture. Pour immediately into the prepared pan and bake until the cake is golden brown and starting to pull away from the sides of the pan, 20 to 25 minutes. Run a knife or small metal spatula around the edges and remove the sides of the pan. Invert the cake onto a wire rack and carefully remove the bottom of the pan. Cool the cake completely on the rack. Then cut the cake in half horizontally with a long sharp knife to make two layers.

6. Combine the remaining ¼ cup plus 1½ teaspoons sugar and the water in a small saucepan with a tight-fitting lid. Heat to a rapid boil. Cover, and remove from the heat. Cool completely while covered.

7. Stir the liqueur into the cooled sugar syrup. Sprinkle this mixture over the bottom and top of both layers. Ice the bottom and top layers with Chocolate Buttercream Frosting. Do not ice the sides.

Serves 8

Chocolate Buttercream Frosting

4 ounces sweet chocolate
¼ cup water
1 teaspoon vanilla extract
9 tablespoons unsalted butter, at room
   temperature
1 egg yolk
⅓ cup confectioners' sugar
1 teaspoon dark rum

1. Melt the chocolate with the water and vanilla in the top of a double boiler over simmering water. Stir until smooth, and set aside to cool.

2. Beat the butter in the large bowl of an electric mixer until light. Add the egg yolk, and beat until light and fluffy. Beat in the chocolate, sugar, and rum.

Makes enough for a 9-inch cake

GRITS AND HOMINY

Acquired Tastes That Are Rich in Protein

I am a true grits and hominy lover. North of the Mason-Dixon line, however, you will be hard put to find many others who share the predilection. I have even met denizens of the Deep South who shuddered at the thought of dipping a spoon into a bowlful of either. For grits and hominy are acquired tastes—but they are so highly nutritive and protein-rich that the tastes are eminently worthy of acquisition.

Try telling that to a person of prejudiced palate! Actually, I did try once, and got tossed out on my ear.

In the 1940s and '50s, the most outspoken star of the American theater was indubitably Tallulah Bankhead. A legend in her time, Tallulah (as everyone called her) was a tempestuous personality judged more for her performances off-stage than on. But if you will accept a firsthand opinion, that was a terrible canard. When I saw her, Bankhead's talent was so mesmerizing that most of the audience was red-eyed and snuffling into handkerchiefs by the final curtain, though she was playing the part of an unmitigated vixen. Southern, of course, like Bankhead herself.

Tallulah was touring the South in her greatest hit, *The Little Foxes*. To attend opening night in Richmond, Virginia, I had to cut half a day's college classes, travel by trolley and bus from Williamsburg, and worst of all, catch a milk train back. But it was an experience worth twice the adversity. I sat in the last row of the second balcony, very high up, but even from afar the lady's gift was formidable. I cried too.

As the theater emptied, still under the actress's spell, I found myself wandering to the stage door.

"Where you goin', boy?" A burly old man stood guard, blinking in the dark.

"Interview with Miss Bankhead," I lied, flipping open a college newspaper press card he never glanced at.

"To the right and down the steps. But take yo' turn. There's a passel of others waitin' fo' her already."

In the dim light I could make out about a dozen men and women, awkwardly queued outside a dressing room. The door was unmarked and tightly shut, but a trail of rose petals on the floor and a whiff of expensive perfume in the air firmly established that *she* was behind it. If one had further doubt, a deep Alabama growl reverberated inside.

"I said *no* interviews and I meant it. Get rid of them!"

The assembled group heard what Bankhead said, yet no one moved. If anything, a few hardy souls bent closer to the doorway as her decibels rose.

"Don't give me that crap about the power of the press, darling." *Dahl-ling* is how it came out, but no term of endearment was ever less benign. "I am sick of playing jerkwater towns, giving the performance of my life, only to have some local yokel ask me if I sleep in the nude! Send them away—"

She was still shouting as the door opened. A highly flushed man held it ajar. We could all plainly see the lady inside, wearing what appeared to be only a fur coat and panties. Legs crossed, she was seated at a dressing table, drinking whiskey.

The functionary stumbled as he spoke. "Ladies . . . gentlemen . . . you must forgive. Y'see, she's been under a severe strain preparin' for this openin'. Actually a migraine headache . . ." His voice trailed unhappily. "Can we set up another time for interviews? Tomorrow afternoon maybe?"

One gray-haired matron removed an enormous bouquet from behind her back and with deadly aim tossed it through the open door, barely missing Tallulah's head. Bankhead did not flinch. Picking up a loose blossom, she handed the rest to her maid.

"How sweet," she muttered grimly. "How welcoming . . ."

The crowd surged forward, but the star rose and we retreated again.

"Darlings . . . darlings," she sputtered, "I can't tell you how touched I am by this sign of your affection. But—" She gave a slight gargle that became a hacking cough. "It's been a *bad* day."

The group responded at once: "You were riveting." "Brilliant." "Enthralling."

The woman who had thrown the flowers was less effusive: "My deadline for feature stories in the *News Leader* is tomorrow. Nine a.m."

"Oh?" Holding the mink together with one hand, Bankhead managed to pour herself another drink with the other. "Well . . . just what did you want to know, darling?" she said like a trouper,

shaking her long hair back.

Before the woman could answer, a very fat man with a high-pitched voice called out from the rear.

"Tell us yo' favorite Southern dishes, honey."

She stared at him with ill-conceived contempt. "Southern Comfort—on the rocks!"

"What? No grits, no hominy?"

Tallulah rocked on her heels before answering. "The only good thing about *grits*," she seethed, "is that it rhymes with Ritz, where I go for my favorite dishes. And as for *harmony*, I'd rather starve!"

She was slightly drunk and decidedly livid. The crowd sensed it and dispersed, moving backward down the hall.

I can never explain why I said it, but as we were shuffling away, I turned to the person closest and shook my head. "She doesn't know the vitamins she's missing," I said.

Bankhead's voice roared like thunder. "And you," she cried, "don't know the tongue-lashing you've missed, Buster!"

The interview was over. But for years after I could not eat grits or hominy without remembering the terrible swift sword of her voice, and blushing.

The Grain's Genesis

Since grits and hominy are both essentially kernels from the same cob that produced cornmeal, one would assume they all shared the same forkful of food history. Not so, however.

Long, long before Columbus's raffish boatmen brought corn back from the New World and the first European miller decided the dried kernels would grind up to a usable flour, hominy and grits were staples in the American diet. Eaten by whom? The Indians, of course, who invented them both.

Algonquin history, in fact, tells how northeastern tribes managed to stay alive during hard winters because they had discovered the secret of storing and preparing *tackhummin,* "corn without skin."

What the Algonquins did to make *tackhummin* (a name which in time evolved to *hummin* and then through Pilgrim misrendering to *hominy*) was to hull dried corn by soaking it in water mixed with wood ashes. After a day's stint in the drink, the bleached kernels puffed up so considerably that the hulls burst and developed a decidedly non-corn flavor that was so addictive, the braves ate it three times a day without complaint—most probably because the plump kernels added a healthy jolt of complex carbohydrates, fats, iron, and thiamine to their otherwise dreary rations of dried deer and berries.

But that's not the whole story... Dried hulled hominy was also pounded by dutiful Indian squaws into a coarse mix (rougher than cornmeal) that was boiled and eaten hot by their braves. It was this pounded homespun cereal, gifted to them by the Indian tribes in Plymouth, that kept the earliest American colonists alive during the first terrible winters of their immigration. The Pilgrims accepted the Indians' bounty against their will, for they were a starchy lot, given to extreme conservatism in their diet. But hunger overcame pride in the end. They ate and survived.

It is inscribed in a diary of one of the *Mayflower* expedition that a certain colonial housewife, after first tasting the dubious porridge, shook her head vigorously and declared it to be equal to any bowl of groats she had ever tasted, and worthy of the Lord's benediction.

Groats she dubbed it and groats it remained for over a half century, until some footloose Massachusetts pioneer made his way to Virginia with a sack of the stuff over his shoulder.

After tasting hominy groats for the first time, a young denizen of the James

River country mispronounced it as *grits.* "Good grits" is reputedly his actual quote.

Grits is probably the most popular dining adjunct (after yams) below the Mason-Dixon line today. And I am happy to report, it has never lost its Southern accent!

GRITS

Some Plain Grain Talk

*T*hough still sometimes referred to as "hominy grits" in certain rustic parts of the South, grits as we know them are no longer derived from boiled, slaked whole hominy.

Technically, I guess one might call grits a residual grain, since they are milled as part of cornmeal before being separated and graded. What is left is a coarse cereal high in carbohydrates, made of dried, hulled, and ground corn kernels from which the bran and sometimes the germ is removed.

For the record, there are grits and *grits* in the marketplace. Like cornmeal, grits are not only processed and packaged by large commercial flour mills but also produced in lesser volume by a clutch of small, dedicated millers in outlying geography whose stone-ground output differs greatly from the commercial brands in nutritive value, appearance, and, let's face it, price.

However, whether you mail-order "speckled-heart grits" (see Calloway Gardens Country Store in the source list at the back of the book) or simply pick up a package close at hand in the supermarket, grits have a decided place in your grain lexicon. It is a high-fiber food, well endowed with protein, that may be combined with eggs, vegetables, cheese, or chicken to supply the maximum requirements of vitamins and minerals for a balanced diet.

And besides all that, take it from me, grits are utterly delicious!

How to Buy Them

*T*here are several options when buying grits.

Consumers may purchase the well-known brands that are available on supermarket shelves or search out the stone-ground varieties found only at gourmet groceries, natural foods stores, or by mail order.

There are differences (aside from price) between commercially produced grits and the grits that are actually ground between millstones, the old-fashioned way. For one thing, all stone-ground grits are organic; which is to say it is rougher in texture and more naturally nutritive than any fine-milled graded grits that are mass-produced.

However, that commendation comes with a cavil. Stone-ground grits are decidedly less smooth when cooked and will not produce the silky feel that commercially milled grits brings to a soufflé, roulade, or popover.

My advice: Try both and experiment!

Instant grits are another dish of cereal entirely. This product is precooked and then redried before it is packaged. One "recooks" the grits by adding boiling water. In my opinion, much is lost in the translation.

How to Store Them

*S*tone-ground grits have an exceedingly brief shelf life, and it will usually take less than a month for the paper package to become a breeding ground for un-wanted pantry pests. The only sterile environment for storing stone-ground grits is the refrigerator or freezer. I keep the package in an airtight plastic bag and figure a shelf life of four to five months in the fridge and up to a year in the freezer. Commercially produced grits may also be kept in the refrigerator, but any cool pantry shelf will do in a pinch. However, remember to seal the carton well (I use paper masking tape) after every use!

How to Cook Them

My way of cooking grits is somewhat unorthodox and decidedly *not* the method prescribed by either commercial manufacturers or stone-ground mills.

The instructions on most packaged grits are almost invariably the same: *"Bring the water to a boil. Slowly stir in the grits and cook covered over low heat 15–20 minutes. Then let stand off heat (covered) for a few minutes."* Stone-ground grits come with basically the same recommendation but the grits are cooked longer, 20 to 30 minutes.

Greene's technique, as you will ob-serve, is abbreviated: Bring the liquid to a boil first, then reduce the heat. Whisk the grits into the barely simmering water so the grains separate, and cook the mixture, uncovered, stirring occasion-ally, for about 10 minutes. No longer. The accelerated cooking time, I find, is an insurance policy against blobs,

lumps, and mush.

Brands of stone-ground grits vary considerably in coarseness of grind and often require a longer cooking period—about 20 minutes—to obtain the desired consistency of texture. Grits should be smooth and mollifying to the tongue, never rough or contentious!

STONE-GROUND VS COMMERCIALLY MILLED GRITS

Stone-ground grits are milled of dried hulled corn kernels and always include the heart (or germ) of the corn, which is exceedingly high in niacin, iron, and riboflavin.

Mass-produced grits are steamed to loosen the tough outer shell be-fore the grains are dried and split and the hull, bran, and germ are removed, leaving only the endo-sperm (tissue formed inside the seed's embryo sac) as a nutritive en-dowment.

However, it must be noted that both stone-ground and commer-cially manufactured grits are "forti-fied" with added vitamins and min-erals. And the word "Enriched" is emblazoned on each and every package!

SCROLLED, FILLED GRITS

A baked-and-souffléed cheese roll wrapped to capacity with ham and shrimp. I call it a "scroll" but it is actually a roulade—adapted from Nathalie Dupree's *New Southern Cooking*.

FOR THE ROULADE

½ cup plain yogurt
½ cup milk
¼ cup hominy grits
⅓ cup freshly grated Parmesan cheese
⅓ cup grated Swiss or Jarlsberg cheese
4 egg yolks
½ teaspoon salt
¼ teaspoon freshly ground black pepper
6 egg whites

FOR THE FILLING

4 tablespoons (½ stick) unsalted butter
3 large scallions, finely chopped
1 clove garlic, minced
½ cup chopped cooked ham
½ pound shrimp, shelled and deveined
¼ teaspoon chili powder
Hot pepper sauce
2 tablespoons all-purpose flour
½ cup homemade chicken stock (see page 376) or canned broth
½ cup plus 2 tablespoons heavy or whipping cream
1 teaspoon fresh lemon juice
Salt and freshly ground black pepper to taste

1. Preheat the oven to 350°F. Grease a 10½ by 15½-inch jelly roll pan, then grease a piece of wax paper and line the pan with it, greased side up.

2. Make the roulade: Combine the yogurt and milk in a medium-size heavy saucepan. Bring to boiling over medium heat, stirring frequently. Reduce the heat, stir in the grits, and cook, stirring constantly, over low heat until creamy in texture, about 10 minutes. Remove from the heat.

3. Stir both cheeses into the grits mixture. Then beat in the egg yolks, one at a time, beating thoroughly after each addition. Add the salt and pepper.

4. Beat the egg whites until stiff, and fold them into the grits mixture. Pour the mixture into the prepared jelly roll pan, and smooth it out evenly in the pan. Bake until firm, 15 to 20 minutes. The top should spring back lightly when touched. Invert the roulade onto a sheet of aluminum foil. Remove the pan and peel off the wax paper. Reduce the oven temperature to 300°F.

5. Make the filling: Melt 2 tablespoons of the butter in a large heavy skillet over medium heat. Add the scallions; cook 1 minute. Add the garlic and cook 4 minutes longer. Stir in the ham, toss to coat, and then add the shrimp. Sprinkle with the chili powder and a dash of hot pepper sauce. Toss until the shrimp turn pink, about 3 minutes. Remove from the heat and set aside.

6. Melt the remaining 2 tablespoons butter in a medium-size saucepan over medium-low heat. Stir in the flour. Cook, stirring constantly, 2 minutes. Whisk in the chicken stock and cream. Cook, stirring constantly, until very thick, about 5 minutes. Add the lemon juice, ⅛ teaspoon hot pepper sauce, and salt and pepper to taste. Combine with the ham and shrimp mixture.

7. Spread the filling evenly over the grits roulade, and roll it up like a jelly role using the foil to help with the rolling. Arrange the roulade on an ovenproof serving platter. (The dish can be prepared ahead to this point; keep it covered in the refrigerator.) Bake for 10 minutes before serving.

Serves 6

TOP DRAWER GRITS AND SPINACH SOUFFLE

A second soufflé guaranteed to please at brunch, lunch, dinner, or any time something puffed and tasty seems appropriate. Midnight perhaps—this light and lovely dish has great after hours appeal.

2½ tablespoons unsalted butter
6 tablespoons freshly grated Parmesan
    cheese
1 shallot, minced
10 ounces fresh spinach, rinsed, stems
    removed, finely chopped
1½ cups homemade chicken stock (see page
    376) or canned broth
½ cup hominy grits
4 egg yolks
¼ cup heavy or whipping cream
1 teaspoon freshly grated nutmeg
Freshly ground black pepper to taste
6 egg whites

1. Preheat the oven to 400°F. Rub a 1-quart soufflé dish with ½ tablespoon of the butter and sprinkle with 1 tablespoon of the cheese.

2. Melt the remaining 2 tablespoons butter in a medium-size heavy saucepan over medium-low heat. Add the shallot; cook 2 minutes. Stir in the spinach and cook, covered, until the spinach is slightly wilted, about 3 minutes.

3. Add the chicken stock to the spinach mixture, and heat to boiling. Reduce the heat, stir in the grits, and cook, stirring constantly, over low heat until creamy in texture, about 10 minutes. Reduce the heat to low and beat in the egg yolks, one at a time, beating well after each addition. Do not allow the mixture to boil.

4. Transfer the grits mixture to a large bowl. Stir in the cream, nutmeg, 4 tablespoons of the cheese, and pepper to taste.

5. Beat the egg whites until stiff but not dry. Stir a third of the whites into the grits mixture. Fold in the remaining whites. Pour into the prepared soufflé dish and sprinkle the top with the remaining 1 tablespoon cheese. Bake until golden and firm, 30 to 35 minutes. Serve immediately.

Serves 6

LAYING ON THE GRITS

Precisely because it is so "down homey" in character, grits are a grain whose name produces a smile all across the map of America. In the theater, for instance, "grits-eater" is a kinder epithet than "mush-mouth" for an actor who does not enunciate clearly. Likewise in the Deep South, the expression "laying on the grits" is considered to be a more polite form than "greasing the palm" when one is speaking of dealings with a politician on the take. And while we are on the subject, did you know that migratory corn-pickers always refer to a red rash that affects some newcomers to their ranks as "grits zits"? And so it goes . . . In a factory town, the "big grits" is always a pay boss. In poor urban areas, "dumb grits" means a welfare worker.

BACON AND CHEESE GRITS SOUFFLE

*E*lizabeth David said it about omelets, but with a slight amendment, it makes a perfect introduction to this grits show-stopper: "Everyone knows there is only one infallible recipe for the perfect soufflé . . . your own!"

That having been said, here is one of mine—definitely infallible, composed of grits, eggs, and hot air plus some highly arresting flavorings. I guarantee it will rise like high hopes in your oven!

1½ tablespoons unsalted butter
¼ cup freshly grated Parmesan cheese
4 strips bacon
1 small white onion, finely chopped
1 small clove garlic, minced
1 cup milk
1 cup water
½ teaspoon salt
½ cup hominy grits
4 egg yolks
⅛ teaspoon freshly grated nutmeg
½ cup grated Jalapeño Monterey Jack
   cheese
¼ cup heavy or whipping cream
Freshly ground black pepper to taste
5 egg whites

1. Preheat the oven to 400°F. Rub a 1-quart soufflé dish with ½ tablespoon of the butter and sprinkle with 1 tablespoon of the Parmesan cheese.

2. Sauté the bacon in a heavy skillet until crisp. Drain on paper towels, and remove all but 2 tablespoons bacon drippings from the skillet.

3. Add the onion to the bacon drippings in the skillet; cook over medium-low heat 1 minute. Add the garlic; cook until both the onions and garlic are golden, about 3 minutes longer. Set aside.

4. Combine the milk, water, and salt in a medium-size saucepan, and heat to boiling. Reduce the heat, stir in the grits, and cook, stirring constantly, over low heat until creamy in texture, about 10 minutes. Add the remaining 1 tablespoon butter. Reduce the heat to low and beat in the egg yolks, one at a time, beating well after each addition. Do not allow to boil.

5. Transfer the grits mixture to a large bowl. Crumble the bacon and add it to the grits along with the reserved onion mixture, the nutmeg, Jack cheese, 2 tablespoons of the Parmesan cheese, the cream, and pepper to taste.

6. Beat the egg whites until stiff but not dry. Stir a third of the whites into the grits mixture. Fold in the remaining whites. Pour into the prepared soufflé dish, and sprinkle the top with the remaining 1 tablespoon Parmesan cheese. Bake until golden and firm, 30 to 35 minutes. Serve immediately.

Serves 6

GRITS-CRUSTED TAMALE PIE

Zanne Zakroff, food editor of *Gourmet* magazine, is truly a gem of a cook—and a gem of a person. She once told me that every year one of her Christmas presents to her younger brother is a dinner for him and his friends, at which her tamale pie has become a mainstay. I have substituted grits for cornmeal in her recipe.

FOR THE FILLING

2 tablespoons vegetable oil
1 large onion, chopped
1 large clove garlic, minced
2 medium green bell peppers, cored, seeded, and chopped
1 pound ground beef
1 can (8 ounces) tomato sauce
2 tablespoons tomato paste
1 package (10 ounces) frozen corn, thawed
⅓ cup seedless raisins
1 cup sliced Spanish olives
1 tablespoon ground cumin
2 teaspoons unsweetened cocoa powder
½ teaspoon ground allspice
2 teaspoons chili powder
1 tablespoon Worcestershire sauce
1 teaspoon hot pepper sauce
1 tablespoon yellow cornmeal
¼ cup water (if needed)
Salt and freshly ground black pepper to taste

FOR THE TOPPING

3½ cups water
¼ teaspoon salt
¾ cup hominy grits
2 tablespoons unsalted butter
¼ cup yellow cornmeal
2 teaspoons baking powder
1 large egg, lightly beaten

½ cup grated sharp Cheddar cheese
1 can (4 ounces) mild green chiles, chopped

1. Make the filling: Heat the oil in a large heavy skillet over medium-low heat. Add the onion; cook 1 minute. Add the garlic and bell peppers; cook 5 minutes longer. Crumble in the beef and cook over medium heat, stirring to break up lumps, until the meat loses its pink color, about 5 minutes. Stir in the remaining filling ingredients through the cornmeal, and simmer, uncovered, 30 minutes. Add the water if the mixture is too dry. Season with salt and pepper, and spoon into a shallow 2½-quart casserole.

2. Preheat the oven to 400°F.

3. Make the topping: Combine the water and salt in a medium-size heavy saucepan and bring to boiling. Reduce the heat, stir in the grits, and cook, stirring constantly, over low heat until very thick, about 12 minutes. Stir in the butter and remove from the heat. Stir in the remaining topping ingredients, and spoon the mixture over the filling.

4. Bake the tamale pie 10 minutes. Reduce the oven heat to 350°F, and bake 30 minutes longer. Let stand 5 minutes before serving.

Serves 6

OLD-TIME GRITS AND CHICKEN SHORTCAKE

This is an upscale version of chicken hash. The grits cake is topped with a rich chicken mixture, which is easy to put together and can be reheated successfully.

FOR THE SHORTCAKE

5 cups water
½ teaspoon salt
1 cup hominy grits
2 tablespoons unsalted butter
1 small clove garlic, minced
3 eggs, separated
¾ cup grated mild Cheddar cheese

FOR THE CHICKEN TOPPING

2 tablespoons unsalted butter, cut into 6
*   teaspoons*
2 tablespoons plus 2 teaspoons all-purpose
*   flour*
1¼ cups homemade chicken stock (see page
*   376) or canned broth*
2 tablespoons dry sherry
Salt and ground white pepper to taste
2 cups coarsely chopped cooked chicken
1 small onion, halved and thinly sliced
⅔ cup light cream or half-and-half
2 egg yolks
2 tablespoons freshly grated Parmesan
*   cheese*

1. Preheat the oven to 350°F. Rub a 2½- to 3-quart shallow casserole with vegetable oil or butter.

2. Make the shortcake: Combine the water with the salt in a medium-size heavy saucepan and bring to boiling. Reduce the heat, stir in the grits, and cook, stirring constantly, over low heat until very thick, about 12 minutes. Remove from the heat and beat in the 2 tablespoons butter and the garlic. Beat in the egg yolks, one at a time. Fold in the cheese.

3. Beat the egg whites until stiff; fold them into the grits mixture.

4. Pour the grits mixture into the prepared casserole, and place the casserole in a roasting pan. Pour 1 inch hot water into the pan. Bake until the top is golden and the mixture is firm, about 1 hour and 15 minutes.

5. When the shortcake is ready, remove it from the oven and from the roasting pan; let stand 5 minutes. Reduce the oven heat to 225°F.

6. Meanwhile, make the chicken topping: Melt 4 teaspoons of the butter in a medium-size saucepan over medium-low heat. Add the 2 tablespoons flour. Cook, stirring constantly, 2 minutes. Whisk in the chicken stock; heat to boiling. Cook, stirring constantly, over medium heat until thick, about 4 minutes. Stir in the sherry, and add salt and white pepper to taste. Fold in the chicken.

7. Spoon the chicken mixture over the shortcake and place in the low oven to keep warm.

8. Melt the remaining 2 teaspoons butter in a medium-size skillet over medium-low heat. Add the onion; cook 4 minutes. Sprinkle with the remaining 2 teaspoons flour. Cook, stirring constantly, 2 minutes. Whisk in the light cream and cook until slightly thickened, about 3 minutes. Mix 2 tablespoons sauce with the egg yolks in a bowl and stir back into the sauce. Cook over low heat 2 minutes. Do not allow to boil. Season with salt and white pepper to taste, and stir in the cheese. Spoon the mixture over the chicken, and place the dish under a preheated broiler to lightly brown the top.

Serves 6 to 8

BOTTOMLESS GRITS, HAM, AND CUSTARD TART

*T*his dish is almost like a quiche—*sans* crust. It makes wonderful picnic fare, wrapped up and served at room temperature.

2 tablespoons unsalted butter
1 shallot, minced
1 cup diced cooked ham
2 teaspoons Madeira
1 cup milk, heated
1 cup homemade chicken stock (see page 376) or canned broth, heated
½ teaspoon freshly grated nutmeg
½ cup hominy grits
3 eggs, lightly beaten
¼ cup heavy or whipping cream
⅓ cup plus 2 tablespoons grated Gruyère cheese
Freshly ground black pepper to taste

1. Preheat the oven to 400°F. Lightly butter a 10-inch glass or ceramic quiche dish.

2. Melt the butter in a medium-size skillet over medium heat. Add the shallot; cook 2 minutes. Add the ham; cook 2 minutes longer. Stir in the Madeira, and continue to cook until almost all liquid has evaporated, about 5 minutes.

3. Add the hot milk, hot chicken stock, and nutmeg to the ham mixture and heat to boiling. Reduce the heat, stir in the grits, and cook, stirring constantly, over low heat until creamy in texture, about 10 minutes.

4. Remove from the heat and beat in the eggs, cream, and the ⅓ cup Gruyère. Pour the mixture into the prepared quiche dish. Sprinkle with the 2 tablespoons cheese and pepper to taste. Bake until golden, 20 to 25 minutes.

Serves 6 to 8

BLUE CHIP FRIED GRITS

*L*eftovers make the best fried grits, but the second best is indubitably the recipe below. However, it comes with an injunction: For maxium flavor and taste, be sure to make the recipe (prior to the frying pan, of course) at least a day ahead, and refrigerate until it is well chilled.

Incidentally, I call this dish "Blue Chip Fried Grits" because my stock increases every time it is served.

3½ cups water
¼ teaspoon salt
¾ cup hominy grits
5½ tablespoons unsalted butter
1 shallot, finely chopped
1 clove garlic, minced

½ cup chopped cooked smoky ham
½ cup freshly grated Parmesan cheese
1 tablespoon vegetable oil

1. Preheat the oven to 350°F. Lightly butter a shallow casserole.

2. Combine the water and salt in a medium-size heavy saucepan and bring to boiling. Reduce the heat, stir in the grits, and cook, stirring constantly, over low heat until creamy in texture, about 10 minutes. Remove from the heat.

3. Melt 2 tablespoons of the butter in a large heavy skillet over medium-low heat. Add the shallot; cook 1 minute. Add the garlic; cook 2 minutes. Stir in the ham and cook 4 minutes longer.

4. Stir the ham mixture into the grits mixture, then stir in the cheese. Spoon into the prepared casserole. Dot the top of the grits mixture with 1½ tablespoons of the butter. Bake until lightly browned, 25 to 30 minutes. Cool, and then refrigerate until well chilled. Cut into squares.

5. Heat the remaining 2 tablespoons butter with the oil in a large heavy skillet over medium-low heat. Sauté the grits, a few pieces at a time, until golden brown on both sides, about 4 minutes. Keep warm in a 225°F oven until all pieces are sautéed.

Serves 6

BEDEVILED GRITS

*I*n Indian mythology, ants are credited with showing man the bounty of corn. Zuni tribesmen claim that ants first furrowed the soil and then pushed the seed into the open rows, where it took root. Later ants ate the corn stalks so the husks would open and fall to the ground. Ants then chewed the kernels of the fallen cobs to let man know it could be pounded into fine grain. And when ants ate the best of the grain man had stored, man was forced to discover another way to soak and dry the kernels to keep himself alive. So ants were responsible for grits, too.

Ants did all of that for man, and what did they get for their trouble? Only bedevilment! To this day Zunis teach their children to step on ants from the time they are able to walk.

But have a bedevilment here of quite a different stripe: a hot casserole of baked grits, mustard, and crumbs that cries out for a chop or a chicken leg as a broiled dinner partner.

4 tablespoons (½ stick) unsalted butter
1 medium onion, minced
1 small clove garlic, minced
1 cup light cream or half-and-half
1 cup homemade chicken stock (see page 376) or canned broth
2½ teaspoons Dijon mustard
1 teaspoon Hungarian paprika
½ cup hominy grits
Dash of hot pepper sauce
¼ cup freshly grated Parmesan cheese
Freshly ground black pepper to taste
½ cup fresh bread crumbs

1. Preheat the oven to 350°F. Lightly butter a shallow baking dish.

2. Melt 2 tablespoons of the butter in a medium-size heavy saucepan over medium-low heat. Add the onion; cook 2 minutes. Add the garlic; cook 2 minutes longer. Stir in the light cream and chicken stock. Whisk in the mustard and paprika, and heat to boiling. Reduce the heat, stir in the grits, and cook, stirring constantly, over low heat until creamy in texture, about 10 minutes. Remove from the heat and add the hot pepper sauce, cheese, and pepper to taste. Pour into the prepared baking dish.

3. Melt the remaining 2 tablespoons butter in a large heavy skillet over me-dium heat. Stir in the bread crumbs and sauté until golden. Spoon over the grits mixture, and bake 15 minutes.

Serves 4 to 6

"CREAMED AGAIN" GRITS AND GARLIC

*T*his may be rich, but it sure is good! Serve it with chicken dressed in a mild tomato sauce.

2 tablespoons unsalted butter
1 large clove garlic, minced
2 cups heavy or whipping cream
1½ cups homemade chicken stock (see page 376) or canned broth
¾ cup hominy grits
¼ cup cubed cream cheese
¼ cup freshly grated Parmesan cheese
Salt and ground white pepper to taste

1. Melt the butter in a medium-size heavy saucepan over medium-low heat. Add the garlic; cook 2 minutes. Stir in the cream and chicken broth. Heat to boiling, stirring frequently, over medium heat. Reduce the heat, stir in the grits, and cook, stirring constantly, over low heat until creamy in texture, about 10 minutes.

2. Add the cream cheese and Parmesan cheese to the grits mixture. Cook until smooth, 3 to 4 minutes longer. Season with salt and white pepper.

Serves 4 to 6

NATHALIE'S SECOND HELPING GRITS

*N*athalie Dupree is one of the best Southern cooks extant. For further proof catch her P.B.S. television show, "New Southern Cooking," or get her book of the same name. "Second Helping Grits" is what I dub her signature dish—because it's simple, it's sexy, and you always want more!

This rendering calls for Parmesan cheese. Being a free spirit, Nathalie also uses Swiss or Monterey Jack when she feels like it.

2 cups heavy or whipping cream
½ cup stone-ground hominy grits
2 tablespoons unsalted butter
Salt and freshly ground white pepper to taste
½ cup freshly grated Parmesan cheese

1. Heat the cream, stirring frequently, in a medium-size heavy saucepan. Bring it to boiling, then reduce the heat. Stir in the grits and cook, stirring constantly, over low heat until creamy in texture, about 10 minutes.

2. Add the butter to the grits, along with salt and white pepper. Remove from the heat and stir in the cheese.

Serves 4

A RAINBOW QUARTET

In the South, grits are traditionally served as an accompaniment to breakfast; they come to the table puddled with melted butter, followed by frizzled ham, eggs, hash-browned potatoes, and biscuits.

I discovered grits at a less auspicious groaning board, however: the marble counter of a drugstore (long gone now) that occupied a goodly portion of The Duke of Gloucester Street in Williamsburg, Virginia, where I went to college.

Grits were served, unrequested, along with my breakfast order the first day I arrived. And I will tell you, unashamedly, it was love at first bite. But as I implied earlier, not all denizens of the South share my predilection.

The first real friend I made at college was a worldly sophomore from Birmingham, Alabama, who watched my grits consumption at the counter three days in a row before finally commenting on the obvious penchant.

"You really like that stuff?" he inquired in a low voice not meant to be overheard. "Or are you just bein' Yankee polite?"

"No, I love it. Don't you?"

"I hate grits. But you can't admit things like that when you're tenth-generation, Southern-born. It's one notch above spittin' on the Confederate flag or declarin' *War and Peace* is a better book than *Gone with the Wind!*"

"So you don't like grits," I murmured, thoughtfully licking the last bit off my fork. "It tastes so good to me."

"Taste has nothing to do with it," he replied. "It's color. Since I was a little kid I have never been able to stomach white foods!"

The quartet of grits recipes that follow (ever so delicately shaded green, pale blue, and variegated hues by turns) would have made my friend a true grits fan at once. They are all highly flavorsome menu adjuncts to think about when you are planning a lunch, brunch, or dinner party. But *not* breakfast!

Blue Grits

Blue cheese adds a remarkable tang to a "mess of grits." This is one side dish that is a natural with smoky grilled foods.

1 quart water

½ teaspoon salt
1 cup hominy grits
¼ cup heavy or whipping cream
2 ounces creamy blue cheese (such as Cambazola or Bleu Castello), cubed
1 tablespoon unsalted butter
Chopped fresh parsley, for garnish

1. Combine the water and salt in a medium-size heavy saucepan and heat to boiling. Reduce the heat, stir in the grits, and cook, stirring constantly, until creamy in texture, about 10 minutes.

2. Stir the cream into the grits and raise the heat slightly. Continue to cook, stirring constantly, until slightly thickened, about 5 minutes. Add the cheese and butter; cook 2 minutes longer. Sprinkle with parsley before serving.

Serves 6

Confetti Grits

White, green, and red: a toss-up of colorful confetti that goes well with chicken and pork.

2 tablespoons unsalted butter
1 scallion, white bulb and green top, finely chopped
1½ cups water
½ cup milk
½ cup hominy grits (stone-ground, if possible)
1 large plum tomato, seeded and cut into slivers
1 tablespoon chopped fresh basil
Salt and freshly ground black pepper to taste

1. Melt the butter in a medium-size heavy saucepan over medium-low heat. Add the scallion; cook 2 minutes. Stir in the water and milk, and heat to boiling. Reduce the heat, stir in the grits, and cook, stirring constantly, over low heat until creamy in texture, about 10 minutes. Add more milk if the mixture becomes too thick before it is tender. (Stone-ground grits may require ½ cup more milk.)

2. Stir the tomato and basil into the grits. Season with salt and pepper, and serve immediately.

Serves 4

Smoky Green-Peppered Grits

Another grits dish that mates successfully with grilled meats.

1 tablespoon olive oil
1 shallot, minced
2 green bell peppers, roasted (see page 248), peeled, seeded, and chopped
3½ cups homemade chicken stock (see page 376) or canned broth
¾ cup hominy grits
¼ teaspoon crushed dried hot red peppers
Salt to taste

1. Heat the oil in a medium-size heavy saucepan over medium-low heat. Add the shallot; cook 2 minutes. Stir in the peppers and stock, and heat to boiling. Reduce the heat, stir in the grits, and cook, stirring constantly, over low heat until creamy in texture, about 10 minutes.

2. Stir the dried red peppers into the grits, and season with salt.

Serves 4 to 6

Grits Primavera

This is a rich grits complement to a simply broiled chicken breast or sautéed veal scallops.

1 package (10 ounces) frozen peas, thawed
¼ cup heavy or whipping cream
1 tablespoon honey
2 tablespoons unsalted butter
2 large shallots, minced
2 cups homemade chicken stock (see page 376) or canned broth
¾ cup milk
¾ cup hominy grits
Pinch of salt

1. Combine the peas, cream, and honey in the container of a food processor. Process just until finely chopped, and set aside.

2. Melt the butter in a medium-size heavy saucepan over medium-low heat. Add the shallots; cook 2 minutes. Add the stock and milk, and heat to boiling.

Reduce the heat, stir in the grits and salt, and cook, stirring constantly, over low heat until creamy in texture, about 10 minutes.

3. Stir the pea mixture into the grits. Continue to cook until warmed through, 2 to 3 minutes.

Serves 4 to 6

GRITS TRIVIA FROM THE WHITE HOUSE KITCHEN

• The first President to eat grits in public office was James Madison, but he never served it to guests or even to his wife, Dolley. Why? Virginia-born Madison spent most of his political career fighting off the charge that he was a "regionalist," and he went out of his way to eat food from anywhere *but* the South!

• Grits was finally officially served at a presidential table when Ulysses S. Grant took over. Though he defeated the Confederacy, Grant always claimed the South won his appetite—so it was a pyrrhic victory.

• Woodrow Wilson suffered many physical disabilities during his term as President. To alleviate the pain of ulcers, doctors prescribed (and he ate) a small bowl of grits with cream and sugar for lunch daily.

• Franklin Delano Roosevelt admired grits so much, the kitchen staff at Warm Springs, Georgia, had a special bowl designed with a cover—to keep the grits warm when his breakfast was interrupted by phone calls.

• Harry Truman was another grits enthusiast but never ate a bowlful in the White House if he could help it. "Some things just taste better on home territory," he said.

• Gerald Ford was reputed to have tried grits once and pushed the plate away. But it is important to recall that ex-President Ford was also quoted as saying, "Eating and sleeping are both a waste of time!"

• Without a doubt, grits' greatest supporter in the White House was Jimmy Carter. When Carter was President, grits were served up for breakfast every single morning. And if you believe the witnesses, they were entirely polished off before the Chief of State left the table.

GRITS POPOVERS

*T*his recipe came in a "bread and butter" note from a friend after much of an evening was spent discussing grits. She does not know where she got it, but whoever invented it, it is a stunner.

Baker's Secret (see page 42)
1¼ cups milk
¼ teaspoon salt
¼ cup hominy grits
4 strips bacon
2 large eggs
¼ cup bread flour

1. Preheat the oven to 400°F. Rub a muffin tin with Baker's Secret or spray with a vegetable cooking spray.

2. Combine 1 cup of the milk with the salt in a medium-size heavy saucepan and bring to boiling. Reduce the heat, stir in the grits, and cook, stirring constantly, over low heat until very thick, about 12 minutes. Remove from the heat.

3. Meanwhile, sauté the bacon until crisp. Drain it on paper towels, crumble, and reserve. Reserve the bacon drippings.

4. Place the eggs with the remaining ¼ cup milk and the flour in a blender container. Blend until smooth. Add the grits mixture and the bacon drippings. Blend until smooth. Stir in the crumbled bacon.

5. Pour the batter into the prepared muffin cups. They should be two-thirds full. Bake 20 minutes. Slash the sides of the popovers with a knife, return them to the oven, and bake 4 or 5 minutes longer.

Makes 12 small popovers

HOMINY

Some Plain Grain Talk

*L*ike a desperado, whole hominy is known by various aliases around the country: *posole, samp, mote,* and *nixtamal,* to name a few. Actually it is no outlaw grain at all, merely whole corn that has been processed in a water bath liberally dosed with slaked (hydrated) lime or a combination of unslaked lime, calcium carbonate, and lye or wood ash. The corn soaks in this mixture until the kernels swell, loosen from the hulls, and become somewhat puffy. In passing they acquire a distinctive flavor (slightly smoky) that is highly addictive and decidedly un-corn-like.

After the kernels are washed and any residual hulls excised, whole hominy is either canned (processed and packed in water), dried, or frozen.

Whole hominy (or *posole* as it is commonly known in the Southwest, where it is a staple in Mexican households) is a highly malleable ingredient. In my kitchen it has not only been stewed, baked, broiled, and fried but also processed into a creamy mixture not unlike mashed potatoes in texture—which has become a favored stand-in in dumpling and bread recipes.

Whole hominy is a carbohydrate that is high in protein, well endowed with phosphorus, magnesium, zinc, and niacin, *and* relatively low in calories: 156 per cup.

More to the point, the ash it was bathed with is rich in mineral salts that most other corn products lack, so—particularly in its dried state—whole hominy is a highly nutritious food.

How to Buy It

Whole hominy is not an easy ingredient to find. However, it *is* available at Hispanic and Mexican groceries, found mainly in cities with large Spanish-speaking populations—usually in water-packed cans labeled *posole* (or spelled the Mexican way, *pozole*). It is relatively inexpensive.

If you live in an outlying area without "ethnic neighborhood shopping," canned whole hominy may be ordered by mail (see the list of purveyors at the back of the book).

Recently I have noticed dried whole hominy, packaged by the pound like other dried grains, being sold at gourmet groceries and specialty food shops around the country. The dried hominy requires a longer period of cooking time and is decidedly pricier than canned.

In his book *The Feast of Santa Fe*, Huntley Dent advises that fresh-frozen posole may be purchased in supermarkets that stock other Mexican foods. But in all candor, I must confess that I have yet to find a supermarket east of the Pecos that carried a package.

Whole hominy is available yellow or white, but the latter type is most commonly found.

I might add that the flour made of whole hominy is known as *mass harina* and is used for making tortillas by hand.

How to Store It

Canned whole hominy comes in two sizes: a 16-ounce and a 29-ounce can. If you are using less than a full amount for a recipe, be sure to reserve the processing liquid in the can, and repack the remaining hominy, covered with the liquid, in a sterilized jar. It will keep for weeks in a cold refrigerator.

Unused dried posole should be stored in extra-thick self-seal plastic bags or in a storage jar with a tight-fitting closure on the pantry shelf or in a kitchen cabinet. It will keep for months at a moderately low room temperature (45° to 50°F).

Cooked dried posole (left over from a recipe) should be stored in the fridge in an earthenware or glass bowl well covered with plastic wrap. Shelf life is just two or three days.

Cooked whole hominy does *not* freeze, so skip that amenity please.

How to Cook It

There is no hard and fast formula for cooking whole hominy, just a lot of cautions and cavils. Here are some of mine:

• Be sure to drain and rinse canned whole hominy before it is used.

• Canned whole hominy cooks quickly: Thirty minutes is my rule of thumb for most top-of-the-stove preparations. Baking takes longer: 45 to 50 minutes, depending on your oven heat. But always test for doneness before you serve!

• For super-smooth processed whole hominy, always add heavy cream or milk to the container of the food processor.

• Before it is cooked, dried whole hominy must be soaked overnight in cold water. Figure on 2 to 2½ hours of cooking time before the dried hominy approximates the texture and pliability of the canned variety. It is a lot of work, but the flavor is superior to any other posole you will ever sample. (One cup dried posole yields 3 cups cooked.)

URBAN POZOLE VERDE

Pozole is a Mexican peasant dish (cooked up of hog's head and hominy) that the Anglos annexed shortly after the U.S. Government annexed New Mexico back in the 1840s.

Nobody is alive to tell the tale of how Mexican *pozole* survived the border change to New Mexican *posole*, but since it is still consumed frequently (some say once a day) by most of the state's rustic denizens, it is generally agreed to be a helluva dish in any language!

Try my version (totally inauthentic, with chicken in the pot yet) for a highly urban *pozole verde*. You're right, Greene's stew!

1 frying chicken (about 4 pounds)
1 large onion, halved
2 large cloves garlic
1 bay leaf
2 sprigs thyme, or ½ teaspoon dried
3 sprigs parsley
½ teaspoon freshly ground black pepper
1 quart homemade chicken stock (see page 376) or canned broth
1 quart water
1 pound boneless pork loin, cut into thin strips about 2 inches long
2 teaspoons peanut oil
1 medium onion, chopped
1 large green bell pepper, roasted (see page 248), seeded, peeled, and quartered
1 hot green chile pepper, seeded and chopped
1 can (4 ounces) mild green chiles, drained
½ cup hulled toasted pumpkin seeds (see Note)
1 can (13 ounces) tomatillos, drained
2 teaspoons chopped cilantro (Chinese parsley)
1 can (16 ounces) white whole hominy, rinsed and drained

FOR THE GARNISH

1 avocado, peeled, cored, and chopped
1 red onion, chopped
Tortilla chips

1. Place the chicken in a large kettle and add the onion halves, garlic, bay leaf, thyme, parsley, pepper, chicken stock, and water. Heat to boiling. Reduce the heat and simmer, partially covered, 45 minutes.

2. Remove the chicken to a bowl and set aside to cool. Strain the liquid, reserving both liquid and vegetables. Discard the bay leaf.

3. Return 1 cup liquid to the kettle and add the pork. Cook, covered, skimming occasionally, over medium-low heat 30 minutes.

4. Meanwhile, heat the oil in a large heavy skillet over medium-low heat. Add the chopped onion; cook 4 minutes. Add the roasted pepper, the hot green pepper, and the canned chiles. Cook 1 minute. Stir in the pumpkin seeds, tomatillos, and cilantro. Cook 2 minutes longer. Remove from the heat and allow to cool slightly.

5. Place the pepper mixture in the container of a food processor with about ¼ cup of the reserved chicken stock, and add the reserved vegetables. Process until smooth.

6. Remove the skin and bones from the chicken. Cut the chicken meat into chunks.

7. When the pork has cooked 30 minutes, add the puréed mixture, the remaining chicken stock, and the drained hominy. Heat to boiling. Reduce the heat and cook, covered, over medium heat 15 minutes. Stir in the

chicken; cook, covered, 15 minutes longer. Place the garnishes in serving bowls. Serve very hot.

Serves 4 to 6

Note: To toast pumpkin seeds, heat a large heavy skillet over medium heat. When hot, add the seeds and cook, stirring frequently, until golden, 6 to 8 minutes.

HOMINY AND BANGERS

*B*angers are mild British sausages, and hardly the expected partner of hominy. So, imagine my surprise—and delight—when I ran across that unusual combination in the Chelsea area of London. Well, here it is, punched up in flavor and in all its "adapted by Greene" glory.

3 large sweet Italian sausages
2 teaspoons unsalted butter
1 small onion, finely chopped
¼ teaspoon fennel seeds
1 medium hot green pepper, seeded, deveined, and minced
1 small fennel bulb, chopped (about 1¼ cups)
1 can (16 ounces) white whole hominy, rinsed and drained
2 teaspoons Pernod liqueur
Salt and freshly ground black pepper to taste
1 tablespoon chopped fennel fronds
Hot pepper sauce

1. Sauté the sausages in a large oil-rubbed skillet over medium heat until well browned on all sides, about 8 minutes. Remove the sausages. Slice and reserve.

2. Pour off all but 1 tablespoon fat from the skillet. Stir in the butter. Add the onion and fennel seeds. Cook over medium heat until golden, about 4 minutes. Add the hot pepper; cook 2 minutes. Stir in the fennel and hominy. Cook, covered, over medium-low heat 10 minutes. Add the sausages and continue to cook until the fennel and hominy are soft, about 10 minutes longer. Sprinkle with Pernod and salt and pepper, and cook, uncovered, 2 minutes. Garnish with chopped fennel fronds, and pass the pepper sauce on the side.

Serves 4

TWO HOMINY HOMILIES

"Pray for peace and end to this terrible fight. Pray for courage and salvation. And pray that someone back home in Texas don't forget to stir up the hominy."—Anonymous carving on a musket found at Bull Run, 1865

"It's a very curious thing
  Odd as it can be—
  But every spoon of hominy
  I eat . . . ends up as part of me!"
—Attributed to Tiny Alice,
  First Fat Lady of The
    Barnum & Bailey
    Ringling Brothers Circus, 1929

NEW DELHI FRISBEES

*T*his dish is based on a vegetarian croquette—spicy, crisp, and dappled with peanuts—that is a culinary gift of the estimable Indian cook and writer Julie Sahni. Julie's original recipe called for mashed potatoes, but mashed posole was at hand so a substitution was effected. This dish is wonderful in either rendition.

¼ cup minute tapioca

1 cup cooked dried whole hominy (see Note) or rinsed and drained canned hominy

5 to 6 tablespoons heavy or whipping cream

4 hot green chile peppers, seeded, deveined, and minced

3 tablespoons finely chopped cilantro (Chinese parsley)

¼ cup dry-roasted unsalted peanuts, finely chopped

4 small scallions, white bulbs and green tops, chopped

1 small shallot, finely chopped

Peanut oil for frying

Salt

1. Place the tapioca in a fine-mesh strainer and rinse under cold water. Place in a small bowl and cover with 1 inch cold water. Let stand 20 minutes. Drain in a sieve, pressing gently with the back of a spoon. Transfer to a medium-size bowl.

2. Place the hominy in the container of a food processor, and process until finely minced. Then add just enough cream to create a mixture with the consistency of mashed potatoes.

3. Add the processed hominy to the tapioca, along with the peppers, cilantro, peanuts, scallions, and shallot. Mix well.

4. With wet hands, form the mixture into small patties and place them on a plate. Refrigerate for 1 hour.

5. Heat 1½ inches peanut oil in a heavy skillet until hot but not smoking. Fry the croquettes, about five at a time, until golden on both sides, 3 to 4 minutes per side. (Raise heat slightly if not browned enough.) Drain on paper towels, and transfer to a heatproof serving platter. Sprinkle with salt before serving.

6. If necessary, reheat the patties in a 375°F oven for 10 minutes before serving.

Serves 4 to 6

Note: To cook dried hominy, first soak ⅓ cup hominy overnight in cold water. Drain, rinse, and cover again with cold water in a medium-size saucepan. Heat to boiling, reduce the heat, and simmer, covered, 2½ hours. Drain and reserve.

SUPER CREAMY HOMINY AND GREEN CHILES

*I*n the Old West, when dried hominy was plentiful and other social amenities scarce, the grain was often used in ways far from its essential application. There are domestic

records of dried hominy used to anchor pie pastry in the oven, not to mention stuffing sofa cushions or substituting for buckshot. The most bizarre use of dried hominy took place after a local wedding in a small town in Texas, when a newly married bride and groom were pelted black and blue with hominy instead of rice. The couple later sued for "aggrieved and injured emotions."

A less violent use of hominy is limned below—a creamy breakfast/lunch innovation that owes a debt to Huntley Dent, whose cookbook *The Feast of Santa Fe* is awash with posole variations.

1 can (29 ounces) white or golden whole hominy, rinsed and drained
½ cup heavy or whipping cream
3 tablespoons unsalted butter
1 fresh jalapeño pepper, seeded, deveined, and minced
1 can (4 ounces) mild green chiles, chopped
½ cup grated Monterey Jack cheese
Salt and freshly ground black pepper to taste
4 to 6 poached eggs (optional)

1. Place the hominy and the cream in the container of a food processor. Process, using the pulse switch, only until coarsely ground, about 5 seconds.

2. Melt the butter in a heavy skillet over medium-low heat. Add the jalapeño pepper; cook 1 minute. Stir in the mild green chiles and the hominy mixture. Cook, stirring constantly, until the hominy begins to bubble, about 3 minutes. Remove from the heat and stir in the cheese. Add salt and pepper to taste. Serve with poached eggs on top, if desired.

Serves 4 to 6

LITTLE RED HOMINY WITH CHEESE

*T*his tasty side dish is a hit next to barbecued chicken. I have also used it as a first course.

2½ tablespoons unsalted butter
1 medium onion, finely chopped
1 clove garlic, minced
1 cup chopped peeled, seeded tomatoes
½ teaspoon sugar
1 teaspoon tomato paste
1 tablespoon sliced pickled jalapeño pepper
1 can (29 ounces) white or golden whole hominy, rinsed and drained
¼ teaspoon salt
¼ teaspoon freshly ground black pepper
2 cups grated Monterey Jack cheese

1. Preheat the oven to 375°F.
2. Melt the butter in a large heavy skillet over medium-low heat. Add the onion; cook 1 minute. Add the garlic; cook 2 minutes longer. Stir in the tomatoes, sugar, and tomato paste. Cook over medium heat 5 minutes. Add the peppers and cook 5 minutes longer. Stir in the hominy, salt, and pepper. Remove from the heat.

3. Stir 1½ cups of the cheese into the hominy mixture and transfer to a buttered casserole. Sprinkle the top with the remaining ½ cup cheese. Place the casserole in the oven and immediately reduce the heat to 350°F. Bake 45 minutes. Let stand 5 minutes before serving.

Serves 4 to 6

HOMINY DIMPLINGS WITH GREEN SALSA

I call them "dimplings" because these miniatures are too ethereal to be saddled with a "dumpling" label. What's unusual about the "dimplings" is the smoky hominy flavor. It became apparent at first taste that the only suitable blanket would have to be American Indian—hence the very green salsa on the side. Serve as nibbling food with cool drinks or as a spicy accompaniment to grilled chicken.

1 can (16 ounces) white whole hominy, rinsed and drained
½ cup heavy or whipping cream
½ cup all-purpose flour
1 egg yolk, lightly beaten
¼ cup freshly grated Parmesan cheese
¼ teaspoon freshly grated nutmeg
¼ teaspoon hot pepper sauce
6 tablespoons (¾ stick) unsalted butter, melted
Salt and freshly ground black pepper to taste
Green Salsa (recipe follows)

1. Place the hominy in the container of a food processor. Add the cream, and process until smooth. Transfer to a large bowl.

2. With a heavy wooden spoon, stir the flour, egg yolk, cheese, nutmeg, hot pepper sauce, and 2 tablespoons of the butter into the hominy mixture until smooth. Add salt and pepper to taste.

3. Using about ¼ cup at at time, roll the hominy mixture out on a heavily floured board to form thin ropes. Cut into 1-inch pieces, gently pinching down the ends. Cook the dimplings in simmering salted water until they float to the top, about 20 seconds. Remove with a slotted spoon and rest the spoon on paper towels to drain. Then transfer the dimplings to a buttered baking dish. Continue the process until all the batter is used up.

4. Preheat the oven to 400°F.

5. Drizzle the remaining 4 tablespoons melted butter over the dimplings, and bake 10 minutes. Serve with Green Salsa.

Serves 4 to 6

Green Salsa

1 small onion, quartered
3 or 4 large hot green chile peppers, seeded and chopped
8 small cherry tomatoes (preferably underripe)
Juice of ½ lime
2 tablespoons chopped cilantro (Chinese parsley)
1 large sprig parsley, chopped
2 sprigs thyme, chopped
½ cup olive oil
3 tablespoons white wine vinegar
Salt and freshly ground black pepper to taste

Place the onion and hot peppers in the container of a food processor. Process, pulsing, until finely chopped. Add the tomatoes, lime juice, cilantro, parsley, and thyme. Continue to process until chopped. Transfer to a bowl, stir in the oil and vinegar, and season with salt and pepper.

Makes about 1½ cups

HOMINY BREAD WHEEL

*I*f hominy is hard to find nowadays, that was not always the case. The late James Beard, a deep-dyed hominy lover all of his life, told of being a small boy in Portland, Oregon, waiting on the steps of his mother's boardinghouse for the "hominy man" who regularly passed through the neighborhood in a little horse-drawn cart once a week.

"Friendly and pleasant," Beard recalled. "He sold fresh horseradish as well as hominy. And carried all of the town's gossip with him!"

If I had a wish to spare, it would be for the return of the hominy man. I'd have him passing through my street once a week—not for the local gossip, but because I could make my favorite bread recipe more often.

2 packages dry yeast
1 teaspoon sugar
½ cup lukewarm water
1 can (16 ounces) white whole hominy, rinsed and drained
½ cup cold milk
1 cup lukewarm milk
1 teaspoon coarse (kosher) salt
2 tablespoons caraway seeds
1 cup whole-wheat flour
3 cups bread flour (approximately)
1 cup rye flour
1 tablespoon unsalted butter, melted

1. Combine the yeast, sugar, and lukewarm water in a large bowl. Let stand 5 minutes.

2. Place the hominy and the cold milk in the container of a food processor. Process until the mixture is the texture of mashed potatoes.

3. Stir the processed hominy mixture into the yeast mixture. Stir in the lukewarm milk, coarse salt, caraway seeds, whole-wheat flour, and 1 cup of the bread flour. Beat with a wooden spoon until smooth. Cover, and let stand in a warm place 30 minutes.

4. Stir the rye flour into the hominy mixture, and add about ½ cup of the bread flour to form a stiff dough. Scrape out onto a well-floured board, and knead for 10 minutes, incorporating about 1½ cups more bread flour. When the dough is smooth and elastic, transfer it to a well-greased bowl. Cover, and let rise in a warm place until doubled in volume, about 1½ hours.

5. Punch the dough down and return it to a floured board. Knead briefly. Let stand 3 minutes.

6. Place the dough in a well-greased 9-inch springform pan. Cover loosely with a flour-rubbed tea towel. Let stand in a warm place until the dough has risen to the top of the pan, about 1 hour.

7. Preheat the oven to 375°F.

8. Slash the top of the dough in several places with a sharp knife, and brush with the melted butter. Sprinkle the oven with a few drops of water to create steam, then place the pan in the hot oven. Bake until the bread is golden brown on top and sounds hollow when tapped with your finger, about 45 minutes. Cool on a rack for at least 20 minutes before removing bread from the pan.

Makes one 9-inch round loaf

SHARON'S HOMINY HONEYS

Sharon Tyler Herbst, my dear friend and cooking peer, wrote a delightful book, *Breads*. I was thrilled when I saw the recipe on which these were based—a real old-fashioned sweet honey muffin.

Baker's Secret (see page 42) or vegetable cooking spray
1 can (16 ounces) white whole hominy, rinsed and drained
¾ cup milk
2 eggs, lightly beaten
6 tablespoons (¾ stick) unsalted butter, melted
¾ cup honey
2 cups all-purpose flour
1 tablespoon baking powder
½ teaspoon salt
½ cup raisins
½ cup chopped walnuts

1. Preheat the oven to 400°F. Rub a muffin tin with Baker's Secret or spray with a vegetable cooking spray.

2. Combine the hominy with the milk in the container of a food processor, and process until smooth. Transfer to a large bowl.

3. Add the eggs to the processed hominy, along with 4 tablespoons of the butter, ¼ cup of the honey, the flour, baking powder, salt, raisins, and walnuts. Mix thoroughly.

4. Spoon the batter into the prepared muffin cups. They should be two thirds full. Bake until golden brown, 25 to 30 minutes.

5. Meanwhile, combine the remaining ½ cup honey with the remaining 2 tablespoons butter in a small saucepan. Stir over low heat until blended. Transfer to a heatproof bowl.

6. Remove the muffins from the tins and dip the tops into the honey mixture. Place on a plate to cool, or serve while still warm. Serve remaining honey dip with the muffins.

Makes 12 muffins

MILLET

Keeps You Sound of Body and Clear of Mind

My millet memoir is about a remarkable woman named Lavinia Mumphard, who cleaned my apartment once a week back in the 1950s.

What made Mrs. Mumphard remarkable was not her ability to juggle a vacuum cleaner or bend a dust mop to her will—it was her all-pervasive candor.

"I hate cleaning so much, I do it *bad*," she told me once as we surveyed the streaks on a tile floor she'd been assiduously scrubbing. "I should be a cook. Cooking is what I really do good. But I am a *Geechee* in a town where nobody—uptown or down, black or white—got a taste for Geechee food!"

Facing that fact squarely, she cleaned houses badly instead. And traveled all over New York City and its environs to do it, for she had no husband (he was an unmentionable subject) and was the sole support of herself and two daughters.

Greatly admiring Mrs. Mumphard's strength of character, I persuaded many of my friends to hire her as well. And though it was almost immediately apparent that her talents as a "domestic" were marginal, she stayed in their employ for years. As one friend pointed out after her death, "Mrs. M. was a comfort to man and beast alike. Dogs, cats, even second husbands and stepchildren, loved her on sight!" Mrs. Mumphard was also an inspired and generous cook who taught me about the Gullah foods of her forebears.

She always arrived with a worn black oilcloth bag bulging with cleaning clothes, sneakers, rags, duster, and a small iron pot. In this pot there was usually a sack of what she called "millies," a grain she would boil or steam and combine with any leftovers found in my refrigerator, then season with a pinch of some herb or spice she carried in a twist of brown paper.

Mrs. Mumphard believed everyone should eat "millies" once a day. She cooked them wherever she went to clean, for her own lunch and the lucky householder's as well. Her greatest happiness was the times when I was feeling out of sorts and remained in bed, while she went into the kitchen to whip me up "a little curing mess"—which I must admit always had me on my feet the next day.

"This stuff keeps the doctor away from the front *and* the back door," she would state gravely as she spooned the fluffy cooked millet onto our plates.

"And y'know, doctors are like devils: always waiting for a weakness in the flesh. So eat up . . . fast!"

Gullah people, who come from the islands off the coast between Charleston and Savannah, retain many of the mystical notions of their African antecedents. Mrs. Mumphard relayed a healthy quota of these warnings and signs, one of which concerned the millet we ate together religiously: "Millies is good for the body, like fish is good for the brain. But they sure ain't good together. Never mix those two in a pot unless you're looking for big, bad troubles."

As I did not cook millet at all and hardly ever prepared fish at the time, I was not much affected by this injunction. But I remembered it.

Like all mothers, Mrs. Mumphard took great pride in her daughters' accomplishments. From time to time, she would bring pictures in the black bag of one or the other's confirmation or graduation exercise. So when her eldest daughter became engaged, it was really no surprise that she sent wedding invitations to all her clients.

The bride-to-be worked as a typist and had saved her money for years (as her mother was proud to point out). The groom's trade was cloudy. "He calls hisself an advance man, but far as I can see he don't advance much" was his future mother-in-law's evaluation. "But that's just between you and me."

Their wedding reception was held in a large room, ringed with card tables and spruced up with flowers and plants, the ceiling strung with elaborate white paper garlands. My friends and I were among a handful of guests who were seated on the bride's side of the room, where we could clearly observe the receiving line and Mrs. Mumphard, resplendent in icy green satin, regally greeting one and all.

We were the first to sample the buffet, an incredible array of Geechee-Gullah foods, all homemade and brought by friends. There were so many barbecued, fried, roasted, sautéed, and stewed offerings, it made the knees weak just contemplating which to choose first. Among the platters and casseroles, however, one dish caught my eye. It was made of the millet Mrs. Mumphard and I shared so often, but the grains were unmistakably laced with chunks of fish.

As I bid Mrs. Mumphard goodnight afterward, I could not resist mentioning that combination. Her eyes turned heavenward at the query. "Bad luck," she murmured. "We don't know who brang it, but it sure puts a sorry face on this day!"

No matter how I attempted to reassure her that signs and portents were not always followed by dire consequences, she simply would not be mollified. "Bad . . . bad . . . bad luck!"

When she came to clean my apartment a week later, Mrs. Mumphard's face still betrayed the jeremiad.

"What's wrong, Mrs. Mumphard?" I asked.

"Groom took off. Ran away with all the wedding money too. Daughter just cries and cries, night and day. And *you* know why it happened. Millies and fish in the same damn pot!"

The Grain's Genesis

More ancient than any other grain that grows, millet has been around the field and in and out of cook pots since the Neolithic age. Maybe longer. Some agro-scientists actually suggest that millet was one of the grasses that *brontosaurus* and friends chomped a million or so years ago, swishing their weighty tails and reseeding the soil with droppings as they traveled across half the surface of the earth.

Historians disagree on just where millet was first cultivated by man. Most evidence points to Africa or Asia, but a wild strain known as "Job's Tears"— which grows in the Philippines, where native lore insists it sprouted at the dawn of time—has turned the issue somewhat murky. We do know that millet's first official recognition was the *Fan Shen-Chiu Shu* (tables of agricultural dicta compiled in 2800 B.C.), which declared it to be one of China's five sacred crops.

We know millet was cultivated in India during the same era. Shards of temple urns—once filled nightly with food for the gods and recently unearthed by archeological digs at Pratapgarh— reveal infinitesimal seeds of millet glued by time to the pottery's surface.

How millet came to Africa is anyone's guess. The wind may have blown it in that southerly direction, or a stray caravan from China may have spilled some seed along its way to the Middle East. In any case, as it is a grain that flowers in poor sod and worse climate, millet took root in African soil like crabgrass (a weed to which it is faintly related) and grew virtually all over the continent.

Millet swayed from the top of the hanging gardens of Babylon (Herodotus wrote that the millet was so tall, he would not disclose its true height for fear of being disbelieved), and it sprouted between the legs of the Colossus of Rhodes, completely obscuring the base of the statue for some time until Rhodian gardeners were ordered to rip it out. However, do not get the wrong idea. Millet was no mere decorative greenery. The Old Testament in fact referred to it as "the gruel of endurance." And it was assiduously consumed (usually as some porridge or pottage) by the Etruscans, Greeks, Romans, Gauls, Persians, Assyrians, Tartars, and Visigoths too— because they all believed millet kept them sound of body and clear of mind in what was essentially "a naughty world."

The world's no less iniquitous today, but I would hazard a guess that less than 1 percent of health-concerned Americans, and far fewer Western Europeans, have ever considered a spoonful of millet as prandial therapy.

And that, my friends, is an omission to be repaired!

Some Plain Grain Talk

When I stated that few Americans or Europeans had ever tasted a spoonful of millet, I was guilty of an oversight: Birds and beasts on both continents eat it all the time.

As a matter of fact, in the U.S. millet is raised almost exclusively for hay, silage—and birdseed. That is no joke. I am told on the greatest authority that a formerly mum canary will sing its head off when millet is added to its daily diet. But that should come as no surprise when one considers the high vitamin and mineral content of this amazing grain. Rich in phosphorus, iron, calcium, riboflavin, and niacin, the nutritive value of a cup of cooked millet (90 calories) is only a step below wheat on the protein ladder. It is also higher in the amino acid lysine (one of the building blocks in the body's immune system) than rice, corn, or oats. When cooked in combination with any of the above, it will create a monster complex carbohydrate that will rival a sirloin steak! Millet is that good for the body's well-being.

Despite its unfamiliarity in the West, millet is a vital food for at least half a billion diners, including the Africans, Indians, and Chinese, and a serious hedge for survival for many of them. In Africa, according to the late Waverley Root, millet is usually the first crop to grow and the last to yield. In the absence of water, millet hibernates. When it rains, the plant awakens with a start and returns to its growing cycle.

How to Buy It

The bad news about millet, at this point in time, is that in the U.S. it is sold only in natural or health food stores, and by mail order.

The good news, on the other hand, is that millet is a remarkably inexpensive grain—at this writing much less than a dollar per pound. As there is no packaged, branded millet on the market, it is almost always sold in bulk, so a consumer may purchase as little or as much as a recipe requires.

Don't try buying millet at pet shops! The varieties sold as birdseed are often unhulled and are not particularly felicitous in a soup or stew. All millet for cooking purposes has been hulled, stripped of its outer bran layer, which is indigestible to all but our feathered friends.

When millet shopping, look for grains that are a bright gold color. Millet should have little or no aroma in its raw state and ideally will resemble sand. (Do not be dismayed: The tiny seed swells considerably as it cooks.)

How to Store It

Staying power is another of millet's myriad virtues. It is probably the hardiest grain around, neither susceptible to winter's sudden temperature changes nor subject to summer's mold or mildew. It is also highly inhospitable to any household creepies or crawlies.

I usually purchase several pounds of millet at a time and store it in a wide-mouth jar with a tight-fitting or anchor-type closure. (The mouth should be capacious enough to accommodate a small scoop. Millet is a very fine-textured grain and a nuisance to clean up if it spills.) A glass jar is best because it allows an instant survey of what's on hand.

Millet's shelf life is long. Count on six months, or longer if your container is truly secure. Stale millet can be detected at once, because it smells!

How to Cook It

My only offbeat canon for cooking millet comes from a good friend and uncommonly talented food writer, Elizabeth Schneider. She insists that millet is much more flavorsome if the grain is lightly toasted in a heavy skillet for about 5 minutes before it is added to the recipe at hand. And after tasting untoasted millet versus toasted, I think you will concur.

Millet may be pretoasted—but never more than a day in advance, please. And do not be tempted to add butter or oil to the pan; that's sautéing, not toasting!

Millet cooks quickly, about 20 minutes in a covered saucepan until all liquid is absorbed. My ratio of grain to liquid varies with the complexity of the dish being prepared, but a good rule of thumb is ½ cup millet to 1¼ cups liquid. It is also imperative to allow the cooked millet to stand, covered, off the heat for about 10 minutes for the flavors to meld properly.

Toasted cooked millet may be stored in the refrigerator for up to two days. But allow the mixture to fully come to room temperature before proceeding with the recipe.

BASIC COOKED MILLET

What I admire most about millet is its utterly adaptable flavor. Cooked unadorned, the grain has the delicate flavor of toasted cashew nuts. Prepared in conjunction with other stronger seasonings, however, it will take on myriad tinctures without losing that essential character—which is a neat trick, on the stove or off! Here is my basic recipe for preparing millet in all seasons.

½ cup hulled millet seeds
1¼ cups water, homemade chicken stock (see page 376) or canned broth, or vegetable stock (see page 378)
Salt and freshly ground black pepper to taste
Chopped fresh parsley, for garnish

1. Place the millet in a large heavy skillet and stir over medium-high heat until the seeds turn golden, about 5 minutes. The millet will pop slightly as it browns. Remove from the heat.

2. Combine the millet with the water or stock in a medium-size heavy saucepan, and heat to boiling. Reduce the heat, cover, and cook over medium-low heat until the millet is tender and all liquid has been absorbed, about 20 minutes. Remove the pan from the heat and let the millet stand, covered, 10 minutes.

3. Fluff the millet with a fork, and season with salt and pepper. Serve sprinkled with parsley.

Serves 4

SOUR GRASSES AND MILLET SOUP

Sauerkraut is an important ingredient in this hearty millet soup. I love it with sorrel, but it is excellent with any fresh, tender greens.

1 smoked porkette or smoked pork
    tenderloin (about 2 pounds)
7 cups water
1 clove garlic, peeled
½ cup hulled millet seeds
2 quarts homemade chicken stock (see page
    376) or canned broth
3 medium carrots, diced
2 large ribs celery, diced
2 cups canned tomatoes with juice,
    chopped
½ teaspoon caraway seeds, crushed
Pinch of sugar
1 pound sauerkraut, drained
2 large potatoes, peeled and cubed
½ cup coarsely chopped trimmed greens
    (arugula, dandelion, sorrel, or spinach)
½ teaspoon crushed dried hot red peppers
Salt and freshly ground black pepper to
    taste
2 tablespoons gin
Sour cream, for garnish

1. Place the porkette with 5 cups of the water and the garlic clove in a saucepan. Heat to boiling. Reduce the heat and simmer until the meat is tender, about 50 minutes. Remove the pork and allow it to cool slightly. Then remove the casing and set the meat aside to cool thoroughly.

2. Coarsely chop half the pork (or more if you want a richer soup), and reserve. Reserve the remaining pork for another use.

3. Place the millet in a large heavy skillet and stir over medium-high heat until the seeds are golden, about 5 minutes. The millet will pop slightly as it browns. Remove from the heat.

4. Combine the chopped porkette with the millet in a large heavy saucepan. Stir in 6 cups of the chicken stock, the remaining 2 cups water, the carrots, and the celery. Heat to boiling. Reduce the heat, cover, and simmer over medium-low heat 20 minutes.

5. Add the tomatoes to the soup mixture along with the caraway seeds, sugar, and sauerkraut. Cook, covered, 20 minutes longer.

6. Add the remaining 2 cups chicken stock, potatoes, greens, and dried red peppers to the soup and continue to cook, partially covered, 20 minutes. Season with salt and pepper. Stir in the gin and cook, uncovered, 2 minutes. Serve in soup bowls with a dab of sour cream in the center of each.

Serves 6 to 8

PAPA'S STEW-SOUP

I have never been to the Himalayas, so I cannot verify for certain that the long-lived Hunzan people who make their home in those mountains are really as strong and muscular as they are reputed to be. But I will tell you as gospel that their diet is based

on millet. According to mountain climbers of my acquaintance, Hunzan housewives cook the grain with a small amount of meat for flavoring one day, and add vegetables to the pot (along with more millet, of course) for the next six.

This millet prescription, a one-dish dinner, is a variation on that theme.

FOR THE SOUP

1 package (16 ounces) dried white pea
    beans
2 tablespoons olive oil
1 medium onion, chopped
1 shallot, chopped
4 leeks, white parts only, rinsed, dried,
    and chopped
1 clove garlic, minced
1 medium carrot, chopped
1 rib celery, chopped
1 ham bone, or ½ pound chunk ham
2½ quarts water
¼ teaspoon freshly ground black pepper
¼ teaspoon chopped fresh thyme, or a
    pinch of dried
2 tablespoons chopped fresh basil leaves, or
    1½ teaspoons dried
1 bay leaf

FOR THE MEATBALLS

1 pound ground veal
1 small onion, minced
¼ cup fresh bread crumbs
1 egg, lightly beaten
2 tablespoons water
½ teaspoon freshly grated nutmeg
2 tablespoons minced fresh parsley
1½ tablespoons unsalted butter
1½ teaspoons olive oil

¾ cup hulled millet seeds
1 cup chopped seeded tomatoes
½ cup chopped fresh parsley

1. Pick over the beans and remove any debris. Cook the beans in a large pot of boiling water 1 minute. Remove from the heat, cover, and let stand overnight.

2. The next day, heat the oil in a large soup pot over medium heat. Add the onion and shallot; cook 3 minutes. Add the leeks and garlic; cook 1 minute longer. Add the carrot and celery, and stir until coated with the onion mixture. Add the ham bone.

3. Drain the beans and add them to the pot along with the water, pepper, thyme, basil, and bay leaf. Heat to boiling. Reduce the heat, cover, and simmer, skimming the surface occasionally, until the beans are almost tender, about 2½ hours.

4. Meanwhile, make the meatballs: Combine the veal, onion, bread crumbs, egg, water, nutmeg, and parsley in a large bowl. Mix thoroughly and shape into small spheres about 1¼ inches in diameter.

5. Heat the butter with the oil in a heavy skillet over medium-high heat. Sauté the meatballs, a few at a time, until well browned on all sides, 4 to 5 minutes per batch. Remove with a slotted spoon and drain on paper towels. Set aside.

6. Place the millet in a large heavy skillet and stir over medium-high heat until the seeds turn golden, about 5 minutes. The millet will pop slightly as it browns. Remove from the heat, and set aside.

7. When the beans are almost tender, discard the bay leaf and remove the ham bone or chunk of ham. Allow the bone to cool slightly, then pick off any meat and shred it into strips. (Or shred the chunk of meat.) Return the meat to the soup, add the tomatoes, and heat to boiling. Reduce the heat, cover, and cook until the beans are tender, about 15 minutes. Stir in the millet and cook, covered, 20 minutes longer. Remove the pot from the heat, and add the meatballs to the soup. Let stand, covered, 10 minutes. Sprinkle with parsley.

Serves 6 to 8

GINGERED AND GARLICKED LAMB ROAST

Some of the best lamb I've eaten is raised by Jamison Farms in Latrobe, Pennsylvania. I always use ginger in my mustardy marinade. The ginger theme is carried over to a side dish of millet. Simply prepared green vegetables are all this combination needs to make the meal complete.

1 leg of lamb (5½ to 6 pounds)
1 large clove garlic, cut into ½-inch slivers
1-inch chunk fresh ginger root, peeled and
    cut into ½-inch slivers
2 tablespoons Dijon mustard
1 tablespoon soy sauce
¼ cup olive oil
Juice of ½ lemon
Gingered Millet (recipe follows)

1. With a small sharp knife or an ice pick, make a pattern of small deep incisions over the top and sides of the lamb. Place the lamb on a rack in a roasting pan, and fill half the incisions with slivers of garlic, and half with ginger.

2. Combine the mustard, soy sauce, and oil in a small bowl. Whisk until thick and smooth. Whisk in the lemon juice. Spread this dressing over the top and sides of the lamb, and let it stand 2 to 3 hours, uncovered and unrefrigerated, before roasting.

3. Preheat the oven to 450°F.

4. Roast the lamb 15 minutes. Then reduce the heat to 325°F, and continue to roast 1 hour longer for medium-rare. (A well-done roast will need an additional 30 minutes.) Let the lamb stand 15 minutes before carving. Serve with Gingered Millet.

Serves 8

Gingered Millet

1 cup hulled millet seeds
1 tablespoon olive oil
1 large shallot, minced
2½ cups homemade chicken stock (see page
    376) or canned broth
¼ teaspoon ground ginger
¼ teaspoon hot pepper sauce
Salt and freshly ground black pepper to
    taste
1 tablespoon unsalted butter
Chopped fresh parsley, for garnish

1. Place the millet in a large heavy skillet and stir over medium-high heat until the seeds turn golden, about 5 minutes. The millet will pop slightly as it browns. Remove from the heat.

2. Heat the oil in a large saucepan over medium-low heat. Add the shallot; cook until golden, about 4 minutes. Add the chicken stock and millet. Heat to boiling. Reduce the heat, cover, and cook over medium-low heat 20 minutes. Remove from the heat and let stand, covered, 10 minutes. Then fluff the millet with a fork. Add the ginger, hot pepper sauce, and salt and pepper. Dot with butter and sprinkle with parsley.

Serves 8

BRAISED PORK, MILLET, AND EGGPLANT, CAIRO STYLE

This dish, from Cairo, Illinois, makes a hearty winter feast. The millet should be slightly juicy in this case. Serve it with any root vegetables.

2 large cloves garlic
1 boned and rolled pork loin (2½ to 3 pounds)
2 teaspoons olive oil
Salt and freshly ground black pepper
1 tablespoon unsalted butter
2 tablespoons vegetable oil
1 large onion, chopped
1 cup red wine
2 cups canned tomatoes with juice, chopped
1 teaspoon chopped fresh basil, or ¼ teaspoon dried
1 small eggplant (about ¾ pound), cubed
1 cup hulled millet seeds
2½ cups water
1 cup homemade beef stock (see page 377) or canned broth (approximately)
¼ cup chopped fresh parsley

1. Cut 1 of the garlic cloves into slivers. Mince the remaining garlic clove.

2. Using a small sharp knife, poke holes into the pork at 1½-inch intervals on all sides. Insert the slivered garlic into each opening. Rub the pork with the olive oil, then rub it lightly with salt and pepper.

3. Heat the butter with the vegetable oil in a large Dutch oven over medium-high heat. Add the pork loin and brown on all sides, 8 minutes. Remove the pork and discard half the fat from the pan.

4. Add the onion to the pan; cook over medium heat 1 minute. Stir in the minced garlic; cook 1 minute longer. Add the wine and heat to boiling, scraping the bottom and sides of the pan. Stir in the tomatoes and basil. Return the

pork to the pan and cook, covered, over medium-low heat 45 minutes.

5. Meanwhile, place the eggplant in a colander and sprinkle it with salt. Let it stand 30 minutes. Then rinse under cold running water, drain, and set aside.

6. While the eggplant is draining; place the millet in a large heavy skillet and stir over medium-high heat until the seeds turn golden, about 5 minutes. The millet will pop slightly as it browns. Remove from the heat.

7. Combine the millet with the water and ½ teaspoon salt in a medium-size heavy saucepan. Heat to boiling. Reduce the heat, cover, and cook over medium-low heat until the millet is tender and all liquid has been absorbed, about 20 minutes. Fluff the millet with a fork and let it stand, uncovered, until ready to use.

8. When the pork has cooked for 45 minutes, stir in the eggplant and beef stock. Continue to cook, covered, until the pork is tender, about 45 minutes.

9. Transfer the pork to a carving platter and keep warm. Raise the heat under the pan juices and heat to boiling. Reduce the heat to low and stir in the reserved millet. Cook 3 minutes. (The mixture should be slightly wet. Add more stock if it is too dry.) Stir in 3 tablespoons of the parsley.

10. Thinly slice the pork. Spoon the millet and eggplant into a shallow serving dish and place the sliced pork decoratively over the top. Sprinkle with the remaining 1 tablespoon parsley.

Serves 6 to 8

MILANESE MILLET AND VEAL SHANKS

*T*his traditional Italian veal dish is enriched with a helping of millet—and is all the better for it. The meat adds a rich flavoring to the millet, and lightly sautéed summer squash works as a perfect match.

4 pieces veal shank, each about 2 inches thick (3½ to 4 pounds total)
2 tablespoons all-purpose flour
2 tablespoons unsalted butter
2 tablespoons olive oil
2 medium onions, finely chopped
2 cloves garlic, minced
1 rib celery, finely chopped
4 small anchovy filets, chopped
1½ cups homemade chicken stock (see page 376) or canned broth
⅓ cup white wine
¾ cup hulled millet seeds
Finely slivered zest of 1 lemon
½ cup chopped fresh parsley
Salt and freshly ground black pepper to taste

1. Pat the veal shanks dry, and dust them lightly with the flour. Heat the butter with 1 tablespoon of the oil in a large heavy pot over medium heat. Brown the shanks well on both sides, about 4 minutes, then remove them to a plate.

2. Add the remaining 1 tablespoon oil to the pot. Cook the onions over medium-low heat 1 minute. Add the garlic; cook 2 minutes longer. Stir in the celery, anchovies, chicken stock, and wine. Return the veal shanks to the pot and heat to boiling. Reduce the heat, cover, and simmer, turning the shanks once, until tender, about 1 hour and 25 minutes.

3. Meanwhile, place the millet in a large heavy skillet and stir over medium-high heat until the seeds turn golden, about 5 minutes. The millet will pop slightly as it browns. Remove from the heat, and set aside.

4. When the shanks are tender, remove them to a heatproof dish, cover, and keep warm in a 225°F oven.

5. Stir the millet into the cooking juices and heat to boiling. Reduce the heat, cover, and cook over medium-low heat until the millet is tender and all liquid has been absorbed, about 25 minutes.

6. Stir in the lemon zest and all but 1 tablespoon of the parsley. Add salt and pepper. Return the shanks to the mixture; sprinkle with the reserved parsley.
Serves 4

ROMANESQUE STUFFED RED PEPPERS

*B*y and large, Italians are not millet eaters. They prefer rice, which they claim is less trouble to chew.

Once, however, in the raffish Trastevere section of Rome—where the young artists and writers hang out—I saw a small crowd milling around a vendor who was shuffling blistery-hot stuffed peppers on the grill of a charcoal stove. The smell took one's breath away.

I can no longer remember the tariff for this street fare, but I well recall the number I ate: three, one after the other. How could I resist? These peppers were soft inside, filled with wondrous chunks of sausage and garlic, melting with cheese.

Business was brisk and when all the peppers were sold, the street merchant merely covered his grill and began stuffing more, right there on the Po embankment. That's how I discovered that cooked millet was one of the ingredients. My Italian was not good enough to ask for the recipe, but I did watch him carefully. What follows is my oven-baked version.

¼ cup hulled millet seeds
½ cup plus 2 tablespoons water
¾ teaspoon salt
6 medium red bell peppers
8 sweet Italian sausages (about 1¼ pounds total)
1 medium onion, finely chopped
1 clove garlic, minced
1 tablespoon curry powder
½ teaspoon freshly ground black pepper
1 egg, lightly beaten
¼ cup homemade chicken stock (see page 376) or canned broth
3 tablespoons fresh bread crumbs
2 tablespoons freshly grated Parmesan cheese
2 tablespoons olive oil
Chopped fresh parsley, for garnish

1. Place the millet in a large heavy skillet and stir over medium-high heat until the seeds turn golden, about 5 minutes. The millet will pop slightly as it browns. Remove from the heat.

2. Combine the millet with the water and ½ teaspoon of the salt in a medium-size saucepan. Heat to boiling. Reduce the heat, cover, and cook over medium-low heat until the millet is tender and all liquid has been absorbed, about 20 minutes. Remove from the heat and let stand, covered, 10 minutes. Then fluff the millet with a fork and set it aside.

3. Preheat the oven to 375°F.

4. Cut the tops off the peppers, and carefully remove the seeds and membranes. Cook the peppers in boiling salted water 1 minute. Set them aside upside down to drain.

5. Remove the sausage meat from the casings and sauté it in a large skillet over medium-high heat, stirring with a wooden spoon to break up lumps, 5 minutes. Add the onion, garlic, curry powder, the remaining ¼ teaspoon salt, and the pepper. Cook, stirring occasionally, 10 minutes. Drain the mixture in a sieve.

6. Transfer the sausage mixture to a large bowl and combine it with the egg, chicken stock, and millet. Mix well. Stuff the peppers with this mixture, and place them snugly in a shallow ovenproof baking dish. Sprinkle the peppers with the bread crumbs, cheese, and oil. Bake 50 minutes. Sprinkle with parsley before serving.

Serves 6

MILLET-STUFFED ROAST CHICKEN WITH PROSCIUTTO AND GARLIC

*F*ennel and prosciutto are two of my favorite ingredients to stuff in a chicken. Millet is a third. The sage in this stuffing must be fresh.

¼ cup hulled millet seeds
1½ cups plus 2 tablespoons homemade
   chicken stock (see page 376) or canned
   broth
1 large clove garlic, minced
4 fresh sage leaves, chopped, or ½ teaspoon
   dried
¼ pound sliced prosciutto, coarsely
   chopped
¼ teaspoon fennel seeds, crushed
1 whole chicken (about 3½ pounds), well
   rinsed and dried
1 small clove garlic, bruised
3 tablespoons unsalted butter, at room
   temperature
1 cup water
1 tablespoon all-purpose flour
Chopped fresh parsley, for garnish

1. Preheat the oven to 400°F.

2. Place the millet in a large heavy skillet and stir over medium-high heat until the seeds turn golden, about 5 minutes. The millet will pop slightly as it browns. Remove from the heat.

3. Combine the millet with ½ cup plus 2 tablespoons of the chicken stock in a medium-size saucepan. Heat to boiling. Reduce the heat, cover, and cook over medium-low heat until the millet is tender and all liquid has been absorbed, about 20 minutes. Remove from the heat, fluff with a fork, and allow to cool slightly.

4. Place the millet in a medium-size bowl and add the minced garlic, sage, prosciutto, and fennel seeds. Toss well. Stuff the chicken loosely with this mixture. Sew and truss. Place remaining stuffing in an ovenproof dish, cover tightly, and set aside.

5. Rub the chicken with the bruised garlic, then with 2 tablespoons of the butter. Place the chicken on a rack in a roasting pan, and add the water to the pan. Roast 30 minutes.

6. Pour the remaining 1 cup chicken stock over the chicken, reduce the oven heat to 350°F, and roast another 30 minutes, basting occasionally with the pan juices.

7. Place the dish of extra stuffing in the oven. Continue to roast the chicken, basting occasionally with pan juices, 30 minutes longer, or until the meat juices run yellow when pricked with a fork.

8. Remove the strings from the chicken and scoop out the stuffing with a large spoon. Combine the two stuffings and keep warm with the chicken in a 225°F oven.

9. Melt the remaining 1 tablespoon butter in a medium-size saucepan over medium heat. Stir in the flour and cook, stirring constantly, until lightly browned, about 3 minutes. Whisk in the pan juices and cook until slightly thickened, about 2 minutes. Serve the gravy on the side.

Serves 2 to 4

LOW-COUNTRY JAMBALAYA WITH MILLET AND RICE

*T*he Gullah people live on the small chain of barrier islands between Savannah, Georgia, and Charleston, South Carolina. They are a very insular group who speak a dialect not familiar to the ear, even to other black Southerners, for their English is marked with the risings and fallings of the Dahomey land of their African forebears.

As a matter of fact, they grow the same vegetables their ancestors did. They believe in the same superstitions, and they eat the same millet that grew in their homeland for centuries. Which makes them as unique as the Amish in their own way.

This recipe is a variation of Gullah cooking, highly amended by me. I beg purists to forgive the presence of chorizo and Italian sausage in place of Carolina spiced sausage, and Geechees will have to hide their eyes from the sight of shrimp and millet in the same dish!

½ cup hulled millet seeds
1½ pounds sweet Italian sausages
1 pound chorizos (Spanish sausages)
1 tablespoon vegetable oil
1 tablespoon unsalted butter
3 whole chicken breasts, skinned and
    boned, cut into 18 pieces
3 tablespoons all-purpose flour
    (approximately)
Salt and freshly ground black pepper to
    taste
1 large onion, chopped
2 cloves garlic, minced
½ medium red bell pepper, cored, seeded,
    and chopped
1 large poblano pepper, roasted (see page
    249), cored, seeded, and chopped
1 large tomato, peeled, seeded, and
    chopped
1 can (14 ounces) imported plum tomatoes,
    with juice, chopped
1 teaspoon sugar
1 tablespoon chopped fresh basil, or 1
    teaspoon dried
1 teaspoon chopped fresh thyme, or ¼
    teaspoon dried
1 quart homemade chicken stock (see page
    376) or canned broth, heated
½ cup long-grain rice

¾ pound shrimp, shelled and deveined
½ pound okra, sliced
Chopped fresh parsley, for garnish

1. Place the millet in a large heavy skillet and stir over medium-high heat until the seeds turn golden, about 5 minutes. The millet will pop slightly as it browns. Remove from the heat and set aside.

2. Sauté the Italian sausages in a large oil-rubbed heavy pot or Dutch oven over medium heat until well browned on all sides, about 4 minutes. Transfer the sausages to a plate.

3. Add the chorizos to the pot and sauté until well browned on all sides, about 6 minutes. Transfer to the plate with the Italian sausages; slice both and reserve.

4. Add the oil and the butter to the pot. Sprinkle the chicken pieces with the flour, and season with salt and pepper. Sauté the chicken in the same pot until golden on both sides, 4 to 6 minutes. Transfer to the plate with the sliced sausages.

5. Add the onion to the pot and cook until golden, scraping the bottom

and sides of the pot, about 4 minutes. Stir in the garlic and bell pepper. Cook over medium-low heat 5 minutes. Add the poblano pepper, both the fresh and canned tomatoes, the sugar, basil, thyme, and chicken stock. Heat to boiling, and return the sausage slices and sautéed chicken pieces along with any accumulated juices. Stir in the rice and millet. Reduce the heat, cover, and cook over medium-low heat until the rice and millet are tender, about 20 minutes. Remove the cover and cook, stirring occasionally, 10 minutes longer.

6. Stir in the shrimp and okra; cook, tossing gently, 5 minutes longer. Sprinkle with parsley before serving.

Serves 8 to 10

NORTH FORK SCALLOP AND MILLET SALAD

Millet can take the place of bulgur or rice in any summer salad. This one comes from the North Fork of Long Island's east end.

FOR THE SALAD
½ cup hulled millet seeds
1¼ cups water
½ lemon
½ cup white wine
1 clove garlic
1 pound bay scallops
2 medium cucumbers, peeled, seeded, and finely diced
2 shallots, minced
¼ cup chopped canned roasted sweet red peppers
⅛ teaspoon chopped fresh thyme, or a pinch of dried
1 teaspoon chopped fresh tarragon, or ¼ teaspoon dried

FOR THE DRESSING
1 clove garlic, minced
¼ teaspoon coarse (kosher) salt
1 teaspoon Dijon mustard
Juice of ½ lemon
⅓ cup olive oil
Pinch of curry powder

3 tablespoons reserved scallop broth

Salt and freshly ground black pepper to taste
Chopped fresh parsley, for garnish

1. Place the millet in a large heavy skillet and stir over medium-high heat until the seeds turn golden, about 5 minutes. The millet will pop slightly as it browns. Remove from the heat.

2. Combine the millet with the water in a medium-size saucepan. Remove the seeds from the lemon half and squeeze the juice into the liquid, then add the lemon half as well. Heat to boiling. Reduce the heat, cover, and cook over medium-low heat until the millet is tender and all liquid has been absorbed, about 20 minutes. Remove from the heat, and let stand, covered, 10 minutes. Discard the lemon half and fluff the millet with a fork. Set it aside to cool.

3. Meanwhile, place the wine and

the garlic clove in a large noncorrosive saucepan. Heat to boiling. Stir in the scallops and cook, stirring constantly, over high heat 3 minutes. Drain the scallops, reserving the liquid, and set both aside to cool. Discard the garlic clove.

4. Place the cooled millet in a salad bowl and toss in the cucumbers, shallots, red peppers, thyme, tarragon, and cooled scallops. Set aside.

5. Make the dressing: Mash the garlic with the salt in a small bowl until a paste is formed. Stir in the mustard and lemon juice. Slowly whisk in the oil, curry powder, and broth.

6. Pour the dressing over the scallop mixture, and toss well. Add salt and pepper to taste. Serve at room temperature or slightly chilled, sprinkled with parsley.

Serves 6

SOUTH FORK SWORDFISH AND MILLET SALAD

*F*rom Long Island's South Fork, where I spend my summers. I make this whenever the swordfish are running off Montauk.

FOR THE SALAD
¼ cup hulled millet seeds
½ cup plus 2 tablespoons water
½ teaspoon salt
½ cup minced celery
1 small shallot, minced
1½ cups cubed cooked swordfish (about ¾ pound)
3 tablespoons chopped fresh chives

FOR THE DRESSING
½ cup mayonnaise, preferably homemade (see page 379)
½ teaspoon anchovy paste
Juice of 1 lemon
1 teaspoon chopped fresh basil

Salt and freshly ground black pepper to taste

1. Place the millet in a large heavy skillet and stir over medium-high heat until the seeds turn golden, about 5 minutes. The millet will pop slightly as it browns. Remove from the heat.

2. Combine the millet with the water and salt in a medium-size saucepan. Heat to boiling. Reduce the heat, cover, and cook over medium-low heat until the millet is tender and all liquid has been absorbed, about 20 minutes. Remove from the heat and let stand, covered, 10 minutes. Then fluff the millet with a fork and allow it to cool.

3. Place the cooled millet in a salad bowl and toss in the celery, shallot, swordfish, and chives. Set aside.

4. Make the dressing: Beat the mayonnaise with the anchovy paste and lemon juice in a medium-size bowl until smooth. Stir in the basil.

5. Spoon the dressing over the swordfish mixture, and toss well. Season with salt and pepper. Serve at room temperature or slightly chilled.

Serves 4

RED-HOT TEN-SPEED MILLET

Some of my best millet inspirations have been found in cross-cultural kitchens. Red-Hot Ten-Speed Millet, for instance, may seem vaguely Oriental as to ingredients, but I must warn the unsuspecting chef that it is totally American "feisty" in character. Mark it as a dish for Fahrenheit-raising on the next cold night!

½ cup hulled millet seeds
3 tablespoons peanut oil
1 medium onion, minced
2 large cloves garlic, minced
1 small green bell pepper, cored, seeded,
    and minced
1 large red bell pepper, cored, seeded, and
    minced
½ teaspoon sugar
3 tablespoons chopped canned roasted
    sweet red peppers
1¼ cups homemade chicken stock (see page
    376) or canned broth
1 tablespoon hot chili oil
1 teaspoon red wine vinegar
1 teaspoon dark sesame oil
1 cup chopped cooked chicken (optional)
Salt to taste
Chopped fresh parsley, for garnish

1. Place the millet in a large heavy skillet and stir over medium-high heat until the seeds turn golden, about 5 minutes. The millet will pop slightly as it browns. Remove from the heat.

2. Heat the oil in a medium-size saucepan over medium heat. Add the onion; cook 1 minute. Add the garlic and both bell peppers; cook 2 minutes. Sprinkle with the sugar and stir in the millet, the sweet peppers, and the chicken stock. Heat to boiling. Reduce the heat, cover, and cook over medium-low heat until the millet is tender and all liquid has been absorbed, 20 minutes.

3. Stir in the chili oil, vinegar, and sesame oil. If you are serving the chopped chicken, spoon it over the millet. Remove the pan from the heat, and let it stand, covered, 10 minutes. Then fluff the millet with a fork, and season with salt. Serve sprinkled with parsley.

Serves 4

PARMESAN-FLECKED MILLET WITH PEPPERED TOMATO SAUCE

This dish often takes the place of polenta at my table. Parmesan cheese is tossed into the cooked millet, and the whole is topped with a peppery tomato sauce. This is wonderful with grilled sausages.

½ cup hulled millet seeds
1¼ cups water
3 tablespoons unsalted butter, at room
    temperature

½ cup freshly grated Parmesan cheese
Salt and freshly ground black pepper to
    taste
Peppered Tomato Sauce (recipe follows)

1. Place the millet in a large heavy skillet and stir over medium-high heat until the seeds turn golden, about 5 minutes. The millet will pop slightly as it browns. Remove from the heat.

2. Combine the millet with the water in a medium-size heavy saucepan and heat to boiling. Reduce the heat, cover, and cook over medium-low heat until the millet is tender and all liquid has been absorbed, about 20 minutes. Remove the pan from the heat and let it stand, covered, 10 minutes.

3. Add the butter and Parmesan cheese to the millet, gently tossing with two forks to mix, and season with salt and pepper. Transfer the millet to a serving platter, and spoon some of the Peppered Tomato Sauce over the middle. Pass the remaining sauce.

Serves 4

Peppered Tomato Sauce

3 tablespoons unsalted butter
2 teaspoons olive oil
1 leek, white part and 3 inches of green stem, rinsed, dried, and finely minced
2 large cloves garlic, minced
1 small rib celery, finely chopped
2 medium tomatoes, peeled, seeded, and chopped
2 cups canned tomatoes, with juice, chopped
½ teaspoon chopped fresh thyme, or a pinch of dried
1 tablespoon chopped fresh basil, or 1 teaspoon dried
1 teaspoon sugar
2½ teaspoons finely minced hot green peppers, or ½ teaspoon crushed dried hot red peppers
Salt and freshly ground black pepper to taste

1. Heat 2 tablespoons of the butter with the oil in a large heavy skillet over medium-low heat. Add the leek; cook 5 minutes. Add the garlic; cook 2 minutes longer. Stir in the celery and the fresh and canned tomatoes. Heat to boiling, then reduce the heat. Stir in the herbs, sugar, and peppers. Cook until fairly thick, about 30 minutes.

2. Stir in the remaining 1 tablespoon butter, and season with salt and pepper.

Makes about 2 cups

Millet is officially a member of the Gramineae (grass) family, a group that has lots of offshoots with curious names. *Panicum milliaceum*, the common variety one finds in the U.S., is also known as "Indian grass" or "hog grass," depending upon your geographic frame of reference. *Echinochloa*, consumed in Japan, East Africa, and the Middle East, is dubbed "broomcorn millet," some say because its ear resembles a primitive broom. But that does not explain why *E. frumentacea*, or "Japanese millet," is not to be found in Japan at all but West Africans literally live on the stuff! In northern Italy and southern Germany they eat *Setaria italica*, which is known as "foxtail millet" or "Turkish weed"—take your pick. *Pennisetum spicatum*, known in the parts of Great Britain where it is grown as "bullrush millet," is tagged "candle millet" by the French. The French also call it *P. americanum* when they're being formal—but only they could tell you why, since it never grew over here. In India there are tropical millets and mountain millets. The best known are *Eleusine coracana* and *Pennisetum glaucum*, nicknamed "finger millet" and "cattail millet" respectively.

LOUISIANA MILLET CROQUETTELETTES

In New Orleans, *lagniappe* means a little something extra or an unexpected bequest. So, have a little millet *lagniappe* on me: Besides its other plus factors for the body, this grain has recently been recognized as a remarkable antacid—one that doctors can prescribe as a dietary supplement for colitis and ulcer patients with utter impunity, for it has no side effects whatsoever.

How far can a little seed go, you ask? Lots! As evidence, a Louisiana-style *croquettelette* that will embellish any breakfast, lunch, or dinner menu with amazing grace.

½ cup hulled millet seeds
2 cups water
½ teaspoon salt
1 fresh jalapeño pepper, seeded and minced
1 shallot, minced
1 teaspoon soy sauce
1 egg, lightly beaten
3 strips thick bacon, crisp-fried and
　　crumbled
½ teaspoon baking powder
¼ cup all-purpose flour
3 tablespoons unsalted butter
　　(approximately)
2 teaspoons vegetable oil (approximately)

1. Place the millet in a large heavy skillet and stir over medium-high heat until the seeds turn golden, about 5 minutes. The millet will pop slightly as it browns. Remove from the heat.

2. Combine the millet with the water and salt in a medium-size saucepan. Heat to boiling. Reduce the heat, cover, and cook over medium-low heat until the millet is very tender and all liquid has been absorbed and the millet is mushy, 30 to 35 minutes. Remove from the heat and let stand, covered, 10 minutes. Then fluff the millet with a fork.

3. Preheat the oven to 375°F.

4. Transfer the millet to a bowl and add the pepper, shallot, soy sauce, egg, bacon, baking powder, and flour. Mix thoroughly with a wooden spoon. Using wet hands, form into small meatball shapes and place on a plate. Flatten the balls slightly with a spatula.

5. Heat half the butter with half the oil in a heavy skillet, and sauté the patties over medium heat until golden brown, about 2 minutes per side. Transfer to an ovenproof serving platter. Continue sautéing the patties, adding butter and oil as needed. Bake the patties for 10 minutes before serving.

Serves 4

Note: The patties can be prepared and sautéed ahead of time. Cover and refrigerate; then bake in a preheated 375°F oven before serving.

MILLETY GREENS

Still another pot of Gullah goodness. This is my favorite fall/winter/wet spring dish—long-cooked pork and greens spangled with lots and lots of golden millet. Every forkful seems to put the diner in the pink too.

2 tablespoons vegetable oil
1 large onion, chopped
1 large clove garlic, minced
Pinch of ground cloves
2 pounds smoked pork neck bones or ham hocks
6 cups homemade chicken stock (see page 376) or canned broth
2 pounds greens (such as mustard or collard), trimmed, rinsed, and coarsely chopped
1½ cups hulled millet seeds
Chopped fresh parsley, for garnish

1. Heat the oil in a large pot over medium heat. Add the onion; cook 1 minute. Add the garlic and cloves; cook until lightly browned, about 4 minutes.

2. Add the pork pieces to the onion mixture. Toss to coat, and stir in the chicken stock. Heat to boiling. Reduce the heat, cover, and simmer 1 hour.

3. Add the greens to the pork mixture; cook, covered, 5 minutes. Stir well, re-cover, and continue to cook 25 minutes.

4. Meanwhile, place the millet in a large heavy skillet and stir over medium-high heat until the seeds turn golden, about 5 minutes. The millet will pop slightly as it browns. Remove from the heat.

5. Stir the millet into the greens mixture. Continue to cook, covered, over medium-low heat until the millet is very tender and most liquid has been absorbed, about 30 minutes. Remove the pork bones, and slice the meat from the bones. Return the meat to the pot and cook, uncovered, until all liquid has been absorbed, about 5 minutes longer. Serve sprinkled with parsley.

Serves 6

GOLDEN SMASH

This creamy carrot and millet dish is enriched with a tablespoon of cream cheese just before serving. It goes well with simple broiled meats.

½ cup hulled millet seeds
2 tablespoons unsalted butter
1 medium shallot or small onion, minced
1 clove garlic, minced
4 medium carrots, finely grated (about 2 cups)
¾ cup homemade chicken stock (see page 376) or canned broth

½ cup heavy or whipping cream
1 teaspoon freshly ground nutmeg
Pinch of ground cinnamon
1 tablespoon diced cream cheese
Salt and freshly ground black pepper to taste
Chopped fresh parsley, for garnish

1. Place the millet in a large heavy skillet and stir over medium-high heat until the seeds turn golden, about 5 minutes. The millet will pop slightly as it browns. Remove from the heat.

2. Melt the butter in a medium-size saucepan over medium-low heat. Add the shallot; cook 3 minutes. Add the garlic; cook 2 minutes longer. Stir in the millet, tossing to coat the seeds with the shallot mixture. Add the carrots, chicken stock, cream, nutmeg, and cinnamon. Heat to boiling. Reduce the heat, cover, and cook over medium-low heat until the millet is tender and all liquid has been absorbed, about 20 minutes. Remove from the heat and let stand, covered, 5 minutes. Stir in the cream cheese; let stand covered, 5 minutes longer.

3. Fluff the millet with a fork, and season with salt and pepper. Serve sprinkled with parsley.

Serves 4

MONDAY MEAL TICKET

Monday Meal Ticket is a version of what was reputed to be the best hangover cure in Vercelli, in northern Italy. It is equally salubrious without the headache.

½ cup hulled millet seeds
3 tablespoons unsalted butter
1 tablespoon olive oil
1¼ cups homemade chicken stock (see page 376) or canned broth
1 large onion, chopped
1 clove garlic, minced
Pinch of ground cloves
1½ cups cubed boiled potatoes
1 teaspoon chopped fresh sage, or ¼ teaspoon dried
1 teaspoon hot pepper sauce
Salt and freshly ground black pepper to taste
Chopped fresh parsley, for garnish

1. Place the millet in a large heavy skillet and stir over medium-high heat until the seeds turn golden, about 5 minutes. The millet will pop slightly as it browns. Remove from the heat.

2. Heat 1 teaspoon of the butter with 1 teaspoon of the oil in a medium-size saucepan. Stir in the millet and chicken stock, and heat to boiling. Reduce the heat, cover, and cook over medium-low heat until the millet is tender and all liquid has been absorbed, about 20 minutes. Remove from the heat and let stand, covered, 10 minutes.

3. Meanwhile, melt 2 tablespoons of the butter in a large heavy skillet over medium-low heat. Add the onion; cook 2 minutes. Add the garlic and sprinkle with the cloves; cook 3 minutes longer. Add the remaining 2 teaspoons butter and 2 teaspoons oil, and raise the heat to medium. Stir in the potatoes, sprinkle with the sage, and cook, tossing gently, until the potatoes are slightly golden, about 4 minutes.

4. Fluff the millet with a fork. Reduce the heat under the skillet and add the millet, tossing gently to mix. Add the hot pepper sauce, and season with salt and pepper. Serve sprinkled with parsley.

Serves 4 to 6

H. JOHN MILLET

H. John Millet is a dish that springs from the Gullah country of the Carolinas. Good Southerners will note a resemblance to Hoppin' John, a dish eaten for good luck on New Year's Eve—hence the name. But *you* eat it more than once a year!

1 cup hulled millet seeds
4 strips bacon
1 medium onion, chopped
1 clove garlic, minced
1 package (10 ounces) frozen black-eyed
    peas
2 cups homemade chicken stock (see page
    376) or canned broth
3 tablespoons red wine vinegar
¼ cup chopped fresh chives
2 tablespoons chopped fresh parsley
1 teaspoon unsalted butter (optional)
Salt and freshly ground black pepper to
    taste

1. Place the millet in a large heavy skillet and stir over medium-high heat until the seeds turn golden, about 5 minutes. The millet will pop slightly as it browns. Remove from the heat.

2. Sauté the bacon in a medium-size saucepan until crisp. Drain on paper towels, crumble, and reserve.

3. Add the onion to the bacon drippings. Cook over medium-low heat 1 minute. Add the garlic; cook 2 minutes. Stir in the black-eyed peas, tossing with a wooden spoon until thawed. Add the chicken stock, and heat to boiling. Reduce the heat, cover, and cook over medium heat 10 minutes.

4. Stir in the millet and return to boiling. Reduce the heat, cover, and cook over medium-low heat until the millet is tender and all liquid has been absorbed, about 20 minutes. Remove from the heat and let stand, covered, 10 minutes.

5. Fluff the millet with a fork, then toss in the reserved bacon, the vinegar, chives, parsley, and butter, if desired. Season with salt and pepper to taste.

Serves 6

MILLET BREAD

A whole-wheat and millet bread of such exuberant crunch, you'll be tempted to eat it *sans* butter—the way I do—with a plate of sliced tomatoes and some cheese.

1 cup hulled millet seeds
¾ cup boiling water
1 cup lukewarm water
1 package dry yeast
1 tablespoon honey
3½ cups whole-wheat flour (approximately)
½ cup bread flour
2 tablespoons unsalted butter

1 tablespoon vegetable oil
1 large bunch leeks, white parts only,
    rinsed, dried, and chopped (about
    2 cups)
Pinch of ground cloves
1 teaspoon salt
1 tablespoon unsalted butter, melted

1. Place the millet in a large heavy skillet and stir over medium-high heat until the seeds turn golden, about 5 minutes. The millet will pop slightly as it browns. Remove from the heat and transfer to a medium-size heatproof bowl. Pour the boiling water over the millet. Let stand 15 minutes, stirring often to cool.

2. Pour the lukewarm water into a large bowl. Sprinkle it with the yeast, stir in the honey, and let it stand 5 minutes.

3. Stir 1 cup of the whole-wheat flour and the bread flour into the yeast mixture. Beat until smooth. Stir in the millet mixture. Let stand, covered, in a warm place 45 minutes.

4. Meanwhile, heat the 2 tablespoons butter with the oil in a large skillet over medium-high heat. Add the leeks, and sprinkle them with the cloves. Cook, stirring frequently, until golden, about 10 minutes. Allow to cool slightly.

5. Stir the leek mixture into the flour mixture. Stir in the salt and enough whole-wheat flour (1½ to 2 cups) to form a stiff dough. Scrape the dough out onto a floured board. Knead 10 minutes, adding more whole-wheat flour as needed to form a smooth, elastic dough. Place the dough in a greased bowl, cover with plastic wrap, and let stand in a warm place until doubled in volume, about 1 hour.

6. Punch the dough down and knead it briefly on a floured board. Let it stand 2 minutes. Grease a loaf pan and place the dough in it. Cover the pan loosely with a flour-rubbed tea towel, and let it stand until the dough has risen over the top of the pan, about 1 hour.

7. Preheat the oven to 375°F.

8. Slash the top of the bread down the middle and brush it with the melted butter. Bake until the loaf is well browned and sounds hollow when tapped with your finger, about 45 minutes. Cool on a rack for 5 minutes before removing it from the pan.

Makes 1 loaf

RAJ HALWAH
(Prune, Millet, and Almond Tart)

This recipe hails from Jaipur (the capital of Rajasthan), where the denizens celebrate the arrival of spring by squirting pink water on one another and by throwing clouds of multicolored powders into the air, dyeing the streets mauve and green and saffron.

One of the traditions of the holiday is a dense sweet candy that vendors sell in pie-like wedges. This confection contains fruits and millet, sugar and nuts, and Lord knows what else. I have never found a true recipe for it, so a highly inauthentic version follows. I suggest you serve it on special occasions (minus the waterworks and powder), in tiny slices with lots of whipped cream and black coffee on the side.

½ cup pitted dried prunes
1 small cinnamon stick
1¼ cups water
1 teaspoon vanilla extract
½ cup hulled millet seeds

2 tablespoons unsalted butter
¾ cup firmly packed dark brown sugar
½ cup coarsely chopped almonds
2 tablespoons dark rum

A JAIPUR LEGEND

Millet legends abound in many Eastern cultures, but one from India I cannot resist passing on.

As it is told in Jaipur, once there was no moon. There was only a sulky moon child, married at birth to the sun, who lived in the sky. A mere girl, the moon child's function was to toss a ball of pure cold mountain snow into the heavens nightly, then find it again the next day— a task that made her hands cold and her temper short, particularly with her husband, the sun, who had yet to physically make her his wife, much as he tried. All her waking hours were spent searching the earth until she found the snowball, which only made her husband angrier.

Sometimes he would turn his rays so bright that the ball of snow would start to melt and the poor girl would have to press it together again, shaving a bit here and rounding an edge there before it could be tossed into the night sky once more. By month's end, the ball would have gotten slimmer and slimmer as the moon child grew sulkier and sulkier and her bridegroom more and more impatient.

One day an extraordinary event took place. The sun left the sky at noon to look for his wife. Darkness covered the earth, but eventually he found her, lying utterly exhausted on a bed of plants and covered with bits of melting snow. She looked so beautiful that he made love to her then and there. And she was not sulky anymore.

The snow, melted by their love, fell on a millet plant, which promptly bloomed, bringing grain to Jaipur for the very first time.

It blooms there still, but heck, you know that already. What you really want to know is what happened to the young bride. Well, the sun put her where he'd always wanted her in the first place— behind him in the sky. But now she is called Lady Moon!

1. Combine the prunes, cinnamon stick, water, and vanilla in a medium-size saucepan. Heat to boiling, and boil 5 minutes. Then remove the prunes with a slotted spoon and allow them to cool slightly. Reserve the pan of cooking liquid, adding enough water to make 1¼ cups liquid.

2. While the prunes are cooling, place the millet in a large heavy skillet and stir over medium-high heat until the seeds turn golden, about 5 minutes. The millet will pop slightly as it browns. Remove from the heat.

3. Heat the prune cooking liquid to boiling, stir in the millet, and reduce the heat. Cook, covered, over medium-low heat 20 minutes. Remove from the heat and let stand, covered, 10 minutes longer. Then fluff the millet with a fork, and discard the cinnamon stick.

4. Preheat the oven to 350°F. Butter a 9-inch quiche pan with removable sides.

5. Coarsely chop the cooled prunes. Melt the butter in a medium-size saucepan over medium-low heat. Add the brown sugar, and cook, stirring constantly, until it dissolves. Then stir in the millet, prunes, almonds, and rum. Mix thoroughly, and transfer to the prepared quiche pan. Bake 30 minutes. Cool on a rack before removing the sides.

Serves 8 to 10

APRICOT MILLET SOUFFLE

*T*his warm and creamy apricot and millet soufflé is from Vienna. Runny on the spoon, it is not as rich as it sounds. It is a loving bequest from the doyenne of healthy cooking, Marina Polvay, who used to live on the blue Danube. Now she makes her home on a bluer body of water, the Atlantic Ocean, in Miami Beach.

I serve this soufflé with Mock Crème Fraîche, but purists may opt for a cold custard sauce or sweetened whipped cream. Let your conscience and your waistline be your guide!

¼ cup hulled millet seeds
¾ cup water
1 cup light cream or half-and-half
2 tablespoons unsalted butter
2 tablespoons all-purpose flour
¼ teaspoon salt
⅛ teaspoon freshly grated nutmeg
⅛ teaspoon ground cinnamon
⅔ cup apricot preserves
2 tablespoons sugar
4 egg yolks
3 tablespoons apricot brandy
6 egg whites
Mock Crème Fraiche (recipe follows)

1. Combine the millet with the water in a medium-size saucepan, and heat to boiling. Reduce the heat, cover, and cook over medium-low heat until the millet is very tender and all liquid has been absorbed, about 25 minutes. Remove from the heat and let stand, covered, 10 minutes.

2. Transfer the millet to the container of a food processor. With the motor running, pour the light cream through the feed tube. Process until smooth.

3. Melt the butter in a medium-size saucepan over medium-low heat. Add the flour. Cook, stirring constantly, 2 minutes. Stir in the millet mixture, salt, nutmeg, cinnamon, apricot preserves, and sugar. Cook until thick, about 4 minutes. Remove the pan from the heat and beat in the egg yolks, one at a time, beating thoroughly after each addition. Stir in the apricot brandy.

4. Beat the egg whites until stiff but not dry. Fold them into the apricot mixture.

5. Pour the mixture into a buttered and sugared 2-quart soufflé dish. Bake until golden and firm, 30 to 35 minutes. Serve immediately with Mock Crème Fraîche.

Serves 6 to 8

Mock Crème Fraîche

1 cup heavy or whipping cream
1 tablespoon confectioners' sugar
3 tablespoons sour cream

Beat the cream with the sugar until quite thick. Then beat in the sour cream. Refrigerate, covered, until ready to serve.

Makes about 1¼ cups

MILLET CRUNCH

This confection hails from Edinburgh, Scotland. I tasted a slice in a tea shop, asked for the recipe, and was rewarded before the check arrived. Called Millet Crunch, it is no candy bar but a solid chewy butterscotch brownie, filled with bits of almond and, yes, millet too. Millet in fact gives it the essential crunch! Kids love this cookie. So will you, because it freezes like a charm.

2 tablespoons hulled millet seeds
⅓ cup water
1 cup all-purpose flour
2 tablespoons confectioners' sugar
8 tablespoons (1 stick) unsalted butter, cut into pieces
1 cup firmly packed light brown sugar
½ cup firmly packed dark brown sugar
2 eggs, lightly beaten
1 teaspoon vanilla extract
¾ cup slivered almonds, chopped
Confectioners' sugar

1. Place the millet in a heavy skillet and stir over medium-high heat until the seeds turn golden, about 5 minutes. The millet will pop slightly as it browns. Remove from the heat.

2. Combine the millet with the water in a small saucepan. Heat to boiling. Reduce the heat, cover, and cook over low heat 15 minutes. Remove the cover and continue to cook, stirring fre-quently, 10 minutes longer. Remove from the heat and set aside to cool.

3. Preheat the oven to 400°F.

4. Combine the flour, the confectioners' sugar, and the butter in a large bowl. Blend with a pastry blender until the mixture has the texture of coarse crumbs. Butter a rimmed baking sheet (no larger than 14 by 9 inches), and press the mixture evenly over the bottom. Bake 10 minutes. Set the baking sheet aside to cool. Leave the oven on.

5. Combine the brown sugars with the eggs, vanilla, millet, and almonds in a large bowl. Beat with a wooden spoon until well mixed, and pour over the cooled crust. Bake until a toothpick inserted in the center comes out clean, about 15 minutes. Dust the top with confectioners' sugar. Cool, and cut into squares. Store in an airtight container.

Makes about thirty-six 1-inch squares

FONDENTINA

This final contribution is a Caribbean export, from the small island of St. Lucia, where it is sold in the open market at Castries (the capital) and everywhere else that tourists wander. It is usually offered from open baskets filled with other exotica like dried tree frog, mace eggs, and cinnamon bark 2 feet long. (I long ago rejected admonitions against eating street foods, for how else would one come up with a new recipe?)

In Castries they call this sweetmeat *fondentina*, which means "little fondant" or "broken tooth." Back home when I was trying to reconstruct the recipe, I dubbed them "joyous jawbreakers." They are like dense meringues that melt on the tongue—usually under the influence of coffee.

I serve fondentinas with fresh fruit or on a cookie tray when there's no dessert. But they're very addictive for afternoon nibbling too!

½ cup hulled millet seeds
1 cup cream of coconut (I use Coco Lopez)
¼ cup water
⅛ teaspoon ground ginger
1 cup lightly crushed whole roasted
   almonds (with skins)

1. Place the millet in a large heavy skillet and stir over medium-high heat until the seeds turn golden, about 5 minutes. The millet will pop slightly as it browns. Remove from the heat.

2. Combine the millet with the cream of coconut and water in a medium-size saucepan. Heat to boiling. Boil, stirring vigorously, until the liquid has reduced by a third, 7 or 8 minutes. Reduce the heat, cover, and cook over medium-low heat 15 minutes. (The millet will still be slightly crunchy.) Stir in the ginger, remove from the heat, and let stand, covered, 10 minutes.

3. Transfer the mixture to the container of a food processor or blender. Process on high speed until the mixture is very thick, about 30 seconds. Quickly pour it back into the saucepan (off the heat) and stir in the almonds. With buttered fingers and a tablespoon, form the mixture into small balls and place them on a buttered dish. Allow them to cool, then store in an airtight container.

Makes about 20 pieces

OATS

For a Lower Blood Cholesterol Level

If I wore a hat I would tip it to oats, with a deep bow to oatmeal as well. For it is a cereal that probably saved my life—and certainly salvaged my pride—when I was a kid.

Though it may be hard to believe, I was once a frail child, susceptible to lingering winter colds that almost always settled in the passages of my middle ear, causing great pain and keeping me out of school for weeks at a time.

My parents' room was the largest and warmest in the house, so it was designated as "sick bay." (Where my father and mother slept during my bouts with earache, I never knew.) What I recall most vividly of those throbbing earache days is not the physical torment but the fact that I rode out the storms on their mahogany bed, under a large and comforting eiderdown that became my refuge the instant infection struck.

The pain I endured as a child was usually caused by an abscess. When an earache grew particularly intense or my temperature rose, our family doctor was summoned. And always came, for the danger of septicemia affecting the brain was a constant worry in that long-ago time before antibiotics.

On one occasion, when the infection subsided, a new indignity lay in store. The doctor insisted that when I went back to school I must wear a hat, to cover my ears and protect me from germs. My mother chose a *beret* for this function.

It was made of navy blue felt and had a little corkscrew nib in the dead center, like the handle of a saucepan lid. My mother used it to make sure the beret was pulled down evenly over my ears before I left for school in the morning.

I hated that beret with more passion than I'd ever expended on anything— even abscesses of the middle ear. I would stuff it into my schoolbag the moment I was out of her field of vision, but never in time to escape the taunts of my schoolmates. They found my beret plainly bizarre and an endless source of ribald remarks. The older boys would snatch the hat from my head and swat it high into the air like a shuttlecock, knowing I was too timid to defend my property. The younger ones merely called names: "Here comes Bert the beret," they squealed.

My grandmother, the official and blunt opinion-giver of the family, hated that beret as much as I did. "What a crazy thing to make him wear," she up-braided my mother. "It makes him look like a French waiter, Pauline! No wonder they make fun...those *gonifs!*"

"The doctor said..." my mother be-gan lamely. But my grandmother cut her off.

"If he would eat a hot breakfast in-stead of all that *hozzarei* (meaning the Sugar Pops, Post Toasties, and Rice Kris-pies I doted on), he wouldn't need to wear it!"

"What's a hot breakfast got to do

with my ears?" I asked.

My grandmother gave her daughter a wry look. "Exactly the same thing," she said, "as a funny hat has to do with self-respect! Listen to me. Take this box of oatmeal. Try it on him for a week. Lots of butter, a little sugar and milk in the bowl, and before you know it he'll be as healthy as what's-his-name from the phone booth—"

"Superman!" I piped up.

"*Supermensch!*" my grandmother amended. "You better believe he eats oatmeal too!"

Who could resist the logic? The very next day I ate my first bowl of oatmeal for breakfast, changing the formula slightly to a *lot* of sugar, and cream instead of milk.

Can you doubt that it changed my life? I never had another earache again nor wore the dreaded beret one more time. Oats were clearly the reason for that happy ending.

There is, however, a semi-sweet resid-ual to this tale, one I had not been warned about. Thanks to my sagacious grandmother's change of breakfast, I also got *fat!*

The Grain's Genesis

*T*he oat is one grain that, historically speaking, has never won any popularity contests. Too abrasive a cereal to be chomped for one thing, it had a bad reputation for another, having been used exclusively as horse fodder and cattle silage since the dawn of agriculture. Early Bronze Age farmers are credited with the discovery of oats as animal feed when their oxen formed paths quite on their own, selectively chewing their way through fields of wild grasses and con-suming only the oats, leaving the other stalks unsampled.

Alexander the Great fed his fabled horse Esepheus only oats because, he claimed, that grain, which flourished best in a south wind, passed on the velocity of the sirocco and mistral to his beast's fleet hooves. However, when offered a quaff of oat-and-honey *kykeōn*, which initiates to the Eleusinian mysteries were expected to drink, Alexander resolutely refused to taste a single drop: "I prefer neither to outrun nor to outcopulate my horse," he stated!

When man first added oats to his diet is unknown. In the fifth century A.D., Roman intelligence reported that Attila the Hun fed his barbarian troops only soups of oats, which reputedly turned them fierce as tigers. However, the sybaritic Roman army disdained to even contemplate such a "mean diet" for their foot soldiers—which may have something to do with the fall of Rome, who knows?

What kept oats from catching on as a popular food for centuries was clearly a matter of class distinction at the table. A basic food of the poor—because it flourished in lackluster soil where wheat withered and barley blackened—oats came to be synonymous with the stuff of beggar's bowls. And consequently it was shunned in all forms by the medieval middle class, lest its stamp of poverty be contagious as the plague.

It took the Crusades to first give oats a measure of respectability. A grain that was easy to carry in a saddlebag, could be cooked with minimal fuss over an open fire, and provided a soldier with the muscle to shoot a crossbow a hundred times a day had to be a serious source of energy, it was reasoned. The returning Crusaders planted fields of this grain in all their native lands: Scotland, Ireland, Wales, England, Denmark, Germany, and France—where, I am happy to report, it continues to proliferate with unerring regularity. And as for oats, over the years, it has become as respectable as meat and potatoes.

Some Plain Grain Talk

Perhaps because the oat was tradition-ally a low man on the grain totem pole, it has taken almost twenty centuries for this cereal to be recognized as a lifesaver, nutritionally speaking.

Whole-grain oats, for the record, are crammed with seven B vitamins, vitamin E, and nine minerals including calcium and iron. Oats are also easily digested and reasonably high in protein. Moreover, the quality of that protein is actually head and shoulders above most of the other grains we routinely consume for their value, such as whole wheat!

What gives the oat the horse laugh (if one may bring up its earliest employment) is the degree of soluble fiber in its compound, which helps to substantially lower cholesterol levels in the blood. The American Cancer Institute recommends 20 to 35 grams of fiber in the daily diet. One serving of cooked oats is almost 8 for starters, and a half dozen oatmeal cookies puts you over the top! Oat bran (examined substantially in the chapter on bran) has even been proven to reduce the level of artery-impairing LDL cholesterol after extended periods of daily consumption.

The depressing news about oats' healthful properties is that 85 percent of the crop grown in the U.S. is still used as livestock feed rather than as a cooking ingredient and enters our diet only subliminally in the meat, milk, and eggs we consume.

A fast glance at the oat-inspired recipes that follow will, I hope, serve to change that ratio!

How to Buy Them

Without a doubt, oats are the easiest grain for American cooks to find. The highly visible round red, white, blue and yellow Quaker carton on supermarket shelves is relatively little changed from the time my grandmother stirred up a bowl of cereal and altered my breakfast patterns forever.

Unlike most grains, when oats are

milled, nothing but the inedible hull is removed. The bran and germ are retained *in toto* in the edible kernel, which is known as a "groat," though it has nothing in common with buckwheat groats. A groat is not always a groat, it seems. But an oat groat *is* the basis for all the cereal variations on the market. To wit:

Steel-Cut Oats (sometimes known as "Scotch" or "Irish" oats): These are organic, unrefined oats that are merely dried and rough-sliced. Since they are processed with virtually no heat, steel-cut oats retain most of their original B vitamins, which is a plus. However, they are decidedly on the chewy side and require longer cooking times than any other conventional oat cereal—which could be a minus to the harried homemaker. Irish and Scotch oatmeal do stir up into extremely felicitous (that is to say super-creamy) amalgams, but they are both rather expensive and hard to find except at food specialty shops or from mail-order sources.

All of the oat recipes in this book call for rolled or quick oats, which are more readily available to consumers.

Rolled Oats (sometimes dubbed "old-fashioned oats"): the cereal of my childhood, made by slicing raw oats into a confetti-like mixture which is steamed and then rolled into flakes and dried. Oats sold in natural foods stores are rolled as well, but sometimes known as "table-cut" oats. Not unlike the Quaker packaged variety in flavor, "table-cut" oats are a bit thicker, which makes them chewier in a bowl of oatmeal and crunchier in an "outrageous" Chocolate-Oatmeal Chipper. Cooking time for "table-cut" rolled oats: 8 minutes from stove to bowl. Cooking time for Old Fashioned Quaker Oats: 5 minutes on the nose.

Quick Oats: Not appreciably different from commercial rolled oats in the way they are processed, these oats are sliced finer and rolled into very thin flakes over a heat source, which precooks them marginally. The object is to save kitchen time, but quick-cooking oats lose some nutritive clout and save only 2 minutes. Cooking time: 3 minutes.

Instant Oats: a faster, express variation on the preprocessed theme. Only boiling water is needed to reconstitute these mini-cuts, but they are invariably sugared or artificially flavored and leave a heck of a lot to be desired in a "natural" food. Pass them by, I say.

How to Store Them

Oats are high in unsaturated fats, yet curiously enough have little or no storage requirements because the grain has a rare natural characteristic: an antioxidant that actually delays rancidity. As a matter of fact, before the discovery of chemical preservatives, commercial bakers often added a pinch of ground oats to breads and cakes to stave off early staleness. So it is not surprising that a package of oats should have a life expectancy of up to a year on a pantry shelf, longer still if the temperature is moderately cool.

I always store rolled and quick oats in the cartons in which they were packaged. But I also take the precaution of resealing the lids after every use with a strip of heavy-duty masking tape.

Rolled "table-cut" oats, purchased from natural foods stores, I keep in any wide-mouth jar with a screw-top lid that is absolutely airtight. I also label and date the contents legibly and keep them no longer than one year. You do the same.

How to Cook Them

Preparing oatmeal is a very personal business. I, for one, don't agree with the standardized formula on the carton. When I whip up a batch of breakfast oatmeal for two, I always mix 1 cup of rolled oats with 2 cups of cool water (that is to say, straight from the tap). I place the mixture—without the addition of salt—over moderately low heat for about 5 minutes, stirring the thickening oats from time to time until the mixture boils. I then remove it from the heat, cover the pan, and allow the cereal to rest 2 or 3 minutes longer. The result? Perfect creamy oatmeal every time, merely waiting for butter, sugar, and cream or milk to turn it into an Olympian feed.

Some kitchen savants believe that all oats taste best if they are lightly toasted prior to serious cookery, whether that be for a morning meal or for a midnight snack of oatmeal pancakes. Toasting certainly brings out oats' subtle flavor and it's no big deal to accomplish. Simply spread the oats on a baking sheet and slip them into a preheated 350°F oven for approximately 10 minutes. Remember, however, to turn them often with a wide spatula, so they toast evenly. Golden brown is the color you are seeking. Any excess toasted cereal may be stored in a heavy-duty plastic self-seal bag in the freezer. Add it to bread crumbs when you're low, or substitute a measure for ground nuts when you're stirring up a batch of chocolate chip cookies.

Though its lineage is Old World, the oat is not exactly a johnny-come-lately to the American kitchen. The grain reputedly found its way here in 1602 via a British sea captain with an eye on early retirement in the colonies. Settling on one of the Elizabeth Islands, off Massachusetts, he farmed for the rest of his life, planting fields and fields of oats—which not only survived the brutally cold Atlantic winters but stored well in his silo the rest of the year. In short order, the colonists at Plymouth followed his example and planted oats as well, which caused their livestock to flourish and the cereal to enter the Pilgrim diet with a vengeance.

Even back then, however, sensible cooks realized oats had a greater potential than filling porridge bowls. There is a curious recipe, noted in the yellowed pages of Abigail Bradford's hymnal, for a "hache of oatmeale, suet and onyions bound together with eggs" that was shaped as a fowl, boiled, and eaten on Shrove Tuesday—named "Dry Goose"!

NICE RED PISSALADIERE

*T*his is really a pie, made with oats and a rich tomato sauce, that is covered with olives and baked until crisp. It was influenced by a French recipe that I once tasted in Nice. I always serve it as an appetizer.

1½ to 2 cups Niçoise Tomato Sauce (see page 199)
2 cups rolled oats
2 tablespoons freshly grated Parmesan cheese

1 teaspoon chopped fresh basil, or ½ teaspoon dried
2 tablespoons sliced imported black olives, preferable Niçoise
1 teaspoon olive oil

1. Preheat the oven to 350°F. Lightly grease a 9-inch pie plate.

2. Heat 1½ cups of the tomato sauce in a medium-size saucepan over medium-low heat until warmed through. Stir in the oats, cheese, and basil. Add more tomato sauce if the mixture seems dry.

3. Spoon the mixture evenly into the prepared pie plate. Arrange the sliced olives over the top, and drizzle with the oil. Bake until firm, about 25 minutes.

Serves 6 to 8

OATED HAM AND LAMB LOAF WITH DILL SAUCE

A seriously old-fashioned farm loaf chock full of oaty goodness and flavor. Try it next time you have a hankering for meat loaf.

FOR THE LOAF

2 tablespoons unsalted butter
1 large shallot, minced
1 pound ground lamb
1 pound cooked smoked ham steak, ground
1 teaspoon English dry mustard
½ teaspoon salt
¼ teaspoon freshly ground black pepper
¼ teaspoon ground allspice
2 tablespoons dry sherry
2 tablespoons chopped fresh dill
2 eggs, lightly beaten
2 cups rolled oats
½ cup homemade beef stock (see page 377) or canned broth
1½ tablespoons Dijon mustard
1 teaspoon heavy or whipping cream

FOR THE DILL SAUCE

2 tablespoons unsalted butter
2 tablespoons all-purpose flour
1 cup homemade beef stock (see page 377) or canned broth, warmed
2 tablespoons freshly grated horseradish, or 1½ tablespoons prepared horseradish
1½ tablespoons Dijon mustard
¼ cup sour cream, at room temperature
1 teaspoon fresh lemon juice
2 tablespoons chopped fresh dill

1. Preheat the oven to 375°F.

2. Make the loaf: Melt the butter in a small skillet over medium-low heat. Add the shallot; cook 4 minutes. Remove from the heat.

3. Combine the lamb and ham in a large bowl. Add the shallot, dry mustard, salt, pepper, allspice, sherry, dill, eggs, rolled oats, and beef stock. Mix thoroughly. Form into a loaf on a shallow baking dish.

4. Mix the Dijon mustard with the cream, and spread over the loaf. Bake until golden, 50 to 60 minutes.

5. Meanwhile, make the dill sauce: Melt the butter in a small saucepan over medium-low heat. Whisk in the flour. Cook, stirring constantly, 2 minutes. Whisk in the beef stock, and stir until smooth. Add the horseradish and mustard. Cook 2 minutes.

6. Remove the sauce from the heat and beat in the sour cream. Stir in the lemon juice and dill. Keep the sauce warm for serving with the loaf.

Serves 6 to 8

GREENGROCER'S STEW

Most people think oats' place in the kitchen should be consigned to a cereal bowl or possibly a cookie jar. Not my late grandmother, however. She used the grain to thicken weak gravies and watery stews, and to meld disparate vegetables into wondrous analeptic soups. The one I recall best was called Greengrocer's Borscht, so named because the main ingredients changed according to the produce that was in season. This version was my favorite, and I dedicate it to her equally green memory.

4 tablespoons (½ stick) unsalted butter
1 medium onion, chopped
2 cloves garlic, minced
1 cup rolled oats
1 quart homemade chicken or vegetable stock (see page 376) or canned chicken broth
1 medium potato, cubed
1 fennel bulb (about 1½ pounds), chopped
10 ounces fresh spinach, trimmed, rinsed, and coarsely chopped
½ teaspoon freshly grated nutmeg
⅛ teaspoon ground allspice
Freshly ground black pepper to taste
¾ cup sour cream

1. Melt the butter in a large skillet over medium heat. Add the onion; cook 4 minutes. Add the garlic; cook 1 minute longer. Stir in the oats and raise the heat slightly. Cook, stirring constantly, until all the butter has been absorbed and the oats have turned golden, about 5 minutes. Remove from the heat.

2. Heat the stock to boiling in a medium-size saucepan. Stir in the potato and fennel. Reduce the heat and simmer, uncovered, 12 minutes. Stir in the oatmeal mixture, spinach, nutmeg, and allspice. Cook 10 minutes longer. The mixture will be quite thick. Remove from the heat and allow to cool slightly.

3. Purée the soup, in batches, in a blender or food processor. Transfer it to a medium-size pot and warm it over low heat for 10 minutes before serving. Add pepper to taste, and top each bowlful with a tablespoon of sour cream.

Serves 8 to 10

PARMESAN-AND-OAT-FLECKED CHICKEN

Crispy fried chicken coated in golden oats and cheese. Team up these cutlets with your favorite pasta.

½ cup quick rolled oats
3 tablespoons fine fresh bread crumbs
½ cup freshly grated Parmesan cheese
2 whole boneless, skinless chicken breasts, halved and pounded
Salt to taste

¼ cup all-purpose flour
1 egg
1 tablespoon water
2 tablespoons unsalted butter
1 tablespoon vegetable oil

1. Place the oats in the container of a food processor, and process until fine, 1 minute. Transfer to a shallow bowl, and stir in the bread crumbs and cheese.

2. Sprinkle the chicken breasts with salt and dust lightly with the flour.

3. Beat the egg with the water in a shallow bowl.

4. Dip the chicken breasts into the egg mixture, letting any excess drip off. Then coat with the bread crumb mixture. Stack the prepared chicken between sheets of waxed paper, and let stand 20 minutes.

5. Heat the butter with the oil in a large heavy skillet over medium heat. Sauté the chicken pieces, two at a time, until golden brown on both sides, about 4 minutes per side. Keep warm in a 225°F oven while sautéing the remaining breasts.

Serves 2 to 4

WILD OAT FISH AND PEPPER FRY

A totally 1980s version of fish and chips—minus the chips. Strips of oat-battered, deep-fried hot green peppers stand in for the carbohydrate, and you'll definitely notice the difference!

1 cup quick rolled oats
¼ cup sifted all-purpose flour
2 teaspoons English dry mustard
½ teaspoon freshly grated nutmeg
½ teaspoon salt
4 eggs, separated
2 teaspoons Dijon mustard
1 cup dark beer or ale
2 pounds haddock, cod, or flounder, cut
     into 3-inch pieces
½ cup vegetable oil
¼ cup fresh lemon juice
¼ cup white wine vinegar
Flour
Vegetable oil for frying
12 or more jalapeño peppers, seeded,
     deveined, each cut into 4 strips
     lengthwise
Malt vinegar

1. Place the oats in the container of a food processor, and process until fine, 1 minute. Transfer to a large bowl and whisk in the flour, dry mustard, nutmeg, salt, egg yolks, Dijon mustard, and beer. Refrigerate, covered, 8 hours.

2. Place the fish in a shallow glass or ceramic dish. Combine the ½ cup vegetable oil with the lemon juice and wine vinegar. Pour this over the fish, and let stand, covered, at room temperature for 1 hour.

3. Beat the egg whites until stiff, and fold them into the batter.

4. Drain the fish and pat dry with paper towels. Dust with flour.

5. Heat 2 to 3 inches of oil in a heavy saucepan or deep-fryer until hot but not smoking. Dip the fish into the batter and fry, a few pieces at a time, until golden brown on both sides, about 4 minutes. Drain on paper towels, and keep warm in a 225°F oven.

6. When all the fish is cooked, dust the pepper strips with flour and dip them into the batter. Fry, about 10 pieces at a time, until golden brown on both sides, 2 to 3 minutes. Drain on paper towels, and serve with the fish. Pass the malt vinegar for sprinkling on the fish.

Serves 4 to 6

CASBAH SAUSAGES

One tends to think of oats as a cold-climate crop. Not so. North Africa, and to a lesser extent East Africa too, make good use of this "never say die" grain that is able to extract nutrients from soils that would shrivel and dry barley, rice, or wheat.

One residual of oats' survival pattern is an Algerian dish devised of ground meat, cereal, spices, and lots and lots of garlic—named *kefte, kufta,* or *kefthe,* depending upon the casbah where you first sampled it. In North Africa these spicy sausages are usually grilled on skewers over open braziers under highly unsanitary conditions. Call me "chicken," but I prefer to sauté them at home—in a well-scrubbed pan!

4 tablespoons (½ stick) unsalted butter
1 medium onion, finely chopped
1 clove garlic, minced
1 pound ground lamb
½ pound ground veal
½ cup quick rolled oats
1 egg, lightly beaten
Pinch of ground allspice
¼ teaspoon ground cinnamon
2 tablespoons chopped fresh parsley
Dash of hot pepper sauce
1 tablespoon fresh lemon juice
2 tablespoons water
Salt and freshly gound black pepper to
     taste
1 tablespoon olive oil

1. Heat 2 tablespoons of the butter in a medium-size heavy skillet over medium-low heat. Add the onion; cook 3 minutes. Add the garlic; cook 2 minutes longer. Remove from the heat.

2. Combine the lamb and veal with the oats and beaten egg in a large bowl. Mix well. Add the onion/garlic mixture, allspice, cinnamon, parsley, hot pepper sauce, lemon juice, water, and salt and pepper. Mix thoroughly. Form into small sausage shapes.

3. Heat the remaining 2 tablespoons butter with the oil in a heavy skillet until hot. Add the sausages, about six at a time, and cook over medium-high heat until deep golden on all sides, about 8 minutes per batch. Shake the pan back and forth to turn the sausages. Drain on paper towels, and keep warm in a 225°F oven until all the sausages have been cooked.

Serves 4

Oats have certainly had their detractors over the years, but they have never been Scotsmen. In Scotland oats are prized beyond estate, chattel, and almost but not quite beyond malt whisky! Duels have been fought to defend the grain's honor and heads have rolled when monarchs did not take sufficient pride in the national cereal.

Dr. Samuel Johnson, acknowledged curmudgeon of the eighteenth century, was not an oats lover. When he defined oats in his *Dictionary of the English Language* as "a grain which in England is given to horses but in Scotland supports the people," he caused such civilian unrest in the Highlands that a letter was drafted by the Lord Mayor of Edinburgh, advising him to amend the statement or never consider crossing the Scottish border again.

No such alteration was ever made, and one supposes Johnson never had a change of heart about the oat. But what gastronomic experiences he missed!

OKLAHOMA OAT-FRIED CARROTS

The oat is a grain that is high in flavor and low in calories—a scant 100 per ¼ cup—which makes it an ideal substitute for higher-tabbed bread crumbs in most recipes. Consider one of my favorite oat-dusted vegetable dishes as a prime example.

4 large carrots
1 egg
1 tablespoon heavy or whipping cream
1 chicken bouillon cube, crushed
¼ teaspoon freshly grated nutmeg
1 cup rolled oats (approximately)
2 tablespoons unsalted butter
1 tablespoon vegetable oil
Salt and freshly ground black pepper to
    taste

1. Slice the carrots into 3-inch lengths. Cook them in boiling salted water about 5 minutes, then drain and allow to cool. Slice each piece lengthwise into three pieces.

2. Beat the egg with the cream, crushed bouillon cube, and nutmeg in a shallow bowl. Place the oats in another shallow bowl.

3. Heat the butter with the oil in a large heavy skillet over medium heat. Dip the carrot strips into the egg mixture and then into the oats. Sauté until lightly browned, about 2 minutes per side. Keep warm in a 225°F oven until all the carrots have been sautéed. Sprinkle with salt and pepper, and serve.

Serves 4

SCOTTISH STOVIES

A second oat-dressed vegetable. This time it's pan-roasted potatoes and they hail from Oban, Scotland.

5 tablespoons unsalted butter
3 medium onions, sliced into thin rounds
6 to 8 small russet potatoes, cut in half
    lengthwise
¾ cup water
1 teaspoon salt
¼ teaspoon ground white pepper
Pinch of ground allspice
¼ cup rolled oats
⅛ teaspoon hot Hungarian paprika

1. Melt 4 tablespoons of the butter in a large heavy pot or Dutch oven over medium-high heat. Add the onions and toss lightly to break the rings apart. Add the potatoes, cut side down. Pour the water over the potatoes, and sprinkle with salt, white pepper, and allspice. Heat to boiling, then reduce the heat. Cook, covered, over low heat until the potatoes are tender, 25 to 30 minutes.

2. Preheat the oven to 250°F.

3. Partially remove the cover and raise the heat slightly under the potatoes. Continue to cook until all liquid has been absorbed, 3 to 5 minutes. Transfer to a heatproof serving dish and place in the oven.

4. Melt the remaining 1 tablespoon butter in a small skillet over high heat. Toss in the oats and sprinkle with the

paprika. Cook, tossing constantly, until the oats turn golden, about 2 minutes. Sprinkle them over the potatoes and return to the oven for 5 minutes before serving.

Serves 4 to 6

NIZZA PIZZA

I lived in the south of France at one time, not far from Nice, a city that belonged to Italy hundreds of years ago and still bears it an emotional allegiance—mainly in relation to the foods indigenous to the area, like pizza dappled and drizzled with a wondrous anchovy-tinged tomato sauce. I used to frequent a small stall on the waterfront that stayed open all night, serving a special oat-crusted pizza that everyone called *Nizza*—which was, in fact, the Italian name for Nice those hundreds of years ago.

2½ cups Niçoise Tomato Sauce (recipe
*   follows), warmed*
2 cups rolled oats
1 cup ricotta cheese
1½ cups grated mozzarella cheese
½ to ¾ cup chopped salami or pepperoni,
*   or 7 Casbah Sausages (see page 197),*
*   chopped*

1. Preheat the oven to 400°F. Lightly grease a 12-inch pizza pan.

2. In a mixing bowl, combine 2 cups of the warm tomato sauce with the oats, and stir well. Spread the mixture over the bottom of the prepared pizza pan. Bake until crisp, about 15 to 18 minutes. Set aside to cool. Raise the oven heat to 425°F.

3. Spread the ricotta over the cooled pizza, then sprinkle with the remaining ½ cup tomato sauce. Sprinkle with the mozzarella and then the salami. Bake until bubbly, 12 to 15 minutes.

Serves 4 to 6

Niçoise Tomato Sauce

2 tablespoons unsalted butter
1 tablespoon olive oil
1 medium onion, finely chopped
1 clove garlic, minced

1½ teaspoons anchovy paste
½ cup clam broth
1½ cups chopped, seeded fresh tomatoes
1 cup tomato sauce
½ teaspoon chopped fresh oregano, or ¼
*   teaspoon dried*
¼ teaspoon chopped fresh thyme, or a
*   pinch of dried*
1 tablespoon chopped fresh basil, or 1
*   teaspoon dried*
Salt and freshly ground black pepper to
*   taste*

Heat the butter with the oil in a large saucepan over medium-low heat. Add the onion; cook 1 minute. Add the garlic; cook 2 minutes. Stir in the anchovy paste, clam broth, tomatoes, tomato sauce, and herbs. Heat to boiling. Reduce the heat and simmer, uncovered, until the tomatoes are soft, about 20 minutes. Season with salt and pepper.

Makes about 2½ cups

EIDERDOWN PANCAKES

Oats are not unfamiliar at the breakfast table. But in pancakes? Yes, and delicious as well as healthy.

1 cup all-purpose flour
½ cup quick rolled oats
1 tablespoon baking powder
½ teaspoon salt
1½ cups buttermilk
2 tablespoons vegetable oil
3 eggs, separated
Melted butter
Maple syrup

1. Combine the flour with the oats, baking powder, and salt in a large bowl. Beat in the buttermilk, vegetable oil, and egg yolks.
2. Beat the egg whites until stiff, and fold them into the batter.
3. Heat a lightly greased griddle or heavy skillet over medium heat. Pour about ¼ cup batter for each pancake on the griddle and cook until the underside is golden brown and the top is bubbly, about 2 minutes. Turn over, and lightly brown the other side. Keep warm in a 225°F oven while preparing the remaining pancakes. Serve with melted butter and maple syrup.

Makes about 12 pancakes

GRIDDLE SCONES

Straight from Scotland and another tasty way to add oats to your morning meal.

1 cup quick rolled oats
1 cup all-purpose flour
½ teaspoon salt
2 teaspoons cream of tartar
1 teaspoon baking soda
¼ cup (½ stick) unsalted butter, chilled
⅔ cup heavy or whipping cream

1. Place the oats in the container of a food processor, and process until fine, 1 minute. Transfer to a large bowl and add the flour, salt, cream of tartar, and baking soda. Mix well. Cut in the butter with a knife, and blend with a pastry blender until the mixture has the texture of coarse crumbs. Stir in the cream.
2. Transfer the dough to a lightly floured board, knead briefly, and roll it out to form a circle about ½ inch thick. Cut the dough into six pie-shaped wedges.
3. Rub a 9- to 10-inch cast-iron skillet with flour and place it over medium-low heat for 5 minutes. Then cook the scones in the skillet, three at a time, 8 minutes per side.

Makes 6 scones

EDIE ACSELL'S MUFFIN PAN CRISPIES

*E*die is a good friend, great teacher, and wonderful cook who lives in Denver. Her sweet muffins must be handled gently. They are fragile, but well worth the care.

Baker's Secret (see page 42) or vegetable
  cooking spray
8 tablespoons (1 stick) unsalted butter, at
  room temperature
¼ cup plus ⅓ cup firmly packed light
  brown sugar
¼ teaspoon salt
½ teaspoon baking powder
1 teaspoon vanilla extract
1½ cups quick rolled oats
1 tablespoon milk
⅓ cup raisins, plumped in boiling water to
  cover and drained
¼ cup hot water
¼ teaspoon ground cinnamon
⅛ teaspoon freshly grated nutmeg

1. Preheat the oven to 350°F. Rub a muffin tin (with 2-inch bottoms) with Baker's Secret or spray with a vegetable cooking spray.

2. In the medium-size bowl of an electric mixer, beat 4 tablespoons of the butter with ¼ cup brown sugar at medium speed until smooth. Beat in the salt, baking powder, and vanilla. Then on low speed, beat in the oats and milk until well mixed. Work in the raisins with your hands.

3. Place about 1½ tablespoons batter in each of the prepared muffin cups. Gently smooth the tops with a fork. Bake 15 minutes.

4. Meanwhile, melt the remaining 4 tablespoons butter in a small saucepan over medium-low heat. Stir in the ⅓ cup brown sugar, the hot water, and the cinnamon and nutmeg. Cook 2 minutes, then remove from the heat.

5. Spoon the hot butter mixture over the muffins, about 2 tablespoons per cup. Return to the oven and bake 15 minutes longer.

6. Cool the muffins in the tin on a cake rack for 5 minutes. Then loosen the

OATMEAL THERAPY

Round the world, oats seem to have a singular reputation for homeopathic cures. Why? I have no idea. But here are a few examples.

In Russia, they believe a poultice compounded of equal parts hot oatmeal and hot dry mustard will stave off an imminent case of pneumonia. That is to say, if the patient's epidermis can survive the treatment. From Scotland comes more soothing stuff: There they prescribe a lotion of oats and rosewater for rough hands and knobby knees. In the Swiss Alps, oats and cream pounded to a paste is said to allay chilblains and other snow burns. In Japan, cold oatmeal forced into the nostrils will stop a nosebleed, they say. And in Rio de Janeiro, a facial mask of oatmeal cooked in wine will not only cleanse the pores but give the sinuses a jolt at the same time—at least in my opinion. In Germany, habitual drinkers consume a bowl of oatmeal and fried onions to rid of them of a hangover. And in the French provinces the peasants chew oats—straight from the fields—to sweeten their breath after eating garlic.

edges with a sharp knife and let them stand, still in the tin, until firm, about 10 minutes longer. Invert the muffins onto a parchment- or brown-paper-lined cake rack and allow to cool completely.
Makes 12 muffins

OATED APPLESAUCE MUFFS

O atmeal turns baked products into creamy-textured goods that seem so rich that a dab of honey—without butter—is the only thing one would want to top them with.

Baker's Secret (see page 42) or vegetable
  cooking spray
1¼ cups all-purpose flour
1¼ cups quick rolled oats
¼ cup firmly packed light brown sugar
1 tablespoon baking powder
¼ teaspoon baking soda
¼ teaspoon salt
1 teaspoon ground cinnamon
Pinch of ground cloves
⅛ teaspoon freshly grated nutmeg
1 egg
¾ cup milk
3 tablespoons vegetable oil
1 cup homemade applesauce (see page 40)

1. Preheat the oven to 425°F. Rub a muffin tin with Baker's Secret or spray with a vegetable cooking spray.

2. In a medium-size bowl, combine the flour, oats, brown sugar, baking powder, baking soda, salt, cinnamon, cloves, and nutmeg. Mix well.

3. In a large bowl, combine the egg, milk, oil, and applesauce. Stir in the dry ingredients, and mix well. Spoon the batter into the prepared muffin cups so they are two-thirds full. Bake until firm and golden, 18 to 20 minutes.
Makes 12 muffins

GOLDEN OAT BISCUITS

I warrant that you'll never taste a crumblier biscuit—but it's so good you won't want to leave any of those crumbs either!

1 cup rolled oats
1⅓ cups all-purpose flour
1 tablespoon baking powder
½ teaspoon salt
3 tablespoons unsalted butter, chilled
2 tablespoons lard, chilled
1 cup heavy or whipping cream

1. Preheat the oven to 450°F.

2. Place the oats in the container of a food processor, and process until fine, 1 minute. Transfer to a large bowl, and add the flour, baking powder, and salt. Mix well. Cut in the butter and lard, blending with a pastry blender until the mixture has the texture of coarse crumbs. Stir in the cream. The dough will be slightly tacky.

3. Place the dough on a heavily floured board, and pat it down until it is about ¼ inch thick. Cut out twelve biscuits with a round cutter, and place them on a flour-rubbed baking sheet. Bake until puffed and golden brown, 12 to 15 minutes.

Makes 12 biscuits

Acountry girl from the small town of Czenstochowa in Poland, where the present Pope was also born, my grandmother left her family, friends, and native land the day she turned eighteen and married my grandfather, never looking back nor seeming to regret the rupture.

When I was a small boy, the story of my grandmother's exodus from Europe to America held a magnetic fascination, and I would ply her with question after question about "the old country" and her life on the farm, queries that she would sometimes answer lyrically and at other times refuse to think about.

"It's too long ago . . . Who remembers?" She would shake her head. "Besides, it's a mistake to think about that old stuff. The past is past."

But my mind was suffused with images of ancestral connections—borrowed no doubt from pastoral movies in which peasants frolicked happily all day long—that would not be dismissed. So my questioning went on.

One day when we were having lunch together, I abruptly put down my fork. "Did you really leave Poland with nothing but the clothes you had on, Grandma?"

She thought about it for a while before speaking. "Listen, we weren't rich, but I left with a trunk. It wasn't a big trunk, but it held my wedding dress, two changes of underwear, and two sheets and pillowcases. Sheets I sewed by hand when I was your age."

"And that was all?"

My grandmother nodded. Then, remembering something, she went to the dresser where all the important family papers were kept. From a bottom drawer filled with lace napkins and damask cloths, she extracted a small tissue-wrapped package. I watched as she folded back the paper. Inside was a small gilt-bordered card—or what must once have been gilt, since it was now broken in many places and tarnished with age. In the center was pinned a brittle clump of dried flowers that on careful scrutiny appeared to be a bunch of grains with most of the spikelets missing.

"My mother gave this to me the day I left her house." My grandmother spoke very softly, holding the card away from my hands. "It's a barometer made of oats. If you hold it upside down, the little branches shake to one side or another, and you can tell if the weather will be good or bad."

"Hold it upside down, Grandma," I cried. She did, and sure enough there was an involuntary tremor—or so it seems now—to the left.

We both laughed with delight.

"But what does it mean? Rain or shine?"

My grandmother did not answer, for she was preoccupied, replacing the card in its tissue covering.

"Listen," she said at last, "this all happened over fifty years ago, and the truth is *I can't remember!*"

GOOD-FOR-WHAT-AILS-YOU BREAD

My grandmother made a wonderful bread compounded of rye, wheat, chopped nuts, and oats of course. It was simply known as Good-For-What-Ails-You Bread—and so it was.

¾ cup quick rolled oats
1¾ cups lukewarm water
2 tablespoons unsalted butter
1 package dry yeast
Pinch of sugar
½ cup rye flour
½ cup whole-wheat flour
2½ to 3 cups bread flour
¼ cup slivered blanched almonds, toasted
    (see Note) and chopped
¼ cup walnut halves, chopped
1 tablespoon unsalted butter, melted

1. Combine ½ cup of the oats with 1 cup of the lukewarm water in a medium-size saucepan. Heat to boiling, then remove from the heat. Stir in the 2 tablespoons butter, and let cool to lukewarm.

2. Meanwhile, sprinkle the yeast over ¼ cup of the lukewarm water in a large bowl. Stir in the sugar, and let stand 5 minutes.

3. Stir the lukewarm oat mixture into the yeast mixture along with the remaining ½ cup lukewarm water, the rye flour, whole-wheat flour, and enough bread flour to make a stiff dough, about 2 cups. Transfer to a floured board and

knead for 10 minutes, working in more bread flour as needed. Transfer the dough to a lightly greased bowl, cover with plastic wrap, and let rise in a warm place until doubled in volume, about 1 hour.

4. Punch the dough down and transfer it to a floured board. Knead in the almonds, walnuts, and remaining ¼ cup oats. Let stand 2 minutes.

5. Grease a standard-size loaf pan and place the dough in it. Cover the pan loosely with a flour-rubbed tea towel, and let it stand until doubled in volume, about 1 hour.

6. Preheat the oven to 375°F.

7. Slash the top of the dough with a sharp knife, and brush with the melted butter. Bake until the bread is golden brown and sounds hollow when tapped with your finger, about 45 minutes. Cool in the pan on a rack.

Makes 1 loaf

Note: To toast slivered almonds, heat a dry small skillet over medium heat. Toast, stirring frequently, until golden, 6 to 8 minutes.

MELTED CHEESE BATTER BREAD

This is an easy recipe for bread that is made in a 9 by 13-inch pan. It's a great party dish. Cut the pieces about ½ inch thick, and then in half across. I often fry the leftover bread in olive oil for toast fingers.

1 cup milk, lukewarm
2 teaspoons sugar
1 package dry yeast
½ cup heavy or whipping cream, lukewarm
3½ cups all-purpose flour
3 eggs, lightly beaten
1 teaspoon salt
½ teaspoon freshly ground black pepper
½ teaspoon hot Hungarian paprika
9 tablespoons unsalted butter, melted and cooled to lukewarm
1½ cups grated sharp Cheddar cheese
1¼ cups rolled oats (approximately)

1. Place ¼ cup of the lukewarm milk in a large bowl. Sprinkle it with the sugar and yeast, and let stand 5 minutes. Stir in the remaining milk, the lukewarm cream, and 1½ cups of the flour. Cover with plastic wrap and let rise in a warm place 45 minutes.

2. Stir the eggs into the yeast mixture. Then stir in the remaining 2 cups flour, the salt, pepper, paprika, and 8 tablespoons of the melted butter. Mix thoroughly, and stir in the cheese and 1 cup of the oats. Transfer the batter to a lightly greased 9 by 13-inch baking pan. Lightly brush the top with the remaining 1 tablespoon butter, and sprinkle with the remaining 3 to 4 tablespoons oats. Let stand, uncovered, until doubled in volume, about 1½ hours.

3. Preheat the oven to 375°F.

4. Bake until the bread is golden on top, about 30 minutes. Serve slightly warm.

Serves 8

OHIO OLD-FASHIONED OAT CAKE

Jim Fobel is a young baker with a good memory and some fine family recipes. This devise, adapted from his *Old Fashioned Baking Book*, is a moist and spicy single-layer oat cake topped with a super-crunchy (more oats) frosting that is broiled till bubbly. It's a cake that makes friends every time it's served.

FOR THE CAKE
1 cup rolled oats
1¼ cups boiling water
1½ cups all-purpose flour
1 teaspoon ground cinnamon
½ teaspoon baking powder
½ teaspoon baking soda
½ teaspoon salt
8 tablespoons (1 stick) unsalted butter, at room temperature
¾ cup firmly packed dark brown sugar
½ cup granulated sugar
2 large eggs
1 teaspoon vanilla extract

FOR THE TOPPING
4 tablespoons (½ stick) unsalted butter
⅓ cup evaporated milk
½ cup firmly packed dark brown sugar
½ cup rolled oats
½ cup shredded sweetened coconut
½ cup chopped walnuts
½ cup chopped pecans

1. Make the cake: Preheat the oven to 350°F. Lightly butter and flour a 9-inch springform pan.

2. Place the oats in a medium-size heatproof bowl and pour the boiling water over them. Stir until well mixed, then allow to cool to lukewarm.

3. Combine the flour, cinnamon, baking powder, baking soda, and salt in a bowl. Set aside.

4. In the large bowl of an electric mixer, beat the butter until light and fluffy. Slowly beat in the two sugars. Then beat in the eggs, one at a time, beating thoroughly after each addition. Beat in the vanilla.

5. On low speed, add the dry mixture to the butter mixture in three batches, alternating with three batches of the oatmeal. Beat only until mixed—do not overbeat.

6. Pour the mixture into the prepared pan. Place the pan in the center of the oven and bake until firm, 30 to 35

minutes. Cool on a rack, then remove the sides of the springform pan. Transfer the cake to a baking sheet.

7. Make the topping: Preheat the broiling unit.

8. Combine the butter and evaporated milk in a medium-size saucepan. Heat slowly to a simmer, stirring to melt the butter. Add the brown sugar, and stir until dissolved. Remove the pan from the heat, and stir in the oats, coconut, walnuts, and pecans. Spoon this mixture over the top of the cake. Heat the cake under the broiler until the topping is bubbling and golden brown, about 2 minutes. (Be careful, as the topping burns easily.) Let the cake stand until cool.

Serves 8 to 10

VERY BERRY CRISP

*T*he sweet-toothed have always had an affinity for oats, it seems. The ancient Greeks made a dessert called *pilakous* that was oats, flour, cheese, and honey whipped together, and considered it such a delicacy it was served only on holidays and occasions of national celebration. The Gauls, being of simpler tastes, combined oats with sugar and suet and baked the mixture into hard flat rectangular cakes that they ate after every meal. These sweets were known as *seuils* (or "doorsteps"). In Henry VIII's time, when cockfighting was a royal sport, British cooks invented a sweet punch of oatmeal, port, beer, sugar, molasses, and, yes, minced oysters. This drink was dubbed "cock ale," which some food snoops believe may just be the precursor of the "cocktail," but I, for one, hope not. In our own country during the American Revolution, when milled flour was scarce, thrifty housewives made bottomless pies of fruit covered with a mixture of oats, sugar, and butter, which were variously known as *grunts*, *crumbles*, or *crisps*, depending upon the baker's place of origin.

FOR THE TOPPING
½ cup firmly packed dark brown sugar
6 tablespoons all-purpose flour
6 tablespoons rolled oats
¼ teaspoon ground cinnamon
Pinch of salt
4 tablespoons (½ stick) unsalted butter, chilled

FOR THE FILLING
1 pint blueberries or other berries, rinsed, dried, and stems removed
½ cup granulated sugar
Finely slivered zest of 1 orange
1 tablespoon all-purpose flour
1 tablespoon orange liqueur

1. Preheat the oven to 350°F. Butter a 9-inch glass pie plate.

2. Make the topping: Combine the sugar, flour, oats, cinnamon, and salt in a medium-size bowl, and mix well. Cut in the butter with a knife, and mix with your fingers until it has the texture of coarse crumbs. Set aside.

3. Prepare the filling: Combine all the filling ingredients in a medium-size bowl, and mix well. Pour into the prepared pie plate.

4. Spread the crumb topping evenly over the berry filling. Bake 30 minutes. Serve slightly warm.

Serves 6 to 8

OUT-OF-THIS-WORLD PECAN PIE

Oats not only go in the crust but are toasted and added to a traditional pie filling, to make for a very untraditional and wonderful dessert. I serve it with sweetened whipped cream.

1 Rummed Oat Crust (recipe follows)
¼ cup rolled oats
3 eggs
½ cup honey
½ cup granulated sugar
1 cup firmly packed light brown sugar
⅛ teaspoon freshly ground black pepper
2 tablespoons unsalted butter, melted
¼ cup heavy or whipping cream
½ teaspoon vanilla extract
1 cup broken pecan pieces

1. Roll out the Rummed Oat Crust dough on a lightly floured board, and line a 9-inch pie plate with it. Trim and flute the edges.

2. Preheat the oven to 400°F.

3. Place the oats in a medium-size skillet over medium heat. Cook, stirring constantly, until lightly toasted, about 5 minutes. Allow to cool.

4. Lightly beat the eggs in a large bowl. Beat in the honey, both sugars, pepper, butter, cream, and vanilla. Stir in the oats and the pecan pieces. Pour into the pie shell, and bake 10 minutes. Reduce the heat to 325°F and continue to bake until the filling is firm, about 30 minutes longer. Serve warm.

Serves 8

Rummed Oat Crust

⅓ cup rolled oats
¾ cup all-purpose flour
1 teaspoon sugar
½ teaspoon salt
6 tablespoons solid vegetable shortening, chilled
1 egg yolk, beaten
1 to 2 tablespoons dark rum

1. Place the oats in the container of a food processor, and process until fine, 1 minute.

2. Transfer the ground oats to a large bowl and stir in the flour, sugar, and salt. Cut in the shortening with a knife, then blend with a pastry blender until the mixture has the texture of coarse crumbs. Mix in the egg yolk with a fork, and add enough rum to form a soft dough. Wrap in plastic wrap and refrigerate 1 hour before using.

Makes one 9- to 10-inch crust

COFFEE TOFFEE CRUNCH PIE

*T*he oats are combined with chocolate to make a crust for this special pie. Ever since I ran this in the old *Cuisine* magazine, people have been writing for this recipe. It always seems someone lost it, or lent it, and can't live without it. I quite agree.

1 Chocolate Oat 'n' Nut Crust (recipe
    follows)
8 tablespoons (1 stick) unsalted butter, at
    room temperature
¾ cup firmly packed light brown sugar
1 ounce unsweetened chocolate, melted
2 teaspoons instant coffee powder
2 eggs
1¼ cups heavy or whipping cream
2 tablespoons strong brewed coffee, chilled
1 tablespoon confectioners' sugar
¼ teaspoon vanilla extract
Chilled semi-sweet chocolate for chocolate
    curls

1. Make sure the Chocolate Oat 'n' Nut Crust has cooled before proceeding with the recipe.

2. Beat the butter with the brown sugar in the large bowl of an electric mixer until light. Beat in the chocolate and instant coffee powder. Then add the eggs, one at a time, beating 5 minutes after each addition. Spoon into the prepared crust, and refrigerate at least 6 hours.

3. No more than 2 hours before serving, beat the cream until fairly stiff. Beat in the brewed coffee, confectioners' sugar, and vanilla. Spoon this over the pie filling. Using a vegetable peeler to make chocolate curls, scrape a piece of semi-sweet chocolate over the pie. Refrigerate until ready to serve.

Serves 8 to 10

Chocolate Oat 'n' Nut Crust

½ cup rolled oats
½ cup whole roasted almonds
⅓ cup sugar
⅓ cup unsalted butter, melted
½ ounce (½ square) unsweetened
    chocolate, melted

1. Preheat the oven to 375°F.

2. Place the oats and the almonds in the container of a food processor, and process until finely ground, 1 minute. Transfer to a bowl, and stir in the sugar, butter, and chocolate. Mix well. Pat over the bottom and sides of a 9-inch pie plate. Bake 5 minutes. Set the pie plate on a rack to cool.

Makes one 9-inch crust

CHERRY OAT DELIGHTS

*O*atmeal cookies! They deserve a chapter all to themselves, if truth be told. To me the oatmeal cookie (soft, fragmentary, filled with fruit or nutty nubbins) is the quintessential reason for remaining an adolescent forever.

2 ounces dried pitted cherries
4 teaspoons dark rum
8 tablespoons (1 stick) unsalted butter, at
    room temperature
1 cup firmly packed dark brown sugar
1 egg
Finely grated zest of 1 orange
¾ cup all-purpose flour
½ teaspoon baking powder
½ teaspoon baking soda
¼ teaspoon salt
1½ cups quick rolled oats

1. Preheat the oven to 375°F. Lightly grease, then line with foil, two or more baking sheets.

2. Place the cherries in a small bowl, sprinkle with the rum, and set aside.

3. Beat the butter with the brown sugar in the large bowl of an electric mixer until smooth. Beat in the egg and orange zest.

4. Combine the flour with the baking powder, baking soda, and salt. Slowly add to the butter mixture. Then stir in the oats and the cherries with the rum.

5. Place spoonfuls of dough on the prepared baking sheets, about 1½ inches apart. Do not crowd, as the dough will spread. Bake until golden brown, 8 to 10 minutes. Cool completely before peeling off the foil.

Makes about 2 dozen

"OUTRAGEOUS" CHOCOLATE-OATMEAL CHIPPER

The name of these triple chocolate cookies says it all—or almost. Serve them only to guests who you don't want to have leave—ever!

1½ cups rolled oats
8 tablespoons (1 stick) unsalted butter, at
    room temperature
½ cup granulated sugar
½ cup firmly packed light brown sugar
1 egg
1 teaspoon vanilla extract
1 cup all-purpose flour
½ teaspoon baking powder
½ teaspoon baking soda
¼ teaspoon salt
2 ounces semi-sweet chocolate chips (about
    ⅓ cup)
3 ounces milk chocolate, chopped (about
    ½ cup)
3 ounces white chocolate, chopped (about
    ½ cup)
½ cup chopped blanched almonds

1. Preheat the oven to 375°F.

2. Place 1¼ cups of the oats in the container of a food processor, and process until fine, 1 minute.

3. Beat the butter with both sugars in the large bowl of an electric mixer until smooth. Beat in the egg and vanilla.

4. Combine the processed oats with the flour, baking powder, baking soda, and salt. Slowly add to the butter mixture. Then stir in the remaining ¼ cup oats, the chocolates, and the almonds.

5. Drop the dough by spoonfuls onto ungreased baking sheets, and bake until golden brown, about 10 minutes. Cool slightly on the sheets before removing.

Makes about 40 cookies

LA VENA NUZMAN'S HUMONGOUS OATMEAL COOKIES

La Vena Nuzman is a Kansas City chum who bakes an oatmeal cookie that can stand in for a Frisbee, or just possibly a beach umbrella if push comes to shove. The funny thing about her cookies is the bigger they bake, the better they taste! Share one with a friend. On second thought, make that two.

1 cup (2 sticks) unsalted butter, at room
    temperature
1 cup granulated sugar
1 cup firmly packed light brown sugar
2 eggs
1 teaspoon vanilla extract
1½ cups all-purpose flour
½ teaspoon baking powder
½ teaspoon salt
1 teaspoon ground cinnamon
1 teaspoon ground allspice
1 teaspoon ground cloves
½ teaspoon ground ginger
3 cups quick rolled oats
1 cup soft (very fresh) raisins

1. Beat the butter with both sugars in the bowl of an electric mixer until smooth. Beat in the eggs and vanilla.

2. Combine the flour with the baking powder, salt, and spices. Slowly add this to the butter mixture, then stir in the oats. Let stand, covered, at room temperature 1 to 2 hours. Stir in the raisins.

3. Preheat the oven to 375°F. Lightly grease two or more baking sheets.

4. Place ¼ cup dough for each cookie on the prepared baking sheets—no more than four per sheet. Flatten them with your fingers, and bake until golden brown, about 10 minutes. Cool on the baking sheet for a few minutes before removing to cake racks to cool completely. Store in an airtight container.

Makes 16 huge cookies

MILDRED SCHULZ'S CHOCOLATE DREAMS

I consider a Mildred Schulz recipe to be a talisman of good luck, for I have never written a cookbook that did not have one of her signature dishes tucked safely between its covers. Mildred, who lives in Golden, Colorado, is one of the great unsung home cooks of America but hates to have me say it. Oh, well. Certainly her Chocolate Dreams won't sully the Schulz reputation a jot!

6 ounces semi-sweet chocolate, broken into
    bits
2 cups rolled oats
½ cup firmly packed light brown sugar

4 tablespoons (½ stick) unsalted butter,
    melted
¼ cup dark corn syrup

1. Preheat the oven to 350°F. Generously butter a 7 by 11-inch baking pan (preferably not glass).

2. Melt the chocolate in the top of a double boiler over hot (not simmering) water.

3. Combine the oats with the brown sugar in a large bowl, and mix thoroughly. Pour the melted butter over the top, then stir in the melted chocolate and the corn syrup. Mix thoroughly once more.

4. Spoon the chocolate/oats mixture into the prepared pan. Smooth with a spatula. Bake until the top bubbles up, 15 to 20 minutes. Let the pan cool on a rack 10 minutes. Then cut the cookie into small bars and let them cool in the pan until they can hold their shape. Remove the bars from the pan and cool the pieces thoroughly on a cake rack.

Makes about 2 dozen bars

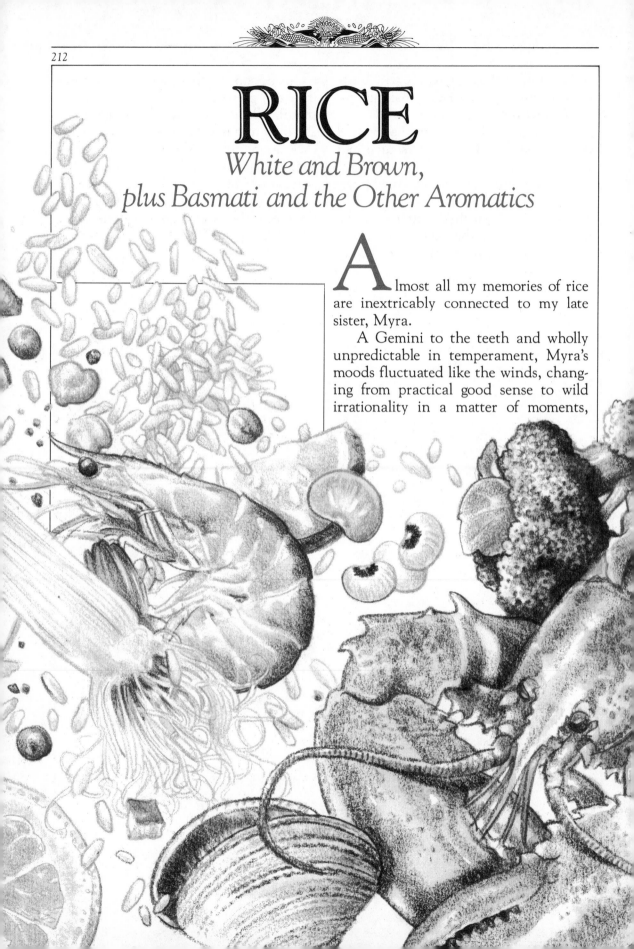

RICE

White and Brown, plus Basmati and the Other Aromatics

Almost all my memories of rice are inextricably connected to my late sister, Myra.

A Gemini to the teeth and wholly unpredictable in temperament, Myra's moods fluctuated like the winds, changing from practical good sense to wild irrationality in a matter of moments,

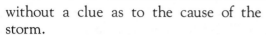

without a clue as to the cause of the storm.

At one time or another both my mother and my father were recipients of my sister's mood changes. But not I, her junior by five years (and a Libran, the mirror image of her astrological sign). She indulged me extravagantly and unstintingly all of her life and I am certain watches over me still.

Half a century ago, rice was not a grain universally consumed and had only very recently come into our diet. We ate it every Thursday night, in fact, for that was the evening my mother worked late at Macy's and allotted her children the princely sum of a dollar to eat out.

In my sister's wisdom this stipend was best invested in two "special" dinners at The Palace, a remarkably dark and dingy Chinese restaurant two flights above our local movie theater. Despite its sobriquet, The Palace had very few regal items on the bill of fare. But dining there was certainly an exercise in economics. For a mere forty cents we each had a soup, entrée, and dessert, leaving a dividend of twenty cents, which we always left as tip for the very ancient waiter.

We did not order rice at The Palace, but like tea it came to the table in an endless relay of replenishment which, according to your point of view, was considered either a premium or a penance. Even my sister, a worldly adolescent who prided herself on the measure of sophistication she'd acquired vetting endless Norma Shearer movies, never permitted me to swallow a mouthful of chicken chow mein without a helping of rice alongside on the fork.

One Thursday night at The Palace I made a bold request. I asked my sister if I could order *fried* rice for a change. Myra was dubious.

"I don't know. Will it cost more?" She sounded remarkably like our mother.

"Why should it?" I countered. "All they do is fry the stuff instead of boiling it!"

Of course I had no idea what fried rice was, but intrigued by its appearance—sizzling and golden under a small metal lid—the question of any supplementary cost never entered my mind. Myra, on the other hand, fully expected the worst.

When the bill came her fears proved not unfounded. There, scrawled in pencil on the check, was an additional tariff of twenty cents (half the price of a "special dinner") for one à la carte portion of rice. Fried.

Over a cup of cold tea, we immediately charted a course of action, while the old waiter—actually the only one in The Palace's employ—stood a discreet distance from our table.

Emptying both my pockets and her change purse on the tablecloth, we counted out a scant eight cents and one rhinestone button.

"Can we possibly leave such a tip?" I whispered, struck at last by the enormity of my extravagance.

"Of course," replied my sister, rising to the occasion and discreetly placing a folded dollar bill over the small pile of change.

When we left The Palace that evening, descending the narrow stairwell to the street, I was certain I heard a curse (in broken English but quite loud) following us down the steps. But my sister, the soul of hauteur, was oblivious to any slur.

"Don't feel guilty, kiddo," Myra counseled. "Developing one's taste is worth a little sacrifice."

"By whom?" I thought but did not ask. "The waiter or me?"

The Grain's Genesis

No one knows for sure how old rice really is, but it is *old*! Botanists place its first cultivation in the Orient about

5,000 years before the birth of Christ. However, it was consumed long, long before that. Recent archeological digs in China unearthed sealed jars filled with rice that had been harvested almost 7,000 years ago. And despite a touch of mildew and a few petrified moths, the grain was deemed still edible.

In India, the earliest rice was the grain of a wild grass known as *newaree*, which grew in swampy patches and had to be separated from weeds, leeches, and water snakes by hand. Slaves or women usually picked this vestigial rice, for it was considered to be the lowliest of household employments. It is reported in Malaysian lore, for instance, that if a new wife was disobedient all a husband need do to curb her temper was to suggest a stroll past the viper-infested marshes where rice bloomed.

Even when rice was domesticated, Chinese farmers were so superstitious about how and why the grain grew that they would stand at the water's edge and cast handfuls of seed into the bog, praying to the god of harvest that germination would take place.

This kind of hit-or-miss rice agriculture went on for centuries until China's Emperor Shen Nung devised a plan for flooding arable fields to create controlled rice paddies. Shen himself celebrated the initial planting with a ceremony in which he dropped the first few seeds into the ground. His touch was obviously green as jade, for the rice not only sprouted, it flourished wildly in China forever after. In 2800 B.C. it was named one of the Five Sacred Crops (along with soybeans, wheat, millet, and barley).

The Chinese were very proprietary about rice and zealously guarded the secrets of both its agriculture and its cookery. Of a consequence—though rice cultivation spread all over the East in no time at all—no two Asian nations ever grew or prepared it in quite the same way.

Rice came to Japan as the spoils of a small border skirmish between a Chinese warlord and a Japanese shogun. As a result, the Japanese have always consumed less of it than the Chinese. Nonetheless, rice was deemed such a status symbol in feudal Japan that a rich man's land was assessed not by acreage but rather by the amount of rice he paid his samurai to protect it.

It is a mystery how Oriental rice spread to the Middle East, but more than likely Indian traders took it there. In India, where rice grows on a third of all tillable land, it is a staple for half the population (barley being the top grain in the north). Both rice and barley are held to be immortal cereals and are referred to in the Koran as "twin sons of heaven."

By contrast, in 1326 Osman I, founder of the Ottoman Empire, declared rice to be a profane food, insisting that its consumption led to indolence, venery, and prurient behavior. As a consequence, rice fields were burned and cooked rice in any form whatsoever was banished from Turkish kitchens for over a century. (Though, it must be told, contraband rice was often eaten on the sly. And the very word *pilau*—originally an acronym for the Greek word for "plate" and the Latin for "to praise"— implied that free-thinkers ate as they pleased.)

In time the rice dictum ended, but so did the Ottoman Empire. By then, rice had found its way to the wet shores of the Po Valley in Italy and to the high marshes of Spain—where the last of the invading Moors discovered it and returned rice to its rightful place in the Middle East once more. Or at least that's how one cloudy version of the story goes.

Some Plain Grain Talk

Rice may not be the most nutritional grain in the world, but it is still the grain most of the world eats to survive. In

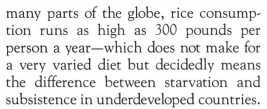

many parts of the globe, rice consumption runs as high as 300 pounds per person a year—which does not make for a very varied diet but decidedly means the difference between starvation and subsistence in underdeveloped countries.

Rice supplies 55 percent of man's daily food requirements, and one pound (which is a heck of a lot of rice at anyone's table) delivers four times the food energy of a like amount of potatoes or pasta.

Rice is primarily carbohydrate, composed of 80 percent starch and 12 percent water. Yet it provides enough protein, thiamine (B$_1$), phosphorus, and potassium to be a significant factor in the diet, particularly when it is combined with other carbohydrates in a saucepan.

Over 7,000 varieties of rice are grown around the world. In America, we eat two kinds. The most conspicuously consumed (by 98 percent of the population) is long-grain and medium-grain white rice. A mere 2 percent eat brown rice.

To set the matter straight, all rice is brown to begin with. It goes through a complex transformation process that strips the kernel of its husk, bran, and germ to achieve pristine and polished whiteness—leaving only the endosperm and very little else in the way of nutritional fiber.

How to Buy It

In the U.S. there are three basic types of rice available to consumers: long-grain, medium-grain, and short-grain.

Long-Grain Rice. The most popular of the long-grain varieties is *regular-milled white rice*. The kernel is about five times as long as it is wide, and the cooked grain is unusually fluffy and separates easily. Most regular milled white rice on supermarket shelves is "enriched," which means it has been spiked with iron, calcium, and assorted B-complex vitamins to make up for the deficiencies caused by removal of the husk, bran, and germ. Enriched rice comes ready to cook, so don't wash it or the enrichment will go down the drain. *Converted white rice*, sometimes dubbed "parboiled," is rice that has been steamed and pressure-cooked before milling—a process that forces residual nutrients into the kernel's heart, making it a tad higher in vitamin content than regular milled rice. Converted rice has drawbacks, however. It takes longer to cook and loses its light texture when held on the stove for a period of time. *Instant or "precooked" white rice* has been partially cooked and dehydrated, so the kernels reconstitute quickly in very little water. It's the least nourishing form of white rice and also the most expensive!

Brown long-grain rice is the whole unpolished grain minus the outer husk. It's decidedly chewier than white rice because each kernel is cloaked in a delicate layer of high-fiber bran. Bran adds a golden-tan color, a distinctive flavor (somewhat on the nutty side), plus a jot more vitamins, minerals, and trace elements. But fiber is the main reason to include brown rice in your diet.

Basmati long-grain rice is a highly aromatic variety imported from the Punjab, in the foothills of the Himalayas. Basmati kernels are somewhat unricelike: long, thin strands that have been aged to decrease the moisture content and increase the extraordinary bouquet, which to my non-Hindu nose translates as "spicy-flowery."

Texmati long-grain rice is a hybrid grown in the U.S. It has neither the assertive flavor of a true basmati nor the fluffiness of a conventional domestic long-grain. But it makes a pleasant change on a dinner plate from time to time. There are other white and brown aromatic rices grown in America (notably in the Southwest and California). Of varying bouquet, all are tabbed well below the price of basmati.

Medium-Grain Rice. As its name implies, medium-grain rice, whether white or brown, is a compromise kernel. Shorter and plumper than long-grain varieties, it is neither as dense nor as glutinous as traditional short-grains, yet may be substituted for the latter in many recipes. Immediately after cooking, medium-grain rice is moist and tender. However, since it contains a high concentration of amylopectin (a starch with gelatin components), the kernels tend to mass and become sticky as the rice cools.

Short-Grain Rice. The rice with the highest degree of cohesion (amylopectin), short-grain rice's viscosity is obviously a matter of taste. In Japan and China, where it is known as *glutinous rice*, this short-grain rice is starchy as the dickens, but despite its name, gluten-free. Opaque, oval-shaped, and chalky white where most other rices are translucent, it is best when the rice is young and the kernels lose their identity and mass quickly. Ideal for a chopstick but hard on a Western knife and fork, glutinous rice has a highly curtailed stove-life in most kitchens. California rice growers do produce a middle-of-the-road short-grain, but it is not easy to find (note the mail-order sources at the back of this book). *Italian arborio short-grain rice*, on the other hand, is a highly kinetic kernel. This grain, cutivated exclusively in the northern Po and Ticino valleys, is unique in that it is used only in the preparation of risotto, one of the great masterpieces of classic Italian cuisine. The varieties—arborio, vialone, nano, and canaroli—have shorter, rounder kernels than any other short-grain rice, with the precise degree of starch in their composition needed to render the creamy texture of this exquisite dish.

How to Store It

By and large, rice is a hardy grain that will keep for an indefinite time on a pantry shelf, as long as the package remains sealed. However, there are some basic tips on rice storage that are worth noting.

Contents of opened packages should be transferred to airtight jars. Glass or ceramic containers with secure screw-top or vacuum-seal lids are the ideal receptacles.

Rice should always be stored in a cool, dry, and if possible, semi-dark place. Coolness inhibits insect infestation, dryness wards off mold, and darkness limits vitamin loss.

By contrast with regular milled white rice, brown rice is *not* a pantry perennial. The oxidation of the oil in the bran causes rancidity and dictates a highly abbreviated shelf life: six months, if you're lucky. Refrigerating or freezing brown rice in self-seal plastic bags will extend that storage time considerably, but make sure to check the contents regularly. The bags must be completely airtight or moisture buildup will occur inside the packet. If you freeze brown rice, it is sensible to allow the kernels to defrost before proceeding with a recipe.

How to Cook It

I have grouped the recipes according to the basic rice types—long-grain, medium-grain, and short-grain—with their individual cooking characteristics.

It is important to note, however, that many of the recipes are interchangeable in terms of type of rice. If, for instance, a high-fiber advocate or an aromatics aficionado wishes to substitute brown rice or basmati rice for regular-milled white rice in a dish, it may usually be adapted to meet that culinary quirk—with appropriate adjustments in cooking time and seasoning.

Check out the Rice Cooking Chart (page 218) for specific information.

LONG-GRAIN WHITE RICE

A good kitchen rule to file away is that this rice triples as it cooks. One-third cup raw rice will produce 1 cup of steam- ing cooked rice, 1 cup raw will produce 3 cups cooked, and so on.

BASIC COOKED RICE

The easiest and most accepted way to prepare regular-milled long-grain white rice is the fail-safe method that follows. It may be prepared on top of the stove in approximately 15 minutes.

If you prefer to cook the rice in the oven (a method neither particularly energy-efficient nor time-saving), boil the liquid before combining it with the other ingredients. Stir once, cover tightly, and bake in a preheated 350°F oven for 25 to 30 minutes.

Converted white rice requires more liquid (2 to 2½ cups to 1 cup rice) and a longer cooking time (20 to 25 minutes) on top of the stove, but the end result will be greater: 3 to 4 cups cooked rice. It can be used in any of the recipes in this section.

1 cup long-grain white rice
2 cups liquid (water, broth, consommé,
  vegetable juice)
½ teaspoon salt
1 tablespoon unsalted butter

1. Combine the rice, liquid, salt, and butter in a medium-size saucepan and heat to boiling. Stir once or twice, and reduce the heat. Cover, and simmer 15 minutes.
2. If the rice is not quite tender or the liquid is not entirely absorbed, replace the lid and cook 2 to 4 minutes longer. Fluff with a fork before serving.
Makes 3 cups

All rice is divided by weather, it seems:

The *Indica* variety, which grows in a cold climate, is a hardy long-grain rice with a firm bite to the kernel.

The *Japonica* variety, on the other hand, which blooms in warm weather and moist atmospheric conditions, is a short-grain rice that cooks soft and loses its kernels' identity in a rice bowl.

RICE COOKING CHART

1 Cup Uncooked Rice	Basic Technique	Steamed Boiled Technique	Yield
Long-grain white	Heat rice and 2 cups liquid to boiling; reduce heat. Cook covered 15 minutes.	Boil in 3 or 4 quarts water 12 minutes. Drain. Place over simmering water. Cover with paper towel. Steam 15 minutes.	3 cups
Long-grain brown	Heat rice and 2½ cups liquid to boiling; reduce heat. Cook covered 45 to 50 minutes (or soak overnight to reduce time).	Boil in 3 or 4 quarts water 30 minutes (or soak overnight to reduce time). Drain in colander. Place over simmering water. Cover with paper towel. Steam 20 minutes.	3 to 4 cups
Basmati	Rinse well. Soak in water 30 minutes. Boil in 3 or 4 quarts water 5 minutes. Drain.	Rinse. Soak in 2 cups water. Drain into a saucepan. Heat drained water to boiling. Stir in rice. Reduce heat. Cook partially covered 10 minutes. Cover and place on flame tamer 10 minutes. Let stand 5 minutes.	3 cups
Texmati and other aromatics	Heat rice and 1¾ cups liquid to boiling; reduce heat. Cook covered 15 minutes.	Boil in 3 or 4 quarts water 12 minutes. Drain. No need to steam.	3 cups

1 Cup Uncooked Rice	Basic Technique	Steamed Boiled Technique	Yield
Brown aromatics	Heat rice and 2 cups liquid to boiling; reduce heat. Cook covered 40 to 45 minutes (or soak overnight to reduce time).	Boil in 3 or 4 quarts water 30 minutes (or soak overnight to reduce time). Drain in colander. Place over simmering water. Cover with paper towel. Steam 20 minutes.	3½ cups
Medium-grain white	Heat rice and 1½ cups liquid to boiling; reduce heat. Cook covered 15 minutes.	Boil in 3 or 4 quarts water 15 minutes. Drain in colander. Place over simmering water. Cover with paper towel. Steam 15 minutes.	3 cups
Medium-grain brown	See long-grain brown.	See long-grain brown.	3 cups
Short-grain white	Rinse well. Soak with 1 cup plus 2 tablespoons water in saucepan 10 minutes. Heat to boiling; reduce heat. Cook covered 5 minutes. Raise heat 30 seconds. Let stand off heat 10 minutes.	Does not apply.	2 cups
Italian arborio	Stir rice into reduced wine and onion mixture. Slowly add 2½ to 3 cups simmering liquid, stirring until creamy, 25 minutes.	Does not apply.	2½ to 3 cups
Short-grain brown	See long-grain brown (use only 2 cups liquid).	See long-grain brown.	2¼ cups

STEAMED BOILED RICE

My alternative—and favorite—way of cooking long-grain rice is a tad eclectic. This version may be a jot less vitaminized because of the parboiling, but the ease of cookery makes up for the nutritional slack. The rice is prepared in under a half hour's time and can then be kept over minimal heat for several hours—with every grain still separate and intact whenever the rice is finally served.

1 cup long-grain white rice
3 quarts boiling salted water

1. Add the rice to the boiling water. Stir once with a wooden spoon, so the rice does not stick to the bottom of the pot, and when the water returns to boiling, reduce the heat. Simmer, uncovered, until just tender, about 12 minutes.

Drain in a colander.

2. Place the colander over 2 inches of simmering water in another pot. (Do not let the bottom of the colander touch the water.) Cover the rice with a single layer of paper towels. Steam for at least 15 minutes. The rice can be held this way for several hours without harm.

Makes 3 cups

FRESH AND SPLIT PEA POTTAGE

A hearty bowl of fresh-and-dried pea soup cooked to a turn with herbs, pink nubbins of ham, and rice, of course. The lineage? Southern most probably, but then most of my best dishes are seasoned with *déjà vu*.

1½ tablespoons unsalted butter
1 medium onion, chopped
1 clove garlic, minced
1 pound dried split peas
1 carrot, peeled and broken in half
1 sprig fresh mint, or ¼ teaspoon dried
1 sprig fresh thyme, or a pinch of dried
1 ham bone, or ½ pound smoked ham
2 quarts plus 2½ cups homemade chicken
  stock (see page 376) or canned broth
1 quart water
2 cups dry white wine
½ cup long-grain white rice
1 package (10 ounces) frozen peas, thawed
Freshly ground black pepper to taste
½ teaspoon chopped fresh mint
1 tablespoon chopped fresh parsley
Garlic-rubbed croutons (see Note)

1. Melt the butter in a large pot over medium-low heat. Add the onion; cook 1 minute. Add the garlic; cook 5 minutes longer. Stir in the split peas.

2. Tie the carrot, mint, and thyme together in a cheesecloth bag. Add this to the pot along with the ham bone, all the chicken stock, water, and wine. Heat to boiling. Then reduce the heat, cover partially, and simmer, stirring occasionally, until the split peas are tender, about 1 hour.

3. Remove the cheesecloth bag from the soup and discard it. Remove the ham bone from the soup and cut off any meat. Chop the meat fine, and set it aside.

4. Return the soup to boiling and add the rice. Reduce the heat, cover, and simmer 15 minutes. Add the chopped ham and thawed peas. Cook 5 minutes longer, and season with pepper.

5. Combine the chopped mint and parsley, and sprinkle over the soup. Serve with garlic-rubbed croutons.

Serves 8

Note: To make garlic-rubbed croutons: Bake 8 thin slices of bread in a 400°F oven until crisp and brown, about 5 minutes. Rub with a split clove of garlic and brush with ¼ cup melted butter. Cut into squares.

COLD GREEN CREAM

A pale green broccoli, lettuce, and rice bisque that should be served on the chilly side. Add an even chillier liter of Chardonnay, a loaf of warm sourdough bread, and a ripe cheese, and voilà, it's California cuisine.

1 small stalk broccoli (½ to ¾ pound)
2 tablespoons unsalted butter
2 leeks, white bulbs and 1 inch of stems, rinsed, dried, and chopped
1 clove garlic, minced
1 small hot green pepper, seeded and minced
½ cup long-grain white rice
6 cups homemade chicken stock (see page 376) or canned broth
1 small head lettuce, such as Boston, rinsed and chopped (about 2½ cups)
¼ teaspoon freshly grated nutmeg
1 tablespoon fresh lemon juice
Salt and freshly ground black pepper to taste
½ cup sour cream

1. Trim the broccoli stem and cut the head into flowerets. Peel and coarsely chop the stalk.

2. Melt the butter in a large heavy saucepan over medium-low heat. Add the leeks; cook 2 minutes. Add the broccoli, garlic, hot pepper, and rice. Toss to coat, add the chicken stock, and heat to boiling. Reduce the heat and simmer, uncovered, over medium-low heat 15 minutes. Add the lettuce and nutmeg. Cook 10 minutes longer. Set aside to cool slightly, then add lemon juice and salt and pepper. Cool to room temperature.

3. Place the soup, in batches, in the container of a food processor and purée. Pour into a bowl and stir in the sour cream. Serve well chilled.

Serves 6 to 8

SIASCONSET CLAM 'N' RICE 'N' EVERYTHING NICE CHOWDER

This chowder originated on the northern edge of Nantucket Island. Please observe that the rice here is a subtle tie that binds.

2 to 2½ quarts chowder clams (quahogs),
  well scrubbed under cold running
  water
1 cup water
½ cup white wine
6 tablespoons (¾ stick) unsalted butter
3 sprigs parsley
1 bay leaf
1 small onion stuck with 1 whole clove
4 strips thick-sliced bacon
1 teaspoon olive oil
1 large onion, minced
1 large clove garlic, minced
1 rib celery, minced
2 tablespoons minced red bell pepper
1 large baking potato (about ¾ pound),
  peeled and cubed
2 cups milk
2 cups heavy or whipping cream
5 whole allspice, crushed
⅓ cup long-grain white rice
¼ teaspoon chopped fresh thyme, or a
  pinch of dried
Dash of Worcestershire sauce
Dash of hot pepper sauce
Salt and freshly ground black pepper to
  taste
1 cup corn kernels (3 medium ears)
Chopped fresh parsley, for garnish

1. Place the clams in a pot with the water, wine, 2 tablespoons of the butter, parsley sprigs, bay leaf, and onion stuck with a clove. Cover and heat to boiling. Reduce the heat and simmer over medium-low heat until the clams open, about 8 minutes. (Clams may have to be fully opened with a clam knife.)

2. Remove the clams from the shells, straining any juices back into the clam broth. Chop the clams coarsely and reserve. Strain the clam broth and reserve; you should have about 1¾ cups.

3. Cook the bacon in boiling water 5 minutes. Drain, and pat dry with paper towels.

4. Rub a heavy skillet with the oil, and sauté the bacon in it until crisp. Drain the bacon on paper towels. Dis-

card all but 1 tablespoon drippings from the pan, and stir in 2 tablespoons of the butter.

5. Add the minced onion to the skillet, and cook over medium heat 2 minutes. Add the garlic; cook 4 minutes longer. Stir in the celery and bell pepper; cook 5 minutes. Add the potato and stir for 1 minute.

6. Transfer the mixture to a large pot and add the bacon, 1 cup of the reserved clam broth, the milk, and the remaining 2 tablespoons butter. Heat to boiling. Stir in the cream and allspice, and cook

Rice has been one of the United States' prandial pleasures for over three hundred years, but how the silken grain came to America in the first place is a matter of conjecture. Romantics insist it was a gift from a grateful British sea captain whose vessel, blown off course in a mid-Atlantic squall, was given safe harbor in Charleston, South Carolina. In gratitude, it was reported, he presented the citizenry with a sack of rice ready for planting. And the rest, as they say, is casserole history!

Nonromantics take a less elevated view of rice's arrival, insisting that its agriculture was simply an extension of slavery. Since most of the slaves in the Carolinas came from the West African coast south of the Sahara, where rice had flourished for hundreds of years, slave owners merely kept their busy farm hands even busier planting and harvesting rice—until the Civil War ravaged the rice fields and dissipated the industry, which in time moved south, southwest, and west by turns. In California, Texas, Arkansas, Mississippi, and Missouri, almost 19 billion pounds of rice are raised yearly.

over medium-low heat 4 minutes.

7. Add the rice to the chowder, and heat the mixture to boiling. Reduce the heat, and add the thyme, Worcestershire, and hot pepper sauce. Simmer uncovered until the rice and potatoes are tender, about 25 minutes. Season with salt and pepper.

8. Stir the corn into the chowder and continue to cook over medium-low heat until thick, about 5 minutes. Stir in the reserved clams and remaining ¾ cup clam broth. Cook 5 minutes longer. Sprinkle with parsley before serving.

Serves 6 to 8

GOLD COAST CHOWDER

A bounteous chowder from the south of France and perfect for dinner accompanied by plenty of crusty bread. Skip the cream (no need to add more stock) for a lighter version.

4 tablespoons (½ stick) unsalted butter
1 large onion, finely chopped
1 large clove garlic, minced
¼ cup all-purpose flour
1 can (28 ounces) imported plum tomatoes, crushed, with juice
2 tablespoons curry powder
1 teaspoon ground turmeric
¼ teaspoon ground allspice
6 cups fish stock (see page 377), heated
½ cup long-grain white rice
1½ pounds white fish filets (such as flounder or sole), cut into 1-inch pieces
1 cup heavy or whipping cream, at room temperature
Salt and freshly ground black pepper to taste
Chopped fresh parsley, for garnish

1. Melt the butter in a large saucepan over medium-low heat. Add the onion; cook 4 minutes. Add the garlic; cook 3 minutes longer. Do not allow to brown.

2. Whisk the flour into the onion mixture. Cook, stirring constantly, 2 minutes. Whisk in the tomatoes, curry, turmeric, allspice, and fish stock. Heat to boiling. Add the rice and stir until the mixture returns to boiling. Then reduce the heat and simmer, uncovered, 15 minutes.

3. Reduce the heat under the saucepan to medium-low. Add the fish, and cook 5 minutes. Slowly add the cream, and heat to boiling. Remove the pan from the heat, and season with salt and pepper. Garnish with parsley.

Serves 6

ALL RIGHT CLAM AND RICE PIE

*A*bout twenty five years ago, I spent a lot of time visiting Cape Cod, where there was a small restaurant that served a wildly rich clam pie. When one of my band of fellow travelers would suggest going out for some clam pie, the reaction was always the same: "All *right*, now you're talkin'." This is my version, from memory.

FOR THE CRUST

1¼ cups plus 1 teaspoon all-purpose flour
1 teaspoon sugar
½ teaspoon salt
6 tablespoons lard, chilled
1 egg yolk
1 teaspoon red wine vinegar
1 to 2 tablespoons cold water

FOR THE FILLING

2 tablespoons unsalted butter
1 tablespoon olive oil
1 large onion, finely chopped
1 clove garlic, minced
¼ teaspoon chopped fresh thyme, or ⅛ teaspoon dried
1 cup chopped raw or canned clams with their broth
1 cup grated zucchini, lightly pressed to remove water
1½ cups cooked long-grain white or brown rice, heated
1 teaspoon minced seeded jalapeño pepper
2 eggs
¼ cup heavy or whipping cream
3 whole allspice, finely crushed
¼ cup freshly grated Parmesan cheese
4 ounces mozzarella cheese, thinly sliced

Niçoise Tomato Sauce (see page 199)

1. Make the crust: Combine 1¼ cups flour, the sugar, and the salt in a medium-size bowl. Cut in the lard, and blend with a pastry blender until the mixture has the texture of coarse crumbs. Lightly beat the egg yolk with the vinegar and water. Using a fork, cut the liquid into the flour mixture to form a soft dough. (Do not overwork.) Sprinkle the dough with 1 teaspoon flour. Wrap in plastic wrap and refrigerate 1 hour before using.

2. Preheat the oven to 400°F.

3. Butter a 9-inch loose-bottom tart or quiche pan. Roll out the chilled dough on a lightly floured board, and line the prepared pan with the dough. Trim and flute the edges. Line the crust with foil, and weight it with rice or beans. Bake 5 minutes. Remove the foil and weights, and bake 4 minutes longer. Remove the crust from the oven and set aside. Reduce the oven heat to 350°F.

4. Make the filling: Heat the butter with the oil in a large heavy skillet. Add the onion; cook 2 minutes. Add the garlic and thyme; cook 3 minutes longer. Stir in the clams and zucchini; cook 2 minutes longer. Stir in the rice and pepper. Transfer the mixture to a large bowl.

5. Beat the eggs with the cream and allspice until smooth. Toss into the rice/clam mixture, and stir in the Parmesan cheese. Spoon the mixture into the prepared crust. Place the mozzarella slices over the top. Bake 30 minutes. Let stand 5 minutes before serving with Niçoise Tomato Sauce.

Serves 6 to 8

STAR-SPANGLED SCALLOPS WITH BLUE CHEESE RICE

From Love Point in Chesapeake Bay, where the scallops are sweet and inventive chefs "cream" their rice with blue cheese. This is a wonderful brunch dish.

FOR THE SCALLOPS

1 pound bay scallops
3 tablespoons all-purpose flour
2 tablespoons vegetable oil
4 teaspoons unsalted butter
8 scallions, white bulbs and green tops
    chopped separately
1 clove garlic, minced
1 medium red bell pepper, blanched,
    seeded, and finely chopped
½ cup diced smoky country ham
¼ cup dry white wine
¼ cup homemade chicken stock (see page
    376) or canned broth
1 tablespoon chopped fresh basil

FOR THE RICE

¼ cup heavy or whipping cream
⅛ teaspoon crushed dried hot red peppers
3 tablespoons creamy blue-type cheese
    (Bleu Castello or Cambazola)
2 cups cooked long-grain white rice, heated
Chopped fresh parsley, for garnish

1. Preheat the oven to 350°F.
2. Pat the scallops dry with paper towels and dust with the flour.
3. Heat the oil with 2 teaspoons of the butter in a heavy noncorrosive skillet over medium heat. Sauté the scallops, about a third at a time, until golden, about 3 minutes. Using a slotted spoon, transfer the scallops to a bowl and set aside.
4. Add the remaining 2 teaspoons butter to the skillet, and sauté the scallion bulbs 1 minute. Add the garlic; cook 2 minutes. Stir in the bell pepper and ham; cook 3 minutes longer. Add the wine and stock, scraping the sides and bottom of the pan with a wooden spoon. Heat to boiling, and boil until slightly thickened, about 1 minute. Return the scallops to the pan and toss with the basil. Transfer to an ovenproof serving dish, sprinkle with the scallion tops, and bake for 10 to 15 minutes.
5. Meanwhile, make the rice: Heat the cream to boiling in a medium-size saucepan. Reduce the heat, and add the hot peppers and cheese. When the cheese has melted, add the cooked rice and stir until warmed through, about 4 minutes. Sprinkle with parsley, and serve with the Spangled Scallops.

Serves 4

WEST SIDE POT-ROASTED CHICKEN WITH RICE

The West Side of Manhattan is a real melting pot of the world's population. This dish, created in that teeming borough, reflects its roots—French-style pot-roasted chicken is flavored with Italian hard sausage. Long-grain rice binds it together.

1 chicken (about 4 pounds), well rinsed
    and dried
4 sprigs parsley
2 fresh sage leaves, or a pinch of dried
1 large clove garlic, bruised
1½ tablespoons olive oil
1 tablespoon unsalted butter
1 medium onion, finely chopped

1 teaspoon minced hot red pepper
¼-inch-thick slice of hard Italian salami or
    sopressata, chopped
2 cups homemade chicken stock (see page
    376) or canned broth
½ cup dry white wine
1 cup long-grain white rice
Chopped fresh parsley, for garnish

1. Rinse the chicken and pat dry with paper towels. Stuff the cavity with the parsley sprigs and sage. Sew and truss. Rub the chicken with the bruised garlic, then mince the garlic and reserve.

2. Heat the oil in a large saucepan or Dutch oven over medium-high heat. Add the chicken and brown well on all sides, about 12 minutes.

3. Remove the chicken from the pan, and wipe out the pan. Add the butter, and cook the onion over medium-low heat 1 minute. Add the reserved garlic and the red pepper; cook 4 minutes longer. Stir in the salami.

4. Return the chicken to the pot, breast side up. Pour the stock and wine over the chicken, and heat to boiling. Reduce the heat and simmer, covered, 1 hour.

5. Stir in the rice, around the chicken, and continue to cook, covered, until all liquid has been absorbed, about 15 minutes.

6. To serve, carve the chicken and place on a platter. Surround with rice and sprinkle with chopped parsley.

Serves 4

ALMOND-CRISPED CORNISH HENS WITH JAMBALAYA DRESSING

The stuffing is based on a rendering I sampled in Abbeville, Louisiana. The crust for the bird, made of ground almonds, garlic, brandy, and sweet butter to hold it together, is a new twist on an old northern trick of coating roasts with bread crumbs to keep the birds moist. The nutty, crackling skin makes a great dish even better.

6 small Cornish game hens
Jambalaya Dressing (recipe follows)
8 tablespoons (1 stick) unsalted butter, at
    room temperature
1 large clove garlic, crushed
½ cup ground blanched almonds
2 tablespoons brandy
1 quart homemade chicken stock (see page
    376) or canned broth
1 clove garlic
1 medium rib celery, chopped
3 sprigs parsley
¼ teaspoon salt
8 black peppercorns
1½ tablespoons unsalted butter
1½ tablespoons all-purpose flour
¼ cup heavy or whipping cream
Salt and freshly ground black pepper to
    taste

1. Wipe the Cornish hens inside and out with damp paper towels. Reserve the giblets. Spoon the Jambalaya Dressing into the cavities. Sew and truss.

2. Beat the 8 tablespoons butter with the crushed garlic in a medium-size bowl until smooth. Beat in the ground almonds and the brandy. Spread this mixture evenly over the hens. Place the hens on racks in roasting pans, and let stand 30 minutes.

3. Meanwhile, preheat the oven to 425°F.

4. Place the hens in the oven, and roast 1 hour.

5. While the hens are roasting, combine the giblets (not the liver) with the chicken stock in a saucepan, and add the whole clove of garlic, celery, parsley

sprigs, salt, and peppercorns. Heat to boiling. Reduce the heat and simmer, uncovered, until reduced by one third, about 25 minutes. Strain.

6. After they have cooked for an hour, pour the chicken stock around the hens. Continue roasting until the juices run yellow when the hens are pricked with a fork, about 30 minutes longer. Transfer the hens to a serving dish, remove the strings, and keep warm. Degrease the pan juices.

7. Melt the 1½ tablespoons butter in a medium-size saucepan over medium heat. Add the flour and cook, whisking constantly, 2 minutes. Stir in the pan drippings and the cream. Simmer 5 minutes. Thin the sauce with additional chicken stock if it is too thick, and season with salt and pepper. Serve with the hens.

Serves 6

I n China there are two words for rice. The Cantonese *mai* means "agriculture," while the Mandarin *mee* means "culture." In Japan, where they reduce everything to basics, there is a very basic word for rice as well: *gohan*. It denotes "a full meal." In India, a Sanskrit equivalent, *vrihih*, bespeaks of rice as a "life-giving seed." Thailand's name for rice translates as "food with wings to fly." In Korea, the word for rice means "god's tears," or, some aver, "god's fears." Take your pick!

Oddly enough, the Greeks, who were never great rice fanciers, gave the grain its botanical handle. They called it *Oryza sativa*—*sativa* being the word for "sown" and *oryza* simply a tag that states "of Oriental origin."

Jambalaya Dressing

1 teaspoon olive oil
2 sweet italian sausages (about ½ pound)
2 tablespoons unsalted butter
1 medium onion, chopped
1 clove garlic, minced
¼ cup diced green bell pepper
¼ cup diced red bell pepper
1 cup chopped, peeled, seeded tomatoes
¼ teaspoon sugar
¼ cup homemade chicken stock (see page 376) or canned broth
1 tablespoon chopped fresh basil, or 1 teaspoon dried
½ teaspoon finely grated lemon zest
¼ teaspoon ground chili powder
Pinch of dried thyme
5 ounces shrimp, shelled and deveined
½ cup chopped cooked ham
2¼ cups cooked long-grain white rice
Salt and freshly ground black pepper to taste

1. Rub a heavy skillet with the oil, and sauté the sausages over medium heat until golden brown on all sides, 6 to 8 minutes. Transfer to a plate, and cut into ¼-inch-thick slices. Set aside.

2. Discard all grease from the skillet, and melt the butter in the skillet over medium-low heat. Add the onion; cook, scraping the bottom and sides of the pan with a wooden spoon, 3 minutes. Add the garlic and both bell peppers; cook 3 minutes longer. Then stir in the tomatoes, sugar, stock, basil, lemon zest, chili powder, and thyme. Simmer, uncovered, 5 minutes. Add the shrimp and cook 1 minute more.

3. Transfer the tomato-shrimp mixture to a large bowl. Stir in the ham, sausage slices, and rice. Mix well, and season with salt and pepper.

Makes enough dressing for 6 Cornish hens

INDONESIAN FRIED RICE AND CHICKEN WITH GADO GADO SAUCE

*T*his dish, an Indonesian concoction, is devised of rice fried with chicken under a blanket of super-spicy peanut butter and pepper sauce. Use either white or brown rice and any leftover chicken in the fridge. But do not attempt to make it unless fresh cilantro (Chinese parsley) is on hand for seasoning!

4 cups cooked long-grain white or brown rice
2 cups cubed cooked chicken
1 tablespoon chopped fresh cilantro (Chinese parsley)
2 teaspoons chopped fresh parsley
3 tablespoons mayonnaise, preferably homemade (see page 379)
½ teaspoon salt
¼ teaspoon freshly ground black pepper
1 tablespoon unsalted butter
3 tablespoons peanut oil
Gado Gado (recipe follows), heated

1. Place 2½ cups of the cooked rice in a large bowl and add the chicken, cilantro, parsley, mayonnaise, salt, and pepper. Mix well.

2. Heat the butter with the oil in a 10-inch skillet (preferably non-stick) over medium heat. Spread the remaining 1½ cups rice over the bottom of the skillet. Press lightly with the back of a wooden spoon. Then spoon the chicken mixture over the rice. Reduce the heat to medium-low and cook, uncovered, until the bottom of the bottom layer of rice is very crispy, 25 to 30 minutes. Shift the pan occasionally if it is larger than the burner. Raise the heat slightly if the mixture is not crisp enough, but watch carefully.

3. When the bottom layer of rice is crisp, remove the skillet from the heat and let it stand 3 or 4 minutes. Invert onto a serving platter, and serve with Gado Gado on the side.

Serves 4

Gado Gado

¼ cup peanut oil
1 small onion, finely chopped (about ¼ cup)
1 clove garlic, minced
½ teaspoon minced fresh ginger
½ teaspoon crushed dried hot red peppers
½ cup chunky peanut butter
¼ cup soy sauce
¼ cup fresh lime juice
1 cup water

1. Heat the oil in a medium-size saucepan over medium heat. Add the onion and cook until golden, about 4 minutes. Stir in the garlic, ginger, and dried red peppers. Cook 2 minutes.

2. Reduce the heat to medium-low and slowly stir in the peanut butter, soy sauce, lime juice, and water. Heat to boiling. Reduce the heat and simmer, uncovered, until thickened, 10 minutes.

Makes about 2 cups

*I*n China, losing or quitting a job is known as "breaking the rice bowl"—probably because of the effect such an event has on one's eating habits. On the other hand, getting a good job is known as "buying heavy rice."

COLD BAYOU RICE

A cool, soothing rice salad for a hot, hot day. The dressing is a homemade mayonnaise. If you substitute store-bought, thin it with a little milk and add some mustard and vinegar for flavor.

4½ cups cooked long-grain white rice, chilled
1 cup diced cooked ham
½ cup chopped fresh parsley
4 scallions, white bulbs and green tops, finely chopped
2 teaspoons capers
2 eggs yolks, at room temperature
Juice of 1 lemon
1 tablespoon Dijon mustard
⅔ cup olive or vegetable oil, or a combination of both
¼ cup red wine vinegar
1 teaspoon salt
½ teaspoon freshly ground black pepper

1. In a large bowl, combine the rice with the ham, parsley, scallions, and capers. Toss with two forks to mix.

2. Beat the egg yolks with the lemon juice and mustard in a small bowl until slightly thickened. Beat in the oil, a few drops at a time. Then beat in the vinegar, salt, and pepper.

3. Pour the egg yolk mixture over the rice mixture and toss with two forks until well mixed. Chill for 3 hours before serving.

Serves 6

RED, RED RICE

A smoky red pepper gives this rice its wonderful flavor. I often sauté a batch of sausages and slice them over the top, then toss a green salad together, for a light supper.

1 large red bell pepper
3 tablespoons unsalted butter
1 teaspoon olive oil
¼ cup thinly sliced scallion bulbs
3 cups cooked long-grain white rice, heated
Salt and freshly ground black pepper to taste
Chopped fresh parsley, for garnish

1. Char the pepper over a gas flame, under a broiler, or on a preheated grill. Wrap the charred pepper in paper towels and place in a plastic bag for 5 minutes. Rub off the charred skin with paper towels. Seed the pepper and chop.

2. Heat 2 tablespoons of the butter with the oil in a large skillet. Add the scallions; cook 2 minutes but do not brown. Add the chopped roasted pepper and cook 1 minute longer. Transfer the mixture to the container of a food processor, and process until smooth.

3. Melt the remaining 1 tablespoon butter in the skillet, and toss in the rice. Add the processed pepper mixture and toss until well mixed. Season with salt and pepper, and sprinkle with parsley before serving.

Serves 4

DOUBLE-QUICK TOMATO RICE

This is a quick side dish for broiled chicken or chops. Serve it with a healthy green vegetable like broccoli.

3 tablespoons unsalted butter
1 shallot, minced
1 small rib celery, minced
1 cup Bloody Mary mix or V-8 juice
1 cup homemade chicken stock (see page 376) or canned broth
¼ teaspoon salt
1 cup long-grain white rice

Melt the butter in a medium-size saucepan over medium heat. Add the shallot and celery and cook until the vegetables lose their color, 3 to 4 minutes. Add the Bloody Mary mix, stock, and salt. Cover and quickly heat to boiling. Stir in the rice and reduce the heat to low. Cook, covered, until tender, about 15 minutes. Raise the heat slightly if the rice is too wet.

Serves 4

GREEN HERBED RICE

This bowl of rice adds color to any broiled or roasted food. I use fresh basil, which is available at most supermarkets year-round these days. But experiment with other herbs by all means.

¾ cup chopped fresh parsley
¼ cup chopped fresh basil
2 tablespoons chopped green scallion tops
¼ cup olive oil (approximately)
3 cups cooked long-grain white rice, heated
Salt and freshly ground black pepper to taste
1 tablespoon unsalted butter
Freshly grated Pamesan cheese, for garnish (optional)

1. Place the parsley, basil, and scallion tops in the container of a food processor. With the machine running, add just enough oil through the feed tube to make a smooth purée.

2. Toss the puréed mixture into the hot rice, along with salt and pepper and the butter. Serve immediately or keep warm in a 225°F oven. Sprinkle with cheese, if desired, before serving.

Serves 4

NUTTY RICE

I particularly like this spicy rice dish with grilled or broiled seafood.

3 tablespoons unsalted butter
¼ to ½ teaspoon crushed dried hot red
*   peppers*
⅓ cup chopped macadamia nuts
3 cups cooked long-grain rice, heated

Melt the butter in a large skillet over medium heat. Stir in the dried red peppers (according to taste) and macadamia nuts. Cook, stirring constantly, until the nuts begin to turn golden, 3 to 4 minutes. Reduce the heat and lightly toss in the cooked rice. Serve immediately or keep warm in a 225°F oven.

Serves 4

PRALINE PANCAKES

*P*ecan-flecked rice pancakes—in the best of all possible worlds dappled with a plentitude of warm praline syrup—from Baton Rouge, Louisiana, where a sweet tooth is considered to be every citizen's birthright.

FOR THE SYRUP

1 cup sugar
⅔ cup hot water
2 teaspoons vanilla extract

FOR THE PANCAKES

4 egg yolks
1½ cups milk
4 tablespoons (½ stick) unsalted butter,
*   melted*
1 teaspoon vanilla extract
2 teaspoons brandy
1 cup all-purpose flour
2 teaspoons baking powder
2 tablespoons sugar
½ teaspoon salt
⅛ teaspoon ground cinnamon
½ cup coarsely chopped pecan halves
1 cup cooked long-grain white rice, chilled

1. Make the Caramel Syrup: Heat the sugar in a medium-size skillet over medium heat until it begins to melt and turns golden, about 1½ minutes. Continue to cook, stirring constantly, until the sugar caramelizes (turns a deep golden color). Quickly and very carefully, stir in the hot water all at once. Stir until any lumps are dissolved. Remove from the heat and add the vanilla. Set aside.

2. Make the Praline Pancakes: Beat the egg yolks in a large bowl until light. Stir in the milk, butter, vanilla, brandy, flour, baking powder, sugar, salt, and cinnamon. Beat well, and then beat in the pecans and rice.

3. On a preheated hot, greased griddle or cast-iron skillet, pour about ½ cup batter for each pancake. Cook until bubbles form on the top and the undersides are lightly browned, about 1 minute. Turn cakes over and lightly brown the other side. Keep warm in a 225°F oven while cooking the remaining pancakes. Serve with syrup drizzled over the cakes.

Makes about 16 pancakes

ULTIMATE RICE VELVET WITH RASPBERRIES AND VANILLA SAUCE

My adaptation of an Alice B. Toklas original. I have been making various versions of this dish for well over twenty years—with not one complaint. Feel free to add a little amaretto, kirsch, even brandy to the custard—at your whim.

½ cup plus 1 tablespoon long-grain white
  rice
1 quart milk
Pinch of salt
8 egg yolks
1 cup sugar
5 tablespoons all-purpose flour
2 cups milk, scalded
1 teaspoon vanilla extract
3 egg whites
1 pint fresh raspberries
Classic Vanilla Sauce (see page 105)

1. Combine the rice, 1 quart milk, and salt in the top of a double boiler. Cook, uncovered, over hot water, stirring occasionally, until the rice is tender, about 1 hour. Transfer the mixture to a heatproof bowl.

2. Preheat the oven to 350°F.

3. Beat the egg yolks in the large bowl of an electric mixer until light. Sift the sugar with the flour and gradually add to the egg yolks. Beat on medium-low speed for 10 minutes. Beat in the scalded milk. Transfer to the top of a double boiler and cook over hot water, stirring frequently, until thick enough to coat a wooden spoon, about 25 minutes. Strain into a large bowl.

4. Add the vanilla to the egg yolk mixture. Drain the rice and add it to the mixture. Beat the egg whites until stiff, and fold into the rice mixture.

5. Pour the rice mixture into a buttered 2-quart soufflé dish, and bake 25 to 30 minutes. The center should be a bit wet. Serve slightly warm, at room temperature, or chilled, with fresh raspberries and Classic Vanilla Sauce.
Serves 6 to 8

The history of rice pudding is obviously a matter of being in the wrong soup at the right time. It all started with the Roman centurions, who quaffed an "aqueous brew of rice and water" to clear their brains after battle.

When the Gauls won a few skirmishes, they celebrated the victory by adding cream to the centurions' broth—giving body to the bisque and a few pounds to Roman waistlines in passing.

However, it took the good-living Benedictine monks to give the soup its true character during the Middle Ages. They first added dried fruits; then honey, eggs, and brandy; and seasoned the pot with cinnamon, cloves, and mace before it was served. Indeed the mixture was often so thick, the sensible brothers consumed it with a fork and knife instead of a spoon.

The soup's metamorphosis came about during a visit of a young abbot from Rome. Being served the Benedictine soup, he tasted it carefully before making a comment.

"This may be the worst soup ever made," he stated forthrightly. "But it is also the best pudding I have ever tasted!"

CHOCOLATE RICE RUINATION

Call it cocoa overkill if you must, but to my jaded tongue this is the best dessert I've tasted since I was ten years old and learned to melt Nestlé bars in their foil wrappers and eat the contents with a demitasse spoon. If you ask about the dessert's pernicious cognomen, I will tell you this: Like those Nestlé bars, a single spoonful of this pudding is the start of utter dietary decadence.

1 can (14 ounces) condensed milk
2 ounces semi-sweet chocolate, chopped
4 tablespoons (½ stick) unsalted butter
½ cup milk
2 egg yolks
3 teaspoons vanilla extract
2 cups steamed, boiled long-grain white rice (see page 220)
1 cup heavy or whipping cream
1 teaspoon confectioners' sugar
Piece of semi-sweet chocolate, chilled

1. Preheat the oven to 325°F. Butter a shallow soufflé dish.

2. Combine the condensed milk with the chocolate in a medium-size saucepan over low heat. Cook, stirring constantly, until the chocolate has melted, 5 minutes. Gradually add the butter, and stir until melted. Remove the pan from the heat.

3. Whisk the milk into the chocolate mixture. Beat in the egg yolks and 2 teaspoons of the vanilla. Then stir in the rice. Pour the mixture into the prepared soufflé dish, and bake 30 minutes. The middle will be slightly loose. Cool on a wire rack. Refrigerate, covered, until well chilled.

4. Before serving, beat the cream in a large bowl until slightly thickened. Add the remaining 1 teaspoon vanilla and the confectioners' sugar, and beat until stiff. Pile the whipped cream on top of the pudding. Using a vegetable peeler, scrape the piece of semi-sweet chocolate over the top to make chocolate curls. Refrigerate until ready to serve.

Serves 8

LONG-GRAIN BROWN RICE

Despite its high fiber content and heady flavor, too few cooks are willing to undertake the preparation of brown rice. And not because of any "health food" stigma attached to its consumption, either. They are simply intimidated by the time it requires to cook the stuff!

Traditionally, brown rice must cook for 45 to 50 minutes before a grain is deemed fork-tender. However, a recent breakthrough cooking technique speeds up that process considerably: presoaking the grains in the liquid in which they are to be cooked for 8 to 10 hours, or preferably overnight. By presoaking brown rice in this manner, it is possible to slice the actual stove time in half, to 22 minutes flat!

BASIC COOKED BROWN RICE

1 cup brown rice
2½ cups liquid (water, broth, consommé)
    (approximately)
1 teaspoon salt
1½ tablespoons butter

1. Combine the rice, liquid, salt, and butter in a heavy saucepan and heat to boiling. Stir once or twice, reduce the heat, cover, and cook 45 to 50 minutes (see Note).

2. If the rice is not tender, add more liquid and continue to cook, covered. Fluff with a fork before serving.
    Makes 3 to 4 cups.

Note: To save time, soak brown rice in the liquid overnight, and reduce cooking time to 20 to 22 minutes.

STEAMED BOILED BROWN RICE

1 cup brown rice
4 quarts boiling salted water

1. Add the rice to the boiling water. Stir once with a wooden spoon, so that the rice does not stick to the bottom of the pot. When the water returns to boiling, reduce the heat and simmer, uncovered, until just tender, about 30 minutes (see Note). Drain in a colander.

2. Place the colander over 2 inches of boiling water in another pot. Do not let the bottom of the colander touch the water. Cover the rice with a single layer of paper towels, and steam at least 20 minutes. Brown rice can be held this way for several hours without harm.
    Makes 3 to 4 cups

Note: To save time, soak brown rice in the liquid overnight. Drain it in a fine sieve, reserving the liquid. Bring the liquid to a boil, add the rice, and reduce the initial cooking time to 17 minutes.

HOPPIN' JOHN SOUP

*F*rom St. Landry parish to Atchafalaya Basin (or anywhere else in the South, for that matter), it's a bleak, black year that does not dawn with a pot of rice and black-eyed peas bubbling away on the stove. That's Hoppin' John. And while my version is somewhat on the slurping side, it will still work wonders for the imbiber—as a talisman or a tonic!

1 tablespoon unsalted butter
2 tablespoons olive oil
1 large onion, minced
1 large clove garlic, minced
1 pound dried black-eyed peas, picked over
1 ham bone, or ½ pound chunk smoked ham
½ teaspoon chopped fresh thyme, or ¼ teaspoon dried
1 bay leaf
1 quart homemade chicken stock (see page 376) or canned broth (approximately)
1 quart water
½ cup brown rice
Juice of 1 lemon
1 teaspoon grated lemon zest
Salt and freshly ground black pepper to taste
1 teaspoon chopped fresh chives

1. Heat the butter with the oil in a large pot over medium-low heat. Add the onion; cook 1 minute. Add the garlic; cook 5 minutes. Stir in the black-eyed peas, then add the ham bone, thyme, bay leaf, chicken stock, and water. Heat to boiling. Reduce the heat and simmer, partially covered, 1 hour.

2. Stir the rice into the soup and continue to cook, partially covered, until black-eyed peas and rice are tender, about 30 minutes longer. If the soup is too thick, add more stock.

3. Remove the ham bone from the soup. Cut off any meat from the bone and chop it fine.

4. Add the ham meat to the soup, and cook 2 minutes. Stir in the lemon juice and lemon zest. Add salt and pepper, and sprinkle with chives.

Serves 6 to 8

VIVA BROWN RICE

Brown rice has certainly had its share of public defenders and detractors.

Aimee Semple McPherson, the evangelist, ate brown rice because she claimed it was toughening her to face adversity. Charles Atlas, the bodybuilder, ate brown rice at age eighty because he was certain it would keep his physical appearance close to the way it had been when he was eighteen!

George Bernard Shaw, who insisted that a brown rice diet was responsible for his mental prowess, wrote a play when he turned ninety-five. After it had been badly reviewed by the press, the comic W. C. Fields quipped: "He probably thought he'd been eating brown *lice* all along!"

Fidel Castro is a true brown rice buff. Expressing a desire to celebrate the grain with the creation of a national dish, he desisted only when the members of his cabinet pointed out that the Cuban word for rice, *arroz*, sounds suspiciously like the Russian word for rifles, *ruzhyo!*

JODY'S INCREDIBLE STUFFED PORK CHOPS

Jody Gillis is a letter-writing fan from Santee, California, who has become something more: a precious friend and a perfervid recipe donor. Her contribution to this grains collection is a solid winner: a savory pork chop crammed to the nines with herbed rice and baked in a sauce that up to now has been a deep dark family secret.

The recipe was sent to me with a query: "Do you want the white or brown version? I prefer the brown myself, possibly because it is the only brown rice dish that I have ever gotten Larry [Jody's husband] to eat without the threat of divorce proceedings!"

Consider Jody Gillis's offering a cure-all for all such intractable spouses.

1 teaspoon salt
¼ teaspoon freshly ground black pepper
¼ teaspoon chopped fresh thyme
¼ teaspoon chopped fresh sage
4 double pork chops, with a pocket cut in each
7 tablespoons unsalted butter
1 onion, finely chopped
1 small rib celery, finely chopped
2 ounces mushrooms, chopped
⅔ cup cooked brown rice
¼ cup dry white wine
¼ cup strong homemade chicken stock (see page 376)
1 cup sour cream, at room temperature
Chopped fresh parsley, for garnish

1. Combine the salt, pepper, thyme, and sage in a small bowl. Mix well and rub the chops, inside the pocket and out, with this mixture.

2. Melt 4 tablespoons of the butter in a heavy skillet over medium heat. Add the onion and celery; cook 5 minutes. Add the mushrooms; cook 3 minutes longer. Reduce the heat to low and stir in the cooked rice. Mix well. Remove the skillet from the heat and allow to cool slightly.

3. Preheat the oven to 350°F.

4. Fill the pockets of the pork chops with the rice mixture. Secure the openings with toothpicks.

5. Melt the remaining 3 tablespoons butter in a large skillet over medium heat. Brown the chops well on both sides. Transfer to a casserole.

6. Pour the wine and stock over the chops, cover, and bake 1 hour.

7. Transfer the chops to a shallow serving dish. Stir the sour cream into the pork juices and pour over the chops. Sprinkle with parsley before serving.

Serves 4

BROWN RICE IN A BUNDLE OF VEAL

*T*his is actually a love letter to brown rice—wrapped in an envelope of tender veal and wild mushrooms. And postmarked Rome, where I came upon the recipe.

4 tablespoons olive oil
1 cup sliced fresh wild mushrooms (such as shiitake or porcini)
1 medium onion, finely chopped
1 medium carrot, diced
2 tablespoons dry white wine
1 cup homemade chicken stock (see page 376) or canned broth
1 cup cooked brown rice

2 ounces thinly sliced prosciutto, chopped
1 large slice top round of veal (about 1 pound), butterflied and pounded thin
2 tablespoons unsalted butter, melted
2 tablespoons dry sherry
Chopped fresh parsley, for garnish

1. Preheat the oven to 375°F.

2. Heat 2 tablespoons of the oil in a

large heavy skillet over medium-high heat. Add the mushrooms and cook, tossing constantly, until lightly browned, about 4 minutes. Using a slotted spoon, transfer the mushrooms to a bowl and set aside.

3. Add the remaining 2 tablespoons oil to the skillet. Add the onion; cook 3 minutes. Stir in the carrot and the mushrooms. Sprinkle with the wine and cook until all liquid has evaporated, about 4 minutes. Stir in ¼ cup of the chicken stock and continue to cook until the carrot is fairly tender and almost all liquid has evaporated, about 5 minutes. Stir in the cooked rice. Remove from the heat and stir in the prosciutto.

4. Lay the veal open flat on a piece of cheesecloth large enough to enclose it. Spread the rice mixture over the veal, and roll it closed, using the cheesecloth to help roll. Tie securely to keep the meat from falling apart while cooking.

5. Spread 1 tablespoon of the melted butter over the bottom of a shallow baking dish. Place the meat seam side down in the butter. Drizzle the remaining 1 tablespoon butter over the top, and roast 30 minutes.

6. Meanwhile, combine ¼ cup stock with the sherry. Baste the meat after it has cooked for 10 minutes, and continue to baste every 10 minutes. After 30 minutes, pour the remaining stock around the meat and roast, basting once with pan juices, until the meat is tender, about 15 minutes longer.

7. Remove the meat from the dish and carefully remove the cheesecloth. Slice the veal roll into ½-inch-thick slices. Transfer them to a serving platter and pour the pan juices over the top. Serve sprinkled with parsley.

Serves 4

HOT CUBANO CHICKEN 'N' RICE

Certainly no national dish, this recipe is still worthy of a ten-gun salute or at least the dip of a Havana panatella from time to time.

1 large eggplant (about 1 pound), cut into
    ½-inch cubes
Salt
12 chicken wings
1 tablespoon hot pepper sauce
1 pound Italian sausages
2 tablespoons unsalted butter
½ pound smoked ham, cubed
1 large onion, chopped
2 cloves garlic, minced
1 medium red bell pepper, cored, seeded,
    and chopped
2 hot red peppers, seeded, deveined, and
    minced
1 can (14 ounces) imported plum tomatoes,
    with juice, chopped

1 tablespoon chopped fresh basil
⅛ teaspoon dried thyme
1 cup brown rice
2½ cups homemade chicken stock (see page
    376) or canned broth
Freshly ground black pepper to taste
1 cup corn kernels (3 medium ears)
1 package (10 ounces) frozen baby lima
    beans, thawed
Chopped fresh parsley, for garnish

1. Place the eggplant cubes in a colander. Sprinkle with salt, and let stand 30 minutes. Then rinse with cold water and squeeze dry. Sprinkle the chicken wings with hot pepper sauce. Set chicken wings and eggplant aside.

2. Place the sausages in a large heavy pot. Sauté over low heat until grease begins to render. Then raise the heat to medium and sauté until golden brown on all sides, about 15 minutes. Remove the sausages to a plate, cool slightly, and cut into ½-inch-thick slices.

3. Drain all but 2 tablespoons fat from the pot. Add the butter and sauté the chicken wings over medium heat until well browned. Transfer the wings to the plate with the sausages.

4. Add the ham cubes to the pot and sauté 5 minutes. Transfer to the plate with the wings and sausages.

5. Add the onion to the pot; cook 2 minutes. Add the garlic; cook 1 minute longer. Reduce the heat under the pot to medium-low and stir in the bell pepper, hot peppers, and eggplant cubes. Cook, stirring occasionally, 5 minutes.

6. Stir the tomatoes into the onion/pepper mixture, and add the basil, thyme, rice, and chicken stock. Heat to boiling. Reduce the heat, cover, and cook over medium-low heat 25 minutes. Season with salt and pepper.

7. Preheat the oven to 350°F.

8. Add the ham, chicken wings, sausages, corn, and lima beans to the rice mixture. Stir once, cover, and bake until the rice is tender, about 20 minutes. Sprinkle with parsley before serving.

Serves 4 to 6

CIRCASSIAN CHICKEN WITH BROWN RICE

A bequest from Mother Russia, this is reputedly one of the Empress Catherine's favorite picnic foods, and she often decorated it herself with precious jewels as garnish. I'll take parsley, thank you all the same. The dish makes dandy summer party fare—serve it with bread and salad on the side.

2 small chickens (2½ to 3 pounds each),
    well rinsed
1 medium onion, unpeeled, stuck with 2
    whole cloves
1 medium rib celery, coarsely chopped
1 medium carrot, coarsely chopped
4 sprigs parsley
4 sprigs dill
1 sprig thyme
10 peppercorns
1 quart homemade chicken stock (see page
    376) or canned broth
2 tablespoons unsalted butter
1 medium onion, chopped
½ cup hazelnuts, roasted and skinned (see
    Note)

Pinch of cayenne pepper
Salt and freshly ground black pepper to
    taste
2 teaspoons unflavored gelatin
3 cups cooked brown rice
Chopped fresh dill, for garnish

1. Place the chickens in a large pot and add the onion stuck with cloves, celery, carrot, parsley, dill, thyme, peppercorns, and stock. Heat to boiling. Reduce the heat and simmer, partially covered, until the chickens are tender, about 50 minutes.

2. Preheat the broiler.

3. Remove the chickens from the

stock and carefully cut into serving pieces. Return the backs to the pot, heat the stock to boiling, and reduce to about 2¼ cups, 15 minutes. Strain.

4. Broil the reserved chicken pieces, skin side up, until golden, about 5 minutes. Set aside.

5. Melt the butter in a medium-size skillet over medium-low heat. Add the chopped onion and cook until soft, about 5 minutes. Transfer the onions to the container of a food processor, and add the hazelnuts and 2 cups of the chicken stock. Being very careful, process until smooth. Add cayenne pepper, and salt and black pepper.

6. Dissolve the gelatin in ¼ cup of the chicken stock in a small bowl. Place the bowl over simmering water and stir until the gelatin has dissolved. Stir this mixture into the sauce.

7. Spread the rice over the bottom of a 2-inch-deep serving platter. Arrange the chicken pieces over the rice, and pour the sauce over the chicken. Garnish with chopped dill. Refrigerate until the gelatin sets and the dish has chilled, about 3 hours.

Serves 6 to 8

Note: To roast hazelnuts, spread them evenly on a baking sheet, and place in a 400°F oven for 5 minutes. Carefully wrap the nuts in paper towels and place in a plastic bag and let stand until cool enough to handle. Rub the hazelnuts in paper towels to remove the skins.

CROCCHETTA DI SPINACI

*T*he ultimate vegetable croquettes come from a tiny trattoria in Calabria, where they were served as a first course prior to pasta. Light, crisp, and highly addictive, this is the kind of finger food that can make a cocktail party, or break it if the hostess runs short before the guests have had second (or third) helpings!

1 cup cooked brown rice
2 packages (10 ounces each) frozen chopped spinach, thawed and squeezed dry
2 eggs, lightly beaten
⅓ cup freshly grated Parmesan cheese
½ teaspoon freshly grated nutmeg
½ teaspoon salt
¼ teaspoon freshly ground black pepper
¼ teaspoon hot pepper sauce
½ to ¾ cup fresh bread crumbs
2 tablespoons unsalted butter
4 tablespoons olive oil (approximately)

1. Preheat the oven to 350°F.

2. Place the cooked rice in a large bowl and add the spinach, eggs, cheese, nutmeg, salt, pepper, and hot pepper sauce. Mix well.

3. Using a soup spoon, form the mixture into rounds and drop them into the bread crumbs. Using the tips of your fingers, lightly roll the rounds to coat with crumbs.

4. Heat the butter with 2 tablespoons of the oil in a large skillet over medium heat. Sauté the croquettes, a few at a time, until golden brown on both sides, about 3 minutes per side. Drain on paper towels, and arrange on an ovenproof platter. Continue to sauté croquettes until all the mixture is used up, adding more oil as needed. Bake for 10 minutes before serving.

Serves 4 to 6

BROWN RICE WITH GREEN PEAS

*T*his amalgam of vegetable and grain calls for *cooked* brown rice. When I am making a dish with cooked brown rice, I generally prepare it the day before and keep it refrigerated until the penultimate moment. I know there is a rumor that cooked brown rice spoils faster than cooked regular-milled white rice, but it simply ain't so! Keeping any cooked rice for several days is no problem if you store it in an airtight self-seal bag or a plastic storage container with a tight-fitting lid, so the grains neither dry out nor absorb the flavor of other foods in the fridge.

1 tablespoon unsalted butter
1 large shallot, minced
2 pounds fresh peas, shelled (about 2 cups), or 1 package (10 ounces) frozen peas, thawed
¼ cup heavy or whipping cream
⅓ cup homemade chicken stock (see page 376) or canned broth
3½ cups cooked brown rice, heated
Salt and freshly ground black pepper to taste
1 teaspoon chopped fresh chives

1. Preheat the oven to 350°F. Lightly oil a medium-size baking dish.

2. Melt the butter in a medium-size saucepan over medium-low heat. Add the shallot; cook 1 minute. Stir in the peas. Cook, covered, until just tender—about 5 minutes for fresh, less for frozen.

3. Place half the pea mixture in the container of a food processor, and add the cream and stock. Process until fine.

4. Return the purée to the saucepan and add the remaining pea mixture, the rice, and salt and pepper. Transfer to the prepared baking dish and bake, loosely covered, 15 minutes. Sprinkle with chives before serving.

Serves 4 to 6

BROWN RICE WITH ZUCCHINI

*T*his is one side dish that is full of flavor. A bit of goat cheese makes all the difference. I sometimes just add a cup of cooked chicken and eat it for lunch.

2 tablespoons unsalted butter
1 small onion, chopped
1 clove garlic, minced
1 large or 2 small zucchini, grated (1⅓ cups)
2 tablespoons chopped fresh basil
1 tablespoon strong chicken stock (see Note) or bouillon
1¾ cups cooked brown rice, heated

3 tablespoons dry goat cheese, such as Montrachet
2 tablespoons heavy or whipping cream
Dash of hot pepper sauce
Salt and freshly ground black pepper to taste

1. Preheat the oven to 350°F.
2. Melt the butter in a large skillet

over medium-low heat. Add the onion; cook 2 minutes. Add the garlic; cook 1 minute longer. Stir in the zucchini, basil, and chicken stock; cook 4 minutes longer.

3. Stir the cooked rice into the zucchini mixture. Add the goat cheese, cream, and hot pepper sauce. Cook 1 minute, then season with salt and pepper. Transfer to an ovenproof serving dish, and bake for 12 minutes.

Serves 4

Note: If you do not have strong chicken stock on hand (see page 379), reduce ¼ cup canned chicken broth to 1 tablespoon by simmering for 10 minutes.

STIRRED-UP BROWN RICE WITH WILD MUSHROOMS AND FENNEL

A rustic dish that is all the better when permitted to slow-cook over low heat, so that the rice may absorb the rich and earthy flavor of its collaborators in the pot.

2 tablespoons unsalted butter
1 teaspoon olive oil
2 large shallots, minced
1 clove garlic, minced
¼ cup sliced fresh wild mushrooms (such as shiitake or porcini)
1 cup brown rice
1 small fennel bulb (about ½ pound), chopped
3 cups homemade chicken stock (see page 376) or canned broth
½ cup chopped fresh parsley

1. Heat the butter with the oil in a medium-size saucepan over medium heat. Add the shallots; cook 2 minutes. Add the garlic; cook 1 minute longer. Stir in the mushrooms, rice, and fennel, stirring to coat with the shallot mixture.

2. Add the chicken stock and heat to boiling, then reduce the heat. Cook, covered, over medium-low heat until the rice is tender and all liquid has been absorbed, 45 to 50 minutes. Stir in the parsley before serving.

Serves 4 to 6

ST. LUCIAN BROWN RICE AND EGGPLANT

I had a version of this dish in St. Lucia, one of the most spectacularly beautiful (and non-touristy) islands in the Caribbean. Nutmeg trees grow all over the islands. Mace is the lacey coating of the nutmeg seed. They serve this dish with hearty fish, such as dolphin, swordfish, or tuna.

1 eggplant (½ to ¾ pound), sliced
Salt
½ cup all-purpose flour
¼ teaspoon ground mace
4 to 6 tablespoons olive oil
2 tablespoons unsalted butter
1 medium onion, finely chopped
1 clove garlic, minced
¼ cup finely chopped red or green bell
    pepper
¾ to 1 cup chopped seeded tomatoes
Pinch of sugar
Pinch of thyme
1 cup brown rice
2½ cups homemade chicken stock (see page
    376) or canned broth
Freshly ground black pepper to taste
Chopped fresh parsley, for garnish

1. Place the eggplant slices in a colander and sprinkle with salt. Let stand 30 minutes, then rinse and pat dry. Cut the slices in half.

2. Combine the flour with the mace on a plate. Dust the eggplant slices with this mixture.

3. Heat 4 tablespoons oil in a heavy skillet over medium heat. Sauté the eggplant slices, a few pieces at a time, until golden brown on both sides. Drain on paper towels. Add more oil as needed.

4. Heat the butter with ½ teaspoon oil in a medium-size saucepan over medium-low heat. Add the onion; cook 1 minute. Add the garlic and pepper, tossing to coat. Stir in the tomatoes, sugar, thyme, and rice. Cook 1 minute. Stir in the eggplant slices and the chicken stock, and heat to boiling. Reduce the heat and cook, covered, over medium-low heat until the rice is tender and all liquid has been absorbed, 45 to 50 minutes. Add salt and pepper, and sprinkle with parsley.

Serves 4 to 6

Toward the end of the first century B.C., religious laws in the Orient and the Middle East reached such epic proportions that thousands of believers starved to death rather than consume "impure" foods.

To the Hebrews, unclean or impure foods included any meat cut by a sword; flesh of excessively hairy or hairless beasts; meat of animals with humps (like camels) and meat of seafood with shells (like shrimp). Also verboten were vegetables and fruits that had been sullied by insects, and rice grains from markets where they had been sniffed by dogs, cats, or housewives.

In China it was forbidden for the poor to eat brown rice from public granaries, because rats were reportedly seen on the premises. When the public granaries were burned down, however, the rats ran away and the poor usually caught and ate them. But they never got a sniff at the brown rice.

India had other problems. In that country, white rice was considered impure by high-caste Brahmins because it was always husked by low-caste "untouchables." Consequently Brahmins ate only brown rice for a hundred years, until some religious leader—who was obviously a pragmatist—determined that all impure foods could be purified by the judicious sprinkling of a little holy water or ghee (clarified butter).

RUSSET RICE

Another dish that benefits from slow-cooked rather than presoaked rice.

2 tablespoons unsalted butter
1 leek (white part only), well rinsed and
    finely chopped
3 scallions, white bulbs and green tops,
    finely chopped
1¼ cups chopped seeded fresh tomatoes
½ teaspoon tomato paste
Pinch of sugar
Pinch of thyme
¾ cup brown rice
2 cups homemade chicken stock (see page
    376) or canned broth, heated
Chopped fresh parsley, for garnish

1. Melt the butter in a medium-size saucepan over medium-low heat. Add the leek and scallions; cook 5 minutes.

2. Stir the tomatoes into the onion mixture, and add the tomato paste, sugar, and thyme. Cook 1 minute. Add the rice and stir until well coated with the mixture, then add the chicken stock. Heat to boiling. Reduce the heat and cook, covered, over medium-low heat until the rice is tender and all liquid has been absorbed, 45 to 50 minutes. Sprinkle with parsley before serving.

Serves 4 to 6

BASMATI, TEXMATI, AND OTHER AROMATIC LONG-GRAIN RICES

Basmati. There is only one true basmati rice. Grown in the north of India and Pakistan, it is imported to America in fairly small quantities, which makes it expensive. But like many other luxury foods, it is worthy of serious kitchen attention.

Traditionally basmati rice is sold in bulk and must be carefully washed before it is cooked. The water bath not only removes residual dirt particles, it also releases a measure of starch that would otherwise make cooked basmati rice sticky. More important, since basmati rice expands in length as it cooks, repeated washing and soaking keeps the kernels from breaking or splitting apart.

There are two methods that I use for preparing basmati rice, both borrowed from my friend Julie Sahni, author of *Classic Indian Cooking* and *Classic Indian Vegetarian and Grain Cooking*. Even a novice who can't boil water can master the art of cooking basmati rice in minutes.

Texmati and other domestic aromatic rices. I admire foods with strong flavor. To my tongue, Texas Texmati rice and the other well-known American aromatics, like Louisiana's "popcorn" and wild pecan rice or California's Calmati and Wehani rice, have little in common with the bouquet, taste, or texture of true basmati rice. There is even some question whether basmati was ever crossbred into these varieties, as is alleged. Della rice, the daddy of all scented U.S. varieties—developed almost twenty years ago—is thought to be a strain of Indochinese and Indonesian rices grafted onto local long-grain rootstock in Louisiana.

But in the final analysis, a rice's antecedance is of scant importance at the stove. A domestic aromatic like Tex-mati rice may not be as uniquely flavored as basmati, but it is still mighty good to eat, less than half the price, and a lot easier to prepare.

(For instructions on preparing brown aromatic rices, see the cooking chart on page 218.)

BASIC COOKED BASMATI RICE

What makes a rice *aromatic?*

The Indians who lived in the foothills of the Himalayas believed it was a gift of the god Veda. Early rice farmers in Louisiana and Texas thought it might be the result of acid rain. Both were wild surmises, as it turns out. In 1982 two members of the U.S. Department of Agriculture, along with a fellow scientist from the Rice Research Institute of Manila, identified the substance that gives cooked aromatic rice its characteristic fragrance: known as 2-acetyl-1-pyroline, it is a chemical found in all rice. A higher concentration in basmati and other aromatics gives them their quintessential scent.

1 cup basmati rice
4 quarts water

1. Wash the rice by placing it in a large bowl and adding cold water to cover; when the water turns milky, about 3 minutes, pour off the water. Repeat several times, until the water remains clear. Drain. Cover the rice once more with cold water, and let stand 30 minutes. Drain.

2. Heat 4 quarts unsalted water to boiling. Stir in the rice, and return to boiling; cook 5 minutes. Drain the rice. Before serving, fluff gently with a fork, being careful not to break the kernels.

Makes about 3 cups

Though basmati rice comes from northern India, few of the populace who live there consume it. Essentially bread-eaters who like their loaves on the wheaten side, Punjabis hardly ever touch rice—aromatic or otherwise.

TRADITIONAL STEAMED BASMATI RICE

1 cup basmati rice
Water

1. Wash the basmati rice by placing it in a large bowl and adding cold water to cover; when the water turns milky, in about 3 minutes, pour off the water. Repeat several times until the water remains clear. Drain. Cover the rice with 2 cups of cold water, and let stand 30 minutes. Drain the rice in a colander over a medium-size ovenproof saucepan.

2. Heat the water in the saucepan to boiling. Stir in the rice, and return to boiling. Reduce the heat and cook, parti-ally covered, over low heat until the water is almost absorbed, 10 minutes.

3. Cover the saucepan tightly and either steam the rice on a flame tamer set over very low heat for 10 minutes, or place the covered saucepan on the middle rack of a preheated 300°F oven for 25 minutes. Remove from the heat and let stand, covered, 5 minutes. Before serving, fluff gently with a fork, being careful not to break the kernels.

Makes about 3 cups.

BASIC COOKED TEXMATI RICE

*I*n my kitchen, there are two ways to cook Texmati rice. The first is merely to add a cupful of rice to 3 quarts of boiling water, stir once, and cook for 12 minutes. Drain and serve.

The second method, which follows, takes a bit longer, but the extra time that the rice stands after cooking seems to allow the flavor to fully coalesce.

1 cup Texmati rice
1¾ cups water
1 teaspoon salt
1 teaspoon unsalted butter

Combine the rice, water, salt, and butter in a medium-size saucepan and heat to boiling. Stir once or twice and reduce the heat. Cover, and cook 15 minutes. Remove from the heat and let stand, covered, 5 minutes. Fluff with a fork before serving.

Makes 3 cups

ROAST CHICKEN WITH PESTO RICE

*L*ittle Italy is where the notion for a pesto rice stuffing came into my head. Needless to say, make it only when fresh basil is bountiful.

2 small roasting chickens (2½ to 3 pounds each), well rinsed and dried
1 clove garlic, bruised
3 cups cooked basmati, Texmati, or other aromatic rice
½ cup Pesto Sauce (recipe follows)
¼ cup pignolia (pine) nuts
2 tablespoons unsalted butter, at room temperature
Salt and freshly ground black pepper to taste
½ cup plus 1 tablespoon homemade chicken stock (see page 376) or canned broth
1 cup water
1 tablespoon all-purpose flour
¼ cup heavy or whipping cream
1 egg yolk, lightly beaten
1 tablespoon chopped fresh basil

1. Preheat the oven to 400°F.

2. Rub the chicken inside and out with the bruised garlic. Combine the cooked rice, Pesto Sauce, and pignolia nuts in a mixing bowl. Stuff each chicken with half the mixture. Sew and truss.

3. Rub each chicken with 1 tablespoon of the butter, and sprinkle with salt and pepper. Roast on a rack in a baking pan, 30 minutes.

4. Reduce the oven heat to 350°F. Pour ½ cup chicken stock over the chicken, and add the water to the pan. Continue to roast, basting occasionally, until the juices run yellow when the chicken is pierced with a fork, about 1 hour longer.

5. Place the chickens on a serving platter and remove the strings. Keep warm while making the sauce.

6. Skim the fat from the pan juices.

Strain the juices through a fine sieve into a saucepan and heat to boiling. Mix the flour with the remaining 1 tablespoon chicken stock and stir this into the juices. Simmer 5 minutes. Stir in the cream and continue to simmer until slightly thickened, about 5 minutes longer. Remove from the heat.

7. Whisk 2 tablespoons of the sauce with the egg yolk in a small bowl. Stir this mixture back into the sauce, and cook over very low heat 2 minutes. Do not allow it to boil. Stir in the basil. Spoon ¼ cup of the sauce over the chickens, and pass the remaining sauce.

Serves 6 to 8

Pesto Sauce

2 cups coarsely chopped fresh basil leaves
½ cup chopped fresh parsley
1 teaspoon coarse (kosher) salt
½ teaspoon freshly ground black pepper
2 large cloves garlic, chopped
¾ cup olive oil
¼ cup pignolia (pine) nuts
½ cup freshly grated Romano or Parmesan cheese

Place all the ingredients except the cheese in the container of a food processor or blender. Blend until smooth, about 2 minutes. (You might have to start and stop the blender several times in the beginning.) Transfer the mixture to a bowl and stir in the cheese.

Makes about 1½ cups

Note: Pesto Sauce can be kept refrigerated in a tightly covered jar for several weeks, or frozen for several months, but it is always best not to stir in the cheese until just before serving.

OPELOUSAS' PAELLA

A Cajun version of a Spanish paella crammed with seafood, sausages, and rice, of course.

1 sprig thyme, or ¼ teaspoon dried
1 bay leaf
2 sprigs parsley
1 pound hot Italian sausages
1½ tablespoons olive oil
1 medium onion, chopped
2 cloves garlic, minced
4 scallions, white bulbs and green tops,
    chopped
1 medium rib celery, minced
½ green bell pepper, cored, seeded, and
    minced
1 small hot red pepper, seeded, deveined,
    and minced
½ cup dry white wine
½ cup clam juice or broth
12 or more littleneck clams, well scrubbed
    under cold running water
2 cups (approximately) homemade chicken
    stock (see page 376) or canned broth
1¼ cups presoaked basmati rice, or natural
    Texmati or other aromatic rice
1½ teaspoons filé powder
1 tablespoon unsalted butter
½ pound or more medium-size shrimp,
    shelled and deveined
Salt and freshly ground black pepper to
    taste
Chopped fresh parsley, for garnish

1. Make an herb bouquet by tying the thyme, bay leaf, and parsley sprigs in a cheesecloth bag, and set aside.

2. Sauté the sausages in a large oil-rubbed heavy pot or Dutch oven until well browned on all sides, 8 to 10 minutes. Remove the sausages, cut them into ½-inch-thick slices, and reserve.

3. Discard all but 1 tablespoon fat from the pot and add the olive oil. Add the onion; cook over medium-low heat 4 minutes. Add the garlic; cook 2 minutes longer. Stir in the scallions, celery, green bell pepper, and the hot pepper. Cook, stirring occasionally, 10 minutes.

4. Meanwhile, combine the white wine and clam juice in a medium-size saucepan and heat to boiling. Add the clams, cover, and reduce the heat to medium. Cook until the clams open, about 5 minutes. Remove the clams, in their shells, with a slotted spoon and reserve.

5. Measure the clam broth in the pan, and add enough chicken stock to make 2 cups if using basmati rice, 2½ cups for other aromatic rice. Return the liquid to the pan and heat to boiling.

6. Stir the rice into the vegetable mixture. Stir in the filé powder, the reserved sausage slices, and the boiling broth. Add the herb bouquet and heat to boiling. Reduce the heat to medium-low and simmer, covered, 10 minutes for basmati rice, 15 minutes for Texmati or other aromatic rice. Discard the herb bouquet.

7. Stir the butter and shrimp into the rice mixture. Continue to cook, covered, 5 minutes. Then season with salt and pepper.

8. Turn off the heat and tuck the reserved clams (in their shells) into the rice mixture. Let stand, covered, 5 minutes. Sprinkle with parsley before serving.

Serves 4 to 6

SAUSAGE-RICE STUFFED TOMATOES

*U*se small tomatoes when you want to serve this as a tasty starter for six. With larger tomatoes, it will make a fine light meal for four. These can be served hot, at room temperature—even cold, sprinkled with a little vinegar and olive oil.

6 small or 4 large firm, ripe tomatoes
Salt and freshly ground black pepper to taste
3 sweet Italian sausages (about ¾ pound)
1 tablespoon unsalted butter
1½ teaspoons olive oil
1 small onion, finely chopped (¼ cup)
1 clove garlic, minced
½ teaspoon sugar
½ teaspoon beef bouillon powder
2 teaspoons red wine vinegar
1 cup cooked basmati, Texmati, or other aromatic rice
2 tablespoons chopped fresh parsley
1 tablespoon chopped fresh basil
3 tablespoons pignolia (pine) nuts
¼ cup freshly grated Parmesan cheese
1 egg, lightly beaten

1. Preheat the oven to 375°F.

2. Cut the tops off the tomatoes and discard. Gently squeeze the tomatoes over a bowl; reserve the juice and pulp (use a spoon to scoop out pulp if necessary). Sprinkle the scooped-out tomatoes with salt and pepper. Drain upside down on paper towels.

3. Remove the sausage meat from the casings, and coarsely chop.

4. Heat the butter with the oil in a large heavy skillet over medium-low heat. Add the onion; cook 1 minute. Add the garlic; cook 2 minutes longer. Add the sausage meat and cook, breaking up any lumps with a wooden spoon, until the sausage loses its pink color, 4 minutes. Add the reserved tomato juice and pulp; sprinkle with the sugar and bouillon powder. Raise the heat to medium-high and cook, stirring frequently, until all liquid has evaporated, 8 minutes.

5. Sprinkle the meat mixture with the vinegar and reduce the heat. Stir in the cooked rice, the parsley, basil, pignolia nuts, half the Parmesan cheese, and the beaten egg. Mix well, and remove from the heat.

6. Spoon the mixture into the tomatoes, mounding the tops. Place in a greased shallow baking dish (the tomatoes should fit snugly), and sprinkle with the remaining Parmesan cheese. Bake 30 minutes. Serve hot, at room temperature, or cold.

Serves 4 to 6

TUNA AND WARM GINGERED RICE SALAD

I am lucky to live part of the year where the tuna is fresh and remarkably sweet, so this salad often finds its way onto my summertime menus. However, if you can't get fresh, this smoky peppery salad is equally tonic with canned tuna packed in water.

1 small clove garlic, minced
¼ teaspoon ground ginger
2 teaspoons soy sauce
Juice of 1 small lemon
¼ cup olive oil
1 cup cooked basmati, Texmati, or other
    aromatic rice, heated
2 large scallions, white bulbs and green
    tops, chopped
1 large red bell pepper, roasted, peeled,
    cored, and chopped (see Note)
1¼ cups cooked fresh or canned (drained
    water-packed) tuna, broken into
    chunks)

1. Using the back of a spoon, mash the garlic with the ginger in a small bowl until a paste is formed. Whisk in the soy sauce, lemon juice, and olive oil.

2. Combine the hot cooked rice with the scallions, roasted bell pepper, and tuna in a medium-size bowl. Pour the dressing over and toss well. Serve immediately.

Serves 4

Note: To roast a pepper, cook it over a gas flame or under a broiler until charred all over. Then carefully wrap the pepper in paper towels and place it in a plastic bag. Let it stand until cool. Remove the core and rub off the charred skin with paper towels.

CHILLY RADISH, RICE, AND SHRIMP SALAD

Aromatic rice and seafood seem such a natural together that I couldn't resist adding some cooked shrimp to my favorite rice and radish salad. Another quick brunch or light supper offering.

2 cups cooked basmati, Texmati, or other
    aromatic rice, chilled
1 shallot, minced
8 to 10 large radishes, trimmed, thinly
    sliced (about 1½ cups)
¼ cup thinly sliced imported black olives
½ pound cooked shrimp, shelled, deveined,
    and halved
1 small cucumber, peeled, seeded, and
    minced
1 tablespoon finely chopped fresh basil
1 teaspoon finely chopped fresh parsley
1 teaspoon finely slivered lemon zest
½ cup Vinaigrette Dressing (recipe follows)
Salt and freshly ground black pepper to
    taste

Combine all ingredients through the lemon zest in a large bowl. Toss lightly. Pour the vinaigrette dressing over, and toss well. Add salt and pepper to taste. Chill slightly before serving.

Serves 4 to 6

Vinaigrette Dressing

1 small clove garlic, crushed
½ teaspoon coarse (kosher) salt
1 teaspoon Dijon mustard
Juice of 1 lemon
⅓ to ½ cup olive oil
2 teaspoons red wine vinegar
¼ teaspoon freshly ground black pepper

Using the back of a spoon, mash the garlic with the salt in a small bowl until a paste is formed. Stir in the mustard and lemon juice. Whisk in the oil, vinegar, and pepper.

Makes about ½ cup

PERSIAN RICE CAKE WITH CRISPY POTATOES AND DILL

This is one of my favorite rice dishes. It is a vegetable cake of Persian derivation, and much dependent upon a flavored rice to fuse the odd ingredients (onions, potatoes, lima beans) together. If you are using basmati rice in this recipe, do not presoak it first (but do wash it), for broken kernels are not amiss here.

1 quart water
1 teaspoon salt
1 cup unsoaked basmati rice, or natural
    Texmati or other aromatic rice
8 tablespoons (1 stick) unsalted butter
1 small onion, finely chopped
½ teaspoon crushed dried hot red peppers
Pinch of ground cloves
1 package (10 ounces) frozen lima beans,
    thawed
½ cup chopped fresh dill
1 medium baking potato (½ pound)

1. Heat the water and ½ teaspoon of the salt to boiling in a medium-size saucepan. Stir in the rice. Boil 7 minutes for basmati rice, about 10 minutes for Texmati or other aromatic rice. The rice should be slightly firm at the center. Drain, and set aside.

2. Melt 4 tablespoons of the butter in a large heavy skillet over medium heat. Stir in the onion and dried red peppers. Cook, stirring constantly, until lightly golden, about 3 minutes.

3. Sprinkle the onion with the cloves, and stir in the lima beans. Reduce the heat to medium-low and cook, stirring occasionally, 4 minutes. Remove from the heat.

4. Add the cooked rice to the onion mixture, tossing with two forks until well mixed. Toss in the dill.

5. Melt 2 tablespoons of the butter over low heat in a 10-inch skillet (preferably non-stick) with a cover. Remove from the heat. Peel the potato and cut into ⅛-inch-thick slices. Lay the slices, just

Aromatic rice is said to develop its characteristic perfume from two things: the soil in which it is planted and the climate during its growing season.

Though *basmati* literally means "queen of fragrance," it is an erratic realm at best. There are fields in the state of Punjab where the rice grows jasmine-scented, while others have a heliotrope or tulip fragrance—and no one really knows why.

In Alvin, Texas, where Texmati rice is grown, the workers who run the heavy-duty planting and threshing machines call different fields by different names. The one traditionally known as "Yellow Rose" always yields the largest and most fragrant kernels. Go figure nature out!

barely overlapping, over the bottom of the skillet.

6. Place the skillet over medium heat and spoon the rice mixture over the potatoes, pressing down lightly. Dot with the remaining 2 tablespoons butter. Cook 5 minutes. Reduce the heat to medium-low, cover, and continue to cook, moving the pan occasionally so that its edges are, at some point, over the heat, 45 minutes. Let stand 4 minutes before inverting onto a serving platter.

Serves 6

LEMON RICE

This is always a hit when I teach it in cooking classes. Add hot peppers to your taste. It goes very well with spicy (though not fiery hot) stews of all sorts.

3 sprigs parsley
2 fresh sage leaves, or ¼ teaspoon dried
2 sprigs thyme, or ¼ teaspoon dried
1 cup presoaked basmati rice, or natural Texmati or other aromatic rice
2 tablespoons unsalted butter
1 teaspoon seeded, deveined, and minced hot green pepper
¼ cup strong homemade chicken stock (see Note)
Finely slivered zest of 1 lemon
Juice of 1 medium lemon
Salt and freshly ground black pepper to taste
Chopped fresh parsley, for garnish

1. Tie the parsley sprigs, sage, and thyme in a cheesecloth bag, and place in a large pot of boiling salted water. Add the rice, stir once with a wooden spoon so it does not stick to the bottom of the pot, and return to boiling. Reduce the heat slightly and simmer, uncovered, until tender, 5 minutes for basmati rice, about 12 minutes for Texmati or other aromatic rice.

2. Meanwhile, melt the butter in a medium-size saucepan over medium-low heat. Stir in the minced pepper, and cook 2 minutes.

3. Drain the rice and add it to the pepper. Toss to mix, and add the chicken stock, lemon zest, and lemon juice. Toss the rice over medium-low heat until all the excess liquid has evaporated, about 5 minutes. Add salt and pepper to taste, and sprinkle with parsley.

Serves 4 to 6

Note: If you do not have strong chicken stock on hand (see page 379), reduce ½ cup canned chicken broth to ¼ cup by simmering for 10 minutes.

CHICORY RICE

You can use any hearty green in this creamy side dish. Keep the main dish on the simple side.

1 bunch (about ½ pound) chicory (curly endive)
3 tablespoons olive oil
2 large shallots, finely chopped
1 large clove garlic, minced
1 cup presoaked basmati rice, or natural Texmati or other aromatic rice
2 teaspoons tomato paste
1½ cups strong chicken stock (see Note) for basmati, or 2 cups for other rice

Salt and freshly ground black pepper to taste
Freshly grated Pecorino or Parmesan cheese

1. Cut the root off the chicory and discard. Rinse the chicory and dry it well. Chop the stems and place in a bowl. Chop the leaves and place in a separate bowl.

2. Heat the oil in a medium-size

saucepan over medium heat. Add the shallots; cook 2 minutes. Add the garlic; cook 1 minute. Stir in the chicory stems and cook 2 minutes longer.

3. Stir the rice and tomato paste into the shallot mixture, and toss until well mixed. Add the chicken stock. Heat to boiling, and stir in the chicory leaves. Reduce the heat and cook, covered, stirring occasionally, over medium-low heat until the rice is tender, about 10 minutes for basmati, 15 minutes for Texmati or other aromatic rice. (Remove the cover and raise the heat slightly if the mixture is too wet.) Add salt and pepper to taste, and serve with cheese on the side.

Serves 4 to 6

Note: If you do not have strong chicken stock on hand (see page 379), reduce 3 cups canned chicken broth to 1½ cups by simmering for 15 minutes.

It has been claimed that the custom of pelting newlywed couples with rice is Indian in origin. And while Western anthropologists assume the practice was just a fertility rite, Indian philosophers do not wholly agree.

If it was an aromatic rice, they state with some authority, the bride would gather it up in her veil and the groom would be assured of a good wedding dinner. And then, being a contented man afterward, he would teach his wife the art of love, rather than mere baby-making!

POT OF TEA PILAF

I once read about an Indian pilaf that was made in a pot of tea. The exotic idea piqued my taste buds, and my version follows. I serve it with grilled chicken or pork.

3 tablespoons olive oil
2 medium onions, finely chopped
1 clove garlic, minced
½ teaspoon minced fresh ginger
1 piece (1 inch) cinnamon stick
½ teaspoon chili powder
¼ teaspoon ground cumin
⅛ teaspoon ground turmeric
1⅓ cups unsoaked basmati rice or natural Texmati rice
2½ cups brewed Chinese black tea
3 tablespoons unsalted butter
1 teaspoon salt
½ teaspoon freshly ground black pepper
1 cup frozen peas, thawed

1. Heat the oil in a medium-size saucepan over medium heat. Add half the onions; cook 1 minute. Add the garlic and ginger; cook 3 minutes longer. Stir in the cinnamon, chili powder, cumin, and turmeric. Reduce the heat and cook, uncovered, over medium-low heat 10 minutes.

2. Stir the rice into the onion mixture, tossing gently to coat. Add the tea and heat to boiling, stirring once. Reduce the heat and cook, covered, over medium-low heat until the rice is fairly tender and all liquid has been absorbed, about 10 minutes for basmati, 15 minutes for Texmati or other aromatic rice. Turn off the heat.

3. Meanwhile, melt the butter in a

medium-size skillet over medium heat. Stir in the remaining onion and cook, stirring constantly, until crisp and golden, about 5 minutes. Remove from the heat.

4. Discard the cinnamon stick from the rice mixture, and toss in the salt, pepper, and peas. Let stand, covered, 5 minutes. Transfer the rice mixture to a bowl and sprinkle with the sautéed onions.

Serves 6

MEDIUM-GRAIN RICE

Medium-grain rice requires no more cooking time than conventional long-grain varieties. However, as medium-grain kernels are shorter and plumper and have a higher degree of amylopectin starch, this rice is at its best (tender and moist) when eaten soon after it is prepared.

In my kitchen, medium-grain rice is a first choice for rice-stuffed vegetable dishes and meat loaves, where substance is a decided requirement. Years ago I learned that medium-grain rice makes a salubrious filling—when amended with pork, herbs, scallions, chili peppers, and Lord knows what other seasonings—for the pale but pungent Cajun sausages known as *boudin blanc*.

Medium-grain rice is also a natural for soups, since it adds an imperceptible measure of starch to thicken an anemic broth, yet the grains remain neat and separate in every bowl.

Medium-grain rice cooks in less liquid than long-grain rice—which makes sense, since the grain itself is considerably shorter.

For instructions on preparing medium-grain *brown* rice, see the chart on page 218 or follow the instructions for preparing long-grain brown rice on page 233. You may use it in the Insalata di Riso on page 257 or in any of the recipes in the brown rice section that call for precooked rice.

BASIC COOKED MEDIUM-GRAIN RICE

1 cup medium-grain white rice
1½ cups liquid (water, broth, consommé, vegetable juice)
½ teaspoon salt
1 tablespoon unsalted butter

1. Combine the rice, liquid, salt, and butter in a medium-size saucepan and heat to boiling. Stir once or twice, reduce the heat, cover, and simmer 15 minutes.

2. If the rice is not tender or the liquid is not entirely absorbed, replace the lid and cook 2 to 4 minutes longer. Fluff with a fork before serving.

Makes about 3 cups

GREEK LEMON SOUP

*T*here is a curious story that takes some of the polish off medium-grain rice. According to some food historians, Theophrastus, Alexander the Great's advisor and confidant, knew about rice being grown in the Orient—but he never made any attempt to have rice plants brought to the Mediterranean because his informants claimed it was a grain that was too white and far too sticky for Greek tastes!

Tempus fugit a few centuries, and the Greeks invented one of the great contributions to gastronomy: *sopa avgolemono*, which translates to "lemon soup" and is much dependent upon medium-grain rice for body.

This soup, I might add, has a double life in my household. In winter it is a hearty brew as limned, but in summer I make it a day ahead and chill it. Skipping the amenity of whipped cream and Parmesan cheese, I merely garnish the bowl with peeled paper-thin lemon slices and a sprinkling of minced chives.

⅓ cup medium-grain white rice
3 cups homemade chicken stock (see page 376) or canned broth
3 cups lamb stock
½ cup heavy or whipping cream
2 tablespoons grated lemon zest
1 tablespoon freshly grated Parmesan cheese
2 egg yolks
Juice of 1 large lemon

1. Wash the rice in a colander under cold running water to remove excess starch. Drain.

2. Combine the chicken and lamb stocks in a medium-size saucepan, and heat to boiling. Stir in the rice and reduce the heat. Cook, uncovered, over medium heat until the rice is tender, 15 to 20 minutes. Remove from the heat.

3. Meanwhile, whip the cream with the lemon zest and Parmesan cheese until stiff. Transfer to a serving bowl and keep in a cool place.

4. When the rice is tender, beat the egg yolks with the lemon juice in a medium-size bowl until light. Slowly beat in 1 cup broth, then slowly stir the egg mixture into the rice and broth mixture. Continue to stir for 1 minute. Serve immediately with the flavored whipped cream.

Serves 6

MARY SURINA'S SARMA

*I*n Slavic households, where rice is a prerequisite in most larders, it was a tradition for a firstborn son's cradle to be adorned with a small pillow filled with raw rice. If the child did not cry at the pillow's hardness, the family rejoiced because they knew the boy would grow to manhood able to survive any adversity. And to celebrate they always made a dish of cabbage stuffed with meat and rice.

If he cried, they ate the same dish—but worried a lot more!

This Yugoslavian dish is a donation from one of the best cooks of my acquaintance, Mary Surina of San Pedro, California. Mary's Sarma comes with a requirement: these stuffed cabbage rolls must be prepared and refrigerated at least a day before they are to be cooked. And it's a good idea to let them come to room temperature before cooking. Some treats, like vintage wines, simply must age before they're served!

1 loose-leafed cabbage (about 1½ pounds)
1¼ pounds ground lean pork
3 sweet Italian sausages (about ¾ pound)
4 cloves garlic, crushed
1 egg, lightly beaten
⅓ cup medium-grain white rice
½ teaspoon salt
¼ teaspoon freshly ground black pepper
2 strips bacon, chopped
1 medium onion, finely chopped
*3 pounds sauerkraut, drained but not
    rinsed*
1 small ham bone (about ½ pound)
*1¾ cups homemade chicken stock (see page
    376) or canned broth*
1 cup water

1. Place the cabbage in a large pot of boiling water. With a wooden fork and spoon, pull the leaves apart as it cooks. Cook until the leaves are wilted but not mushy, about 2 minutes (depending on the looseness of the cabbage). Drain. Trim the large ribs of the cabbage so the shape is even, and shave off the thick part with a sharp knife so the thickness is the same as the leaf. You should have 12 large leaves. Shred the remaining cabbage.

2. Place the pork in a large bowl. Remove the sausage meat from the casings and add it to the pork along with the garlic, egg, rice, salt, and pepper. Mix well.

3. Place about 2 tablespoons meat filling on one side of each cabbage leaf and roll up, tucking in the sides.

4. Render the bacon in a large pot over medium-low heat until soft. Add the onion; cook until golden, about 4 minutes. Stir in the shredded cabbage, and cook 1 minute longer. Remove from the heat.

5. Place a layer of sauerkraut over the cabbage mixture, and place the ham bone in the center of the pot. Arrange a layer of cabbage rolls around the bone, and top with sauerkraut. Continue to layer, ending with sauerkraut. Pour the stock and water over the top. Refrigerate, covered, overnight.

6. Allow the dish to come to room temperature. Place the pot, covered, over medium heat and heat to boiling. Reduce the heat and simmer, covered, 1 hour.

Serves 6

GREENHORN RICE

*B*ecause of its high amylopectin content, medium-grain rice is recommended for ulcer patients and those suffering with like stomach disorders. One painless way to consume this rice is the following dish.

Known as Greenhorn Rice, it may seem slightly familiar; I offered it in an earlier recipe collection called *Honest American Fare*. It is retrieved here because it is one of the most frequently requested rice recipes I have ever logged.

3 tablespoons unsalted butter
1 tablespoon olive oil
1 medium onion, finely chopped
3 shallots, finely chopped
1 clove garlic, minced
1 cup medium-grain white rice
¾ cup homemade chicken stock (see page
376) or canned broth
½ teaspoon salt
¼ teaspoon freshly ground black pepper
¼ teaspoon freshly grated nutmeg
3 sprigs thyme, chopped, or
⅛ teaspoon dried
1 pound fresh spinach, trimmed, rinsed,
and finely chopped
½ cup heavy or whipping cream

1. Preheat the oven to 375°F.

2. Heat the butter with the oil in a Dutch oven over medium-low heat. Add the onion; cook 2 minutes. Stir in the shallots, garlic, and rice. Cook, stirring constantly, until the rice turns milky in color, about 4 minutes. Add the chicken stock, salt, pepper, nutmeg, thyme, and spinach. Stir over medium-high heat until boiling.

3. Cover the pot, transfer it to the oven, and bake until the rice is tender and all liquid has been absorbed, about 15 minutes. Remove the pot from the oven and toss in the cream. Return it, covered, to the oven for another 5 minutes.

Serves 4

BOUDIN BLANC SAUSAGES

Medium-grain rice, which is grown in Louisiana, is a solid staple of Cajun cuisine.

Now you will find Cajun dishes on lots of menus across the country, and Cajun ingredients in loads of gourmet shops, but I promise you will never find this dish anywhere beyond Vermilion Bay and Catahoula Lake. Because it simply won't travel! I am speaking of *boudin blanc*, the peppery local sausages that gastronomes have been known to kill for.

Unlike many of my cooking confederates, I am not addicted to sausage making. It's too messy and too maverick an operation. However, if one were going that route once in a lifetime I would advice *boudin blanc*...

2 pounds boneless pork shoulder with fat,
cut into 1½-inch cubes
2 large onions, chopped (about 2¼ cups)
4 scallions, white bulbs and green tops,
chopped
8 peppercorns
3 whole cloves
3 teaspoons salt
1 bay leaf
2 green bell peppers, cored, seeded, and
chopped
1 hot green pepper, seeded, deveined, and
chopped
1 dried hot red pepper, crushed
2 cloves garlic, finely chopped
1 cup chopped fresh parsley
1 teaspoon chopped fresh basil, or
½ teaspoon dried
2½ cups cooked medium-grain white rice
1 teaspoon ground allspice
1 teaspoon cayenne pepper
½ teaspoon freshly ground black pepper
¼ teaspoon ground mace
4 to 6 sausage casings, 2 inches wide and
12 inches long (available from Italian
or German butchers)

1. Place the pork in a large pot, cover with cold water, and heat to boiling. Drain, and rinse under cold running water. Wipe out the pot and return the pork. Add 1 cup of the chopped onion, one fourth of the chopped scallions, the peppercorns, cloves, 1 teaspoon of the salt, and the bay leaf. Cover with 2 inches of water, and heat to boiling. Reduce the heat and simmer, partially covered, until the pork is tender, about 1½ hours. Drain, and discard the bay leaf, peppercorns, and cloves.

2. Transfer the pork to a large bowl and add the remaining onions and scallions, the green peppers, dried pepper, garlic, parsley, and basil. Mix well. Grind the mixture in a meat grinder, or process in a food processor until fairly smooth. Return it to the bowl and add the rice, allspice, cayenne pepper, black pepper, remaining 2 teaspoons salt, and the mace. Mix well.

3. Rinse the sausage casings in cold water. Hold each casing under the faucet and let the water run through to check for leaks. Tie one end of each casing. Stuff the pork mixture into the casings with the sausage-stuffing attachment of a meat grinder, or using a pastry bag fitted with a ½-inch plain tube. Tie the open ends of the sausages.

4. Cook the sausages in boiling water to cover for 3 minutes. Drain. Cool, wrap in plastic wrap, and refrigerate for 24 hours before serving. (Sausages will keep, tightly wrapped, in the refrigerator for 5 to 6 days.)

5. To serve, either poach the sausages in simmering water for 20 minutes, or prick with a fork and sauté in butter until golden brown on all sides.

Serves 6 to 8

INSALATA DI RISO

An estimable dish from Bari, Italy, located practically in the Adriatic Sea.

1½ cups cooked medium-grain white or brown rice
2 small scallions, white bulbs and green tops, finely chopped
2 fresh shiitake mushroom caps, halved and thinly sliced
5 canned artichoke hearts, sliced
2 ounces Fontina cheese, cut into 1-inch-long julienne strips
1 clove garlic, minced
¼ teaspoon coarse (kosher) salt
¼ cup olive oil
3 tablespoons fresh lemon juice
⅛ teaspoon anchovy paste
Salt and freshly ground black pepper to taste
1 teaspoon chopped fresh chervil, or
¼ teaspoon dried mixed with 1 teaspoon chopped fresh parsley
4 large lettuce leaves

1. Place the rice in a large bowl and gently toss in the scallions, mushrooms, artichokes, and cheese.

2. Using the back of a spoon, mash the garlic with the salt in a small bowl until a paste is formed. Whisk in the oil, lemon juice, and anchovy paste.

3. Pour the dressing over the salad and toss gently to mix. Add salt and pepper, and sprinkle with the chervil. Serve on lettuce leaves.

Serves 4

FUNGO DOLCE (HAZELNUT AND RICE MACAROONS)

From the Piedmont section of Italy, the addition of toasted rice turns this dry hazelnut macaroon into a chewy coconut candy-like bar.

⅔ cup hazelnuts
¾ cup cooked medium-grain white rice
4 egg whites, at room temperature
Pinch of salt
1¼ cups sugar

1. Preheat the oven to 400°F.
2. Spread the hazelnuts out on a baking sheet, and bake 5 minutes. Carefully wrap the nuts in paper towels and place in a plastic bag. Let stand until cool enough to handle. Reduce oven heat to 350°F.
3. Spread the rice out on a baking sheet, and bake, stirring once, 5 minutes. The rice will be slightly crisp. Set aside to cool.
4. Rub the hazelnuts in paper towels to remove the skins. Finely chop half the nuts. Coarsely chop the remaining nuts.
5. Beat the egg whites with the salt in the large bowl of an electric mixer until soft peaks form. Slowly add the sugar on high speed, and continue to beat until thick and shiny. Fold in the nuts and rice.

6. Transfer the mixture to a large heavy saucepan. Cook, stirring constantly, over medium-low heat until the mixture becomes less glossy and thickens, about 15 minutes. (Humidity will determine actual time.) The mixture is ready when it resembles the stage at which fudge is ready to be poured into a pan. Do not overcook, because like fudge, it hardens quickly. (If dough becomes too stiff, add an extra egg white and quickly beat back to semi-soft consistency.) Let cool slightly.
7. Using your fingers and a tablespoon, form the mixture into balls and place them on parchment-lined baking sheets. Bake until crisp and lightly browned, about 10 minutes. Cool slightly before peeling the paper from the macaroons. Cool completely before storing in an airtight container.

Makes about 20 macaroons

SHORT-GRAIN RICE

The first thing to explain about short-grain rice is its maddening diversity. There are three different types on the market: *round* or *pearl* short-grain rice, Italian *arborio* short-grain rice, and Oriental *glutinous* short-grain rice.

Round rice is so called because each grain is almost as wide as it is long. Since this variety is also heavy with amylopectin starch, the cooked kernels have con-

siderable cling. (The shorter the grain, the stickier the stuff in your bowl!) Japanese and Caribbean cooks prefer round rice because of this massing quality.

Arborio short-grain rice is grown only in northern Italy. Though it is high in starch as well, arborio rice has the ability to absorb its cooking liquid to an unusual degree. Developing a creamy consistency that Italians call *all'onda* (waviness), each kernel manages to stay afloat and firm in a virtual sea of flavor.

Oriental glutinous short-grain rice, sometimes known as "sweet rice," can be found only in Asian markets. It is used in China to stuff chicken or duck, and in both China and Japan it is pounded into a sticky dough that is the basis of incredibly sweet pastries and a savory rice soup-stew known as *congee*, with which many Asians start their day.

I must confess I do not cook round or glutinous short-grain rice, but I have good friends who do. The following recipe is borrowed from Elizabeth Andoh, author of the brilliant *An Ocean of Flavor: The Japanese Way with Fish and Seafood.*

(For instructions on preparing short-grain brown rice, see the chart on page 233, or follow the instructions for long-grain brown rice on page 233. For cooking brown glutinous rice, see the instructions for Basic Cooked Brown Rice, page 234.)

BASIC COOKED SHORT-GRAIN RICE

1½ cups round or glutinous short-grain rice
1¾ cups cold water (see Note)

1. Place the rice in a bowl and cover with cold water. Stir vigorously until the water turns cloudy, then drain. Repeat several times, until the water remains clear. Drain. (The rice will be somewhat opaque and will have started to absorb water.)

2. Place the rice with 1¾ cups cold water in a medium-size saucepan with a tight-fitting lid. Let stand 10 minutes.

3. Place the saucepan over medium-high heat and heat to boiling, 3 to 5 minutes. Do not remove the lid. When the water reaches the boiling point and steam begins to escape from under the lid, reduce the heat and continue to cook without removing the lid until all water has been absorbed, about 5 minutes longer. (The pan will start to sizzle when all the water is absorbed.) Then raise the heat to high and cook 30 seconds longer, to dry the rice, and remove from the heat. Let stand, covered, 10 minutes.

Makes about 3 cups

Note: According to Elizabeth Andoh, newly harvested rice is the most sought after (and the most expensive) in Japan. The same holds true for California short-grain rice, which is harvested in late October and early November. If you can locate *shin mai* (new rice), use equal quantities of rice and water in the saucepan: 1½ cups water to 1½ cups rice. As rice ages, more water is required.

CLASSIC RISOTTO WITH RED WINE

A great risotto is dependent upon four things: the correct short-grain rice to begin with, combined with sweet butter and/or olive oil and minced onion, some tonic seasonings, and finally a hot strong broth that is slowly stirred, and stirred, into the dish.

I usually serve risotto as a first course or luncheon dish with salad after. As it is rich, I find that 1 cup of uncooked arborio rice makes enough for four diners. If risotto is to be a main course, double the recipe!

This risotto with red wine and beef broth is a classic rendering. Serve it with additional Parmesan cheese at the table.

3½ tablespoons unsalted butter
1 small onion, finely chopped
1 small clove garlic, minced
1 medium carrot, peeled and chopped
Salt and freshly ground black pepper to
    taste
¼ cup red wine
1 cup Italian arborio rice
2½ to 3 cups homemade beef stock (see
    page 377) or canned broth, simmering
3 tablespoons chopped fresh parsley
Freshly grated Parmesan cheese

1. Melt 2½ tablespoons of the butter in a heavy skillet over medium-low heat. Add the onion; cook 1 minute. Add the garlic and carrot; cook 2 minutes longer. Sprinkle with salt and pepper to taste, and add the wine. Raise the heat slightly and cook, stirring constantly, until almost all the liquid has evaporated, 4 minutes.

2. Stir the rice into the onion/carrot mixture until well coated. Add 1 cup of the simmering beef stock and cook, stirring frequently, until almost all liquid has been absorbed. This should take 10 minutes. Reduce the heat if it is cooking too fast.

3. Add another cup of stock and continue to cook, stirring frequently, until almost all liquid has been absorbed, about 10 minutes.

4. Add ½ cup stock to the rice and continue to cook, stirring frequently, until the rice is tender, 5 to 10 minutes longer. Add more stock if needed. Stir in the remaining butter, sprinkle with parsley, and pass the cheese on the side.

Serves 4

LOBSTER NEWBURG RISOTTO

For years, Lobster Newburg was the top of culinary fashion. A dish that has almost been forgotten will have a fine comeback when it is turned into a creamy rich risotto. Serve this one as a first course to a simple meal.

1 live lobster, 1 to 1¼ pounds
2½ tablespoons unsalted butter
2 shallots, minced
¼ teaspoon tomato paste
2 tablespoons Madeira wine
1 cup Italian arborio rice
1 cup clam broth, simmering
2 to 2½ cups homemade chicken stock (see
    page 376) or canned broth, simmering
⅓ cup heavy or whipping cream
1 teaspoon chopped fresh chives

1. Cook the lobster in boiling water to cover until firm, 5 to 7 minutes. Drain, and set aside to cool.

2. Crack the lobster shell with a nutcracker and remove the meat from the tail and claws. Coarsely chop. You should have about 1 cup. (If there is roe, reserve it, if desired.)

3. Melt the butter in a heavy enameled skillet over medium-low heat. Add the shallots; cook until soft, about 4 minutes. (Add a small amount of roe, if desired.) Stir in ⅓ cup of the lobster meat, the tomato paste, and the Madeira. Add the rice. Stir until it is well coated with the mixture. Then add the simmering clam broth and cook, stirring frequently, until almost all the liquid has been absorbed. This should take 10 minutes. Reduce the heat if it is cooking too fast.

4. Add 1 cup of the simmering chicken stock and continue to cook, stirring frequently, until almost all liquid has been absorbed, about 10 minutes.

5. Add another cup of chicken stock and the remaining lobster. Continue to cook, stirring frequently, until the rice is tender, about 10 minutes longer. Add more chicken stock, if needed.

6. Meanwhile, beat the cream until stiff and fold in the chives. Transfer to a serving bowl and stir into the risotto at the table before serving.

Serves 4

RADICCHIO RISOTTO

Do not be dismayed when the radicchio loses its lustrous red color—it is used to enhance the flavor of this creamy dish. A generous sprinkling of parsley helps make it more eye-appealing.

3½ tablespoons unsalted butter
2 large shallots, minced
¼ pound radicchio (Italian red lettuce), or
    any strong-flavored lettuce, cored and
    chopped
Salt and freshly ground black pepper to
    taste
¼ cup dry white wine
1 cup Italian arborio rice
2½ to 3 cups homemade chicken stock (see
    page 376) or canned broth, simmering
½ cup freshly grated Parmesan cheese
3 tablespoons chopped fresh parsley

1. Melt 2½ tablespoons of the butter in a heavy skillet over medium-low heat. Add the shallots; cook until golden, about 5 minutes. Add the radicchio and sprinkle with salt and pepper; cook 1 minute. Stir in the wine. Raise the heat slightly and cook, stirring constantly, until almost all the liquid has evaporated, 4 minutes.

2. Stir the rice into the radicchio mixture until well coated. Add 1 cup of the simmering chicken stock and cook, stirring frequently, until almost all liquid has been absorbed. This should take 10 minutes. Reduce the heat if it is cooking too fast.

3. Add another cup of stock and continue to cook, stirring frequently, until almost all liquid has been absorbed, about 10 minutes.

4. Add ½ cup stock to the rice and continue to cook, stirring frequently, until the rice is tender, 5 to 10 minutes longer. Add more stock, if needed. Stir in the remaining butter and the cheese and toss in the parsley.

Serves 4

My sister, Myra, made her first trip to Europe armed with enthusiasm and not much money. During the first months of her stay, she toured England, France, and Belgium, managing to ferret out friends of friends, odd relatives, and sometimes utter strangers who not only invited her to dine but often kept her as a house guest for weeks on end.

When she arrived in Rome, a letter announced that this city would probably be her last stop unless she could "wangle a green card," an unlikely prospect in light of Italy's unemployment.

"I don't know a soul here," she wrote with some finality. "But I'd sure like to. Roman men are *very* sexy!"

She stayed there a year, returning home with a Roman coiffure, Roman slang in her speech, Roman lira in her purse, and an impressive bracelet of aquamarines and sapphires on her wrist.

My sister never outgrew her love of things Italian. She brought back the first espresso maker I'd ever seen and a case of Campari, which like a true Roman she sipped every afternoon. For me she produced a small bag filled with arborio rice.

As I had not the slightest clue what this rice was nor how to cook it, my sister undertook the assignment with a prodigal's good grace, insisting that the flame on her gas stove be lowered to the precise degree of blue brevity before she began.

"This dish," she announced gravely, "is called *ri-sotto*, and it is like no other rice you have ever tasted in your life."

Myra was not the greatest cook in the world, but the flavor of her homey risotto (creamy without a drop of cream) altered my taste buds irrevocably. I have eaten many other risottos since, in great hostelries and little trattorias in Milan, Venice, and Rome, but none has ever tasted better. The first forkful cooked up in a tiny apartment in Greenwich Village back in the 1950s remains as green in my memory as my sister herself. And that's saying a lot.

SMOKY SMITHFIELD HAM RISOTTO

Smithfield ham, smoked and cured, is the traditional ham of Virginia. However, it lends itself here as if it were any fine Italian smoked ham.

3½ tablespoons unsalted butter
2 large shallots, minced
¼ pound mushrooms, thinly sliced
½ cup Smithfield ham, slivered
Freshly ground black pepper to taste
¼ cup dry white wine
1 cup Italian arborio rice
2½ to 3 cups homemade chicken stock (see
    page 376) or canned broth, simmering
Freshly grated Parmesan cheese

1. Melt 2½ tablespoons of the butter in a heavy skillet over medium-low heat. Add the shallots; cook 1 minute. Stir in the mushrooms and ham. Sprinkle with pepper and wine. Raise the heat slightly and cook, stirring constantly, until almost all the liquid has evaporated, 4 minutes.

2. Stir the rice into the shallot/ham mixture until well coated. Add 1 cup of the simmering chicken stock and cook, stirring frequently, until almost all the liquid has been absorbed. This should take 10 minutes. Reduce the heat if it is cooking too fast.

3. Add another cup of stock and continue to cook, stirring frequently, until almost all liquid has been absorbed, about 10 minutes.

4. Add ½ cup stock to the rice and continue to cook, stirring frequently, until the rice is tender, 5 to 10 minutes longer. Add more stock, if needed. Stir in the remaining butter and pass the cheese on the side.

Serves 4

RISOTTO WITH GOAT CHEESE

This is a creamy side dish that is enhanced by paper-thin rounds of zucchini tossed in at the last minute. The zucchini will soften slightly in the hot rice, but should not be cooked. It offers a counterbalance to the smooth-textured rice.

2½ tablespoons unsalted butter
2 large shallots, minced
¼ cup dry white wine
1 cup Italian arborio rice
2½ to 3 cups homemade chicken stock (see
    page 376) or canned broth, simmering
¼ pound goat cheese, cut into chunks
1 small zucchini (about 3 ounces), cut into
    thin rounds
Salt and freshly ground black pepper to
    taste

1. Melt the butter in a heavy skillet over medium-low heat. Add the shallots; cook 1 minute. Sprinkle with the wine. Raise the heat slightly and cook, stirring constantly, until almost all the liquid has evaporated, 4 minutes.

2. Stir the rice into the shallot mixture until well coated. Add 1 cup of the simmering chicken stock and cook, stirring frequently, until almost all liquid has been absorbed. This should take 10

Do not allow yourself to be persuaded to use any short-grain rice (American or otherwise) that is not clearly labeled "Arborio Superfino." "Superfino" is the indication that the rice you are using is a *large* short-grained variety.

For shopping sources and mail order information, check the resource pages in the back of the book.

minutes. Reduce the heat if it is cooking too fast.

3. Add another cup of stock and continue to cook, stirring frequently, until almost all liquid has been absorbed, about 10 minutes.

4. Add ½ cup stock to the rice and continue to cook, stirring frequently, until the rice is tender, 5 to 10 minutes longer. Add more stock, if needed. Stir in the goat cheese until melted. Toss in the zucchini, and season with salt and pepper.

Serves 4

RISOTTO WITH BACON AND STRING BEANS

This hearty side dish is as wonderful with grilled chicken as it is with roast pork. As the rice cooks, the beans will soften and become an integral part of the dish's flavor.

2 strips bacon, chopped
1 medium white onion, chopped
¼ cup dry white wine
1 cup Italian arborio rice
½ cup finely chopped string beans
2½ to 3 cups homemade chicken stock (see
    page 376) or canned broth, simmering
⅓ cup freshly grated dry Monterey Jack,
    Pecorino, or Parmesan cheese
1 tablespoon unsalted butter
Chopped fresh parsley, for garnish

1. Sauté the bacon in a heavy skillet over medium-low heat until all grease is rendered. Stir in the onion; cook 2 minutes. Sprinkle with the wine. Raise the heat slightly and cook, stirring constantly, until almost all the liquid has evaporated, 4 minutes.

2. Stir the rice and string beans into the bacon/onion mixture until well coated. Add 1 cup of the simmering chicken stock and cook, stirring frequently, until almost all liquid has been absorbed. This should take 10 minutes. Reduce the heat if it is cooking too fast.

3. Add another cup of stock and continue to cook, stirring frequently, until almost all liquid has been absorbed, about 10 minutes.

4. Add ½ cup more stock to the rice and continue to cook, stirring frequently, until the rice is tender, 5 to 10 minutes longer. Add more stock, if needed. Stir in the cheese and the butter. Sprinkle with parsley.

Serves 4

SEMOLINA
The Quick-Cooking Grain with Endless Possibilities

The cord that binds me to semolina, a very Italian grain, is a silver one—linked to a very American lady, my mother.

Paula Greene was a woman always itching for enterprise. A born visionary, her rise in the world of finance was marred by a flaw fatal: she lacked courage in her convictions.

During the pivotal years of the Depression, I recall my mother scanning the financial sections of the newspapers for hours. Separating columns of gray type headed "Business Opportunities" from "Help Wanted" or "Real Estate," she would pore over each advertisement scrupulously, intent on finding some offering that would propel our family of slender means into solid gold affluence.

In time she found what was deemed an optimum venture. It was a peanut farm. "Peanuts grow like weeds, but on bushes. You don't have to bend to pick 'em," her sales pitch went (for my father had an untrustworthy vertebra). "And it's a steal besides..."

My mother's enthusiasm seemed well founded. Her discovery was a 250-acre spread, not far from Atlanta, that yielded 500 tons of peanuts per harvest. Besides the groves, there was a house, two barns, and innumerable outbuildings on the property.

"It's a steal," my mother announced jubilantly after an initial phone call. "And we can get it for at least a third less if we pay in cash!" She had a nose for horse trading too.

We didn't have any cash, but that seemed a minor impediment and had no effect on my mother's enthusiasm. Borrowing a book on George Washington Carver from the library, she immediately began calculating how to diversify such a remarkable output of goobers. However, neither my father nor her's (whose financial assistance was needed to float a loan) shared her zeal for peanut farming.

"Who eats peanuts?" my grandfather inquired with hard-edged sarcasm. "A few guys at a ball game maybe?"

"Pa!" My mother hated doomsayers. "Just think about peanut butter. Or Mr. Goodbars and peanut clusters. Think about peanut oil and Smithfield ham..."

"I'm thinking, I'm thinking," he replied with a flick of cigarette ash. "And the conclusion is: I'm against it."

"But why, Pa?" his daughter wailed.

"Because, Paulie, I never heard of a successful Jewish farmer." My grandfather spoke in the tones of an oracle. "But I certainly heard of the Ku Klux Klan!"

My mother believed in the promise of peanuts all her days, but she did not press the dream for herself because she could not override an adverse opinion.

There were other aborted opportunities. Once she conceived of a shop that would sell only greeting cards, and even made a down payment on a lease. But she backed out because some clouded-crystal-ball-gazers warned she'd go bankrupt the day after Christmas. Another brainstorm was a health farm—a place in the country where overeaters would pay to diet in rustic seclusion, and where meals would be no more substantial than lettuce leaves and vegetable juice. Pessimists convinced her no one would diet in a group. So she relinquished that iron in the fire too. Giving in, she claimed it was "the hard luck of the Greenes not to have staunch supporters." A family motto I resolutely refused to inherit.

When I opened The Store in Amagansett on borrowed capital, my mother was at first skeptical, then frankly astounded at the degree of attention and praise paid to my skills at the stove.

"I'm not worrying about your future any more," she announced. But in truth she never completely stopped.

When she was seventy, my mother went to Europe for the first time. For three months the only word of her journey was postcards scrawled with descriptions of dishes she ate—to inspire similar versions at my hands.

When she returned, I met her at the airport. With no sign of jet lag, she collared me the very moment she passed through Customs.

"Have I got a great idea..." she began, lowering her voice when she became aware others were listening. "Remember how we almost got rich peanut farming? Well"—my mother winked—"this guy I met in Rome told me an even *better* way to make a killing. A wheat farm in Italy. I know one we could have for a *song!*"

"Mother." I tried hard not to sound reproving. "Wheat grows all over. Why Italy?"

"Why not?" demanded my parent. "Listen, I'm not talking any wheat. I'm talking *semi-lena,* the stuff they use to make macaroni. Think how much macaroni the world eats; multiply that a thousand times and you'll see we're talking big bucks. In Italy they bake *semi-lena;* they fry it; they eat it as cereal; they even put it into soup. I ate *semi-lena* from one end of the boot to the other and I'm telling you the stuff has a future!"

"Sounds good," I began weakly. "But why *buy* a farm?"

My mother could not believe her ears. "To get in on the ground floor!" she fairly shouted. Then, realizing I was no longer her child, she tried to mollify me instead. "With your abilities and my sharp pencil, we could make millions!"

Knowing her son's ambivalence, my mother did not pursue the matter further. But as we gathered her luggage she could not resist a final parry. "You'll have to agree it's something to think about anyway."

"I'll think about it."

"And try *semi-lena.*" My mother gave a little yelp. "I almost forgot, I brought you some." Opening her topcoat, she pointed to a plastic sack of grain, carefully safety-pinned to the lining.

"Mother! You didn't smuggle that in?"

"Nah!" She replied with just a shade too wide-eyed innocence. "I just didn't bother to declare it."

Seating herself in my car, she handed me the package.

"Just remember the peanut farm," my mother said, "and you'll thank me for this someday."

I did not buy a wheat farm in Italy. But I thank her for semolina more times than I can ever calculate, nonetheless.

The Grain's Genesis

*I*f I had listened to my mother, I would have learned that semolina is no grain at all but the roughly milled endosperm (or nutritive tissue) of durum wheat. And that this wheat *(Triticum durum)* is the hardest in the world. It is used almost exclusively in the manufacture of commercially dried pasta.

"Almost" is the key word, for the semolina that does not end up as a twirl of spaghetti will most probably find itself converted into a pile of golden couscous in some North African household.

Hard durum wheat has a long and checkered past. Some botanists claim that it was the first upwardly mobile grain. Man ate it, they aver, because it was a wild plant that grew in every path he chose to take. Hard wheat is probably an offshoot of *einkorn,* an early spring grain that bore a single kernel per stem, and *emmer,* a wild and wooly weed impervious to weather changes. Whatever its forebears, *Triticum durum* certainly proliferated fast, even blooming in northern climes where little else survived.

Wishful thinkers suggest that durum is a miracle grain, for it spread from the North to the East and West, literally in man's footsteps.

There are those who maintain that semolina is actually the "kussemet" mentioned in the Bible. They say that when the children of Israel are instructed in Ezekiel to "take thou also unto thee golden wheat, barley and beans... put them into a vessel and make thee bread thereof," the wheat was plainly hard durum, just as the bread was unleavened. It cannot have been a pleasure to eat, but then the Bible also states "A tooth for a tooth" somewhere else along the line.

Cultivation of hard durum wheat— and its conversion to semolina, which changed the ancient world's diet—took

place in the ninth millennium B.C., when the grain's popularity spread from Asia Minor to North Africa, the French Pyrenees, and the Swiss Lake settlements.

In the Swiss Lake settlements, residues of meal and bread dough made with what appears to be milled semolina flour have recently been unearthed by food-snooping archeologists.

If my mother had been there to witness the event, I can imagine her reaction: "Didn't I tell you this stuff had a future? Well, it had a past too!"

Some Plain Grain Talk

Right off the bat, let's get one thing straight: semolina is not just another pretty grain in the kitchen! The milled "innards" of hard durum wheat does have three distinct faces, however.

Durum semolina is the most commonly known. It is used for the manufacture of commercially dried pasta (known as *pasta secca* in Italy) and commercially produced couscous. This semolina is a sandy substance, pale yellow in color and highly granular if you rub it between your fingers. It contains an extraordinarily high percentage of gluten, which is what makes a spaghetti strand stretch, not break apart in the cooking process.

Durum semolina's gluten content is responsible for its high protein level as well. An average serving of cooked semolina contains 10 to 12 grams of protein, 42 grams of carbohydrate, and 1 gram of dietary fiber—with less than 1 percent fat and no cholesterol whatsoever. Which is reason enough to include some in your daily diet allowance.

Actually, semolina's only drawback is calories. Figure 210 calories per cupful. But that's not really bad, considering the grain's gratification level.

Granular semolina is simply a lower-graded milling of the wheat, with the crushed endosperm thinned out with flour. By law, durum semolina is re-

stricted to no more than 3 percent flour in its composition. Granular semolina is permitted to contain anywhere from 3 to 10 percent flour as an additive. But not to worry—in the U.S. granular semolina is sold only to commercial pasta makers.

Semolina flour is not to be confused with durum flour. The latter is a powdery residue left over after the processing of semolina. Semolina flour is a superfine grind of flour produced for cooking and baking only. Semolina flour has a high ash content and a delicate pale gold color. It is also sometimes mysteriously labeled "Extra Fancy Semolina Patent Flour," which is the guarantee of high-quality milling that the Department of Agriculture insists upon in all imported semolina packaging.

Durum semolina and semolina flour are interchangeable in all of the recipes that follow.

How to Buy It

Semolina, I regret to say, is not an easy product to come by in America. Supermarkets do not regularly stock it on their shelves, and even specialty "fancy food" shops and gourmet groceries have a tendency to dismiss this grain as "exotica" and keep it in short supply. Those who live in urban areas with varied ethnic populations have a better chance of finding semolina. Italian markets and delicatessens usually carry it in packaged form, and Middle Eastern groceries often sell it boxed or in bulk, labeled *couscous*. Natural foods stores sometimes sell semolina in bulk as well. Make sure the stuff you purchase is fresh, however. Stale semolina has a tell-tale smell, like over-the-hill oil, and has lost much of its store of vitamins and essential amino acids.

While others may suggest substituting commercial Farina or Cream of Wheat for semolina in a recipe, I resolutely do not! For mail-order sources, check the listing at the back of the book.

How to Store It

Semolina absorbs odors, so it is wise to store it in an airtight glass container rather than a plastic bag.

Hard durum semolina and semolina flour both have considerable staying power and are capable of a long shelf life (up to half a year) in a cool, dry place. When the grain is past its prime, it takes on a washed-out sickly color and a decidedly rancid smell.

Some cooks store semolina in the freezer, where it will keep indefinitely if well insulated. The maximum duration in the refrigerator would be nine to twelve months, but check for moisture from time to time.

Bring semolina to room temperature after a stint in the cooler. It may have absorbed moisture—even in a glass container—and should be kept open for an hour or so before it is used.

How to Cook It

A good Italian cook of my acquaintance calls semolina *il ingrediente perfetto,* "the perfect ingredient." It's a kitchen trust not misplaced—semolina is a quick-cooking grain of endless possibilities.

How much do I love thee, semolina? Let me count the culinary ways! In small amounts, semolina will thicken a soup, give body to a stew, or enrich a watery sauce. Boiled briefly with the liquid of your choice and amended with butter and cheese or herbs, semolina becomes a side dish that is a heck of a lot less caloric than instant mashed potatoes and a lot less trouble than instant rice! And leftover cooked semolina may be sliced, breaded, and fried (like polenta) for lunch the next day.

Then there is couscous. A diner of good appetite could dwell on the infinite possibilities of that North African-inspired dish for meals on end. And semolina is the basis of all couscous, whether it is sold over the counter or made from scratch. (See page 285 for more on couscous.)

Malleable semolina is dense enough to be the base of a soufflé and delicate enough to stand in for cornstarch or conventional flour in a pie crust, pudding, or cake. Ingredients come and go, but this one (as my mother said) is really a steal!

The Latin word for what we call semolina was *semideus*—literally "demi-god," though some semolina lovers insist that "food of the gods" is what the Romans really had in mind.

LATTUGA ZUPPA
(Italian Lettuce Soup)

A chicken soup of Italian extraction, one that all farmers' daughters learn to make, this dish is made of strong broth, thickened with semolina and dappled with chopped green garden lettuce—and that's all!

1 chicken, 3½ to 4 pounds, well rinsed
1 large onion, unpeeled, quartered
1 large clove garlic, lightly crushed
2 whole cloves
10 peppercorns
2 medium carrots, peeled and chopped
2 medium ribs celery, chopped
1 medium white turnip, peeled and
    chopped
1 medium parsnip, peeled and chopped
4 sprigs parsley
1 teaspoon red wine vinegar
2 tablespoons semolina
1 cup shredded Boston or butterhead
    lettuce, or arugula
½ cup freshly grated Parmesan cheese

1. Place the chicken in a large kettle and add the onion, garlic, cloves, peppercorns, carrots, celery, turnip, parsnip, parsley, and vinegar. Add water to cover, and heat to boiling. Reduce the heat, skim any foam that has floated to the top of the pot, and simmer, partially covered, 1 hour. Continue skimming as necessary. Remove the chicken and allow it to cool slightly.

2. Remove the skin and bones from the chicken, and return them to the soup. (Reserve the chicken meat for another use.) Continue to cook the soup, uncovered, 20 minutes. Strain.

3. Pour 1 quart strained chicken stock into a medium-size saucepan, and heat to boiling. Stir in the semolina. Reduce the heat to medium-low and gently simmer 10 minutes. Stir in the lettuce; cook 1 minute. Stir in the cheese, and serve.

Serves 4

SUPER-CRUNCHY GRILLED CHICKEN

I love grilled chicken. This one is super-crunchy, thanks to the "gold dust" in the marinade. Don't worry if a bit drops into the fire. The chicken will still be crispy.

½ teaspoon anchovy paste
½ teaspoon tomato paste
6 tablespoons olive oil
3 tablespoons freshly grated Parmesan
    cheese
¼ cup semolina
½ teaspoon salt
¼ teaspoon freshly ground black pepper
1 chicken (about 3½ pounds), well rinsed,
    dried, and cut into serving pieces

1. Combine the anchovy paste, tomato paste, olive oil, cheese, semolina, salt, and pepper in a large bowl. Mix well. Add the chicken, and rub the mixture into the chicken pieces with your hands. Let stand, uncovered, 2 hours.

2. Prepare a barbecue grill (with cover) or preheat the broiler. If you are cooking the chicken on a grill, set up a drip pan in the center, and surround it with the hot coals.

3. Place the chicken over the drip pan, cover the grill, and grill until almost tender, about 20 minutes, turning once. Then place the chicken directly over the coals, and grill uncovered until crisp and cooked through, about another 10 minutes.

In the broiler, the chicken will take about 20 minutes per side.

Serves 2 to 4

TUNA FLUMMERY

Neither a pudding nor a cake, this moist and airy bit of bakery is a wondrous amalgam of both, with a surprising ingredient straight off the pantry shelf. It's the kind of dish that will make a drab brunch brighter, and a so-so supper super!

2 tablespoons olive oil
1 medium onion, finely chopped
2 cloves garlic, minced
1 large can (35 ounces) imported Italian
    tomatoes, chopped, with juice
Pinch of sugar
1 tablespoon chopped fresh basil
¼ teaspoon ground allspice
½ teaspoon salt
¼ teaspoon freshly ground black pepper
½ teaspoon anchovy paste
1 cup semolina
2 egg yolks
1 large can (12½ ounces) tuna, drained,
    broken into chunks
3 egg whites
1 tablespoon unsalted butter, melted
3 tablespoons freshly grated Parmesan
    cheese

1. Heat the oil in a medium-size saucepan over medium-low heat. Add the onion; cook 3 minutes. Add the garlic; cook 2 minutes longer. Stir in the tomatoes, sugar, basil, allspice, salt, and pepper. Heat to boiling. Reduce the heat and simmer until reduced to about 3½ cups, about 20 minutes.

2. Preheat the oven to 375°F. Butter a 10-inch glass or ceramic quiche dish.

3. Stir the anchovy paste into the tomato mixture. Then stir in the semolina and reduce the heat. Cook, stirring constantly, over low heat until thickened but not stiff, 1 to 2 minutes. Transfer to a heatproof bowl, and beat in the egg yolks, one at a time, beating vigorously after each addition. Stir in the drained tuna.

4. Beat the egg whites until stiff, and fold into the semolina mixture. Transfer the mixture to the prepared quiche dish. Brush the top with the melted butter and sprinkle with the cheese. Bake until golden, 20 to 25 minutes.

Serves 6 to 8

TORTA DI SPINACI RUSTICANA

A rustic luncheon pie (which makes a tonic picnic dish) baked in the tenderest semolina crust you have ever set a tooth to. The recipe (very homey) stems from the little town of Vercelli (even homier) in Italy. It is a dish that workmen and children wrap in paper bags for lunch, and it may be eaten hot, cold, or anywhere in between!

3 tablespoons olive oil
2 large onions, finely chopped
1½ to 2 pounds spinach or Swiss chard, trimmed
3 smoked pork chops (about 1½ pounds), 1 inch thick, trimmed and diced
1½ cups freshly grated Parmesan cheese
1 cup ricotta cheese
4 eggs, lightly beaten
Salt and freshly ground black pepper to taste
Double recipe Semolina Short Crust Pastry (recipe follows)
1 egg white, lightly beaten

1. Heat the oil in a large heavy skillet over medium-low heat. Cook the onions until soft, 8 minutes; do not brown. Transfer to a large bowl.

2. Wash the spinach or chard and place it, with just the water that clings to the leaves, in a medium-size saucepan. Cover, and cook over medium-low heat, stirring occasionally, until wilted, about 4 minutes (longer for chard). Drain, pressing out excess liquid with the back of a spoon. Chop.

3. Add the chopped greens, diced smoked pork, both cheeses, and eggs to the onions. Mix well, and season with salt and pepper.

4. Preheat the oven to 425°F.

5. Divide the pastry in half. Roll out one half on a lightly floured board, and line a 10-inch glass or ceramic quiche dish with it. Brush the pastry with some of the beaten egg white. Spoon the pork and cheese filling into the pastry shell.

Roll out the remaining pastry and cover the filling. Seal and crimp the edges. Cut a steam hole in the center. If desired, cut decorative leaves from pastry trimmings and place around the steam hole. Brush the top lightly with egg white. Bake until golden, about 40 minutes. Let stand 10 minutes before serving. Serve hot or at room temperature.

Serves 8

Semolina Short Crust Pastry

A pie crust that travels. Use it on your favorite sweet and savory tarts, tortes, or pot pies when the occasion arises.

½ cup semolina
½ cup cake flour
¼ teaspoon salt
4 tablespoons (½ stick) unsalted butter, chilled
1½ tablespoons solid vegetable shortening, chilled
2 to 2½ tablespoons cold water

Combine the semolina with the cake flour and salt in a bowl. Cut in the butter and shortening with a pastry blender until the mixture has the texture of coarse crumbs. Add just enough cold water to form a soft dough. Knead briefly, wrap in plastic wrap, and chill 1 hour before using. Allow to soften slightly before rolling out.

Makes enough for one 9- to 11-inch single-crust pie

"THINK PINK" SOUFFLE

A fire-roasted pepper turns this soufflé lightly pink, and blue cheese turns it elegant beyond belief. I serve this with just a green salad for a light pick-up meal.

3 tablespoons plus 1 teaspoon unsalted
    butter
2 tablespoons freshly grated Parmesan
    cheese
¼ cup semolina
1¼ cups milk, heated
4 egg yolks
1 roasted red bell pepper, seeded and
    chopped (see Note, page 249)
2 ounces blue cheese, chopped
½ teaspoon salt
¼ teaspoon freshly ground black pepper
Pinch of cayenne pepper
⅛ teaspoon freshly grated nutmeg
6 egg whites

1. Preheat the oven to 400°F. Rub a 1½-quart soufflé dish with the 1 teaspoon butter. Sprinkle the dish with 1 tablespoon of the Parmesan cheese.

2. Melt the 3 tablespoons butter in a medium-size saucepan over medium-low heat. Whisk in the semolina; cook, stirring constantly, 2 minutes. Add the hot milk all at once; whisk until smooth and thick, about 1 minute. Remove the pan from the heat and beat in the egg yolks, one at a time, beating vigorously after each addition. Stir in the roasted bell pepper, blue cheese, salt, black and cayenne peppers, and nutmeg. Transfer to a bowl.

3. Beat the egg whites until stiff, and fold into the semolina mixture. Pour into the prepared soufflé dish, sprinkle with the remaining Parmesan cheese, and place in the oven. Immediately reduce the oven heat to 375°F. Bake until the soufflé is puffed and firm, about 30 minutes. Serve immediately.

Serves 4

BAKED FENNEL PUDDING

*I*n this polenta-like pudding, semolina is the chief ingredient rather than cornmeal. Try it with any grilled fowl or fish.

1 small fennel bulb (about ½ pound),
    trimmed and chopped
1 medium onion, chopped
2 cups homemade chicken stock (see page
    376) or canned broth
¾ cup milk (approximately)
1 cup semolina
2 tablespoons unsalted butter
2 eggs, lightly beaten
1 tablespoon Pernod liqueur
Salt and freshly ground black pepper to
    taste
1 teaspoon unsalted butter, melted

1. Combine the fennel, onion, and chicken stock in a medium-size saucepan, and heat to boiling. Reduce the heat and simmer, covered, until the fennel is tender, about 10 minutes. Cool slightly.

2. Preheat the oven to 350°F. Butter a shallow 9-inch baking dish.

3. Transfer the fennel mixture to the container of a food processor or blender, and process until smooth.

4. Measure the fennel mixture and pour it into a medium-size saucepan. Add enough milk to make 3 cups. Heat to boiling. Then stir in the semolina and reduce the heat. Cook, stirring constantly, over low heat until thick, 1 to 2 minutes. Remove from the heat and beat in the butter, eggs, and Pernod. Season with salt and pepper.

5. Transfer the semolina to the prepared baking dish. Smooth it out to fit the dish, and brush the top with the melted butter. Bake until golden, 20 to 25 minutes. Cut into wedges and serve.

Serves 6 to 8

SAVORY SEMOLINA CHEESECAKE

Not a cheesecake in the conventional sense, yet guaranteed to knock your socks off at the first bite! This meld of semolina and Fontina is just what the doctor ordered for a case of "pallid palate."

2 medium carrots, peeled and chopped
1 large shallot, chopped
6 cups (approximately) homemade chicken
*   stock (see page 376) or canned broth*
2 cups semolina
4 tablespoons (½ stick) unsalted butter
3 eggs, lightly beaten
¼ teaspoon freshly grated nutmeg
½ teaspoon salt
¼ teaspoon freshly ground black pepper
2 cups grated Fontina cheese (about ½
*   pound)*
1 teaspoon unsalted butter, melted
3 tablespoons freshly grated Parmesan
*   cheese*

1. Combine the carrots, shallot, and 2 cups of the stock in a medium-size saucepan, and heat to boiling. Reduce the heat, cover, and simmer over medium-low heat until the carrots are tender, about 10 minutes. Cool slightly, and then place the carrots with some of the liquid in a food processor or blender container. Blend until smooth (carefully, as hot liquid will expand).

2. Preheat the oven to 375°F. Butter a 9-inch springform pan.

3. Combine the blended mixture with the remaining liquid in which the carrots were cooked. You should have about 2½ cups. Return it to the saucepan, and add enough chicken stock to make 6½ cups total. Heat to boiling, then stir in the semolina and reduce the heat. Cook, stirring constantly, until thick, 1 to 2 minutes. Remove the pan from the heat and beat in the butter, eggs, nutmeg, salt, and pepper.

4. Spoon one third of the semolina mixture over the bottom of the prepared springform pan. Sprinkle with half the Fontina cheese, leaving about an ⅛-inch border around the edge. Repeat with another third of the semolina mixture and the remaining Fontina. Spread the remaining semolina mixture over the top.

5. Brush the top of the cake with the melted butter, and sprinkle with the Parmesan cheese. Bake 20 minutes, then run under a broiler to lightly brown the top. Cool on a wire rack for 15 minutes. Run a knife around the edge of the cake and remove the sides of the pan. Let the cake stand 15 minutes longer before serving.

Serves 10 to 12

PAKET
(Crusty Fried Eggplant and Tomatoes)

*T*his combination of eggplant and semolina was inspired by a Turkish dish with a wonderful name, *paket*, which means "a package of groceries."

2 small eggplants (about ½ pound each), cut into ¼-inch-thick slices
Salt
¼ cup all-purpose flour (approximately)
2 eggs, lightly beaten
½ cup semolina
1½ teaspoons ground allspice
¼ teaspoon freshly ground black pepper
5 to 7 tablespoons vegetable oil
1 tablespoon unsalted butter
2 medium firm tomatoes, sliced
¼ cup freshly grated Parmesan cheese

1. Place the eggplant in a colander and sprinkle with salt. Let stand 30 minutes. Then rinse with cold water and pat dry.

2. Preheat the oven to 400°F.

3. Place the flour on a plate. Pour the eggs into a shallow bowl. Combine the semolina, allspice, 1 teaspoon salt, and pepper on another plate.

4. Heat 4 tablespoons of the oil with the butter in a heavy skillet over medium heat until hot but not smoking. Dip each eggplant slice in the flour, shaking off any excess. Then dip in the beaten egg, shaking off any excess. Finally dip in the semolina mixture, coating well. Sauté the eggplant slices, a few at a time, until golden brown on both sides. Drain on paper towels.

5. Raise the heat under the skillet slightly, adding more oil if needed, and repeat the process with the tomatoes. Do not overcook the tomatoes; they should remain firm.

6. Arrange the eggplant, occasionally overlapping with tomatoes, in a shallow baking dish. Sprinkle with the cheese. Bake until the vegetables are warmed through and the cheese has melted, 5 to 8 minutes.

Serves 4 to 6

ANNA TERESA CALLEN'S SEMOLINA SHELLS WITH ARUGULA

*I*n Italy, hard durum wheat pasta is almost inevitably factory-made. But here's an exception to the rule, from the mistress of fine Abruzzo cooking, Anna Teresa Callen. A delicate rolled dough shell (known as *cavatelli*), this pasta is flattened out like a noodle, and poached with fresh greens until tender. Getting the knack of rolling and flattening the dough takes practice, so test the first few in boiling water before proceeding with the recipe. They should be on the light side, not rubbery. The multi-accomplished Mrs. Callen serves her shells in a bath of tomato sauce with a shower of grated Pecorino cheese over all. I prefer merely melted butter and Parmesan, but exercise your own option in the matter.

1¼ cups all-purpose flour
¾ cup semolina
Pinch of salt
½ cup plus 2 to 3 tablespoons lukewarm water
4 cups torn, trimmed arugula leaves
4 tablespoons (½ stick) unsalted butter
½ cup freshly grated Parmesan cheese

1. Combine the flour with the semolina and salt in a large bowl. Stir in ½ cup of the lukewarm water and add more, 1 tablespoon at a time, until a stiff dough is formed. Transfer the dough to a lightly floured board and knead 10 minutes. Cover with a bowl and let stand 20 minutes.

2. Pull off pieces of dough and roll them into ropes. Slice the ropes into ⅛- to ¼-inch-thick rounds. Flatten the slices, and pushing with your thumb, form each round into a little (1-inch) shell shape by folding up one side of the circle slightly. (Keep the board lightly floured at all times to make the dough easier to work with, and keep the main batch of dough covered at all times to prevent it from drying out.) Place the formed shells on cloth-lined baking sheets. Let stand until dry, 4 hours. (The shells become easier to form into shapes as they dry.)

3. Cook the shells with the arugula in a large pot of boiling salted water until the shells are tender, about 25 minutes. Drain in a colander.

4. Wipe out the pot and add the butter. Melt the butter over medium heat, and stir in the cooked shells and arugula. Toss to coat. Stir in the cheese, and serve.

Serves 4 to 6

SEMI VEGGIE PIE

*T*his is borrowed from friend Julie Sahni—an Indian dish with some very American modifications. Julie calls the original version a spicy pilaf.

1 small eggplant, cubed (about 1¼ cups)
Salt
5 tablespoons vegetable oil
⅓ cup sliced almonds
1 cup semolina
1 teaspoon mustard seeds
½ teaspoon crushed dried hot red peppers
1 medium onion, chopped
1½ teaspoons minced fresh ginger
1 small baking potato, peeled and cubed (about 1 cup)
2 cups strong homemade vegetable or chicken stock (see Note)
1 teaspoon sesame oil

½ teaspoon salt
¼ teaspoon freshly ground black pepper
½ cup shelled peas, lightly blanched if fresh, thawed if frozen
2 teaspoons fresh lemon juice
2 tablespoons chopped fresh cilantro (Chinese parsley)

1. Place the eggplant in a colander and sprinkle with salt. Let stand 30 minutes. Then rinse with cold water and pat dry.

2. Meanwhile, heat 1 tablespoon of the vegetable oil in a large ovenproof

skillet (with cover) over medium heat. Stir in the almonds and cook, stirring constantly, until golden, about 3 minutes. Transfer to a bowl.

3. Wipe out the skillet and heat another tablespoon of the oil over medium heat. Stir in the semolina, and cook, stirring constantly, until the grains separate and turn golden, about 5 minutes. Transfer to a separate bowl.

4. Wipe out the skillet and heat the remaining 3 tablespoons oil over medium heat. Add the mustard seeds and cover the pan. The mustard seeds will pop as they sauté. Shake the pan occasionally to prevent burning. When the seeds are golden brown (about 3 minutes), add the dried red peppers and cook 15 seconds. Stir in the onion and ginger; cook 2 minutes longer.

5. Add the eggplant and potato cubes to the onion mixture. Cook over medium-low heat, uncovered, stirring occasionally, until the vegetables soften, about 10 minutes. Then add the stock, sesame oil, salt, pepper, and reserved semolina. Heat to boiling, and reduce the heat. Cook, stirring and folding the mixture over on itself with a wooden spatula, for 10 minutes. Add the peas and continue to cook, stirring and folding, for 5 minutes. Stir in the lemon juice, cilantro, and reserved almonds. Keep the pilaf warm in a 225°F oven until ready to serve.

Serves 6

Note: If you do not have strong vegetable or chicken stock on hand (see page 379), reduce 4 cups canned chicken broth (there is no readily available canned vegetable broth) to 2 cups by simmering for 20 minutes.

Semolina is most definitely a grain with Italian connections.

In the north of Italy it is called *malinconia maccheroni* ("melancholy macaroni") because almost all of the hard durum wheat is purchased by pasta factories before it is harvested.

Wheat growers in the south and westerly regions of Italy have a happier name for semolina. They tag it *polvere d'oro*, or "gold dust," because the hard durum wheat that is grown in those parts is milled into semolina flour—which brings a higher price and a sweeter jingle to the pocketbook.

RICOTTA GNOCCHI WITH WILD MUSHROOMS

*T*hough I have studied Italian cooking with some formidable culinary "heavies" in that country, I must confess that I learned to make gnocchi on Manhattan Island, in a kitchen no bigger than a Checker cab. The secret of ethereal gnocchi is speed: make them as quickly as possible. And, since the dough is very buttery and fragile, use a heavy dusting of flour on the board, your knife, and your hands. That will keep the mixture workable.

My trick is to prepare gnocchi a day or so in advance. I poach and drain them, and freeze them until an hour before serving time. Then I merely place the semi-frozen dumplings on a buttered heatproof platter, drizzle them with melted butter, and bake 15 to 20 minutes in a 400°F oven while the mushrooms cook. It's easy, fast, and the results are delicious.

2 cups milk
¾ cup semolina
2 egg yolks
6 tablespoons (¾ stick) unsalted butter, melted
¼ cup freshly grated Parmesan cheese
⅓ cup ricotta cheese
¼ teaspoon freshly grated nutmeg
½ teaspoon salt
2 teaspoons finely chopped fresh basil, or ⅔ teaspoon dried
⅛ teaspoon finely chopped fresh oregano, or a pinch dried
⅛ teaspoon finely chopped fresh thyme, or a pinch dried
3 tablespoons unsalted butter
¼ pound fresh wild mushrooms (such as shiitake), thinly sliced
½ cup heavy or whipping cream

1. Place the milk in a saucepan and heat slowly to boiling (do not scorch). Reduce the heat and slowly whisk in the semolina. Cook over low heat, stirring constantly, until thick, about 5 minutes. Transfer to a bowl.

According to the *Arabian Night's Dream Book*, a little-known turn-of-the-century volume:

Grain is a symbol of *prosperity*.
Eggplant is a sign of *endurance*.
To dream of an eggplant growing in a field of wheat means guaranteed success but also hard work.
To dream of a dish of roasted eggplant surrounded by grains of wheat means a windfall of gold... with no exertion whatsoever!

2. Beat the egg yolks, one at a time, into the semolina, beating thoroughly after each addition. Beat in 4 tablespoons of the melted butter, both cheeses, and the nutmeg, salt, and herbs.

3. Place a large spoonful of gnocchi dough on a heavily floured board. With floured hands, roll the dough into a rope. Cut into 1-inch pieces with a floured knife, gently squeezing the centers. (Keep board, hands, and knife well floured at all times.)

4. Preheat the oven to 400°F. Butter a large baking dish.

5. Cook the gnocchi in a large pot of boiling salted water for 30 to 45 seconds. (You should be able to roll out and cut the next batch while one batch of gnocchi is cooking.) Remove the gnocchi with a slotted spoon and rest the spoon on paper towels. Then place the drained gnocchi in the prepared baking dish in one layer. Continue this process until all dough is used up. Drizzle the remaining 2 tablespoons melted butter over the finished gnocchi.

6. Melt the 3 tablespoons butter in a large heavy skillet over medium heat. Add the mushrooms and sauté, tossing constantly, until golden, about 3 minutes. Remove the pan from the heat and let the mushrooms cool slightly.

7. Bake the gnocchi for 10 minutes. Meanwhile, place the mushrooms over medium-low heat and stir in the cream. Cook, stirring frequently, until smooth, about 3 minutes. Serve over the gnocchi.

Serves 4 to 6

SEMI BAVARIAN CREAM

One rarely thinks of semolina as the basis of delicate desserts, but perhaps this ethereal meal closure will change a few opinions on the subject.

1½ teaspoons unflavored gelatin
¼ cup water
¼ cup semolina
½ cup sugar
2 cups milk
1 teaspoon vanilla extract
1 tablespoon kirsch liqueur
1 cup heavy or whipping cream
3 egg whites
Red-Letter Purée (recipe follows)

1. Combine the gelatin and water in a small bowl, and let soften, 3 to 4 minutes.

2. Combine the semolina, sugar, and milk in a medium-size saucepan. Heat slowly, whisking constantly, to boiling (about 4 minutes). Remove the pan from the heat and whisk in the softened gelatin. Transfer to a bowl. Whisk in the vanilla and kirsch, and set aside to cool to room temperature.

3. Beat the cream until stiff, and fold into the semolina mixture. Beat the egg whites until stiff, and fold into the semolina mixture. Pour into a 6-cup mold, and refrigerate until firm, 3 hours.

4. To unmold, place the mold in a pan of hot water for a few seconds, and then invert it onto a large serving platter. Serve with Red-Letter Purée.

Serves 6 to 8

Red-Letter Purée

1 cup fresh strawberries, hulled
1 cup fresh or frozen raspberries, thawed
½ cup confectioners' sugar
1 tablespoon fresh orange juice
1 teaspoon kirsch liqueur

Place all ingredients in the container of a food processor or blender, and process until smooth. Mash through a fine strainer to remove the seeds. Serve chilled.

Makes about 2 cups

THE SEMI CHOCOLATE CHALLENGE

A remarkable dessert anomaly: half baked chocolate pudding, half baked chocolate tart. Totally irresistible!

8 tablespoons (1 stick) unsalted butter
2 ounces semi-sweet chocolate
2 cups brewed coffee
1 cup heavy or whipping cream
⅓ cup granulated sugar
¼ teaspoon salt

1 cup semolina
2 eggs, lightly beaten
1 egg yolk, lightly beaten
Confectioners' sugar
1 cup heavy or whipping cream
1 tablespoon rum

1. Preheat the oven to 375°F. Butter and flour a 9-inch springform pan.

2. Melt the butter and chocolate together in a small saucepan over low heat, stirring frequently until smooth. Set aside.

3. Combine the coffee and cream in a medium-size saucepan. Heat slowly to boiling, then reduce the heat and stir in the sugar and salt. Slowly stir in the semolina and cook, stirring constantly, 10 minutes. Transfer to a large bowl.

4. Stir the chocolate mixture into the semolina mixture, and beat in the eggs and egg yolk. Pour the mixture into the prepared springform pan. Bake 1 hour. Cool completely on a wire rack. Loosen the edge of the pan with a knife, and remove the sides. Dust with confectioners' sugar.

5. In a small mixing bowl, whip the cream with the rum until the cream holds stiff peaks, 5 minutes. Serve the pudding tart slightly warm or chilled, with the rum-flavored whipped cream.

Serves 10 to 12

APPLE CUSTARD TART WITH TWO HATS

*T*his custardy apple pie, thickened with semolina, rests in a semolina crust. A lattice top crust is crowned with a meringue that sends guests back for more of this "two-hatted" dessert.

Finely grated zest of 1 orange
Finely grated zest of 1 large lemon
3 tablespoons fresh orange juice
1 tablespoon fresh lemon juice
2 tablespoons semolina
2½ pounds green apples (5 medium)
1¾ cups sugar
2 eggs, lightly beaten
Semolina Short Crust Pastry (see page 272)
2 tablespoons whipping cream
5 egg whites

1. Preheat the oven to 450°F.

2. Combine the orange zest, lemon zest, orange juice, lemon juice, and semolina in a large bowl.

3. Peel the apples and grate them directly into the bowl. Stir in 1½ cups of the sugar and the lightly beaten eggs. Mix well.

4. Roll about two thirds of the pastry on a lightly floured board until very thin. Line a 9-inch pie plate with it, and trim and flute the edges. Add the trimmed dough to the remaining third of dough and roll out. Cut into strips.

5. Pour the apple mixture into the pie shell. Place the dough strips in a lattice pattern over the top, and press the ends into the edges of the pie shell. Brush the top with the cream, and place the pie on an aluminum-foil-lined baking sheet. Bake 10 minutes. Reduce the oven heat to 350°F and bake until done, about 35 minutes longer. Cool completely on a wire rack.

6. Preheat the broiler. Beat the egg whites in the large bowl of an electric mixer until almost stiff. Slowly add the remaining ¼ cup sugar, 1 tablespoon at a time, beating until the mixture becomes stiff and glossy. Spread the meringue over the top of the pie, and run it under the broiler until the top is golden brown, about 1 minute.

Serves 8

SEMI-BAKED SNOW

This is one of my favorite desserts of all time—smooth, velvety, loaded with taste. It can be made a day in advance and kept refrigerated in the mold. I usually offer a choice of sweet dessert sauces, but one or the other will do just as well.

1 quart milk
½ cup sugar
5 tablespoons unsalted butter
1 cup semolina
Generous pinch of ground cinnamon
1½ teaspoons vanilla extract
1 tablespoon dark rum
4 eggs, separated
Boiling water
Blue and Red Plum Sauce or Drop Dead
    Chocolate Sauce (recipes follow)

1. Combine the milk, sugar, and 3 tablespoons of the butter in a medium-size saucepan. Heat slowly, stirring occasionally, to boiling; do not scorch. Reduce the heat to low, and slowly whisk in the semolina. Cook, stirring occasionally, 25 minutes. Stir in the cinnamon, vanilla, rum, and remaining 2 tablespoons butter. Transfer to a large bowl.

2. Preheat the oven to 350°F. Butter a 10-cup non-stick mold.

3. Beat the egg yolks, one at a time, into the semolina mixture, beating thoroughly after each addition. Beat the egg whites until stiff, and fold into the mixture. Pour into the prepared mold.

4. Place the mold in a roasting or other large deep pan, and pour boiling water into the pan so that it comes halfway up the mold. Bake 30 minutes. Remove the mold from the hot water and cool 10 minutes before inverting onto a serving plate. Refrigerate to chill, then serve with your choice of sauce.

Serves 10

Blue and Red Plum Sauce

This recipe may be doubled.

8 purple (Italian) plums, pitted and
    roughly chopped (about 1 cup)
½ cup raspberry jam
3 tablespoons sugar
¼ cup dry red wine

Combine all ingredients in a small saucepan and heat to boiling. Reduce the heat to medium and cook, stirring occasionally, until plums are soft, 10 to 12 minutes. Mash through a fine-mesh strainer. Serve slightly warm.

Makes about 1¼ cups

Drop Dead Chocolate Sauce

8 ounces semi-sweet chocolate
5 tablespoons unsalted butter, cut into
    small pieces
¼ cup milk, at room temperature
¼ cup heavy or whipping cream, at room
    temperature
2 tablespoons dark rum

Melt the chocolate in the top of a double boiler over hot, but not simmering, water. Stir in the butter, bit by bit. Stir in the milk, cream, and rum. Stir until smooth. Cool, and store in a tightly covered jar in the refrigerator. Reheat slightly over warm water before serving.

Makes about 2 cups

THE BOZO CAKE

My mother was a remarkable baker with a very special gift. She could look at a recipe once, toss away the cookbook, and produce a flawless version. "It's like sight-reading music," she would offer by way of explanation—as if it were an ability anyone could develop with practice. However, as she grew older she became less and less interested in cake making—with one notable exception. She returned from Italy with the memory of a cake: it was made of semolina and resembled a pound cake, but it was denser. The aroma was lemon, while the flavor was decidedly almond.

"What was the name of this cake?" I quizzed.

"Who knows?" said my mother. "Something Italian. It sounded like *bozo.*"

"Bozo cake?"

"Something like that."

On odd occasions afterward, my mother would drop by my apartment, and she'd take inventory of her old baking equipment, which I kept stashed in a cabinet. My mother would smile ruefully. "Maybe one day we'll try to make bozo cake."

"Without a recipe?" (for none of my Italian cookbooks produced a cake of even the faintest resemblance).

"We could wing it!" my mother replied.

And in time we did. One afternoon I ground nuts and separated eggs while she beat semolina, sugar, and the yolks together into a golden froth. As we scraped the mixture from a bowl into a buttered pan, my mother slapped her forehead. "Yipes. I just remembered. This cake was dome-shaped on top."

"Too late to worry about that," I said. But my mother worried anyway.

"I think I've lost my touch," she murmured as we tasted the still-warm cake. "Or maybe just my memory..."

"What's wrong? I think it's delicious."

"Yeah," my mother agreed, "but it's just not the bozo cake I ate in Italy!"

She nibbled a crumb more. "I suspect chocolate would make a difference too."

"What chocolate?"

"You see, I forgot to tell you. It had a frosting."

PAROZZO DI PAPA
("the Pope's hat")

When I began to compile semolina recipes for this book—twenty years after sampling my mother's bozo cake—my friend Anna Teresa Callen mentioned a semolina cake of her Abruzzo girlhood, a cake known as *parozzo di Papa'* ("the Pope's hat"). As soon as I heard the name, even before I glanced at the ingredients list, I knew it had to be my mother's "bozo" cake (see box). Here's the authentic version.

FOR THE CAKE

6 eggs, separated
1½ cups sugar
1 cup blanched almonds, toasted and

ground (see Note)
1 cup semolina
Finely grated zest of 1 orange
1 tablespoon fresh orange juice

FOR THE ICING

4 ounces semi-sweet chocolate
2 to 3 tablespoons unsalted butter
White chocolate for chocolate curls

1. Preheat the oven to 375°F. Butter a 9-inch (2-quart) round glass ovenproof bowl.

2. Make the cake: Beat the egg yolks in the large bowl of an electric mixer until light. Slowly add the sugar and beat until light and fluffy. Beat in the almonds, semolina, orange zest, and orange juice. The mixture will be very thick.

3. Beat the egg whites until stiff. Stir one third of the whites into the cake mixture with a wooden spoon. Fold and stir the second third of the whites into the mixture. Fold in the remaining whites.

4. Pour the batter into the prepared bowl. Bake until a toothpick inserted in center of the cake comes out clean, about 1 hour. Cool for 10 minutes on a wire rack. Carefully loosen the edges of the cake, pushing gently toward the center, with a long flexible spatula. Invert the cake onto a wire rack, and cool.

5. Make the icing: Melt the chocolate in the top of a double boiler set over hot water. Stir in enough butter to make a very smooth mixture. (Chocolate may seize slightly in the beginning.) Spread the icing over the cake. Make chocolate curls by scraping the white chocolate with a vegetable peeler over the cake.

Serves 8 to 10

Note: To toast almonds, spread them evenly on a baking sheet, and place in a 350°F oven, stirring occasionally, 10 minutes. Grind in a food processor, pulsing on and off to avoid turning the nuts into a paste.

BOZO CAKE

O nly dimly remembered, but delicious.

6 eggs, separated
1½ cups sugar
1½ cups blanched almonds, toasted and ground (see Note, above)
1 cup semolina
Finely grated zest of 1 lemon
2 teaspoons fresh lemon juice

1. Preheat the oven to 375°F. Butter and flour a 9-inch springform pan.

2. Beat the egg yolks in the large bowl of an electric mixer until light. Slowly add the sugar and beat until light and fluffy. Stir in the almonds, semolina, lemon zest, and lemon juice. The mixture will be stiff.

3. Beat the egg whites until stiff. Stir one third of the whites into the cake mixture with a wooden spoon. Fold and stir the second third of the whites into the mixture. Fold in the remaining whites.

4. Pour the batter into the prepared springform pan. Bake until a toothpick inserted in the center comes out clean, about 30 minutes. Cool completely on a rack before removing the sides of the pan.

Serves 8 to 10

MARION'S SEMOLINA SEED CAKE

*T*he next of the semolina desserts is hardly the least of that grain's endowments. But come to think of it, I cannot summon up a happier ending to the subject. It is a nutty sunflower-seed cake—straight out of the head of Marion Cunningham, author of *The Fanny Farmer Book of Baking.*

¼ cup solid vegetable shortening
4 tablespoons (½ stick) unsalted butter, at
    room temperature
1¼ cups sugar
2 eggs
1 cup semolina
1 cup all-purpose flour
1½ teaspoons baking powder
½ teaspoon salt
1 cup milk
1 teaspoon vanilla extract
1 teaspoon finely grated lemon zest
½ cup toasted sunflower seeds (see Note)

1. Preheat the oven to 350°F. Butter and flour a 9-inch springform pan.

2. Beat the shortening with the butter in the large bowl of an electric mixer until light. Slowly add the sugar and beat until light and fluffy. Beat in the eggs, one at a time, beating thoroughly after each addition.

3. In another bowl, combine the semolina, flour, baking powder, and salt. Add this to the egg mixture in thirds on low speed, alternating with thirds of the milk. Then beat in the vanilla, lemon zest, and sunflower seeds.

4. Pour the mixture into the prepared springform pan. Bake until a toothpick inserted in the center comes out clean, about 35 minutes. Cool completely on a rack. Remove pan sides before serving.

Serves 8 to 10

Note: To toast sunflower seeds, spread the seeds evenly in a skillet and place them over medium heat, stirring several times until they turn golden brown, 6 to 8 minutes.

PEACH UPSIDE-DOWN CAKE

I have always been fond of any upside-down cake. It suits my sweet tooth to a "T." But when the cake is made with downy semolina and topped with fresh juicy peaches, upside-down cake takes a step toward immortality.

½ cup milk
2 tablespoons unsalted butter
½ cup semolina
½ cup firmly packed dark brown sugar
2 large ripe peaches, peeled and sliced
    (about 2 cups)
2 tablespoons plus ½ cup granulated sugar

1 egg, well beaten
2 egg yolks, lightly beaten
½ cup cake flour
1 teaspoon baking powder
¼ teaspoon salt
1 teaspoon vanilla extract

1. Preheat the oven to 425°F. Butter an 8-inch square non-stick cake pan.

2. Place the milk with the butter in a small saucepan. Heat over medium heat just until the butter melts.

3. Place the semolina in a large bowl. Pour the milk mixture over it, stir well, and let stand 10 minutes.

4. Press the brown sugar over the bottom of the prepared cake pan. Layer the peach slices over the brown sugar. Sprinkle the peaches with 2 tablespoons granulated sugar. Drizzle the beaten egg over the top.

5. Stir the egg yolks into the semolina mixture. Then stir in the cake flour, ½ cup granulated sugar, baking powder, salt, and vanilla. Pour this over the peaches, transfer to the oven, and bake until a toothpick inserted in the center comes out clean, about 25 minutes. Cool on a rack for 5 minutes before inverting onto a serving platter.

Serves 6 to 8

COUSCOUS

(It's Semolina too!)

After dried pasta, couscous is the most widespread form of semolina.

And what is couscous? A kitchen anomaly in fact, but one you'll be glad you discovered. At Berber stoves, "couscous" originally meant the grains of steamed semolina, traditionally served with North African stews known as *tagines*. However, in the fullness of time, couscous became such a ubiquitous partner to a tagine that even a deep-dyed Moroccan will call the combination "couscous" these days.

Paula Wolfert, doyenne of Middle Eastern food, has another theory. In her book *Couscous and Other Good Foods from Morocco*, she claims the word *couscous* is actually onomatopoeic, a verbal approximation of steam hissing its way through a mess of grains!

In a Moroccan kitchen, couscous is made by hand: hard durum semolina is moistened with water and a fine coating of flour, then rolled back and forth onto itself until tiny pellets are formed. These bits of wheat are later steamed and stirred and steamed again until they become soft and fluffier than rice.

Being able to roll semolina into couscous is considered a great gift. In cities like Rabat, Fez, and Marrakech, a woman will often spend her entire adolescence mastering the art of couscous-making. And a female who is an adept couscous maker may come to a prospective husband with a reduced dowry, but there will be no complaints because her skills are more highly prized than gold. Or so a few knowing Moroccans have said.

Unfortunately, the durum semolina that is most available in this country is not granular enough to make authentic Moroccan couscous from scratch. But packaged couscous makes an admirable substitute in the recipes that follow.

How to Buy It

Couscous is available in cartons in supermarkets, fancy food shops, and natural foods stores everywhere. The best for the money, in my opinion, is the couscous sold in bulk at Middle Eastern groceries. But you have to search it out.

Have a caution when choosing packaged couscous. Do not buy boxes that are labeled "instant" or "precooked" because the contents are not only tasteless but often gluey into the bargain.

How to Cook It

To make couscous the right way takes time, even if you have bought a packaged product; 60 minutes is the optimum steaming cycle.

Many boxed couscous cartons bear instructions for abbreviated cooking periods. Ignore them, please! In most cases the directions require the grain and liquid to be cooked together over direct heat, rather than steaming the grain over the liquid. As a result the grain absorbs all the liquid quickly (like instant rice), which does not yield a particularly felicitous or fluffy kernel of couscous!

If a quick pot of couscous is absolutely necessary, consider the method developed by Marilyn Harris on page 290. It's fail-proof and feasible too.

Traditionally, couscous requires three steamings, optimally accomplished in a pot known as a *couscousière*, which has a tight-fitting colander inside and a heavy cover overall.

If you do not have a *couscousière*, you can use any heavy-duty pot that has a cover and will accommodate a shallow colander. Make sure, however, that the colander fits into the pot snugly. If the colander's openings are too large, line it with a dampened cheesecloth.

BASIC COOKED COUSCOUS

1 cup couscous
1 tablespoon olive oil
Simmering water or stock
½ cup cold water
¼ teaspoon salt
½ cup hot water

1. Combine the couscous with the oil in a medium-size bowl. Stir well, and then pour into the steam pan of a couscousière or a prepared colander. Steam over simmering water or stock for 20 minutes.

2. Return the couscous to the bowl and stir in the cold water, breaking up all lumps with a fork. Return the mixture to the steam pan or colander and steam 20 minutes longer.

3. Transfer the couscous to the bowl once more, and stir in the salt and hot water, breaking up any lumps with a fork. (At this stage, the couscous is the "partially steamed couscous" called for in the recipes that follow.)

4. Place the couscous in a steamer or

colander, set it over the stew, and continue to steam for 20 minutes. Or, if you are using the couscous for another dish such as a salad, return it to the pot of simmering water or stock and continue to steam until tender, 20 minutes. (See Note.) Fluff with a fork.

Makes 3 cups; serves 4 to 6

Note: For the final 20 minutes of cooking time the couscous ideally will be steamed over a stew to absorb the dish's flavor. However, many dishes (like the Tunisian tuna tagine on page 291) cook so briefly that it is necessary to steam the couscous for the full 60 minutes in advance.

TAGINE AID EL KEBIR
(Moroccan Lamb Stew)

North African stews vary as greatly as North American dialects. This one comes from Fez, where it is consumed in great quantities by the faithful at the festival of Aid el Kebir. A tagine of lamb, it commemorates the Prophet Abraham, who sacrificed a sheep in place of his son. My advice is to serve this stew over couscous, with a smidgen of *harissa* sauce on the side (you won't be able to take more). Harissa is a fiery condiment that most Moroccans agree "wakes up the organs!"

1 leg of lamb (about 5½ pounds), meat cut into 1½-inch cubes
Salt and freshly ground black pepper to taste
5 tablespoons olive oil
12 tablespoons (1½ sticks) unsalted butter
5 large yellow onions, coarsely chopped
½ teaspoon ground ginger
⅛ teaspoon saffron, or to taste, crumbled
½ teaspoon ground cinnamon
½ teaspoon ground turmeric
½ teaspoon freshly grated nutmeg
4 sprigs parsley
3 sprigs cilantro (Chinese parsley)
7 cups lamb stock (see page 378)
3 medium turnips, peeled and cut into 1½-inch pieces
5 medium carrots, peeled and cut into 2-inch strips
4 medium tomatoes, seeded and coarsely chopped

¼ cup dark honey
½ cup raisins
3 medium zucchini, cut into 2-inch strips
1½ recipes partially steamed Basic Cooked Couscous (see facing page)
Harissa (recipe follows)
1 can (6 ounces) chick-peas, drained, skins removed
1½ cups toasted whole blanched almonds (see Note)
Chopped fresh parsley, for garnish

1. Sprinkle the lamb cubes with salt and pepper. Heat 3 tablespoons of the oil in a large heavy skillet over medium-high heat. Sauté the lamb, a few pieces at a time, until well browned, about 8 minutes per batch. Transfer to the bottom of a couscousière or a large heavy pot.

2. Add 8 tablespoons (1 stick) of the butter to the lamb. Place the pot over medium heat and add 2 chopped onions, the ginger, saffron, ¼ teaspoon of the cinnamon, the turmeric, and nutmeg. Tie the parsley and cilantro sprigs in a cheesecloth bag and add to the pot. Stir in the lamb stock, and heat to boiling. Reduce the heat and simmer, covered, 30 minutes. Add the turnips and carrots and continue to cook, covered, 20 minutes longer.

3. Meanwhile, heat the remaining 2 tablespoons oil in a large heavy skillet over medium heat. Stir in the remaining 3 chopped onions; cook until golden, about 8 minutes. Sprinkle with the remaining ¼ teaspoon cinnamon, and add the tomatoes, honey and raisins. Raise the heat slightly and cook until all liquid has evaporated, 20 minutes.

4. Stir the tomato mixture into the stew, and add the zucchini. Heat to boiling; reduce the heat. Place the partially steamed couscous in the couscousière steam pan or in a colander that fits tightly in the pot. Cook over medium heat 25 minutes.

5. To serve, place the couscous in the center of a large serving dish and dot with the remaining 4 tablespoons (½ stick) butter. Stir 1 tablespoon Harissa, the chick-peas, and the almonds into the stew and strain the stew, reserving the broth. Arrange the meat and vegetables around the couscous. Sprinkle with pars-ley. Serve each diner a bowl of broth with which to moisten their couscous. Pass the stew and the remaining Harissa.

Serves 6 to 8

Note: To toast almonds, spread them evenly on a baking sheet, and place in a 350°F oven, stirring occasionally, 10 minutes.

Harissa

2 cloves garlic, minced
2 hot green peppers, seeded and coarsely chopped
1 teaspoon crushed dried hot red peppers
4 teaspoons caraway seeds
1 teaspoon ground cumin
1 teaspoon ground coriander
1 teaspoon salt
½ teaspoon freshly ground black pepper
Olive oil

Lightly mash the garlic with the fresh and dried peppers in a small bowl. Transfer to the container of a blender, and add the caraway seeds, cumin, coriander, salt, pepper, and enough olive oil to cover. Blend until smooth. Store in a jar with a tight-fitting lid in the refrigerator for up to a month.

Makes about ½ cup

COUSCOUS WITH LAMB BAKED IN A TOMATO BLANKET

A second North African lamb stew is of French Algerian derivation. Half tagine, its other half is a classic ragoût—a culinary marriage made in heaven. This dish bakes partially in the oven and then is finished on top of the stove, with couscous absorbing all the aromatic steam.

4 pounds boneless lamb shoulder or breast,
    cut into 1½-inch cubes
¼ cup all-purpose flour
¼ cup vegetable oil
2 large yellow onions, finely chopped
1 large clove garlic, minced
Pinch of saffron
½ teaspoon ground cinnamon
½ cup dry white wine
3½ cups fresh or canned peeled, seeded,
    chopped tomatoes (drained if canned)
1 cup homemade chicken stock (see page
    376) or canned broth
1 tablespoon sugar
3 tablespoons unsalted butter
2 teaspoons slivered orange zest
3 tablespoons cognac, warmed
1½ recipes partially steamed Basic Cooked
    Couscous (see page 286)
Chopped fresh parsley, for garnish

1. Preheat the oven to 375°F.

2. Dust the lamb cubes with the flour. Heat the oil in a Dutch oven (for which you have a tight-fitting colander) over medium heat. Sauté the lamb cubes, a few pieces at a time, until dark brown on all sides, 8 minutes per batch. Transfer to a plate. When all pieces are sautéed, reduce the heat to medium-low and return all the meat, with any juices that have accumulated. Sprinkle with any leftover flour and stir well. Stir in the onions; cook 4 minutes. Add the garlic, saffron, and ¼ teaspoon of the cinnamon; cook 2 minutes longer. Stir in the wine, tomatoes, and chicken stock. Sprinkle with the sugar. Heat to boiling, then cover and transfer to the oven. Bake 1 hour.

3. Melt 1 tablespoon of the butter in a small saucepan over medium-low heat. Add the orange zest and the remaining ¼ teaspoon of the cinnamon; cook 3 minutes. Add the cognac, and carefully set aflame. When the flame has died down, stir this mixture into the stew.

4. Place the Dutch oven on a burner over medium heat and heat to boiling. Then reduce the heat, and place the partially steamed couscous in a colander that fits tightly in the pot. Cook, covered, over medium-low heat 25 minutes. (Stir the stew once or twice to prevent sticking.) Serve, sprinkled with parsley, in individual bowls, placing a spoonful of couscous on top of each serving of stew.

Serves 6 to 8

MARILYN HARRIS'S CHICKEN AND VEGETABLE TAGINE

The following couscous dish is only vaguely connected to North Africa, but do not let that deter you, please, for it is wonderful!

It stems from a territory somewhat dearer and closer to my heart than Morocco—Cincinnati, Ohio, believe it or not. The donor is Marilyn Harris, one of the fine American cooks *not* hiding her light under a bushel. Marilyn is a cooking teacher, food consultant, TV personality, and the host of her own radio show, called *Cooking with Marilyn*, on WCKY in Cincinnati. Her cookbook of the same name will be published soon by Paxton Press. Marilyn's chicken and vegetable tagine is a miracle

of good taste, and her quick and easy couscous could possibly convert a Moroccan to her cause.

¼ cup raisins
¼ cup dry sherry
1 chicken (about 4 pounds), well rinsed, dried, and cut into pieces
Salt and freshly ground black pepper to taste
3 to 4 tablespoons all-purpose flour
1 tablespoon unsalted butter
2 tablespoons olive oil
1 medium onion, halved and sliced
1 large clove garlic, minced
1 can (14 ounces) plum tomatoes, chopped, with juice
1 medium carrot, peeled and cut into 2-inch julienne
1 medium rib celery, cut into 2-inch julienne
1 small turnip, peeled and cut into 2-inch julienne
¼ teaspoon salt
Dash of hot pepper sauce
⅛ teaspoon ground cinnamon
Marilyn's Quick and Easy Couscous (recipe follows)
2 tablespoons chopped fresh parsley

1. Combine the raisins with the sherry in a small saucepan. Heat to boiling; remove from the heat and reserve.

2. Sprinkle the chicken with salt and pepper. Dredge with flour.

3. Heat the butter with the oil in a heavy skillet (with cover) over medium heat. Sauté the chicken pieces, half at a time, until well browned on both sides, 8 to 10 minutes per batch. Transfer to a plate.

4. Add the onion to the skillet; cook 2 minutes. Add the garlic; cook 2 minutes longer. Stir in the tomatoes, carrot,

celery, and turnip, and heat to boiling. Reduce the heat and return the chicken to the skillet. Cook, covered, 30 minutes.

5. Stir the raisins and sherry, the salt, hot pepper sauce, and cinnamon into the chicken juices. Cook, partially covered, over low heat 10 to 15 minutes longer.

6. To serve, place the couscous on a platter and spoon the chicken mixture over the top. Sprinkle with parsley.

Serves 4

Marilyn's Quick and Easy Couscous

2 tablespoons olive oil
1½ cups medium-grain couscous
2 cups homemade chicken stock (see page 376) or canned broth
½ teaspoon salt
¼ teaspoon freshly ground black pepper
¼ teaspoon ground allspice
⅛ teaspoon ground mace
2 tablespoons unsalted butter

1. Preheat the oven to 375°F.

2. Heat the oil in a large skillet over medium-low heat. Stir in the couscous; cook 2 minutes. Stir in the stock, salt, pepper, allspice, and mace. Cook, tossing gently with two forks, until all liquid has been absorbed, about 2 minutes. Stir the butter into the couscous, and transfer to a heatproof serving dish. Bake for 5 minutes.

Serves 4

COUSCOUS AND FRESH TUNA, TUNISIAN STYLE

*F*ish tagines are part of every North African cook's repertoire, but you will not find the next dish in any medina from one end of Tunis to the other. The chief ingredient of this stew is straight out of the Atlantic Ocean, even though the cooking method is influenced by the Gulf of Hammamet. Eat couscous and fresh tuna in the summer, when the yellowfin are running.

¼ cup olive oil
2 medium onions, halved and sliced
2 cloves garlic, minced
1 medium green bell pepper, cored, seeded, and cut into strips
1 medium red bell pepper, cored, seeded, and cut into strips
1 medium yellow bell pepper, cored, seeded, and cut into strips
1 fresh jalapeño pepper, seeded, deveined, and minced
1 tablespoon semolina
¼ teaspoon chopped fresh thyme, or a pinch of dried
½ teaspoon anchovy paste
3 large tomatoes, peeled, seeded, and coarsely chopped
1½ cups fish stock (see page 377)
1 recipe partially steamed Basic Cooked Couscous (see page 286)
1 large zucchini, cut into ½-inch cubes
1½ pounds fresh tuna, cut into ½-inch-thick slices
2 tablespoons unsalted butter
1 cup chopped fresh parsley
½ cup sliced oil-cured black olives
Harissa (see page 288)

1. Heat the oil in a large heavy skillet (with cover) if you are using a couscousière, or in a Dutch oven, over medium heat. Add the onions; cook 1 minute. Add the garlic; cook 2 minutes longer. Stir in all the peppers and reduce the heat. Cook, covered, over medium-low heat 5 minutes. If you are using a couscousière, transfer the mixture to the stew pot.

2. Whisk the semolina into the pepper mixture. Cook, stirring constantly, 2 minutes. Stir in the thyme, anchovy paste, tomatoes, and fish stock, and heat to boiling. Reduce the heat to medium-low and cook, uncovered, 5 minutes. Place the partially steamed couscous in the couscousière steam pan or in a colander that fits tightly in the Dutch oven. Cover, and cook 10 minutes longer.

3. Add the zucchini to the stew and return the couscous. Cover and cook 8 minutes. Stir the fish into the stew and return the couscous. Cover, and cook 7 minutes longer. Remove the couscous from the steamer or colander and toss it with the butter. Keep warm. Stir the parsley and olives into the stew.

4. To serve, spoon the stew into individual soup bowls, and place a large scoop of couscous in the center. Pass the Harissa.

Serves 4 to 6

ROASTED GARLIC COUSCOUS SALAD

*B*ack in 16th-century England, a salad was described as "odds and ends of very common kitchen furniture." Can that mean leftovers, do you suppose? If so, let us muse on the infinite possibilities of day-after couscous in a salad bowl.

1 large head garlic, whole (about 20 to 25 cloves)
Salt
6 to 7 tablespoons olive oil
1 tablespoon red wine vinegar
3 cups Basic Cooked Couscous, warm or at room temperature (see page 286)
Freshly ground black pepper to taste
¼ cup chopped fresh parsley

1. Preheat the oven to 400°F.
2. Place the garlic on an oven proof dish, and roast it in the oven until the skin begins to blacken, 30 to 35 minutes.

Cool slightly. Then, using a sharp knife, cut the head apart. Using a spoon and your fingers, squeeze the individual garlic cloves from their skins into a medium-size bowl. Mash with a fork.

3. Add ¼ teaspoon salt to the mashed garlic, and mash with the back of a spoon. Slowly whisk in the oil and vinegar until smooth. Toss with the couscous in a bowl, and season with salt and pepper. Sprinkle with parsley before serving.

Serves 4 to 6

BASIL AND TOMATO COUSCOUS SALAD

*T*his salad of tomatoes flecked with bleu cheese is best served at room temperature. It is terrific with cold chicken, broiled or even fried.

2 cups Basic Cooked Couscous (see page 286)
½ cup lightly crushed cooked or canned tomatoes with juice
1 small clove garlic, crushed
¼ teaspoon salt
2 ounces blue cheese
1 teaspoon Dijon mustard
¼ cup olive oil
Juice of ½ lemon
Freshly ground black pepper to taste
2 teaspoons chopped fresh basil

1. Combine the couscous with the tomatoes in a large bowl. Lightly toss.
2. Mash the garlic with the salt and bleu cheese in a small bowl until smooth. Stir in the mustard. Whisk in the oil and lemon juice. Pour over the couscous and lightly toss until mixed. Add pepper, and sprinkle with the basil.

Serves 4

CUCKOO CHICKEN SALAD

*T*his recipe does wonders for leftover turkey as well. A luncheon or light supper dish.

2 cups Basic Cooked Couscous (see page 286)
1 rib celery, minced (about ½ cup)
1 small shallot, minced
1 cup cooked chicken chunks
¾ cup cubed cooked ham
1 small hot green pepper, seeded, deveined, and minced
½ cup frozen peas, thawed
¼ teaspoon minced fresh sage leaves, or a pinch of dried
⅓ cup mayonnaise, preferably homemade (see page 379)
⅓ cup sour cream
1 teaspoon Dijon mustard
¼ cup plus 1 tablespoon strong beef stock (see Note)
Salt and freshly ground black pepper to taste
Chopped fresh parsley, for garnish

1. Combine the couscous with the celery, shallot, chicken, ham, hot pepper, peas, and sage in a large bowl. Lightly toss.

2. Whisk the mayonnaise with the sour cream in a medium-size bowl. Whisk in the mustard and beef stock. Pour over the couscous mixture and lightly toss until mixed. Add salt and pepper, and sprinkle with parsley.

Serves 4

Note: If you do not have strong beef stock on hand (see page 379), reduce ½ cup plus 2 tablespoons canned beef broth to ¼ cup plus 1 tablespoon by simmering for 10 minutes.

WHEAT

*The Berry, the Germ, and the Flour,
Whole-Wheat Style*

I live on a street in Manhattan, an artery for truckers, bicyclists, joggers, and somewhat privileged pre-schoolers, that I tend to think of as Wheat Street. No grain grows there, but it is the street where I first learned to make bread. It is also the street where the gentleman who inspired my bread-making lived.

Some "foodies" call my thoroughfare the Street of Good Cooks, for it is inhabited by a remarkable clutch of kitchen practitioners. East to west: Anna Teresa

Callen, Madhur Jaffrey, Mimi Sheraton, and slightly off course, Lydie Marshall. Strategically in the middle of our tree-lined street was the home of my baking mentor, James Beard. A well-polished marker on the facade keeps him a neighbor to us all, in perpetuity.

I would on occasion meet Mr. Beard on the street, usually when he was taking his pug dog, Percy, for a nightly airing. Together we would walk along the darkened sidewalks and hold some kind of colloquy about the state of food in America, and more specifically the eating places on our own turf. Although in actuality it was never much of a dialogue. Beard spoke and I assented.

"Terrible!" was his opinion of the new restaurants that were gradually replacing all the homey, long-established businesses in the vicinity. "But, I suppose you must give them credit for optimism. Like a phoenix, one opens on the very site where another failed a month before. Now that is *optimism!*"

Beard was once an actor, and he knew how to hit a vowel so it could be heard around a street corner. "*Un*-less, of course, you call it lack of *imagination!*"

Later, he confided, "When I was a young man, taking over a bankrupt business was considered bad luck. But I guess there were more pessimists around in those days."

Actually, James Beard and I first met at the nether end of Long Island. A friend brought him into my take-out food shop there (The Store in Amagansett) almost twenty years ago, when the shine was still on the stove and I hadn't the slightest notion of writing about food for a living. My happiness in those days was merely cooking it.

I remember Mr. Beard in my store that day—a wholly generous giant, glowing and glowering by turns, with an endless supply of recipes at his command that he rattled off along with some hard-edged advice.

"In this business one must keep changing—constantly," he advised after a cursory glance at The Store's menu (top-heavy with quiche and crêpes). "Because even your most dedicated food-loving customer today will turn out to have the attention span of a fruit fly tomorrow!"

Several decades later, as we meandered along our shared Manhattan street with Percy between us, I reminded him of that remark. To his credit, he neither recalled nor disavowed the statement but turned the idea over in his mind before answering. "A food lover," he said, "as opposed to someone who merely enjoys good food, is virtually a Casanova—always looking for the perfect meal that will whet his appetite for another, and another after that. But not me. Too many perfect meals give me a stomach ache!"

The only foods he talked about with any real sensuality were dishes so homespun and elemental they would never bear recognition in a Michelin or Mobil Guide: fried eggs, crisp home-cured bacon, and good chewy bread.

Bread was a particular bond he and I shared. Beard grew up in his mother's boardinghouse in Portland, Oregon, where fresh loaves were set in the oven at sunrise daily. Bread baking did not come into my life, however, until I was past forty and fairly stodgy about expanding culinary horizons. I only baked my first loaf because a friend gave me a copy of *Beard on Bread*.

I should have gotten him to sign it the first time we met. To my regret, I was too embarrassed to ask. Instead I paid him a dubious compliment. "You are my disciple of bread baking, Mr. Beard," I blurted out.

If he took offence at my gaffe, you would never know it. Patting me on the shoulder instead, he winked. "Only time will tell if you've got that wrong way round or not."

When he learned that I had recently been to some obscure American town, Mr. Beard would always quiz me about the dishes I'd eaten there. "Was the bread any good?" he would ask. "If the bread is chewable and the butter is unsalted, there's still hope!"

Hope was an essential ingredient of the Beard persona, although he experienced many physical setbacks and equally awesome recuperations at the end of his life. We had not met on the street for several months when I ran into him one night; he looked somewhat the worse for a recent hospital stay but was still jauntily outfitted, wearing a bow tie and carrying a malacca walking stick.

"I've just been on the town, Bert," he informed me, "to Sally's restaurant around the corner." (Sally being Sally Darr, the chef-owner of La Tulipe, a small but splendid restaurant.) "That girl really knows how to orchestrate a meal," he ruminated. "And the bread is *very* chewy. I'm bringing home a slice for Percy." He held up a small crusty end. "Like us, he likes bread with bite to it!"

Wheat Street has not been the same since James Beard left it.

The Grain's Genesis

*I*t's a sobering thought, but wheat, which has been around on this planet longer than man, stands a pretty good chance of outlasting him here too. Faced with immutable odds, man crumbles. Wheat, on the other hand, merely adapts; and has been doing so successfully for millennia!

The first wheat was wild grass. Not all the grass seeds were tasty or even good to eat, but man consumed them greedily because they were there. Unlike plants that had to be dug up or wild things that had to be hunted or trapped, these grains required no effort whatsoever. If he was hungry (and early man usually was), he merely stretched out his

fingers and helped himself to a handful of breakfast, lunch, or dinner.

Paleolithic peoples were nomads, but wheat gave them roots. Somewhere in the broad expanse of Asia—stretching from the slopes of the Himalayas to the shores of the Mediterranean—the leader of a tribe that was forever on the prowl for food stopped short. Before him was a stand of ripening cereal grasses, no different from any field he and his kinsmen had picked over in the past. But on this day he did not order it to be picked over. Instead he bid his family take only half the wild wheat for provender and—here's the switch—plant the rest in the ground nearby. Which necessitated raking, furrowing, seeding, watering, and most important of all, remaining in the territory for the harvest. Which, in loftier terms, is considered to be the birth of agrarian society.

Wheat-growing changed the complexion and digestive system of the ancient world. The Tigris and Euphrates valley, then known as "the fertile crescent" but now dry as a bone, was once covered with endless rows of golden grain—stalks so high that mothers kept small children out of the fields lest they become lost forever in the waving maze.

Sheaves were woven into thatch for roofs and lacings for sandals; large canes kept residents warm in winter and small canes fired their stoves year-round. More important, perhaps, wheat was consumed in a multitude of ways: roasted as cereal, boiled into soup, braised with meat and vegetables as stew, and crushed into flour for bread.

Shards of cooking vessels dating back to 6700 B.C. have been found containing the remnants of cooked wheat in one form or another. And a team of eager archeologists recently unearthed rough implements for grinding seeds (if not precisely wheat, close enough) that were in use 50,000 years before that.

Wheat is obviously a grain that

brought civilization to the world. Because of it, human beings began to pair (two could glean as cheaply as one) and live in communities. Not to mention domesticating animals, building homes, inventing wheels, and making wars upon one another.

But that, if I may be forgiven a pun, is too wheaty a subject to get into here!

Some Plain Grain Talk

There are virtually endless types of wheat. A scientist in the Soviet Union recently logged over 30,000 different varieties—and, worse luck, he named them all!

Happily, all 30,000 belong to fourteen basic wheat species. And just one of those, *Triticum aestivum*, or common wheat, makes up 95 percent of the crop grown and consumed in the U.S. Agronomists refer to wheat strains as "winter wheat" or "spring wheat," depending upon the time of year the seed is planted. Wheat also comes in two botanical nominations, "hard wheat" and "soft wheat," that indicate the volume of gluten in the grain's cellular structure.

Hard common wheat has 10 to 13 percent protein content. The kernels are resilent and tough to mill.

Soft common wheat has 6 to 10 percent protein content. It is also starchier and more malleable than its hard wheat counterparts.

Hard durum wheat (or semolina) represents the remaining 5 percent of wheat grown in the U.S. It is also the toughest wheat of all. But by now you have all the information about semolina you will ever need, so we can skip it here!

In America, hard spring wheat is raised in the coldest parts of the North and Northwest. Hard winter wheat grows in the Central Plains. Soft winter wheat springs from the South and Midwest.

Hard wheat, with its high gluten content and ability to absorb liquid easily, is deemed the ideal grain for bread baking. Soft wheat, with a relatively low amount of gluten in the grain, is adjudged best for cookies, cake, and pastry.

This chapter is concerned with "whole wheat" in a holistic sense, in three very basic and highly nutritious forms: wheat berries, wheat germ, and whole-wheat flour.

WHEAT BERRIES

The name may seem unfamiliar. It's relatively new nomenclature for what used to be known as unprocessed whole wheat. My grandmother used to buy whole wheat in bulk and grind it herself (in a coffee mill) whenever she felt the urge to make a loaf of cracked-wheat bread. (Bulgur is cracked wheat berries.)

Nowadays commercial wheat berries usually come from organically grown wheat and have a culinary identity distinct from cracked wheat. Like all "drieds," they must be presoaked and then precooked before they're used in a recipe. Even then, wheat berries have a decided *al dente* crunch, so be forewarned before setting a molar to a mouthful.

Wheat berries are very good for you. They are high in protein, carbohydrates, B vitamins, and seven amino acids that provide the body with energy: 335 units of protein per cooked half cup. And low in calories: 55 for the same amount.

How to Buy Them

I am sorry to say wheat berries are not generally found on supermarket shelves. They may be obtained at any natural foods store around the country, however, or by mail order (see the resource list at the back of the book).

Wheat berries are very inexpensive. Health food shops sell whole wheat loose (in bulk) and packaged. Bulk sales are cheapest and more sensible in the long run, since wheat berries have a rather long shelf life.

Most wheat berries sold over the counter are hard (red) wheat. Ideally the grains are a uniform deep russet-brown color. There should be no undersized kernels or any hint of husk attached. Wheat husks, unlike bran coverings, are inedible. If it is possible, run your fingers through a batch of wheat berries before you buy them. No chaff should be visible, and they should feel smooth and dry to the touch. Pass over any damp or spotted grains—they're on the way to spoilage.

How to Store Them

*A*s wheat berries are relatively inexpensive and within my normal shopping sphere, I generally buy them only when I have a specific need—never more than a pound or two at a time. I store the unused portion in a glass container with a screw-top lid, in the pantry. Wheat berries keep best in a dry, relatively low-humidity environment, optimally at a temperature that hovers in the low 60s. If your kitchen area is considerably warmer, I suggest you stow the berries in the refrigerator, where they will keep forever. As wheat berries are fairly self-contained, they are not prone to any insect invasion. If you do notice unwanted visitors, however, an overnight stint in the freezer will destroy them at once.

How to Cook Them

*T*o prepare wheat berries for use in the recipes that follow, they first must be soaked overnight. Then, depending upon their further use, either partially or fully cooked.

Partially cooked (or parboiled) wheat berries save time and absorb the essential flavor of the dish they finish in. Fully cooked wheat berries may be eaten as is, amended with a dressing, tossed with vegetables in a salad, or used to bind meats in loaves and croquettes. I even add cooked wheat berries to certain breads for texture.

PRECOOKED WHEAT BERRIES

*W*heat berries double in volume when they are cooked so that 1 cup dried yields 2 cups cooked.

1 cup wheat berries
3½ cups cold water

1. Combine the wheat berries and cold water in a saucepan. Cover, and soak overnight.

2. Boil the wheat berries in their soaking water for 15 minutes for parboiled wheat berries; 50 to 60 minutes for fully cooked wheat berries. Add more water if necessary as they cook.

3. Drain and cool thoroughly. Store in the refrigerator, in a container with a lid or in a self-seal, airtight plastic bag. Parboiled wheat berries will keep for 3 to 4 days, fully cooked berries for up to a week. (Do not freeze; they will turn mushy.)

Makes 2 cups

HARSCHO

*T*his is a version of a hearty Georgian dish—from Russia, not below the Mason-Dixon line. A combination soup-stew, flavored with every herb that grows (at least in my garden), it is said to bring color to the diner's cheeks after the first sip.

2 tablespoons vegetable oil
1 beef chuck roast (3 pounds), about 2 inches thick
1 clove garlic, bruised
1 large onion, quartered and sliced
1½ quarts homemade beef stock (see page 377) or canned broth
1 clove garlic, minced
¼ cup pearl barley
1 cup parboiled wheat berries (see page 298)
2 cups chopped cabbage
1 cup water
1 large turnip (½ pound), peeled and cut into ½-inch cubes
2 large carrots, peeled and cut into ¼-inch-thick slices
2 medium potatoes (1 pound), peeled and cut into ¾-inch cubes
Dash of hot pepper sauce
Salt and freshly ground black pepper to taste
1 cup frozen peas, thawed
¼ cup chopped fresh parsley
1 teaspoon chopped fresh basil
1 teaspoon chopped fresh cilantro (Chinese parsley)
1 teaspoon chopped fresh dill
1 teaspoon chopped fresh tarragon
1 teaspoon chopped fresh chives

1. Preheat the oven to 350°F.

2. Heat the oil in a large heavy pot or Dutch oven over medium-high heat. Rub the meat with the bruised garlic, and cook it in the hot oil until well browned on all sides, 6 minutes. Remove the meat to a plate and add the onion to the pot; cook 1 minute. Place the meat on top of the onions, cover, and transfer to the oven. Bake for 1 hour.

3. Remove the pot from the oven and add 1 quart of the stock, the minced garlic, barley, parboiled wheat berries, and cabbage. Heat to boiling on top of the stove, then cover, return to the oven, and bake 45 minutes.

4. Remove the pot from the oven and add the remaining 2 cups beef stock, the water, turnip, carrots, and potatoes. Heat to boiling on top of the stove, then cover, return to the oven, and cook until the meat and vegetables are tender, about 45 minutes.

5. Remove the pot from the oven. Transfer the meat to a carving board. Add hot pepper sauce to the stew in the pot, and season with salt and pepper. Stir in the peas. Let stand, covered, 5 minutes.

6. Carve the meat into serving pieces. Combine the herbs and stir into the stew. Return the meat to the stew, and serve.

Serves 6 to 8

WHEAT BERRY CAVIAR

You might call this "poor man's caviar." The puréed olives turn the wheat berries as black as the best caviar. It makes a wonderful first course.

2 small cloves garlic
1 cup California "small" pitted black olives
¼ teaspoon salt
¼ teaspoon Dijon mustard
¼ cup olive oil
1½ cups fully cooked wheat berries (see page 298), chilled
Chopped fresh chives, for garnish

1. Turn on a food processor and drop the garlic through the feed tube.

Process until minced. Add the olives, salt, mustard, and oil, and process until the olives are finely minced.

2. Place the cooked wheat berries in a serving bowl. Add the processed olive mixture, and toss gently to mix. Sprinkle with chives.

Serves 4

INCAN-STYLE PORK

Originally from Peru, this spicy amalgam of meat and grain is influenced by the fine cooking style of Felipe Rojas-Lombardi. Felipe makes it with quinoa (see "The New Grains"), but I prefer the crunch of wheat berries in his stew. Serve with a plate of plain boiled potatoes.

2 pounds lean boneless pork shoulder, cut into 1-inch cubes
1 tablespoon olive oil
1 tablespoon red wine vinegar
1 shallot, minced
3 cloves garlic, minced
1 teaspoon salt
½ teaspoon freshly ground black pepper
¼ teaspoon ground cumin
2 dried ancho peppers, seeded and coarsely chopped
2 hot green peppers, seeded, deveined, and chopped
6 tablespoons vegetable oil
1 hot Italian sausage or Spanish chorizo, finely chopped
2 large onions, finely chopped

1 cup V-8 or tomato juice
½ cup (approximately) homemade chicken stock (see page 376) or canned broth
1 cup parboiled wheat berries (see page 298)
2 tablespoons chopped fresh cilantro (Chinese parsley)
Boiled potatoes, heated

1. Place the pork in a large bowl and add the olive oil, vinegar, shallot, 2 cloves of the garlic, salt, pepper, and cumin. Mix well with your hands. Let stand, covered, 2 hours.

2. Meanwhile, place the ancho and hot green peppers in a bowl. Cover with hot water; let soak 3 minutes. Drain.

Repeat this process three times. Then cover with hot water and let stand 15 minutes. Drain, and combine with 2 tablespoons of the vegetable oil in the container of a food processor or blender. Process until smooth.

3. Heat the remaining 4 tablespoons vegetable oil in a large heavy pot or Dutch oven over medium-high heat. Sauté the pork, in about four batches, until well browned, 6 minutes per batch. Transfer to a plate using a slotted spoon. Reduce the heat to medium.

4. Add the sausage to the pot; cook 1 minute. Add the onions and the remaining garlic; cook until golden, about 4 to 5 minutes. Reduce the heat to medium-low and stir in the puréed pepper mixture; cook 5 minutes.

5. Return the pork to the pot and stir well. Add the V-8 and the chicken stock, and heat to boiling. Stir in the

A ccording to grain guru E. J. Kahn, "more of the globe's arable surface is given over to wheat than any other crop grown"—about 600,000,000 acres. Indeed, says Kahn, there are parts of the world where one could fly a small plane over wheat fields and run out of gas long before the wheat ran out of sight!

wheat berries and reduce the heat. Cook, stirring occasionally, partially covered, until the meat is tender, about 1 hour. Add more chicken stock if the mixture becomes too dry. Sprinkle with cilantro, and serve with boiled potatoes.

Serves 6

ELBA'S KIPPES

*T*his dish—an utterly delicious meat and wheat berry croquette, filled with ham or chicken—comes from the Dominican Republic by way of a young woman named Elba Trinidad. Elba serves *kippes* (pronounced keep-ess) hot or cold, as the mood strikes her. I must confess I prefer them warm, with sour cream on the side. If the cream seems too bland, season it with a splash of lemon juice.

½ pound ground beef
½ pound ground veal
¼ pound ground pork
1 large onion, finely chopped
2 hot green peppers, seeded, deveined, and minced
1½ cups fully cooked wheat berries (see page 298)
¼ cup chopped fresh parsley
½ teaspoon salt
¼ pound cooked chicken or ham, ground (about 1¼ cups)
Vegetable oil for deep-frying

1. Combine the beef, veal, and pork in a large bowl and mix well. Add the onion, green peppers, cooked wheat berries, parsley, and salt. Mix well. Form into 20 meatballs.

2. Place the meatballs on a work surface and press to make meat cakes. With your fingers, poke a well in the center of each cake. (They will look a little like birds' nests.) Place about 1 teaspoon ground chicken or ham in each well, and sprinkle with a few drops of water. Press the filling down gently and fold the edges of the meat over the top. Smooth once again into meat cakes.

3. Heat 2 inches oil in a deep heavy skillet or shallow saucepan. Fry the meat cakes, about five at a time, until golden and crisp on both sides, about 6 minutes. Drain well on paper towels. Serve hot or at room temperature.

Makes 20 meat cakes (serves 4)

HEALTHY FARMER'S WIFE'S POT-ROASTED CHICKEN

*T*his is basically a good old-fashioned farm-style pot-roasted chicken. The addition of wheat berries makes it not only heartier, but healthier as well.

¼ pound salt pork, diced (about ½ cup)
12 small white onions
1 chicken (3½ to 4 pounds), well rinsed and dried
1 clove garlic, bruised
1 tablespoon unsalted butter, at room temperature
4 tablespoons unsalted butter
2 medium potatoes (about 1 pound), peeled and diced
1 large carrot, peeled and diced
½ cup parboiled wheat berries (see page 298)
2 teaspoons green peppercorns, or more to taste
4 sprigs parsley
½ bay leaf
2 small sprigs thyme
Chopped fresh parsley, for garnish

1. Preheat the oven to 325°F.

2. Cook the salt pork in boiling water to cover for 2 minutes. Drain and pat dry.

3. Peel the onions, and cut an "X" in the root end of each one. Set aside.

4. Rub the chicken with the garlic, inside and out. Sew and truss the chicken; rub with 1 tablespoon butter.

5. Sauté the salt pork in a large heavy pot or Dutch oven over medium-low heat until crisp and rendered of grease. Using a slotted spoon, transfer to a bowl.

6. Raise the heat slightly and add the chicken to the pot. Brown the chicken well on all sides, 12 minutes. Carefully transfer to a plate.

7. Add the onions to the pot and sauté, stirring frequently, until golden brown, 8 to 10 minutes. Transfer to a bowl.

8. Pour off all grease from the pot and add the 4 tablespoons butter. Stir over medium-low heat, scraping the bottom and sides of the pot with a wooden spoon. Add the potatoes and carrot, stirring well to coat the vegetables. Add the reserved salt pork, wheat berries, and green peppercorns.

9. Push the potato mixture to the edges of the pot and place the chicken in the center. Tie the herbs in a cheesecloth bag, and place in the pot. Cover, and transfer to the oven. Cook until the chicken is tender, about 1 hour and 15 minutes.

10. To serve, carve the chicken and place on a platter. Discard the herb bag, then spoon the vegetable mixture with all the juices into a serving bowl. Sprinkle vegetables and chicken with parsley, and serve.

Serves 3 or 4

ZUCCHINI, TOMATO, AND WHEAT BERRY SLAW

*F*ully cooked wheat berries add a remarkable bite to salads that must be tasted to be believed.

2 cups fully cooked wheat berries (see page 298), chilled
1 large shallot, minced
2 thin medium zucchini, cut into very thin slices
16 to 20 cherry tomatoes, cut into ¼-inch-thick rounds
2 tablespoons chopped fresh basil
1 clove garlic, minced
¼ teaspoon salt
½ teaspoon Dijon mustard
1 tablespoon fresh lemon juice
1 tablespoon red wine vinegar
1 tablespoon strong beef stock (see Note)
¼ cup olive oil

1. Combine the cooked wheat berries with the shallot, zucchini, tomatoes, and basil in a serving bowl. Toss gently to mix.

2. Using the back of a spoon, mash the garlic with the salt in a small bowl until a paste is formed. Whisk in the mustard, lemon juice, vinegar, beef stock, and olive oil. Pour over the salad and toss gently to mix. Let stand 15 to 20 minutes before serving.

Serves 6

Note: If you do not have strong beef stock on hand (see page 379), reduce ¼ cup canned beef broth to 1 tablespoon by simmering for 5 minutes.

SANDRA DAY'S WHEAT BERRY WALDORF SALAD

*M*y good friend Sandra Day, former food editor of the *New Orleans Times-Picayune*, now lives and writes in Lafayette, Louisiana. She also sends me wonderful recipes from time to time. Here is her latest. "If you can't get fennel, and I haven't seen any fresh since I got here," Sandra imparts, "use two stalks of celery instead!"

1 cup fully cooked wheat berries (see page 298), chilled
2 small fennel bulbs (6 ounces each), trimmed and finely chopped (about 1 cup)
¼ cup mayonnaise, preferably homemade (see page 379)
2 teaspoons Dijon mustard
2 tablespoons fresh lemon juice
½ teaspoon fennel seeds, crushed
1 sweet red apple
½ cup walnut halves, toasted (see Note) and coarsely chopped
Lettuce leaves

1. Combine the wheat berries and

the fennel in a bowl. Toss to mix.

2. Combine the mayonnaise with the mustard, lemon juice, and fennel seeds in a small bowl. Pour over the wheat and fennel, and toss well.

3. Core the apple and dice it, tossing the cubes in the salad as you work to prevent discoloring. Toss in the walnuts. Serve on lettuce leaves.

Serves 4

Note: To toast walnuts, spread them evenly on a baking sheet and place in a 350°F oven, stirring occasionally, for 10 minutes.

BEAN AND BERRY BAKE

A variation of Boston's finest buzz-food, and a bounty wherever it turns up geographically. The best way to bake this dish is in an old-fashioned bean pot. If you have to substitute a Dutch oven, be forewarned: the dish will probably cook faster, necessitating more liquid along the way.

1 pound dry white beans
2 teaspoons unsalted butter
1 clove garlic, bruised
1 cup parboiled wheat berries (see page 298)
1 large onion, finely chopped
3 strips bacon, fried crisp and crumbled
4 slices Canadian bacon, chopped
2 tablespoons dark brown sugar
2 teaspoons Worcestershire sauce
¼ cup molasses
5 tablespoons chili sauce
1 tablespoon English dry mustard
1 teaspoon curry powder
¼ teaspoon hot Hungarian paprika
1½ teaspoons salt
½ cup dark rum
2 cups V-8 juice or tomato juice
3 strips raw bacon

1. Pick the beans over, discarding any debris, and place in a large pot. Cover with cold water. Heat to boiling; boil 2 minutes. Remove from the heat and let stand, covered, 1 hour.

2. Preheat the oven to 275°F.

3. Rub a bean pot with the butter. Then rub it well with the bruised garlic.

4. Drain the beans and transfer to a large bowl. Add the wheat berries, onion, crumbled bacon, and the Canadian bacon.

5. In a small bowl, combine the sugar, Worcestershire sauce, molasses, chili sauce, mustard, curry powder, paprika, salt, and dark rum. Pour over the bean mixture. Add ½ cup of the V-8 juice. Mix well and transfer to the prepared bean pot. Place the raw bacon strips over the top. Bake, covered, 7 hours or more, adding more V-8 juice as the beans dry out, about every 30 minutes. If all the V-8 juice is absorbed before the beans are tender, add water as needed.

Serves 6 to 8

SALLY'S CRAZY HEALTH BREAD

This recipe was sent to me by a woman who calls herself "an ex-hippie who is alive and well in Brattleboro, Vermont."

"I came of age during 'the molar movement' at a farm commune in the mid-sixties," she explained. "It was a time when anything that could possibly be chewed or chawed without deleterious effect on the digestive system went into all my recipes. Most of them were tossed in the Disposall when I turned thirty. But this bread holds up. Make it with only *cooled* cooked whole wheat!"

And that's all she wrote.

1 cup lukewarm water
1 package dry yeast
1½ tablespoons molasses
2 tablespoons honey
Pinch of ginger
½ cup fully cooked wheat berries (see page 298), at room temperature
¼ cup pumpkin seeds, toasted and chopped (see Note)
2 tablespoons semolina
2 tablespoons unprocessed bran
1 teaspoon caraway seeds
¼ teaspoon anise seeds
2¾ teaspoons salt
½ cup rye flour
¼ cup buckwheat flour
2½ to 3 cups whole-wheat flour
1 egg white
2 teaspoons sesame seeds
¼ teaspoon freshly ground black pepper

1. Place ¼ cup of the lukewarm water in a large bowl. Sprinkle it with the yeast, then stir in the molasses, honey, and ginger. Let stand until bubbly, 8 to 10 minutes.

2. Add the remaining water to the yeast mixture, along with the cooked wheat berries, pumpkin seeds, semolina, bran, caraway seeds, anise seeds, and ¾ teaspoon of the salt. Mix well, and stir in the rye flour, buckwheat flour, and about 1½ cups whole-wheat flour, enough to form a soft dough.

3. Transfer the dough to a floured

Early Romans called whole wheat *spelt*. Caesar's diary of the Gallic Wars is weighted with the problem of acquiring *spelt* on foreign shores, as K-rations for his legions. These days, Italians call whole wheat *frumento*, but it still turns up as *spelt* in old kitchen tracts and documents written prior to the 14th century.

The French borrowed *frumento* and altered it to *froment*, which in time became *pain de froment*, their word for "bread" as well. During the reign of Louis XIV, when the French disdained coarse bread for croissants and brioche, the name of the grain was altered once again, to *blé*. *Blé*, which sounds like the French verb *blêmir* (to grow pale), had a nice white sound to it. White has been the scourge of whole wheat for centuries. The English word *wheat*, in fact, is derived from the old English *hwit* (white). However, the health-minded Portuguese rejected the blanched moniker entirely. They call wheat *trigo*, which means "hard to handle." Polish farmers dub whole wheat *pszenica*. It means "under the teeth," which is closer to the mark. And it's all wholly wheat round the world, no matter how it's *spelt*. Ouch!

board and knead, adding more whole-wheat flour as needed, until smooth and elastic, about 12 minutes. Transfer to a lightly greased bowl. Cover with plastic wrap and let rise in a warm place until doubled in volume, about 1½ hours.

4. Punch the dough down. Knead briefly and return it to the bowl. Cover again with plastic wrap and let rise in a warm place until doubled in volume, about 1 hour.

5. Generously oil a 9 by 5 by 3-inch loaf pan.

6. Punch the dough down once more, and transfer it to a floured board. Knead 5 minutes. Let it rest 2 minutes, and then roll and stretch the dough into a rope about 15 inches long. Flatten it with your hands and fold it over on itself in thirds. Gently stretch the dough so that it will fit snugly into the loaf pan. Before placing the dough in the pan,

brush the dough with the egg white and sprinkle each side with sesame seeds. Place the dough, folded side down, into the prepared pan, pressing down gently to fill the bottom of the pan. Sprinkle the remaining 2 teaspoons salt and the pepper over the top. Cover with a flour-rubbed tea towel and let rise in a warm place until the dough comes over the top of the pan, about 1 hour.

7. Preheat the oven to 350°F.

8. Bake the bread until it is golden brown and sounds hollow when tapped with your finger, about 45 minutes. Loosen the bread in the pan, and cool it in the pan on a rack.

Makes 1 loaf

Note: To toast pumpkin seeds, heat a small skillet over medium heat. Add the seeds and toast, stirring frequently, until golden, 6 to 8 minutes. Cool before chopping.

BAREFOOT CONTESSA'S WHOLE-WHEAT BERRY BREAD

No, the Barefoot Contessa was not an old flame of mine. It is the moniker of a highly innovative and often intoxicating gourmet emporium in East Hampton, Long Island. I admired their whole-wheat berry bread for years and when I requested the recipe, the owner, Ina Garten (who certainly wears shoes at her store), presented it to me with panache. And so I pass it along to you.

1 cup lukewarm water (115°F)
1 package dry yeast
¼ cup honey
Pinch of ground ginger
½ cup unprocessed bran
1 cup fully cooked wheat berries (see page 298), at room temperature
1 teaspoon salt

1¼ cups whole-wheat flour
1¼ cups unbleached all-purpose flour (approximately)
Cornmeal

1. Place the lukewarm water in a large bowl. Sprinkle the yeast over it, and then stir in the honey and ginger.

Let stand until bubbly, about 5 minutes.

2. Stir in the bran, parboiled wheat berries, and salt. Stir in the whole-wheat flour, and add about ¾ cup of the all-purpose flour, enough to make a stiff dough.

3. Transfer the dough to a lightly floured board and knead, adding more all-purpose flour as needed, until it is smooth and elastic, about 15 minutes.

4. Divide the dough in half, and form each portion into a round loaf.

Place the loaves on a cornmeal-sprinkled baking sheet, and cover with a flour-rubbed tea towel. Let stand in a warm place until doubled in volume, 1½ to 2 hours.

5. Preheat the oven to 350°F.

6. Bake the bread until the loaves are browned and sound hollow when tapped with your finger, about 45 minutes. Cool on a rack.

Makes 2 loaves

WHEAT GERM

Wheat germ is the natural, untreated embryo of the wheat berry. A pale gold substance of crumblike texture and nutty taste, it adds considerable salubrity to the daily diet while sparking up vittles at the same time. For evidence, note the variety of recipes that follow—everything from wheat germ pancakes to wheat germ roasted potatoes.

Wheat germ is a healthy seasoning, sky high in potassium (240 mg per quarter cup), thiamine, niacin, zinc, and riboflavin. Also well endowed with protein and carbohydrates, it contains no sodium or cholesterol whatsoever.

How to Buy It

Wheat germ is a highly visible product on supermarket and grocers' shelves everywhere in the U.S. You will find it next to the packaged cereals. The brand most in evidence is Kretschmer, manufactured by Quaker Oats. Kretschmer wheat germ is sold two ways: plain toasted and honey-flavored. Skip the latter version, as its use (even in desserts) is limited by the added sweetening.

How to Store It

Wheat germ is a highly fragile product, given to fast spoilage once the vacuum-sealed jar is opened. The label on wheat germ containers clearly states that the contents must be refrigerated after opening because the germ (which contains nutritive oils) will turn rancid quickly at room temperature. So why take chances? Refrigerated wheat germ will keep up to six months.

How to Cook It

There are no hard and fast rules for cooking or baking with wheat germ, except for one: do not go overboard. I find, for instance, that wheat germ makes a dandy replacement for half the nuts in a nut cake or half the bread crumbs coating a pork chop, but is not compatible as a total replacement for the original ingredient called for in most recipes. It's too heavy, for one thing, and the fiber content is generally too hard on the alimentary canal, for another.

CRADLED EGGPLANT

An American original: eggplant-stuffed eggplant, garlanded with onion, tomato, anchovy, herbs, cheese, and, oh yes, wheat germ.

2 small eggplants (13 to 14 ounces total)
3 tablespoons olive oil
1 small onion, finely chopped
1 small clove garlic, minced
1 small tomato (3 to 4 ounces), peeled, seeded, and chopped
½ teaspoon anchovy paste
½ teaspoon Worcestershire sauce
Salt and freshly ground black pepper to taste
1 egg, lightly beaten
3 tablespoons toasted wheat germ
¼ cup freshly grated Parmesan cheese
1 tablespoon chopped fresh basil, or 1 teaspoon dried
3 tablespoons buttered bread crumbs (see Note)

1. Cut the stems from the eggplants, and slice each in half lengthwise. Scoop out the flesh with a spoon or grapefruit knife, leaving a shell about ⅛ inch thick. Chop the scooped-out flesh.

2. Heat the oil in a large heavy skillet over medium-low heat. Add the onion; cook 1 minute. Stir in the garlic and cook 4 minutes longer. Raise the heat slightly and stir in the chopped eggplant. Cook, stirring frequently, until the eggplant is tender, about 4 minutes. Add the tomato, anchovy paste, and Worcestershire sauce. Cook 3 minutes longer. Season with salt and pepper, and remove from the heat.

3. Preheat the oven to 350°F.

4. Stir the beaten egg, wheat germ, cheese, and basil into the eggplant mixture. Fill each eggplant half with this mixture, and sprinkle with the buttered bread crumbs.

5. Place the eggplant in a shallow baking dish, and add about ¼ inch hot water to the dish. Bake 45 minutes. Check occasionally, adding more water, if necessary.

Serves 2 to 4

Note: To make buttered bread crumbs, lightly sauté 3 tablespoons fresh bread crumbs in 1 tablespoon melted butter until lightly toasted, 2 minutes.

PATCHWORK ROASTED POTATOES

Another terrific recipe from home cook Mary Surina. This tastes as if it takes hours to make. The secret is, it doesn't!

3 tablespoons toasted wheat germ
3 tablespoons fine fresh bread crumbs
3 tablespoons freshly grated Parmesan cheese
Generous pinch of freshly grated nutmeg

4 tablespoons (½ stick) unsalted butter
2 baking potatoes (about 1 pound)
Salt and freshly ground black pepper to taste

1. Preheat the oven to 400°F. Lightly butter a baking dish.

2. Combine the wheat germ, bread crumbs, cheese, and nutmeg in a shallow bowl.

3. Melt the butter in a medium-size saucepan. Remove from the heat.

4. Peel the potatoes and cut each in half lengthwise. Then cut each half lengthwise into four crescents (a total of 8 slices per potato).

5. Pat the potatoes dry with paper towels, and toss them in the melted butter until well coated. Then roll the potatoes in the wheat germ mixture, and place on the prepared baking dish. Bake until very crisp and tender, 45 to 50 minutes. Sprinkle with salt and pepper, and serve.

Serves 4

HUDSON VALLEY APPLE-BUTTER BREAD

*T*his is a recipe that makes a diner ask, "Which came first, the butter or the bread?" Try making a loaf without the velvety brown-gold apple butter, and you'll never ask the question again.

1 cup lukewarm water
1 package dry yeast
1 teaspoon sugar
Pinch of ground ginger
⅓ cup Homemade Apple Butter (recipe follows)
2 tablespoons unsalted butter, melted
1 tablespoon honey
½ teaspoon salt
¼ cup toasted wheat germ
1 cup whole-wheat flour
2 to 2½ cups bread flour (approximately)
Cornmeal
1 egg
1 teaspoon water

1. Place ¼ cup of the lukewarm water in a large bowl. Sprinkle with the yeast, then stir in the sugar and ginger. Let stand until bubbly, about 5 minutes.

2. Add the remaining lukewarm water to the yeast mixture, and stir in the apple butter, melted butter, honey, salt, wheat germ, whole-wheat flour, and about 1 cup of the bread flour, enough to form a soft dough.

3. Transfer the dough to a floured board and knead, adding more bread flour as needed, until smooth and elastic, about 10 minutes. Transfer to a lightly greased bowl, cover with plastic wrap, and let rise in a warm place until doubled in volume, about 1 hour.

4. Punch the dough down and knead briefly on a floured board. Form the dough into a round loaf and place on a cornmeal-sprinkled baking sheet. Cover with a flour-rubbed tea towel, and let rise until doubled in volume, about 1 hour.

5. Preheat the oven to 425°F.

6. Beat the egg and 1 teaspoon water together, and brush the dough with the mixture. Place the dough in the oven, along with a small pan of water. Bake 10 minutes. Reduce the heat to 375°F and bake until the bread sounds hollow when tapped with your finger, about 20 minutes longer. Cool on a rack.

Makes 1 large loaf

Homemade Apple Butter

2 pounds medium, tart apples (Winesap,
    Jonathan, Jona-Reds)
1 cup apple juice
1 cup firmly packed dark brown sugar, or
    less if desired
1½ teaspoons ground cinnamon
¼ teaspoon ground allspice
⅛ teaspoon ground cloves
1 tablespoon fresh orange juice

1. Wash the apples and remove the stems. Quarter them, and place the apples and the apple juice in a large saucepan, tossing the apples to coat with the juice. Heat to boiling. Reduce the heat and simmer, covered, until the apples are almost soft, about 15 minutes. Then simmer partially covered until very soft, about 10 minutes longer. Turn off the heat and let stand, partially covered, 45 minutes. The mixture should be very thick.

2. Mash the fruit thoroughly through a fine-mesh strainer into another saucepan. Discard skins and seeds. Add the brown sugar, spices, and orange juice. Heat to boiling, and remove from the heat. Pour into sterilized jars and seal.

Makes about 2 pints

WHEATED BENNE PENNIES

I learned to make benne wafers, a favorite southern cookie, when I attended school in the South. I now add toasted wheat germ to the batter—not so much to make them wholesome as for the flavor it imparts.

1 egg
½ teaspoon vanilla extract
6 tablespoons (¾ stick) unsalted butter,
    melted
¾ cup firmly packed light brown sugar
¼ cup all-purpose flour
¼ cup pecans, chopped
¼ cup toasted wheat germ
½ cup sesame seeds, toasted (see Note)

1. Preheat the oven to 400°F. Line baking sheets with aluminum foil and lightly butter the foil.

2. Beat the egg with the vanilla in the medium-size bowl of an electric mixer. Slowly beat in the melted butter. Add the brown sugar, and beat until smooth. Beat in the flour, in three batches. Then stir in the pecans, wheat germ, and toasted sesame seeds.

3. Drop large teaspoonfuls of cookie batter onto the prepared baking sheets, placing them far apart. There should be only six cookies on each baking sheet, as they spread considerably. Bake until golden brown, about 5 minutes. Cool completely before peeling the cookies off the foil. Repeat until all the batter is used up.

Makes 24 cookies

Note: To toast sesame seeds, heat a small skillet over medium heat. Add the seeds and toast, stirring frequently, until golden, about 5 minutes.

POPPY-SEED HOT SHOTS

*P*ancakes with a difference, from one of my favorite American cooks, Clara B. Less— a lady with a good memory and an inexhaustible supply of great dishes.

½ cup all-purpose flour
¼ cup toasted wheat germ
1½ teaspoons poppy seeds
1½ teaspoons sugar
½ teaspoon baking powder
¼ teaspoon baking soda
¼ teaspoon salt
1 egg
1 cup buttermilk
1 tablespoon unsalted butter, melted

1. Combine the flour, wheat germ, poppy seeds, sugar, baking power, baking soda, and salt in a large bowl. Mix well.

2. Whisk the egg with the butter-milk and melted butter in another bowl. Pour this over the flour mixture and stir just until mixed.

3. Heat a lightly greased cast-iron skillet or griddle over medium heat until hot but not smoking. Cook the pancakes, a few at a time, using about 2 large tablespoons per pancake. When lightly browned, about 2 minutes, turn over and cook the other side for 1 minute. Transfer to a serving platter and keep warm in a 225°F oven while cooking the remaining pancakes. Reduce the heat if the cakes brown too quickly.

Makes about twelve 2- to 3-inch pancakes

SNIPPY GINGER SNAPS

I grew up a ginger freak. The gingerier the snap, the more I liked it. Wheat germ adds not only a richer taste but also a crunch that I can't seem to do without.

4 tablespoons (½ stick) unsalted butter, at
*   room temperature*
¼ cup sugar
2 tablespoons molasses
¾ teaspoon ground ginger
½ teaspoon ground cinnamon
¼ teaspoon ground cloves
¼ teaspoon baking soda
Pinch of salt
½ cup all-purpose flour
¼ cup toasted wheat germ

1. Beat the butter in the medium-size bowl of an electric mixer until light and fluffy. Slowly beat in the sugar. Beat in the molasses, ginger, cinnamon, cloves, baking soda, and salt. Add the flour, 2 tablespoons at a time. Stir in the wheat germ and mix thoroughly. Refrigerate the dough, covered, 4 hours.

2. Preheat the oven to 325°F.

3. Shape the dough into a roll about 1½ inches thick. Cut across with a sharp knife into ⅛-inch-thick slices. Place the slices on lightly buttered baking sheets, and bake until lightly browned, about 8 minutes. Cool on the baking sheets before removing.

Makes about 32 cookies

CRACKERJACK CRANBERRY TART

*T*his is half crumble, half tart. The wheat germ adds a good-for-you touch to a fine old-fashioned dessert. I always serve it with ice cream or sweetened whipped cream.

1 cup pecan halves
1 cup walnut halves
1 cup cranberries, picked over
½ cup granulated sugar
¼ cup fresh orange juice
1 teaspoon finely slivered orange zest
1 teaspoon vanilla extract
½ cup toasted wheat germ
¾ cup firmly packed light brown sugar
8 tablespoons (1 stick) unsalted butter,
    chilled and cut into small pieces
Vanilla ice cream or sweetened whipped
    cream (see Note)

1. Preheat the oven to 350°F. Butter and flour a 10-inch glass or ceramic quiche pan.

2. Spread out the nut halves on a baking sheet, and toast them in the oven, turning once, for 5 minutes. Set aside to cool.

3. Combine the cranberries, granulated sugar, and orange juice in a medium-size saucepan. Heat to boiling. Add the orange zest and vanilla. Boil until the cranberries begin to pop, about 1 minute. Remove from heat and set aside to cool.

4. Place the nuts in the container of a food processor, and process until ground. Combine with the wheat germ and brown sugar in a medium-size bowl, and mix well. With your fingers or a pastry blender, work the butter into the dry ingredients until the mixture resembles coarse crumbs.

5. Press half of the nut mixture over the bottom and sides of the prepared quiche pan. Cover with the cooled cranberry mixture. Sprinkle the top with the remaining nut mixture. Bake until the top is a deep golden color, 40 to 45 minutes. Cool on a rack. Serve slightly warm, with vanilla ice cream or sweetened whipped cream.

Serves 8 to 10

Note: To make sweetened whipped cream, whip 1 cup heavy or whipping cream with 1 tablespoon confectioners' sugar.

GROVE TART

I ate something similar to this tart in the Florida Keys—oranges and lemons, picked fresh from the tree. If you are not lucky enough to have your own grove, store-bought does just fine.

FOR THE CRUST:

½ cup firmly packed light brown sugar
1 cup all-purpose flour
¼ cup toasted wheat germ
¼ cup ground pecans
7 tablespoons unsalted butter, chilled

FOR THE FILLING:

2 eggs
1 cup granulated sugar
1 teaspoon finely grated lemon zest
1 teaspoon finely grated orange zest
1 tablespoon fresh lemon juice
2 tablespoons fresh orange juice
2 tablespoons all-purpose flour
½ cup pecan halves

Confectioners' sugar
Sweetened whipped cream (optional; see
    Note, facing page)

1. Preheat the oven to 350°F. Lightly butter a 10-inch round glass or ceramic pie plate or quiche pan.

2. Make the crust: Combine all the ingredients for the crust in a large bowl. Blend with a pastry blender until the mixture has the texture of cornmeal. Remove ½ cup of this mixture and set aside. Pat the remaining mixture over the bottom and sides of the prepared pie plate. Bake 10 minutes. Cool on a rack.

3. Make the filling: Beat the eggs with the sugar in the large bowl of an electric mixture until light. Beat in the lemon and orange zests, the juices, and the flour. Pour into the cooled pie shell. Sprinkle the remaining crust mixture over the top, then arrange the pecan halves over that. Bake until set, 25 to 30 minutes. Cool on a rack and dust with confectioners' sugar before serving. Top with the whipped cream if you like.

Serves 8

CAUGHT-IN-THE-CRUNCH TART

This recipe was inspired by a tart I once tasted at a party. The original is the handiwork of John Sedlar, chef extraordinaire in Southern California. Wheat germ adds a decided flavor note. It is definitely a non-calorie-counter's dessert.

FOR THE PASTRY

1 egg yolk
⅓ cup sugar
8 tablespoons (1 stick) unsalted butter, at
    room temperature
1¾ cups all-purpose flour
2 tablespoons ice water

FOR THE FILLING

1 cup sugar
½ cup heavy or whipping cream, heated
¾ cup (1½ sticks) unsalted butter, cut into
    12 pieces
½ cup toasted wheat germ

¾ cup pecan halves, toasted and coarsely
    chopped (see Note)
¾ cup walnut halves, toasted and coarsely
    chopped (see Note)

FOR THE TOPPING

1½ ounces semi-sweet chocolate, coarsely
    chopped
¼ cup heavy or whipping cream
¼ teaspoon vanilla extract

1. Make the pastry: Beat the egg yolk in the large bowl of an electric mixer until light. Slowly add the sugar, and beat until light and fluffy. Beat in the butter. On low speed, beat in the flour until the mixture is crumbly. Add the ice water, and continue to beat until the dough cleans the sides of the bowl. Wrap in plastic wrap and refrigerate 1 hour.

2. Preheat the oven to 375°F.

3. Roll out the pastry (between two sheets of wax paper, if necessary), and line a 10- to 11-inch loose-bottom tart pan or glass or ceramic quiche pan. Trim and flute the edges. Line the pastry with foil; weight it with rice or dried beans. Bake 10 minutes. Remove the foil and weights, and bake until golden, about 8 minutes longer. Cool completely on a rack.

4. Make the filling: Place the sugar in a heavy skillet or saucepan. Cook over medium-high heat, without stirring, until the edges begin to melt. Reduce the heat to medium and continue to cook, stirring constantly, until the sugar caramelizes to a deep tan color. Reduce the heat to low and carefully stir in the cream. (The mixture will bubble up.) Stir until it is completely smooth. Then stir in the butter, three pieces at a time, until smooth. Remove the pan from the heat, and stir in the wheat germ and nuts. Immediately pour into the cooled crust and spread evenly over the bottom. Cool completely.

5. Make the topping: Melt the chocolate in the top of a double boiler over hot water. Stir in the cream and vanilla until smooth. Transfer to a bowl, place it in a larger bowl filled with ice, and stir until cool. Pour evenly over the entire top of the tart. Let set for 2 hours before serving.

Serves 10 to 12

Note: To toast the nuts, heat a large skillet over medium heat. Add the nuts and toast, stirring frequently, until golden, 6 to 8 minutes. Cool before chopping.

THE FLOURING OF THE GRAIN

*T*here are flours and flours on grocers' shelves, and they are all confusing to non-cognoscenti cooks!

To set the matter straight: all flour is made of wheat, but not all of it is very nutritious. White flour isn't. Whole-wheat flour is! Primarily because whole-wheat flour is milled of the entire wheat kernel. Yes, the endosperm, germ, and bran too! One can actually see the tiny brown flecks in every slice of bread or cake that you bake with whole-wheat flour. That is your assurance that the flour is crammed to the nines with vitamins, minerals, and trace elements. But it is also a warning of this flour's vulnerability. Because of its high nutrients, whole-wheat flour has a brief shelf life.

The two primary proteins in flour (any flour) are known as *gliadin* and *glutenin*. When these proteins combine with a liquid (any liquid), they mutate into a super-protein called *gluten*. Gluten in dough forms a kind of cellular spider's web. Taut to begin with, when the dough is kneaded and punched down, the strands of the web loosen and stretch. If you are baking with yeast, enzymes in the yeast cause the sugar in the dough to ferment. Fermentation in turn releases carbon dioxide, which makes the dough rise. It rises because the carbon dioxide fills the strands of the gluten web with air. So, the bread or rolls come out of your oven high, wide, and handsome!

In some of the recipes for bread, cake, and rolls that follow, whole-wheat flour is combined with all-purpose flour or soft wheat cake flour. The reason for the merger is simple as pie: a reduced amount of gluten is desirable for light-textured baked goods.

For the record, other types of flour available are *all-purpose flour* (a blend of hard and soft wheats with medium gluten content and 10 percent protein); *cake flour*, also known as soft wheat flour (a flour made entirely of soft wheat, often with the addition of cornstarch to lighten the starch level, and with a scant 6 percent protein content); and *bread flour* (a pure hard wheat flour, with 14 percent protein content).

How to Buy It

Whole-wheat flour is available to consumers two ways: stone ground and commercially milled. The nutrient levels of both flours depend entirely on how the grains were milled and processed. The most nutritious and best-flavored whole-wheat flours are indubitably the output of small independent millers around the country. These flours, labeled "Stone-Ground Whole Wheat," can always be found at natural foods stores, where organic stone-ground whole-wheat flours are available as well. Stone-ground flour is ground on rotating millstones, and the texture and flavor may vary somewhat

from milling to milling, but it is a wonderful ingredient and worth the higher price tag in my opinion.

Unbleached commercial whole-wheat flour can be found at supermarkets everywhere. It is a perfectly acceptable alternative to stone-ground whole-wheat flour, though decidedly less coarse in texture. On occasion commercial flours contain additives like ground barley as filler; check the label before you buy. And the aging process of the wheat is sometimes artificially speeded up with the addition of potassium bromate. Look carefully at the package; if it is called "bromated whole-wheat flour," you may wish to pass it by. Incidentally, all flours (whole wheat and otherwise; commercial and stone ground) are "enriched" by U.S.D.A. mandate these days. So accept the vitamin supplement with good grace—whether it is good for you or not, you can't avoid it!

How to Store It

All flour absorbs odors, so it is best to stash it in an airtight container. Glass, rather than plastic, is my preference. Whole-wheat flour, because it contains a high ratio of wheat germ and its essential oils, spoils rapidly, and plastic containers seem to quicken the process. Beyond-the-pale whole-wheat flour has a terrible odor, like stale olive oil. I keep whole-wheat flour in the refrigerator, where it remains in prime condition for about three months. Do not keep whole-wheat flour in its original package, even if it is insulated in airtight plastic bags. Paper absorbs oil and will hasten its demise, in the fridge or out!

WHOLESOME WHOLE-WHEAT NOODLES

Unlike the Italians, who eschew any ingredients other than flour and egg yolks in their pasta, I leaven these noodles with a tad of oil and a splash of water. They roll more felicitously after the addition, I find. But I *am* a purist in the matter of pasta machines: mine is a small stainless-steel hand-cranked model, known as an "Atlas," that outperforms any electric invention on the market.

Whole-wheat noodles are very low in calories (100 per generous cupful), so I feel I have the right to burn a few when it comes to toppings. You let your conscience be your own guide in the matter!

2 cups whole-wheat flour
½ teaspoon salt
1 tablespoon vegetable oil
2 egg yolks
½ cup water (approximately)

1. Combine the flour with the salt in a large bowl.

2. Combine the oil, egg yolks, and ½ cup water in another bowl. Pour this over the flour mixture and work with your fingers to form a soft dough. Add 1 to 2 tablespoons more water if needed.

3. Transfer the dough to a lightly floured board and knead 10 minutes. Cover the dough with a bowl and let rest 1 hour.

4. Divide the dough into four pieces. Run them through a pasta machine, or roll out into a thin dough and cut into noodles. Dry for 1 hour before using.

Makes about 1 pound

HOLD EVERYTHING WHOLE-WHEAT NOODLES WITH CLAMS

I call this "hold everything" because that is what I do when my friends on Long Island call me up and say they are dropping off some clams they just plucked from the bay. I put everything else on hold—and enjoy.

2 sweet Italian sausages (about ½ pound),
*   finely chopped*
2 sprigs parsley
1 sprig thyme, or a pinch of dried
1 sprig oregano, or a pinch of dried
3 tablespoons unsalted butter
1 small onion, finely chopped
1 clove garlic, minced

36 clams, washed well
1 cup dry white wine
1 teaspoon all-purpose flour
½ cup heavy or whipping cream
1 pound fresh whole-wheat noodles (see
*   above)*
¼ teaspoon crushed dried hot red peppers
1 tablespoon chopped fresh parsley

1. Sauté the sausages in a lightly oiled heavy skillet over medium heat until rendered of all fat and crisp, 8 minutes. Drain on paper towels.

2. Tie the parsley, thyme, and oregano in a cheesecloth bag to make a bouquet garni, and set aside.

3. Melt 2 tablespoons of the butter in a large saucepan over medium-low heat. Add the onion; cook 1 minute. Add the garlic; cook 2 minutes longer. Add the bouquet garni to the pan, along with the clams and white wine. Heat to boiling. Cover, and cook over medium-high heat until the clams open, about 10 minutes.

4. Remove the clams from the saucepan with a slotted spoon. Discard the bouquet garni and any clams that did not open, reserving the broth.

5. Remove the meat from the clams.

Chop and reserve.

6. Melt the remaining 1 tablespoon butter in a medium-size saucepan over medium-low heat. Add the flour; cook, stirring constantly, 2 minutes. Whisk in 1½ cups reserved clam broth and the cream. Heat to boiling, and boil until slightly thickened, about 10 minutes.

7. Meanwhile, drop the pasta into a large pot of salted boiling water and boil until just tender, 3 to 5 minutes.

8. While the pasta is cooking, add the dried red peppers, the chopped clams, and the sausage bits to the cream sauce; cook 2 minutes longer.

9. Drain the pasta and place in a serving dish. Pour the clam and sausage mixture over the top. Toss well, and sprinkle with the parsley.

Serves 4

SAUSAGE-AND-FENNEL-TOPPED NOODLES

As in the previous recipe, I often add sausage meat to white sauces as well as red, to perk up the flavor of the other ingredients. This time its partner is fresh fennel, straight from the farmer's market.

2 stalks fennel
½ pound sweet Italian sausages
2 tablespoons unsalted butter
1 onion, finely chopped
1 clove garlic, minced
1 teaspoon fennel seeds, lightly crushed
2 egg yolks
⅓ cup homemade chicken stock (see page 376) or canned broth
¾ pound fresh whole-wheat noodles (see facing page)
⅓ cup freshly grated Parmesan cheese
¼ cup chopped fresh parsley

1. Cook the fennel in boiling salted water to cover for 2 minutes. Rinse under cold running water and drain. Finely chop the fennel (you should have about ½ cup), and set aside.

2. Remove the sausages from their casings and sauté, breaking up the lumps, in an oil-rubbed large heavy skillet over medium heat until crisp and well browned, about 5 minutes. Using a slotted spoon, transfer to a bowl.

3. Pour off all grease from the skillet and add 1 tablespoon of the butter. Add the onion, and cook over medium-low heat 1 minute. Add the garlic, fennel seeds, and fennel. Cook, stirring occasionally, 3 minutes. Add the sausage, and cook 2 minutes longer. Reduce the heat to low.

4. Combine the egg yolks and chicken stock in a bowl. Cook the noodles in a large pot of boiling salted water until just tender, 3 to 5 minutes. Drain. Return the noodles to the pan they cooked in, and toss with the remaining 1 tablespoon butter.

5. Add the noodles to the sausage mixture and gently toss until mixed.

Pour the egg mixture over the top, and add the Parmesan cheese and 3 tablespoons of the parsley. Cook, tossing gently, over low heat 2 minutes. Do not allow to boil. Sprinkle with the remaining 1 tablespoon parsley before serving.

Serves 4

TICKER-TAPE NOODLE HASH

*L*eftover lamb makes a wonderful base for a hash. Instead of potatoes, I use wholewheat noodles. With very tonic results, I might add.

½ pound whole-wheat noodles, fresh (see page 316) or packaged
4 tablespoons olive oil
1 large onion, finely chopped
¼ pound thinly sliced pancetta or smoky bacon, finely chopped
5 cloves garlic, minced
2½ cups cooked lamb, cut into ½-inch cubes
1 teaspoon chopped fresh thyme, or ½ teaspoon dried
1 tablespoon chopped fresh basil, or 1 teaspoon dried
¼ teaspoon ground cumin
⅛ teaspoon ground turmeric
⅓ cup heavy or whipping cream
Salt and freshly ground black pepper to taste
2 tablespoons chopped fresh parsley

1. Cook the pasta in a large pot of boiling salted water until barely tender (3 minutes for homemade; longer for commercially packaged). Drain. Return the noodles to the pan they cooked in, and toss with 1 tablespoon of the oil. Keep warm over low heat.

2. Heat 2 tablespoons of the oil in a large heavy saucepan over medium heat. Add the onion and pancetta; cook until the onion is golden, about 5 minutes. Add the garlic; cook 2 minutes longer. Stir in the lamb, thyme, basil, cumin, and turmeric. Continue to cook, stirring constantly, 4 minutes.

3. Add the remaining 1 tablespoon oil to the lamb mixture, and add the pasta and cream, tossing lightly until well mixed. Continue to toss until warmed through. Season with salt and pepper, and sprinkle with the parsley.

Serves 6

EMBARRASSMENT OF ONIONS TART

A n onion quiche, if you will. Serve it as a side dish with any meat or fish. Or do as I do, and eat it as a main course with a salad, with no embarrassment whatsoever.

100% or 50% Whole-Wheat Pastry (see pages 327 and 328)
4 strips bacon
2 tablespoons unsalted butter
4 medium leeks, white bulbs only, rinsed well and chopped
1 medium onion, chopped
1 shallot, minced
1 clove garlic, minced
Pinch of ground cloves
½ teaspoon chopped fresh thyme, or a pinch of dried
2 eggs
½ cup sour cream
½ cup heavy or whipping cream
¼ cup milk
2 teaspoons Dijon mustard
½ teaspoon salt
¼ teaspoon freshly ground black pepper
1 cup grated Jarlsberg cheese
2 teaspoons chopped fresh chives

1. Preheat the oven to 400°F.

2. Line a 10-inch glass or ceramic quiche dish with the pastry, and trim and flute the edges. Line the pastry with foil, making sure the edges are covered, and weight with rice or dried beans.

Bake 15 minutes. Remove the foil and weights, and bake another 5 minutes. Cool on a rack. Reduce the oven temperature to 375°F.

3. Sauté the bacon in a large heavy skillet until crisp. Drain on paper towels, crumble, and reserve.

4. Pour off all but 2 tablespoons bacon drippings from the skillet. Melt the butter in the drippings over medium-low heat. Stir in the leeks, onion, shallot, and garlic. Cook 2 minutes. Sprinkle with the cloves and thyme. Cover, and cook, stirring occasionally, until the onions are tender, about 30 minutes. Remove from the heat.

5. Lightly beat the eggs in a medium-size bowl. Beat in the sour cream, heavy cream, milk, mustard, salt, and pepper. Stir in the onion mixture, the reserved bacon, and the cheese. Pour into the cooled pie shell, and sprinkle the top with the chives. Bake until slightly puffed and golden, 25 to 30 minutes. Let stand for 10 minutes before serving.

Serves 6

WELL-BRED WHOLE-WHEAT LOAF

M y friend Sharon Tyler Herbst, who has appeared in this book already, is a wonderful food writer and a caring person—we share a bond when it comes to the concerns of the food industry and the world at large. One of my truest joys in life has

been breaking bread with Sharon and her husband, Ron—particularly when it is this bread, made by her own two hands.

½ cup lukewarm water
2 packages dry yeast
¼ cup plus 3 teaspoons malt syrup or
    honey
1 cup cottage cheese, at room temperature
2 tablespoons molasses
5 to 5½ cups whole-wheat flour
¼ cup vegetable oil
2 eggs, lightly beaten, at room temperature
2½ teaspoons salt
½ cup toasted wheat germ
1 tablespoon water

1. Place the lukewarm water in the large bowl of an electric mixer, and sprinkle with the yeast. Stir in 1 teaspoon of the malt syrup. Let stand until bubbly, 5 to 10 minutes. Then add the cottage cheese, ¼ cup malt syrup, molasses, and 1½ cups of the flour. Beat at medium speed 2 minutes. Scrape down the sides of the bowl, cover with plastic wrap, and let stand in a warm place until bubbly and tripled in volume, about 1 hour.

2. Stir the oil into the dough along with the eggs, salt, and wheat germ. Stir in enough of the remaining flour to make a soft dough. Turn the dough out onto a floured board and knead, adding more flour as needed, until smooth and elastic, about 10 minutes. Transfer the dough to a greased bowl, cover with a damp towel, and let rise in a warm place until tripled in volume, about 1 hour.

3. Punch down the dough and divide it in half. Place each portion in a greased 8 by 4 by 3-inch loaf pan, and cover with a flour-rubbed tea towel. Let rise until doubled in volume, about 45 minutes.

4. Combine the remaining 2 teaspoons malt syrup with the 1 tablespoon water. Slash the tops of the loaves, if desired, and brush them with the malt syrup glaze. Place the bread in a cold oven, and turn the heat on to 375°F. Bake until the bread sounds hollow when tapped with your finger, 30 to 35 minutes. Remove the loaves from the pans, and cool on racks.

Makes 2 loaves

MILDRED SCHULZ'S WHOLE-WHEAT BATTER BREAD

Mildred Schulz, mother of my friend and collaborator, Phillip S. Schulz, has always appeared in my books. She brings me good luck. Her batter bread is not only easy but delicious as well—a lucky find for any home breadmaker.

1½ cups lukewarm water
1 package dry yeast
2 tablespoons honey
2 cups whole-wheat flour
1 cup all-purpose flour
1 teaspoon salt

2 tablespoons unsalted butter, at room
    temperature

1. Place the lukewarm water in the large bowl of an electric mixer. Sprinkle with the yeast, and stir in the honey. Let

stand until bubbly, about 5 minutes.

2. On medium speed, beat in 1 cup of the whole-wheat flour, ½ cup of the all-purpose flour, the salt, and the butter. Beat 2 minutes, scraping the sides of the bowl often. On low speed, beat in the remaining flours. Cover the bowl, and let the dough rise in a warm place until doubled in volume, about 1 hour.

3. Stir the dough down by beating 25 strokes with a wooden spoon. Spread the dough into a greased 9 by 5 by 3-inch loaf pan. Cover loosely with a flour-rubbed tea towel, and let rise in a warm place until the dough comes to the top of the pan, about 1 hour.

4. Preheat the oven to 400°F.

5. Bake until the bread is golden brown and sounds hollow when tapped with your finger, about 30 minutes. Remove from the pan and cool on a rack.

Makes 1 loaf

DARLENE SCHULZ'S COST-CONSCIOUS COTTAGE CHEESE BUNS

Another Schulz—this time Phillip's sister-in-law. I first ate these scrumptious buns in Brownsville, Wisconsin, when I spent a memorable Christmas weekend in a part of the country where the food is hearty, healthy, and generously apportioned.

1½ cups cottage cheese
2 tablespoons unsalted butter
4 teaspoons honey
1 teaspoon molasses
½ teaspoon salt
½ cup lukewarm water
2 packages dry yeast
¼ teaspoon sugar
2 eggs, lightly beaten
4½ cups whole-wheat flour (approximately)
Cornmeal

1. Combine the cottage cheese, butter, honey, molasses, and salt in a small saucepan. Stir over medium-low heat until the butter has melted. Remove from the heat and allow to cool to lukewarm.

2. Place the lukewarm water in a large bowl, and sprinkle with the yeast. Stir in the sugar. Let stand until bubbly, about 5 minutes.

3. Add the eggs to the cottage cheese mixture, and then add this mixture to the yeast mixture. Stir in about 3 cups of the flour, enough to make a soft dough. Transfer the dough to a floured board and knead, adding more flour as needed, 10 minutes.

4. Place the dough in a lightly greased bowl. Cover with plastic wrap, and let rise in a warm place until doubled in volume, about 1 hour.

5. Punch the dough down and knead briefly on a floured board. Divide the dough into fourteen equal portions. Shape each portion into a roll, tucking any cracks underneath. Place the rolls, seven per sheet, on two cornmeal-sprinkled baking sheets. Cover with flour-rubbed tea towels, and let rise until doubled in volume, or until almost roll size, about 35 minutes.

6. Preheat the oven to 375°F.

7. Bake until the rolls are nicely browned, about 15 minutes. Cool on a rack.

Makes 14 hamburger-size rolls

MARYBETTE SLUSARSKI'S RED-FACED TOMATO BREAD

MaryBette Slusarski lives in Ackworth, Iowa, and produces a newsletter called *Food for Thought*. Her tomato-laced bread is one of the best whole-wheats I have ever chomped.

1½ pounds ripe tomatoes
½ cup lukewarm water
2 packages dry yeast
1 teaspoon plus 2 tablespoons honey
⅛ teaspoon ground ginger
2 tablespoons vegetable oil
1 teaspoon salt
1 tablespoon chopped fresh basil
4 to 5 cups stone-ground whole-wheat flour
Cornmeal

1. Peel and seed the tomatoes. Process in a food processor or blender to make a purée. You should have 1½ cups. Heat the purée in a saucepan to lukewarm.

2. Place the lukewarm water in a large bowl and sprinkle with the yeast. Stir in 1 teaspoon honey and the ginger. Let stand until foamy, about 5 minutes.

3. Add the puréed tomatoes to the yeast mixture, along with the 2 tablespoons honey, oil, salt, basil, and 2 cups of the flour. Then stir in 1½ to 2 more cups flour, enough to form a soft dough. Scrape the dough out onto a floured board and knead, adding more flour as needed, 10 minutes. Transfer the dough to a lightly greased bowl and cover with plastic wrap. Let stand in a warm place until doubled in volume, about 1 hour.

4. Punch the dough down and knead briefly on a floured board. Divide the dough in half and form into round loaves. Place the loaves on a cornmeal-sprinkled baking sheet. Cover with a flour-rubbed tea towel, and let rise in a warm place until doubled in volume, about 1 hour.

5. Preheat the oven to 325°F.

6. Bake until the bread sounds hollow when tapped with your finger, 45 to 50 minutes. Cool on a rack.

Makes 2 loaves

SKY-HIGH WHEAT BISCUITS

I once sampled a similar recipe in New Iberia, Louisiana, at a place named simply "Helen's." Whole-wheat flour, added to the recipe, makes it a healthier bite and tastier too.

1 cup whole-wheat flour
1 cup cake flour
1 tablespoon baking powder
½ teaspoon baking soda
2 teaspoons sugar
½ teaspoon salt
5⅓ tablespoons (⅓ cup) unsalted butter, chilled
¾ cup buttermilk
2 tablespoons unsalted butter, melted

1. Preheat the oven to 450°F. Lightly butter a 9-inch round cake pan.

2. Combine the flours with the baking powder, baking soda, sugar, and salt in a large bowl. Cut in the butter with a knife, and blend with a pastry blender until the mixture has the texture of coarse crumbs. Stir in the buttermilk to form a soft dough.

3. Transfer the dough to a floured board. Knead briefly, and roll out about ¾ inch thick. Using a biscuit or cookie cutter, cut into 2½- to 3-inch circles. Place the biscuits in the prepared cake pan, and brush the tops with the melted butter. Bake until golden brown and firm, about 25 minutes.

Makes 8 or 9 biscuits

WHIRLIGIGS

I hate to admit that it never seemed possible to me to make bread sticks at home. I was wrong. These bread sticks can be made ahead and frozen, for up to two months, and served whenever the whim strikes.

1½ cups warm water (110°F)
1 package dry yeast
1 teaspoon honey
2 cups stone-ground whole-wheat flour
1 teaspoon salt
1½ to 2 cups all-purpose flour
2 tablespoons olive oil (approximately)
Coarse (kosher) salt

1. Place ¼ cup of the warm water in a large bowl. Sprinkle the yeast over it, and stir in the honey. Let stand until bubbly, about 5 minutes.

2. Add the remaining warm water to the yeast mixture, and stir in the whole-wheat flour, salt, and about 1¼ cups of the all-purpose flour. The dough will be slightly sticky. Transfer to a well-floured board and knead, adding more flour as needed, until smooth and elastic, about 10 minutes. Place the dough in a greased bowl, cover with plastic wrap, and let rise in a warm place until doubled in volume, about 1 hour.

3. Punch the dough down, cover, and let rise once more until doubled in volume, about 45 minutes.

4. Preheat the oven to 450°F.

5. Brush four baking sheets with some of the olive oil, and sprinkle with coarse salt.

6. Punch the dough down once more. With floured hands, scrape a heaping tablespoon of dough onto a well-floured board. Roll the dough into a thin rope no more than ½ inch thick and about 12 inches long. Place on a prepared baking sheet. Repeat with the remaining dough. Brush each dough stick with more olive oil and sprinkle with coarse salt. Bake until golden and crisp, about 20 minutes. Cool on a rack.

Makes about 24 bread sticks

BLACK 'N' BLUE BLUEBERRY MUFFINS

These muffins were invented by an Ohio woman who had an overstock of whole-wheat flour one summer, when the blueberries were going crazy in her Columbus backyard.

1 cup blueberries
2 tablespoons sugar
1 teaspoon finely slivered lemon zest
⅓ cup all-purpose flour
¾ cup whole-wheat flour
1 teaspoon baking soda
½ teaspoon salt
1 egg
2 tablespoons honey
½ cup milk
2 tablespoons unsalted butter, melted

1. Preheat the oven to 400°F. Lightly grease 9 muffin cups.

2. Pick over the blueberries, discarding any stems, and place in a colander. Rinse with cold water, shake off the excess, and place in a bowl. Sprinkle with the sugar and lemon zest.

3. Combine the flours in a large bowl, and add the baking soda and salt. Mix well.

4. Lightly beat the egg in a medium-size bowl. Then beat in the honey, milk, and melted butter. Stir this into the flour mixture, and add the blueberries.

5. Fill the prepared muffin cups half full with the batter. Bake until golden brown and firm, 15 to 20 minutes. Loosen the muffins, but allow to cool in the pan on a rack.

Makes 9 muffins

SINFUL CINNAMON-PECAN COFFEE CAKE

The next recipe is old-fashioned yet remarkably streamlined in execution and came my way from the talented hand of Karen Haram, the food editor of the San Antonio *Express-News*.

FOR THE TOPPING

3 tablespoons whole-wheat flour
3 tablespoons all-purpose flour
3 tablespoons unsalted butter, chilled
1½ teaspoons ground cinnamon
⅔ cup chopped pecans
¼ cup firmly packed light brown sugar

FOR THE CAKE

¾ cup whole-wheat flour

1 cup all-purpose flour
Pinch of salt
1 teaspoon baking soda
1 teaspoon baking powder
1½ teaspoons ground cinnamon
¾ cup firmly packed light brown sugar
¾ cup granulated sugar
8 tablespoons (1 stick) unsalted butter, at
    room temperature
1 large egg
1⅓ cups buttermilk

1. Preheat the oven to 350°F. Lightly butter a 9 by 13-inch cake pan.

2. Make the topping: Combine the two flours in a medium-size bowl. Cut in the butter with a knife, and then blend with a pastry blender until the butter is totally incorporated into the flour. Add the cinnamon, pecans, and brown sugar, mixing well with your fingers. Set aside.

3. Make the cake: Combine the two flours with the salt, baking soda, baking powder, and cinnamon in a bowl. Set aside.

4. Place the two sugars with the butter in the large bowl of an electric mixer, and beat until smooth. Add the egg, and continue to beat until light. Stir the flour mixture into the butter mixture in three batches, alternating with three batches of the buttermilk.

5. Pour the batter into the prepared cake pan. Sprinkle the topping evenly over the batter. Bake in the center of the oven until a toothpick inserted in the center comes out clean, 35 to 40 minutes. Cool on a rack before serving.

Serves 12

SUGAR-CRUSTED WHOLE-WHEAT CRULLERS

*I*n South Dakota, where these spring from, whole wheat is an ingredient in three out of four entries in every farmer's recipe book.

1 egg
1¼ cups plus 2 tablespoons sugar
½ cup sour cream
1 tablespoon unsalted butter, melted
¾ cup stone-ground whole-wheat flour
½ cup all-purpose flour
1 teaspoon baking powder
½ teaspoon baking soda
¼ teaspoon salt
⅛ teaspoon freshly grated nutmeg
⅛ teaspoon ground mace
1 teaspoon ground cinnamon
Vegetable oil for deep-frying

1. Beat the egg in the large bowl of an electric mixer until light. Slowly add ¼ cup plus 2 tablespoons of the sugar, and continue to beat until light and fluffy. Beat in the sour cream and melted butter. Stir in the flours, baking powder, baking soda, salt, nutmeg, and mace. Scrape the mixture into a small bowl (the dough will be quite sticky). Cover and refrigerate 45 minutes.

2. Transfer the chilled dough to a well-floured board. Using about 3 tablespoons of dough, roll out a rope about ¾ inch thick and about 5 inches long. Transfer to a floured surface, and repeat with the remaining dough. When all the crullers are formed, cover with a flour-rubbed tea towel and let rest 20 minutes.

3. Meanwhile, combine the remaining 1 cup sugar and the cinnamon on a plate.

4. Heat 2 to 3 inches of oil in a heavy skillet until hot. Cook the crullers, no more than three at a time, until golden brown, 2 to 3 minutes per side. Roll them on paper towels and then immediately roll in the sugar/cinnamon mixture. Place on a rack while frying the remaining dough. Serve warm or at room temperature.

Makes about 10 crullers

WHITLING BUTTERMILK WHEAT CAKES

*T*hese wondrous wheat cakes are worthy of a toast with strong coffee the next time you linger over breakfast.

1 cup plus 2 tablespoons stone-ground whole-wheat flour
1 tablespoon sugar
1½ teaspoons baking soda
½ teaspoon salt
1 egg
1½ cups buttermilk
1 tablespoon vegetable oil

1. Combine the flour with the sugar, baking soda, and salt in a medium-size bowl. Mix well.

2. Whisk the egg with the buttermilk and oil in another bowl. Pour over the flour mixture and stir just until mixed.

3. Heat a lightly greased cast-iron skillet or griddle over medium heat until hot but not smoking. Cook the pancakes, a few at a time, using about 3 tablespoons batter per pancake. When lightly browned, about 2 minutes, turn over and cook the other side for 1 minute. Transfer to a serving platter and keep warm while cooking the remaining cakes. Reduce the heat if the cakes brown too quickly.

Makes about eighteen 2- to 3-inch pancakes

DUMMERSTON APPLESAUCE TART

*I*n Dummerston, Vermont, one need only to pass through an old covered bridge to smell the apple orchards. This tart is hearty and healthy, like all the good denizens who live there.

100% Whole-Wheat Pastry (recipe follows)
5 tart green apples
1 tablespoon unsalted butter
½ teaspoon ground cinnamon
⅓ cup firmly packed light brown sugar
1 tablespoon dark rum
1½ tablespoons finely slivered orange zest
2 tablespoons fresh orange juice
¼ cup honey
½ teaspoon vanilla extract
⅓ cup apricot preserves

1. Preheat the oven to 400°F.

2. Press the pastry over the bottom and sides of a lightly buttered 9-inch loose-bottom quiche or tart pan. Line with foil; weight with rice or dried beans. Bake 15 minutes. Remove the foil and weights, and bake 5 minutes longer. Cool on a rack. Reduce the oven temperature to 375°F.

3. Peel, core, and coarsely chop 3 of the apples. Melt the butter in a heavy saucepan over medium-low heat. Add the apples and cook, stirring frequently, 5 minutes. Add the cinnamon, brown sugar, rum, and orange zest. Cook until the apples are soft, about 20 minutes. Mash until thick. Set aside to cool.

4. Peel, core, and cut the remaining 2 apples into ⅛-inch-thick slices. Combine with the orange juice, honey, and vanilla in a bowl. Let stand 10 minutes. Drain, reserving 2 tablespoons of the juice.

5. Spoon the applesauce mixture over the bottom of the prepared shell. Cover with a neat layer of overlapping sliced apples.

6. Combine the apricot preserves with the reserved 2 tablespoons juice in a small saucepan. Heat to boiling, then reduce the heat and cook, breaking up the lumps with a spoon, 2 minutes. Spoon over the apples. Bake until the top is golden and the apples are tender, about 40 minutes. Serve slightly warm.

Serves 8

100% Whole-Wheat Pastry

1¼ cups stone-ground whole-wheat flour
¼ teaspoon salt
½ cup lard
1 egg yolk
1 teaspoon red wine vinegar
2½ tablespoons cold water (approximately)

1. Combine the flour and salt in a medium-size bowl. Cut in the lard with a knife, and blend with a pastry blender until the mixture has the texture of coarse crumbs.

2. Combine the egg yolk, vinegar, and cold water in a small bowl. Cut this into the pastry mixture with a knife or fork to form a soft dough. Knead briefly before using.

Makes one 9- to 10-inch single crust

olumbus did it!

They say he brought wheat to the New World on his second voyage—but it was only a handful of grain and it promptly withered when he went on his way. But don't blame him. The man might have been a heck of a navigator, but he knew beans about agriculture.

Wheat came this way again in 1620, with the founders of the Plymouth Colony. Bartholomew Gosnold planted grain on Cuttyhunk Island, near Martha's Vineyard, where it "took" that time around. Wheat grew, Gosnold's family even managed to produce a few loaves of bread, but it certainly was not the "amber waves of grain" celebrated in story and song.

America did not become beautiful with wheat until a couple of centuries later, when Swedish, Norwegian, German, and Russian immigrants drifted in this direction. Once they took a look at the cities of the Atlantic coastline, they picked up their belongings, bought wagons, and headed west, where they had heard the landscape went on forever. That's true wheat country, you see.

By the mid-1800s Ohio, Pennsylvania, upper New York State, and Virginia all produced bumper wheat crops. By the turn of the century, Kansas and Iowa's output totaled the entire yield of the Ukraine, and inventive second-generation cooks were cramming whole wheat into more dishes than one could shake a stick at.

APROPOS APRICOT TART

*T*his one is sinful—a creamy custard topped with fresh apricots. Other fresh fruits, such as oranges, peaches, or sweet berries, work as well.

FOR THE CRUST

50% Whole-Wheat Pastry (recipe follows)
½ cup sugar
3 tablespoons water

FOR THE FILLING

3 egg yolks
¼ cup sugar
¼ teaspoon vanilla extract
1½ tablespoons cornstarch
¾ cup milk, scalded
½ cup heavy or whipping cream

FOR THE TOPPING

10 to 12 very ripe apricots, peeled and
    quartered or halved
½ cup red currant jelly
1½ tablespoons sugar
1½ tablespoons orange liqueur, such as
    Grand Marnier

1. Preheat the oven to 400°F.
2. Line a 10-inch loose-bottom tart pan with the pastry, and trim and flute the edges. Line the pastry with foil; weight with rice or dried beans. Bake 15 minutes. Remove the foil and weights, and bake 10 minutes longer or until lightly browned. Cool on a rack.
3. Place the sugar and the water in a small saucepan. Cook, stirring constantly, until the sugar melts and turns golden. Drizzle over the bottom of the cooled crust.
4. Make the filling: Beat the egg yolks with the sugar in the top of a double boiler until light. Stir in the vanilla, and whisk in the cornstarch until smooth. Whisk in the milk. Cook, stirring constantly, over simmering water

until thick, about 12 minutes. Transfer to a bowl, cool, then refrigerate for 30 minutes.
5. Beat the cream until stiff, and fold into the chilled custard. Spoon this mixture into the prepared shell.
6. Make the topping: Arrange the apricots over the custard in a decorative pattern. Refrigerate.
7. Combine the currant jelly, sugar, and orange liqueur in a small saucepan. Heat to boiling, then reduce the heat and cook over medium-low heat 5 minutes. Drizzle over the apricots. Refrigerate until ready to serve.

Serves 8

50% Whole-Wheat Pastry

⅔ cup whole-wheat flour
⅔ cup cake flour
¼ teaspoon salt
4 tablespoons (½ stick) unsalted butter,
    chilled
2 tablespoons solid vegetable shortening,
    chilled
2½ to 3 tablespoons cold water

Combine the flours with the salt in a bowl. Cut in the chilled butter and shortening with a knife, then blend with a pastry blender until the mixture has the texture of coarse crumbs. Add just enough water to make a soft dough, and knead briefly. Wrap in plastic wrap and refrigerate for 1 hour before using.

Makes one 9- to 11-inch single crust

WILD RICE

The Luxury Grain That's Rich in B Vitamins

I have never truly enjoyed the flavor of any comestible endowed with the label *wild*. That goes for wild turkey, wild grapes, wild boar, wild duck, and shame the devil, wild strawberries too. Why? Because they are all just a tinge over-pungent for my domesticated taste. The proscription list does have one notable exception, however, and that is wild rice.

Wild rice (no rice at all, in fact, but a seed) is a fairly recent predilection of mine, which I can trace to a Thanksgiving dinner—one of the worst I can recall ever having eaten.

In the mid-1950s my first play was produced Off-Broadway, and I became—all too briefly—an object of some small celebrity. My picture appeared twice on the drama page of the *New York Times*; I was the subject of interviews in *Variety*, *Vogue*, and the *Village Voice*. I was certain I had arrived. A well-known theatrical agent left me his card, and I acquired a small coterie of loyal fans, one of whom was a writer whose counsel I have never forgotten.

"On paper," she advised at our first meeting, "be yourself until it hurts!"

This woman's critique was not to be taken lightly, for she moved in a circle of literary lions, all of whom heeled like lap dogs whenever she held forth about their work. Her name was Judith, and as the French say, she was a lady of a certain age—probably the sunny side of sixty when we met. She had been married to a successful novelist for years and had recently left him because, as she told anyone within earshot, he had sold his soul to the devil or to David O. Selznick—they were interchangeable in her view—to become the highest-paid screenwriter in Hollywood.

Judith was equally liberal with her analysis of dramaturgy and with show-biz gossip, but the price one paid for her erudition was usually a headache—and more often a hangover. She drank constantly (always vodka straight up) and was never without a lit cigarette clamped between her teeth.

Early one fall, Judith invited me to spend Thanksgiving at her Bucks County farmhouse. "It's a wonderful old house, but like a vampire it needs young blood once in a while," she said, roaring with laughter and tossing down her fifth or sixth Stolichnaya of the evening. "So come and be a victim."

When I explained that traditionally I spent Thanksgiving with my sister, Judith became positively expansive. "Bring her along. We have bedrooms enough to accommodate the Continental Army!"

All that fall I heard nothing more about Thanksgiving. A cable from London advised me the theater season was "lousy," and a postcard from L.A. revealed that her husband's latest film was even worse. But neither missive referred to the upcoming holiday.

My sister, who was never exactly Judith's ardent admirer, was furious. "What a nut," Myra railed. "If you don't pin her down soon, I'm ordering a turkey!"

I managed to track Judith down in San Francisco.

"Oh my God!" she cried. "Don't tell me. Thanksgiving! Don't worry, I'll send a map. Come at noon."

"Thursday?"

"When else? I'm flying home Wednesday night."

If I had a nagging doubt about when and where she would shop for dinner, it was promptly put out of mind. Not knowing the length of our stay was disconcerting enough.

The drive through the crisp November countryside was worth all the vagaries of the expedition. A thin plume of smoke was swirling from the chimney when we arrived, and Judith announced that her husband was in residence, "to keep the home fires burning!"

He was welcoming, but they had both obviously been drinking all morning and were growing short-tempered. A brief tour of the house confirmed my misgivings: It was a splendid showplace but striped with mildew and unbrushed cobwebs. There was neither fresh linen in the guest rooms nor any sign of dinner on the stove.

Hours of enervating Hollywood stories and endlessly refilled Bloody Marys passed before I stole a glance at my watch. Judith must have seen me, for she rose, unsteadily. "I guess it's time to think about the bird," she declared, stifling a yawn.

About time, I would have said.

Offering help, I was delighted when Judith refused assistance. But I could not focus on any conversation because of the sound of running water from the kitchen—a clear sign the bird was either being defrosted forcibly or, worse yet, parboiled.

When she returned, Judith commented brusquely, "This is going to be a simple meal. I hate tricky holiday foods, don't you?" Clearly there was no option.

The evening star had already deepened in the sky by the time dinner was ready. Candles provided little light at the table, which was provident, for the turkey was totally resistant to being carved. After several hopeless attempts with a knife, Judith's husband tore the carcass apart with his bare hands. The meat was tough and stringy, and there were no accompanying vegetables to fill the slack, except for a plate of canned sweet potatoes that Judith had obviously neglected to warm in the oven. No bread. No cranberries. No salad. Actually nothing to eat at all, except the turkey's stuffing, which she had miraculously concocted out of wild rice, herbs, and sausages.

Until that dinner I had never fully appreciated the flavor and fragrance of wild rice, but it was then the sole reason for giving thanks. We consumed every kernel.

The Grain's Genesis

*I*f it's not rice, then what is it?

Diners have asked that question about wild rice for almost three hundred years. The answer, then and now, is: an aquatic seed, *Zizania aquatica.*

Wild rice is the preserve of Native Americans. Chippewas and Winnebagos who live along the freshwater lakes and brackish swamps of upper Michigan, Minnesota, and Wisconsin are wild rice's official harvesters. U.S. law protects their title rights on reservation waters. But long before the first white man set a muddy foot on the territory, they tended the crop just as assiduously, for wild rice sustained the tribes in fallow hunting seasons.

Traditionally, Indian women pick the wild rice. Two to a canoe, they navigate their weedy way through the plants. One sits in the stern of the craft, paddling very slowly, while the other uses two long pointed sticks (like batons) to very gently shake the pale green stalks. She shakes and bends the stem until it releases its seed, which is gathered in the bottom of the boat. On a good day the women go home with a canoe crammed with wild rice. But more often than not, all kernels are not ripe at the same time, so it will take two or even three trips in the canoe to gather a full crop.

That is how wild rice is harvested by the Indians today, and that is how it was harvested three centuries back—which explains why it is sometimes called "the caviar of grains." Good things are inevitably hard to come by.

Some Plain Grain Talk

*N*o doubt about it, wild rice is very expensive stuff. But as described, all truly wild wild rice is harvested by Indians, and they do it the hard way. After picking, the rice is cured over smoke fires and then spread on the ground, where traditionally—though probably not as much now, if at all—young Indian males dance on the cooling grains to loosen the hulls. Finally the rice is sifted through blankets so the chaff blows off and the finished kernels (now a burnished black-brown color) are graded for packaging. All that labor adds up to a premium price in the marketplace.

In an attempt to turn wild rice into a mass-market product, controlled-irrigation farms (in California, Idaho, and Washington) are producing a hearty hybrid; one that can be picked by mechanical threshers and processed by mechanical parchers and winnowers, all of which do the job faster and should reduce the price tag. Unfortunately, this not-really-wild rice is not much cheaper, and it is a good deal less pungent and flavorsome.

Wild rice is one of the few luxury foods that is actually good for you. A high-carbohydrate grain (72.2 mg per cup), it contains healthy doses of phosphorus, magnesium, potassium, and zinc as well as thiamine, riboflavin, and niacin, all elements of B vitamins. More important (to dieters, anyway), a cupful of cooked wild rice contains a scant 130 calories.

How to Buy It

It is nice to be able to report that wild rice is available in supermarkets, gourmet groceries, and natural foods stores. But a chary consumer will do well to make a note of the various grades of wild rice before shopping.

Giant (long-grain) wild rice is the *ne plus ultra*, the blue-ribbon variety. Every grain is perfectly matched in size and never measures less than an inch in length. Long-grain wild rice has an earthy, dark flavor that makes it a favored partner to wild game. It's top restaurant chefs' first choice!

Fancy (medium-grain) wild rice is what most average cooks deem "a choice top-quality ingredient." The grains are also graded—equal in size, unbroken, and evenly matched in color. Fancy wild rice is what I think of as all-purpose. Though it is not appreciably cheaper than the giant variety, there is a price difference.

Select (short-grain) wild rice is low man on the grain scale. The kernels are not uniform in size and they are sometimes broken as well. It's a fine rice for soup or pancakes, but a roasted quail will quake at the prospect of having a spoonful of select in its dressing!

How to Store It

Wild rice manufacturers claim that this grain will keep indefinitely if it is stored in a tightly covered container in a cool, dry place. However, wild rice has a moisture level of from 7.9 to 11.2 percent. If humid, wild rice is capable of developing mold, or worse yet, maggots. In warm weather keep it refrigerated, or at least take the precaution of turning the jar upside down from time to time, to keep the rice from developing mildew. Cooked wild rice may be refrigerated (in an airtight self-seal plastic bag) for a week. Other cooks freeze uncooked wild rice. I do not, because a subtle textural change that occurs makes such storage uneconomical in the long run.

How to Cook It

Unlike white or brown rice, it is almost impossible to chart a cooking time for wild rice. A short-grained variety, for instance, will cook relatively quickly (35 to 40 minutes), while a long-grained variety will take half again as long (50 to 60 minutes).

Cooked wild rice should have bite, like *al dente* pasta. If it is cooked too long, the grain becomes mushy and the taste, like the nutrients, goes up in steam!

Wild rice is not as tricky to control during the cooking process as ordinary rice. If the rice is cooking too fast, add cold water or ice cubes to retard the boiling. A wise cook will also uncover the pot every so often to test a kernel for doneness.

Although cooking instructions on a package of wild rice usually state that 1 cup of uncooked rice yields 3 cups cooked, I often end up with 3½ or even 4 cups, depending upon the brand. It's a good idea to make a note of the quantity you get for future reference!

BASIC COOKED WILD RICE

1 cup wild rice
1 teaspoon salt
3 cups water (approximately)

Rinse the rice under cold water and drain it. Then place it in a saucepan with the salt and 3 cups water and heat to boiling. Reduce the heat to medium-low, and simmer, covered, for 35 to 60 minutes, adding more water, if necessary. Drain, if necessary.

Makes 3 to 4 cups

WILDER BEET TOP SOUP

*T*he addition of wild rice is the perfect amendment to my good friend Mildred Schulz's classic Colorado Beet Top Soup.

3 tablespoons unsalted butter, at room
    temperature
1 small yellow onion, minced
3 tablespoons wild rice
4½ cups homemade chicken stock (see page
    376) or canned broth
1½ pounds beet tops (from 2 large
    bunches)
1 pound potatoes, peeled and diced
1 cup light cream or half-and-half
1 tablespoon cornstarch
⅛ teaspoon ground allspice
Dash of hot pepper sauce
Salt and freshly ground black pepper to
    taste

1. Melt 1 tablespoon of the butter in a medium-size saucepan over medium-low heat. Add the onion; cook 3 minutes. Stir in the rice and 2 cups of the stock, and heat to boiling. Reduce the heat to medium-low, cover, and cook for about 20 minutes.

2. Meanwhile, wash the beet leaves well, discarding the stems. Cook the leaves in boiling water for 5 minutes. Rinse under cold running water, drain well, and chop.

3. Add the beet leaves, potatoes, and the remaining 2½ cups chicken stock to the soup. Heat to boiling. Then reduce the heat and cook, covered, over medium-low heat 25 minutes longer.

4. Stir the cream into the soup; simmer uncovered 5 minutes.

5. Stir the remaining 2 tablespoons butter and the cornstarch together in a small bowl until smooth. Stir this into the soup and cook until slightly thickened, 4 to 5 minutes. Add the allspice and hot pepper sauce, and season with salt and pepper.

Serves 6

GOLD-STANDARD STUFFED SQUASH

A solid gold appetizer or party "finger food." These squashes stuffed with chicken, ham, and wild rice are good hot or at room temperature.

4 small yellow squash (10 ounces total)
1 tablespoon unsalted butter
1 shallot, minced
⅛ teaspoon chopped fresh rosemary, or a
  pinch dried
⅛ teaspoon cayenne pepper
½ teaspoon all-purpose flour
¼ cup cooked wild rice (see page 333)
¼ cup finely chopped cooked chicken
¼ cup finely chopped smoky cooked ham
2 tablespoons heavy or whipping cream
1½ tablespoons freshly grated Parmesan
  cheese

1. Preheat the oven to 400°F. Lightly butter an ovenproof serving dish.

2. Cut the squash in half lengthwise. Cook, cut side down, in boiling water for 4 minutes. Drain on paper towels and allow to cool slightly.

3. Scoop out the insides of the squash with a spoon, leaving the shell ⅛ to ¼ inch thick. Drain the squash shells on paper towels. Finely chop the scooped-out pulp.

4. Melt the butter in a small skillet over medium-low heat. Add the shallot; cook 2 minutes. Add the rosemary, cayenne pepper, and chopped squash pulp. Cook, stirring occasionally, until all liquid has evaporated, about 5 minutes. Sprinkle the mixture with the flour, then stir in the cooked wild rice, chicken, ham, and cream. Remove the skillet from the heat.

5. Fill the squash shells with the rice mixture, mounding each squash high. Sprinkle with Parmesan cheese, and place in the prepared serving dish. Bake 10 minutes before serving.

Serves 4 as an appetizer

O f all the wild rice raised in the U.S., 85 percent is still produced by Native Americans. State laws regulate and monitor the industry, determining the length of the picking season and generally protecting Indians' rights, since most of the waters where the rice is grown are on reservation property.

In Minnesota wild rice may be harvested only by residents with permits; interlopers are punished, and fines are high. The picking season is brief—three weeks at most and powerboats are not permitted on rice waters.

These days the majority of rice pickers sell their crops to commercial processors, for the male tribe members are no longer interested in "dancing" in their moccasins on the cured rice. But the real enemy of the old-time wild rice tradition is time, and cost-effectiveness.

Paddy rice growers are the invaders—big business combines that are artificially seeding wetlands with wild rice and polluting the waters with herbicides and pesticides to grow a uniformly marketable crop. Despite protests of environmentalists and the Minnesota Department of Natural Resources, wild rice soon may not be very wild at all, and the sensual earthy flavor of the grain will be replaced by a blander taste, as plastic as the credit card that more than likely purchases it!

ROAST TURKEY WITH TWO RICE AND THREE SAUSAGE DRESSING

The stuffing is reminiscent of that fateful Thanksgiving I spent in Pennsylvania. The turkey is *my* method for roasting the bird—not a hint of stringy toughness anywhere!

1 fresh turkey (about 20 pounds) with
    giblets
2 large cloves garlic, bruised
Salt and freshly ground black pepper to
    taste
Two Rice and Three Sausage Dressing
    (recipe follows)
3 strips bacon
⅓ cup dry white wine
1 quart water
1 medium onion, unpeeled
1 medium rib celery, broken in half
3 sprigs parsley
¼ teaspoon salt
4 peppercorns
1½ tablespoons unsalted butter
1½ tablespoons all-purpose flour
¼ cup heavy or whipping cream

1. Preheat the oven to 325°F.

2. Remove the giblets from the turkey, and reserve them. Wipe the turkey out with a damp cloth. Rub it well, inside and out, with one of the garlic cloves, and with salt and pepper to taste. Stuff the cavity with the dressing. Sew and truss. Place the turkey on a rack in a roasting pan, and lay the bacon strips over the breast. Cut a piece of cheesecloth to fit over the turkey, dip it in the wine, and place it over the turkey. Pour the excess wine over the cheesecloth, and roast the turkey for 30 minutes.

3. Meanwhile, combine the reserved giblets (but not the liver), water, onion, celery, remaining clove of garlic, parsley sprigs, salt, and peppercorns in a large saucepan. Heat to boiling, reduce the heat, and simmer until reduced to 2 cups, 25 minutes. Strain.

4. Continue to roast the turkey, basting it with stock every 30 minutes, until the legs move freely and the juices run clear when the inner thigh is pierced with a fork, about 6 hours in all. For the last 30 minutes, increase the heat to 375°F and remove the cheesecloth (basting as you peel it off). Transfer the turkey to a carving board and let it stand 15 minutes.

5. Meanwhile, strain the turkey

A species of wild rice called *kaw-sun* (*Zizania latifolia*) grows in northern China and Tibet. The funny thing about this Oriental wild rice is its status, which is low. The Chinese do not consider it a delicacy. They don't even eat it. The truth is, they feed it to fowl. In the past, however, this rice was used like tea leaves, to tell fortunes.

In bygone days a seer would sit at the side of a road and scrawl the characters for "love," "wealth," "fame," and "fertility" in the dust. On each character he would place a grain of wild rice.

After someone produced a yen, the fortune-teller would release a hungry fowl onto the ideogram. As the chicken, duck, or turkey pecked away, a rosy future was assured.

drippings, removing the excess fat. Melt the butter in a medium-size saucepan over medium-low heat. Stir in the flour and cook, stirring constantly, 2 minutes. Whisk in the drippings and cream; simmer 5 minutes. Add salt and pepper to taste. Serve the gravy with the turkey and dressing.

Serves 8 to 10

Two Rice and Three Sausage Dressing

2¾ cups water
Salt to taste
⅔ cup wild rice, rinsed
⅔ cup long-grain white rice
½ pound sweet Italian sausage, sliced
¼ pound Spanish chorizos (or other spicy sausage), quartered lengthwise and sliced
1 Italian sopressata (about ¼ pound), diced
1 large onion, finely chopped
½ medium red bell pepper, cored, seeded, and chopped
2 tablespoons unsalted butter
2 tablespoons chopped fresh parsley
¼ teaspoon chopped fresh marjoram or oregano, or a pinch dried
⅛ teaspoon chopped fresh thyme, or a pinch dried
¼ teaspoon hot pepper sauce

1. Heat the water to boiling, add salt, and add the wild rice. Return to boiling, then reduce the heat to medium-low and simmer, covered, until tender, 35 to 60 minutes, depending on the rice. Remove the cover and raise the heat slightly if the rice is too wet. Set the cooked rice aside.

2. Meanwhile, cook the long-grain white rice, stirring once, in a large pot of boiling salted water for 12 minutes. Drain in a colander. Place the colander over 2 inches of boiling water in the same pot (do not let the bottom of the colander touch the water). Cover the rice with a single layer of paper towels, and steam for at least 15 minutes to dry it out.

3. While the rice is cooking, sauté the Italian sausage in a lightly oiled large heavy skillet until lightly browned, 6 to 8 minutes. Remove with a slotted spoon to a large bowl. In the same skillet, sauté the chorizos until lightly browned, about 8 minutes. Transfer to the bowl. Sauté the soprassata in the same skillet until crisp, about 8 minutes, and transfer to the bowl.

4. Discard all but 2 tablespoons grease from the skillet. Add the onion and bell pepper; cook over medium-low heat 5 minutes. Stir in the butter, parsley, marjoram, thyme, and hot pepper sauce.

5. Add the onion/pepper mixture to the sausages. Then add both rices and mix well. Allow to cool before stuffing the turkey.

Makes enough for a 20- to 22-pound turkey

RACY, RICEY MEAT LOAF

If I don't eat meat loaf every other week, I feel cheated. Definitely comfort food, and with the addition of wild rice, it takes on a hearty, gutsy flavor. This loaf is best served hot or at room temperature.

1 tablespoon unsalted butter
2 shallots, minced
1½ pounds ground beef
1 pound ground veal
¾ ground pork
1 hot green pepper, seeded and minced
1 cup cooked wild rice (see page 333)
2 eggs, lightly beaten
½ cup tomato juice
½ cup milk
1 tablespoon chopped fresh parsley
2 teaspoons chopped fresh basil, or ¾
    teaspoon dried
¼ teaspoon chopped fresh thyme, or a
    pinch of dried
3 tablespoons chili sauce
2 teaspoons Dijon mustard
⅛ teaspoon hot Hungarian paprika
2 strips bacon

1. Preheat the oven to 375°F.

2. Melt the butter in a small skillet over medium-low heat. Add the shallot; cook 4 minutes. Remove the skillet from the heat.

3. Combine the beef, veal, and pork in a large bowl. Mix well and add the reserved shallots, hot green pepper, cooked wild rice, eggs, tomato juice, milk, parsley, basil, and thyme. Mix thoroughly. Shape into a loaf on a shallow baking dish.

4. Whisk the chili sauce, mustard, and paparika together in a bowl, and spread over the meat loaf. Lay the bacon on top. Bake until the juices run fairly clear when the loaf is pricked with a fork, about 1½ hours. Reduce the heat if the loaf is getting too brown. Let it stand 5 minutes before serving.

Serves 6 to 8

MOORS AND MARTYRS STEW

The original version of this Caribbean dish is made with black beans and rice and is called Moors and Christians. My version, with wild rice, is dubbed Moors and Martyrs. But the only martyrdom involved is in not receiving a second helping.

½ pound (½ package) dried black beans
2 strips bacon, chopped
1 tablespoon butter
1 medium onion, finely chopped
1 clove garlic, minced
½ medium rib celery, finely chopped
½ cup chopped cooked ham
½ teaspoon salt
¼ teaspoon freshly ground black pepper
1 bay leaf
½ teaspoon ground allspice
⅓ cup wild rice
5 cups (approximately) homemade chicken
    stock (see page 376) or canned broth
⅛ teaspoon hot pepper sauce

1 pound smoked Polish sausage (kielbasa),
    cut into 1½-inch pieces
1½ cups cooked long-grain white rice,
    heated
⅛ cup finely chopped green scallion tops

1. Place the beans in a medium-size pot, and cover with cold water. Heat to boiling; boil 2 minutes. Remove from the heat and let stand, covered, 1 hour. Drain.

2. Meanwhile, sauté the bacon in a large heavy pot or Dutch oven until almost crisp. Add the butter and onion; cook over medium heat 1 minute. Reduce the heat to medium-low and add the garlic; cook 2 minutes longer. Then stir in the celery and ham. Cook, stirring occasionally, 10 minutes.

3. Add the salt to the onion mixture along with the pepper, bay leaf, and allspice. Stir in the drained beans and the wild rice, tossing to coat with the onion mixture. Add the chicken stock, and heat to boiling. Reduce the heat and simmer, partially covered, until the beans and rice are almost tender, about 1 hour.

4. Scoop out ¼ cup of the stew and place it in the container of a food processor. Process until smooth, adding more chicken stock if needed. Return the processed mixture to the stew, and add the hot pepper sauce and sausage. Cook, covered, until the beans and rice are very tender, 30 to 45 minutes longer.

5. Pour the stew into a large shallow serving dish. Mound the white rice in the center and sprinkle with the scallion tops. Stir each portion of rice into the stew as you serve.

Serves 4 to 6

WILD RICE PATTIES

Be sure you do not pass this recipe by. It's an excellent croquette, which came to me from a friend. The sour cream and caviar embellishment is strictly my own.

¼ cup wild rice
1 cup water
1 teaspoon salt
½ pound baking potatoes, peeled and diced
2 egg yolks
1 tablespoon sour cream
4 strips bacon, chopped
2 large scallions, white bulbs and green
    tops, minced
1½ tablespoons chopped fresh parsley
Pinch of dried marjoram
⅛ teaspoon freshly grated nutmeg
⅓ cup fresh bread crumbs
1 tablespoon freshly grated Parmesan
    cheese
Freshly ground black pepper to taste
3 to 4 tablespoons unsalted butter
Sour cream
Caviar

1. Combine the wild rice with the water and salt in a small saucepan, and heat to boiling. Reduce the heat to medium-low and simmer, covered, until the rice is very tender, 40 to 60 minutes. Remove the cover and raise the heat slightly if the rice is too wet.

2. Meanwhile, cook the potatoes in boiling salted water to cover until tender, 15 minutes. Drain, and mash the potatoes until smooth. Beat in the egg yolks and sour cream. Combine with the rice in a medium-size bowl, and set aside.

3. Sauté the bacon in a medium-size skillet over medium heat until crisp. Add the scallions, parsley, and marjoram, and cook 3 minutes. Cool slightly, and add to the rice/potato mixture. Add the nutmeg, bread crumbs, cheese, and salt and pepper to taste. Mix well, and refrigerate, loosely covered, for 1 hour.

4. Form the wild rice mixture into small balls. Press into patties.

5. Melt 3 tablespoons butter in a heavy skillet over medium heat. Sauté the patties, about six at a time, until golden brown on both sides, about 2 minutes per side. Drain on paper towels, and transfer to an ovenproof serving dish. Keep the patties warm in a 225°F oven while sautéing the remainder. Continue to fry patties until all the rice mixture is used up.

6. Top each one with dabs of sour cream and caviar before serving.

Serves 6 to 8

WILD RICE WITH BRUSSELS SPROUTS AND BANGERS

*T*here is a saying that there are three vegetables in England: cabbage, cabbage, and cabbage. Since Brussels sprouts belong to the cabbage family, they make a great partnership when teamed with bangers (the English handle for sausages) and wild rice.

10 ounces Brussels sprouts
2 cups water (approximately)
½ teaspoon salt
⅓ cup wild rice
½ pound sweet Italian sausage
1 tablespoon butter
1 large shallot, minced
1 clove garlic, minced
1 hot green pepper, seeded and minced
1 teaspoon soy sauce

1. Trim the Brussels sprouts, and cut a small "X" in the root end of each one.

2. Heat the water to boiling in a medium-size saucepan. Add the salt and Brussels sprouts, cover, and cook 3 minutes. Remove the sprouts with a slotted spoon, and reduce the heat to medium-low.

3. Add the wild rice to the water. Cover and cook until tender, adding more water if necessary, 35 to 60 minutes, depending on the rice. Remove the cover and raise the heat slightly if the mixture is too wet.

4. Meanwhile, sauté the sausages in an oil-rubbed heavy skillet over medium heat until well browned, about 8 minutes. Remove the sausages to a plate. Cut the Brussels sprouts crosswise into ¼-inch-thick slices. Cut the sausages into ¼-inch pieces.

5. Wipe out the skillet and melt the butter in it over medium-low heat. Add the shallot; cook 1 minute. Add the garlic, hot green pepper, and sausage slices. Cook until the vegetables are lightly browned and the sausages are cooked through, about 5 minutes. Sprinkle with the soy sauce and add the wild rice. Toss until well mixed, about 1 minute. Add the Brussels sprouts and continue to cook, tossing gently, until the sprouts are warmed through, about 4 minutes.

Serves 4

MARY CASSETTI'S WILD RICE FRITTATA

Mary lives in upstate New York and happens to be a very good cook. A frittata, sometimes called an Italian omelet, is often baked in the oven, but the traditional method calls for cooking the entire dish stove-top. I serve it for lunch or a late supper.

1 tablespoon olive oil
¼ cup finely chopped scallions, white
*   bulbs and green tops*
1 small clove garlic, minced
1 large fresh shiitake mushroom (1 ounce),
*   halved and sliced*
½ cup Canadian bacon in thin strips
*   (about 6 slices)*
1 tablespoon chopped fresh parsley
6 eggs
¼ cup heavy or whipping cream
½ cup cooked wild rice (see page 333)
½ cup grated Jarlsberg cheese
¼ cup freshly grated Parmesan cheese
4 teaspoons unsalted butter
Salt and freshly ground black pepper to
*   taste*

1. Heat the oil in a medium-size skillet over medium heat. Add the scallion; cook 1 minute. Add the garlic; cook 2 minutes. Add the mushroom and Canadian bacon. Cook, stirring constantly, 3 minutes. Then stir in the parsley and remove from the heat.

2. Beat the eggs in a large bowl. Beat in the cream. Stir in the mushroom mixture, the cooked wild rice, the Jarlsberg cheese, and 2 tablespoons of the Parmesan cheese.

3. Melt 3 teaspoons of the butter in a 9-inch skillet (preferably non-stick) over medium heat until foamy. Pour in the egg mixture, and reduce the heat to medium-low. Cook without stirring for 20 minutes.

4. Rub another skillet of the same size with the remaining teaspoon of butter. Place it over medium heat for 1

The first Europeans to taste wild rice in the New World were French settlers from Brittany. Having an affinity for the familiar white *riz*, they did not enjoy wild rice at all.

As the story goes, they disliked the stuff so much they spat it out (behind the Indians' backs) after a first bite. And though they knew the Chippewa name for the grain—*mahnomen*, which means "seeds from the wild"—the Frenchmen privately called it *folle avoine* ("crazy oats").

In time, the Frenchmen developed a taste for wild rice. The sensible Breton women mixed the wild rice with vegetables and served it cold after Sunday mass. The settlers liked it so much they called it a *salade* and in time invited the Indians to share it.

After a first bite the Chippewa braves spat the food out (behind the Frenchmen's backs of course!), and they gave it a name of their own: *paolsu mizin* ("sick food")!

minute, then place it upside-down over the skillet with the frittata, and invert. Sprinkle the top of the frittata with the remaining 2 tablespoons Parmesan cheese, and season with salt and pepper. Return to low heat for 3 minutes.

Serves 4 to 6

WILD ABOUT CHICKEN SALAD

*L*eftover chicken, fennel, and wild rice make an intriguing combination. I add a touch of peanut butter to the dressing for a good nutty flavor.

2 small fennel bulbs (6 ounces each) with fronds
2 cups cooked wild rice (see page 333)
2 scallions, white bulbs and green tops, finely chopped
2 cups cooked chicken in bite-size pieces
½ cup walnut oil
2 tablespoons white wine vinegar
2 teaspoons Dijon mustard
2 teaspoons chunky-style peanut butter
¼ cup walnut pieces, toasted (see Note)
Salt and freshly ground black pepper to taste

1. Trim the fennel bulbs and discard the stems. Chop and reserve the fronds. Cut the bulbs in half lengthwise, remove and discard the cores, and cut across into very thin slices. Place the slices in a large bowl, and add the cooked wild rice, scallions, and chicken.

2. Whisk the walnut oil with the vinegar in a small bowl. Then whisk in the mustard and peanut butter. Pour the dressing over the salad and toss well. Add the walnuts, and season with salt and pepper. Serve at room temperature, sprinkled with the reserved fennel fronds.

Serves 6

Note: To toast the walnuts, heat a small skillet over medium heat. Add the nuts and toast until golden, stirring frequently, 6 to 8 minutes.

CABBAGE PATCH SLAW

A one-dish meal: cole slaw studded with wild rice and tuna. A great picnic dish.

1½ cups cooked wild rice (see page 333)
2 cups shredded cabbage
1 cup flaked cooked tuna, or drained canned water-packed tuna
1 large shallot, finely chopped
¼ teaspoon anchovy paste
1 tablespoon fresh lemon juice
1 teaspoon red wine vinegar
¼ cup olive oil
⅛ teaspoon chopped fresh rosemary, or a pinch dried
Salt and freshly ground black pepper to taste

1. Combine the cooked wild rice, cabbage, tuna, and shallot in a large bowl. Toss gently to mix.

2. Stir the anchovy paste, lemon juice, and vinegar together in a small bowl until smooth. Whisk in the oil and rosemary. Pour the dressing over the salad and toss. Season with salt and pepper, and serve.

Serves 4

SHOCKING-PINK WILD RICE

Grated beets turn this salad shocking pink. I serve it with cold broiled chicken and a plate of sliced tomatoes.

1¼ to 1½ pounds fresh beets with 1-inch
  stems, unpeeled
1 large shallot, minced
1 cup cooked wild rice (see page 333)
1 cup plus 2 tablespoons sour cream
1½ tablespoons prepared horseradish
2 tablespoons strong beef stock (see Note)
3 tablespoons heavy or whipping cream
Salt and freshly ground black pepper to
  taste
3 tablespoons chopped fresh parsley

1. Place the beets in a saucepan, cover with cold water, and heat to boiling. Reduce the heat and simmer, uncovered, until barely tender, about 25 minutes. Drain under cold water. Remove the skins and grate the beets into a large bowl. Add the shallot and cooked wild rice.

2. Combine the sour cream, horseradish, beef stock, and cream in a small bowl. Whisk until smooth. Combine all but 2 tablespoons of the sour cream mixture with the beet mixture. Toss well, and season with salt and pepper. Transfer to a serving bowl, place the remaining sour cream mixture in the center of the salad, and ring with the parsley. Serve chilled or at room temperature.

Serves 4 to 6

Note: If you do not have strong beef stock on hand (see page 379), reduce ¼ cup canned beef broth to 2 tablespoons by simmering for 5 minutes.

BETTER TIMES SALAD

My mother used to make a version of this lentil salad with white rice in the days of the Depression. It's cheap and hearty. Better times call for more expensive wild rice, which turns the salad into a celebration.

⅔ cup lentils
1 cup cooked wild rice (see page 333)
⅓ cup finely sliced red radishes (about
  2 ounces)
⅓ cup finely sliced white radishes (about
  2 ounces)
¼ cup finely chopped green scallion tops
2 pickled jalapeño peppers, finely sliced
1 clove garlic, crushed
¼ teaspoon salt

2 tablespoons fresh lime juice
2 teaspoons country-style Dijon mustard
  (with seeds)
¼ cup olive oil
Chopped fresh parsley, for garnish

1. Cook the lentils in boiling salted water until tender, about 20 minutes. Drain, and set aside to cool.

2. Combine the cooled lentils with

the cooked wild rice, radishes, scallion tops, and peppers in a bowl. Toss well.

3. Using the back of a spoon, mash the garlic with the salt in a small bowl until a paste is formed. Whisk in the lime juice, mustard, and oil. Pour the dressing over the rice mixture and toss well. Serve at room temperature, sprinkled with parsley.

Serves 4 to 6

STRIP POTATO MAYONNAISE

Made with grated, barely cooked potatoes, this elegant salad graces the table at many of my parties.

2 large potatoes (1 pound)
2 tablespoons fresh lemon juice
1 cup cooked wild rice (see page 333)
¼ pound sliced prosciutto, chopped
2 fresh shiitake mushroom caps, halved and thinly sliced
¼ pound Fontina cheese, diced
¾ cup Homemade Mayonnaise (see page 379)
¼ cup sour cream
½ teaspoon salt
¼ teaspoon freshly ground black pepper
1 tablespoon chopped fresh parsley
1 teaspoon chopped fresh chives

1. Peel the potatoes and run them through the coarse shredder of a food processer. (They will look a little like spaghetti.) As you shred them, place the potatoes in a large bowl of cold water containing 1 tablespoon of the lemon juice. Drain the potato shreds, and cook in boiling salted water until crisp-tender, about 3 to 4 minutes. Rinse under cold running water, drain, and pat dry with paper towels.

2. Place the potatoes in a large bowl. Add the cooked wild rice, prosciutto, mushrooms, and cheese. Toss well.

3. Whisk the mayonnaise with the sour cream in a bowl. Add the remaining tablespoon of lemon juice, the salt, pepper, and parsley. Pour the dressing over the potato/rice mixture, and toss gently until well mixed. Serve at room temperature, sprinkled with the chives.

Serves 4

As I have mentioned, foods that pleased the Native American did not always sit well below his guests' belts.

Lewis and Clark complained of having to eat raw deer heart, a meal that Sacajawea, their intrepid female Indian guide, proclaimed to be "a great delicacy."

John Bartram, America's first naturalist, who logged all the foods the Indians ate, wrote of consuming *misickquatash* with the Sioux, *mausamp* with the Iroquois, and *rockahominy* with the Crows—and never feeling "right" again afterward.

On the other hand, in 1807 Peter Pond, a fur trader, wrote to his wife about eating wild rice with the Indians of Wisconsin: "When it is Cleaned fit for youse thay Boile it as we do Rise and Eat it with Bairs Greas and Sugar.... And it did very well."

PECAN RICE PILAF

*F*or any holiday—or non-holiday—meal on your agenda, consider wild rice instead of potatoes. I like it best, I think, baked into a pilaf, as in this tonic pecan version created by my friend Marilyn Harris.

2 tablespoons unsalted butter
1 large shallot, minced
⅓ cup wild rice
1¼ cups water
½ cup long-grain white rice
¾ cup homemade beef stock (see page 377)
    or canned broth
¼ cup dry white wine
1 small bay leaf
Dash of hot pepper sauce
½ cup frozen peas, thawed
2 tablespoons chopped fresh parsley
¼ cup pecan halves, toasted and coarsely
    chopped (see Note)
1 teaspoon chopped fresh mint (optional)

1. Melt the butter in a medium-size saucepan over medium heat. Add the shallot; cook 2 minutes. Stir in the wild rice and the water, and heat to boiling.

Reduce the heat to medium-low and simmer, covered, 30 minutes.

2. Add the white rice, beef stock, wine, bay leaf, and hot pepper sauce to the wild rice. Heat to boiling, then reduce the heat to medium-low. Simmer, covered, until both rices are tender and almost all liquid has been absorbed, about 25 minutes. Discard the bay leaf. Stir the peas into the mixture; cook, covered, 5 minutes longer. Remove the cover and raise the heat slightly if the mixture is too wet. Toss in the parsley and pecans, and sprinkle with the mint, if you like.

Serves 4

Note: To toast the pecans, heat a small skillet over medium heat. Add the nuts and toast until golden, stirring frequently, 6 to 8 minutes.

PILAF OF WILD RICE WITH WILDER MUSHROOMS

*T*his recipe comes from Haiti, where its creator had the wild rice smuggled into Port-au-Prince, stashed inside the shoes that she had sent to New York to be repaired!

½ ounce dried wild mushrooms
¾ cup hot water
1 tablespoon peanut oil
1 strip bacon, chopped
1 small onion, halved and sliced
1 clove garlic, minced
¼ teaspoon crushed dried hot red peppers

Pinch of cloves
¼ teaspoon chopped fresh tarragon, or a
    pinch dried
⅓ cup wild rice
½ cup (approximately) homemade chicken
    stock (see page 376) or canned broth
Chopped fresh parsley, for garnish

1. Place the mushrooms in a small bowl, cover with the hot water, and let stand until soft, about 20 minutes. Strain, reserving ½ cup liquid. Coarsely chop the mushrooms.

2. Heat the oil in a medium-size saucepan over medium-low heat. Add the bacon; cook until almost crisp, about 3 minutes. Add the onion; cook 1 minute. Stir in the garlic and dried red peppers; continue to cook until the onion and garlic are very dark brown but not burned, 4 to 5 minutes longer. Sprinkle with the cloves and tarragon. Then stir in the reserved mushroom liquid, mushrooms, rice, and chicken stock.

Heat to boiling. Reduce the heat to medium-low and simmer, covered, adding more stock if needed, until the rice is tender, 35 to 60 minutes, depending on the rice. Remove the cover and raise the heat slightly if the mixture is too wet. Sprinkle with parsley before serving.

Serves 3 or 4

WILD CRIMSON RICE

A baked rice dish that goes well with all kinds of fowl and pork. It is delicious at room temperature as well, but because the tomatoes have a tendency to get juicy when the dish sits, you might wish to add a teaspoon or so of flour to the tomato mixture.

2 tablespoons unsalted butter
1 medium onion, finely chopped
1 clove garlic, minced
3 cups chopped, seeded ripe tomatoes
1 teaspoon sugar
½ teaspoon salt
¼ teaspoon freshly ground black pepper
1 tablespoon chopped fresh basil,
    or 1 teaspoon dried
1 teaspoon chopped fresh oregano,
    or ¼ teaspoon dried
½ teaspoon whole allspice, crushed
1 cup cooked wild rice (see page 333)
½ cup heavy or whipping cream
1 tablespoon freshly grated Parmesan
    cheese
1 cup grated mozzarella cheese

1. Melt the butter in a medium-size saucepan over medium-low heat. Add the onion; cook 1 minute. Add the garlic; cook 2 minutes longer. Add the tomatoes, sugar, salt, pepper, basil, oregano, and allspice. Cook, uncovered, stirring occasionally, until very thick, about 30 minutes.

2. Preheat the oven to 350°F. Butter an 8- or 9-inch shallow ovenproof serving dish.

3. Stir the cooked wild rice into the tomato mixture, then add the cream and Parmesan cheese. Spoon into the prepared serving dish. Bake 30 minutes.

4. Sprinkle the mozzarella over the baked tomato mixture, and return the dish to the oven until the cheese melts, 3 or 4 minutes. Let stand a few minutes before serving.

Serves 6

WILDERNESS BREAD

*S*eptember is the month of the Wild Rice Moon, a festival of Indian foods named for a harvest moon round and golden as a tub of fresh butter. Which brings to mind a highly appropriate accompaniment that is one of my favorite recipes: a crisp and crusty loaf of wheat and wild rice bread.

½ cup milk
2 tablespoons unsalted butter
½ teaspoon salt
1½ cups cooked wild rice (see page 333)
¼ cup lukewarm water
1 package dry yeast
1 tablespoon dark brown sugar
Pinch of ground ginger
1 cup whole-wheat flour
1¾ cups bread flour (approximately)
1 teaspoon unsalted butter, melted

1. Combine the milk, 2 tablespoons butter, and salt in a medium-size saucepan over medium-low heat, and heat until the butter melts. Remove the pan from the heat, and stir in the cooked wild rice. Allow to cool to room temperature.

2. Place the lukewarm water in a large bowl, and sprinkle it with the yeast. Then stir in the sugar and ginger. Let stand until bubbly, 8 to 10 minutes. Stir in the rice mixture, whole-wheat flour, and about 1 cup of the bread flour, enough to make a stiff dough.

3. Scrape the dough out onto a well-floured board and knead, adding more bread flour as needed, until soft and elastic, about 12 minutes. Transfer the dough to a greased bowl, cover with plastic wrap, and let rise in a warm place until doubled in volume, about 1 hour.

4. Punch the dough down. Knead it briefly and place in a greased 9 by 5 by 3-inch loaf pan. Cover loosely with a flour-rubbed tea towel, and let rise in a warm place until the bread reaches over the top of the pan, about 1 hour.

5. Preheat the oven to 350°F.

6. Make a slash down the center of the bread with a sharp knife, and brush with the melted butter. Bake 35 minutes. Then raise the heat to 400°F and bake until the bread is golden brown and sounds hollow when tapped with your finger, about 10 minutes longer. Gently loosen the bread from the pan, but allow it to cool completely in the pan on a rack.

Makes 1 loaf

*I*ndians who grow it claim to be able to spot wild rice half a mile away. The pale green plumes and the purplish blossoms give it away.

Uncooked wild rice has a purple-black color, and a wise Indian can tell if it will be flavorsome or not by holding a handful close to his nose. Dried wild rice at its best should have a faint but distinct smoky perfume.

If you find that smokiness too intense for your taste, rinse it several times in cold water prior to cooking. I like wild rice just the way it comes, "with a taste that fights back," which is an Ojibwa expression for a properly cured and cooked batch.

WILD RICE AND DATE MUFFINS

W ild rice and dates make these muffins very special. A word of warning, however: These are best served hot from the oven, because wild rice has a tendency to get heavy as it sits.

1 ¼ cups all-purpose flour
1 tablespoon baking powder
½ teaspoon salt
5 tablespoons unsalted butter, melted
1 cup milk
2 eggs, lightly beaten
3 tablespoons maple syrup
1 cup cooked wild rice (see page 333)
½ cup chopped dates

1. Preheat the oven to 425°F. Lightly grease a 12-cup muffin tin.
2. Combine the flour, baking powder, and salt in a large bowl. Make a well in the center, and add the melted butter, milk, eggs, and maple syrup. Using a wooden spoon, stir the liquid into the flour until smooth. Then stir in the cooked wild rice and the dates.
3. Spoon the batter into the muffin cups (the cups will be very full). Bake until golden brown and firm to the

T he Ojibwa (who harvest wild rice) do not believe in war or war dances. This tribe never tortured their prisoners, and it is said they looked down on other more aggressive tribes (like the Iroquois) who did.
  Perhaps the Ojibwa people's pacific nature was related to the food they ate. Ojibwas were vegetarians; eating no meat whatsoever—only greens and grains. Notably wild rice.

touch, 15 to 18 minutes. Serve immediately.
  Makes 12 muffins

JILL GARDNER'S WILD RICE AND WALNUT FLAPJACKS

J ill Gardner is a talented food writer who lives in San Francisco. These pancakes are her creation, and she serves them at elegant lunches. I serve them to weekend guests for brunch, with a side of sausage and plenty of Vermont maple syrup.

½ cup all-purpose flour
½ teaspoon baking powder
¼ teaspoon salt
Pinch of freshly ground black pepper
½ cup coarsely ground walnuts
1 egg

½ cup sour cream
½ cup milk
1 cup cooked wild rice (see page 333)
4 tablespoons (½ stick) unsalted butter, melted

1. Combine the flour, baking powder, salt, pepper, and walnuts in a medium-size bowl. Mix well.

2. Combine the egg, sour cream, and ¼ cup of the milk in a small bowl. Whisk until smooth. Then, using a wooden spoon, stir into the flour mixture. Let stand 10 minutes.

3. Stir the remaining ¼ cup milk into the batter. Stir in the cooked wild rice and melted butter.

4. Heat a lightly greased cast-iron skillet or griddle over medium heat until hot but not smoking. Cook the pancakes, a few at a time, using about 3 tablespoons batter per pancake. When lightly browned, about 2 minutes, turn over and cook the other side for 1 minute. Transfer to a serving platter and keep warm in a 225°F oven while cooking the remaining pancakes. Reduce the heat under the skillet if the pancakes brown too quickly.

Makes about sixteen 2½- to 3-inch pancakes

LOW-MAN-ON-THE-TOTEM-POLE PORRIDGE

*T*his can be a dessert, or a breakfast or brunch dish. Sweet but not too sweet. The notion was told to me by its inventor, Arthur Schwartz, the food editor and restaurant critic of the New York *Daily News.*

Arthur makes this dish with broken (select) wild rice. He claims the lowest grade stirs up into the best porridge. If you can't find a broken batch, smash a few with a hammer. I did.

¼ cup wild rice
1 cup milk
⅛ teaspoon ground cinnamon
½ cup blueberries
Maple syrup
Heavy or whipping cream

1. Combine the rice, milk, and cinnamon in a medium-size saucepan and heat to boiling. Reduce the heat to medium-low, cover, and cook until the rice is very tender, 50 to 60 minutes. Remove the cover and raise the heat for a few minutes if the mixture is too wet. The rice should be creamy.

2. Divide the rice between two serving bowls. Add ¼ cup blueberries to each bowl, along with generous amounts of maple syrup and cream.

Serves 2

*S*candinavian homesteaders in the upper territory of Minnesota in the late 19th century would trade whatever they could spare from their fields or dwindling store supplies for wild rice from the local Indian tribes.

The Swedes used to call wild rice *ficka pendar* ("pocket money"), not because it was then so marketable but because a small amount represented dinner for a family of five or six. No matter how empty the cupboard or how slim the wallet, everyone ate when there was pocket money—for wild rice triples or quadruples as it cooks!

THE NEW GRAINS

Amaranth, Quinoa, and Triticale

When I was a small kid, going to the theater was the most exciting event of my life—specifically vaudeville, because it was not only fast-paced but also wildly flamboyant. Vaudeville disappeared almost immediately with the onset of the Depression, but it was certainly a delirious experience while it lasted.

In our household, vaudeville was always a family outing, a dispensation viewed by both parents with justifiable apprehension. My sister, five years my senior, was charged with the onerous responsibility of keeping me from crying, shouting, or jumping up and down on my seat during a performance. Not an easy task, as I was an excitable child.

Vaudeville had a fixed formula. There were always five or six acts on the program, a gilt-edged sign proclaiming each name before the curtain rose. At the top of the bill came the jugglers—who managed to toss dozens of plates and glittering balls in the air without ever ceasing to smile, even as latecomers rustled programs, coughed, or talked through their performance. Next came the tap dancers. In pairs, trios, or quartets, these talented hoofers brought the audience to life, and their trickiest footfalls were often matched by waves of applause and demands for encores. Animal acts followed on their heels. Sometimes the trainer would bring out a pack of dogs, dressed in trousers and skirts, who walked on their hind legs, smoked cigarettes, and danced the Charleston. At other times the animals were trained seals who managed to squeak out familiar tunes on horn-bugles for a promised herring or sardine. On one occasion I recall a totally different animal act: a flock of trained doves that plucked chiffon scarves from the near-naked bosom and limbs of an "exotic dancer." As I recollect, my father bid me *not* to look at that animal act. But I did anyway.

Animal acts were generally followed by tumblers or acrobats. The following next-to-closing spot was always eagerly awaited; sometimes it was a famous comedian or a popular singer, at other times a pair of ballroom dancers. The act I remember best was a world-renowned magician who proceeded to saw a shrieking woman in half. It was not necessary to caution me not to look at that!

The closing act was always a "stellar attraction," very often world-famous. On one occasion it was the great dancer Pavlova; on another the star was Gertrude Ederle, who swam the English Channel and promised a demonstration of her famous backstroke in a tank as wide as the proscenium arch.

I was taken to see many stellar performers in my young life as a vaudeville-goer, but in all candor I must tell you that I never actually saw a closing act. I always fell fast asleep before that moment arrived. All the way home, I would complain about what I had missed until Myra (a bit of a show-off herself) would re-create the closing act secondhand, in the back of our family car.

"Why do they always put the good things last?" I questioned.

"To keep you waiting and wanting, kiddo," said my sister.

Who am I to fly in the face of tradition? Now that you've waited and waded through this book for so long, here at last are my thoughts on the *new grains*. Announcing . . . Amaranth, quinoa, and triticale! Definitely not a tumbling act.

AMARANTH

The Grain's Genesis

Amaranth is a "new" grain that's actually as old as the hills. A seed of mystical attributes, 500 years ago the Aztecs believed that a single spoonful could turn a softie into a hunk; and that a steady diet would produce a race of honest-to-gosh supermen.

As a consequence, Aztecs grew lots

of amaranth. Over 20,000 tons were harvested, chaffed, winnowed, then sent by mule team, ox cart, and broad men's backs to Tenochtitlán (now Mexico City) as a yearly tribute to the emperor Montezuma.

As a source of energy and fortitude, amaranth was as important to the Aztecs as the corn and beans that kept them alive. On holy days, Aztec women pounded amaranth with honey and (ouch!) human blood into a rough dough that they baked in the form of snakes, birds, and other assorted household deities. These cakes were broken apart and consumed religiously to keep the faith in strength and fitness.

When Hernando Cortez, the Spanish conquistador (and a good church-goer despite his bloody reputation), observed these doings for the first time, he was so offended that supposedly he could not speak for a week's time. In Cortez's mind, the Aztec ritual was a mockery of the Christian communion he had been raised to revere, and the only punishment he could conceive of to fit the crime was total obliteration.

Though he had come to Mexico on a self-declared mission of goodwill, Cortez killed Montezuma at once. He commanded his troops to burn every square inch of amaranth that bloomed between the Gulf of California and the Bay of Campeche. What's worse, he also ordered them to cut off the hands of anyone found with a single seed in his possession.

Historians date the pillage of amaranth as the end of the Aztec empire. Dispirited and deprived of their "wonder food," formerly brave warriors became itinerant peasants without a leader or a focus.

General Cortez returned to Spain in triumph of course, but his victory was short-lived. Not only had he terminated amaranth's role as a source of food in the New World, he stemmed the spread of a highly nutritious grain in the Old World as well.

The happy end to this tale is: You can't keep a good seed down! Amaranth survived even if the Aztecs did not, and half a millennium later we are rediscovering its tonic effect on the human body.

Some Plain Grain Talk

Amaranth's name is borrowed from the Greek. It means "not withering," or more literally, "immortal." That's not a randomly bestowed tag, either, for the curious thing about amaranth is its longevity. Other grain kernels, such as corn, wheat, and rice, will not sprout after long intervals; a decade is most plants' time span. Amaranth, on the other hand, sprouts indefinitely. A handful of seed recovered from an Aztec ruin 1,000 years old recently set down taproots at a farm in Pennsylvania. And that, my friends, is immortal enough for all normal purposes!

Immortality is not the reason to include amaranth on your grocery list. Health is! This small grain—only slightly larger than a poppy seed—provides the human system with the most effective balance of protein under the sun. Amaranth's high nutritive bonus to the diet is matched only by milk, and it stands head and shoulders above all other complex carbohydrates because of the enormous jolt of lysine in its composition. Lysine is an amino acid that controls protein absorption in the body.

Amaranth has other pluses: it is exceptionally high in vitamins and minerals; 3½ ounces contain more calcium than a super-thick shake; and ½ cup totals less than 16 calories.

How to Buy It

Amaranth has become available to consumers only recently. Rediscovered by nutritionists and plant breeders in the mid-1970s, this grain was first sold only by mail order. And it was regarded with a raised eyebrow by all but deep-dyed health-food votaries because of its "wonder protein" reputation. But once it was cooked and tasted, amaranth proved to be so delicious (it has a mild toasted-sesame flavor) that health-conscious diners jumped on the band-wagon and created a market demand.

At present, amaranth is sold at natu-ral foods stores, packaged and in bulk. I have also noted its appearance in forward-minded supermarkets as well, particularly those chains in the Pacific Northwest and California where the fit-ness fervor affects impulse buying. A brief survey of "health food" shelves re-cently revealed not only amaranth grain but amaranth cereal (combined with whole wheat), amaranth flour, amaranth crackers, amaranth granola, amaranth pasta, and amaranth chocolate chip cookies! All out there, ready to lure shoppers who cannot resist the "Mystical Grain of the Aztecs" emblazoned on every package.

My advice is to purchase amaranth in bulk if possible, for that's the least expensive (and least hyped) option. Price varies with distribution, of course, but bulk amaranth is relatively inexpensive —about $1 per pound. Since amaranth increases radically in volume as it cooks (like most grains), a buck provides a bucketful of nutrition!

How to Store It

Amaranth has a long, long shelf life and is virtually pest-resistant. However, a wise cook will keep this grain well covered (preferably in a glass container ample enough to keep the seeds from being crushed) on a pantry shelf where the temperature does not exceed 65°F, or refrigerated when the climate is warmer.

In the unlikely case that amaranth spoils, let your nose be the judge: over-the-hill amaranth smells like linseed oil. It won't kill you, but it also won't work wonders either. So dispose of it, please.

How to Cook It

Amaranth is a grain with two culinary alternatives. A mildly spicy seed, it may be cooked in liquid until creamy and served as a side dish. Or it may be tossed in a hot pan until the seeds burst and develop a crackle not unlike seasoned popcorn.

Not much has been written about amaranth cookery. The few cookbooks that have touched on the subject usually call for more liquid than I deem war-ranted. Too much water turns cooked amaranth into gruel. The correct for-mula, in my opinion (a ratio of 2 parts liquid to 1 part grain), will approximate the texture—though certainly not the flavor—of cooked grits. And in fact,

To my totally untrained eye, the most attractive feature of grow-ing amaranth is its lack of conform-ity: it blooms in a rainbow of colors. The plant is rather tall and wavy, with blossoms not unlike celosia top-ping each stalk. The leaves of the amaranth plant are also edible, not dissimilar to spinach in taste and texture. Seed heads are large, and each yields almost a kilo of pure seed after it is cleared of its resplendent chaff.

Farmers are beginning to grow amaranth, and that's a healthy sign for the crop's future. Home garden-ers can grow it in their backyards, too. When you're through cooking, take a moment to check the back of the book for information on how and where to obtain seeds.

many of the grits recipes in this book may, with some minor adjustments, be adapted to its use.

When cooking amaranth, it is advisable to use a non-stick pan to keep the seeds from becoming cohesive. Amaranth doubles when cooked: ½ cup dry becomes 1 cup cooked.

BASIC COOKED AMARANTH

½ cup amaranth
1 cup water, broth, or vegetable juice
1 teaspoon unsalted butter

Combine the amaranth and the liquid in a medium-size saucepan and heat to boiling. Reduce the heat to low, cover, and cook, stirring occasionally, until tender, 20 to 25 minutes. Remove the cover and stir for a few minutes if the mixture seems too watery. Stir in the butter.

Makes 1 cup

BASIC POPPED AMARANTH

"Popped" amaranth is too insubstantial for serious nibblers, but the puffed seeds do offer a lot of possibilities for a nutrition-minded cook, adding texture and tang to soups, stews, waffles, and even a slice of old-fashioned pound cake.

When popping amaranth seeds, use a heavy skillet and pop only 1 tablespoon at a time to prevent scorching. Popped amaranth cannot be stored for any appreciable length of time; it turns rancid.

¼ cup amaranth

Place a heavy skillet over high heat until very hot. Add 1 tablespoon of the amaranth and cook, stirring constantly with a flat wooden spoon or pastry brush, until most of the seeds pop, 10 to 15 seconds. Transfer to a bowl. Continue to pop the remaining amaranth seeds, 1 tablespoon at a time.

Makes slightly more than ¾ cup

BORDERLINE BOURRIDE WITH AIOLI

*P*opping amaranth can be a hazardous job: I suggest wearing a pith helmet as protection from the barrage of fast-flying mini-missiles! It does, however, add a nice firm texture and toasty flavor to soup. This Eurostyle fish pottage, for one; the home-grown tomato soup that follows, for another.

12 clams
12 mussels
¼ teaspoon cornstarch
3 tablespoons amaranth
¼ cup olive oil
1 medium onion, finely chopped
3 small scallions, white bulbs and green
  tops, chopped
2 cloves garlic, minced
1 medium rib celery, finely chopped
½ medium green bell pepper, cored,
  seeded, and chopped
½ teaspoon chopped fresh thyme, or a
  pinch dried
1 bay leaf
1 cup chopped, seeded, peeled fresh
  tomatoes
1 can (14 ounces) plum tomatoes, chopped,
  with juice
1½ cups fish stock (see page 377)
1 cup dry white wine
½ teaspoon fennel seeds, crushed
Pinch of saffron
4 tablespoons chopped fresh parsley
Salt and freshly ground black pepper to
  taste
12 medium-size shrimp, shelled and
  deveined
1 small red snapper (about 1¼ pounds),
  cleaned and cut across into pieces
½ teaspoon anchovy paste
Aioli (recipe follows)

1. Scrub the clams and mussels under cold running water. Pull the beards from the mussels. Place both in a large bowl, cover with cold water, and stir in the cornstarch. Let stand 1 hour. Then rinse several times with cold running water. (This procedure cleans the bivalves effectively.) Let stand in cold water while preparing the dish.

2. Cook the amaranth in a very hot skillet, 1 tablespoon at a time, stirring constantly, until it pops, 10 to 15 seconds per tablespoon. Set aside.

3. Heat the oil in a large heavy pot or Dutch oven over medium-low heat. Add the onion; cook 1 minute. Add the scallions and half the garlic; cook 5 minutes. Add the popped amaranth, celery, bell pepper, thyme, bay leaf, fresh and canned tomatoes, stock, wine, fennel seeds, saffron, and 3 tablespoons of the parsley. Heat to boiling. Reduce the heat and simmer, partially covered, 30 minutes. Discard the bay leaf, then season with salt and pepper.

4. Add the clams to the bourride and cook, covered, over medium heat for 2 minutes. Add the mussels and reduce the heat to medium-low; cook 2 minutes longer. Stir in the shrimp and the fish. Cook, covered, 4 minutes longer. (The bivalves should be open by this point.)

5. Mash the remaining garlic with the anchovy paste, and stir into the bourride. Sprinkle with the remaining 1 tablespoon parsley, and serve with Aioli on the side.

Serves 4

Aioli

1 slice stale homemade white bread, or 2
    slices French bread, ½ inch thick
3 tablespoons milk
6 cloves garlic, crushed
1 egg yolk, at room temperature
¼ teaspoon salt
1 cup vegetable oil
½ cup olive oil
2 tablespoons boiling water
2 tablespoons fresh lemon juice

1. Trim the crusts from the bread, and break the bread into pieces in a small bowl. Add the milk; let stand 10 minutes. Place the milk-soaked bread in the corner of a clean tea towel and squeeze it dry. Transfer the bread to a large bowl.

2. Add the garlic to the bread, and pound them together with the back of a heavy spoon or a pestle until very smooth. Pound in the egg yolk and salt.

3. Whisk in the oils, a drop at a time, until the mixture thickens; then slowly whisk in the remaining oil, 3 tablespoons at a time, until smooth and thick. Whisk in the boiling water and the lemon juice. Refrigerate, tightly covered, until ready to use. It will keep for 4 to 5 days.

Makes 2 cups

CHILLY, MINTY, TOMATOEY BISQUE

Amaranth adds spice to an otherwise traditional cold, creamy tomato soup. Make this soup when the tomatoes are at their freshest.

2 pounds ripe tomatoes
3 tablespoons unsalted butter
1 medium onion, finely chopped
1 clove garlic, minced
½ teaspoon ground allspice
3 cups homemade chicken stock (see page
    376) or canned broth, heated
¼ cup amaranth
Pinch of sugar
½ cup sour cream
Salt and freshly ground black pepper to
    taste
2 tablespoons chopped fresh mint
½ cup chopped seeded cucumber
Sour cream, for garnish

1. Cut the tomatoes into eighths, and set aside.

2. Melt the butter in a medium-size saucepan over medium-low heat. Add the onion; cook 1 minute. Add the garlic and sprinkle with the allspice; cook 4 minutes longer. Stir in the hot stock, amaranth, tomatoes, and sugar. Heat to boiling. Reduce the heat and simmer, partially covered, 25 minutes. Set aside to cool.

3. Transfer the cooled soup, a third at a time, to a blender container. Blend until very smooth. (The amaranth will make the process take longer than normal.) Pour through a fine-mesh strainer into a bowl. Beat in the ½ cup sour cream, and season with salt and pepper. Refrigerate until cold, 2 hours.

4. Just before serving, combine the mint and the cucumbers. Spoon some over each bowl as you serve the soup, and dapple with sour cream.

Serves 4 to 6

CHICKEN DEVILTRY

Amaranth seeds are not only vitamin-high, they're highly versatile. At my table, they've been "popping up" in a multitude of delectable dishes for some time. The newest appearance is really worth taking note of: popped amaranth as a stand-in for bread crumbs when a baked chicken leg or a broiled fish filet is in the offing.

2 tablespoons amaranth
2 scallions, white bulbs and green tops,
    finely chopped
1 clove garlic, minced
2 teaspoons Dijon mustard
2 tablespoons fresh lime juice
¼ teaspoon salt
¼ teaspoon freshly ground black pepper
3 to 4 tablespoons olive oil
1 chicken (about 3½ pounds), cut into
    pieces

1. Preheat the oven to 375°F.

2. Cook the amaranth in a very hot skillet, 1 tablespoon at a time, stirring constantly, until it pops, 10 to 15 seconds per tablespoon. Transfer to a shallow bowl and cool slightly.

3. Add the scallions to the amaranth along with the garlic, mustard, lime juice, salt, pepper, and enough oil to make a smooth mixture.

4. Pat the chicken pieces dry, and coat them with the amaranth mixture. Place on a broiler tray. Bake until the chicken is crunchy and the juices run yellow when pricked with a fork, 50 to 60 minutes.

Serves 2 or 3

BAKED FRESH CORN FLUMMERY

Think of corn as amaranth's bodybuilder, and you'll have the following recipe! It's a custardy vegetable pudding that begs for table room at your next summer social, or whenever the tall corn grows. This is a dish, incidentally, that deserves a moment's grace after its stint in the oven; for a good flummery thickens as it cools.

2 large eggs
1 cup Basic Cooked Amaranth (see page
    353)
1 small hot green pepper, seeded, deveined,
    and minced
1 tablespoon sugar
½ teaspoon salt
⅛ teaspoon freshly ground black pepper
¼ teaspoon ground mace
1 cup heavy or whipping cream
2 tablespoons unsalted butter, melted

2 cups fresh corn kernels (from about 6
    medium ears)

1. Preheat the oven to 350°F. Butter a shallow 1- to 1½-quart baking dish.

2. Lightly beat the eggs in a large bowl. Whisk in all the remaining ingredients.

3. Pour the mixture into the prepared baking dish. Place the dish in a larger pan, and pour in hot water to reach about halfway up the dish. Bake until firm, about 1 hour. Cool slightly before serving.

Serves 6 to 8

COFFEE AND CREAM WAFFLES

Coffee with cream is probably my favorite flavoring combination. In this case, popped amaranth is added to a waffle batter as well. There is not a better waffle in existence, as far as I'm concerned.

2 tablespoons amaranth
1 cup brewed coffee, heated
2 tablespoons sugar
1 teaspoon salt
1 cup heavy or whipping cream
3 eggs, separated
Pinch of ground cinnamon
2 cups all-purpose flour, sifted
1½ teaspoons baking soda
8 tablespoons (1 stick) unsalted butter, melted

1. Preheat the oven to 250°F.

2. Cook the amaranth in a very hot skillet, 1 tablespoon at a time, stirring constantly, until it pops, 10 to 15 seconds per tablespoon. Set aside.

3. Combine the hot coffee, sugar, and salt in a large heatproof bowl. Whisk in the cream, egg yolks, cinnamon, flour, baking soda, popped amaranth, and melted butter. Whisk until smooth.

4. Beat the egg whites until stiff, and fold into the batter.

5. Pour ½ to ⅔ cup batter into an oil-rubbed waffle iron (depending on the size of the waffle iron). Bake until golden and crisp. Keep warm on a rack in the oven until all waffle batter is used up, or serve in relays, hot from the iron.

Makes about 6 large waffles

ALEGRIA

Those ancient Aztecs obviously knew a good thing when they tasted it. In Mexico today, one must make a sortie off the beaten path to find a street vendor who still sells *alegría*, a humane version of the Aztecs' baked offerings, but it's worth the trek. This candy really lives up to its name: "happiness"!

10 tablespoons amaranth
¼ cup honey
¼ cup dark corn syrup
4 tablespoons (½ stick) unsalted butter
½ teaspoon vanilla extract

1. Cook the amaranth in a very hot skillet, 1 tablespoon at a time, stirring constantly, until it pops, 10 to 15 seconds per tablespoon. Transfer to a shallow bowl. You should have about 2 cups.

2. Lightly grease a 9 by 13-inch cake pan (or use Baker's Secret, page 42).

3. Combine the honey, corn syrup, butter, and vanilla in a large heavy skillet, and heat to boiling. Reduce the heat to medium and cook, stirring constantly,

until the mixture turns dark amber and thickens, about 10 minutes. Remove from the heat and immediately stir in the popped amaranth, mixing well with a wooden spoon. Spoon the mixture into the prepared pan, and spread it evenly with a heavy spatula. Cut it into bars and set aside to cool. Once cool, recut the bars, if necessary, and store in a plastic self-seal bag in a cool place for up to 2 days.

Makes 42 bars

AGAINST-THE-GRAIN POUND CAKE

Adding amaranth to a pound cake certainly "runs against the grain" of baking techniques. But the slightly spicy undertaste makes this cake all the better.

4 tablespoons amaranth
1 cup (2 sticks) unsalted butter, at room
*   temperature*
½ cup solid vegetable shortening
2¼ cups sugar
6 eggs
Finely grated zest of 2 limes
1¾ teaspoons vanilla extract
2 cups sifted all-purpose flour
2 teaspoons baking powder
½ teaspoon salt
½ cup milk
¼ cup fresh lime juice

1. Preheat the oven to 350°F. Lightly butter and flour a 10-inch bundt pan.
2. Cook the amaranth in a very hot skillet, 1 tablespoon at a time, stirring constantly, until it pops, 10 to 15 seconds per tablespoon. Set aside.
3. Beat the butter with the shortening in the large bowl of an electric mixer until light and fluffy. Slowly beat in 2 cups of the sugar. Add the eggs, one at a time, beating thoroughly after each addition. Beat in the lime zest and 1½ teaspoons of the vanilla. Stir in the popped amaranth.
4. Sift the flour with the baking powder and salt two times. Add to the batter in three parts, alternating with three parts of the milk. Spoon the batter into the prepared bundt pan.

5. Bake the cake until a toothpick inserted in the center comes out clean, about 1 hour.
6. Meanwhile, combine the remaining ¼ cup sugar with the lime juice and the remaining ¼ teaspoon vanilla in a small saucepan. Cook over medium-low heat until the sugar dissolves. Keep warm.
7. When the cake is done, place the pan on a rack. Prick holes in the cake, and pour the warm lime mixture over. Let the cake cool on the rack for 15 to 20 minutes before unmolding.

Serves 10

No doubt about it, amaranth is a helluva grain! Thriving in virtually any climate (cold or hot, wet or dry), it is subject neither to pestilence nor to any of the plagues that affect the world's grain supply. More pertinently, when it is grown in tandem with other rotation crops, like corn, amaranth not only acts as a deterrent to insects but also strengthens the stalks' resistance to weather changes. Think of amaranth as corn's bodyguard and you won't be far off!

QUINOA

The Grain's Genesis

"KEEN-wah" is the way this calcium-high, vitamin-rich grain is pronounced in the Andes, where it has been in common currency for almost five hundred years, since some Inca farmer tossed a handful of wild seed into a patch of mountainous soil and it came up surprisingly edible.

The Incas dubbed quinoa "the mother grain" because it was an annual plant that was self-perpetuating and ever-bearing. They also deemed the kernels sacred, since a steady diet appeared to ensure long, full lives. The notion is not as improbable as it seems. Like amaranth, this south-of-the-border grain is jam-packed with lysine and healthy amounts of the other amino acids that make a protein complete, besides being a repository for phosphorus, calcium, iron, vitamin E, and assorted B vitamins. All of which sounds like a lifesaver diet no matter how you stir the pot!

The name *quinoa* was reputedly tagged on the innocent grain by Francisco Pizarro himself, shortly after he and his army straggled into the Incas' stronghold at Cuzco in 1532. According to Peruvian lore, once Pizarro tasted a bowl of cooked quinoa, he demanded to see where this seed grew. When he had climbed the Andean plateau and studied the plants' tall stalks and brilliant blossoms lightly dusted with snow, the great conquistador is said to have murmured, *"Quimera!"* ("Fantastic!").

The word was misheard, and misquoted, forever after. Pizarro made another comment about quinoa that was somewhat closer to the cutting edge. He called it "the grain that grows where grass will not."

Some Plain Grain Talk

Quinoa is yet another mini-grain of maxi-purpose in the kitchen. Not quite so diminutive as amaranth, this pale yellowish seed looks like a cross between mustard and millet and bears an ever-so-slight grassy scent that disappears as it cooks.

Technically not a cereal grain at all, agrobotanists dub quinoa a dried fruit, of the *Chenopodium* herb family, whose best-known member is a wild and spicy green known as lamb's quarters. Like lamb's quarters, quinoa's leaves are edible too, and darn good in a salad bowl, but there the culinary resemblance ends. Quinoa is cultivated for its copious seed, which may be prepared whole or blended into creamy (yet relatively low-fat) amalgams. Quinoa is truly crammed with protein, and a cup cooked is equal to a quart of milk in calcium content.

More than merely nutritive, this is a grain of decided savor. Although its culinary capabilities are largely untried by many cooks, happily times and tastes are changing. What was once an exclusive prerogative of the Peruvians and Bolivians is on its way to North American tables today. And while the very best quinoa is still being imported from Bolivia, over 200,000 pounds of this grain were harvested in the Rocky Mountains last year. And grain farmers in New Mexico, Oregon, Washington, and parts of Canada are planting quinoa.

How to Buy It

At the moment, quinoa is sold almost exclusively at natural foods stores or gourmet groceries, but its presence is certainly being felt in the supermarket industry. Cartons of Ancient Harvest brand quinoa have begun to appear in limited quantities on supermarket shelves in the West, Northwest, and Southwest. And more to come, obviously.

All quinoa is *not* the same. There are three main varieties, whose texture, flavor, and color differ dramatically.

The best quinoa is known as *altiplano*. This is a pure strain grown in the altiplano regions of Bolivia and Peru—terraced fields high in the Andes, approximately 12,500 feet above sea level, where the climatic conditions produce a remarkably sweet and succulent seed that is pale ivory in color. Altiplano quinoa is the most expensive in the marketplace: about $4 per pound.

The second-best grade is called *valley variety*. Like the altiplano species, it is also mountain-raised (7,000 to 10,000 feet above sea level) in parts of Peru, Ecuador, and Colombia. Over 1,000 types of quinoa are grown in these areas, and they differ dramatically in taste and tooth. Unfortunately for quinoa shoppers, valley varieties are a mixed bag of the output of several hundred small farmers, whose cultivation methods are often extremely primitive. Of a consequence, the quality varies. Valley variety quinoa is yellow in color and sells for about $3.50 per pound.

The third-grade quinoa is called *sea level*, precisely because that is where it is grown in Chile. The seeds are a darkish tan, and the flavor is somewhat on the bittersweet side. Sea level quinoa sells for $2.50 per pound, but it is no bargain.

Quinoa seeds are naturally coated with saponin, a slightly sticky substance that is somewhat acrid to the tongue and detergent-foamy when wet. All quinoa is presoaked and laboriously scrubbed free of saponin before it is dried and packaged, but in some instances, particularly in the case of mixed-grown quinoa sold in bulk, it is not always entirely free of the saponin residue. So a rinsing is recommended before you proceed with any recipe.

My advice to all uninitiates is to buy the packaged variety sold under the Ancient Harvest label. And as a general rule of thumb, when you buy it in bulk, look for the largest, whitest grains you can find.

How to Store It

Quinoa is sometimes dubbed an "oil seed" because it is extremely rich in plant fat (6.9 milligrams per half pound). This natural oiliness makes it a prime target for spoilage. My suggestion is to store it in an airtight glass container with a screw-top lid. Make sure that the container has been sterilized and well dried before it is filled, and do not pack the quinoa too tightly. Always leave an inch or two between the grain and the cover. Also consider adding a sprig or two of dried mint (tied in cheesecloth) as a deterrent to any creeping or crawling visitors.

Even under the best conditions, quinoa's shelf life is brief—never longer than a month below 65°F, and less if the mercury rises. Storing quinoa in the fridge or freezer is advised in warm weather. But do remember to dry the seeds well after each stint in the cooler, to dispel excess moisture.

How to Cook It

Quinoa is extremely easy to prepare. Its ease, in fact, makes it a true kitchen staple for the working cook. It requires only a scant 12 to 15 minutes' stovetop time.

Toasting quinoa in a dry skillet prior to cooking will add a full-bodied depth of flavor. Make sure the pan is fairly warm (over medium-high heat) before adding the quinoa, and stir the grains often to prevent scorching. Toast only for a few minutes. Toasted quinoa will take on a light golden hue.

Sautéing a small minced onion in a teaspoon or two of oil in the skillet before toasting the quinoa, or adding a finely chopped carrot or a handful of cut herbs, will change its flavor and texture.

I find that quinoa is not enhanced when it is pressure-cooked. And any liquid added to the grain should be hot.

BASIC COOKED QUINOA

1 cup quinoa
2 cups stock, water, or vegetable juice, heated
2 tablespoons butter (optional)

1. Rinse the quinoa under cold running water. Drain.

2. Combine the quinoa and hot stock in a medium-size heavy saucepan, and heat to boiling. Reduce the heat to medium-low, cover, and cook until the liquid is absorbed and the quinoa looks transparent, 12 to 15 minutes. Toss in the butter with a fork.

Makes 3 cups

KEEN AND CREAMY QUINOA- MUSHROOM SOUP WITH SHIITAKE "NOODLES"

A mystical mushroom chowder, heavy on the quinoa.

¼ cup quinoa
2 tablespoons unsalted butter
1 medium onion, chopped
½ pound white mushrooms, chopped
3 cups (approximately) homemade beef stock (see page 377) or canned broth, heated
2 tablespoons dark rum
½ cup heavy or whipping cream
Freshly ground black pepper to taste
4 fresh shiitake mushroom caps (about 2 ounces)
Chopped fresh chives, for garnish

1. Rinse the quinoa under cold running water. Drain.

2. Melt the butter in a medium-size saucepan over medium heat. Add the onion; cook until well browned, about 5 minutes. Add the chopped white mushrooms and cook until the mushrooms are soft, about 5 minutes longer.

3. Stir the quinoa into the mushroom mixture, tossing well to coat each grain. Add 2 cups of the beef stock and heat to boiling. Reduce the heat to medium-low, cover, and cook for 15 minutes. Then stir in the rum and cook, uncovered, 1 minute. Set aside to cool slightly.

4. Blend the mushroom/quinoa mixture, in two batches, in a blender until smooth (be careful, as hot foods expand). Add more beef stock if needed to blend easily. Pour the mixture into a clean saucepan and add the remaining stock and the cream. Cook over low heat until warmed through. Do not allow to boil. Sprinkle with pepper.

5. Meanwhile, with a very sharp knife, slice the shiitake mushroom caps on the diagonal as thin as possible. The slices should be almost paper-thin. Sprinkle them over the top of the soup, and garnish with chives.

Serves 4 to 6

SHRIMP AND QUINOA SALAD WITH GREEN OLIVE SALSA

*C*henopodium *quinoa* is probably the most economical plant that grows.

Prepared whole, the grain makes a whole meal. Ground, it turns into a light gluten-free flour. The tender leaves may be eaten as a green vegetable. The older, tougher leaves make fine animal fodder. The stalk is burned for fuel. And even the saponin-filled rinse water is converted into a shampoo.

To carry the economy a bit further, since thrifty quinoa expands during cooking, it will make less-than-thrifty ingredients stretch. For evidence, sample this shrimp and quinoa dish. A salad, appetizer, hors d'oeuvre—you name it—of extravagant flavor yet restrained outlay.

3 tablespoons olive oil
1 medium onion, chopped
1 clove garlic, chopped
2 tablespoons water
3 tablespoons dry white wine
Pinch of saffron
1 cup fresh parsley leaves
½ cup chopped green olives
3 cups cooked quinoa (see page 361)
½ pound cooked shrimp, shelled and deveined
Lettuce leaves, for serving
Green Olive Salsa (recipe follows)

1. Heat the oil in a medium-size saucepan over medium-low heat. Add the onion; cook 1 minute. Add the garlic; cook 2 minutes longer. Stir in the water, wine, saffron, parsley, and olives. Heat to boiling. Reduce the heat to low, cover, and cook 5 minutes. Set aside to cool slightly.

2. Place the olive mixture in the container of a food processor. Process, starting and stopping the processor, until smooth. (Add about 1 tablespoon water if necessary to blend.)

3. Combine the blended olive mixture with the cooked quinoa in a bowl, and add the shrimp. Toss with two forks until mixed. Transfer to a serving bowl, and chill slightly. Serve on lettuce leaves, and pass the Green Olive Salsa.

Serves 4 to 6

There is a Bolivian saying that is emblazoned on T-shirts, bumper stickers, and dusty walls from Cochabamba to Tarija. Very roughly translated, it goes like this:

If the hand that hoes a field
And pulls the weeds
Also stirs the pot
And seasons a stew,
Give thanks to God.
For that is a hand that has
Forgotten how
To twist a knife,
Pull a trigger,
Or make a fist!

Green Olive Salsa

1 large clove garlic
1/4 teaspoon salt
1/2 teaspoon Dijon mustard
Juice of 1/2 lemon
1/2 cup olive oil
2 tablespoons white wine vinegar
1/2 cup coarsely chopped green olives
1/2 cup finely chopped fresh parsley
Salt and freshly ground black pepper to
    taste

Using the back of a spoon, mash the garlic with the salt in a small bowl until a paste is formed. Stir in the mustard and lemon juice. Whisk in the oil and vinegar. Stir in the olives and parsley, and season with salt and pepper. This will keep in the refrigerator for 4 to 5 days.

Makes about 1 1/4 cups

SCARLET LETTER CHICKEN WITH QUINOA

When it is added to the stewed chicken juices in the pot, the quinoa turns as scarlet as the letter A.

1 chicken (3 1/2 to 4 pounds), cut into
    pieces
1 clove garlic, bruised
Salt and freshly ground black pepper to
    taste
2 tablespoons unsalted butter
1 1/2 teaspoons vegetable oil
1 large shallot, finely chopped
2 tablespoons red wine vinegar

2 ripe medium tomatoes, seeded, and
    chopped
1/2 cup homemade chicken stock (see page
    376) or canned broth
1/2 cup quinoa
1 teaspoon chopped fresh tarragon, or
    1/4 teaspoon dried chopped with the
    parsley
1 tablespoon chopped fresh parsley

1. Rub the chicken with the garlic, and sprinkle with salt and pepper.

2. Heat the butter with the oil in a heavy skillet over medium heat. Sauté the chicken, about half the pieces at a time, until well browned on both sides, about 6 minutes. Transfer to a plate.

3. Pour off all but 1 tablespoon drippings from the skillet. Add the shallot and cook over medium-low heat, scraping the bottom and sides of the pan with a wooden spoon, 2 minutes. Return the chicken pieces to the skillet. Sprinkle the vinegar over the chicken and stir gently until the juices have almost evaporated. Stir the tomatoes around the chicken pieces. Pour the stock over the chicken, and heat to boiling. Reduce the heat and simmer, covered, 30 minutes.

4. Rinse the quinoa under cold running water. Drain.

5. Stir the quinoa into the juices around the chicken. Continue to cook, covered, until the quinoa is tender, about 15 minutes. Sprinkle with the tarragon and parsley.

Serves 4

FORTY-CARAT QUINOA

Pure 40-carat-gold carrots give this side dish its color and taste. As with all grains that are rich with their own flavor, the main dish should be kept simple.

2 tablespoons unsalted butter
2 shallots, chopped
2 small carrots, peeled and chopped (about ½ cup)
1⅔ cups homemade chicken stock (see page 376) or canned broth
⅔ cup quinoa
¼ teaspoon ground cumin
Salt and freshly ground black pepper to taste
Chopped fresh parsley, for garnish

1. Melt the butter in a medium-size saucepan over medium-low heat. Add the shallots; cook 1 minute. Add the carrots; cook 1 minute longer. Stir in ⅔ cup of the chicken stock and heat to boiling. Reduce the heat to medium-low and cook, covered, 15 minutes.

2. Transfer the carrot mixture to the container of a food processor and process until smooth. Transfer to a clean saucepan.

3. Rinse the quinoa under cold running water. Drain.

4. Add the remaining 1 cup stock to the processed carrots, and heat to boiling. Stir in the quinoa and reduce the heat. Simmer, covered, over medium-low heat until the quinoa is tender, 12 to 15 minutes. Then stir in the cumin, season with salt and pepper, and sprinkle with parsley.

Serves 4

The quinoa plant is light-sensitive. Inside its showy green foliage is a biological clock that determines when it is time to flower based on the amount of sunlight it receives. If one plant is in the shade of another, the latter will blossom a day or even a week before the former—which makes harvesting even a small crop a tricky and costly operation, and which explains its somewhat hefty price.

ROMAN HOLIDAY QUINOA

*T*his creamy greens-filled vegetable dish may do double duty as an appetizer. Any greens may be substituted, but make sure they are tenderly cooked before they are processed and tossed with the quinoa.

¾ cup quinoa
1½ cups homemade chicken stock (see page 376) or canned broth, heated
2 tablespoons unsalted butter
1 small head romaine lettuce (½ to ¾ pound)
1 tablespoon all-purpose flour
¼ cup milk
¼ cup heavy or whipping cream
Pinch of cayenne pepper
⅛ teaspoon freshly grated nutmeg
½ teaspoon sugar
Salt and freshly ground black pepper to taste

1. Rinse the quinoa under cold running water. Drain.

2. Combine the quinoa and chicken stock in a medium-size heavy saucepan and heat to boiling. Reduce the heat to medium-low and cook, covered, until all liquid has been absorbed and the quinoa looks transparent, 12 to 15 minutes. Toss in 1 tablespoon of the butter with a fork.

3. Meanwhile, cook the lettuce in boiling salted water 5 minutes. Drain. Transfer to the container of a food processor, and process until smooth.

4. Melt the remaining 1 tablespoon butter in a medium-size saucepan over medium-low heat. Add the flour and cook, stirring constantly, 2 minutes. Whisk in the milk and cream, and cook until very thick, 2 minutes. Add the cayenne pepper, nutmeg, and sugar. Add the lettuce, and cook 1 minute longer.

5. Combine the cooked quinoa with the lettuce mixture and season with salt and pepper.

Serves 4

*H*istorians insist that Pizarro, who named quinoa in the first place, was responsible for its disappearing act in the second.

Like Cortez, Pizarro realized that a highly sophisticated Indian culture represented a threat to Spanish colonization. To defuse the Incas, the conquistador banned the growing of quinoa in the mountains; he had them plant formal vegetable gardens instead. These tender greens shriveled as the first blast of icy Andean wind hit the altiplano, but Pizarro refused to be discouraged. He imported Spanish livestock to graze in the lower valleys so the Incas would learn to eat meat and reject their "God-given" comestibles like potatoes, corn, and quinoa.

But the Incas were strict vegetarians, so the cattle languished and the sheep lay down with llamas. When the Incas could not grow quinoa, they ate wild mushrooms instead. After years of raiding the altiplano, where he suspected quinoa still grew under cover, Pizarro developed weak lungs and a cough that turned his once booming voice into a faint whisper. Wherever he looked, he saw defeat, and eventually he took the remnants of his army and left Peru forever.

The day Pizarro left, it is said, the mountain mushrooms dried up in the valleys and quinoa seeds sprouted in the altiplano.

TRITICALE

The Grain's Genesis

One might say that triticale is a kernel made in heaven. And, in terms of most other graybeard grains around, it is a virtual babe in arms as well. Just over a century old, this toothsome cereal is the man-made progeny of wheat and rye, a grain that inherited the best qualities of each parental gene.

Triticale first came to light in Scotland in 1875. A botanist named Stephen Wilson took a gamble and dusted pollen from a rye plant onto the stamen of a wheat stalk. What Wilson had in mind was a world-beater grain with the high fiber content of the latter fused to the protein-rich qualities of the former. The hybrid he produced looked cute but bore no fruit. All the cross-breedings were either sterile or wildly unpredictable in size and shape.

Somewhat daunted, Wilson named his seed *triticale* (trit-a-KAY-lee), combining the scientific monikers for wheat (*Triticum*) and rye (*Secale*). Then he washed his hands of the matter and went on to develop a rust-free form of oat. *Sic transit* glorious experiment!

The triticale adventure was not entirely in vain. In the late 1930s a band of agroscientists in France took a long hard look at Wilson's barren stalk. The hybrid was treated with every substance known to induce fertility—with a singular lack of success. Triticale refused to reproduce. When the experiment was about to be disbanded once again, an intrepid latecomer to the project, Pierre Givaudon, suggested the plant be coated with a crocus derivative called *colchicine*. This last-ditch attempt did the trick and triticale bore fruit at last.

In the half century that followed, untold amounts of money and manpower have been spent developing a field-hardy, pest-resistant grain that its supporters claim will someday solve the problems of hunger all over the world.

If that day has not exactly arrived, it is not triticale's fault. The grain is nutritious and delicious, but little or nothing has appeared in the media—or in cooking manuals, for that matter—to create a public demand. Even health-food faddists seem unaware of its existence. Without promotion or consumer awareness, major grain growers and small farmers alike have been shy of making a financial commitment to its progress.

Triticale's future is up to you and me!

Some Plain Grain Talk

If you compare triticale to wheat—and they are quite alike physically—you will observe that triticale's kernel is larger than wheat's berry and that, sad to say, there are fewer on the stalk.

In terms of nutrients, triticale has a decided edge over its forebears. The average protein content of wheat is about 12 percent; rye's is lower, about 7 percent; triticale runs about 15 to 17 percent. However, it is the biological value of rye protein that gives this new grain a true shot of wholesomeness. Triticale contains a better balance of amino acids than either of its parents, with twice as much lysine as wheat offers in every spoonful.

Scientists and dieticians are "gung-ho" on the health-giving properties of triticale. According to studies made at the University of Manitoba in Canada and at Texas Tech University in the U.S., the salutary effect of triticale on the body is somewhat greater than soybeans and yogurt combined.

How to Buy It

*T*riticale has a low profile in the marketplace at the moment; it is mainly to be found at natural foods stores in major cities or by mail order. But demand will definitely stimulate supply—so ask for it, please! Arrowhead Mills in Texas is currently the largest distributor of triticale products. See the resource list at the back of the book and write to them for a list of retail purveyors in your area.

Triticale is currently packaged three ways:

Whole triticale berries: Rock-hard in their natural state, these retain a slight crunch even after cooking. Not unlike wheat berries in appearance, they have a decidedly more assertive flavor. Whole triticale berries in bulk sell for under $1 per pound.

Flaked triticale: Not unlike rolled oats, packaged flaked triticale is made by a process that slices the raw berries into chips. These chips are then steamed and flattened (by rollers) into flakes, which are then dried. Flaked triticale can, with some minor adjustments, be substituted in many of the recipes in the "Oats" chapter. It may also be cooked as a somewhat crunchy breakfast cereal.

Triticale flour: Made of milled triticale berries, the flour (unlike rye flour) is not gluten-free. However, it is low in gluten and must not be overhandled or the resultant baked goods will be too dense. My advice is to combine triticale with a high-gluten flour like bread flour for additional rise. But do not overwork the mixture.

How to Store It

*S*ince triticale is hard to find, you should plan to purchase it in bulk and keep the unused portion for future use. My suggestion for storage is a large wide-mouth container, preferably glass with an airtight lid. A square 4-quart apothecary jar with a ground-glass top makes a perfect receptacle, but any well-sealed jar will do in a pinch. Make sure you sterilize and dry it well before adding the grain, to inhibit mold and mealybugs. As triticale is a non-oily grain, it may be safely stored in a cupboard where the temperature does not exceed the mid-60s. If your mercury reading is higher, stash triticale in the refrigerator or freezer instead. The shelf life? At least a year!

How to Cook It

*T*riticale has been dubbed "a groat of great savor and substance" by the late Waverley Root. And it lives up to its reputation. However, note that it takes 40 to 50 minutes to cook.

In my opinion, triticale is improved by a day's "rest" in the fridge after cooking. You may safely store cooked triticale for up to 3 days. Keep it in a bowl, well covered with plastic wrap.

Do not freeze cooked triticale. Freezing destroys the grain's texture and dilutes its taste.

BASIC COOKED TRITICALE BERRIES

1 cup triticale berries
3¼ cups cold water

Combine the triticale and 2¼ cups of the cold water in a medium-size saucepan. Cover, and soak, at room temperature, overnight.

The next day, add the remaining 1 cup water to the pot and heat to boiling. Reduce the heat to medium-low, cover, and cook until tender, 40 to 50 minutes.

Drain the triticale and set it aside to cool. If possible, let it rest in the refrigerator for a day before using. Triticale may be stored up to 3 days in the refrigerator, in a bowl covered with plastic wrap.

Makes 2½ cups

TRITICALE GRAN FARO SOUP

*T*his *zuppa* is called *gran faro.* Nobody—even Italian scholars—seems to know why. The name translates as "great beacon," and it's my private theory that it got that name because some early diner "saw the light" after a first slurp! It can be made with either triticale or wheat berries.

1 cup dried pink beans
3 tablespoons olive oil
¼ pound diced prosciutto (about ¾ cup)
1 large onion, chopped
2 cloves garlic, minced
1 large rib celery, chopped
2 medium carrots, peeled and chopped
¼ cup pearl barley
1 cup cooked triticale berries (see above)
4 fresh sage leaves, chopped, or ¼ teaspoon dried
6 cups homemade chicken stock (see page 376) or canned broth
2 cups water

Chopped fresh parsley, for garnish

1. Cover the beans with 3 inches cold water in a medium-size saucepan and heat to boiling. Boil 2 minutes, then remove from the heat and let stand, covered, 3 hours. Drain.

2. Heat 1 tablespoon of the oil in a large heavy pot or Dutch oven over medium-low heat. Add the prosciutto. Cook until crisp, about 5 minutes. Stir in the onion; cook 1 minute. Add the garlic, and continue to cook until the vegetables are golden brown, about 10 minutes.

3. Add 1 tablespoon oil and the celery and carrots to the onion mixture. Cook 1 minute. Add the remaining tablespoon oil and stir in the barley, drained beans, cooked triticale, and sage. Stir until coated with the vegetable mixture. Add 4 cups of the stock and the water. Heat to boiling. Reduce the heat and simmer, partially covered, until the beans are very tender, about 1 hour and 10 minutes.

4. Place 1 cup of the soup mixture in the container of a blender. Blend until smooth (being careful, as hot liquid will expand). Stir this back into the soup, and add the remaining 2 cups chicken stock. Heat to boiling, and then remove from the heat. Sprinkle with parsley before serving.

Serves 6 to 8

SZMATA

*T*he name of this dish means "rags" in Polish. A curious mixture of sauerkraut, smoked ham, grains, and potatoes, it is a "memory dish" from my Polish Jewish grandmother.

When she was young, she lived on a farm, and all the nearest neighbors were not only non-Jews but pig-farmers.

"I used to dream of eating pink, pink ham," she once confided, "because Polish hams are the best in the whole world. Once, when a friend invited me to stay for dinner, I ate a wonderful dish of cabbage and ham that was forbidden to me. It was probably the devil in me—I never told a living soul I ate it. But here's my secret: I never regretted it either!"

Have some rags. You won't regret it.

2 tablespoons olive oil
1½ pounds pork ribs, cut into 2-inch pieces
½ pound thick ham steak, in one piece
2 small leeks, white bulbs only, rinsed well, dried, and chopped
1 clove garlic, minced
1 cup cooked triticale berries (see facing page)
2 tablespoons gin
2 pounds sauerkraut, with juice
½ teaspoon caraway seeds
½ teaspoon fennel seeds
½ cup homemade chicken stock (see page 376) or canned broth
1 large potato (about 10 ounces)

1. Heat the oil in a large heavy pot or Dutch oven over medium heat. Brown the pork pieces well, 8 minutes, and transfer to a plate. Brown the ham steak, 4 minutes, and transfer to the same plate.

2. Add the leeks to the pot and reduce the heat to medium-low; cook 1 minute. Add the garlic; cook until golden, about 5 minutes longer.

3. Stir the cooked triticale into the leek mixture and add the gin, scraping the bottom and sides of the pot. Add the sauerkraut, caraway seeds, fennel seeds, and stock. Mix well, return the pork and ham to the pot, and heat to boiling.

Reduce the heat to medium-low and cook, covered, 1½ hours.

4. Meanwhile, peel and grate the potato. Keep covered in cold water.

5. Remove the meat and keep warm. Drain the potato and stir into the sauer-kraut mixture. Cook, covered, 20 minutes. Remove the pork from the bones and coarsely chop the ham. Return the meat to the pot and cook 10 minutes longer.

Serves 6

RUFFLED RYE BREAD

There is a saying among seedsmen that goes something like this: "Rye is a parvenu that started life as a weed but ended rich enough to have weeds of its own!"

No joke. Rye actually did force its attention on farmers as a wild thing that invaded plowshares and strangled any stalks that grew in its path. In 17th-century Bavaria, the landed barons paid a penny a pound to peasants who pulled and plucked errant rye plants from their wheat acreage. But it was an exercise in futility: hardier rye grew faster and more furiously every time a handful was hauled from the soil.

Eventually some canny landowner gave up and let rye and wheat grow together—and be threshed and milled together, creating out of inanition a mixture that came in time to be known as rye flour.

The best and airiest loaf of rye bread I have ever tasted is a mixture of rye flour with nubbins of triticale—rye and wheat's highly legitimate offspring.

3 tablespoons vegetable oil
1 medium onion, chopped
1 clove garlic, minced
1 tablespoon caraway seeds
1 teaspoon celery seeds
1 can (12 ounces) beer
½ cup warm water
2 packages dry yeast
3 tablespoons honey
1 egg, lightly beaten
1 envelope (3.2 ounces) dry nonfat milk
⅔ cup cooked triticale berries (see page 368)
1 cup rye flour
4 to 5 cups bread flour

1. Heat the oil in a medium-size saucepan over medium-low heat. Add the onion; cook 1 minute. Add the garlic; cook 5 minutes longer. Stir in the caraway seeds, celery seeds, and beer, and heat to boiling. Boil 2 minutes, then set aside to cool to lukewarm.

2. Place the warm water in a large

A vitamin- and mineral-enriched version of the wheat berry, triticale is capable of acting as stand-in for that grain in many instances. Try it in any of the wheat berry recipes in the "Wheat" chapter.

bowl, and sprinkle with the yeast. Stir in 1 tablespoon of the honey. Let stand until bubbly, about 5 minutes.

3. Stir the remaining 2 tablespoons honey into the yeast mixture, along with the egg, dry milk, cooked triticale, and the beer mixture. Stir in the rye flour and 3½ to 4 cups of the bread flour, enough to make a fairly stiff dough. Scrape the dough out onto a floured board and knead, adding more bread flour as needed, until smooth and elastic, about 10 minutes. Transfer the dough to a lightly oiled bowl, cover with plastic wrap, and let stand in a warm place until doubled, about 1 hour.

4. Punch the dough down and return it to the floured board. Knead briefly, and divide in half. Place each half in a greased 8½ by 4½ by 2½-inch bread pan. Cover with a flour-rubbed tea towel, and let rise until doubled in volume, about 1 hour.

5. Preheat the oven to 350°F.

6. Bake the bread until it is nicely browned and sounds hollow when tapped with your finger, about 45 minutes. Cool completely in the pan on a rack.

Makes 2 loaves

ROASTED EGGPLANT SALAD WITH DILL

A version of a French ratatouille, this hearty vegetable-grain salad is a picnic favorite. It is best slightly chilled.

1 large eggplant (about 1 pound), cut into ¼-inch-thick slices
1 large yellow onion, cut into thin slices
1 large clove garlic, minced
7 tablespoons olive oil
Salt and freshly ground black pepper to taste
¾ cup cooked triticale berries (see page 368), chilled
1 tablespoon red wine vinegar
¼ cup chopped fresh dill
Chopped fresh dill, for garnish

1. Preheat the oven to 450°F. Generously butter a baking sheet.

2. Arrange the eggplant slices on the prepared baking sheet. Place the onion over them. Sprinkle with the garlic, and drizzle with 3 tablespoons of the oil. Sprinkle with salt and pepper. Bake until the eggplant is tender, 35 to 40 minutes.

3. Transfer the eggplant mixture to a cutting board and chop. Transfer the chopped mixture to a serving bowl, toss in the cooked triticale, and add the remaining 4 tablespoons oil, vinegar, and ¼ cup dill. Add salt and pepper to taste, and sprinkle with additional dill. Serve slightly chilled.

Serves 4

OKRA AND TRITICALE SALAD WITH YELLOW TOMATOES

*E*ver since I spent time at school in the South, okra has found its way into many of my favorite foods. In this case the okra is sliced raw, so no offending stickiness is to be found. Sweet yellow tomatoes add color, but red may be substituted if none can be found.

FOR THE SALAD
1½ cups cooked triticale berries (see page 368), chilled
1 shallot, minced
1 fresh jalapeño pepper, seeded, deveined, and minced
¼ pound okra, cut into rounds
1 cup yellow cherry tomatoes, cut into rounds
1 tablespoon chopped fresh mint

FOR THE DRESSING
1 small clove garlic, minced
¼ teaspoon salt
1 teaspoon Dijon mustard

2 tablespoons tomato juice
¼ cup olive oil
¼ teaspoon red wine vinegar

1. Make the salad: Combine all ingredients in a bowl and toss lightly.

2. Make the dressing: Using the back of a spoon, mash the garlic with the salt in a small bowl until a paste is formed. Stir in the mustard and tomato juice. Whisk in the oil and vinegar.

3. Pour the dressing over the salad, and toss gently until well mixed. Serve at room temperature or slightly chilled.
Serves 4

TRITICALE-STUFFED BAKED ONIONS

*T*riticale and rice combine in a stuffing that gives an entirely new dimension to a traditional Thanksgiving side dish.

6 large yellow onions
2 teaspoons unsalted butter
½ cup cooked triticale berries (see page 368)
½ cup cooked long-grain white rice
4 teaspoons chopped fresh basil, or 1 teaspoon dried

⅛ teaspoon ground mace
⅛ teaspoon crushed dried hot red peppers
1 medium tomato, peeled, seeded, and chopped
⅔ cup grated mozzarella cheese
2 tablespoons freshly grated Parmesan cheese

1. Peel the onions and cut an "X" into the root end of each one. Cook them in boiling water to cover for 10 minutes, then drain and allow to cool slightly. Remove the center of the onions with a spoon, leaving a two-layer-thick shell. Chop enough of the scooped-out onion to make 2 tablespoons. (Reserve the remaining scooped-out onions for another use.)

2. Preheat the oven to 400°F.

3. Melt the butter in a medium-size skillet over medium-low heat. Add the chopped onion; cook 1 minute. Add the cooked triticale, cooked rice, basil, mace, dried red peppers, and tomato. Cook 4 minutes longer. Remove the skillet from the heat and stir in the mozzarella. Fill the onion shells with this mixture, and sprinkle the tops with the Parmesan cheese. Place on a lightly buttered oven-proof serving dish, and bake 25 minutes.

Serves 6

A FINAL WORD ABOUT VAUDEVILLE

After the last performer strutted onstage, and the last bow and the last encore were enveloped by applause, a heavy velvet curtain always descended from the top of the proscenium arch. The show was finally over.

As the houselights came up and the audience struggled into coats and hats and straggled up the aisles, a magical thing inevitably occurred. Without fanfare, the velvet curtain rose again, revealing another curtain behind it, painted with a curiously flat and unlived-in street scene. In show-business parlance, I have since learned, this curtain is called "a drop." But I did not know that as a child. The pale avenue of storefronts and brick-faced houses was emblazoned with a scroll that read: *FINIS*.

For years I wondered where Finis actually was, and if I would ever find my way there.

Now I see that I have.

APPENDIX

KITCHEN BASICS

CHICKEN STOCK

4 pounds chicken pieces (backs, necks, and
  wings)
4 quarts water (approximately)
2 medium onions, unpeeled
1 leek, rinsed well, trimmed and chopped
2 cloves garlic
2 medium carrots, peeled and coarsely
  chopped
2 medium ribs celery with leaves, chopped
2 medium turnips, peeled and coarsely
  chopped
2 medium parsnips, peeled and coarsely
  chopped
8 sprigs parsley
4 whole cloves
10 peppercorns
1 teaspoon salt, or to taste
1 small bay leaf
1 teaspoon chopped fresh thyme, or
  ½ teaspoon dried
2 tablespoons red wine vinegar

1. Place the chicken pieces in a large pot and add the water. The chicken should be totally covered, so add more water, if necessary. Heat to boiling; boil 5 minutes, skimming the surface as the scum rises to the top.

2. Add the remaining ingredients with enough water to cover the chicken by 3 inches (add more if necessary). Return to boiling; reduce the heat to low. Simmer, partially covered, skimming the surface occasionally, until the stock is reduced to 1½ quarts, about 3 hours. Strain.

Makes 1½ quarts

The secret to a rich, flavorsome stock is always fresh ingredients plus a long tenure of stove time, for the taste of really good stock depends upon prolonged cooking. Expect to end up with only half the amount of liquid with which you originally began, as the reduction gives the stock its richness. A trick I sometimes indulge in when time is short is to add half canned broth (beef, chicken, or clam juice, as the case may be) instead of all water. If you "beef up" your stock with a canned product, make sure to appreciably reduce the amount of salt called for in the recipe, for most canned broths are high in sodium!

All of these stocks keep for three weeks when stored in the refrigerator, tightly covered. If you wish to keep the stock longer, it is best to reboil it and allow it to cool before returning it to the refrigerator. Freezing stock will keep it usable for at least six months.

BEEF STOCK

4 pounds raw beef bones, including some
    meat
3 large onions, chopped
4 medium carrots, peeled and coarsely
    chopped
4 medium ribs celery with leaves, chopped
2 cloves garlic
6 sprigs parsley
1 bay leaf
4 whole cloves
10 peppercorns
2 teaspoons salt, or to taste
3 quarts plus 2 cups water
2 tablespoons red wine vinegar

1. Preheat the oven to 475°F.

2. Place the bones in a large roasting pan, and bake them, uncovered, until brown, 15 minutes. Turn the bones over and reduce the temperature to 450°F. Continue to bake until the second side is browned as well, another 15 minutes. This step will give color to the stock.

3. Meanwhile, combine the remaining ingredients, except the 2 cups water and the vinegar, in a large heavy pot. Heat to boiling; reduce the heat.

3. Add the browned meat bones to the stock. Pour off the grease in the roasting pan and stir in the 2 cups water, scraping the bottom and sides of the pan with a wooden spoon. Add this liquid to the stock. Heat the stock to boiling again; reduce the heat to low. Simmer, partially covered, skimming the surface occasionally, for 3 hours. Stir in the vinegar, and continue to simmer, partially covered, until reduced to about 1½ quarts, about 2 hours longer. Strain.

Makes 1½ quarts

FISH STOCK

2½ to 3 pounds fish bones, including heads
4 cups water
2 cups dry white wine
3 cups clam juice
2 medium onions, chopped
2 medium ribs celery with leaves, chopped
6 sprigs parsley
1 bay leaf
4 whole cloves
10 peppercorns
1 teaspoon salt
1 lemon, halved

Combine all the ingredients in a large pot. Heat to boiling; reduce the heat to medium-low. Simmer, partially covered, until reduced to about 6 cups, 1 hour. Strain.

Makes 1½ quarts

VEGETABLE STOCK

The following vegetable stock will do in place of chicken or beef stock in any recipe where it is used to add savor to a vegetable as it is braised. Its devise is included for those whose dietary strictures prohibit the use of meat and poultry, but nonvegetarians as well will enjoy the remarkable savor vegetable stock adds to a dish.

4 tablespoons (½ stick) unsalted butter
5 medium onions, chopped
2 cloves garlic
4 medium ribs celery with leaves, chopped
4 medium carrots, peeled and coarsely
    chopped
2 leeks, rinsed well, trimmed, and chopped
½ ounce dried mushrooms
1 bunch parsley
1 teaspoon chopped fresh thyme, or ½
    teaspoon dried
1 fresh sage leaf, or a pinch of dried,
    crumbled
1 bay leaf
1½ teaspoons salt
10 peppercorns, lightly crushed
10 whole allspice, lightly crushed

Pinch of freshly grated nutmeg
4 quarts water
½ teaspoon crushed dried hot red peppers
1 tablespoon red wine vinegar

Melt the butter in a large heavy pot over medium heat. Stir in the onions; cook 5 minutes. Add the remaining ingredients through the water. Heat to boiling; reduce the heat to low. Simmer, partially covered, until reduced to about 2½ quarts, about 2 hours. Add the dried red peppers and vinegar. Simmer, uncovered, 30 minutes longer. Strain, gently pressing the liquid out of the vegetables with the back of a spoon.
    Makes 1½ to 2 quarts

LAMB STOCK

1 teaspoon olive oil
1½ pounds lamb shanks
1 medium onion, sliced
1 clove garlic, minced
3 leeks, rinsed well, trimmed and chopped
1 large carrot, peeled and coarsely chopped
1 medium parsnip, peeled and coarsely
    chopped
1 medium turnip, peeled and coarsely
    chopped
1 medium tomato, halved and seeded
4 or 5 sprigs parsley
1 sprig thyme, or ¼ teaspoon dried

2 fresh basil leaves, or a pinch of dried
10 peppercorns
1 cup homemade chicken stock (see page
    376) or canned broth
3 quarts water
1 tablespoon red wine vinegar
Dash of hot pepper sauce
Salt to taste

    1. Preheat the oven to 450°F.
    2. Place the oil in a Dutch oven and add the lamb shanks. Roast, uncovered, in the oven for 10 minutes. Then turn

the shanks over and cover them with the onion and garlic. Roast until well browned, about 30 minutes.

3. Transfer the pot to the top of the stove and add the remaining ingredients through the water. Heat to boiling, scraping the bottom and sides of the pot with a wooden spoon. Reduce the heat and simmer, covered, 3 hours. Then uncover partially and simmer until the mixture reduces to about 2 quarts, about 1 hour longer. Stir in the vinegar, hot pepper sauce, and salt. Strain, reserving the meat for another use.

Makes about 2 quarts.

MAKING STRONG STOCK

Occasionally recipes call for a strong-flavored stock. Strong stock can be made easily by reducing regular stock by approximately half. So, a general rule of thumb is: If a recipe calls for 1 cup strong stock, make it by reducing 2 cups regular stock in a heavy saucepan over medium heat. The excess liquid will boil away, leaving the remaining stock intensely flavored.

HOMEMADE MAYONNAISE

*A*ll the ingredients (except the boiling water) should be at room temperature.

2 egg yolks
2 teaspoons white wine vinegar
Juice of ½ lemon
½ teaspoon salt
Pinch of ground white pepper
½ teaspoon Dijon mustard
1 cup vegetable oil
½ cup olive oil
Dash of hot pepper sauce
1 tablespoon boiling water

1. Whisk the egg yolks in a large bowl until light. Slowly whisk in the vinegar, lemon juice, salt, white pepper, and mustard until smooth.

2. Whisk in the vegetable oil, a few drops at a time, until ½ cup has been incorporated. (The mayonnaise should be very thick at this point.) Continue to beat in the oil, 2 tablespoons at a time. When all the vegetable oil has been incorporated, whisk in the olive oil 2 tablespoons at a time. Season with hot pepper sauce and, if you like, more salt or lemon juice. Thin with the boiling water.

3. Store, tightly covered, in the refrigerator. Mayonnaise will keep five to six days in the refrigerator, but bring it to room temperature before using.

Makes about 1½ cups, enough for 4 servings.

MAIL-ORDER SOURCES

Adams Mills
Route 1
Midland City, AL 36350
(205) 983-4331
Stone-ground cornmeal and grits.

Arrowhead Mills, Inc.
Box 866
Hereford, TX 79045
(806) 364-0730
Many organically grown whole grains.
Catalog available.

Birkett Mills
P.O. Box 440-A
Penn Yan, NY 14527
(315) 536-3391
Buckwheat groats and flour. Roasted
buckwheat (kasha) available in four
grades. Stone-ground flours. Price list
available.

Burpee Seed Company
Warminster, PA 18974
(215) 674-4915
Vegetable amaranth seeds for the
intrepid gardener. Catalog available.

Butte Creek Mill
Box 561
Eagle Point, OR 97524
(503) 826-3531
Rolled grains, stone-ground flours,
whole grains, bran, grits.

Calloway Gardens Country Store
Highway 27
Pine Mountain, GA 31822
(404) 663-2281, ext. 5100
Stone-ground "speckled heart" hominy
grits. Plain and self-rising water-ground
cornmeal.

Commodities
117 Hudson Street
New York, NY 10013
(212) 334-8330
Whole grains, flours, and "new grains."

Dean & Deluca
110 Greene Street, Suite 304
New York, NY 10012
(800) 221-7714
Wild, basmati, and Texmati rices; dried
posole; and a good selection of whole
grains in general.

Farms of Texas
P.O. Box 1305
Alvin, TX 77512
(713) 331-8245
White and brown Texmati rices.

Garden Spot Distributors
Route 1, Box 729A
New Holland, PA 17557
(717) 354-4936
Shiloh Farms products; see listing.
Catalog available for $1.00 (refundable).

Gray's Gristmill
P.O. Box 422
Adamsville, RI 02801
(617) 636-6075
White and yellow stone-ground cornmeal and a variety of stone-ground
flours.

Great Valley Mills
687 Mill Road
Telford, PA 18969
(215) 256-6648
Full line of stone-ground flours.

Health Valley Natural Foods
700 Union Street
Montebello, CA 90640
(213) 724-2211
Whole grains, bran, cereals.

Kenyon Cornmeal Company
Usquepaugh, RI 02836
(401) 783-4054
Flours and mixes for pancakes, muffins,
and bread.

Lundberg Family Farms
5370 Church Street
Richvale, CA 95974
(916) 882-4551
Organically grown aromatic rice.

Moose Lake Wild Rice
Box 325
Deer River, MN 56636
(218) 246-8143
Minnesota wild rice.

Morgan's Mills
Route 2, Box 115
Union, ME 04862
(207) 783-4054
Large variety of flours.

New Hope Mills, Inc.
RR 2, Box 269A
Moravia, NY 13119
(315) 497-0783
Water-ground flours and cornmeal.

Nu-World Amaranth, Inc.
P.O. Box 2202
Naperville, IL 60540
(312) 369-6819
Whole-grain amaranth, amaranth flour, puffed amaranth, amaranth and wheat-, rye-, or oat-flour blends.

Old Mill of Guilford
1340 NC68 North
Oak Ridge, NC 27310
(919) 643-4783
Water-ground and stone-ground flours, cornmeal, and grits.

Quinoa Corporation
2300 Central Avenue, Suite G
Boulder, CO 80301
(800) 237-2304
Quinoa by the pound.

R & R Limited
Box 752
Smithfield, VA 23430
(804) 357-5730
Surrey and Smithfield hams.

Shiloh Farms
Box 97, Highway 59
Sulphur Springs, AR 92769
(501) 298-3297
Variety of whole grains, meals, flours.

St. Maires Wild Rice Inc.
St. Maires, ID 83861
(800) 225-9453
Idaho-style wild rice.

Vermont Country Store
Weston, VT 05161
(802) 824-3184
Variety of whole grains and flours.

Walnut Acres
Penns Creek, PA 17862
(717) 837-3874
Large selection of whole grains, cereals, and flours. Also amaranth grain and flour. Catalog available.

White Lily Foods Company
P.O. Box 871
Knoxville, TN 37901
(615) 546-5511
Unbleached bread flour, soft wheat flours, cornmeal mix. Price list available.

BIBLIOGRAPHY

Much of the information in this book was garnered from growers, agricultural researchers, and individual grain councils. One organization that is owed a great debt for its generous and unstinting sharing of knowledge on the subject of grains is the Rodale Food Center in Emmaus, Pennsylvania. Other background material was culled from the following sources:

Amaranth, Modern Prospects for an Ancient Crop, by the Advisory Committee on Technology, Innovation Board on Science and Technology. National Academy Press, Washington, D.C., 1984.

American Food: The Gastronomic Story, 2nd edition, by Evan Jones. Vintage Books, New York, 1981.

The American Heritage Cookbook and Illustrated History of American Eating & Drinking, by the Editors of American Heritage Magazine. American Heritage Publishing, New York, 1964.

The Bible Cookbook, by Daniel S. Cutler. William Morrow, New York, 1985.

The Book of Whole Foods, Nutrition and Cuisine, by Karen MacNeil. Vintage Books, New York, 1981.

Bowe's and Church's Food Values of Portions Commonly Used, 13th edition, by Jean A. T. Pennington and Helen Nichols Church. Harper & Row, New York, 1980.

The California Nutrition Book, by Paul Saltman, Joel Gurin, and Ira Mothner. Little, Brown, Boston, 1987.

Classic Indian Vegetarian & Grain Cooking, by Julie Sahni. William Morrow, New York, 1985.

Complete Book of Natural Foods, by Fred Rohe. Shambhala Publications, Boulder, Colorado, 1983.

The Cook's Encyclopedia, by Tom Stobart. Harper & Row, New York, 1981.

Creative Cooking with Grains & Pasta, by Sheryl and Mel London. Rodale Press, Emmaus, Pennsylvania, 1982.

The Dictionary of American Food & Drink, by John F. Mariani. Ticknor & Fields, New Haven and New York, 1983.

Eating in America, by Waverley Root and Richard de Rochemont. William Morrow, New York, 1976.

Fannie Farmer Baking Book, by Marion Cunningham. Alfred A. Knopf, New York, 1984.

Food, by Waverley Root. Simon & Schuster, New York, 1980.

Food in History, by Reay Tannahill. Stein & Day, New York, 1973.

Foods & Nutrition Encyclopedia, Volumes 1 and 2, by Audrey Ensminger, M. E. Ensminger, James Konlande, and John Robson. Pegus Press, Clovis, California, 1983.

Hebrew Myths, by Robert Graves and Raphael Patai. Greenwich House (distributed by Crown Publishers, Inc.), New York, 1983.

The Horizon Cookbook and Illustrated History of Eating and Drinking Through the Ages, by William Harlan Hale and the Editors of Horizon Magazine. American Heritage Publishing, New York, 1968.

James Beard's American Cookery, by James Beard. Little, Brown, Boston, 1972.

Jane Brody's Good Food Book, by Jane Brody. W. W. Norton, New York, 1985.

Jane Brody's Nutrition Book, by Jane Brody. W. W. Norton, New York, 1981.

Joy of Cooking, 1971 edition, by Irma S. Rombauer and Marion Rombauer Becker. Bobbs-Merrill, Indianapolis, 1971.

Natural History Magazine, "A Matter of Taste—The Taming of the Grain," by Raymond Sokolov, January 1981.

The New Nutrition Study Guide and Reader, edited by Paul Saltman and Yvonne Baskin. University Extension, University of California, San Diego, 1987.

Nutrition Almanac, 2nd edition, by John D. Kirschmann with Lavon J. Dunne. McGraw-Hill, New York, 1984.

On Food and Cooking, by Harold McGee. Charles Scribner's Sons, New York, 1984.

The New Yorker, "Profiles—The Staff of Life, I: The Golden Thread," by E. J. Kahn, Jr., June 18, 1984.

The New Yorker, "Profiles—The Staff of Life, III: Fiat Panis," by E. J. Kahn, Jr., December 17, 1984.

Rice, by Maria Luisa and Jack Denton Scott. Times Books, New York, 1985.

The Taste of America, by John L. Hess and Karen Hess. Grossman, New York, 1977.

Tastings, by Jennifer Harvey Lang. Crown, New York, 1986.

The World Encyclopedia of Food, by Patrick Coyle, Jr. Facts On File, New York, 1982.

The World's Best Food for Health and Long Life, by Michael Bateman, Caroline Conran, and Oliver Gillie. Houghton Mifflin, Boston, 1981.

INDEX